Key to map symbols

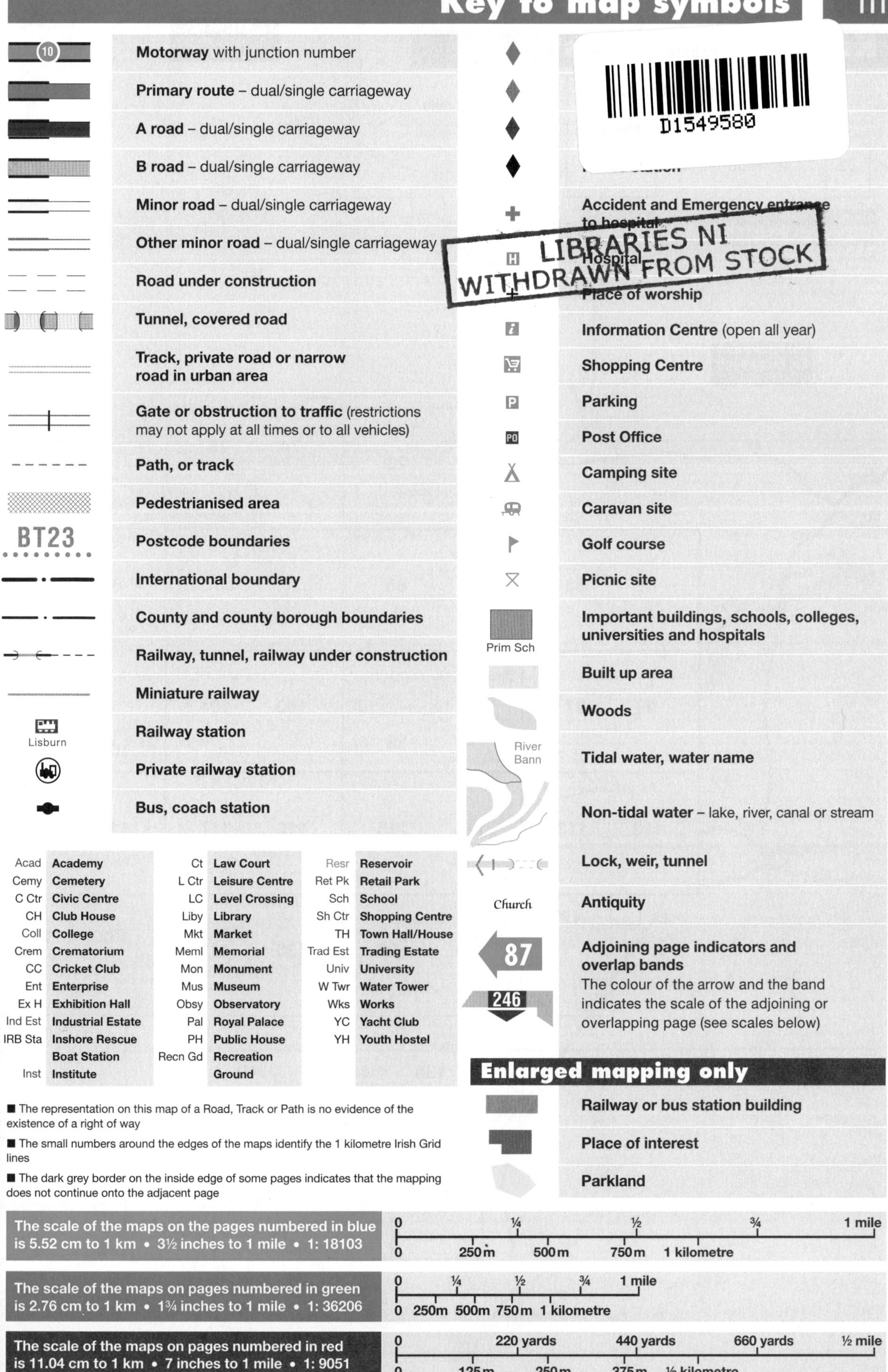

10	**Motorway** with junction number
	Primary route – dual/single carriageway
	A road – dual/single carriageway
	B road – dual/single carriageway
	Minor road – dual/single carriageway
	Other minor road – dual/single carriageway
	Road under construction
	Tunnel, covered road
	Track, private road or narrow road in urban area
	Gate or obstruction to traffic (restrictions may not apply at all times or to all vehicles)
	Path, or track
	Pedestrianised area
BT23	**Postcode boundaries**
	International boundary
	County and county borough boundaries
	Railway, tunnel, railway under construction
	Miniature railway
Lisburn	**Railway station**
	Private railway station
	Bus, coach station

	Accident and Emergency entrance to hospital
	Hospital
	Place of worship
	Information Centre (open all year)
	Shopping Centre
	Parking
	Post Office
	Camping site
	Caravan site
	Golf course
	Picnic site
Prim Sch	**Important buildings, schools, colleges, universities and hospitals**
	Built up area
	Woods
River Bann	**Tidal water, water name**
	Non-tidal water – lake, river, canal or stream
	Lock, weir, tunnel
Church	**Antiquity**
87 / 246	**Adjoining page indicators and overlap bands** The colour of the arrow and the band indicates the scale of the adjoining or overlapping page (see scales below)

Acad	**Academy**	Ct	**Law Court**	Resr	**Reservoir**
Cemy	**Cemetery**	L Ctr	**Leisure Centre**	Ret Pk	**Retail Park**
C Ctr	**Civic Centre**	LC	**Level Crossing**	Sch	**School**
CH	**Club House**	Liby	**Library**	Sh Ctr	**Shopping Centre**
Coll	**College**	Mkt	**Market**	TH	**Town Hall/House**
Crem	**Crematorium**	Meml	**Memorial**	Trad Est	**Trading Estate**
CC	**Cricket Club**	Mon	**Monument**	Univ	**University**
Ent	**Enterprise**	Mus	**Museum**	W Twr	**Water Tower**
Ex H	**Exhibition Hall**	Obsy	**Observatory**	Wks	**Works**
Ind Est	**Industrial Estate**	Pal	**Royal Palace**	YC	**Yacht Club**
IRB Sta	**Inshore Rescue Boat Station**	PH	**Public House**	YH	**Youth Hostel**
Inst	**Institute**	Recn Gd	**Recreation Ground**		

Enlarged mapping only

	Railway or bus station building
	Place of interest
	Parkland

■ The representation on this map of a Road, Track or Path is no evidence of the existence of a right of way

■ The small numbers around the edges of the maps identify the 1 kilometre Irish Grid lines

■ The dark grey border on the inside edge of some pages indicates that the mapping does not continue onto the adjacent page

The scale of the maps on the pages numbered in blue is 5.52 cm to 1 km • 3½ inches to 1 mile • 1: 18103

0 ¼ ½ ¾ 1 mile
0 250 m 500 m 750 m 1 kilometre

The scale of the maps on pages numbered in green is 2.76 cm to 1 km • 1¾ inches to 1 mile • 1: 36206

0 ¼ ½ ¾ 1 mile
0 250m 500m 750m 1 kilometre

The scale of the maps on pages numbered in red is 11.04 cm to 1 km • 7 inches to 1 mile • 1: 9051

0 220 yards 440 yards 660 yards ½ mile
0 125 m 250 m 375 m ½ kilometre

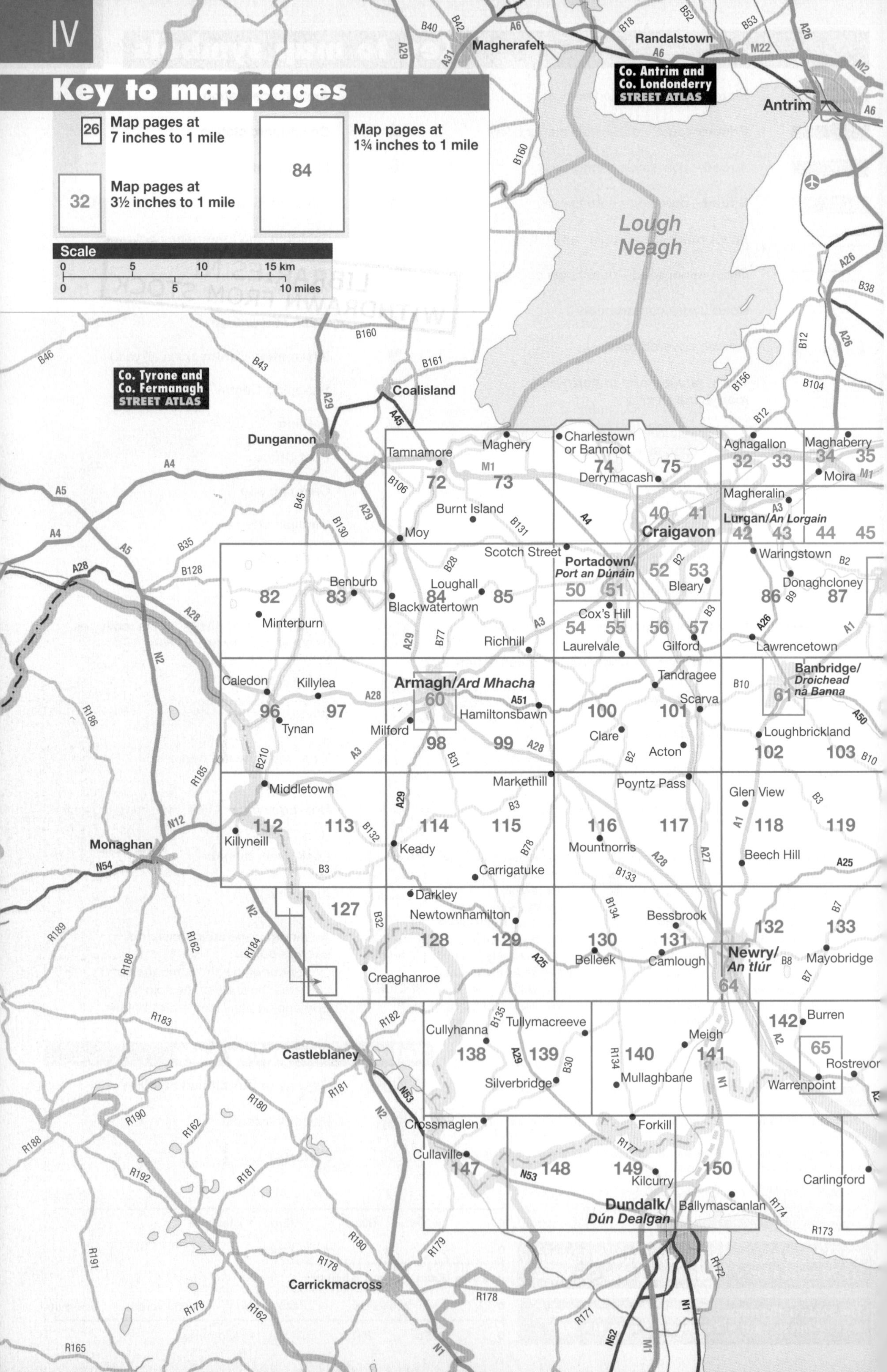
IV
Key to map pages
26 Map pages at 7 inches to 1 mile
32 Map pages at 3½ inches to 1 mile
84 Map pages at 1¾ inches to 1 mile
Scale
0 5 10 15 km
0 5 10 miles
Co. Antrim and Co. Londonderry STREET ATLAS
Co. Tyrone and Co. Fermanagh STREET ATLAS
Magherafelt
Randalstown
Antrim
Lough Neagh
Coalisland
Dungannon
Tamnamore
Maghery
72 73
Burnt Island
Moy
Charlestown or Bannfoot
74 75
Derrymacash
Aghagallon
32 33
Maghaberry
34 35
Moira
Magheralin
40 41
Craigavon
Lurgan/An Lorgain
42 43 44 45
Scotch Street
Portadown/Port an Dúnáin
50 51 52 53
Bleary
Waringstown
Donaghcloney
86 87
Benburb
82 83 84 85
Minterburn
Loughall
Blackwatertown
Cox's Hill
54 55 56 57
Laurelvale
Gilford
Richhill
Lawrencetown
Caledon
Killylea
96 97
Tynan
Armagh/Ard Mhacha
60
Milford
98 99
Hamiltonsbawn
Tandragee
Scarva
100 101
Clare
Acton
Banbridge/Droichead na Banna
61
Loughbrickland
102 103
Markethill
Poyntz Pass
Glen View
Middletown
Killyneill
112 113 114 115 116 117 118 119
Keady
Carrigatuke
Mountnorris
Beech Hill
Monaghan
Darkley
127
Newtownhamilton
128 129 130 131
Belleek
Bessbrook
Camlough
Newry/An tIúr
64
132 133
Mayobridge
Creaghanroe
Cullyhanna
Tullymacreeve
138 139 140 141
Silverbridge
Mullaghbane
Meigh
142 Burren
65
Rostrevor
Warrenpoint
Castleblaney
Crossmaglen
Forkill
Cullaville
147 148 149 150
Kilcurry
Carlingford
Dundalk/Dún Dealgan
Ballymascanlan
Carrickmacross

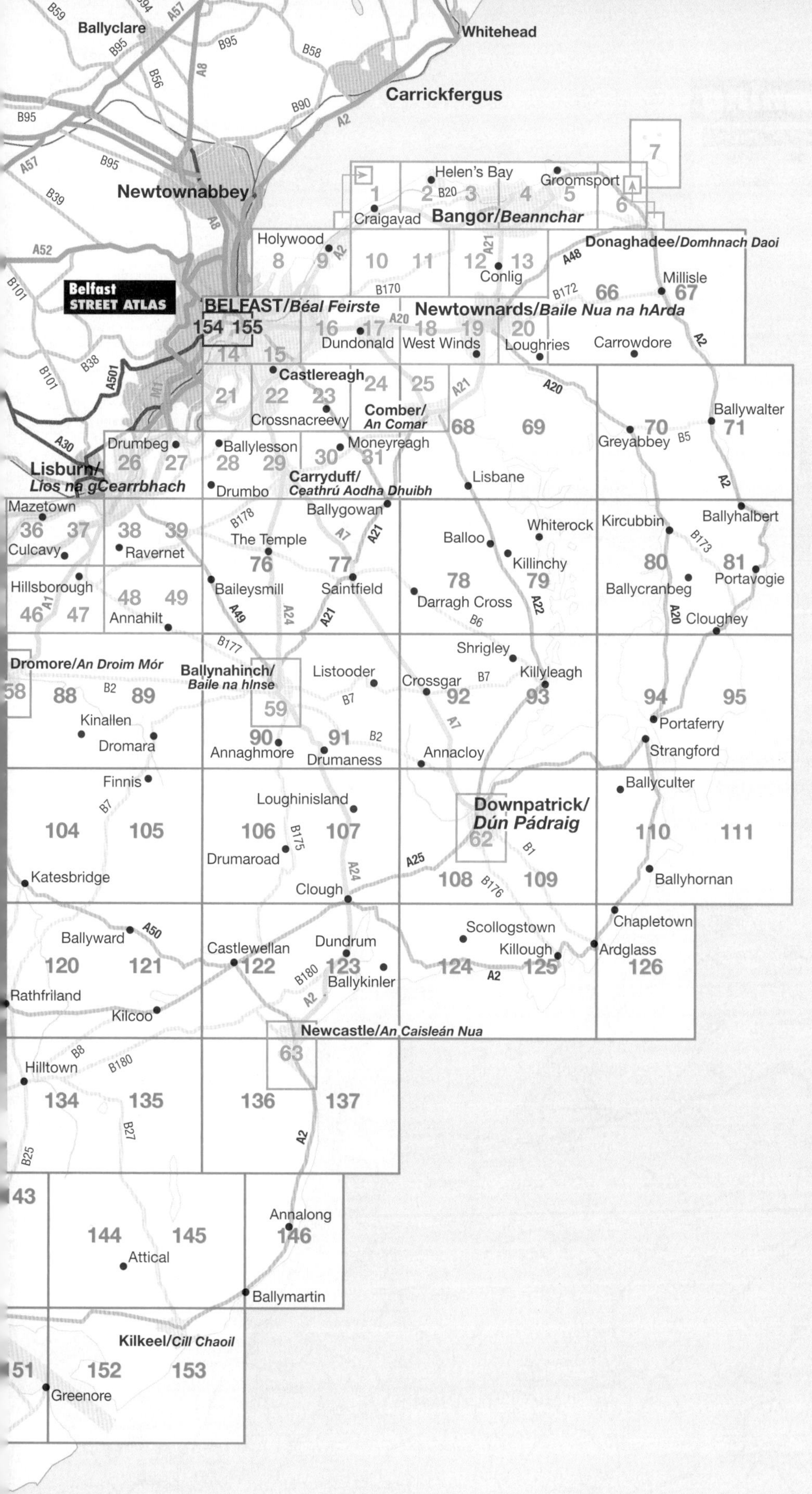
Ballyclare
Whitehead
Carrickfergus
Newtownabbey
Belfast STREET ATLAS
BELFAST/Béal Feirste
154 155
Holywood
Helen's Bay
Groomsport
Craigavad
Bangor/Beannchar
Donaghadee/Domhnach Daoi
Conlig
Millisle
Newtownards/Baile Nua na hArda
Dundonald
West Winds
Loughries
Carrowdore
Castlereagh
Crossnacreevy
Comber/
An Comar
Drumbeg
Ballylesson
Moneyreagh
Lisburn/
Líos na gCearrbhach
Drumbo
Carryduff/
Ceathrú Aodha Dhuibh
Lisbane
Greyabbey
Ballywalter
Mazetown
Culcavy
Ravernet
Ballygowan
The Temple
Balloo
Whiterock
Killinchy
Kircubbin
Ballyhalbert
Portavogie
Hillsborough
Annahilt
Baileysmill
Saintfield
Darragh Cross
Ballycranbeg
Cloughey
Dromore/An Droim Mór
Ballynahinch/
Baile na hInse
Listooder
Crossgar
Shrigley
Killyleagh
Kinallen
Dromara
Annaghmore
Drumaness
Annacloy
Portaferry
Strangford
Finnis
Loughinisland
Downpatrick/
Dún Pádraig
Ballyculter
Drumaroad
Katesbridge
Clough
Ballyhornan
Chapletown
Ballyward
Castlewellan
Dundrum
Scollogstown
Killough
Ardglass
Ballykinler
Rathfriland
Kilcoo
Newcastle/An Caisleán Nua
Hilltown
Annalong
Attical
Ballymartin
Kilkeel/Cill Chaoil
Greenore

Route Planning

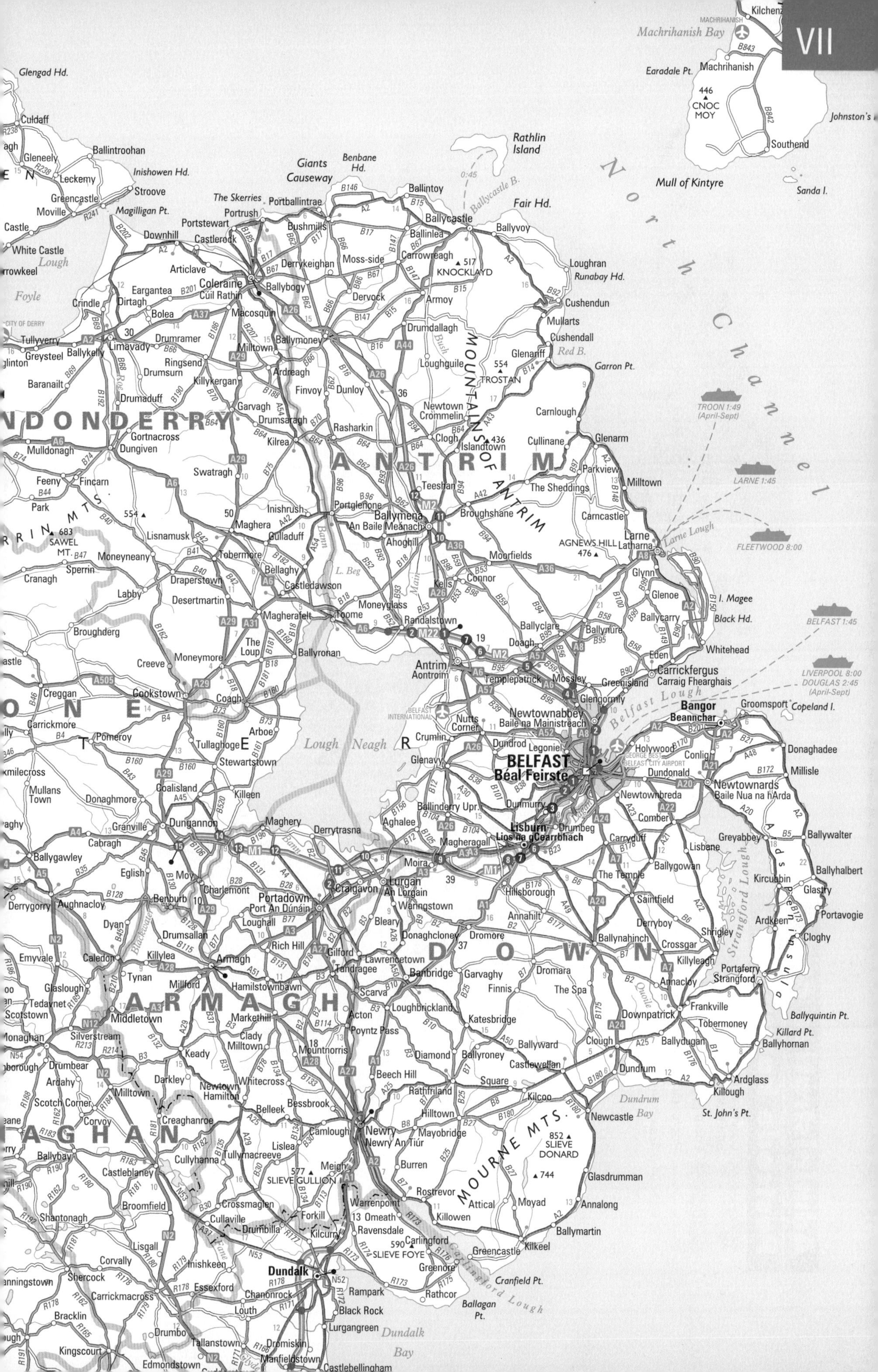
Kilchenzie
Machrihanish Bay
Machrihanish
Eardale Pt.
446 CNOC MOY
Johnston's
Southend
Mull of Kintyre
Sanda I.
Rathlin Island
Fair Hd.
Glengad Hd.
Culdaff
Gleneely
Ballintroohan
Inishowen Hd.
Leckemy
Stroove
Greencastle
Moville
Magilligan Pt.
Castle
White Castle
Lough Foyle
The Skerries
Giants Causeway
Benbane Hd.
Portballintrae
Ballintoy
Ballycastle
Ballyvoy
Portrush
Portstewart
Bushmills
Ballinlea
Downhill
Castlerock
Carrowreagh
517 KNOCKLAYD
Loughran
Runabay Hd.
Derrykeighan
Moss-side
Articlave
Coleraine
Cúil Rathin
Ballybogy
Eargantea
Dervock
Armoy
Cushendun
Crindle
Dirtagh
Bolea
Macosquin
Mullarts
Cushendall
Red B.
Drumdallagh
Tullyverry
Limavady
Drumramer
Ballymoney
Greysteel
Ballykelly
Milltown
Loughguile
Glenariff
Garron Pt.
Ringsend
Drumsurn
Killykergan
Ardreagh
554 TROSTAN
Baranailt
Finvoy
Dunloy
Drumaduff
Garvagh
Drumsaragh
Newtown Crommelin
Carnlough
MOUNTAINS OF ANTRIM
LONDONDERRY
Rasharkin
Gortnacross
Dungiven
Kilrea
Clogh
Islandtown
436
Cullinane
Glenarm
Mulldonagh
ANTRIM
Parkview
Millltown
Feeny
Fincarn
Swatragh
Teeshan
The Sheddings
Park
Portglenone
Ballymena
An Baile Meánach
Broughshane
Carncastle
SPERRIN MTS.
Inishrush
Maghera
Culladuff
Ahoghill
Larne
Latharna
Larne Lough
683 SAWEL MT.
Lisnamusk
Moneyneany
Tobermore
Moorfields
AGNEWS HILL 476
Sperrin
Cranagh
Bellaghy
L. Beg
Kells
Connor
Glynn
Draperstown
Castledawson
Glenoe
I. Magee
Labby
Desertmartin
Moneyglass
Ballycarry
Black Hd.
Magherafelt
Toome
Randalstown
Ballyclare
Ballynure
Broughderg
The Loup
Ballyronan
Doagh
Whitehead
Moneymore
Antrim
Aontroim
Templepatrick
Eden
Carrickfergus
Carraig Fhearghais
Creeve
Mossley
Greenisland
Cookstown
Coagh
Glengormly
Creggan
Belfast Lough
Groomsport
Bangor
Beannchar
Copeland I.
TYRONE
Newtownabbey
Baile na Mainistreach
BELFAST INTERNATIONAL
Nutts Corner
Carrickmore
Pomeroy
Arboe
Tullaghoge
Crumlin
Lough Neagh
Holywood
Conlig
Donaghadee
Dundrod
Legoniel
GEORGE BEST BELFAST CITY AIRPORT
Millisle
Stewartstown
Glenavy
BELFAST
Béal Feirste
Dundonald
Newtownards
Baile Nua na hArda
Sixmilecross
Mullans Town
Coalisland
Killeen
Donaghmore
Newtownbreda
Ballinderry Upr.
Dunmurry
Comber
Aghalee
Granville
Dungannon
Maghery
Derrytrasna
Lisburn
Lios na gCearrbhach
Drumbeg
Greyabbey
Ballywalter
Cabragh
Carryduff
Lisbane
Magheragall
Ballygawley
Moira
39
The Temple
Ballygowan
Ballyhalbert
Eglish
Moy
Lurgan
An Lorgain
Craigavon
Kircubbin
Charlemont
Portadown
Port An Dúnáin
Hillsborough
Saintfield
Glastry
Ards Peninsula
Derrygorry
Aughnacloy
Benburb
Waringstown
Dyan
Loughall
Bleary
Annahilt
Derryboy
Strangford Lough
Ardkeen
Portavogie
Drumsallan
Rich Hill
Donaghcloney
Dromore
Shrigley
Cloghy
Emyvale
Caledon
Killylea
Armagh
Gilford
Lawrencetown
DOWN
Ballynahinch
Crossgar
Tynan
Tandragee
Banbridge
Garvaghy
Dromara
Killyleagh
Portaferry
Strangford
Glaslough
Millford
Hamiltonsbawn
Scarva
Finnis
The Spa
Annacloy
Tedavnet
ARMAGH
Loughbrickland
Quoile
Frankville
Scotstown
Middletown
Markethill
Acton
Poyntz Pass
Katesbridge
Downpatrick
Tobermoney
Ballyquintin Pt.
Monaghan
Silverstream
Clady Milltown
Mountnorris
Killard Pt.
Ballyhornan
Keady
Diamond
Ballyroney
Ballyward
Clough
Ballydugan
Castlewellan
Drumbear
Darkley
Newtown Hamilton
Whitecross
Beech Hill
Square
Dundrum
Ardglass
Ardahy
Milltown
Rathfriland
Kilcoo
Killough
Scotch Corner
Corvoy
Belleek
Bessbrook
Hilltown
Dundrum Bay
St. John's Pt.
Creaghanroe
Camlough
Newry
Newry An Iúir
Mayobridge
Newcastle
MONAGHAN
Lislea
Cullyhanna
Tullymacreeve
Burren
MOURNE MTS.
852 SLIEVE DONARD
Ballybay
Castleblaney
577 SLIEVE GULLION
Meigh
744
Glasdrumman
Broomfield
Crossmaglen
Warrenpoint
Rostrevor
Attical
Moyad
Annalong
Shantonagh
Cullaville
Forkill
Omeath
Killowen
Drumbilla
Ravensdale
Ballymartin
Kilcurry
Carlingford
Kilkeel
Lisgall
590 SLIEVE FOYE
Greencastle
Corvally
Inishkeen
Shercock
Dundalk
Greenore
Cranfield Pt.
Carlingford Lough
Carrickmacross
Essexford
Rampark
Rathcor
Chanonrock
Black Rock
Ballagan Pt.
Louth
Bracklin
Lurgangreen
Dundalk Bay
Drumbo
Tallanstown
Dromiskin
Kingscourt
Manfieldstown
Edmondstown
Castlebellingham
North Channel
TROON 1:49 (April-Sept)
LARNE 1:45
FLEETWOOD 8:00
BELFAST 1:45
LIVERPOOL 8:00
DOUGLAS 2:45 (April-Sept)

Administrative and Postcode boundaries

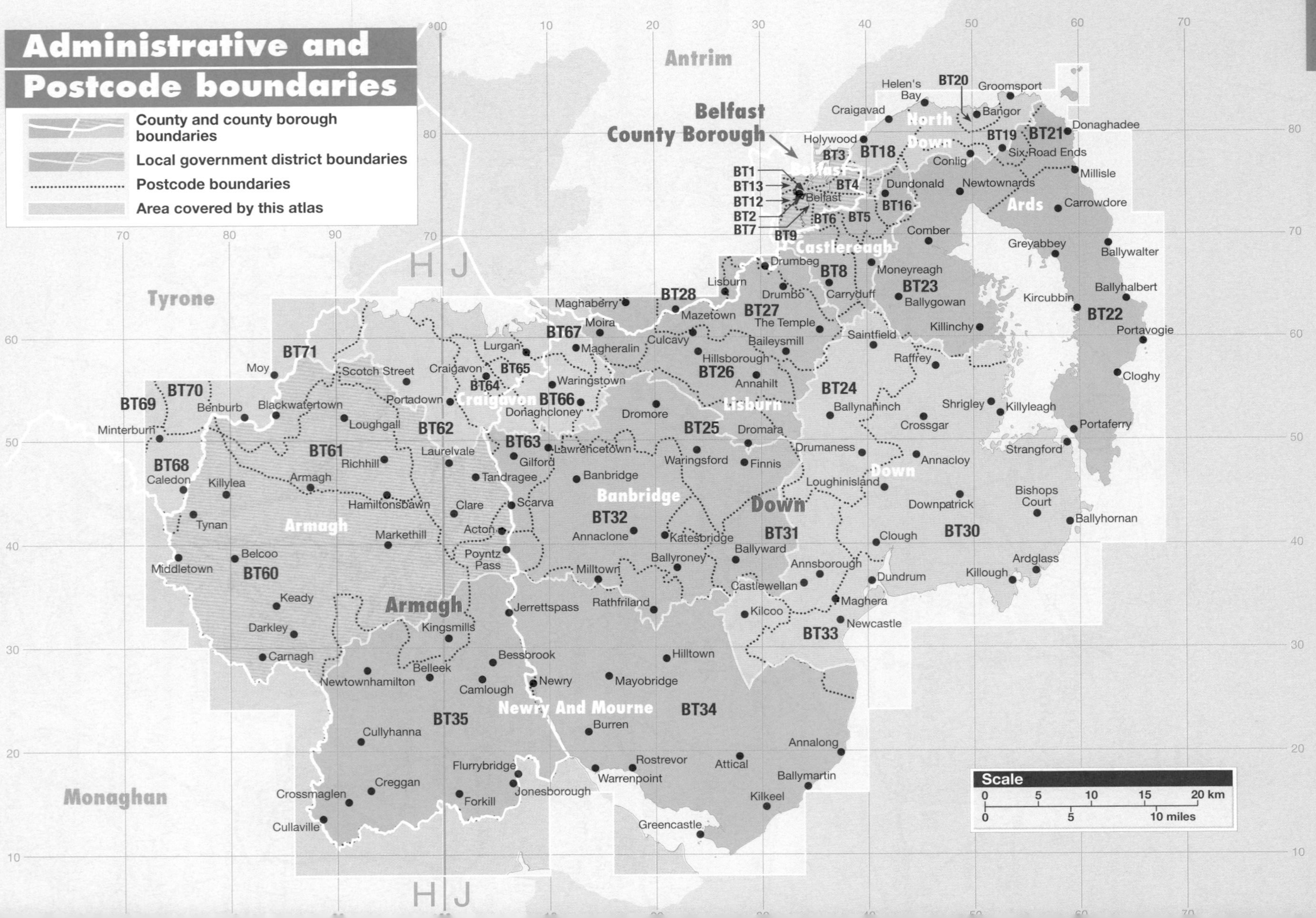

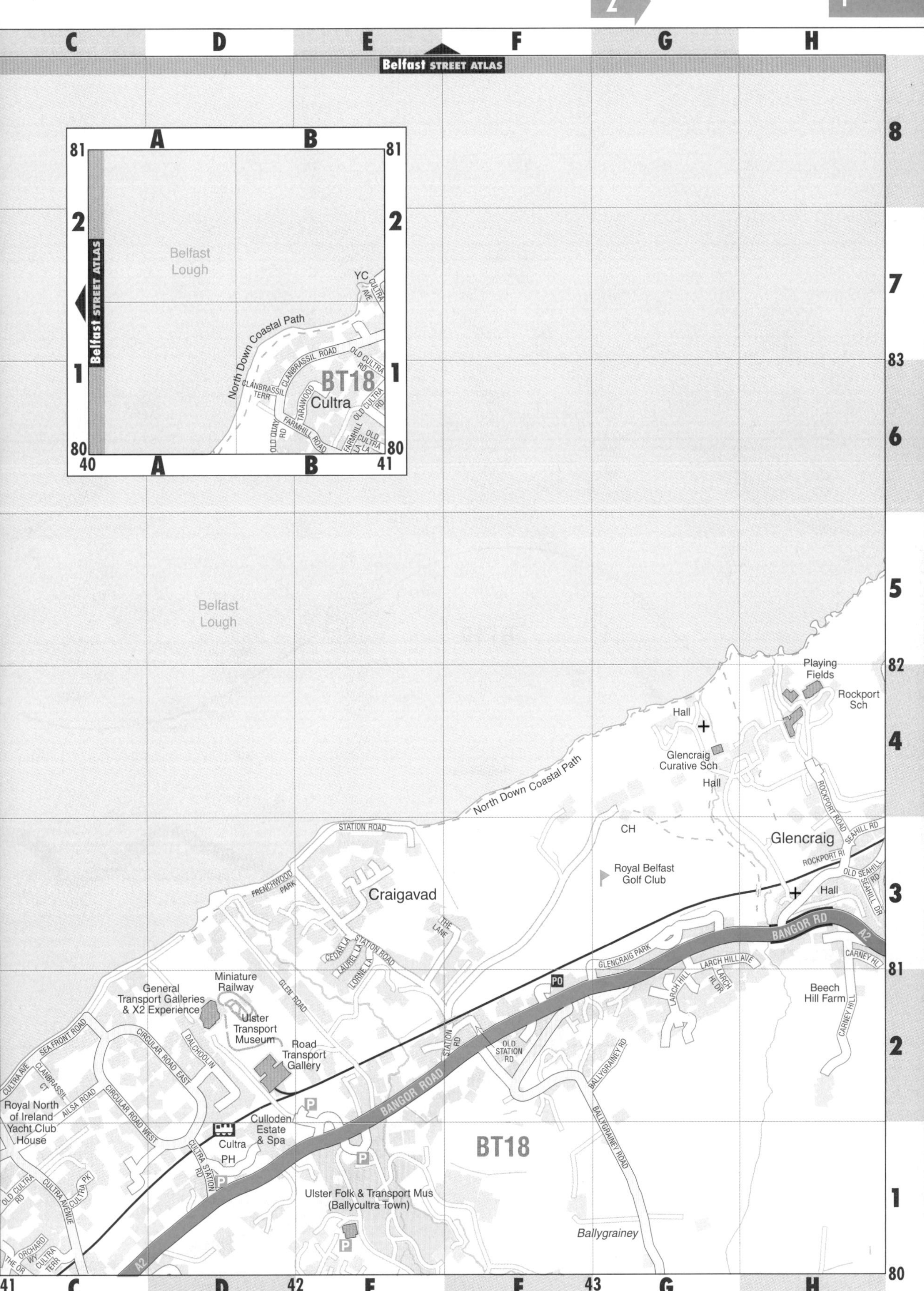
Belfast STREET ATLAS
Belfast Lough
YC
CULTRA AVE
North Down Coastal Path
CLANBRASSIL ROAD
OLD CULTRA RD
BT18
Cultra
CLANBRASSIL TERR
TARAWOOD
OLD CULTRA RD
OLD QUAY RD
FARMHILL ROAD
FARMHILL LA
OLD CULTRA LA
Belfast Lough
Playing Fields
Rockport Sch
Hall
Glencraig Curative Sch
Hall
North Down Coastal Path
ROCKPORT ROAD
STATION ROAD
CH
Glencraig
SEAHILL RD
ROCKPORT RI
OLD SEAHILL RD
SEAHILL DR
Royal Belfast Golf Club
FRENCHWOOD PARK
Craigavad
Hall
THE LANE
BANGOR RD
A2
CEDAR LA
LAUREL LA
STATION ROAD
LORNE LA
GLENCRAIG PARK
LARCH HILL AVE
CARNEY HL
Miniature Railway
GLEN ROAD
PO
LARCH HILL
LARCH HL DR
Beech Hill Farm
General Transport Galleries & X2 Experience
Ulster Transport Museum
CARNEY HILL
SEA FRONT ROAD
CIRCULAR ROAD EAST
DALCHOOLIN
Road Transport Gallery
STATION RD
OLD STATION RD
BALLYGRAINEY RD
CULTRA AVE
CLANBRASSIL CT
AILSA ROAD
CIRCULAR ROAD WEST
BANGOR ROAD
Royal North of Ireland Yacht Club House
P
Culloden Estate & Spa
Cultra
PH
BT18
BALLYGRAINEY ROAD
P
CULTRA STATION RD
P
OLD CULTRA RD
CULTRA AVENUE
CULTRA PK
Ulster Folk & Transport Mus (Ballycultra Town)
Ballygrainey
ORCHARD WY
CULTRA TERR
THE OR
P
A2

1

Belfast Lough
Grey Point
Grey Point Fort
Horse Rock
Helen's Bay
OLD FORT
THE FORT
GREY POINT
Helen's Bay Lawn Tennis Club
Hall
SHERIDAN DRIVE
SHERIDAN GR
Crawfordsburn Country Park
The Sea Park
Quarry Port
Helen's Bay / Cuan Héilin
FORT ROAD
SHERIDAN MANOR
CARRIG DENE
RUSHFIELD
BENNET WOOD
KATHLEEN AVENUE
CHURCH ROAD
Helen's Bay Golf Club
COAST GUARD AVE
KATHLEEN DR
ROCKDENE CT
QUARRY CT
WOODLAND AVENUE
ROCKMOUNT GDNS
CH
North Down Coastal Path
Sewage Works
CARRIAGE MEWS
CHIMERA WOOD
GOLF RD
CAROLSTEEN DR
THE COURTYARD
Ballygrot
BLACKWOOD
CRESCENT
CAROLSTEEN PARK
MOORE DR
Countryside Centre
OLD WINDMILL RD
STATION SQ
BRIDGE RD
DENISE CRES
CAROLSTEEN AVE
CAROLSTEEN GDNS
RHANBUOY PARK
RHANBUOY PK
BT19
Helen's Bay
Sea Hill
RHANBUOY RD
RATHMOYLE PK
BEECHLANDS PARK
SEAHILL
Ballyrobert
Irish Hill
CRAIGDARRAGH ROAD
RHANBUOY PK E
CRAIGDARRAGH PARK
SEAHILL RD E
CRAIGOWEN RD
CRAIGOWEN PK
CRAIGDARRAGH PK EAST
Viaduct
Brookmount
SEAHILL RD
Glencraig Integrated Prim Sch
CRAIGDARRAGH ROAD
Windmills (ruins)
OLD WINDMILL RD
Seahill
Black Hill
The Old Inn
MARTELLO PK
MARTELLO DR
BALLYROBERT ROAD
MARTELLO AVE
Crawfordsburn
Hall
MAIN ST CRAWFORDSBURN
OLD MILL CT
BALLYMULLAN ROAD
MEADOW GROVE
MEADOW PK N
Crawfordsburn Prim Sch
COOTEHALL PK
COOLEEN GDNS
GRAYS PK
COYLE'S LA
MEADOW WAY
MEADOW PK
BURNSIDE PK
A2 BANGOR ROAD
BELFAST ROAD
B20
Edith of Lorne's Glen
CARGOES CR
Culladuff
Ballymullan
COOTEHALL ROAD
Howard's Hill
BT18
BELFAST ROAD
Ballygilbert
Ballydavey Farm
Coach Hill Farm
BALLYMONEY ROAD
A2
A B C D E F
8 7 83 6 5 82 4 3 81 2 1 80
44 45 46

1

11

4

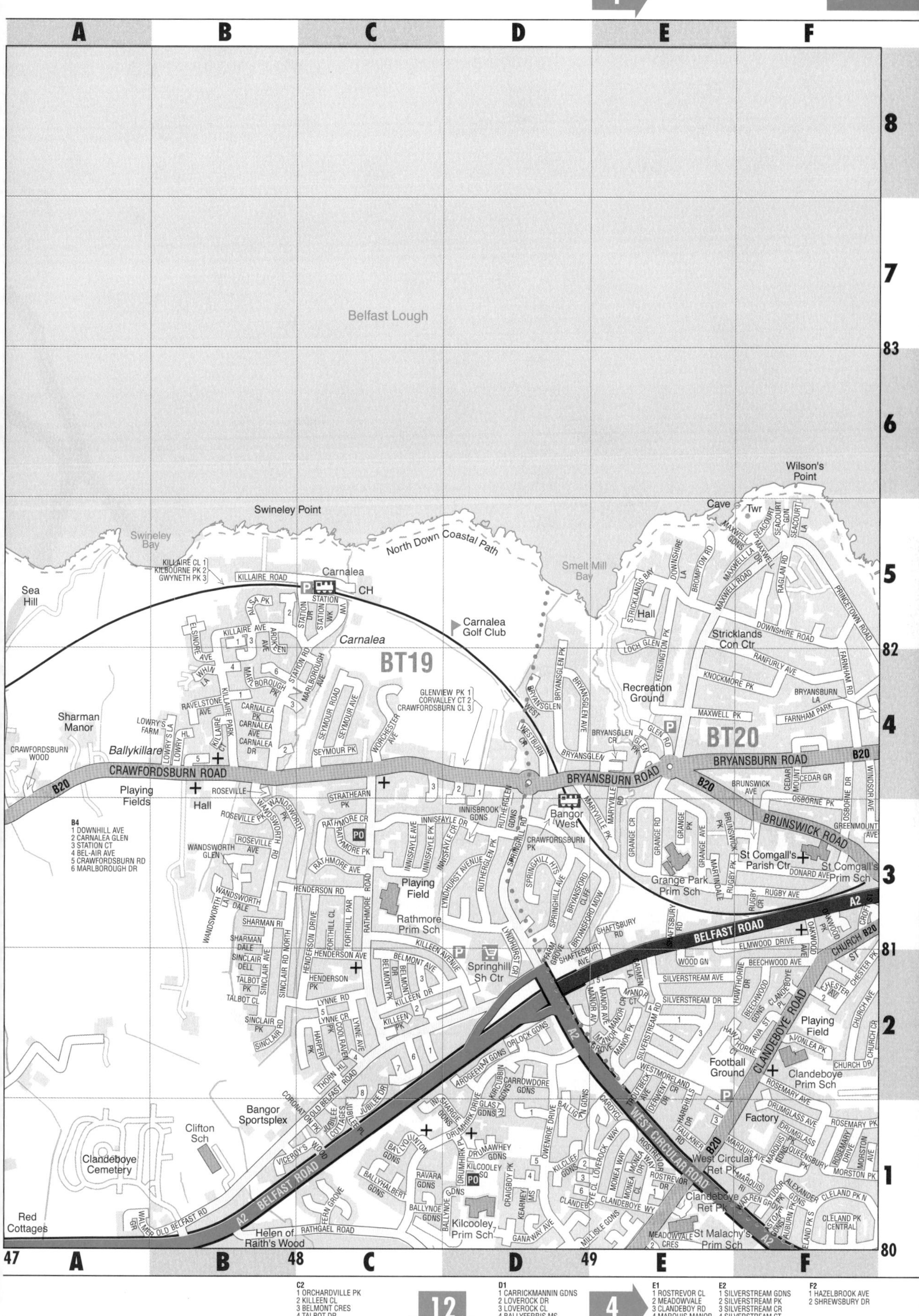

C2
1 ORCHARDVILLE PK
2 KILLEEN CL
3 BELMONT CRES
4 TALBOT DR
5 LYNNE LINK
6 ORCHARDVILLE AVE
7 ORCHARDVILLE GDNS
8 JUBILEE CT

12

D1
1 CARRICKMANNIN GDNS
2 LOVEROCK DR
3 LOVEROCK CL
4 BALLYFERRIS MS
5 BALLYFERRIS WK
6 CLANDEBOYE DR
7 GANAWAY WK

4

E1
1 ROSTREVOR CL
2 MEADOWVALE
3 CLANDEBOY RD
4 MARQUIS MANOR

E2
1 SILVERSTREAM GDNS
2 SILVERSTREAM PK
3 SILVERSTREAM CR
4 SILVERSTREAM CT
5 MANOR MEWS

F2
1 HAZELBROOK AVE
2 SHREWSBURY DR

3

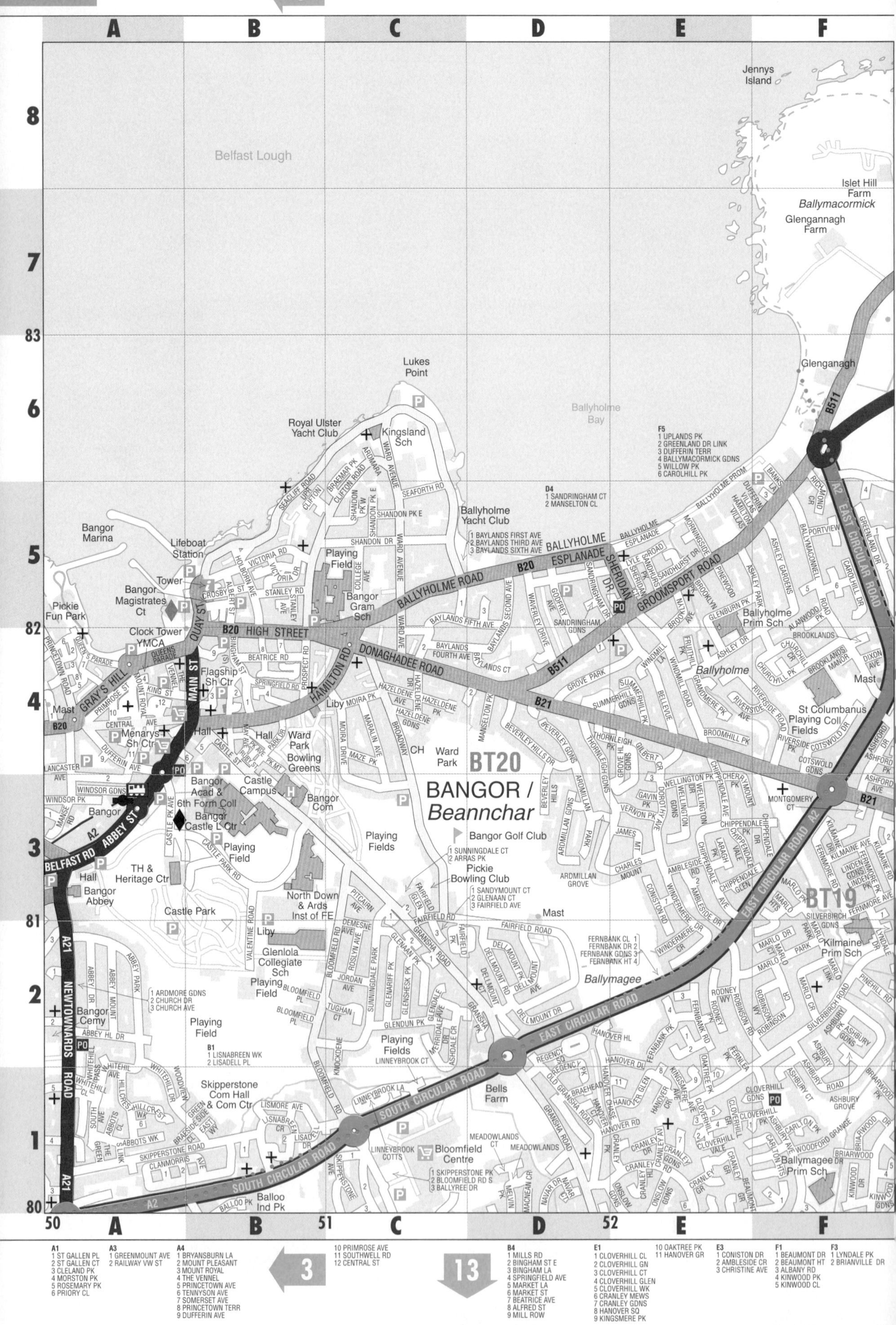

A1
1 ST GALLEN PL
2 ST GALLEN CT
3 CLELAND PK
4 MORSTON PK
5 ROSEMARY PK
6 PRIORY CL

A3
1 GREENMOUNT AVE
2 RAILWAY VW ST

A4
1 BRYANSBURN LA
2 MOUNT PLEASANT
3 MOUNT ROYAL
4 THE VENNEL
5 PRINCETOWN AVE
6 TENNYSON AVE
7 SOMERSET AVE
8 PRINCETOWN TERR
9 DUFFERIN AVE
10 PRIMROSE AVE
11 SOUTHWELL RD
12 CENTRAL ST

3

13

B4
1 MILLS RD
2 BINGHAM ST E
3 BINGHAM LA
4 SPRINGFIELD AVE
5 MARKET LA
6 MARKET ST
7 BEATRICE AVE
8 ALFRED ST
9 MILL ROW

E1
1 CLOVERHILL CL
2 CLOVERHILL GN
3 CLOVERHILL CT
4 CLOVERHILL GLEN
5 CLOVERHILL WK
6 CRANLEY MEWS
7 CRANLEY GDNS
8 HANOVER SQ
9 KINGSMERE PK
10 OAKTREE PK
11 HANOVER GR

E3
1 CONISTON DR
2 AMBLESIDE CR
3 CHRISTINE AVE

F1
1 BEAUMONT DR
2 BEAUMONT HT
3 ALBANY RD
4 KINWOOD PK
5 KINWOOD CL

F3
1 LYNDALE PK
2 BRIANVILLE DR

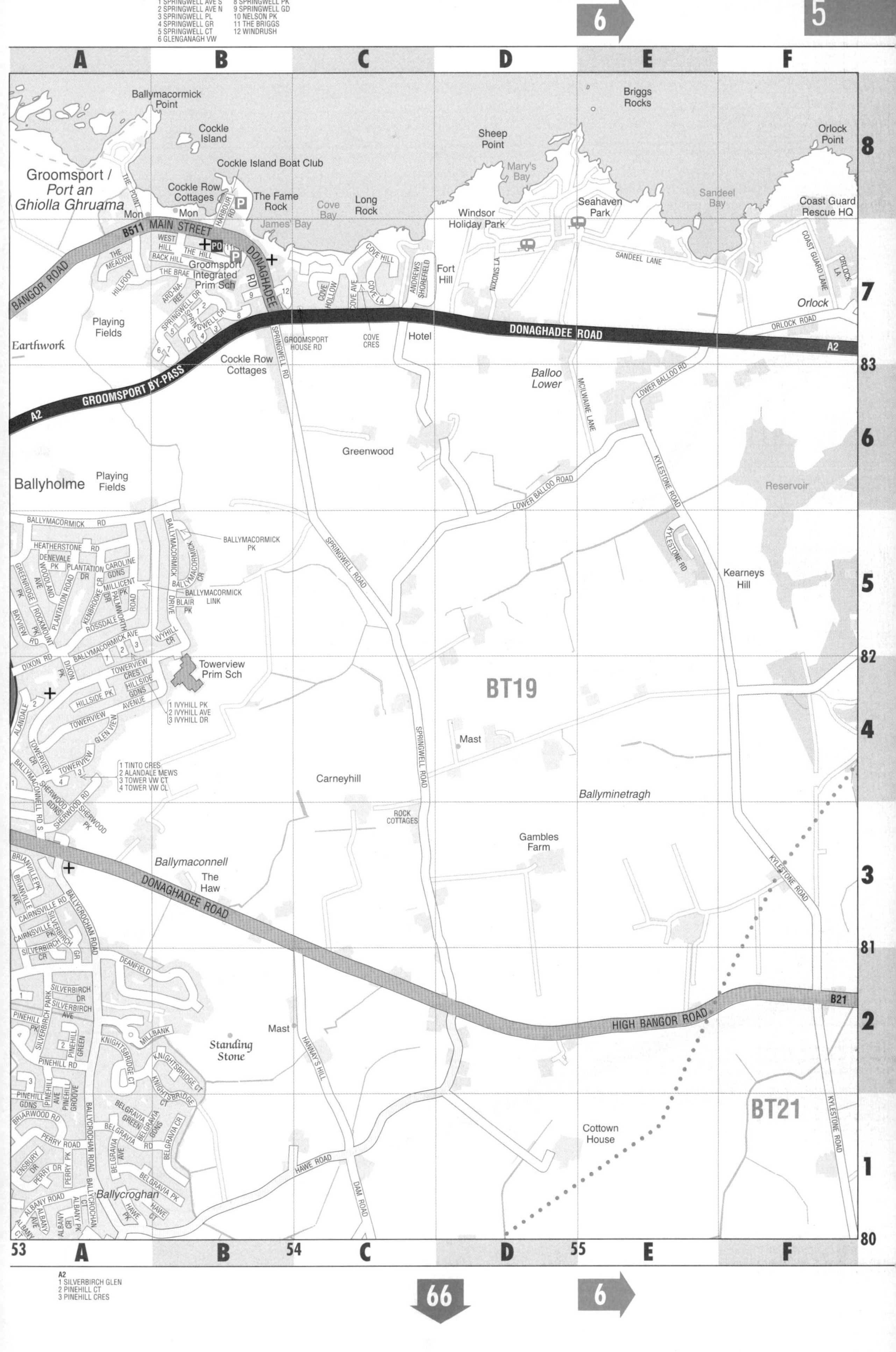
B7
1 SPRINGWELL AVE S
2 SPRINGWELL AVE N
3 SPRINGWELL PL
4 SPRINGWELL GR
5 SPRINGWELL CT
6 GLENGANAGH VW
7 GLENGANAGH PK
8 SPRINGWELL PK
9 SPRINGWELL GD
10 NELSON PK
11 THE BRIGGS
12 WINDRUSH
6
A
B
C
D
E
F
Ballymacormick Point
Cockle Island
Cockle Island Boat Club
Groomsport / Port an Ghiolla Ghruama
Cockle Row Cottages
The Fame Rock
Cove Bay
Long Rock
James' Bay
Mon
Briggs Rocks
Sheep Point
Mary's Bay
Windsor Holiday Park
Seahaven Park
Sandeel Bay
Orlock Point
Coast Guard Rescue HQ
B511 MAIN STREET
BANGOR ROAD
DONAGHADEE RD
HARBOUR RD
THE POINT
WEST HILL
THE HILL
BACK HILL
THE MEADOW
HILLFOOT
THE BRAE
ARD-NA-REE
Groomsport Integrated Prim Sch
COVE HILL
COVE HOLLOW
COVE AVE
COVE LA
ANDREWS SHOREFIELD
Fort Hill
NIXONS LA
SANDEEL LANE
COAST GUARD LANE
ORLOCK LA
Orlock
ORLOCK ROAD
Playing Fields
Earthwork
SPRINGWELL DR
SPRINGWELL CR
GROOMSPORT HOUSE RD
COVE CRES
Hotel
DONAGHADEE ROAD
A2
Cockle Row Cottages
SPRINGWELL RD
A2 GROOMSPORT BY-PASS
Balloo Lower
MCILWAINE LANE
LOWER BALLOO ROAD
Greenwood
Ballyholme
Playing Fields
KYLESTONE ROAD
Reservoir
BALLYMACORMICK RD
HEATHERSTONE RD
DENEVALE PK
WOODLAND AVE
GREENRIDGE PK
PLANTATION DR
PLANTATION ROAD
CAROLINE GDNS
MILLICENT PK
KENBROOKE CR
PALMWORTH DR
ROAD
BAYVIEW RD
ROCKMOUNT PK
ROSSDALE
BALLYMACORMICK DRIVE
BALLYMACORMICK CR
BALLYMACORMICK PK
BALLYMACORMICK LINK
BLAIR PK
SPRINGWELL ROAD
KYLESTONE RD
Kearneys Hill
BALLYMACORMICK AVE
IVYHILL CR
DIXON RD
DIXON PK
TOWERVIEW CRES
HILLSIDE GDNS
HILLSIDE PK
TOWERVIEW AVENUE
Towerview Prim Sch
1 IVYHILL PK
2 IVYHILL AVE
3 IVYHILL DR
BT19
ALANDALE
TOWERVIEW
GLEN VIEW
TOWERVIEW CR
Mast
SPRINGWELL ROAD
1 TINTO CRES
2 ALANDALE MEWS
3 TOWER VW CT
4 TOWER VW CL
Carneyhill
Ballyminetragh
BALLYMACONNELL RD S
SHERWOOD GDNS
SHERWOOD RD
SHERWOOD PK
ROCK COTTAGES
Gambles Farm
Ballymaconnell
The Haw
BRIANVILLE PK
BRIANVILLE AVE
CAIRNSVILLE RD
CAIRNSVILLE PK
SILVERBIRCH GR
SILVERBIRCH CR
BALLYCROGHAN ROAD
DONAGHADEE ROAD
KYLESTONE ROAD
DEANFIELD
SILVERBIRCH DR
SILVERBIRCH AVE
SILVERBIRCH PARK
PINEHILL PK
PINEHILL GREEN
PINEHILL RD
MILLBANK
KNIGHTSBRIDGE CT
Mast
Standing Stone
HANNAY'S HILL
HIGH BANGOR ROAD
B21
PINEHILL AVE
PINEHILL GDNS
PINEHILL GROOVE
BRIARWOOD RD
BELGRAVIA GREEN
BELGRAVIA GDNS
BELGRAVIA CR
BELGRAVIA AVE
BELGRAVIA RD
PERRY ROAD
PERRY DR
PERRY PK
ENSBURY DR
BALLYCROGHAN ROAD
HAWE ROAD
DAM ROAD
Cottown House
BT21
KYLESTONE ROAD
BELGRAVIA PK
ALBANY ROAD
ALBANY PK
ALBANY CR
Ballycroghan
BALLYCROGHAN CT
HAWE PK
HAWE CT
8
83
7
6
5
82
4
3
81
2
1
80
53
54
55
A2
1 SILVERBIRCH GLEN
2 PINEHILL CT
3 PINEHILL CRES
66
6

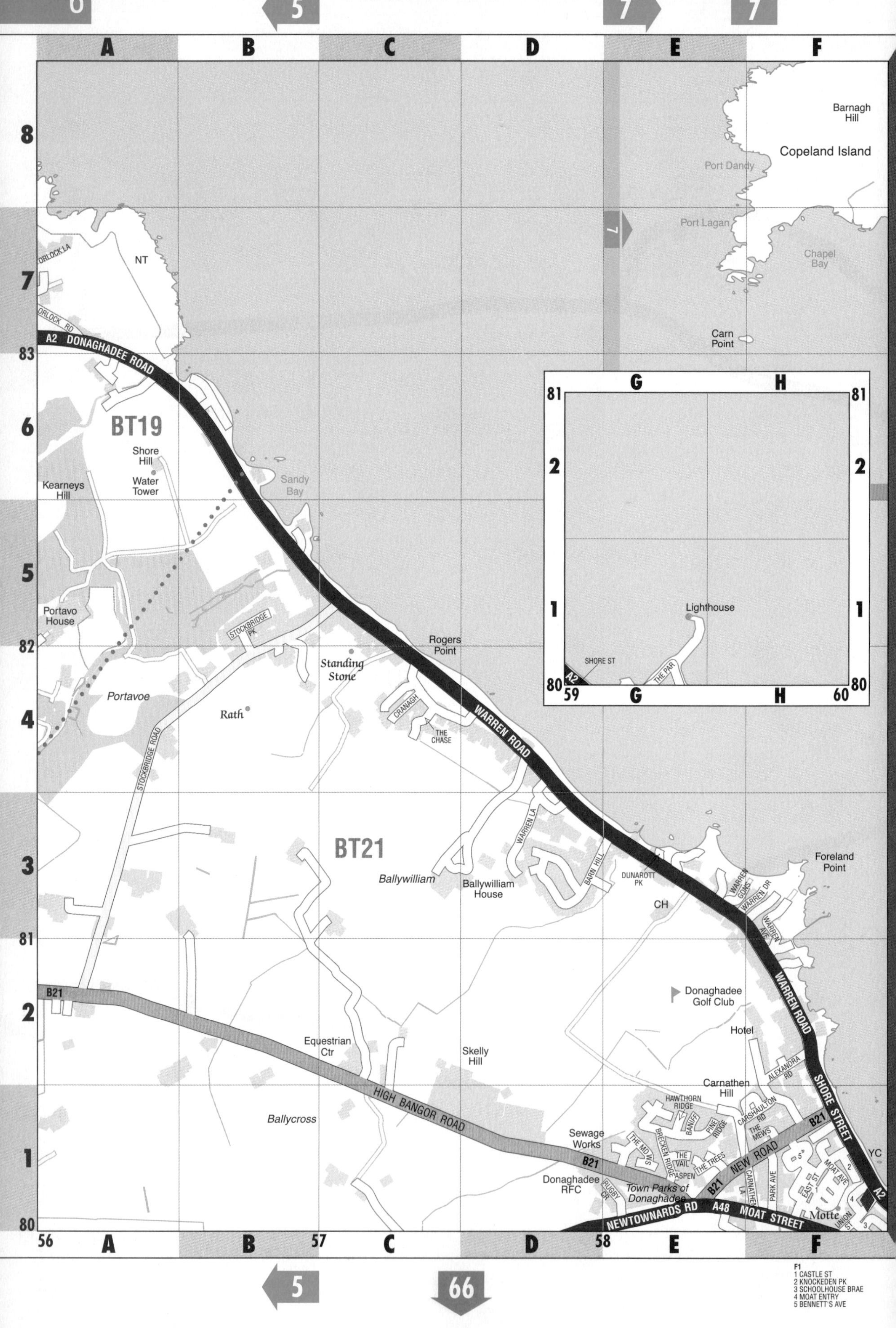

F1
1 CASTLE ST
2 KNOCKEDEN PK
3 SCHOOLHOUSE BRAE
4 MOAT ENTRY
5 BENNETT'S AVE

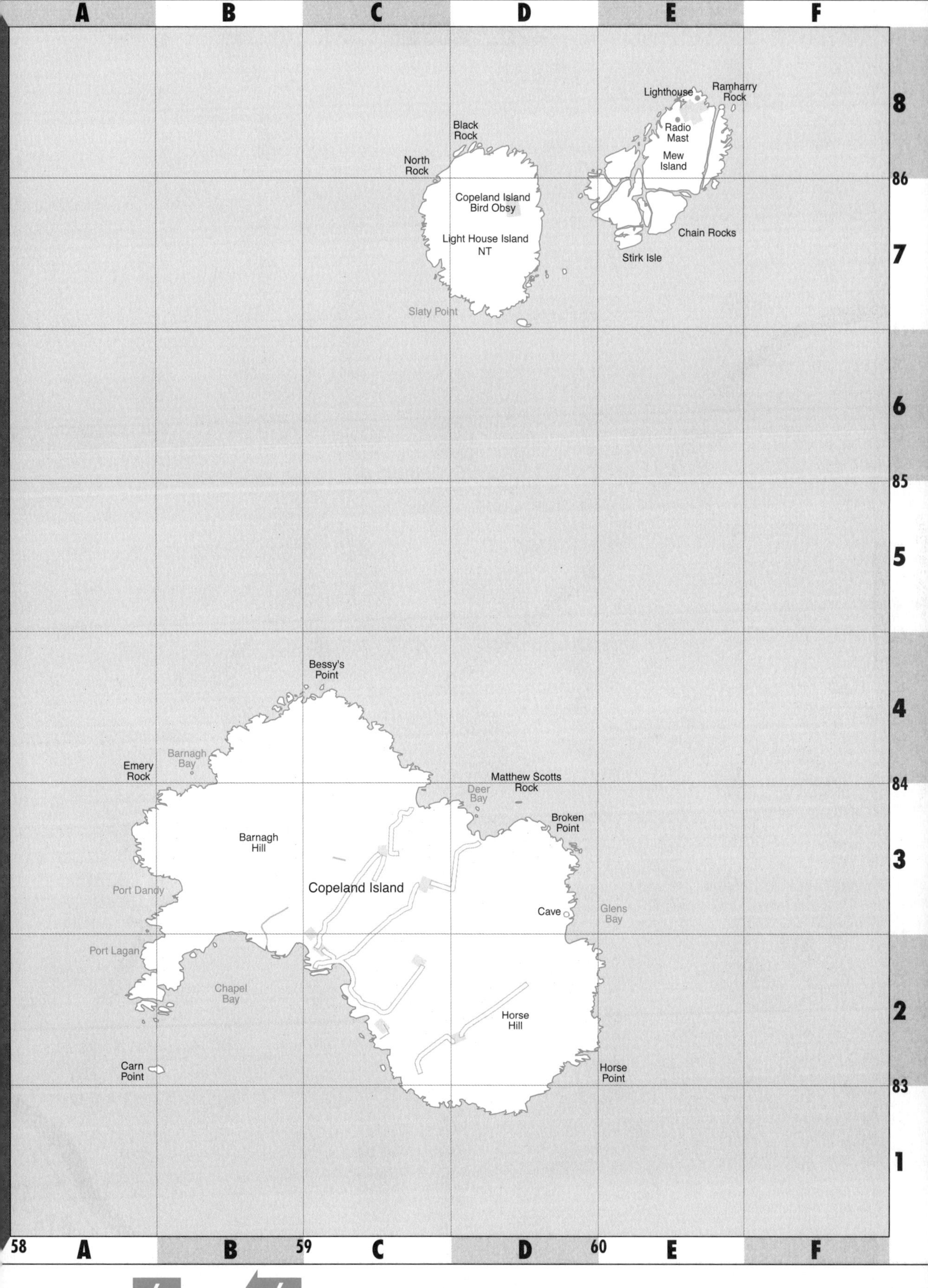
A
B
C
D
E
F
Lighthouse
Ramharry Rock
8
Black Rock
Radio Mast
North Rock
Mew Island
86
Copeland Island Bird Obsy
Light House Island NT
Chain Rocks
Stirk Isle
7
Slaty Point
6
85
5
Bessy's Point
4
Barnagh Bay
Emery Rock
Matthew Scotts Rock
84
Deer Bay
Broken Point
Barnagh Hill
3
Copeland Island
Port Dandy
Cave
Glens Bay
Port Lagan
Chapel Bay
2
Horse Hill
Carn Point
Horse Point
83
1
58
A
B
59
C
D
60
E
F

6
6

Belfast STREET ATLAS
A
B
C
D
E
F
8
7
79
6
5
78
4
3
77
2
1
76
35
36
37
Belfast Lough
Refuse Tip
Low-Wood Intake
DARGAN RD
DARGAN CRESCENT
Round Tower Commericial Park
Council Offices
Fortwilliam Ind Est
Dargan Ind Park
Bayview Ind Park
Loughside Ind Park
DARGAN DRIVE
SEAL ROAD
Quayside Office Park
Graham Ind Park
Somerton Ind Park
Sewage Works
Light Tower
HERDMAN CHANNEL ROAD
Herdman Channel
West Twin Island
MCCAUGHEY ROAD
SINCLAIR RD
STORMONT RD
Tower
Victoria Channel
EDGEWATER ROAD
Edgewater Bsns Pk
WEST BANK DR
WEST BANK CL
WEST BANK WAY
WEST BANK ROAD
Belfast Harbour Ind Est
Westbank Bsns Park
Liverpool Ferry Terminal
Heysham Ferry Terminal
Tower
Mast
WORKMAN ROAD
EAST TWIN ROAD
East Twin Island
WOLFF ROAD
THOMPSON WHARF RD
Musgrave Channel
Mast
AIRPORT ROAD
Works
BT3
Mast
Portside Bsns Park
Belfast Lough Reserve
Harbour Lagoon
AIRPORT ROAD WEST
HERON AVE
HERON VIEW
Sydenham Bsns Park
Tower
Tower
Tower
Loughview Bsns Park
HERON ROAD
MOSCOW ROAD
Sydenham Intake
George Best Belfast City Airport
Works
DEPOT ROAD
Airport Terminal
A2
SYDENHAM BY-PASS
Sydenham Playing Fields
BT4

10

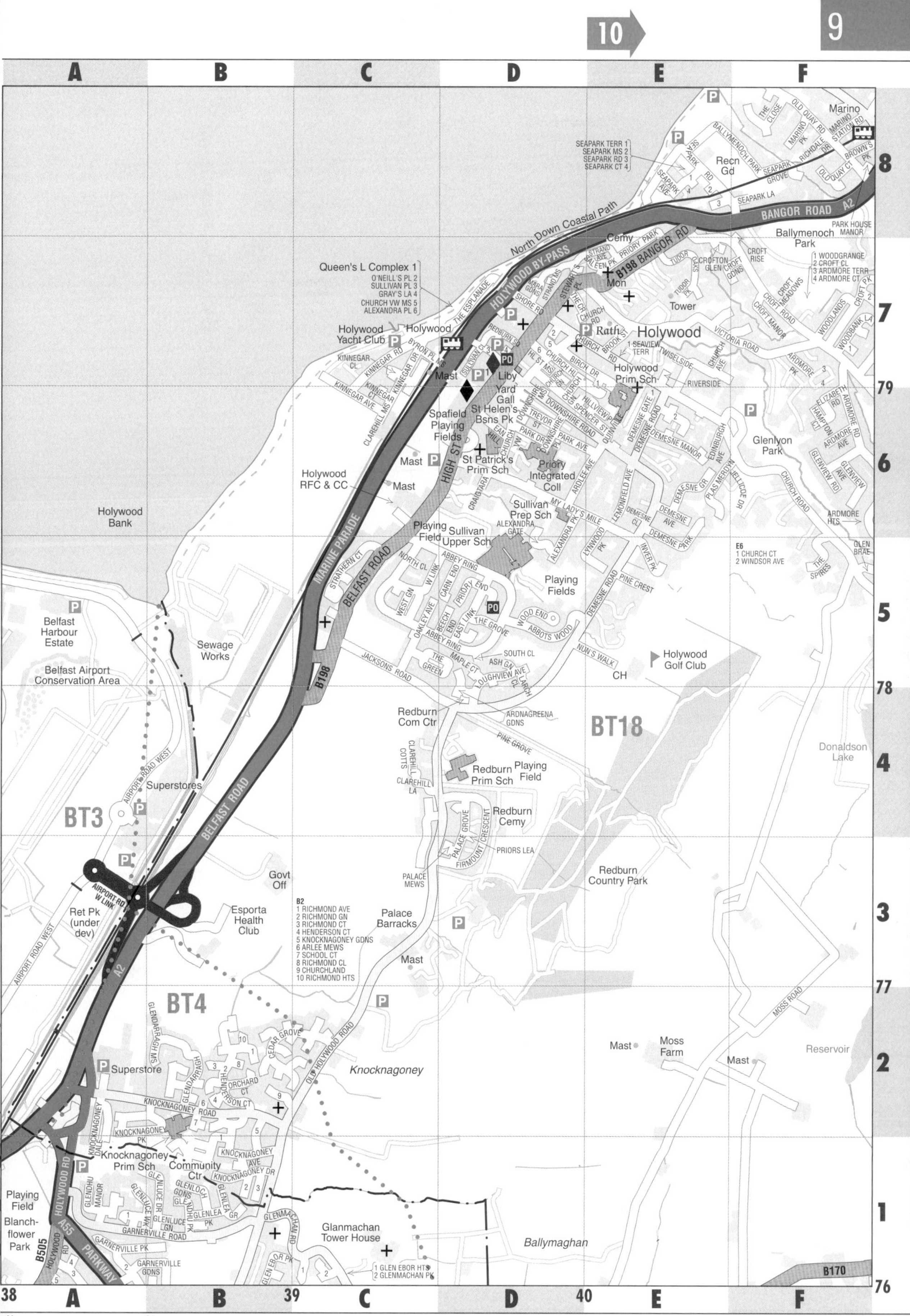

A1
1 GLENDHU GR
2 GARNERVILLE DR
3 TILLYSBURN PK
4 TILLYSBURN DR
5 MARMONT PK

B1
1 KNOCKNAGONEY WY
2 KNOCKNAGONEY GR
3 KNOCKNAGONEY GN

16

10

A8
1 BROWN'S PK
2 OLD CULTRA RD
3 FARMHILL RD
4 THE ORCHARD
5 CULTRA AVE

9
1

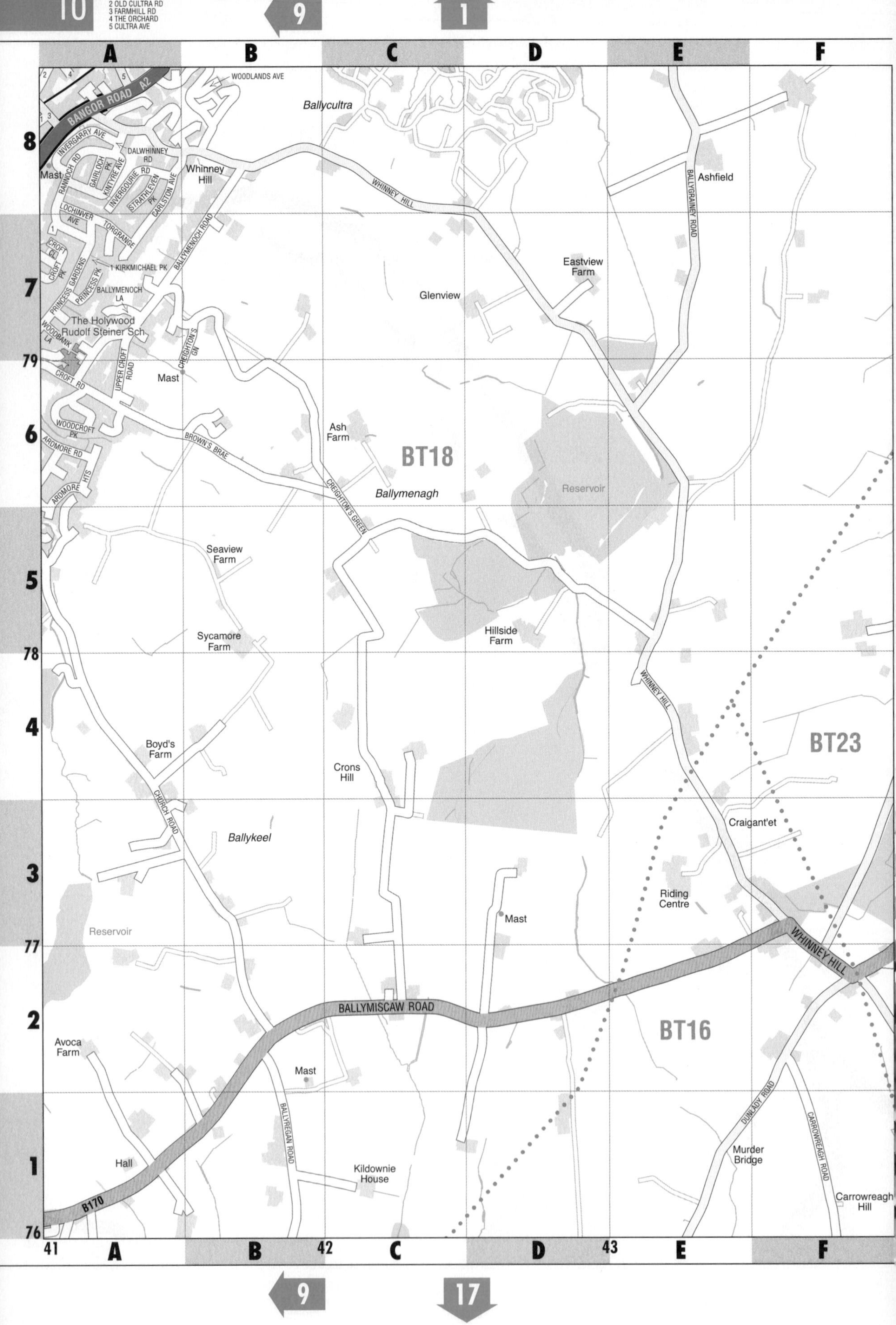

9
17

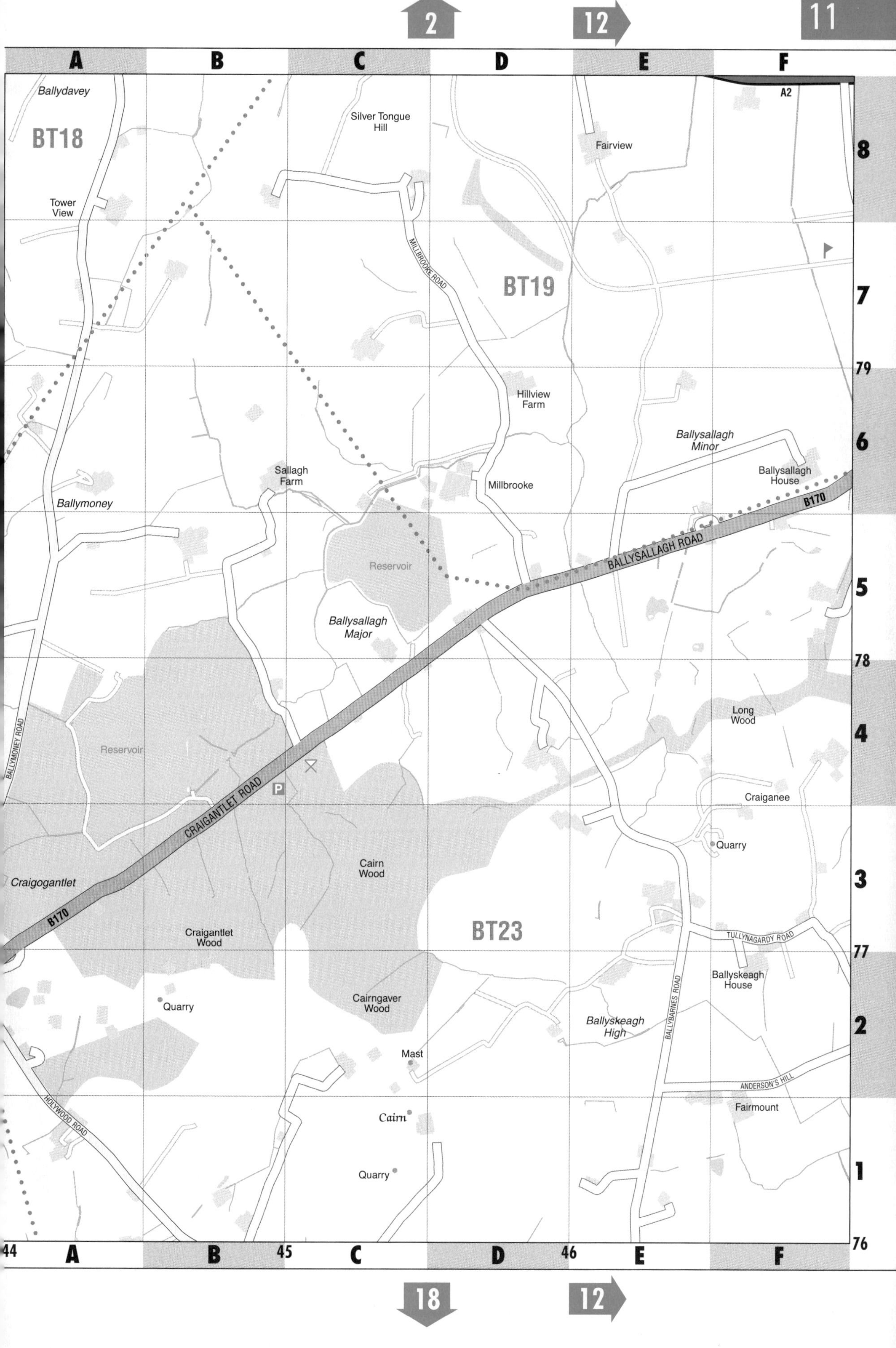
2
12
A
B
C
D
E
F
Ballydavey
BT18
Silver Tongue Hill
Fairview
A2
8
Tower View
MILLBROOKE ROAD
BT19
7
79
Hillview Farm
Ballysallagh Minor
6
Sallagh Farm
Millbrooke
Ballysallagh House
Ballymoney
B170
BALLYSALLAGH ROAD
Reservoir
5
Ballysallagh Major
78
Long Wood
4
BALLYMONEY ROAD
Reservoir
P
CRAIGANTLET ROAD
Craiganee
Quarry
Cairn Wood
3
Craigogantlet
B170
BT23
TULLYNAGARDY ROAD
Craigantlet Wood
77
Ballyskeagh House
Cairngaver Wood
Quarry
BALLYBARNES ROAD
Ballyskeagh High
2
Mast
ANDERSON'S HILL
HOLYWOOD ROAD
Fairmount
Cairn
Quarry
1
44
A
B
45
C
D
46
E
F
76
18
12

11
3
E8
1 MEADOWVALE GDNS
2 MEADOWVALE CL
3 MEADOWVALE LINK
4 MEADOWVALE AVE
5 LAUREL WOOD
F7
1 LORD WARDENS GN
2 LORD WARDENS MS
3 LORD WARDENS DL
4 LORD WARDENS DR
5 LORD WARDENS PK
6 LORD WARDENS CR
7 LORD WARDENS GR
8 HENALTA WOOD
A
B
C
D
E
F
8
7
79
6
5
78
4
3
77
2
1
76
47
48
49
B170
Ursula's Wood
Anna of Glenganagh's Hill
Miss Linley's Hill
Penelope Island
Viceroy's Hill
Lord Price's Wood
CLOISTER AVENUE
Banqueting Hall
Admiral's Island
Ajax Point
Guillaume Tell Island
Ballyvarnet
Gauntlet Hill
BT19
Cloister Wood
BIRCH DR
OWENROE DR
BIRCH PK
AVA FARM
BALLYGOWAN GDNS
B20 CLANDEBOYE RD
MEADOWVALE PK
MEADOWVALE
MEADOWVALE DR
MEADOWVALE CRES
THE BRAMBLES
Free Presbyterian Church & Christian Sch
Clandeboye Business Park
WEST CIRCULAR RD
Playing Field
Rowan Coll (Juvenile Justice Ctr for NI)
BallooTraining & Resource Ctr
Lakewood Specl Sch
Rathgill
RATHGAEL ROAD
Playing Field
LORD WARDENS GLADE
LORD WARDENS HOLLOW
LORD WARDENS CT
LORD WARDENS VIEW
LORD WARDENS PARADE
LORD WARDENS PAR
LORD WARDENS CH
LORD WARDENS GRANGE
LORD WARDENS MANOR
LORD WARDENS MDW
LORD WARDENS AVE
LORD WARDENS RD
BROOK LA
LORD WARDENS VALE 1
LORD WARDENS MT 2
LORD WARDENS GLEN 3
Amenity Site & Council Depot
BALLYSALLAGH ROAD
Fort Robert Wood
Ballyleidy
Sir John's Wood
Tomb Wood
Quebec Wood
Lady Hermione's Hill
Countess Hariot's Wood
Somerset Wood
Chapel Hill
Leinster's Wood
Holly Wood
Lisbane
BEECHFIELD CR
BEECHFIELD DRIVE
BEECHFIELD AVE
BEECHFIELD PK
PH
ESTATE ROAD
Craigforth Hill
Helen of Novar's Wood
Rapier Wood
Lord Terence's Wood
Reservoir
SUMMERFIELD
Clanbrassil Wood
Thora's Fort
Raplock Wood
Temple Wood
Reservoir
Lord Frederick's Wood
Reservoir
THE GREEN
LISBANE PK
TOWER PK
TOWER CL
TOWER RD
CORONATION AVE
HENDERSON AVE
Dane's Wood
Lord James' Wood
Earl Achibald's Wood
Clandeboye Golf Club
Conlig
Barberino Wood
Runestone Hill
Standing Stone
CH
BT23
Conlig Prim Sch
CRAWFORDSBURN ROAD
Tower Lake
Tower Hill Wood
Tower Lake Wood
Helen's Tower
Lower Little Clandeboye Wood
Southland Wood
OLD BANGOR ROAD
Ballyskeagh Low
Cavallo Stud Farm
Helen of Netherby's Wood
Clandeboye Wood
MOUNTAIN ROAD
Whitespots Country Park
Refuse Tip
Ark Open Farm
ANDERSON'S HILL
Dairy Bridge
Cullys Burn
MOUNTAIN ROAD
Somme Heritage Centre
TULLYNAGARDY ROAD
BANGOR ROAD
A21
MOUNTAIN RD
Whitespots
11
19

C8
1 BLOOMFIELD LINK
2 BALLYMINETRAGH GDNS
3 UPRITCHARD CT
4 UPRITCHARD CRES
5 PRIMACY DR

D7
1 WILLOWBROOK PL
2 WILLOWBROOK CR
3 BALMORAL AVE
4 BALMORAL DR
5 BALMORAL CL
6 BALMORAL PK
7 BALMORAL CR
8 BALMORAL CT
9 BALMORAL DL
10 HAMPTON DR
11 THE WILLOWS
12 HAMPTON MS
13 PRIMACY RD

D8
1 GLENDOWAN WY
2 ROSSINVER GDNS

E7
1 ROCKFIELD DL
2 ROCKFIELD GLEN
3 ROCKFIELD DR
4 BROOKVALE CRES
5 HAMPTON LA
6 BROOKVALE PK

4

E8
1 BEXLEY HL
2 CRANLEY GN
3 CRANLEY RD
4 SHAMROCK GLEN
5 ONSLOW AVE
6 ONSLOW CT
7 THE PINES
8 THE CEDARS
9 THE ASHES
10 MALVERN HTS

66

F8
1 STRATFORD GL
2 STRATFORD GR
3 DUNKELD GDNS
4 STRATFORD GDNS
5 STRATFORD RI
6 STRATFORD CT

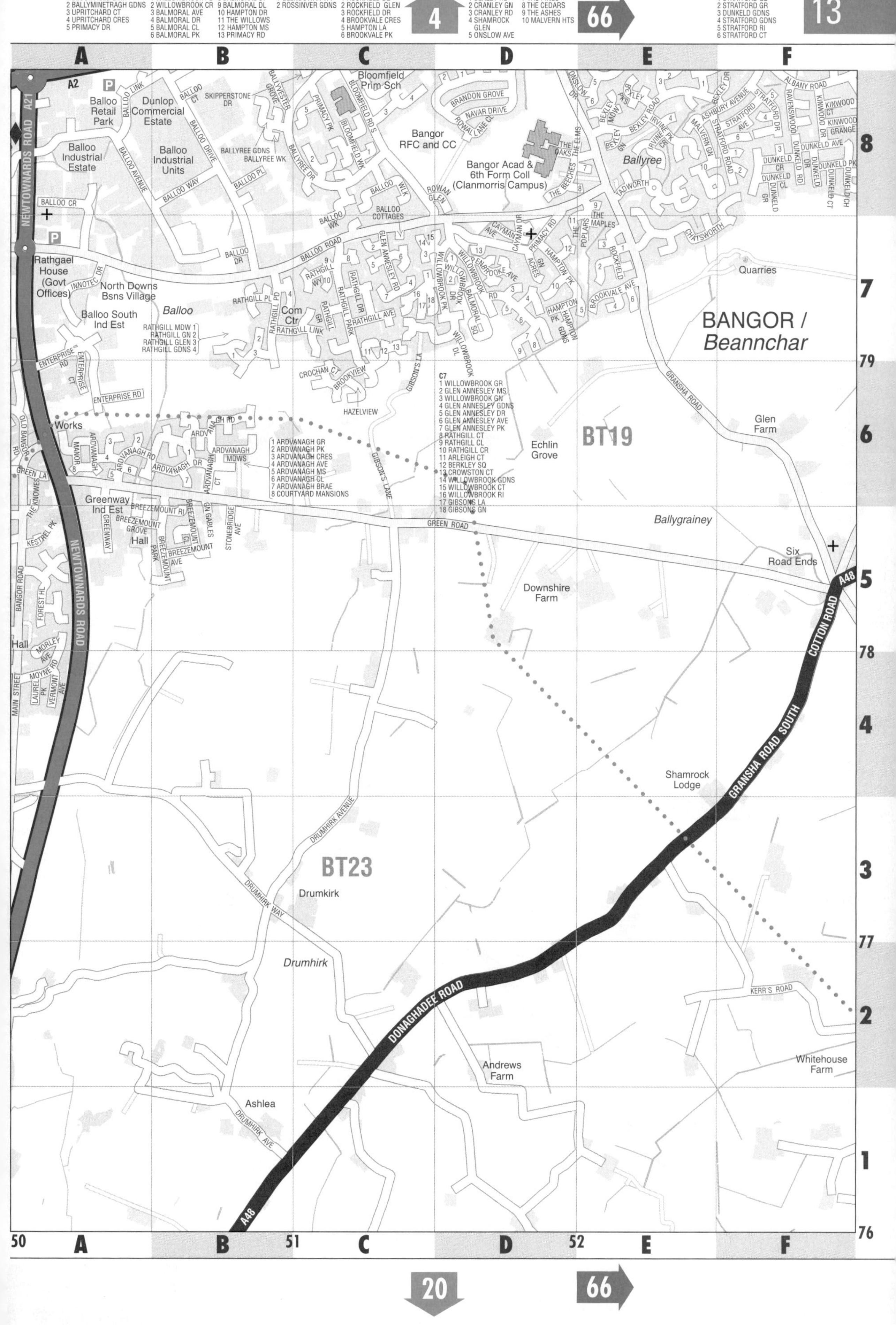

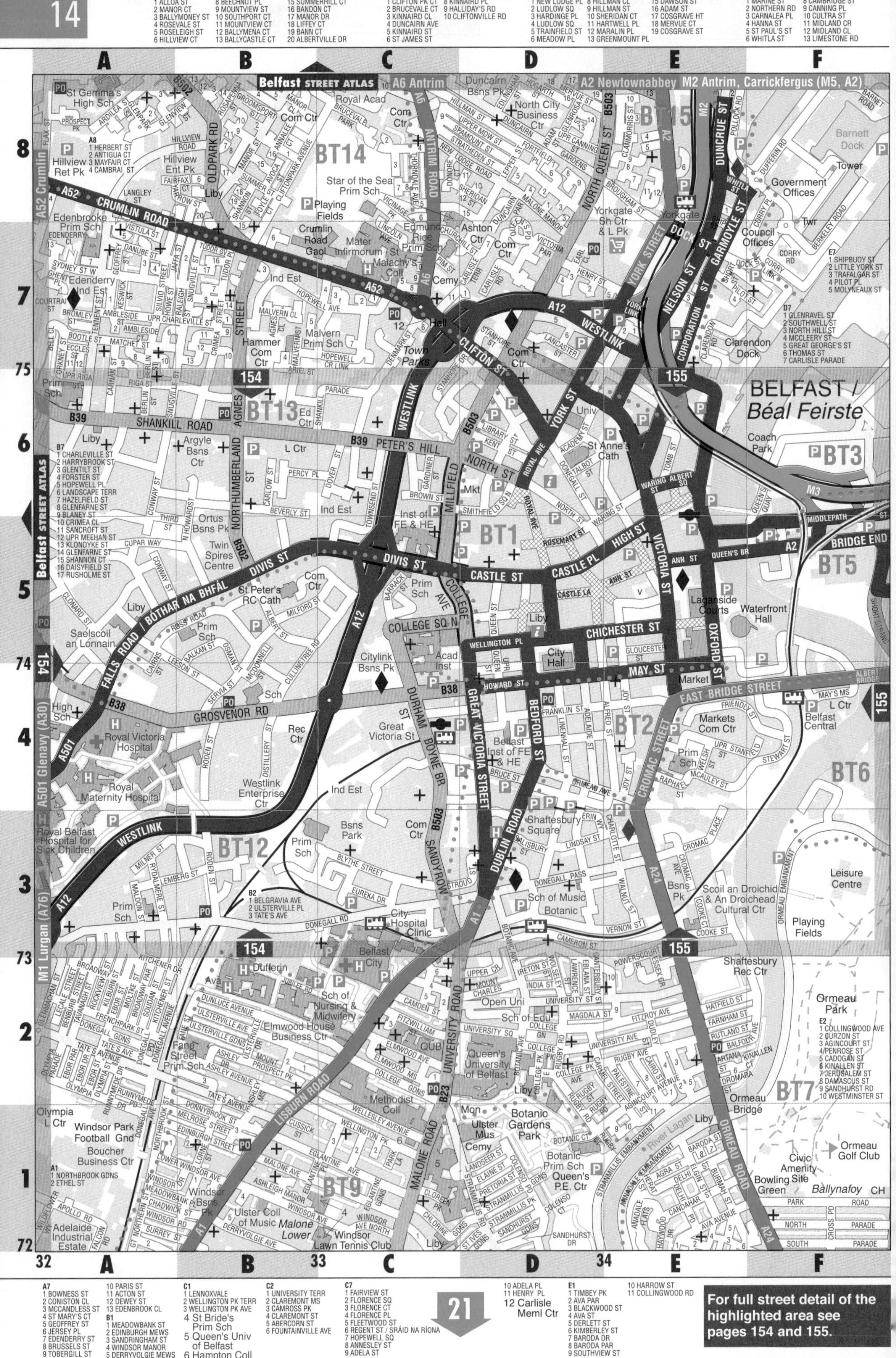
B8
1 ALLOA ST
2 MANOR CT
3 BALLYMONEY ST
4 ROSEVALE ST
5 ROSELEIGH ST
6 HILLVIEW CT
7 BEECHPARK ST
8 BEECHNUT PL
9 MOUNTVIEW ST
10 SOUTHPORT CT
11 MOUNTVIEW CT
12 BALLYMENA CT
13 BALLYCASTLE CT
14 ROSAPENNA CT
15 SUMMERHILL CT
16 BANDON CT
17 MANOR DR
18 LIFFEY CT
19 BANN CT
20 ALBERTVILLE DR
C8
1 CLIFTON PK CT
2 BRUCEVALE CT
3 KINNAIRD CL
4 DUNCAIRN AVE
5 KINNAIRD ST
6 ST JAMES ST
7 KINNAIRD TERR
8 KINNAIRD PL
9 HALLIDAY'S RD
10 CLIFTONVILLE RD
D8
1 NEW LODGE PL
2 LUDLOW SQ
3 HARDINGE PL
4 LUDLOW SQ
5 TRAINFIELD ST
6 MEADOW PL
7 MEADOW CL
8 HILLMAN CL
9 HILLMAN ST
10 SHERIDAN CT
11 HARTWELL PL
12 MARALIN PL
13 GREENMOUNT PL
14 GLENROSA LINK
15 DAWSON ST
16 ADAM ST
17 COSGRAVE HT
18 MERVUE CT
19 COSGRAVE ST
E8
1 MARINE ST
2 NORTHERN RD
3 CARNALEA PL
4 HANNA ST
5 ST PAUL'S ST
6 WHITLA ST
7 BENTINCK ST
8 CAMBRIDGE ST
9 CANNING PL
10 CULTRA ST
11 MIDLAND CR
12 MIDLAND CL
13 LIMESTONE RD
A B C D E F
Belfast STREET ATLAS
A6 Antrim
A2 Newtownabbey
M2 Antrim, Carrickfergus (M5, A2)
A8
1 HERBERT ST
2 ANTIGUA CT
3 MAYFAIR CT
4 CAMBRAI ST
A52 Crumlin
CRUMLIN ROAD
BT14
BT15
BT13
BT12
BT1
BT2
BT3
BT5
BT6
BT7
BT9
St Gemma's High Sch
Royal Acad
Duncairn Bsns Pk
North City Business Ctr
Barnett Dock
Tower
Government Offices
Hillview Ret Pk
Hillview Ent Pk
Star of the Sea Prim Sch
Playing Fields
Crumlin Road Gaol
Mater Infirmorum
Edmund Rice Prim Sch
St Malachy's Coll
Ashton Ctr
Com Ctr
Yorkgate Sh Ctr & L Pk
Yorkgate
Council Offices
Twr
E7
1 SHIPBUOY ST
2 LITTLE YORK ST
3 TEXAS ST
4 PILOT PL
5 MOLYNEAUX ST
D7
1 GLENRAVEL ST
2 SOUTHWELL ST
3 NORTH HILL ST
4 MCCLEERY ST
5 GREAT GEORGE'S ST
6 THOMAS ST
7 CARLISLE PARADE
Edenbrooke Prim Sch
Edenderry Ind Est
Malvern Prim Sch
Hammer Com Ctr
Town Parks
WESTLINK
Clarendon Dock
154
155
BELFAST / Béal Feirste
Coach Park
SHANKILL ROAD
PETER'S HILL
NORTH ST
Argyle Bsns Ctr
L Ctr
Univ
St Anne's Cath
B7
1 CHARLEVILLE ST
2 HARRYBROOK ST
3 GLENTILT ST
4 FORSTER ST
5 HOPEWELL PL
6 LANDSCAPE TERR
7 HAZELFIELD ST
8 GLENFARNE ST
9 BLANEY ST
10 CRIMEA CL
11 SANCROFT ST
12 UPR MEEHAN ST
13 KLONDYKE ST
14 GLENFARNE ST
15 SHANNON CT
16 DAISYFIELD ST
17 RUSHOLME ST
Ortus Bsns Pk
Twin Spires Centre
Ind Est
Inst of FE & HE
Mkt
DIVIS ST
CASTLE ST
CASTLE PL
HIGH ST
VICTORIA ST
QUEEN'S BR
BRIDGE END
MIDDLEPATH
FALLS ROAD / BÓTHAR NA BHFÁL
St Peter's RC Cath
Saelscoil an Lonnain
Prim Sch
COLLEGE SQ N
CHICHESTER ST
City Hall
Laganside Courts
Waterfront Hall
Citylink Bsns Pk
Acad Inst
MAY ST
Market
EAST BRIDGE STREET
OXFORD ST
High Sch
GROSVENOR RD
Royal Victoria Hospital
Royal Maternity Hospital
Great Victoria St
Belfast Inst of FE & HE
Markets Com Ctr
Belfast Central
L Ctr
Westlink Enterprise Ctr
Rec Ctr
GREAT VICTORIA STREET
DUBLIN ROAD
BEDFORD ST
CROMAC STREET
Royal Belfast Hospital for Sick Children
Shaftesbury Square
Bsns Park
Com Ctr
Sch of Music
Botanic
Bsns Pk
Scoil an Droichid & An Droichead Cultural Ctr
Leisure Centre
Playing Fields
City Hospital Clinic
B2
1 BELGRAVIA AVE
2 ULSTERVILLE PL
3 TATE'S AVE
M1 Lurgan (A76)
A501 Glenavy (A30)
Belfast City
Dufferin
Ava
Sch of Nursing & Midwifery
Elmwood House Business Ctr
Open Uni
Sch of Edu
QUB
Queen's University of Belfast
Shaftesbury Rec Ctr
Ormeau Park
E2
1 COLLINGWOOD AVE
2 CURZON ST
3 AGINCOURT ST
4 PENROSE ST
5 CADOGAN ST
6 KINALLEN ST
7 JERUSALEM ST
8 DAMASCUS ST
9 SANDHURST RD
10 WESTMINSTER ST
Fane Street Prim Sch
Methodist Coll
Ormeau Bridge
Olympia L Ctr
Windsor Park Football Gnd
Boucher Business Ctr
Ulster Mus
Botanic Gardens Park
Cemy
Botanic Prim Sch
Queen's P.E. Ctr
River Lagan
Civic Amenity Site
Bowling Green
Ormeau Golf Club
Ballynafoy
A1
1 NORTHBROOK GDNS
2 ETHEL ST
Windsor Bsns Pk
Ulster Coll of Music
Malone Lower
Windsor Lawn Tennis Club
Adelaide Industrial Estate
LISBURN ROAD
MALONE ROAD
UNIVERSITY ROAD
ORMEAU ROAD
32 33 34
A B C D E F
A7
1 BOWNESS ST
2 CONISTON CL
3 MCCANDLESS ST
4 ST MARY'S CT
5 GEOFFREY ST
6 JERSEY PL
7 EDENDERRY ST
8 BRUSSELS ST
9 TOBERGILL ST
10 PARIS ST
11 ACTON ST
12 DEWEY ST
13 EDENBROOK CL
B1
1 MEADOWBANK ST
2 EDINBURGH MEWS
3 SANDRINGHAM ST
4 WINDSOR MANOR
5 DERRYVOLGIE MEWS
C1
1 LENNOXVALE
2 WELLINGTON PK TERR
3 WELLINGTON PK AVE
4 St Bride's Prim Sch
5 Queen's Univ of Belfast
6 Hampton Coll
C2
1 UNIVERSITY TERR
2 CLAREMONT MS
3 CAMROSS PK
4 CLAREMONT ST
5 ABERCORN ST
6 FOUNTAINVILLE AVE
C7
1 FAIRVIEW ST
2 FLORENCE SQ
3 FLORENCE CT
4 FLORENCE PL
5 FLEETWOOD ST
6 REGENT ST / SRÁID NA RÍONA
7 HOPEWELL SQ
8 ANNESLEY ST
9 ADELA ST
10 ADELA PL
11 HENRY PL
12 Carlisle Meml Ctr
21
E1
1 TIMBEY PK
2 AVA PAR
3 BLACKWOOD ST
4 AVA ST
5 DERLETT ST
6 KIMBERLEY ST
7 BARODA DR
8 BARODA PAR
9 SOUTHVIEW ST
10 HARROW ST
11 COLLINGWOOD RD
For full street detail of the highlighted area see pages 154 and 155.

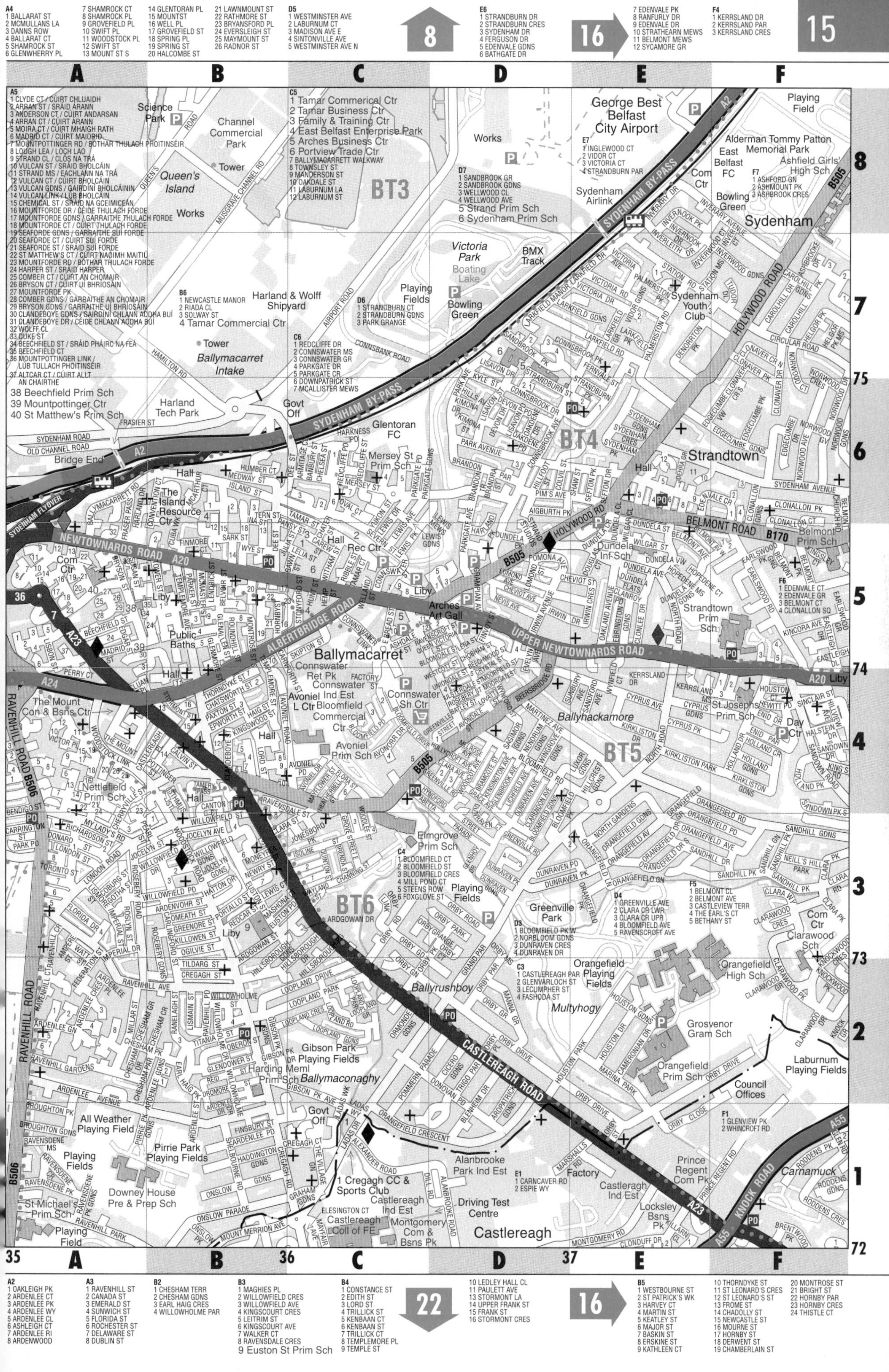

A4
1 BALLARAT ST
2 MCMULLANS LA
3 DANNS ROW
4 BALLARAT CT
5 SHAMROCK ST
6 GLENWHERRY PL
7 SHAMROCK CT
8 SHAMROCK PL
9 GROVEFIELD PL
10 SWIFT PL
11 WOODSTOCK PL
12 SWIFT ST
13 MOUNT ST S
14 GLENTORAN PL
15 MOUNTST
16 WELL PL
17 GROVEFIELD ST
18 SPRING PL
19 SPRING ST
20 HALCOMBE ST
21 LAWNMOUNT ST
22 RATHMORE ST
23 BRYANSFORD PL
24 EVERSLEIGH ST
25 MAYMOUNT ST
26 RADNOR ST
D5
1 WESTMINSTER AVE
2 LABURNUM CT
3 MADISON AVE E
4 SINTONVILLE AVE
5 WESTMINSTER AVE N
8
E6
1 STRANDBURN DR
2 STRANDBURN CRES
3 SYDENHAM DR
4 FERGUSON DR
5 EDENVALE GDNS
6 BATHGATE DR
16
7 EDENVALE PK
8 RANFURLY DR
9 EDENVALE DR
10 STRATHEARN MEWS
11 BELMONT MEWS
12 SYCAMORE GR
F4
1 KERRSLAND DR
2 KERRSLAND PAR
3 KERRSLAND CRES
15
A
B
C
D
E
F
George Best Belfast City Airport
Science Park
Channel Commercial Park
Queen's Island
Tower
Works
BT3
Victoria Park
Boating Lake
BMX Track
Playing Fields
Bowling Green
Harland & Wolff Shipyard
Ballymacarret Intake
Harland Tech Park
Govt Off
SYDENHAM BY-PASS
Glentoran FC
Sydenham Airlink
Sydenham
Alderman Tommy Patton Memorial Park
East Belfast FC
Ashfield Girls' High Sch
Sydenham Youth Club
HOLYWOOD ROAD
BT4
Strandtown
BELMONT ROAD
NEWTOWNARDS ROAD
ALBERTBRIDGE ROAD
UPPER NEWTOWNARDS ROAD
Ballymacarret
Arches Art Gall
Connswater Sh Ctr
Ballyhackamore
BT5
Strandtown Prim Sch
Dundela Inf Sch
St Joseph's Prim Sch
The Island Resource Ctr
Public Baths
Mersey St Prim Sch
Bloomfield Commercial Ctr
Avoniel Prim Sch
Nettlefield Prim Sch
Elmgrove Prim Sch
BT6
Greenville Park
Orangefield Playing Fields
Orangefield High Sch
Grosvenor Gram Sch
Orangefield Prim Sch
Ballyrushboy
Multyhogy
Gibson Park Playing Fields
Harding Meml Prim Sch
Ballymaconaghy
CASTLEREAGH ROAD
RAVENHILL ROAD
All Weather Playing Field
Pirrie Park Playing Fields
Downey House Pre & Prep Sch
St Michael's Prim Sch
Cregagh CC & Sports Club
Castlereagh Ind Est
Castlereagh Coll of FE
Montgomery Com & Bsns Pk
Alanbrooke Park Ind Est
Driving Test Centre
Castlereagh
Locksley Bsns Pk
Prince Regent Com Pk
Council Offices
Laburnum Playing Fields
Carnamuck
KNOCK ROAD
Clarawood Sch
35
36
37
72
73
74
75
8
7
6
5
4
3
2
1
A2
1 OAKLEIGH PK
2 ARDENLEE CT
3 ARDENLEE PK
4 ARDENLEE WY
5 ARDENLEE CL
6 ASHLEIGH CT
7 ARDENLEE RI
8 ARDENWOOD
A3
1 RAVENHILL ST
2 CANADA ST
3 EMERALD ST
4 SUNWICH ST
5 FLORIDA ST
6 ROCHESTER ST
7 DELAWARE ST
8 DUBLIN ST
B2
1 CHESHAM TERR
2 CHESHAM GDNS
3 EARL HAIG CRES
4 WILLOWHOLME PAR
B3
1 MAGHIES PL
2 WILLOWFIELD CRES
3 WILLOWFIELD AVE
4 KINGSCOURT CRES
5 LEITRIM ST
6 KINGSCOURT AVE
7 WALKER CT
8 RAVENSDALE CRES
9 Euston St Prim Sch
B4
1 CONSTANCE ST
2 EDITH ST
3 LORD ST
4 TRILLICK ST
5 KENBAAN CT
6 KENBAAN ST
7 TRILLICK CT
8 TEMPLEMORE PL
9 TEMPLE ST
10 LEDLEY HALL CL
11 PAULETT AVE
13 STORMONT LA
14 UPPER FRANK ST
15 FRANK ST
16 STORMONT CRES
22
16
B5
1 WESTBOURNE ST
2 ST PATRICK'S WK
3 HARVEY CT
4 MARTIN ST
5 KEATLEY ST
6 MAJOR ST
7 BASKIN ST
8 ERSKINE ST
9 KATHLEEN CT
10 THORNDYKE ST
11 ST LEONARD'S CRES
12 ST LEONARD'S ST
13 FROME ST
14 CHADOLLY ST
15 NEWCASTLE ST
16 MOURNE ST
17 HORNBY ST
18 DERWENT ST
19 CHAMBERLAIN ST
20 MONTROSE ST
21 BRIGHT ST
22 HORNBY PAR
23 HORNBY CRES
24 THISTLE CT

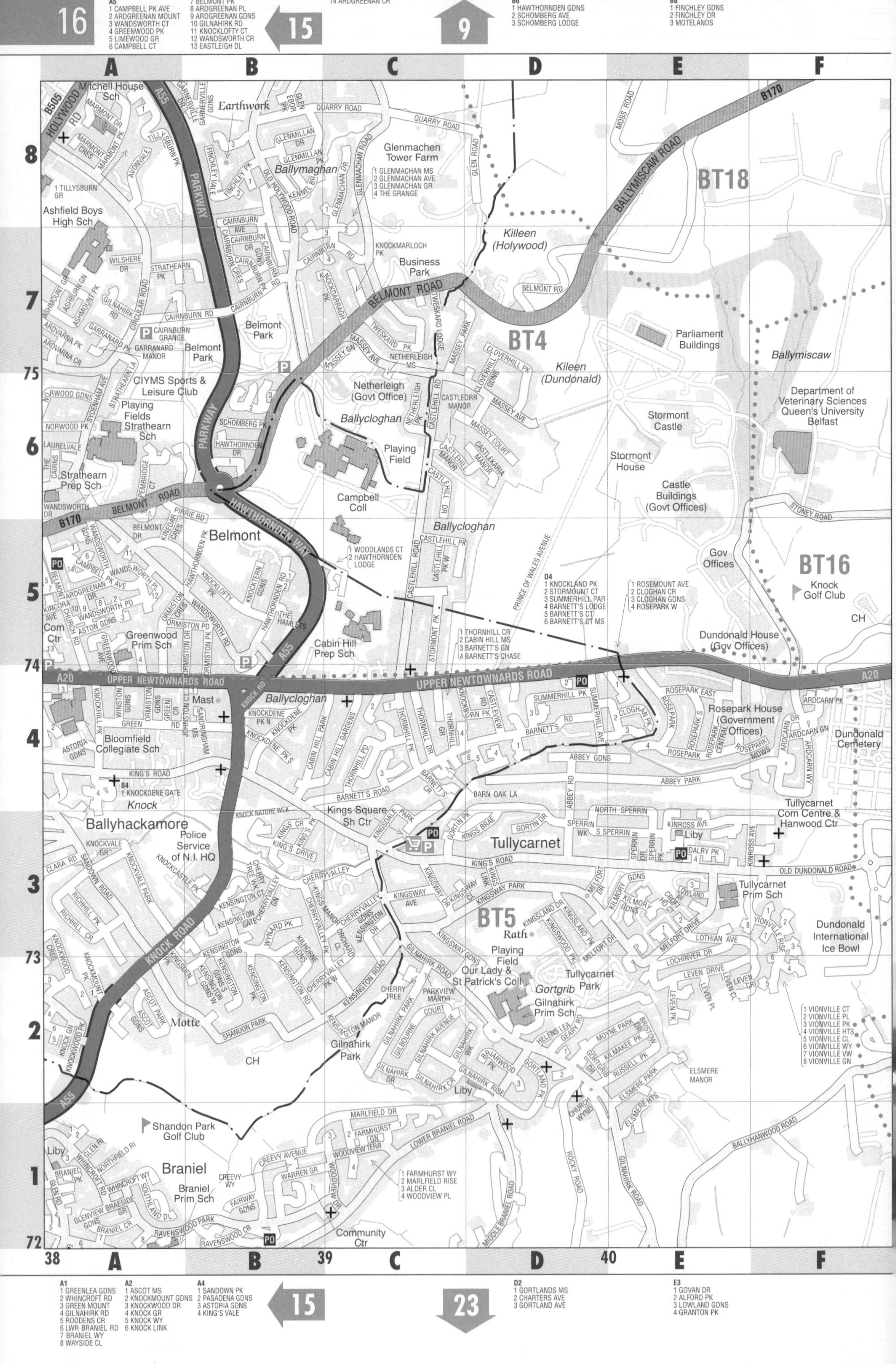
A5
1 CAMPBELL PK AVE
2 ARDGREENAN MOUNT
3 WANDSWORTH CT
4 GREENWOOD PK
5 LIMEWOOD GR
6 CAMPBELL CT
7 BELMONT PK
8 ARDGREENAN PL
9 ARDGREENAN GDNS
10 GILNAHIRK RD
11 KNOCKLOFTY CT
12 WANDSWORTH CR
13 EASTLEIGH DL
14 ARDGREENAN CR
15
9
B6
1 HAWTHORNDEN GDNS
2 SCHOMBERG AVE
3 SCHOMBERG LODGE
B8
1 FINCHLEY GDNS
2 FINCHLEY DR
3 MOTELANDS
A
B
C
D
E
F
8
7
75
6
5
74
4
3
73
2
1
72
38
39
40
BT18
BT4
BT16
BT5
Mitchell House Sch
Earthwork
Ballymaghan
Glenmachen Tower Farm
1 GLENMACHAN MS
2 GLENMACHAN AVE
3 GLENMACHAN GR
4 THE GRANGE
1 TILLYSBURN GR
Ashfield Boys High Sch
Killeen (Holywood)
Business Park
BELMONT ROAD
BALLYMISCAW ROAD
B170
QUARRY ROAD
MOSS ROAD
GLEN ROAD
PARKWAY
Belmont Park
CIYMS Sports & Leisure Club
Playing Fields Strathearn Sch
Strathearn Prep Sch
Netherleigh (Govt Office)
Ballycloghan
Playing Field
Campbell Coll
Parliament Buildings
Kileen (Dundonald)
Ballymiscaw
Stormont Castle
Stormont House
Castle Buildings (Govt Offices)
Department of Veterinary Sciences Queen's University Belfast
STONEY ROAD
Gov Offices
Knock Golf Club
Belmont
HAWTHORNDEN WAY
1 WOODLANDS CT
2 HAWTHORNDEN LODGE
PRINCE OF WALES AVENUE
D4
1 KNOCKLAND PK
2 STORMOUNT CT
3 SUMMERHILL PAR
4 BARNETT'S LODGE
5 BARNETT'S CT
6 BARNETT'S CT MS
1 ROSEMOUNT AVE
2 CLOGHAN CR
3 CLOGHAN GDNS
4 ROSEPARK W
1 THORNHILL CR
2 CABIN HILL MS
3 BARNETT'S GN
4 BARNETT'S CHASE
Greenwood Prim Sch
Cabin Hill Prep Sch
Dundonald House (Gov Offices)
Com Ctr
A20
UPPER NEWTOWNARDS ROAD
Mast
Bloomfield Collegiate Sch
Rosepark House (Government Offices)
Dundonald Cemetery
KING'S ROAD
B4
1 KNOCKDENE GATE
Knock
Ballyhackamore
Police Service of N.I. HQ
Kings Square Sh Ctr
Tullycarnet
Tullycarnet Com Centre & Hanwood Ctr
Liby
OLD DUNDONALD ROAD
Tullycarnet Prim Sch
Rath
Playing Field
Our Lady & St Patrick's Coll
Gortgrib
Tullycarnet Park
Gilnahirk Prim Sch
Dundonald International Ice Bowl
KNOCK ROAD
Motte
Gilnahirk Park
1 VIONVILLE CT
2 VIONVILLE PL
3 VIONVILLE PK
4 VIONVILLE HTS
5 VIONVILLE CL
6 VIONVILLE WY
7 VIONVILLE VW
8 VIONVILLE GN
ELSMERE MANOR
CH
Shandon Park Golf Club
Braniel
Braniel Prim Sch
1 FARMHURST WY
2 MARLFIELD RISE
3 ALDER CL
4 WOODVIEW PL
LOWER BRANIEL ROAD
BALLYHANWOOD ROAD
ROCKY ROAD
GILNAHIRK ROAD
MIDDLE BRANIEL ROAD
Community Ctr
A1
1 GREENLEA GDNS
2 WHINCROFT RD
3 GREEN MOUNT
4 GILNAHIRK RD
5 RODDENS CR
6 LWR BRANIEL RD
7 BRANIEL WY
8 WAYSIDE CL
A2
1 ASCOT MS
2 KNOCKMOUNT GDNS
3 KNOCKWOOD DR
4 KNOCK GR
5 KNOCK WY
6 KNOCK LINK
A4
1 SANDOWN PK
2 PASADENA GDNS
3 ASTORIA GDNS
4 KING'S VALE
15
23
D2
1 GORTLANDS MS
2 CHARTERS AVE
3 GORTLAND AVE
E3
1 GOVAN DR
2 ALFORD PK
3 LOWLAND GDNS
4 GRANTON PK

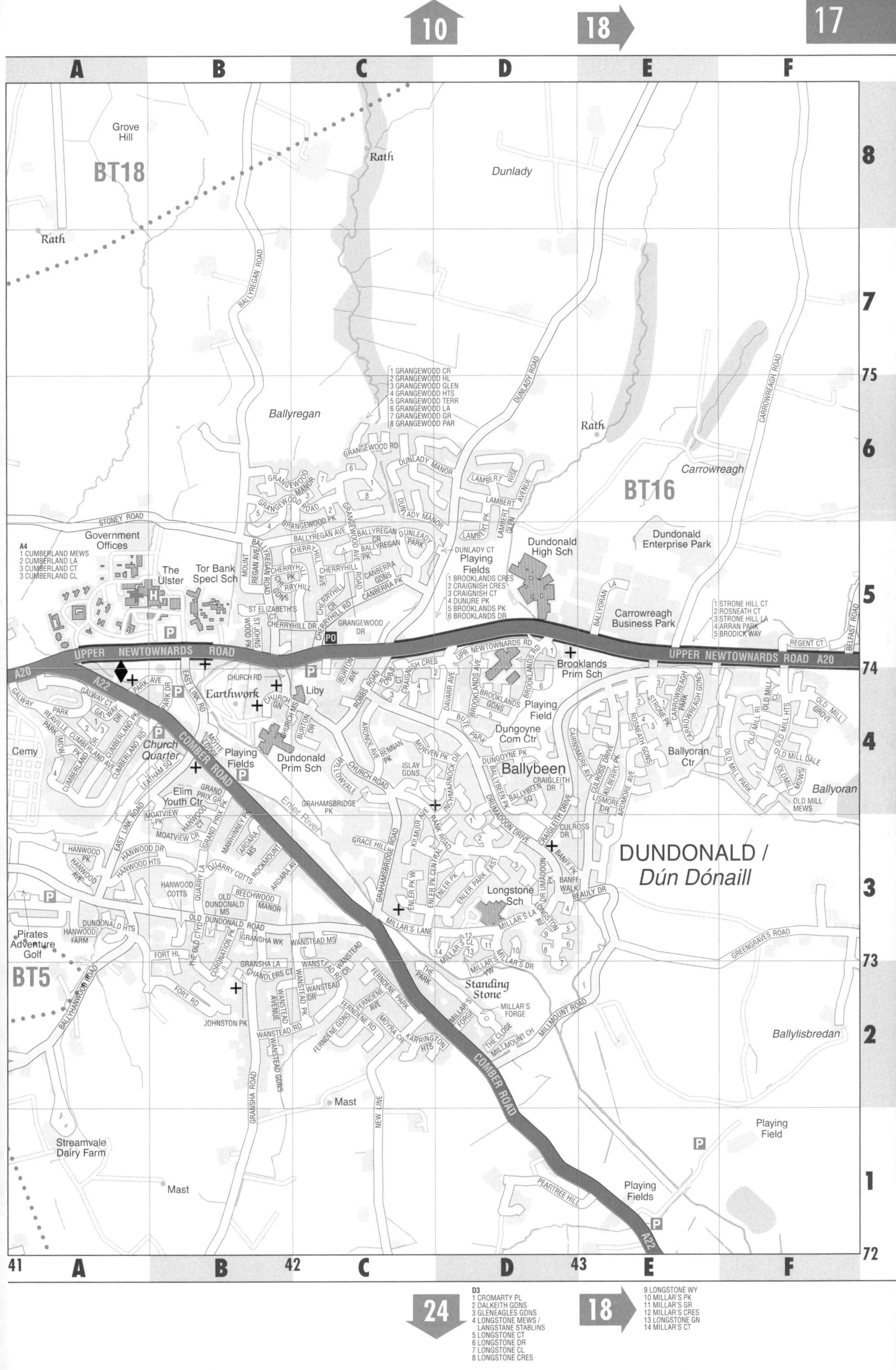
10
18
A
B
C
D
E
F
8
7
75
6
5
74
4
3
73
2
1
72
41
42
43
Grove Hill
BT18
Rath
Dunlady
Ballyregan
Carrowreagh
BT16
1 GRANGEWOOD CR
2 GRANGEWOOD HL
3 GRANGEWOOD GLEN
4 GRANGEWOOD HTS
5 GRANGEWOOD TERR
6 GRANGEWOOD LA
7 GRANGEWOOD GR
8 GRANGEWOOD PAR
BALLYREGAN ROAD
DUNLADY ROAD
CARROWREAGH ROAD
GRANGEWOOD RD
DUNLADY MANOR
LAMBERT RISE
LAMBERT AVENUE
LAMBERT PK
LAMBERT GLEN
STONEY ROAD
Government Offices
A4
1 CUMBERLAND MEWS
2 CUMBERLAND LA
3 CUMBERLAND CT
3 CUMBERLAND CL
The Ulster
Tor Bank Specl Sch
Dundonald High Sch
Dundonald Enterprise Park
Playing Fields
DUNLADY CT
1 BROOKLANDS CRES
2 CRAIGNISH CRES
3 CRAIGNISH CT
4 DUNURE PK
5 BROOKLANDS PK
6 BROOKLANDS DR
BALLYORAN LA
Carrowreagh Business Park
1 STRONE HILL CT
2 ROSNEATH CT
3 STRONE HILL LA
4 ARRAN PARK
5 BRODICK WAY
REGENT CT
BELFAST ROAD
UPPER NEWTOWNARDS ROAD
UPPER NEWTOWNARDS ROAD A20
A20
A22
PO
ST ELIZABETH'S CT
CHERRYHILL DR
GRANGEWOOD DR
Brooklands Prim Sch
CHURCH RD
Earthwork
Liby
Playing Field
Dungoyne Com Ctr
Church Quarter
Cemy
Playing Fields
Dundonald Prim Sch
Ballybeen
Ballyoran Ctr
Ballyoran
OLD MILL MEWS
COMBER ROAD
Elim Youth Ctr
Enler River
GRAHAMSBRIDGE PK
GRAHAMSBRIDGE ROAD
DUNDONALD / Dún Dónaill
Longstone Sch
MILLAR'S LANE
OLD DUNDONALD ROAD
Pirates Adventure Golf
BT5
BALLYHANWOOD ROAD
Standing Stone
MILLAR'S FORGE
MILLMOUNT ROAD
GREENGRAVES ROAD
Ballylisbredan
JOHNSTON PK
GRANSHA ROAD
NEW LINE
Mast
Playing Field
Streamvale Dairy Farm
PEARTREE HILL
A22
24
18
D3
1 CROMARTY PL
2 DALKEITH GDNS
3 GLENEAGLES GDNS
4 LONGSTONE MEWS / LANGSTANE STABLINS
5 LONGSTONE CT
6 LONGSTONE DR
7 LONGSTONE CL
8 LONGSTONE CRES
9 LONGSTONE WY
10 MILLAR'S PK
11 MILLAR'S GR
12 MILLAR'S CRES
13 LONGSTONE GN
14 MILLAR'S CT

17
11

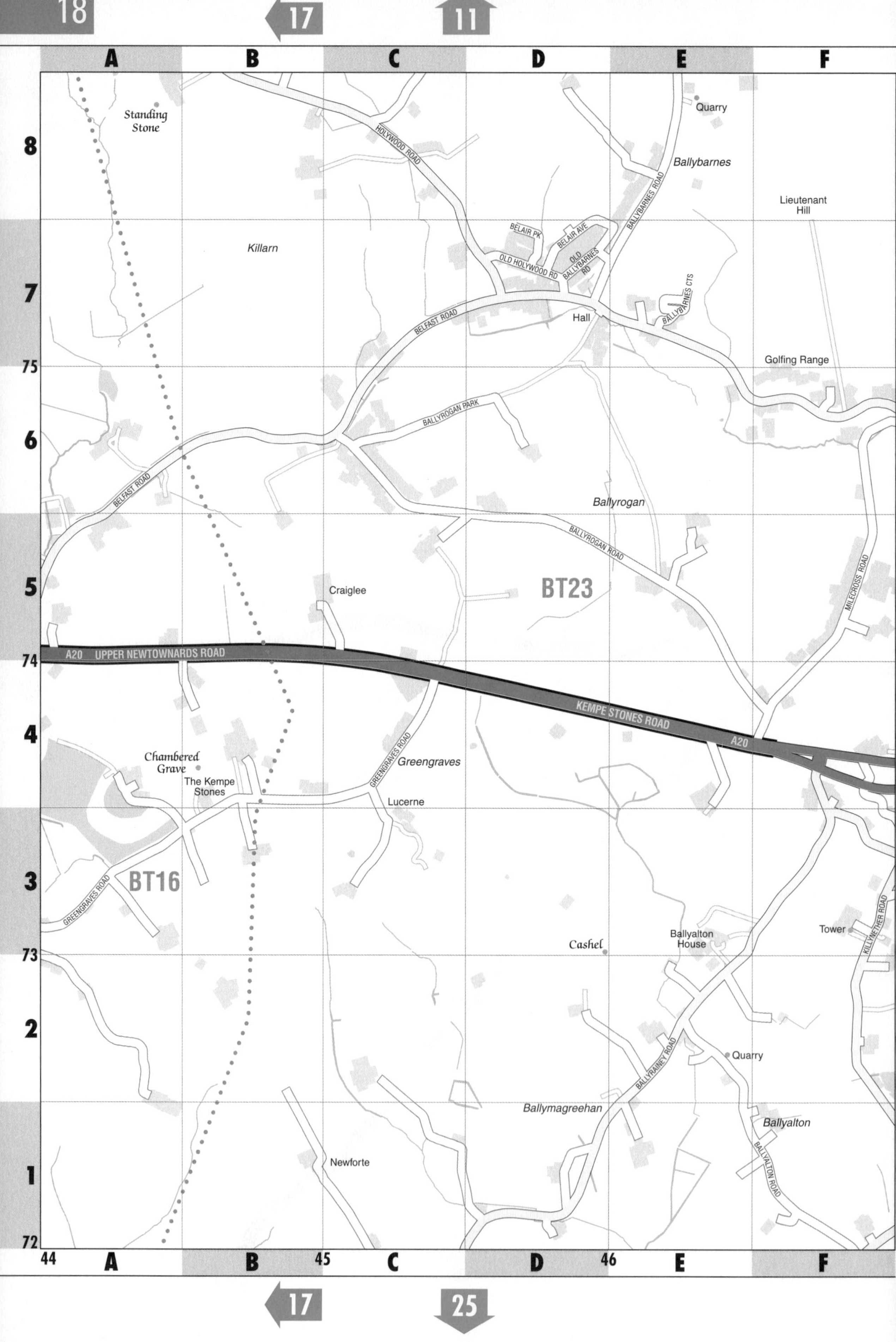
A
B
C
D
E
F
8
7
75
6
5
74
4
3
73
2
1
72
44
45
46
Standing Stone
Quarry
Ballybarnes
HOLYWOOD ROAD
BALLYBARNES ROAD
Lieutenant Hill
Killarn
BELAIR PK
BELAIR AVE
OLD HOLYWOOD RD
OLD BALLYBARNES RD
BALLYBARNES CTS
BELFAST ROAD
Hall
Golfing Range
BALLYROGAN PARK
Ballyrogan
BALLYROGAN ROAD
MILECROSS ROAD
Craiglee
BT23
A20 UPPER NEWTOWNARDS ROAD
KEMPE STONES ROAD
A20
Chambered Grave
The Kempe Stones
GREENGRAVES ROAD
Greengraves
Lucerne
BT16
Tower
KILLYNETHER ROAD
Ballyalton House
Cashel
Quarry
BALLYRAINEY ROAD
Ballymagreehan
Ballyalton
BALLYALTON ROAD
Newforte

17
25

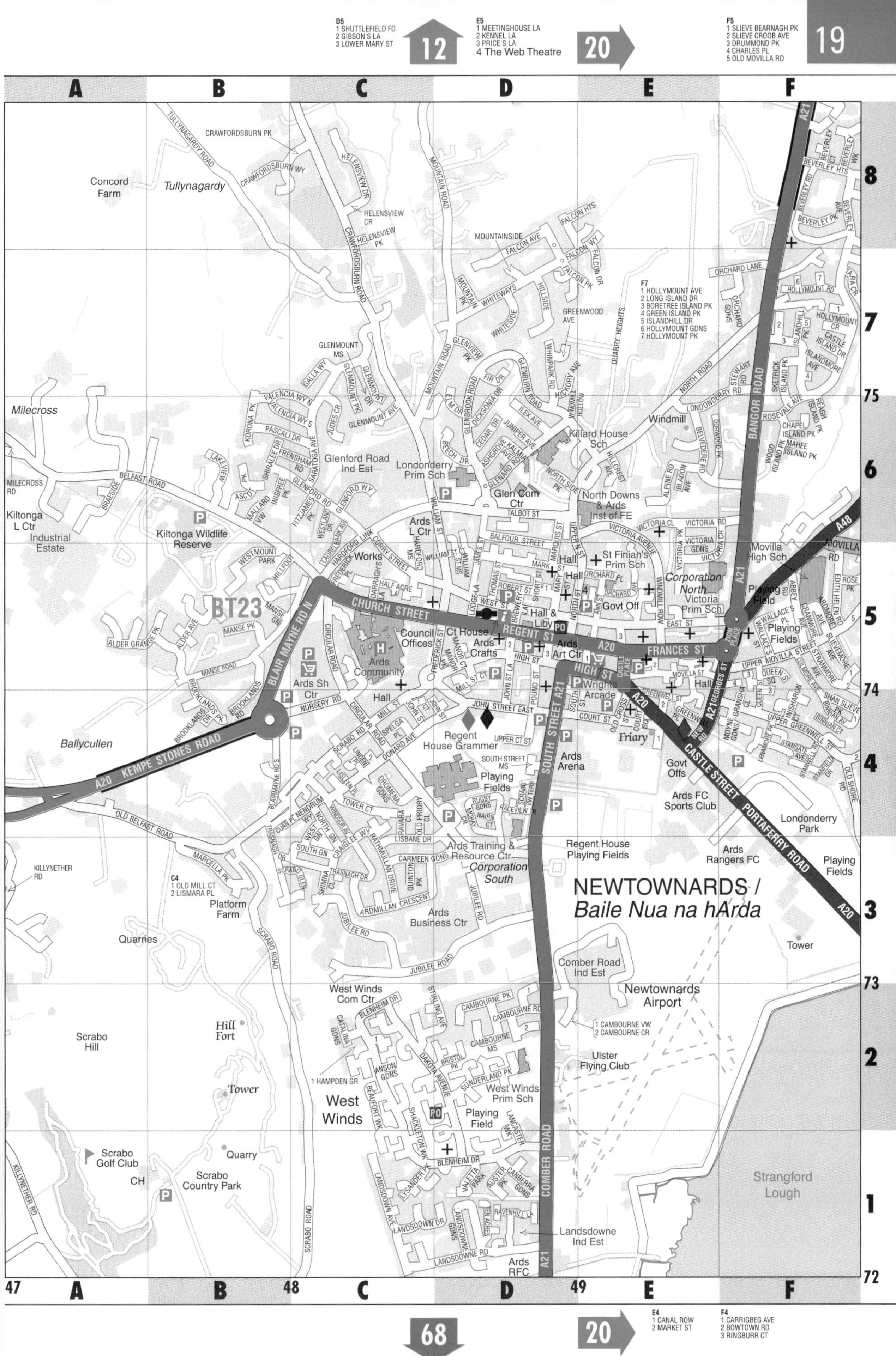
A
B
C
D
E
F
8
7
75
6
5
74
4
3
73
2
1
72
47
48
49
Concord Farm
Tullynagardy
TULLYNAGARDY ROAD
CRAWFORDSBURN PK
CRAWFORDSBURN WY
CRAWFORDSBURN ROAD
HELENSVIEW DR
HELENSVIEW CR
HELENSVIEW PK
MOUNTAIN ROAD
MOUNTAINSIDE
FALCON AVE
FALCON HTS
FALCON WY
FALCON DR
FALCON PK
WHITEWAYS
WHITESIDE
HILLSIDE
GREENWOOD AVE
QUARRY HEIGHTS
F7
1 HOLLYMOUNT AVE
2 LONG ISLAND DR
3 BORETREE ISLAND PK
4 GREEN ISLAND PK
5 ISLANDHILL DR
6 HOLLYMOUNT GDNS
7 HOLLYMOUNT PK
ORCHARD LANE
ORCHARD GDNS
BEVERLEY HTS
BEVERLEY PK
HOLLYMOUNT RD
HOLLYMOUNT CR
CASTLE ISLAND DR
ISLANDMORE AVE
GLENMOUNT MS
GALLA WY
GLENMOUNT PK
GLENMOUNT DR
GLENMOUNT AVE
GLENVIEW PK
FIR DR
GLENBURN ROAD
WHINPARK RD
HICKORY AVE
WINDMILL HOLLOW
NORTH ROAD
LONDONDERRY RD
STEWART RD
BANGOR ROAD
SKETRICK ISLAND PK
ROSEVALE AVE
REAGH ISLAND PK
CHAPEL ISLAND PK
MAHEE ISLAND PK
WOOD ISLAND PK
Milecross
MILECROSS RD
VALENCIA WY N
VALENCIA WY S
KORONA PK
PASCALI DR
JUDES CR
ELM DR
DICKSONIA DR
GLENBROOK ROAD
CEDAR DR
ILEX AVE
JUNIPER AVE
KALMIA AVE
ASHGROVE AVE
GLENARD RD
Killard House Sch
HILLCREST AVE
Windmill
BELVEDERE RD
DORWOOD PK
LAKEVIEW
SHIRALEE DR
FRENSHAM RD
SARATOGA AVE
Glenford Road Ind Est
Londonderry Prim Sch
BEECH DR
NORTH SIDE PK
ALPINE RD
BLADON AVE
BELFAST ROAD
BRAESIDE
ASCOT PK
MALLARD VW
INISFREE PK
GLENFORD RD
FITZJAMES PK
GLENFORD WY
Glen Com Ctr
TALBOT ST
North Downs & Ards Inst of FE
VICTORIA CL
VICTORIA RD
VICTORIA AVENUE
VICTORIA PK
VICTORIA GDNS
VICTORIA CR
Kiltonga L Ctr
Industrial Estate
Kiltonga Wildlife Reserve
Ards L Ctr
BALFOUR STREET
MARQUIS ST
UPPER N ST
Movilla High Sch
MOVILLA RD
A48
WESTMOUNT PARK
HILLPOOL
HARDFORD LINK
CORRY STREET
Works
WILLIAM ST
JAMES ST
MARK ST
Hall
St Finian's Prim Sch
ORCHARD PL
ORCHARD
Corporation North
Victoria Prim Sch
WINDMILL ROW
ABBEY RD
ROSE PK
EDITH HELEN RD
BT23
MANSE GN
MANSE PK
ALDER AVE
ALDER GRANGE PK
MANSE ROAD
BROOKLANDS PK
BROOKLANDS DR
BROOKLANDS RD
BLAIR MAYNE RD N
HALF ACRE LA
CHURCH STREET
THOMAS ST
ROBERT ST
WEST ST
SHORT ST
NORTH ST
ANN'S ST
Govt Off
EAST ST
Playing Field
WALLACE'S PL
CRANMORE AVE
Playing Fields
Council Offices
Ards Community
Ct House
Ards Crafts
REGENT ST
Hall & Liby
PO
Ards Art Ctr
A20
FRANCES ST
ZION PLACE
Ards Sh Ctr
CIRCULAR ROAD
FREDERICK ST
MANOR CT
HIGH ST
CASTLE PLACE
MOVILLA ST
UPPER MOVILLA STREET
QUEEN'S SQ
STRANMORE AVE
GEORGE'S ST
NURSERY RD
MILL ST
JOHN ST
MILL ST CT
JOHN STREET EAST
JOHN ST LA
POUND ST
SOUTH ST
Wrights Arcade
GREENWELL ST
OLD CROSS ST
COURT ST
COURT SQ
Friary
MOYNE GDNS
GRANSHA CL
QUEEN ST
INISHARON
SHAN SLIEVE PK
BINNIAN CL
UPPER GREENWELL ST
STANGATE AVE
STANFIELD DR
OLD SHORE RD
Ballycullen
KEMPE STONES ROAD
SCRABO RD
SPELGA PL
DONARD AVE
Regent House Grammer
UPPER CT ST
SOUTH STREET
South Street MS
Ards Arena
Govt Offs
CASTLE STREET
PORTAFERRY ROAD
Playing Fields
Ards FC Sports Club
Londonderry Park
BLAIRMAYNE RD S
LISLEN PL
DROMENA GDNS
TOWER CT
RUGBY GDNS
NAIRN CT
RACEVIEW TR
OLD BELFAST ROAD
NENDRUM WY
WINDSOR AV
CRAIGLEE WY
RATHMULLAN DRIVE
LISBANE DR
OLD PRIORY CL
RAVARA CL
Ards Training & Resource Ctr
Regent House Playing Fields
Ards Rangers FC
KILLYNETHER RD
MARCELLA PK
C4
1 OLD MILL CT
2 LISMARA PL
SOUTH GN
TRASNAGH DR
CARMEEN GDNS
QUINTON PK
Corporation South
NEWTOWNARDS /
Baile Nua na hArda
Platform Farm
SHIMNA CL
ARDMILLAN CRESCENT
JUBILEE RD
Ards Business Ctr
JUBILEE ROAD
Quarries
SCRABO ROAD
Tower
Comber Road Ind Est
Newtownards Airport
West Winds Com Ctr
BLENHEIM DR
CATALINA GDNS
STIRLING AVE
CAMBOURNE PK
CAMBOURNE RD
CAMBOURNE MS
1 CAMBOURNE VW
2 CAMBOURNE CR
Scrabo Hill
Hill Fort
ANSON GDNS
BRISTOL PK
DAKOTA AVENUE
SUNDERLAND PK
Ulster Flying Club
1 HAMPDEN GR
West Winds Prim Sch
West Winds
BEAUFORT WK
SHACKLETON WK
Playing Field
LANCASTER WK
COMBER ROAD
Scrabo Golf Club
CH
Quarry
Scrabo Country Park
LYSANDER PK
VALETTA PARK
AUSTER PK
CANBERRA GDNS
Strangford Lough
LANSDOWN AVE
LANSDOWN DR
LANSDOWNE GDNS
TEN ACRES
RAVENHILL LA
Landsdowne Ind Est
LANDSDOWNE RD
Ards RFC
A21

A6
1 ST COLUMBAS VALE
2 ST COLUMBA'S DR

A7
1 NEWTOWN DR
2 NEWTOWN WY
3 PARKLAND CR

A8
1 NEWTOWN WY
2 NEWTOWN HTS

19 13 66

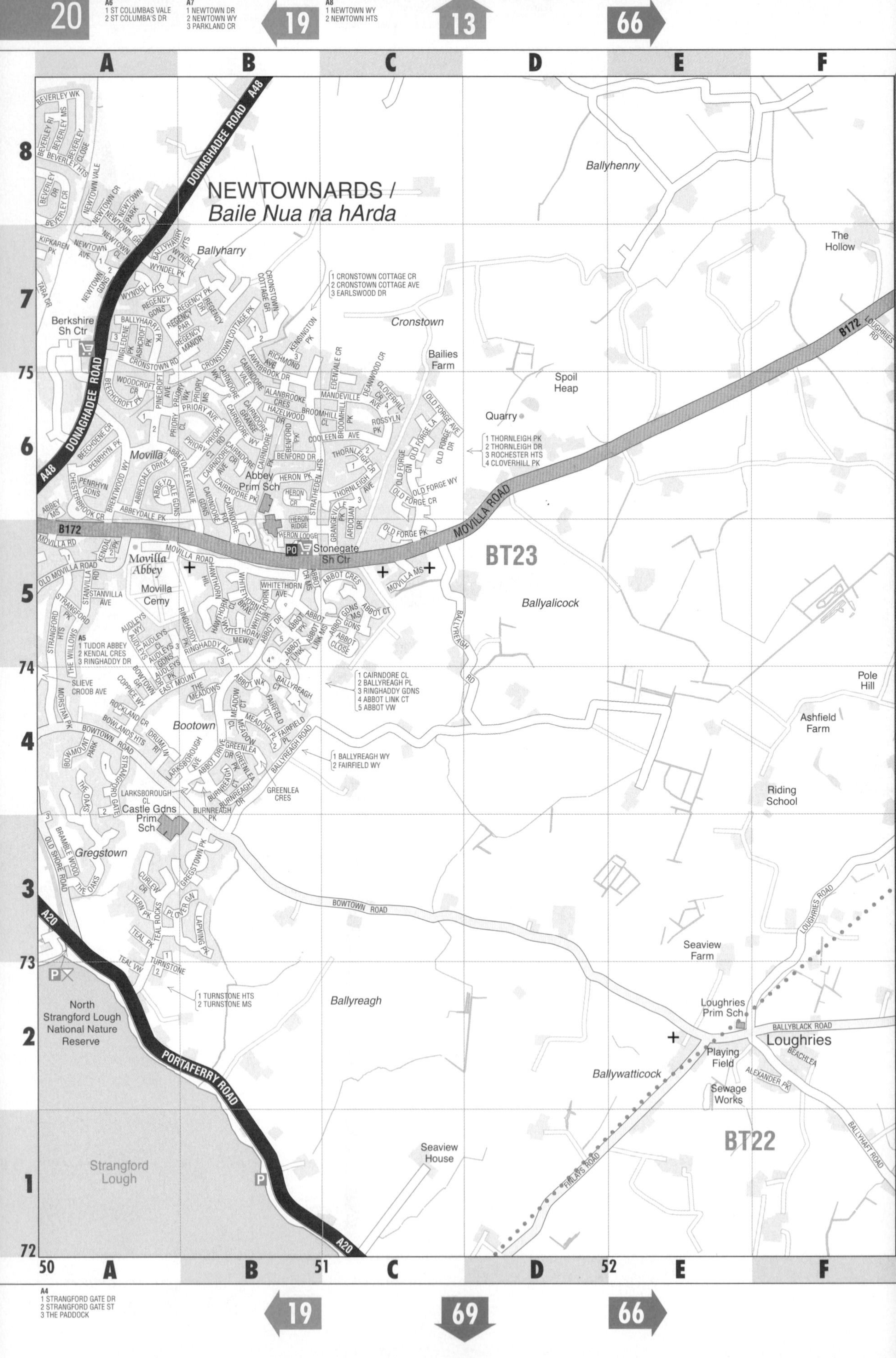

A4
1 STRANGFORD GATE DR
2 STRANGFORD GATE ST
3 THE PADDOCK

19 69 66

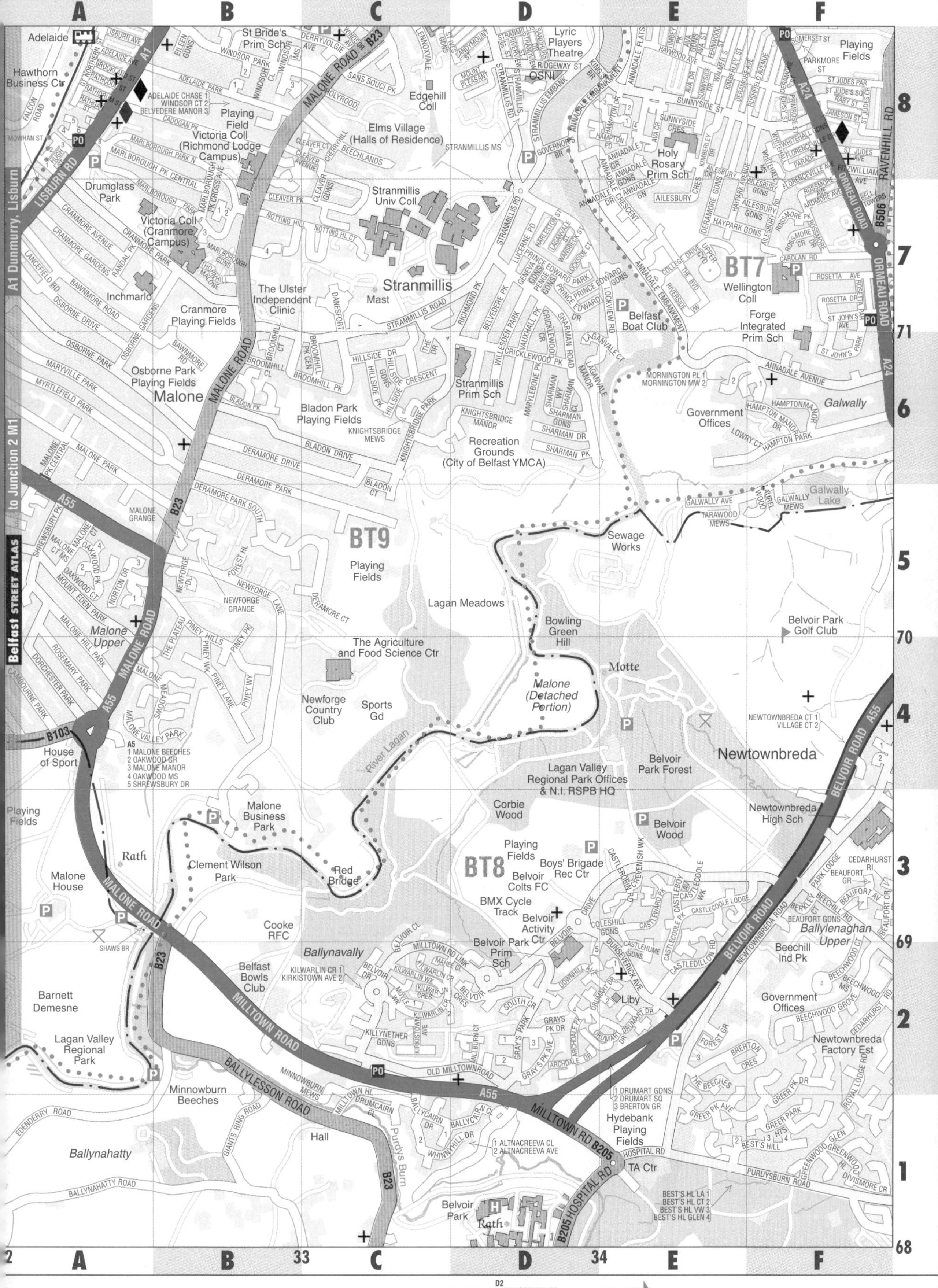
Adelaide
Hawthorn Business Ctr
St Bride's Prim Sch
Lyric Players Theatre
OSNI
Playing Fields
Edgehill Coll
Playing Field
Victoria Coll (Richmond Lodge Campus)
Elms Village (Halls of Residence)
Drumglass Park
Stranmillis Univ Coll
Holy Rosary Prim Sch
Victoria Coll (Cranmore Campus)
Inchmarlo
BT7
Wellington Coll
Stranmillis
The Ulster Independent Clinic
Mast
Cranmore Playing Fields
Belfast Boat Club
Forge Integrated Prim Sch
Osborne Park Playing Fields
Malone
Stranmillis Prim Sch
Bladon Park Playing Fields
Government Offices
Galwally
Recreation Grounds (City of Belfast YMCA)
Galwally Lake
BT9
Sewage Works
Playing Fields
Lagan Meadows
Bowling Green Hill
Belvoir Park Golf Club
Malone Upper
The Agriculture and Food Science Ctr
Motte
Malone (Detached Portion)
Newforge Country Club
Sports Gd
House of Sport
Newtownbreda
Belvoir Park Forest
Lagan Valley Regional Park Offices & N.I. RSPB HQ
Playing Fields
Malone Business Park
Corbie Wood
Newtownbreda High Sch
Belvoir Wood
Rath
Clement Wilson Park
Red Bridge
BT8
Playing Fields
Boys' Brigade Rec Ctr
Belvoir Colts FC
Malone House
BMX Cycle Track
Belvoir Activity Ctr
Cooke RFC
Belvoir Park Prim Sch
Ballylenaghan Upper
Ballynavally
Belfast Bowls Club
Beechill Ind Pk
Barnett Demesne
Liby
Government Offices
Lagan Valley Regional Park
Newtownbreda Factory Est
Minnowburn Beeches
Hydebank Playing Fields
Hall
Ballynahatty
TA Ctr
Belvoir Park
MALONE ROAD
MILLTOWN ROAD
BALLYLESSON ROAD
BELVOIR ROAD
ORMEAU ROAD
STRANMILLIS ROAD
LISBURN RD
A1 Dunmurry, Lisburn
to Junction 2 M1
Belfast STREET ATLAS
A5
1 MALONE BEECHES
2 OAKWOOD GR
3 MALONE MANOR
4 OAKWOOD MS
5 SHREWSBURY DR
1 DRUMART GDNS
2 DRUMART SQ
3 BRERTON GR
1 ALTNACREEVA CL
2 ALTNACREEVA AVE
BEST'S HL LA 1
BEST'S HL CT 2
BEST'S HL VW 3
BEST'S HL GLEN 4
NEWTOWNBREDA CT 1
VILLAGE CT 2
MORNINGTON PL 1
MORNINGTON MW 2
ADELAIDE CHASE 1
WINDSOR CT 2
BELVEDERE MANOR 3
KILWARLIN CR 1
KIRKISTOWN AVE 2

A6
1 DRUMKEEN MANOR
2 BRADFORD PL
3 UPPER GALWALLY RD
4 BRADFORD CT
5 Civic Ctr

A4
1 MOUNT ORIEL
2 ROGERS PL

21

C7
1 DOWNSHIRE PARK CENTRAL

15

C8
1 DOWNSHIRE PK
2 MONTGOMERY CT

D8
1 CARNAMENA GDNS
2 CARNAMENA PK
3 GLENSHARRAGH PK

F8
1 CASAELDONA DR
2 LEAD HILL VW

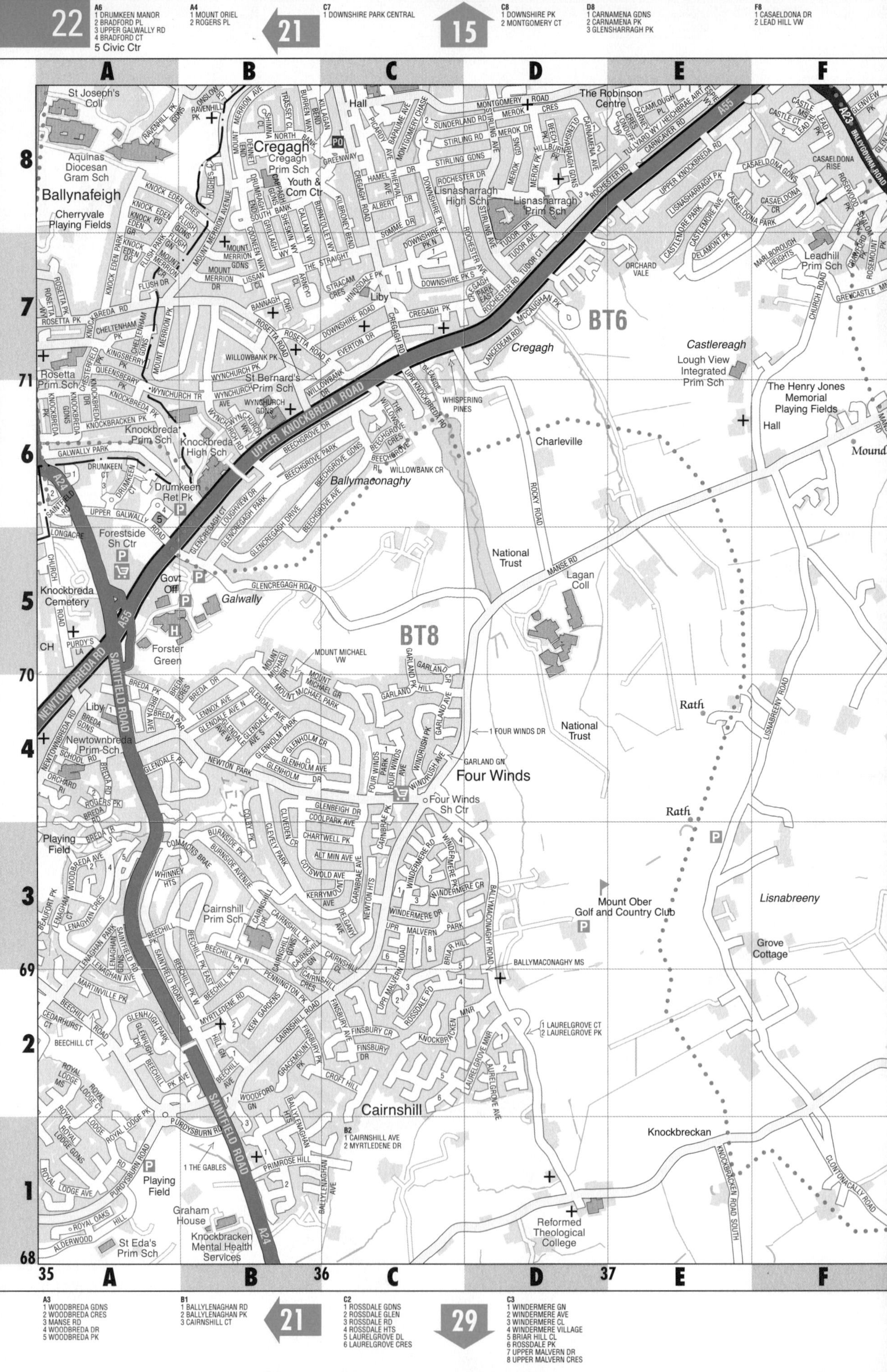

A3
1 WOODBREDA GDNS
2 WOODBREDA CRES
3 MANSE RD
4 WOODBREDA DR
5 WOODBREDA PK

B1
1 BALLYLENAGHAN RD
2 BALLYLENAGHAN PK
3 CAIRNSHILL CT

21

C2
1 ROSSDALE GDNS
2 ROSSDALE GLEN
3 ROSSDALE RD
4 ROSSDALE HTS
5 LAURELGROVE DL
6 LAURELGROVE CRES

29

C3
1 WINDERMERE GN
2 WINDERMERE AVE
3 WINDERMERE CL
4 WINDERMERE VILLAGE
5 BRIAR HILL CL
6 ROSSDALE PK
7 UPPER MALVERN DR
8 UPPER MALVERN CRES

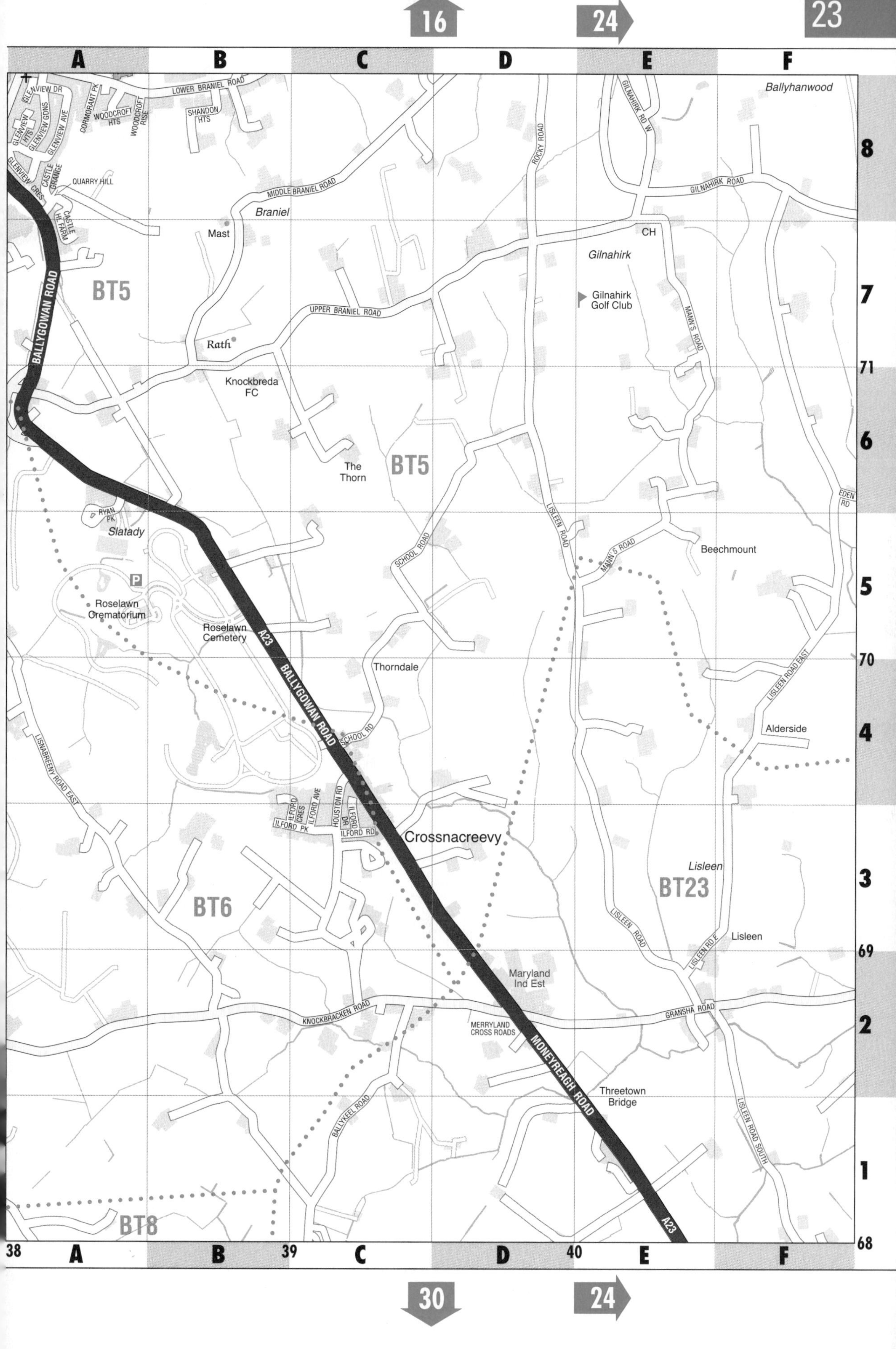
16
24
A
B
C
D
E
F
8
7
71
6
5
70
4
3
69
2
1
68
38
39
40
GLENVIEW DR
GLENVIEW HTS
GLENVIEW GDNS
GLENVIEW AVE
GLENVIEW CRES
CORMORANT PK
WOODCROFT HTS
WOODCROFT RISE
LOWER BRANIEL ROAD
SHANDON HTS
CASTLE GRANGE
QUARRY HILL
CASTLE HILL FARM
MIDDLE BRANIEL ROAD
Braniel
Mast
BT5
BALLYGOWAN ROAD
UPPER BRANIEL ROAD
Rath
Knockbreda FC
ROCKY ROAD
GILNAHIRK RD W
Ballyhanwood
GILNAHIRK ROAD
CH
Gilnahirk
Gilnahirk Golf Club
MANN'S ROAD
The Thorn
BT5
EDEN RD
RYAN PK
Slatady
LISLEEN ROAD
SCHOOL ROAD
MANN'S ROAD
Beechmount
P
Roselawn Crematorium
Roselawn Cemetery
A23
BALLYGOWAN ROAD
Thorndale
LISLEEN ROAD EAST
Alderside
SCHOOL RD
LISNABREENY ROAD EAST
ILFORD CRES
ILFORD AVE
HOUSTON RD
ILFORD DR
ILFORD PK
ILFORD RD
Crossnacreevy
Lisleen
BT6
BT23
LISLEEN ROAD
LISLEEN RD E
Lisleen
Maryland Ind Est
KNOCKBRACKEN ROAD
MERRYLAND CROSS ROADS
GRANSHA ROAD
MONEYREAGH ROAD
Threetown Bridge
BALLYKEEL ROAD
LISLEEN ROAD SOUTH
BT8
A23
30
24

23
17

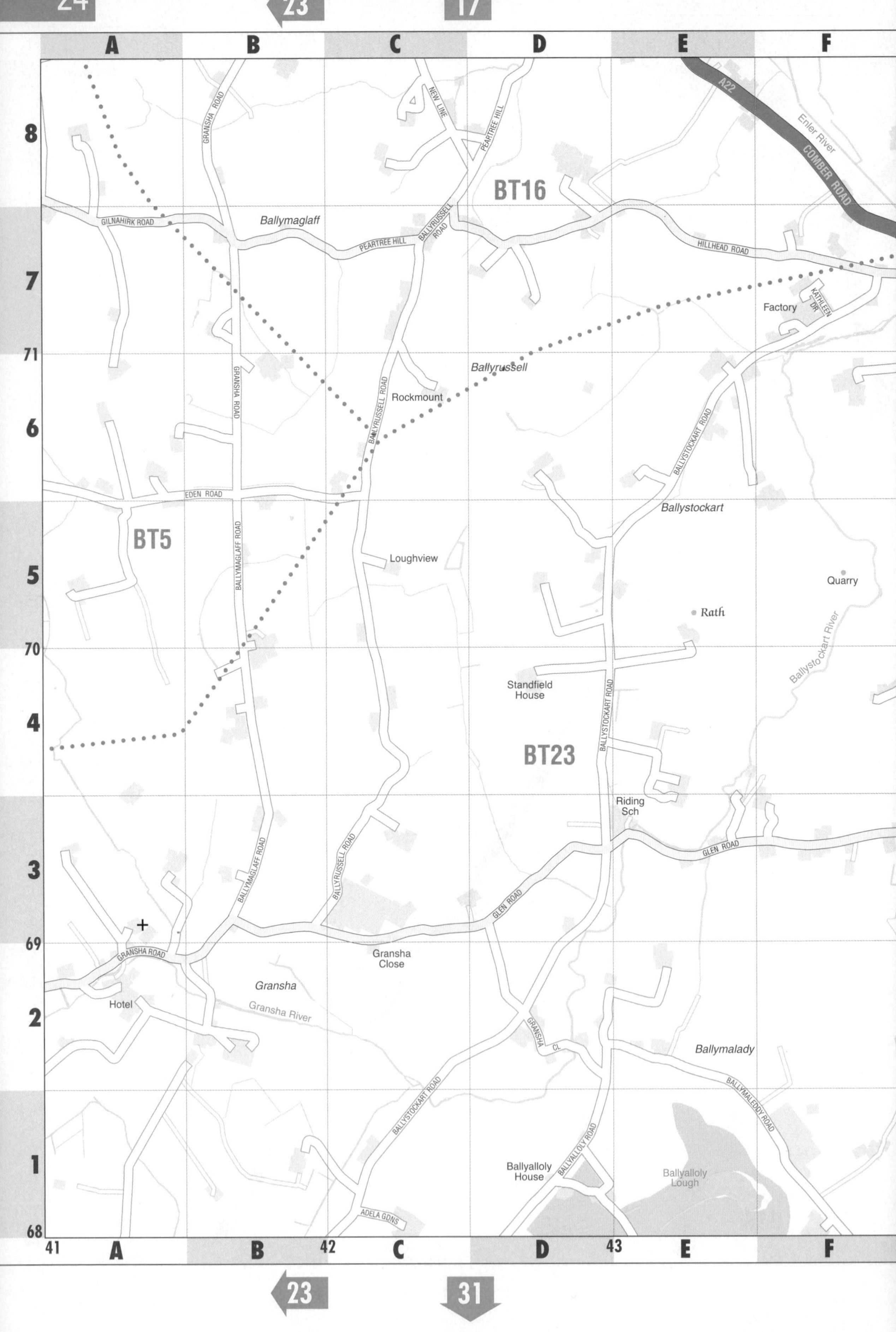
A
B
C
D
E
F
8
7
71
6
5
70
4
3
69
2
1
68
41
42
43
GILNAHIRK ROAD
GRANSHA ROAD
NEW LINE
PEARTREE HILL
BT16
A22
Enler River
COMBER ROAD
Ballymaglaff
PEARTREE HILL
BALLYRUSSELL ROAD
HILLHEAD ROAD
KATHLEEN DR
Factory
Ballyrussell
Rockmount
BALLYRUSSELL ROAD
BALLYSTOCKART ROAD
EDEN ROAD
Ballystockart
BT5
BALLYMAGLAFF ROAD
Loughview
Quarry
Rath
Ballystockart River
Standfield House
BT23
BALLYSTOCKART ROAD
Riding Sch
GLEN ROAD
BALLYMAGLAFF ROAD
BALLYRUSSELL ROAD
GLEN ROAD
GRANSHA ROAD
Gransha Close
Gransha
Hotel
Gransha River
GRANSHA CL
Ballymalady
BALLYMALEDDY ROAD
BALLYSTOCKART ROAD
BALLYALLOLY ROAD
Ballyalloly House
Ballyalloly Lough
ADELA GDNS

23
31

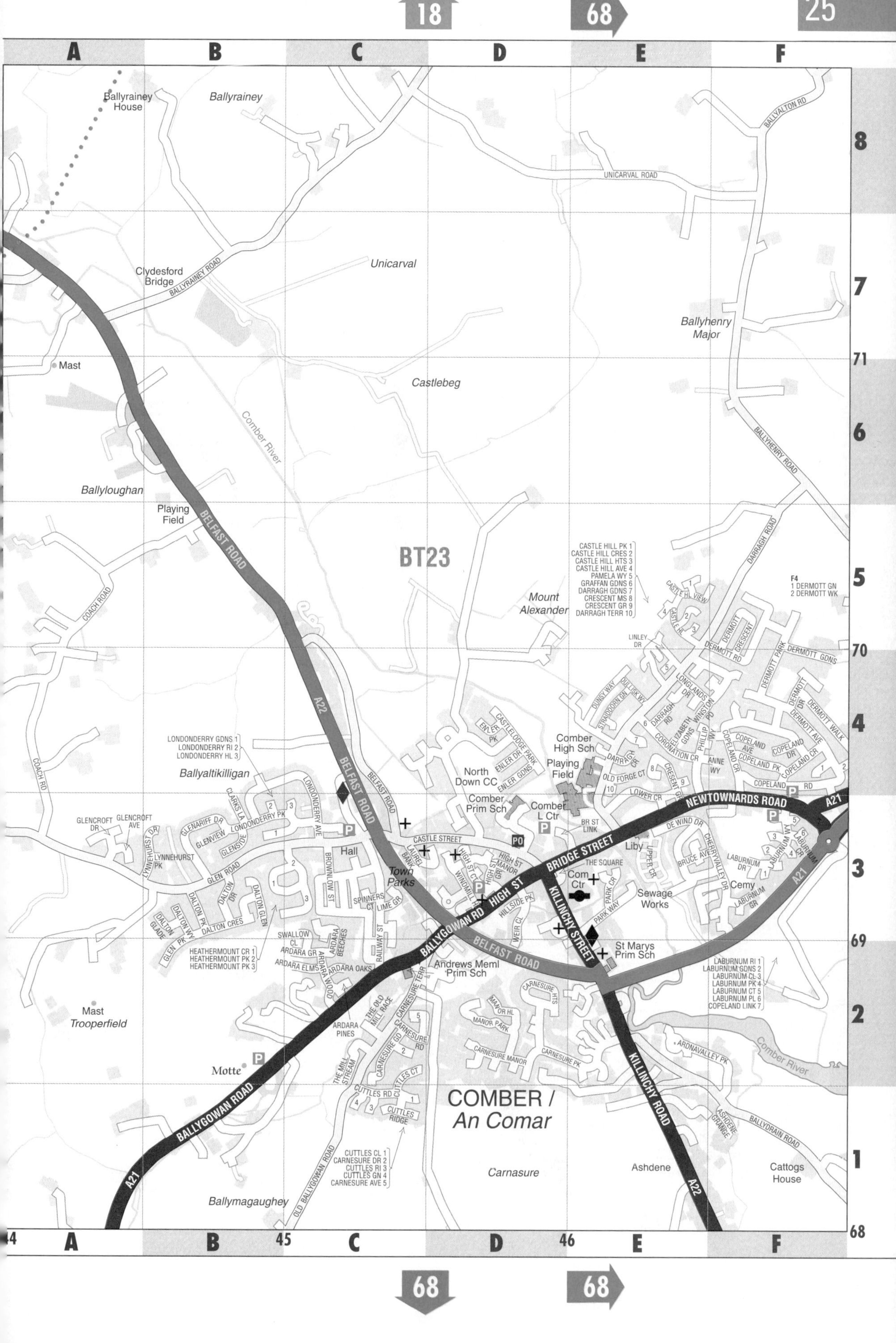
18
68
68
68
A
B
C
D
E
F
8
7
71
6
5
70
4
3
69
2
1
68
44
45
46
Ballyrainey House
Ballyrainey
UNICARVAL ROAD
BALLYALTON RD
Clydesford Bridge
BALLYRAINEY ROAD
Unicarval
Ballyhenry Major
Mast
Castlebeg
Comber River
BALLYHENRY ROAD
Ballyloughan
Playing Field
BELFAST ROAD
BT23
DARRAGH ROAD
COACH ROAD
Mount Alexander
CASTLE HILL PK 1
CASTLE HILL CRES 2
CASTLE HILL HTS 3
CASTLE HILL AVE 4
PAMELA WY 5
GRAFFAN GDNS 6
DARRAGH GDNS 7
CRESCENT MS 8
CRESCENT GR 9
DARRAGH TERR 10
F4
1 DERMOTT GN
2 DERMOTT WK
LINLEY DR
DERMOTT RD
DERMOTT CRESCENT
DERMOTT PARK
DERMOTT GDNS
DERMOTT DR
DERMOTT AVE
DERMOTT WALK
LONGLANDS DR
A22
LONDONDERRY GDNS 1
LONDONDERRY RI 2
LONDONDERRY HL 3
Ballyaltikilligan
CASTLELODGE PARK
ENLER PK
ENLER DR
ENLER GDNS
North Down CC
Comber High Sch
Playing Field
COPELAND AVE
COPELAND DR
COPELAND PK
COPELAND CR
COPELAND RD
ANNE WY
CORONATION CR
OLD FORGE CT
LOWER CR
NEWTOWNARDS ROAD
A21
Comber Prim Sch
Comber L Ctr
BR ST LINK
GLENCROFT DR
GLENCROFT AVE
GLENARIFF DR
LONDONDERRY PK
LONDONDERRY AVE
CLARKS LA
GLENVIEW
GLENSIDE
LYNNEHURST DR
LYNNEHURST PK
GLEN ROAD
Hall
CASTLE STREET
PO
BRIDGE STREET
Liby
DE WIND DR
THE SQUARE
BRUCE AVE
CHERRYVALLEY DR
LABURNUM DR
LABURNUM WY
LABURNUM GR
Cemy
Com Ctr
Sewage Works
Town Parks
BROWNLOW ST
DALTON DR
DALTON GLEN
DALTON PK
DALTON WY
DALTON GLADE
GLEN PK
DALTON CRES
SPINNERS CT
LIME GR
HIGH ST
HILLSIDE PK
KILLINCHY STREET
PARK WAY
PARK CR
WINDMILL
WEIR CL
BALLYGOWAN RD
HEATHERMOUNT CR 1
HEATHERMOUNT PK 2
HEATHERMOUNT PK 3
SWALLOW CL
ARDARA GR
ARDARA ELMS
ARDARA BEECHES
ARDARA OAKS
ARDARA WOOD
RAILWAY ST
Andrews Meml Prim Sch
St Marys Prim Sch
LABURNUM RI 1
LABURNUM GDNS 2
LABURNUM CL 3
LABURNUM PK 4
LABURNUM CT 5
LABURNUM PL 6
COPELAND LINK 7
Mast
Trooperfield
ARDARA PINES
THE OLD MILL RACE
CARNESURE TERR
CARNESURE HTS
MANOR HL
MANOR PARK
CARNESURE MANOR
CARNESURE PK
ARDNAVALLEY PK
Comber River
Motte
THE MILL STREAM
CARNESURE GD
CARNESURE RD
CUTTLES CT
CUTTLES RD
CUTTLES RIDGE
KILLINCHY ROAD
BALLYGOWAN ROAD
COMBER /
An Comar
ASHDENE GRANGE
BALLYDRAIN ROAD
CUTTLES CL 1
CARNESURE DR 2
CUTTLES RI 3
CUTTLES GN 4
CARNESURE AVE 5
OLD BALLYGOWAN ROAD
Carnasure
Ashdene
Cattogs House
Ballymagaughey

F8
1 ELM CORNER
2 OAKLAND WY
3 WILLOW CT
4 Kilmakee Activity Ctr

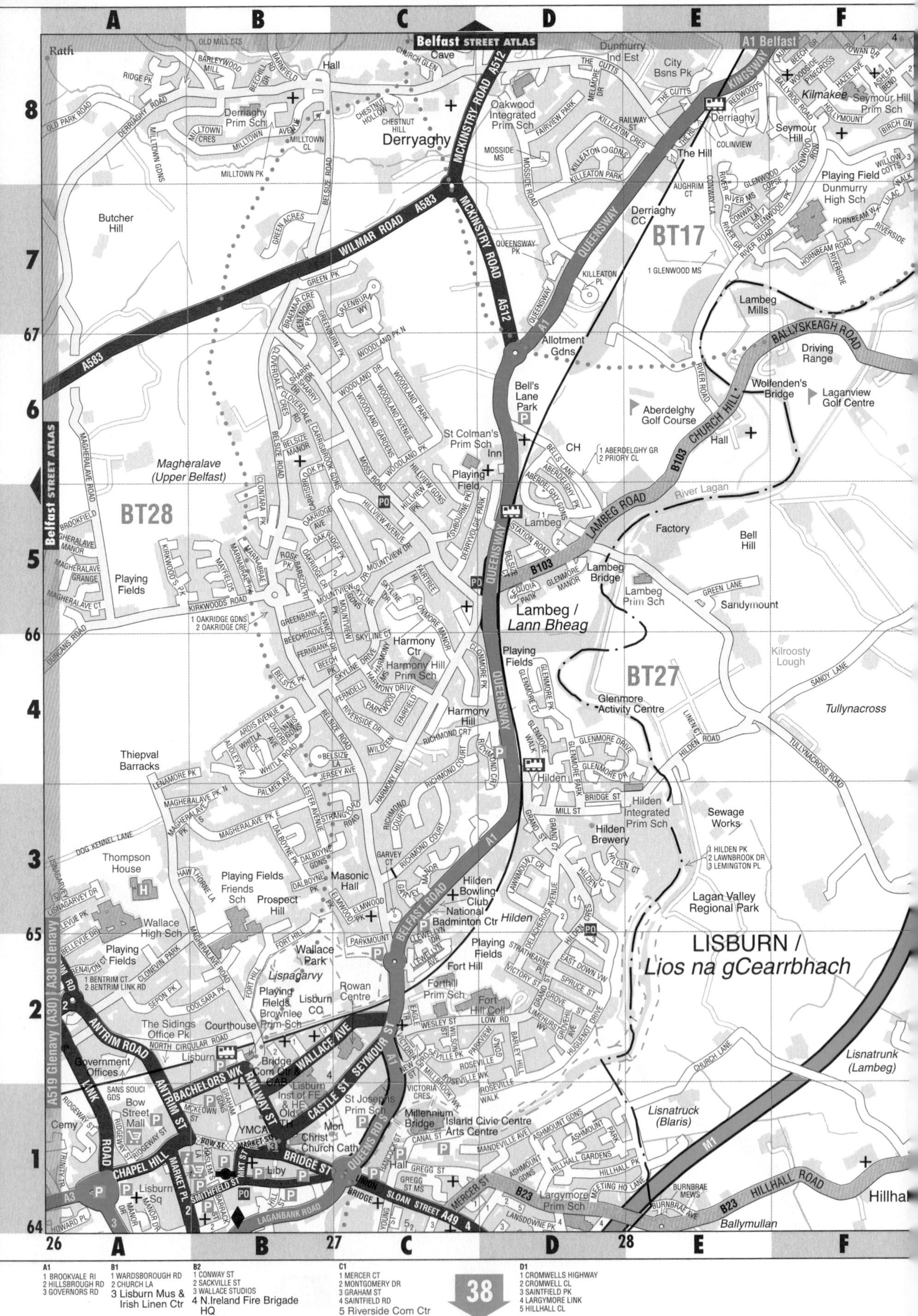

A1
1 BROOKVALE RI
2 HILLSBROUGH RD
3 GOVERNORS RD

B1
1 WARDSBOROUGH RD
2 CHURCH LA
3 Lisburn Mus & Irish Linen Ctr

B2
1 CONWAY ST
2 SACKVILLE ST
3 WALLACE STUDIOS
4 N.Ireland Fire Brigade HQ

C1
1 MERCER CT
2 MONTGOMERY DR
3 GRAHAM ST
4 SAINTFIELD RD
5 Riverside Com Ctr

D1
1 CROMWELLS HIGHWAY
2 CROMWELL CL
3 SAINTFIELD PK
4 LARGYMORE LINK
5 HILLHALL CL

38

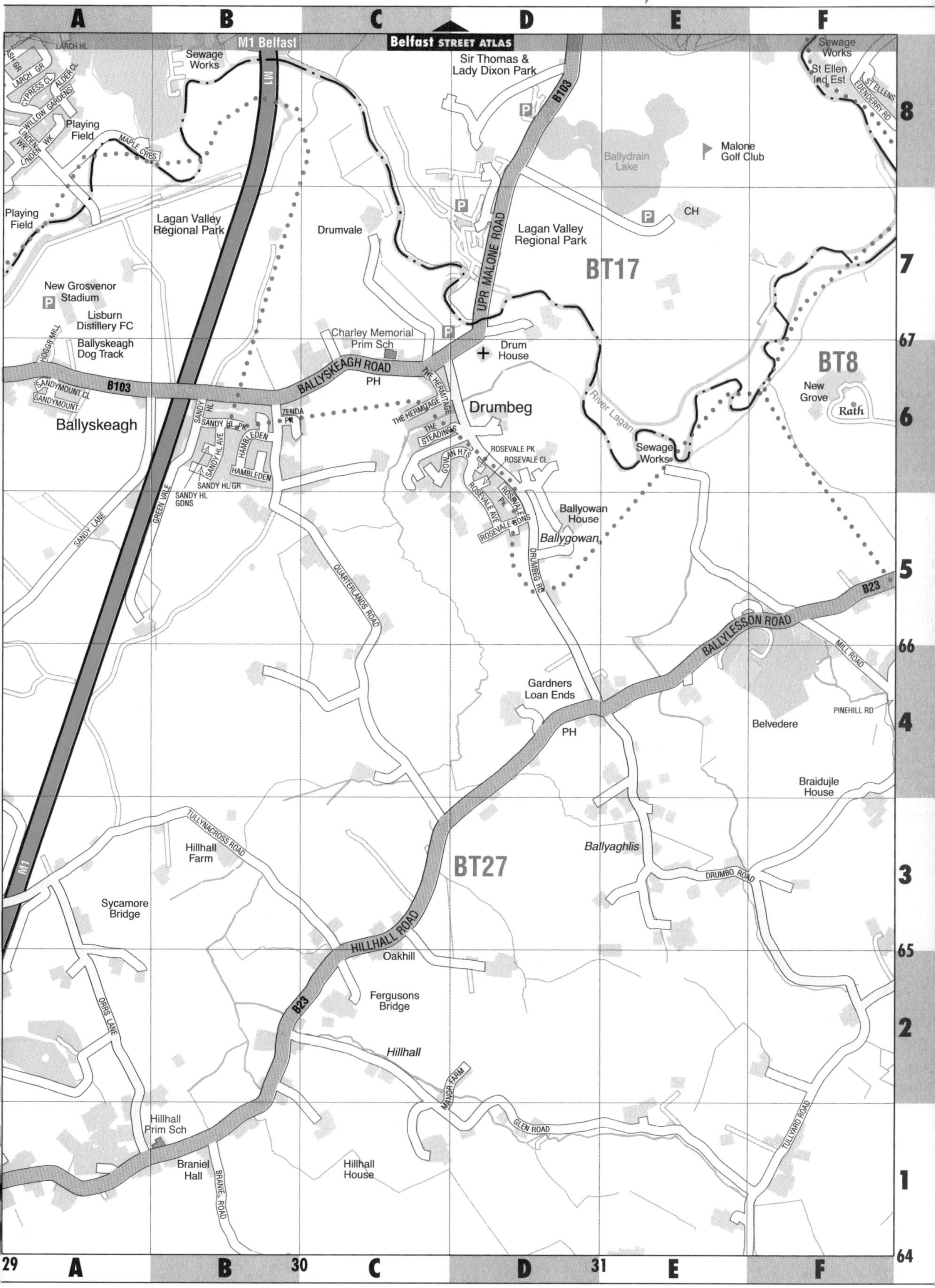

A B C D E F
M1 Belfast
Belfast STREET ATLAS
Sewage Works
Sir Thomas & Lady Dixon Park
B103
Playing Field
MAPLE CRES
Ballydrain Lake
Malone Golf Club
St Ellen Ind Est
Lagan Valley Regional Park
Drumvale
UPR MALONE ROAD
BT17
CH
New Grosvenor Stadium
Lisburn Distillery FC
Ballyskeagh Dog Track
Charley Memorial Prim Sch
Drum House
BALLYSKEAGH ROAD
PH
B103
Drumbeg
River Lagan
BT8
New Grove
Rath
Ballyskeagh
SANDY LANE
GREEN VALE
QUARTERLANDS ROAD
ROSEVALE PK
ROSEVALE CL
Ballyowan House
Ballygowan
DRUMBEG RD
B23
BALLYLESSON ROAD
MILL ROAD
Gardners Loan Ends
PINEHILL RD
Belvedere
Braidujle House
TULLYNACROSS ROAD
Hillhall Farm
Ballyaghlis
BT27
DRUMBO ROAD
Sycamore Bridge
HILLHALL ROAD
Oakhill
Fergusons Bridge
ORRS LANE
Hillhall
MANOR FARM
GLEN ROAD
TULLYARD ROAD
Hillhall Prim Sch
Braniel Hall
BRANIEL ROAD
Hillhall House
8 7 67 6 5 66 4 3 65 2 1 64
29 30 31

27
21

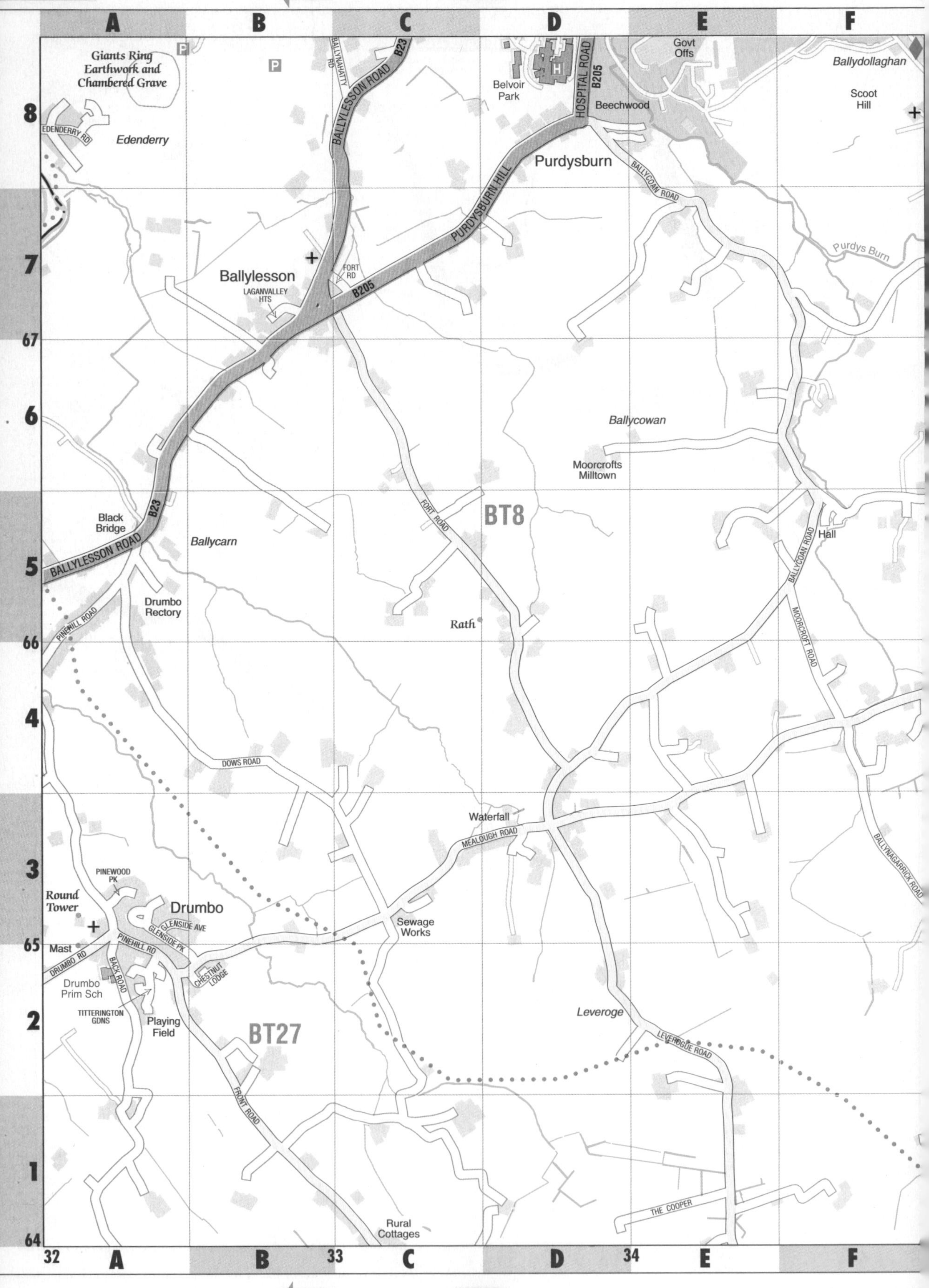
A
B
C
D
E
F
Giants Ring Earthwork and Chambered Grave
Edenderry
EDENDERRY RD
BALLYHAHATTY RD
BALLYLESSON ROAD
B23
Belvoir Park
HOSPITAL ROAD
B205
Govt Offs
Beechwood
Ballydollaghan
Scoot Hill
Purdysburn
PURDYSBURN HILL
BALLYCOAN ROAD
Purdys Burn
Ballylesson
LAGANVALLEY HTS
FORT RD
Ballycowan
Moorcrofts Milltown
BT8
FORT ROAD
Black Bridge
Ballycarn
Hall
BALLYCOAN RD
MOORCROFT ROAD
Drumbo Rectory
PINEHILL ROAD
Rath
DOWS ROAD
Waterfall
MEALOUGH ROAD
BALLYNAGARRICK ROAD
PINEWOOD PK
Round Tower
Drumbo
GLENSIDE AVE
GLENSIDE PK
Sewage Works
Mast
DRUMBO RD
PINEHILL RD
BACK ROAD
CHESTNUT LODGE
Drumbo Prim Sch
TITTERINGTON GDNS
Playing Field
BT27
Leveroge
LEVEROGUE ROAD
FRONT ROAD
THE COOPER
Rural Cottages
8
7
67
6
5
66
4
3
65
2
1
64
32
33
34

27
76

22
30

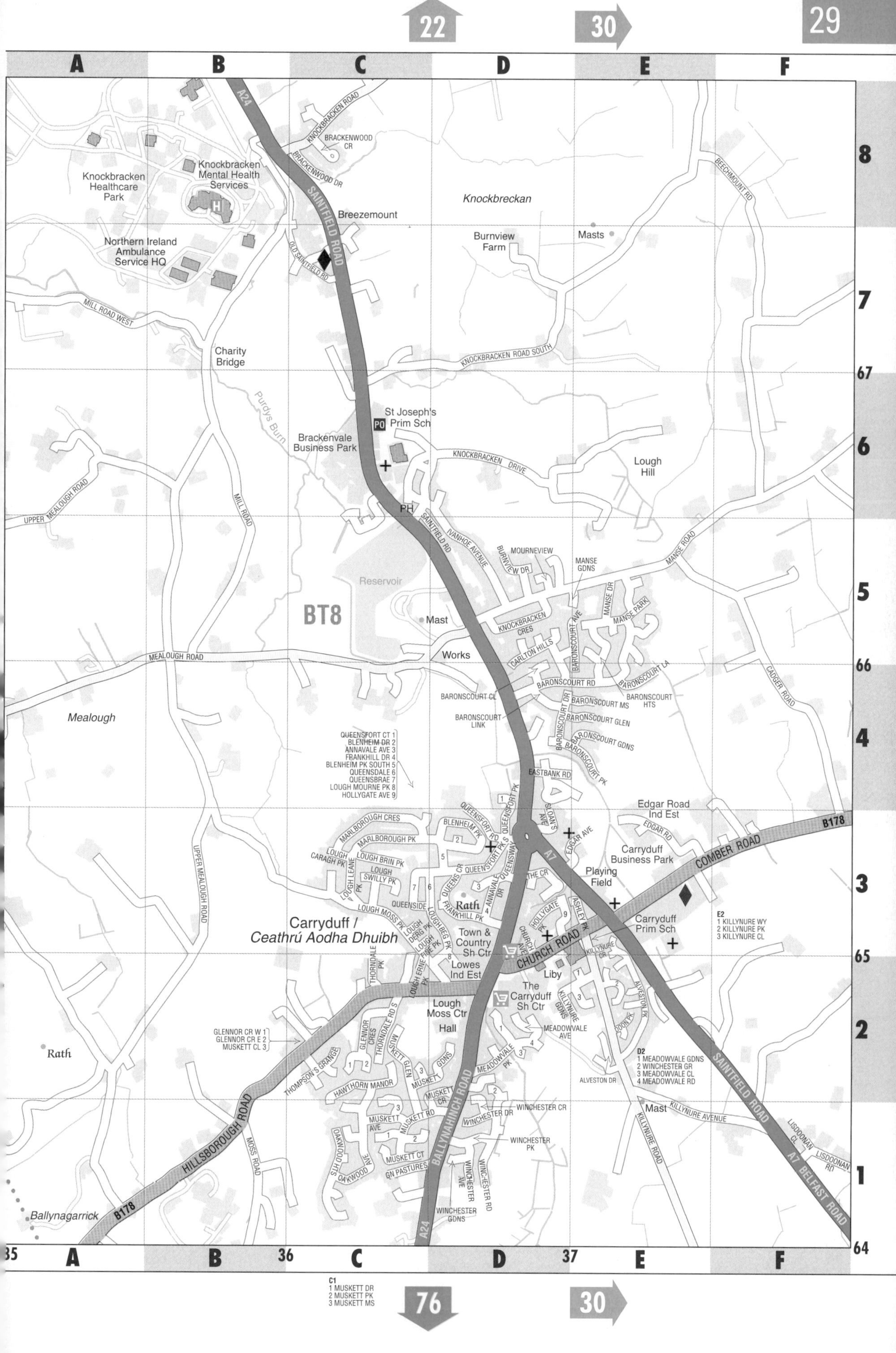

C1
1 MUSKETT DR
2 MUSKETT PK
3 MUSKETT MS

76
30

29
23

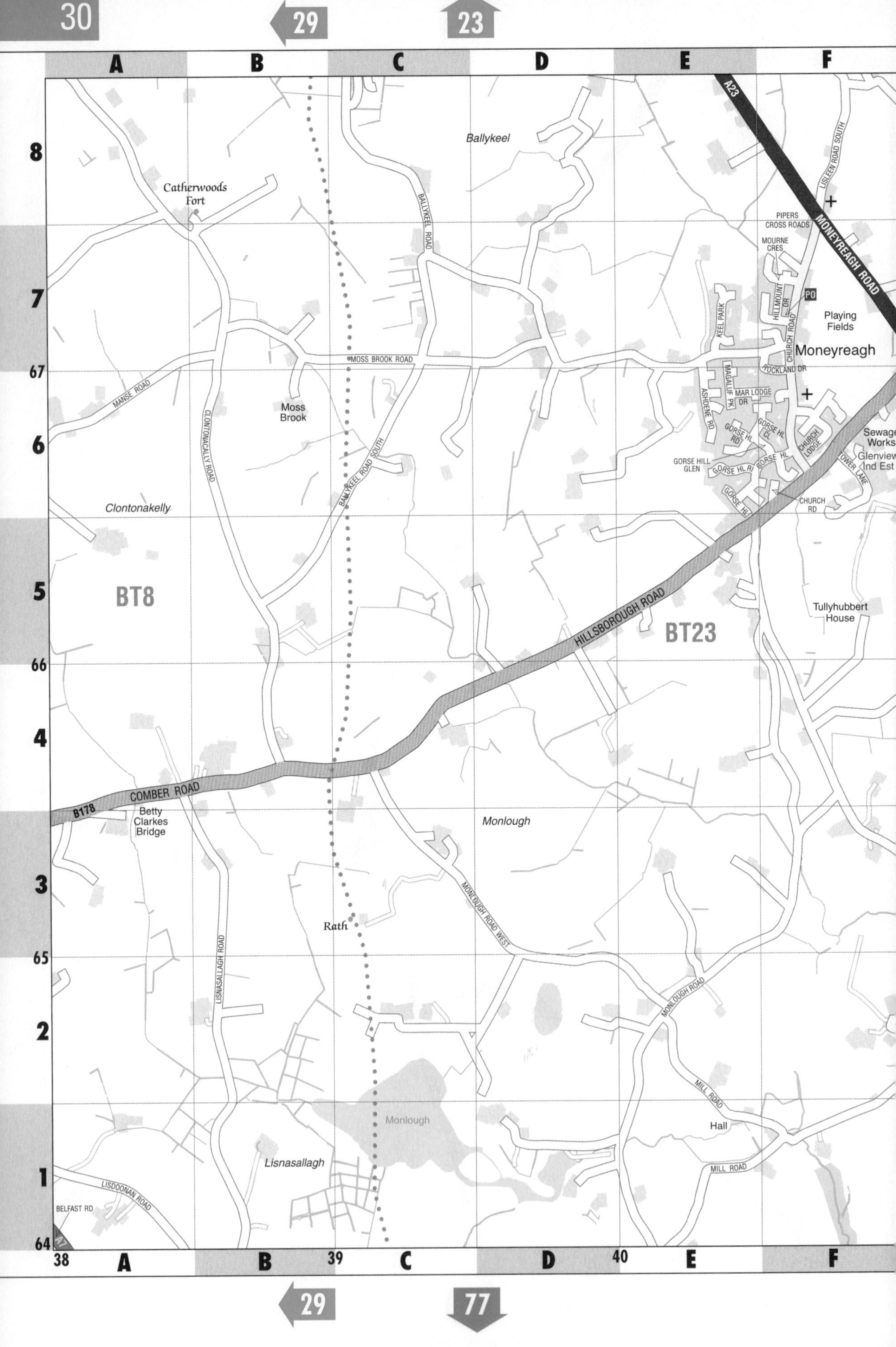
A
B
C
D
E
F
8
7
67
6
5
66
4
3
65
2
1
64
38
39
40
Ballykeel
Catherwoods Fort
BALLYKEEL ROAD
A23
MONEYREAGH ROAD
LISLEEN ROAD SOUTH
PIPERS CROSS ROADS
MOURNE CRES
HILLMOUNT DR
CHURCH ROAD
PO
Playing Fields
KEEL PARK
Moneyreagh
MOSS BROOK ROAD
ROCKLAND DR
MANSE ROAD
MAGALUF PK
MAR LODGE DR
Moss Brook
ASHDENE RD
GORSE HL RD
GORSE HL CL
CHURCH LODGE
Sewage Works
Glenview Ind Est
CLONTONACALLY ROAD
BALLYKEEL ROAD SOUTH
GORSE HILL GLEN
GORSE HL RI
GORSE HL
TOWER LANE
CHURCH RD
Clontonakelly
BT8
HILLSBOROUGH ROAD
Tullyhubbert House
BT23
COMBER ROAD
B178
Betty Clarkes Bridge
Monlough
MONLOUGH ROAD WEST
Rath
LISNASALLAGH ROAD
MONLOUGH ROAD
MILL ROAD
Monlough
Hall
Lisnasallagh
MILL ROAD
LISDOONAN ROAD
BELFAST RD
A7

29
77

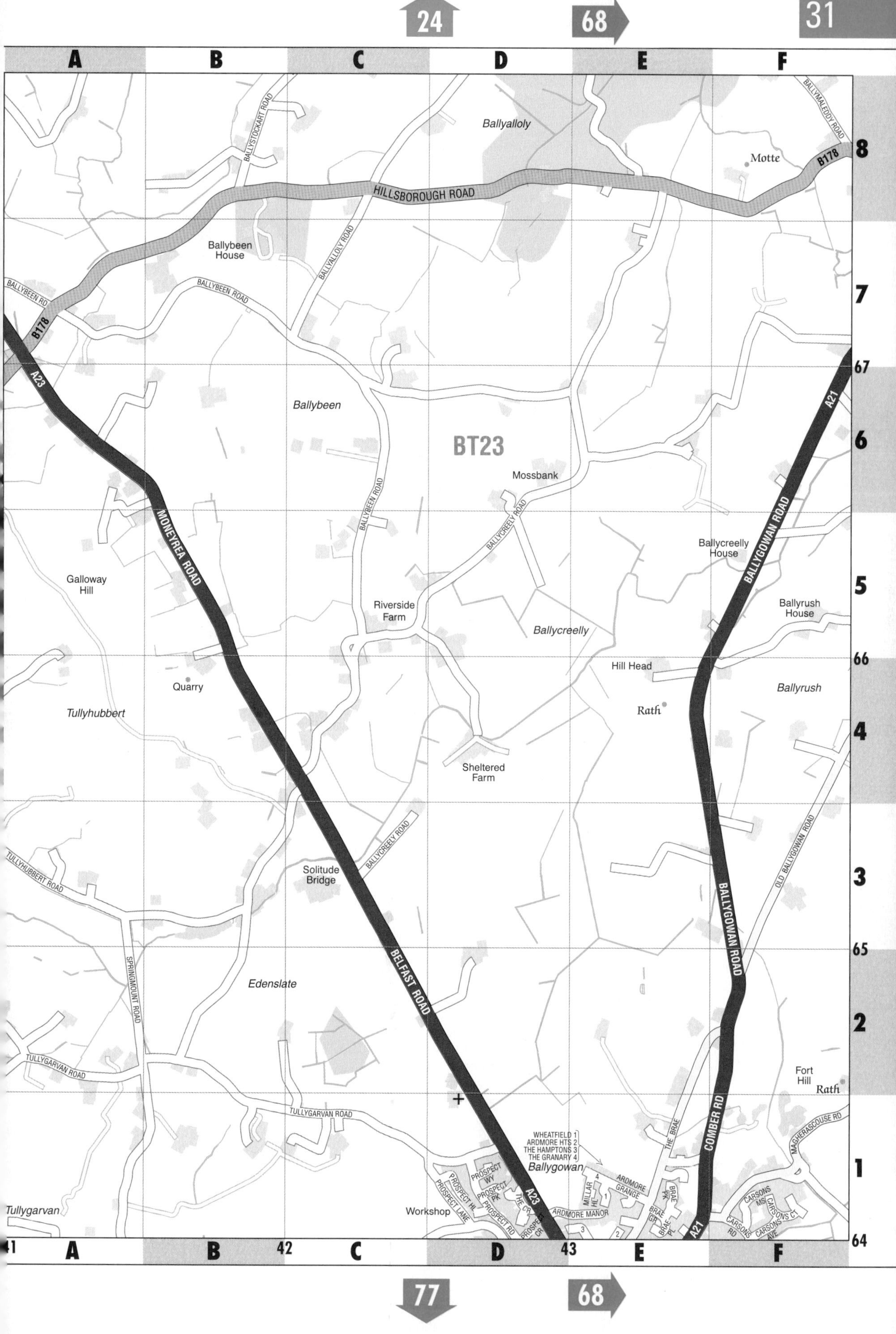
24
68
A
B
C
D
E
F
Ballyalloly
BALLYSTOCKART ROAD
BALLYMALEDDY ROAD
Motte
B178
HILLSBOROUGH ROAD
Ballybeen House
BALLYALLOLY ROAD
BALLYBEEN RD
BALLYBEEN ROAD
B178
A23
Ballybeen
BT23
Mossbank
A21
BALLYBEEN ROAD
MONEYREA ROAD
BALLYCREELY ROAD
BALLYGOWAN ROAD
Ballycreelly House
Galloway Hill
Riverside Farm
Ballycreelly
Ballyrush House
Hill Head
Quarry
Ballyrush
Tullyhubbert
Rath
Sheltered Farm
OLD BALLYGOWAN ROAD
BALLYCREELY ROAD
TULLYHUBBERT ROAD
Solitude Bridge
BALLYGOWAN ROAD
SPRINGMOUNT ROAD
BELFAST ROAD
Edenslate
TULLYGARVAN ROAD
Fort Hill
Rath
TULLYGARVAN ROAD
COMBER RD
MAGHERASCOUSE RD
THE BRAE
WHEATFIELD 1
ARDMORE HTS 2
THE HAMPTONS 3
THE GRANARY 4
Ballygowan
PROSPECT WY
PROSPECT HI
PROSPECT LANE
PROSPECT PK
THE CR
PROSPECT RD
PROSPECT CR
A23
MILLAR HL
ARDMORE GRANGE
ARDMORE MANOR
BRAE PK
BRAE GR
BRAE PL
A21
CARSONS MS
CARSONS CT
CARSONS AVE
CARSONS RD
Tullygarvan
Workshop
8
7
67
6
5
66
4
3
65
2
1
64
41
42
43
77
68

75

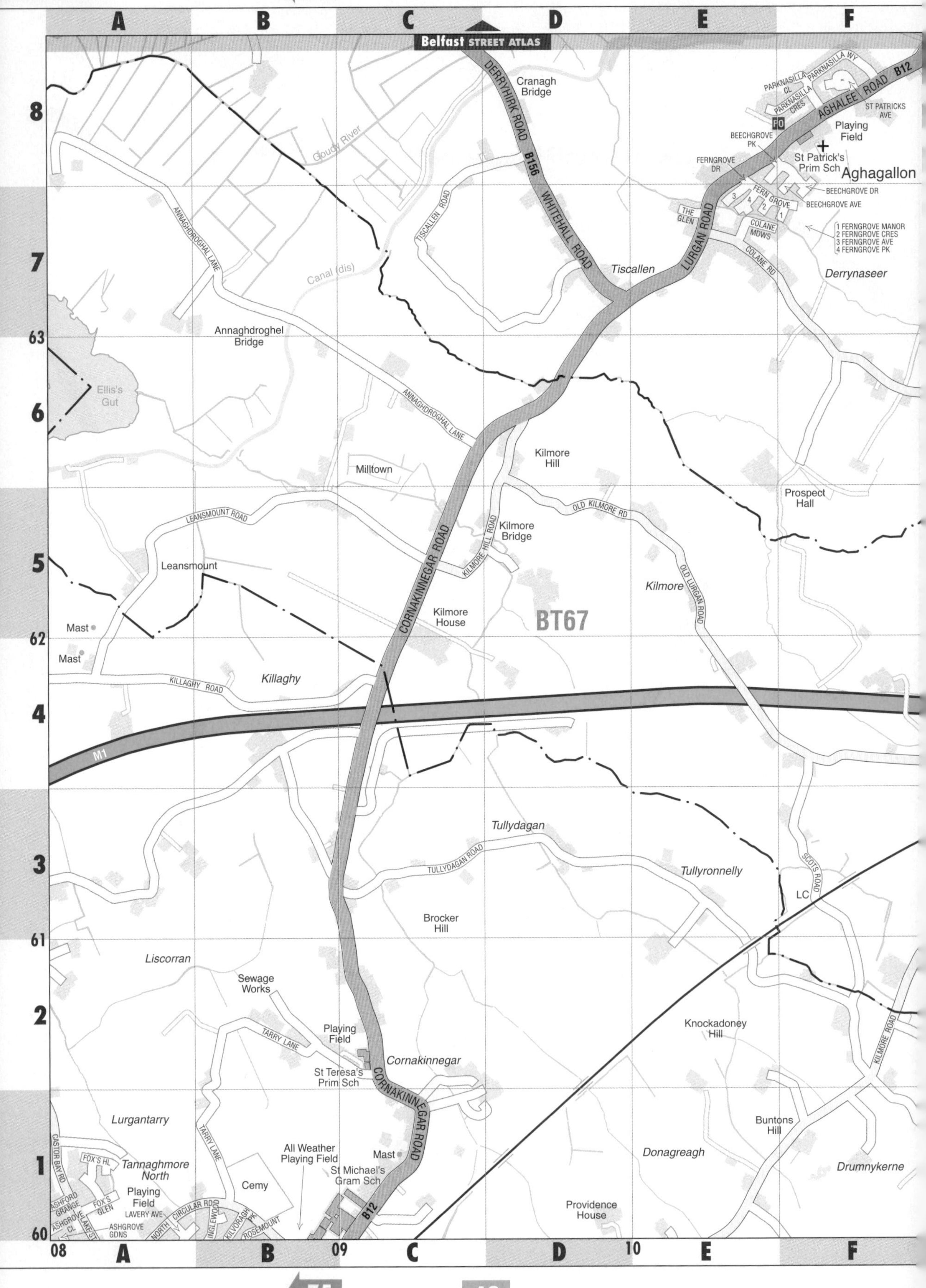
A
B
C
D
E
F
Belfast STREET ATLAS
8
7
63
6
5
62
4
3
61
2
1
60
08
09
10
Cranagh Bridge
DERRYHIRK ROAD
B156
WHITEHALL ROAD
PARKNASILLA CL
PARKNASILLA WY
PARKNASILLA CRES
AGHALEE ROAD
B12
ST PATRICKS AVE
PO
Playing Field
BEECHGROVE PK
FERNGROVE DR
St Patrick's Prim Sch
Aghagallon
BEECHGROVE DR
FERN GROVE
BEECHGROVE AVE
THE GLEN
COLANE MDWS
1 FERNGROVE MANOR
2 FERNGROVE CRES
3 FERNGROVE AVE
4 FERNGROVE PK
COLANE RD
LURGAN ROAD
Tiscallen
Derrynaseer
Goudy River
ANNAGHDROGHAL LANE
TISCALLEN ROAD
Canal (dis)
Annaghdroghel Bridge
Ellis's Gut
ANNAGHDROGHAL LANE
Kilmore Hill
Milltown
Prospect Hall
LEANSMOUNT ROAD
OLD KILMORE RD
Kilmore Bridge
KILMORE HILL ROAD
CORNAKINNEGAR ROAD
Leansmount
OLD LURGAN ROAD
Kilmore
Mast
Kilmore House
BT67
Mast
Killaghy
KILLAGHY ROAD
M1
Tullydagan
TULLYDAGAN ROAD
Tullyronnelly
SCOTS ROAD
LC
Brocker Hill
Liscorran
Sewage Works
Knockadoney Hill
KILMORE ROAD
Playing Field
TARRY LANE
Cornakinnegar
St Teresa's Prim Sch
CORNAKINNEGAR ROAD
Lurgantarry
Buntons Hill
CASTOR BAY RD
FOX'S HL
Tannaghmore North
TARRY LANE
All Weather Playing Field
Mast
Donagreagh
Drumnykerne
St Michael's Gram Sch
Playing Field
Cemy
ASHFORD GRANGE
FOX'S GLEN
ASHGROVE CL
LAVERY AVE
CIRCULAR RD
INGLEWOOD
KILVORAGH PK
ROSEMOUNT
NORTH CIRCULAR RD
ASHGROVE GDNS
LAKE ST
Providence House
B12

75

42

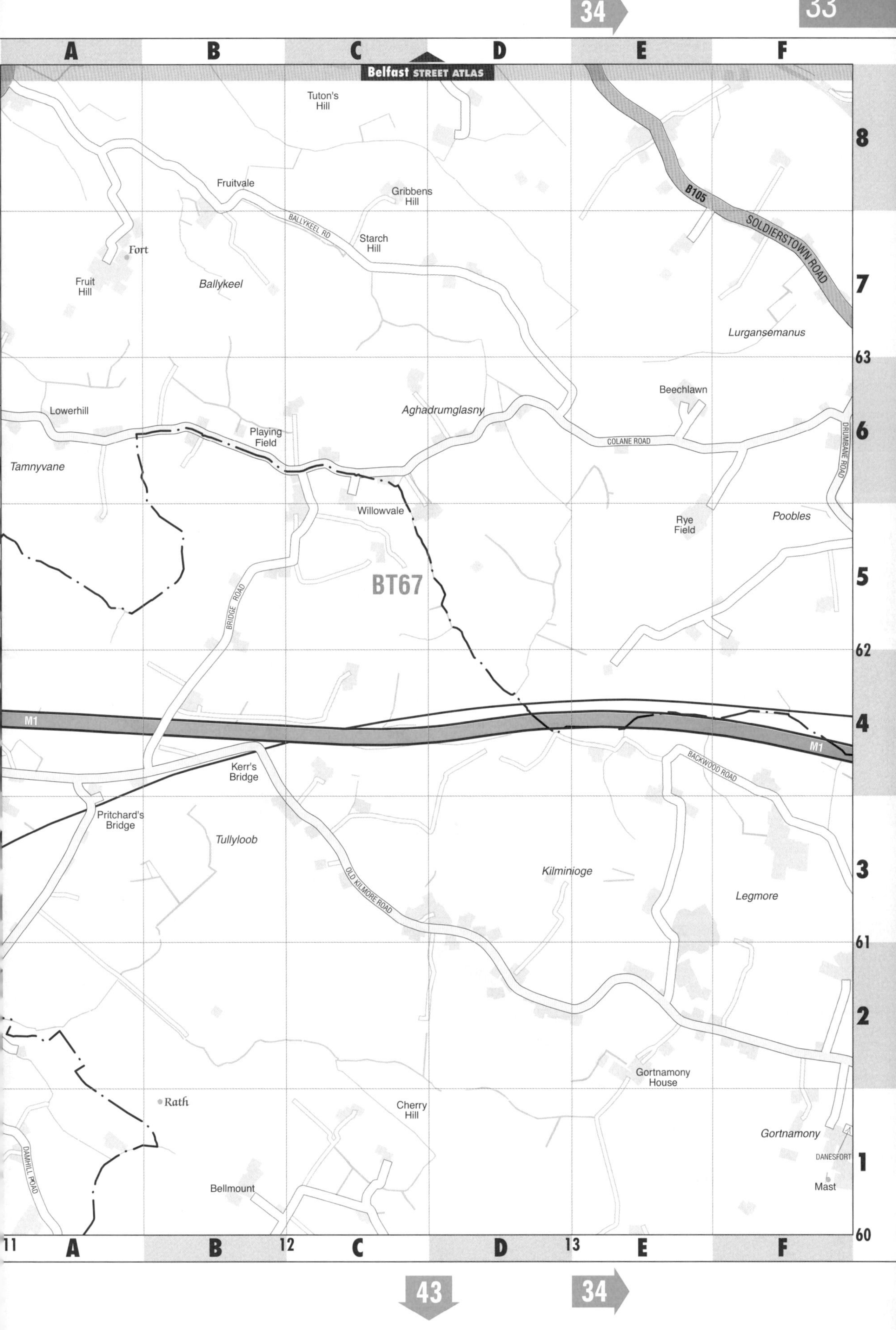
A
B
C
D
E
F
Belfast STREET ATLAS
Tuton's Hill
Fruitvale
Gribbens Hill
BALLYKEEL RD
Starch Hill
Fort
Fruit Hill
Ballykeel
B105
SOLDIERSTOWN ROAD
Lurgansemanus
Beechlawn
Lowerhill
Aghadrumglasny
Playing Field
COLANE ROAD
DRUMBANE ROAD
Tamnyvane
Willowvale
Rye Field
Poobles
BT67
BRIDGE ROAD
M1
Kerr's Bridge
BACKWOOD ROAD
Pritchard's Bridge
Tullyloob
OLD KILMORE ROAD
Kilminioge
Legmore
Gortnamony House
Rath
Cherry Hill
Gortnamony
DANESFORT
Mast
Bellmount
DAMHILL ROAD
8
7
63
6
5
62
4
3
61
2
1
60
11
12
13

33

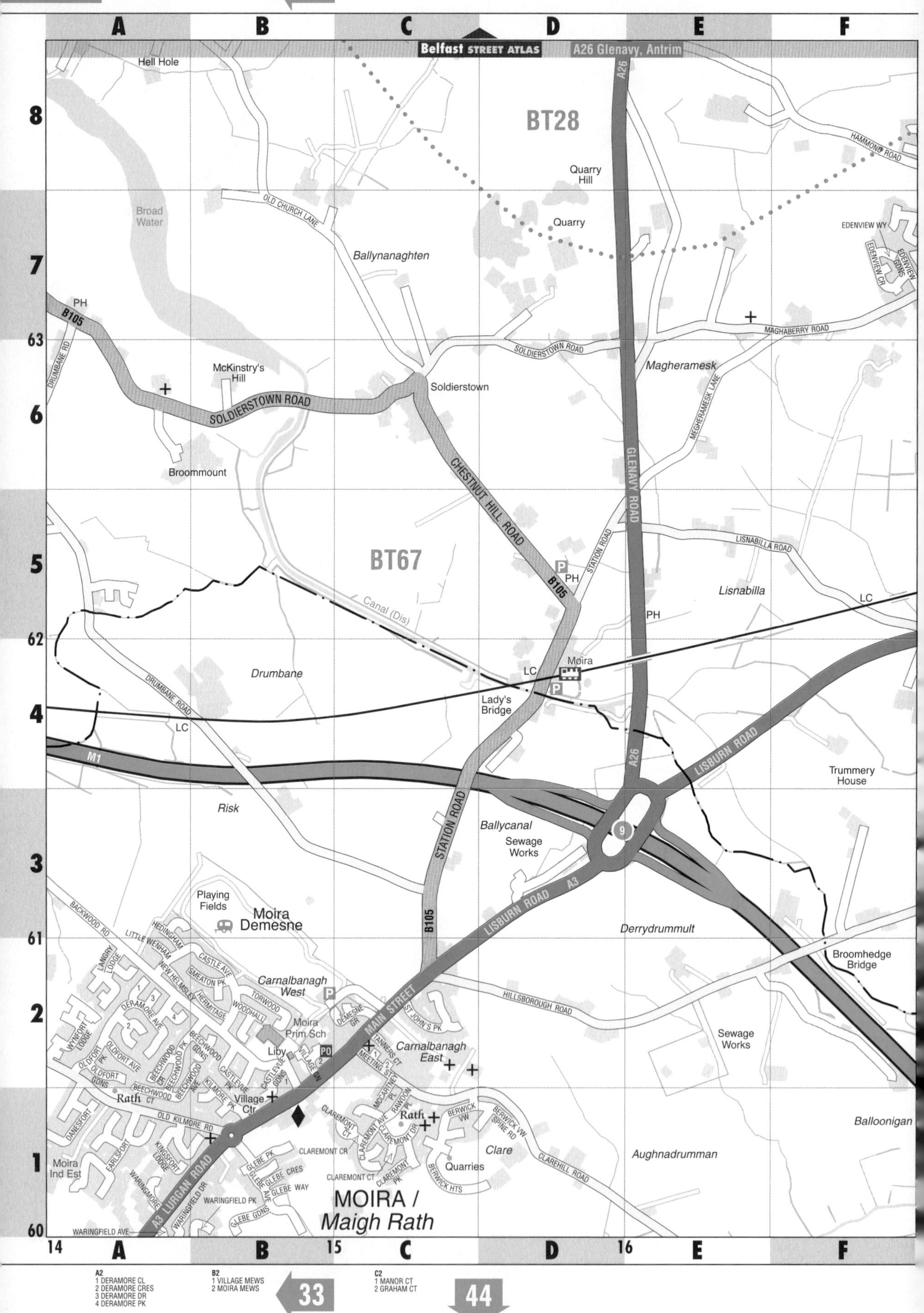

A2
1 DERAMORE CL
2 DERAMORE CRES
3 DERAMORE DR
4 DERAMORE PK

B2
1 VILLAGE MEWS
2 MOIRA MEWS

C2
1 MANOR CT
2 GRAHAM CT

33
44

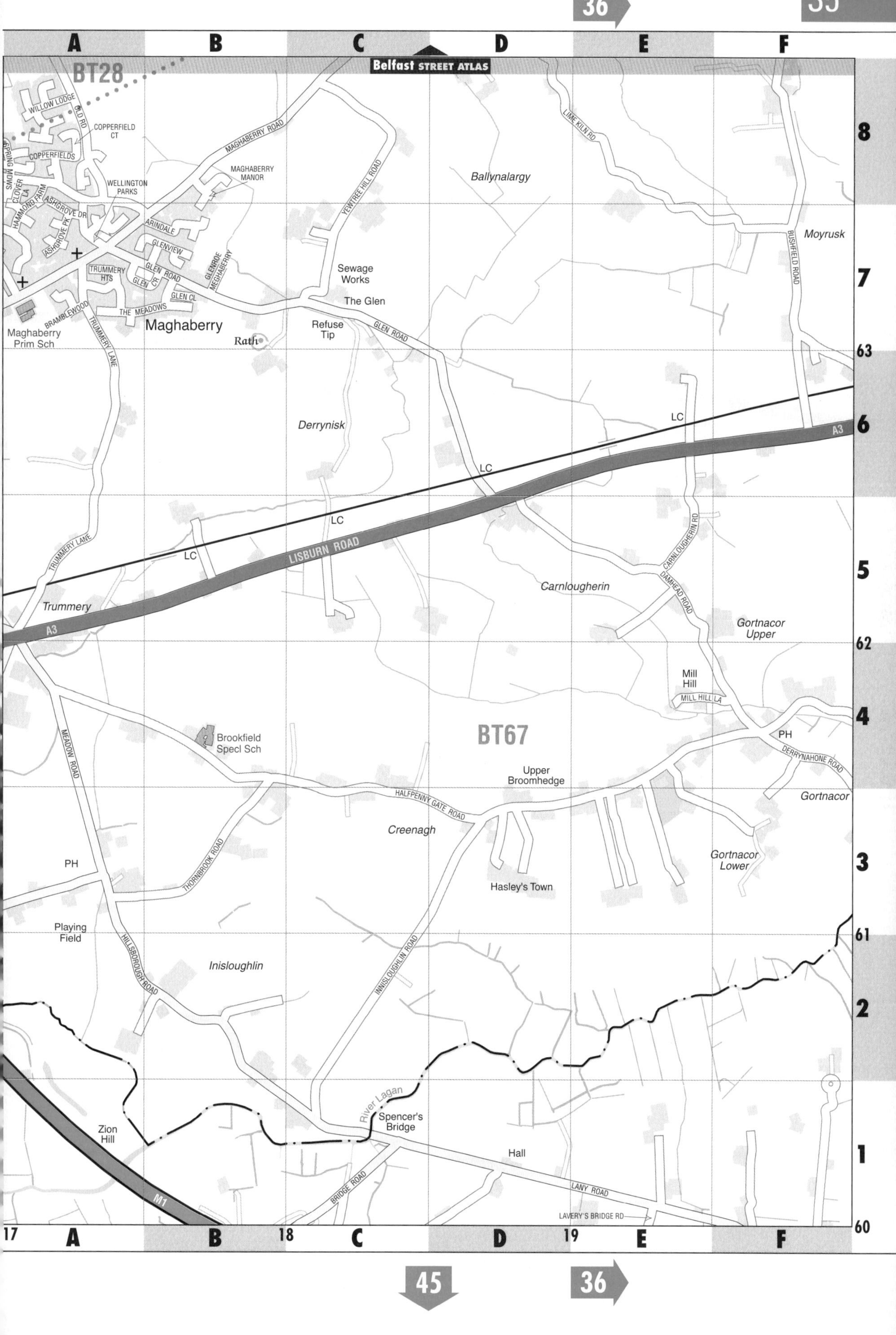
Belfast STREET ATLAS
BT28
BT67
Maghaberry
Maghaberry Prim Sch
Ballynalargy
Moyrusk
Sewage Works
The Glen
Refuse Tip
Rath
Derrynisk
Carnlougherin
Trummery
Gortnacor Upper
Mill Hill
Brookfield Specl Sch
Upper Broomhedge
Gortnacor
Creenagh
Gortnacor Lower
Hasley's Town
Playing Field
Inisloughlin
Zion Hill
Spencer's Bridge
River Lagan
Hall
LISBURN ROAD
A3
M1
MAGHABERRY ROAD
YEWTREE HILL ROAD
LIME KILN RD
BUSHFIELD ROAD
GLEN ROAD
TRUMMERY LANE
CARNLOUGHERIN RD
DAMHEAD ROAD
MILL HILL LA
DERRYNAHONE ROAD
HALFPENNY GATE ROAD
MEADOW ROAD
THORNBROOK ROAD
HILLSBOROUGH ROAD
INNISLOUGHLIN ROAD
BRIDGE ROAD
LANY ROAD
LAVERY'S BRIDGE RD
WILLOW LODGE
OLD RD
COPPERFIELD CT
COPPERFIELDS
SPRING MDWS
CLOVER LA
HAMMOND FARM
ASHGROVE DR
ASHGROVE PK
MAGHABERRY MANOR
WELLINGTON PARKS
ARINDALE
GLENVIEW
GLENROE
MEGHABERRY
TRUMMERY HTS
GLEN CR
GLEN CL
THE MEADOWS
BRAMBLEWOOD
LC
PH
A B C D E F
8 7 63 6 5 62 4 3 61 2 1 60
17 18 19

35

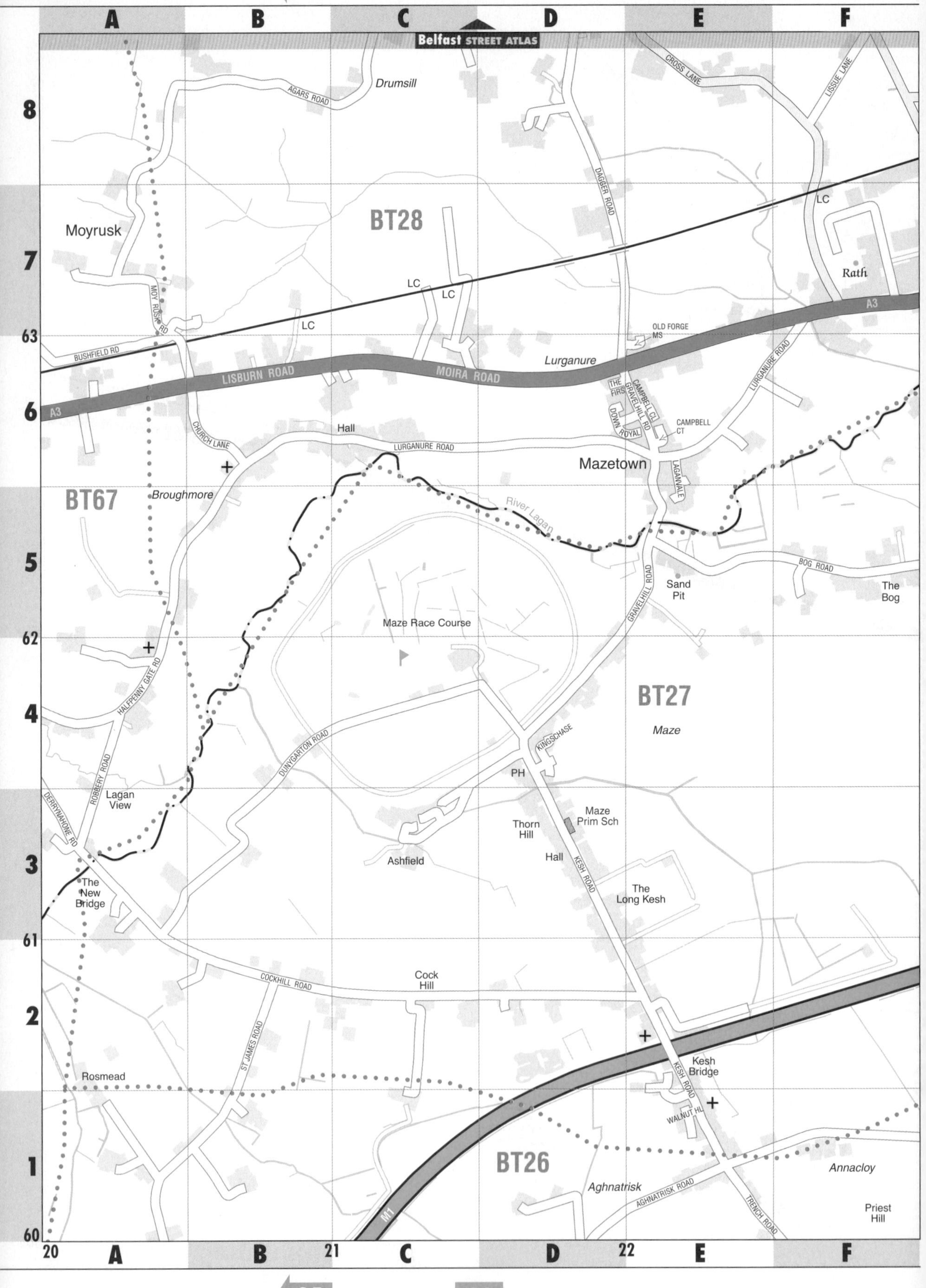
Belfast STREET ATLAS
A
B
C
D
E
F
8
7
63
6
5
62
4
3
61
2
1
60
20
21
22
Drumsill
AGARS ROAD
CROSS LANE
LISSUE LANE
BT28
Moyrusk
DAGGER ROAD
LC
Rath
A3
MOY RUSK RD
BUSHFIELD RD
LISBURN ROAD
MOIRA ROAD
Lurganure
OLD FORGE MS
LURGANURE ROAD
THE FIRS
CAMPBELL CL
GRAVELHILL RD
DOWN ROYAL
CAMPBELL CT
CHURCH LANE
Hall
Mazetown
LAGANVALE
BT67
Broughmore
River Lagan
BOG ROAD
Sand Pit
The Bog
GRAVELHILL ROAD
Maze Race Course
HALFPENNY GATE RD
BT27
KINGSCHASE
Maze
DUNYGARTON ROAD
ROBBERY ROAD
PH
Lagan View
DERRYNAHONE RD
Maze Prim Sch
Thorn Hill
Ashfield
Hall
KESH ROAD
The New Bridge
The Long Kesh
Cock Hill
COCKHILL ROAD
ST JAMES ROAD
Kesh Bridge
Rosmead
WALNUT HL
BT26
M1
Annacloy
Aghnatrisk
AGHNATRISK ROAD
TRENCH ROAD
Priest Hill

35
46

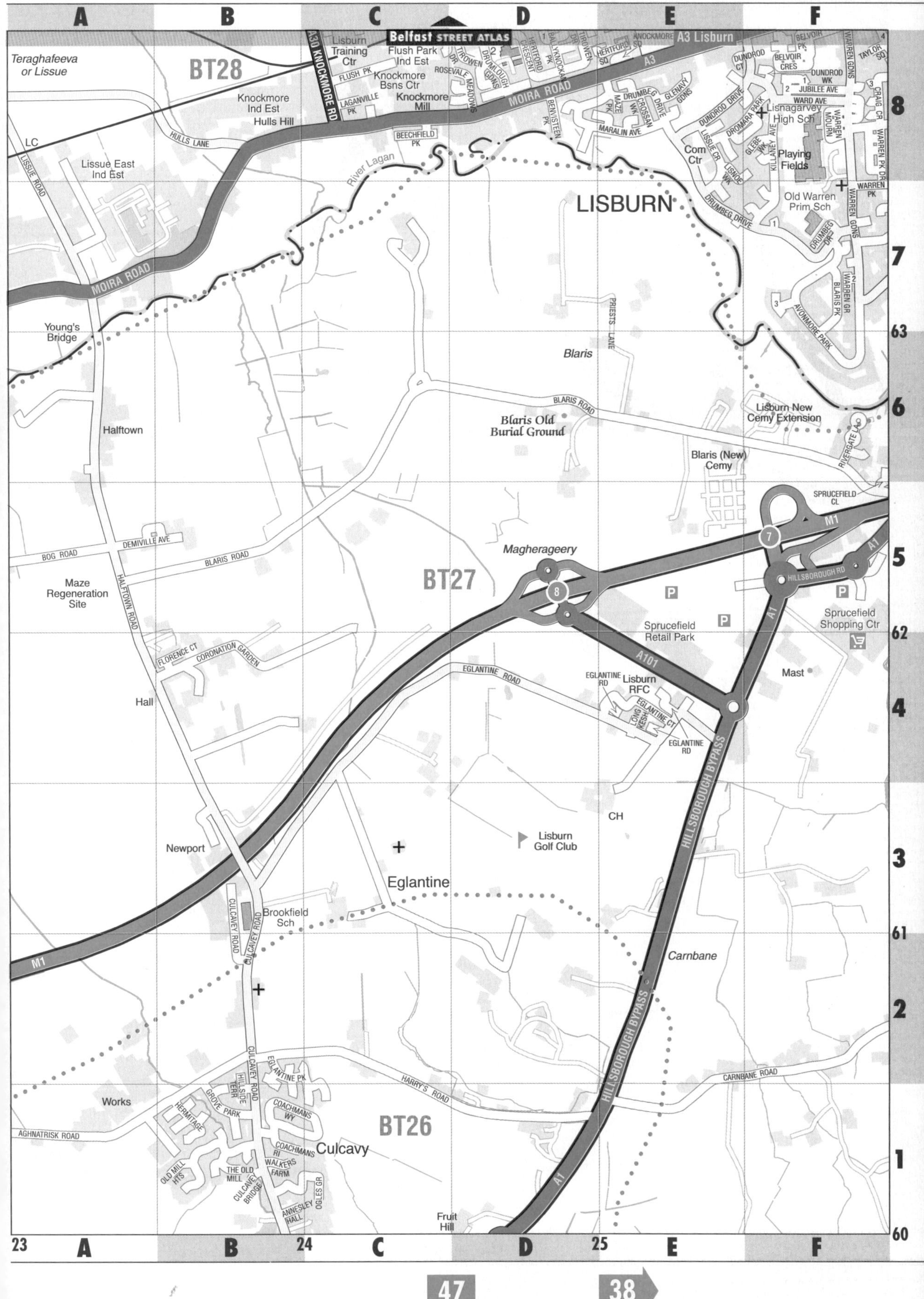
A
B
C
D
E
F
Belfast STREET ATLAS
BT28
BT27
BT26
Teraghafeeva or Lissue
Lisburn Training Ctr
Flush Park Ind Est
Knockmore Bsns Ctr
Knockmore Ind Est
Knockmore Mill
Hulls Hill
HULLS LANE
A30 KNOCKMORE RD
FLUSH PK
LAGANVILLE PK
ROSEVALE MEADOWS
BEECHFIELD PK
MOIRA ROAD
A3 Lisburn
A3
LC
LISSUE ROAD
Lissue East Ind Est
River Lagan
LISBURN
Young's Bridge
Halftown
BOG ROAD
DEMIVILLE AVE
BLARIS ROAD
Maze Regeneration Site
HALFTOWN ROAD
FLORENCE CT
CORONATION GARDEN
Hall
Newport
Brookfield Sch
CULCAVEY ROAD
Eglantine
Lisburn Golf Club
CH
Carnbane
Works
AGHNATRISK ROAD
HARRY'S ROAD
CARNBANE ROAD
Culcavy
EGLANTINE PK
HILLSIDE TERR
GROVE PARK
HERMITAGE
COACHMANS WY
COACHMANS RI
WALKERS FARM
OLD MILL HTS
THE OLD MILL
CULCAVEY BRIDGE
ANNESLEY HALL
OGLES GR
Fruit Hill
A1
HILLSBOROUGH BYPASS
M1
A101
Magherageery
Sprucefield Retail Park
Sprucefield Shopping Ctr
Mast
EGLANTINE ROAD
EGLANTINE RD
Lisburn RFC
EGLANTINE CT
LONG KESH
SPRUCEFIELD CL
HILLSBOROUGH RD
Blaris
PRIESTS LANE
Blaris Old Burial Ground
Blaris (New) Cemy
Lisburn New Cemy Extension
RIVERGATE LA
AVONMORE PARK
BLARIS PK
WARREN GR
DRUMBEG DR
DRUMBEG DRIVE
Old Warren Prim Sch
WARREN GDNS
WARREN PK
WARREN PK DR
Playing Fields
Lisnagarvey High Sch
Com Ctr
LISSUE CR
DROMARA PARK
DUNDROD DRIVE
DUNDROD CT
GLEBE WK
KILLANEY AVE
LISNOE WK
WARD AVE
JUBILEE AVE
DUNDROD WK
BELVOIR CRES
BELVOIR PK
TAYLOR SQ
CRAIG CR
MOURN
MARALIN AVE
MAZE PK
DRUMBEG WK
CROSSAN WK
DRUMBEG DRIVE
GLENAVY GDNS
BENVISTEEN PK
HERTFORD SQ
HERTFORD CRESCENT
BALLYKNOCKAN PK
TROWEN DR
DRUMLOUGH GDNS
KNOCKMORE
8
7
63
6
5
62
4
3
61
2
1
60
23
24
25

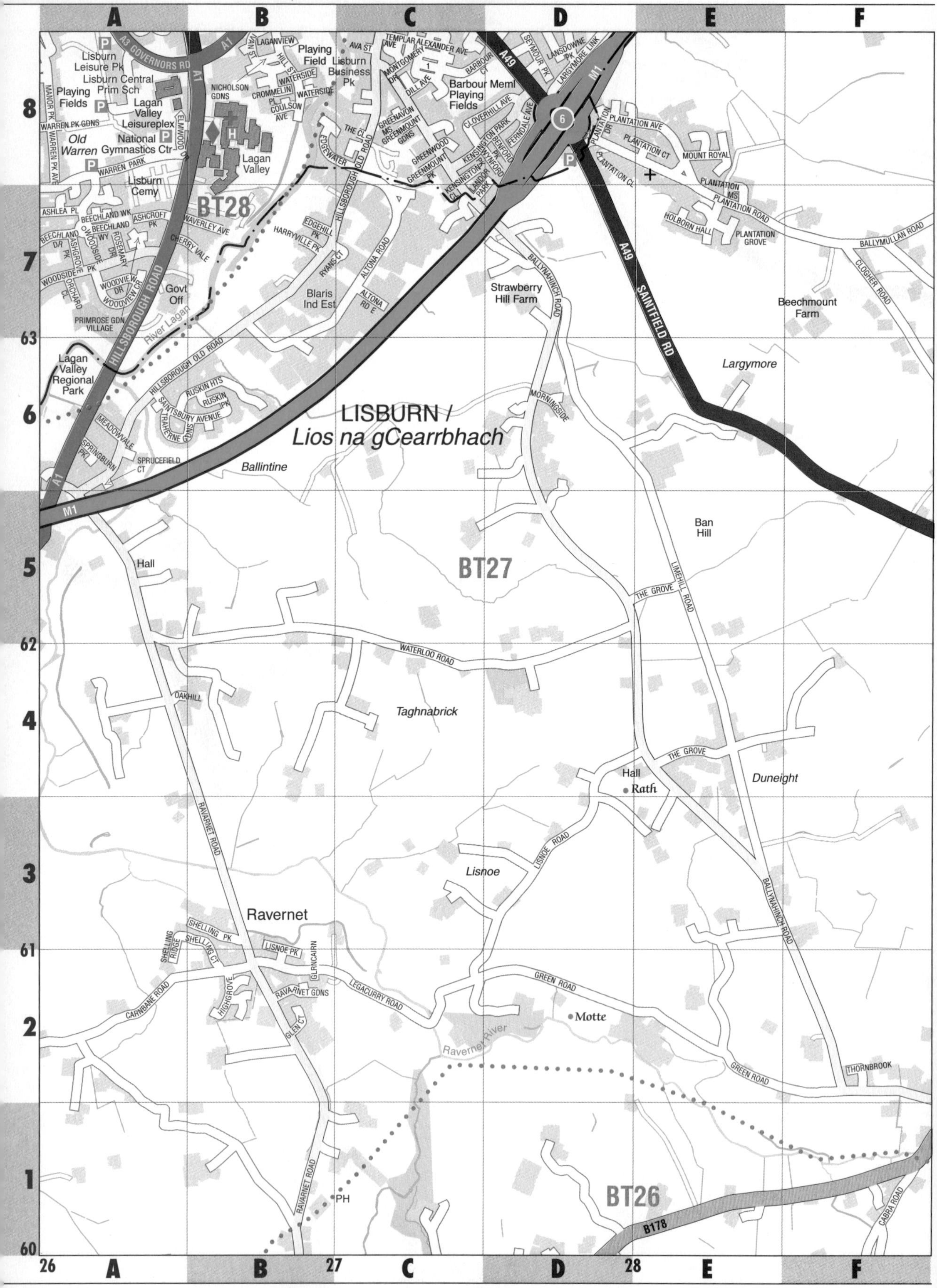

37
C8
1 ALANBROOKE AVE
26

A B C D E F

8
7
63
6
5
62
4
3
61
2
1
60

Lisburn Leisure Pk
Lisburn Central Prim Sch
Playing Fields
Lagan Valley Leisureplex
Old Warren
National Gymnastics Ctr
Lisburn Cemy
Lagan Valley
BT28
Playing Field
Lisburn Business Pk
Barbour Meml Playing Fields
Govt Off
Blaris Ind Est
River Lagan
Lagan Valley Regional Park
Strawberry Hill Farm
Beechmount Farm
Largymore
LISBURN /
Lios na gCearrbhach
Ballintine
Ban Hill
BT27
Hall
Taghnabrick
Hall
Rath
Duneight
Lisnoe
Ravernet
Motte
Ravernet River
PH
BT26

A3 GOVERNORS RD
A1
M1
A49
SAINTFIELD RD
B178
HILLSBOROUGH ROAD
HILLSBOROUGH OLD ROAD
ALTONA ROAD
BALLYNAHINCH ROAD
LIMEHILL ROAD
WATERLOO ROAD
RAVARNET ROAD
LISNOE ROAD
GREEN ROAD
LEGACURRY ROAD
CARNBANE ROAD
PLANTATION ROAD
BALLYMULLAN ROAD
CLOGHER ROAD
CABRA ROAD
THE GROVE
MORNINGSIDE
OAKHILL
THORNBROOK
SHELLING PK
SHELLING CT
SHELLING RIDGE
LISNOE PK
GLENCAIRN
RAVARNET GDNS
HIGHGROVE
GLEN CT
MANOR PK
WARREN PK GDNS
WARREN PK AVE
WARREN PARK
ASHLEA PL
BEECHLAND WK
BEECHLAND PK
BEECHLAND DR
ASHCROFT PK
ASHGROVE PK
WOODSIDE
ROSEMARY
WOODSIDE CL
ORCHARD CL
WOODVIEW DR
WOODVIEW CR
PRIMROSE GDN VILLAGE
WAVERLEY AVE
CHERRY VALE
HARRYVILLE PK
EDGEHILL PK
RYANS CT
ALTONA RD E
ELMWOOD DR
NICHOLSON GDNS
LAGANVIEW
CROMMELIN PL
COULSON AVE
WATERSIDE
AVA ST
TEMPLAR AVE
ALEXANDER AVE
MONTGOMERY DR
DILL AVE
BARBOUR CT
SEYMOUR PK
LANSDOWNE PK
LARGYMORE LINK
GREENAVON MS
GREENMOUNT GDNS
GREENWOOD
GREENMOUNT PK
GLOVERHILL AVE
KENSINGTON PARK
KENSINGTON CL
LANDOR PARK
FERNDALE AVE
THE CL
EDGEWATER
PLANTATION DR
PLANTATION AVE
PLANTATION CT
PLANTATION CL
PLANTATION MS
MOUNT ROYAL
HOLBORN HALL
PLANTATION GROVE
RUSKIN HTS
RUSKIN PK
SAINTSBURY AVENUE
TRAHERNE GDNS
MEADOWVALE
SPRINGBURN PK
SPRUCEFIELD CT

26 A B 27 C D 28 E F

37
48

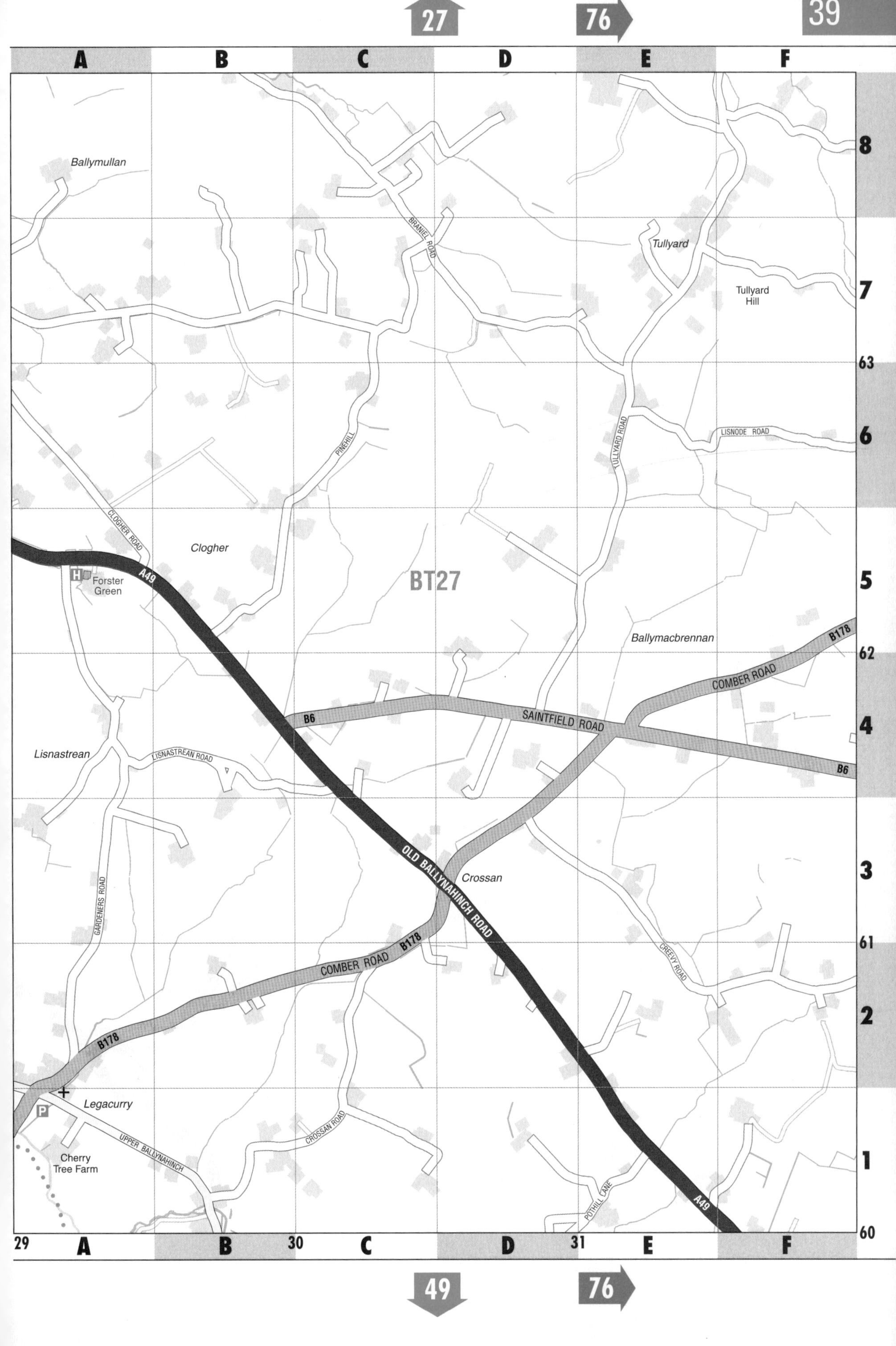
27
76
A
B
C
D
E
F
8
7
63
6
5
62
4
3
61
2
1
60
29
30
31
49
76
Ballymullan
Tullyard
Tullyard
Hill
BRANIEL ROAD
LISNODE ROAD
TULLYARD ROAD
PINEHILL
CLOGHER ROAD
Clogher
A49
Forster
Green
BT27
Ballymacbrennan
B178
COMBER ROAD
B6
SAINTFIELD ROAD
Lisnastrean
LISNASTREAN ROAD
OLD BALLYNAHINCH ROAD
Crossan
GARDENERS ROAD
CREEVY ROAD
B178
Legacurry
UPPER BALLYNAHINCH
CROSSAN ROAD
Cherry
Tree Farm
POTHILL LANE

74
75

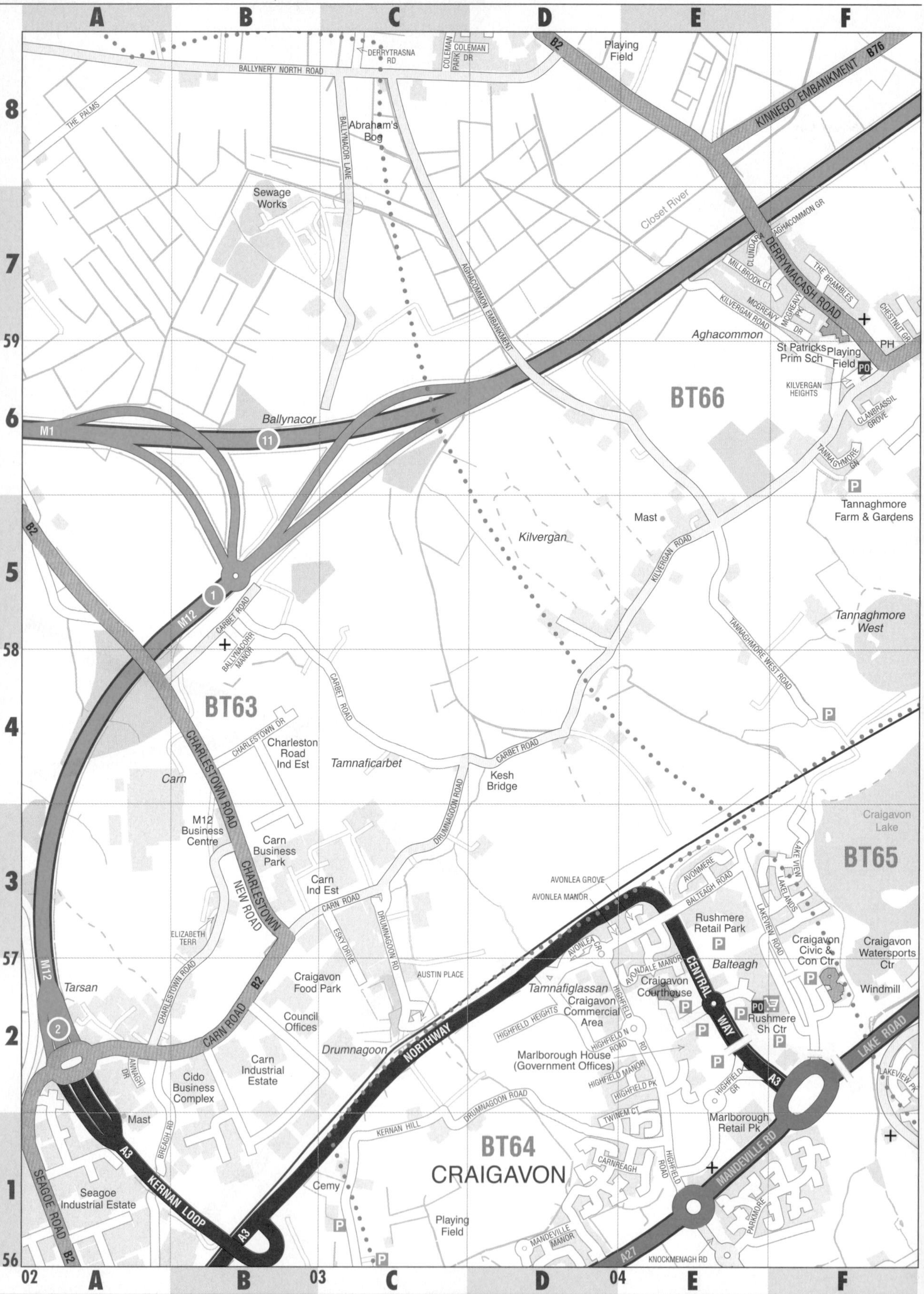

A B C D E F

8
7
59
6
5
58
4
3
57
2
1
56

BALLYNERY NORTH ROAD
DERRYTRASNA RD
COLEMAN PARK
COLEMAN DR
B2
Playing Field
B76
KINNEGO EMBANKMENT
THE PALMS
BALLYNACOR LANE
Abraham's Bog
Sewage Works
Closet River
AGHACOMMON GR
CLUNDAR
DERRYMACASH ROAD
THE BRAMBLES
MILLBROOK CT
MCGREAVY DR
MCGREAVY PK
KILVERGAN ROAD
CHESTNUT GR
AGHACOMMON EMBANKMENT
Aghacommon
St Patricks Prim Sch
Playing Field
PO
PH
KILVERGAN HEIGHTS
CLANBRASSIL GROVE
TANNAGHMORE GN
BT66
M1
Ballynacor
11
Tannaghmore Farm & Gardens
Mast
Kilvergan
KILVERGAN ROAD
B2
1
M12
CARBET ROAD
BALLYNACORR MANOR
Tannaghmore West
TANNAGHMORE WEST ROAD
BT63
CARBET ROAD
CHARLESTOWN DR
Charleston Road Ind Est
Tamnaficarbet
CARBET ROAD
Kesh Bridge
CHARLESTOWN ROAD
Carn
DRUMNAGOON ROAD
M12 Business Centre
Carn Business Park
Craigavon Lake
BT65
CHARLESTOWN NEW ROAD
Carn Ind Est
AVONLEA GROVE
AVONLEA MANOR
AVONMERE
BALTEAGH ROAD
LAKE VIEW
LAKELANDS
LAKEVIEW ROAD
CARN ROAD
ESKY DRIVE
DRUMNAGOON RD
ELIZABETH TERR
Rushmere Retail Park
Craigavon Civic & Con Ctr
Craigavon Watersports Ctr
CHARLESTOWN ROAD
AVONLEA CR
AVONDALE MANOR
CENTRAL WAY
Balteagh
M12
Tarsan
Craigavon Food Park
AUSTIN PLACE
Tamnafiglassan
Craigavon Courthouse
Windmill
B2
CARN ROAD
Council Offices
Craigavon Commercial Area
HIGHFIELD RD
PO
Rushmere Sh Ctr
2
NORTHWAY
HIGHFIELD HEIGHTS
HIGHFIELD N ROAD
LAKE ROAD
ANNAGH DR
Drumnagoon
Marlborough House (Government Offices)
Carn Industrial Estate
Cido Business Complex
HIGHFIELD MANOR
HIGHFIELD PK
A3
LAKEVIEW PK
HIGHFIELD GR
DRUMNAGOON ROAD
Mast
BREAGH RD
KERNAN HILL
TWINEM CT
Marlborough Retail Pk
A3
BT64
CRAIGAVON
CARNREAGH
HIGHFIELD ROAD
MANDEVILLE RD
KERNAN LOOP
SEAGOE ROAD
Seagoe Industrial Estate
Cemy
Playing Field
PARKMORE
A3
MANDEVILLE MANOR
A27
KNOCKMENAGH RD
B2

02 A B 03 C D 04 E F

74
52

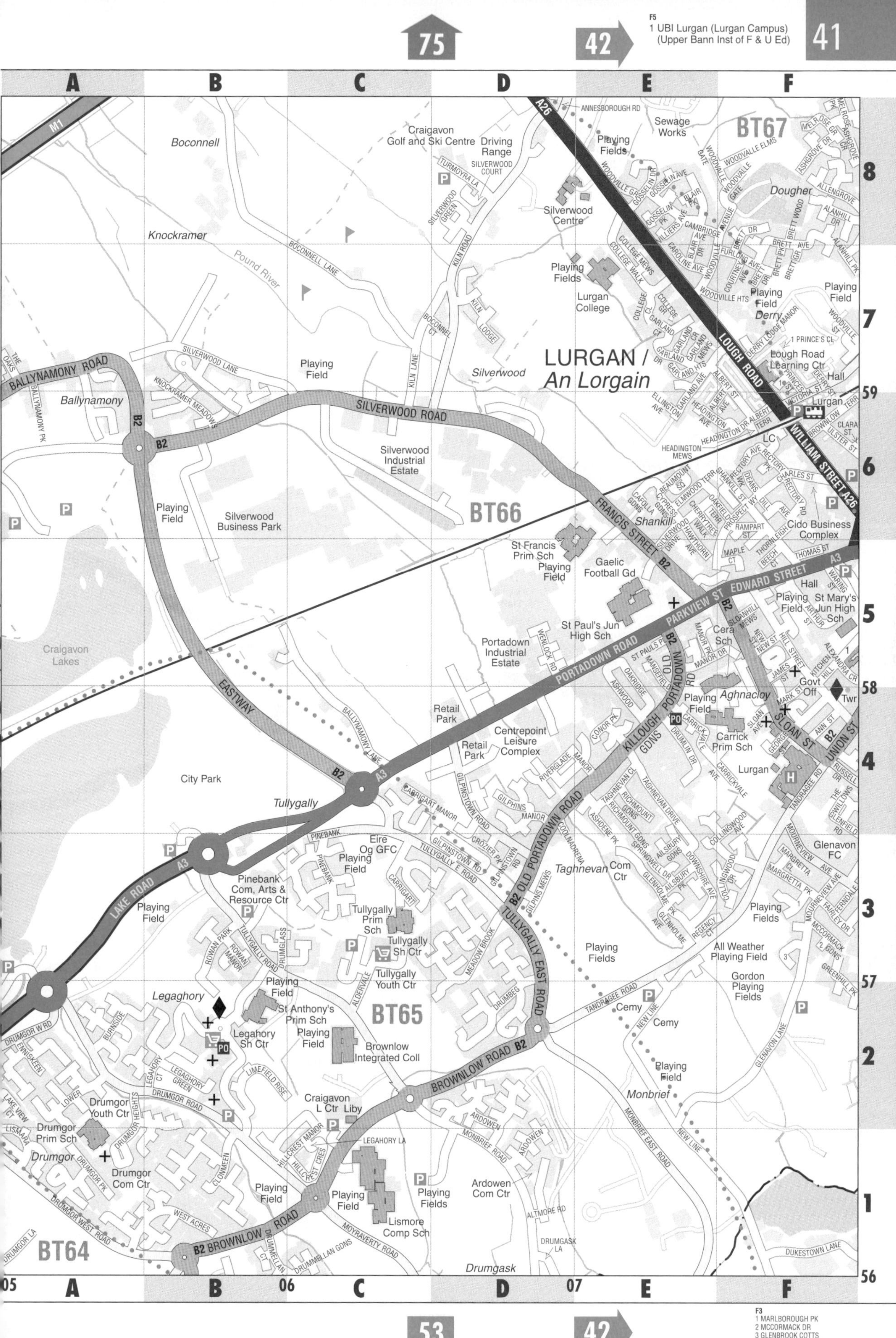
A B C D E F
8 7 59 6 5 58 4 3 57 2 1 56
05 06 07
LURGAN /
An Lorgain
BT67
BT66
BT65
BT64
Boconnell
Knockramer
Ballynamony
BALLYNAMONY ROAD
SILVERWOOD ROAD
Craigavon Golf and Ski Centre
Driving Range
Silverwood Centre
Lurgan College
Silverwood
Silverwood Industrial Estate
Silverwood Business Park
Craigavon Lakes
City Park
Tullygally
EASTWAY
LAKE ROAD
PORTADOWN ROAD
FRANCIS STREET
PARKVIEW ST
EDWARD STREET
LOUGH ROAD
WILLIAM STREET A26
Sewage Works
Dougher
Derry
Shankill
St Francis Prim Sch
Gaelic Football Gd
St Paul's Jun High Sch
Portadown Industrial Estate
Retail Park
Centrepoint Leisure Complex
Aghnacloy
Carrick Prim Sch
Lurgan
Taghnevan
Glenavon FC
All Weather Playing Field
Gordon Playing Fields
Cemy
Monbrief
Pinebank Com, Arts & Resource Ctr
Eire Og GFC
Tullygally Prim Sch
Tullygally Sh Ctr
Tullygally Youth Ctr
Legaghory
St Anthony's Prim Sch
Legahory Sh Ctr
Brownlow Integrated Coll
BROWNLOW ROAD
Craigavon L Ctr
Liby
Drumgor Youth Ctr
Drumgor Prim Sch
Drumgor
Drumgor Com Ctr
Lismore Comp Sch
Ardowen Com Ctr
Drumgask
Cido Business Complex
Lough Road Learning Ctr
St Mary's Jun High Sch
Govt Off
Twr

41
32

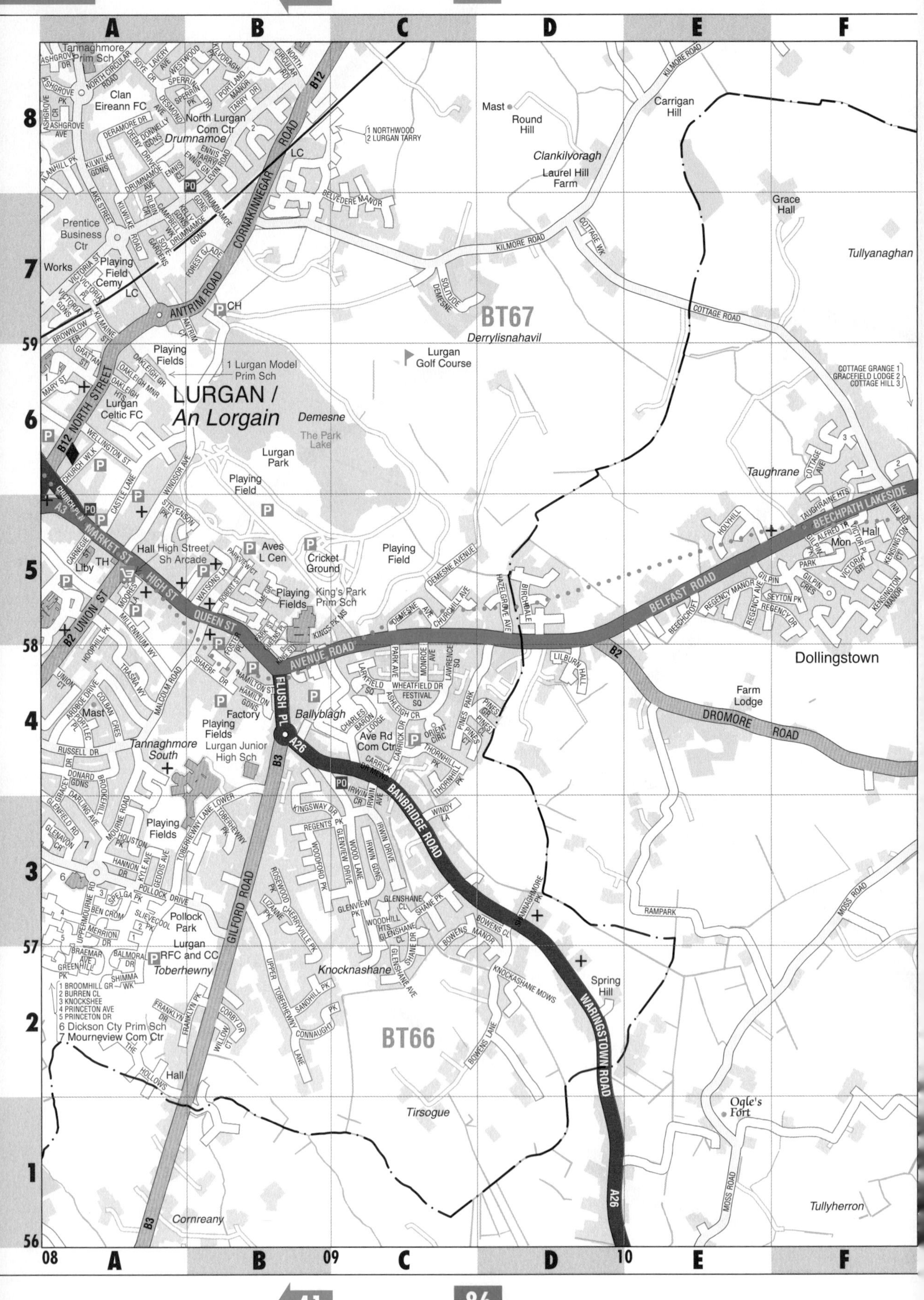
A
B
C
D
E
F
LURGAN /
An Lorgain
BT67
BT66
Dollingstown
Derrylisnahavil
Clankilvoragh
Taughrane
Tullyanaghan
Tullyherron
Knocknashane
Tirsogue
Cornreany
Toberhewny
Ballyblagh
Drumnamoe
Tannaghmore South
Demesne
Lurgan Park
The Park Lake
Lurgan Golf Course
Carrigan Hill
Round Hill
Laurel Hill Farm
Grace Hall
Farm Lodge
Spring Hill
Ogle's Fort
Mast
Clan Eireann FC
North Lurgan Com Ctr
Prentice Business Ctr
Lurgan Celtic FC
Pollock Park
Lurgan RFC and CC
Lurgan Junior High Sch
King's Park Prim Sch
Cricket Ground
Aves L Cen
Ave Rd Com Ctr
High Street Sh Arcade
KILMORE ROAD
COTTAGE ROAD
BELFAST ROAD
BEECHPATH LAKESIDE
DROMORE ROAD
AVENUE ROAD
BANBRIDGE ROAD
WARINGSTOWN ROAD
GILFORD ROAD
ANTRIM ROAD
CORNAKINNEGAR ROAD
NORTH STREET
UNION ST
MARKET ST
HIGH ST
QUEEN ST
FLUSH PL
MOSS ROAD
1 NORTHWOOD
2 LURGAN TARRY
1 Lurgan Model Prim Sch
COTTAGE GRANGE 1
GRACEFIELD LODGE 2
COTTAGE HILL 3
1 BROOMHILL GR
2 BURREN CL
3 KNOCKSHEE
4 PRINCETON AVE
5 PRINCETON DR
6 Dickson Cty Prim Sch
7 Mourneview Com Ctr
8
7
59
6
5
58
4
3
57
2
1
56
08
09
10

41
86

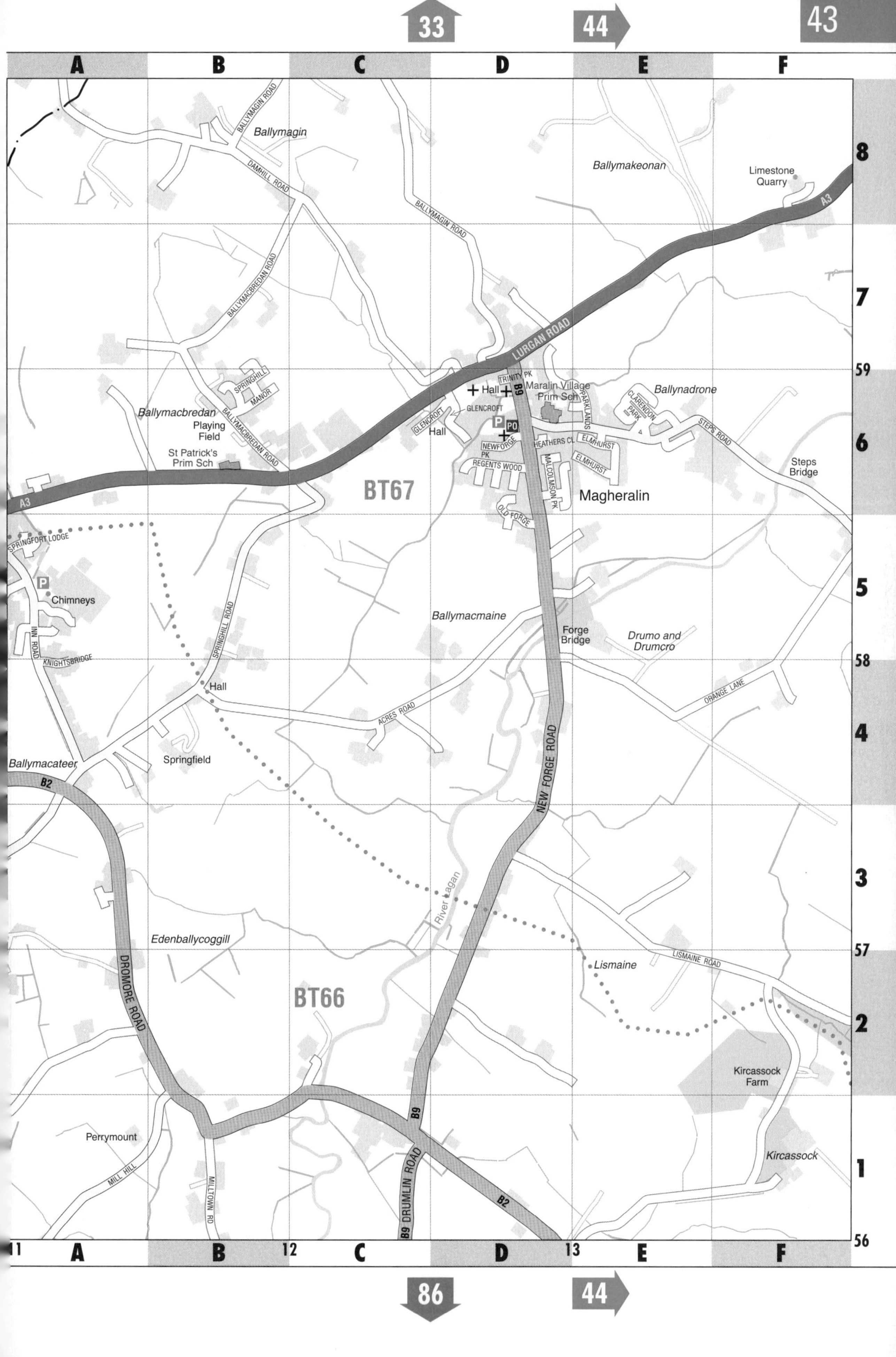
A
B
C
D
E
F
Ballymagin
BALLYMAGIN ROAD
DAMHILL ROAD
BALLYMAGIN ROAD
Ballymakeonan
Limestone Quarry
A3
8
7
BALLYMACBREDAN ROAD
LURGAN ROAD
59
SPRINGHILL MANOR
TRINITY PK
Hall
Maralin Village Prim Sch
PARKLANDS
Ballynadrone
CLARENDON PARK
B9
GLENCROFT
GLENCROFT
Hall
P
PO
Ballymacbredan
Playing Field
St Patrick's Prim Sch
BALLYMACBREDAN ROAD
NEWFORGE PK
HEATHERS CL
ELMHURST
ELMHURST
STEPS ROAD
REGENTS WOOD
MALCOLMSON PK
6
Steps Bridge
A3
BT67
Magheralin
OLD FORGE
SPRINGFORT LODGE
P
Chimneys
SPRINGHILL ROAD
5
Ballymacmaine
Forge Bridge
Drumo and Drumcro
INN ROAD
KNIGHTSBRIDGE
58
Hall
ACRES ROAD
ORANGE LANE
4
Springfield
Ballymacateer
B2
NEW FORGE ROAD
3
River Lagan
Edenballycoggill
57
Lismaine
LISMAINE ROAD
DROMORE ROAD
BT66
2
Kircassock Farm
B9
Perrymount
MILL HILL
MILLTOWN RD
DRUMLIN ROAD
B9
B2
Kircassock
1
56
11
A
B
12
C
D
13
E
F

A8
1 WARINGFIELD GDNS
2 WARINGFIELD MS
3 LAGANVALE
4 WARINGFIELD CL

B8
1 WARINGFIELD PK
2 THE WALLED GDN
3 WARINGFIELD GRANGE

43
34

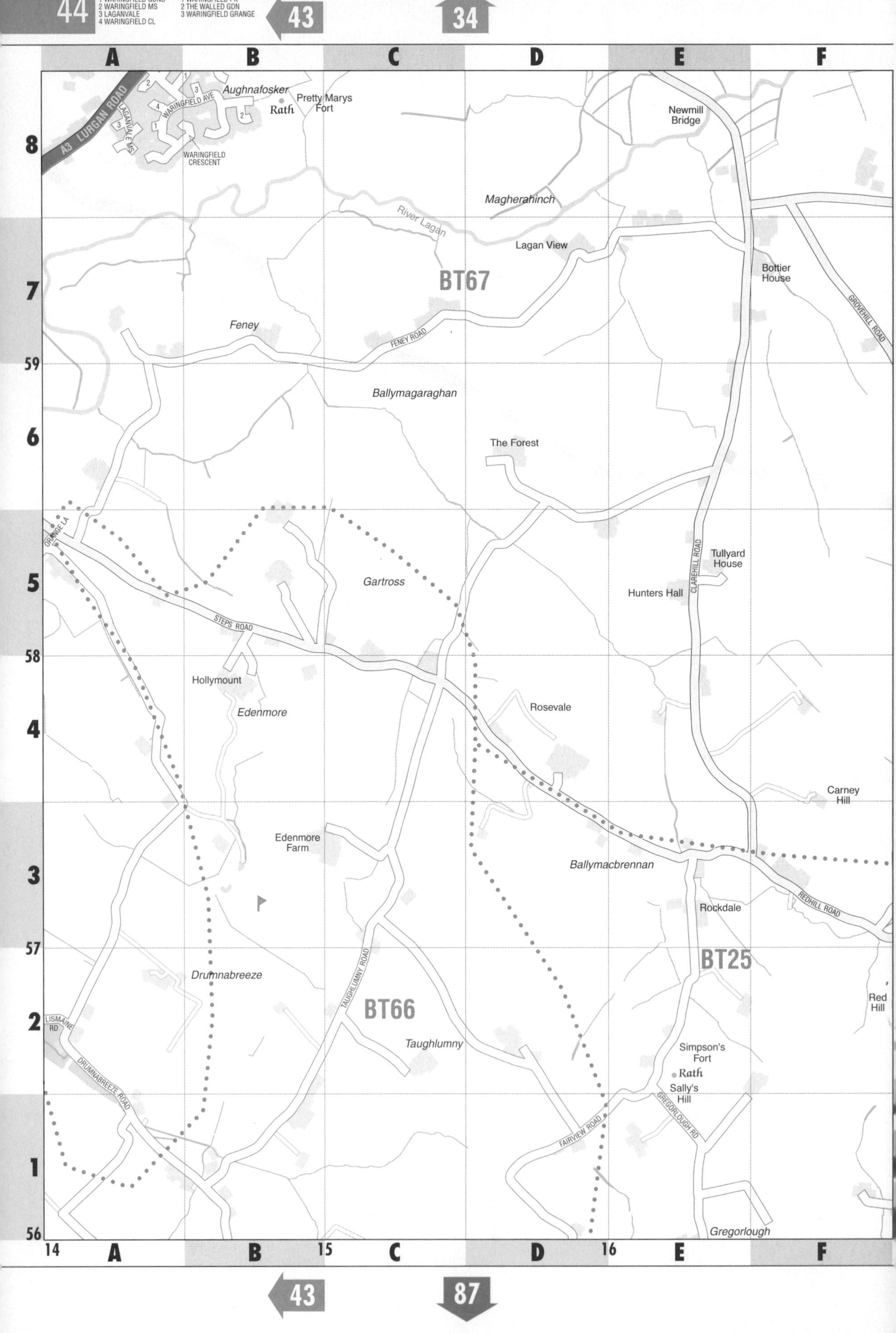

43
87

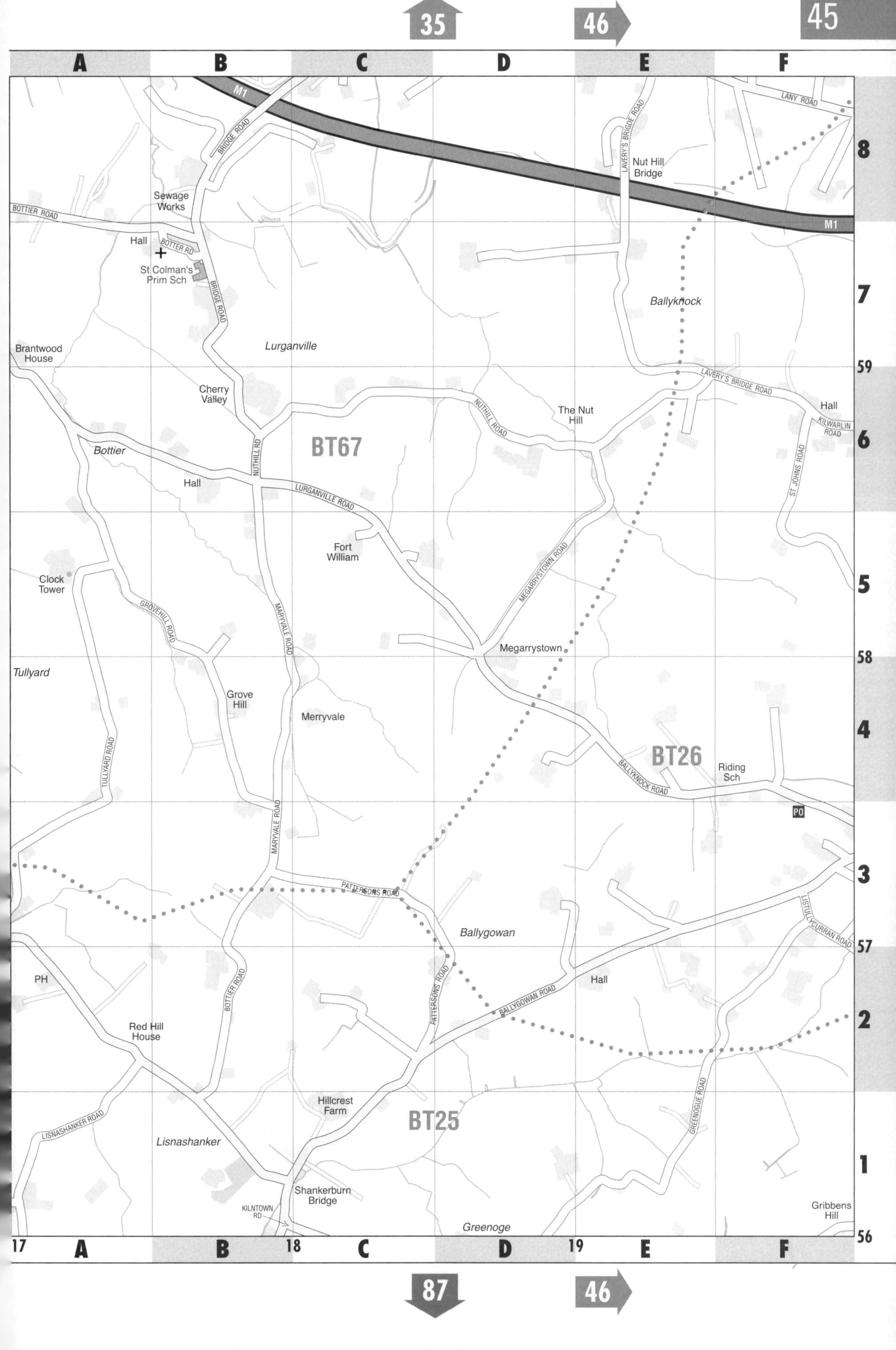
35
46
A
B
C
D
E
F
M1
LANY ROAD
BRIDGE ROAD
LAVERY'S BRIDGE ROAD
Nut Hill Bridge
Sewage Works
BOTTIER ROAD
Hall
BOTTER RD
St Colman's Prim Sch
Ballyknock
Lurganville
Brantwood House
Cherry Valley
LAVERY'S BRIDGE ROAD
NUTHILL ROAD
The Nut Hill
Hall
KILWARLIN ROAD
ST JOHNS ROAD
BT67
Bottier
NUTHILL RD
Hall
LURGANVILLE ROAD
Fort William
Clock Tower
MEGARRYSTOWN ROAD
GROVEHILL ROAD
MARYVALE ROAD
Megarrystown
Tullyard
Grove Hill
Merryvale
TULLYARD ROAD
BT26
Riding Sch
BALLYKNOCK ROAD
PO
MARYVALE ROAD
PATTERSONS ROAD
Ballygowan
LISTULLYCURRAN ROAD
PH
BOTTIER ROAD
PATTERSONS ROAD
BALLYGOWAN ROAD
Hall
Red Hill House
GREENOGUE ROAD
Hillcrest Farm
BT25
LISNASHANKER ROAD
Lisnashanker
Shankerburn Bridge
KILNTOWN RD
Greenoge
Gribbens Hill
8
7
59
6
5
58
4
3
57
2
1
56
17
18
19
87
46

45
36

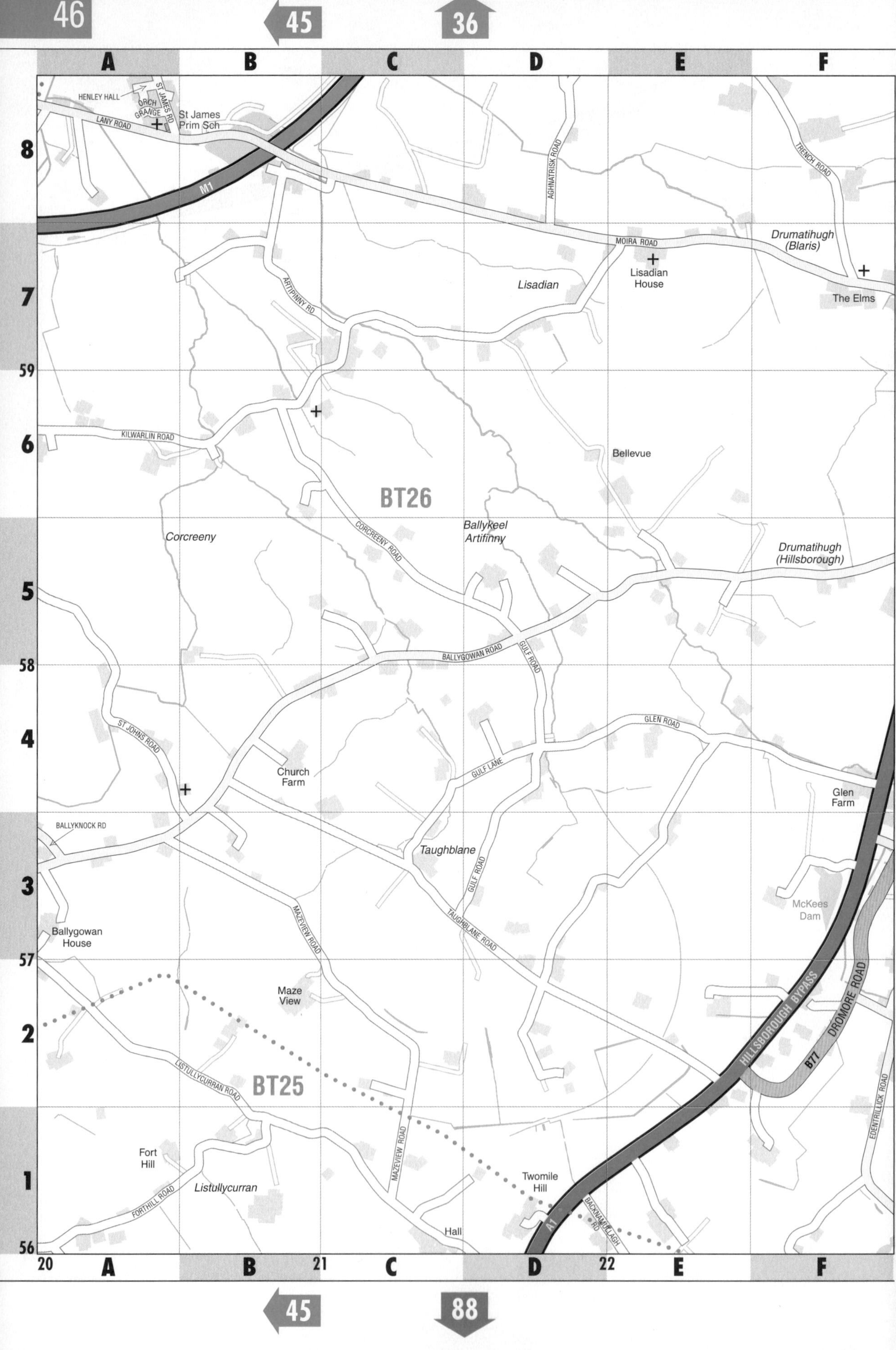
A
B
C
D
E
F
HENLEY HALL
ORCH GRANGE
ST JAMES RD
St James Prim Sch
LANY ROAD
M1
AGHNATRISK ROAD
TRENCH ROAD
MOIRA ROAD
Drumatihugh (Blaris)
Lisadian House
Lisadian
The Elms
ARTIFINNY RD
KILWARLIN ROAD
Bellevue
BT26
CORCREENY ROAD
Corcreeny
Ballykeel Artifinny
Drumatihugh (Hillsborough)
BALLYGOWAN ROAD
GULF ROAD
GLEN ROAD
ST JOHNS ROAD
GULF LANE
Church Farm
Glen Farm
BALLYKNOCK RD
Taughblane
GULF ROAD
McKees Dam
Ballygowan House
MAZEVIEW ROAD
TAUGHBLANE ROAD
Maze View
HILLSBOROUGH BYPASS
DROMORE ROAD
B77
LISTULLYCURRAN ROAD
BT25
EDENTRILLICK ROAD
MAZEVIEW ROAD
Fort Hill
Twomile Hill
Listullycurran
FORTHILL ROAD
BACKNAMULLAGH RD
A1
Hall
8
7
59
6
5
58
4
3
57
2
1
56
20
21
22

45
88

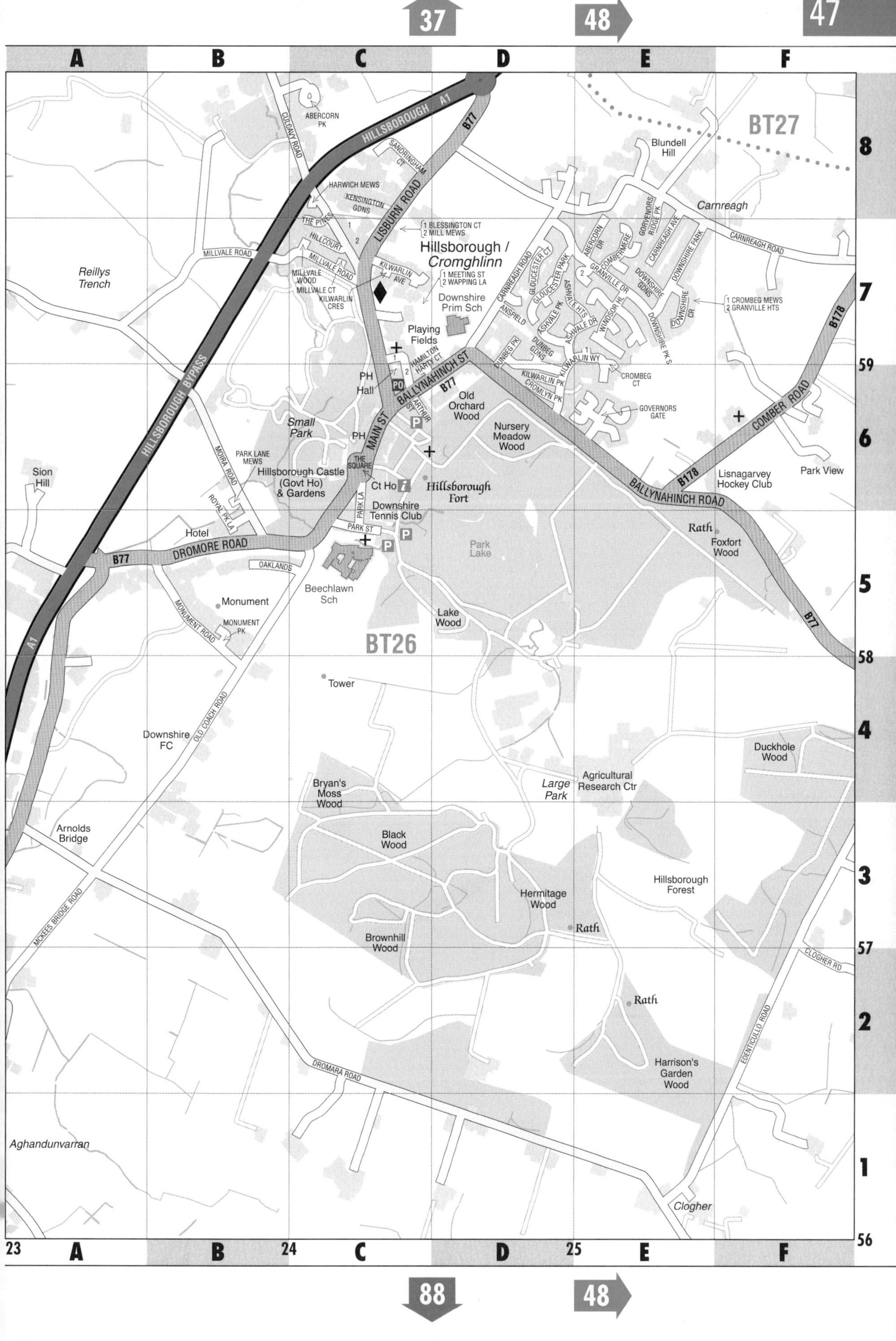
37
48
A
B
C
D
E
F
8
7
59
6
5
58
4
3
57
2
1
56
23
24
25
BT27
BT26
Hillsborough /
Cromghlinn
HILLSBOROUGH A1
HILLSBOROUGH BYPASS
A1
B77
B178
ABERCORN PK
CULCAVY ROAD
SANDRINGHAM CT
LISBURN ROAD
HARWICH MEWS
KENSINGTON GDNS
THE PINES
HILLCOURT
1 BLESSINGTON CT
2 MILL MEWS
MILLVALE ROAD
KILWARLIN AVE
1 MEETING ST
2 WAPPING LA
MILLVALE WOOD
MILLVALE CT
KILWARLIN CRES
Downshire Prim Sch
Playing Fields
Blundell Hill
Carnreagh
CARNREAGH ROAD
GORVENORS RIDGE PK
CARNREAGH AVE
ABERCORN DR
COMBERMERE
DOWNSHIRE PARK
GLOUCESTER CT
GLOUCESTER PARK
GRANVILLE DR
DOWNSHIRE GDNS
ASHVALE HTS
ASHVALE PK
ASHVALE DR
WINDSOR HL
DOWNSHIRE CR
DOWNSHIRE PK S
1 CROMBEG MEWS
2 GRANVILLE HTS
ANSFIELD
DUNBEG PK
DUNBEG GDNS
KILWARLIN WY
KILWARLIN PK
CROMLYN PK
CROMBEG CT
GOVERNORS GATE
HAMILTON HARTY CT
BALLYNAHINCH ST
PH
Hall
PO
ARTHUR ST
Old Orchard Wood
Nursery Meadow Wood
Reillys Trench
Small Park
MAIN ST
THE SQUARE
PARK LANE MEWS
MOIRA ROAD
Hillsborough Castle (Govt Ho) & Gardens
Ct Ho
Hillsborough Fort
Sion Hill
ROYAL PK LA
PARK LA
Downshire Tennis Club
PARK ST
Hotel
DROMORE ROAD
OAKLANDS
Beechlawn Sch
Park Lake
BALLYNAHINCH ROAD
COMBER ROAD
Lisnagarvey Hockey Club
Park View
Rath
Foxfort Wood
Monument
MONUMENT ROAD
MONUMENT PK
Lake Wood
Tower
Downshire FC
OLD COACH ROAD
Duckhole Wood
Agricultural Research Ctr
Large Park
Bryan's Moss Wood
Black Wood
Arnolds Bridge
Hillsborough Forest
MCKEES BRIDGE ROAD
Hermitage Wood
Brownhill Wood
CLOGHER RD
EDENTICULLO ROAD
Harrison's Garden Wood
DROMARA ROAD
Aghandunvarran
Clogher
88
48

47
38

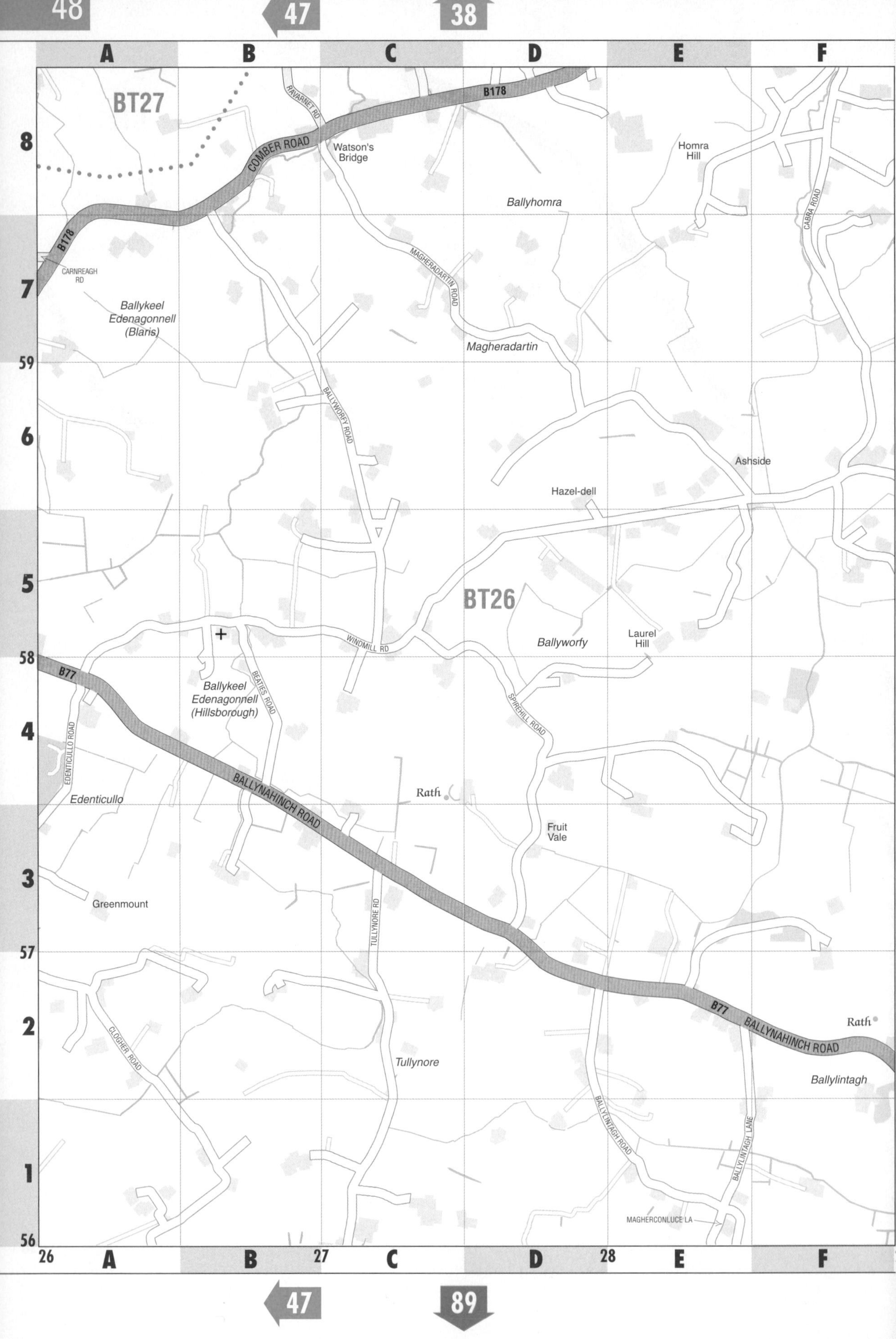
A
B
C
D
E
F
BT27
B178
COMBER ROAD
RAVARNET RD
Watson's Bridge
Homra Hill
Ballyhomra
CABRA ROAD
CARNREAGH RD
MAGHERADARTIN ROAD
Ballykeel Edenagonnell (Blaris)
Magheradartin
BALLYWORFY ROAD
Ashside
Hazel-dell
BT26
Ballyworfy
Laurel Hill
WINDMILL RD
B77
Ballykeel Edenagonnell (Hillsborough)
BEATIES ROAD
SPIREHILL ROAD
EDENTICULLO ROAD
BALLYNAHINCH ROAD
Rath
Edenticullo
Fruit Vale
Greenmount
TULLYNORE RD
CLOGHER ROAD
Tullynore
BALLYNAHINCH ROAD
Rath
Ballylintagh
BALLYLINTAGH ROAD
BALLYLINTAGH LANE
MAGHERCONLUCE LA
8
7
59
6
5
58
4
3
57
2
1
56
26
27
28

47
89

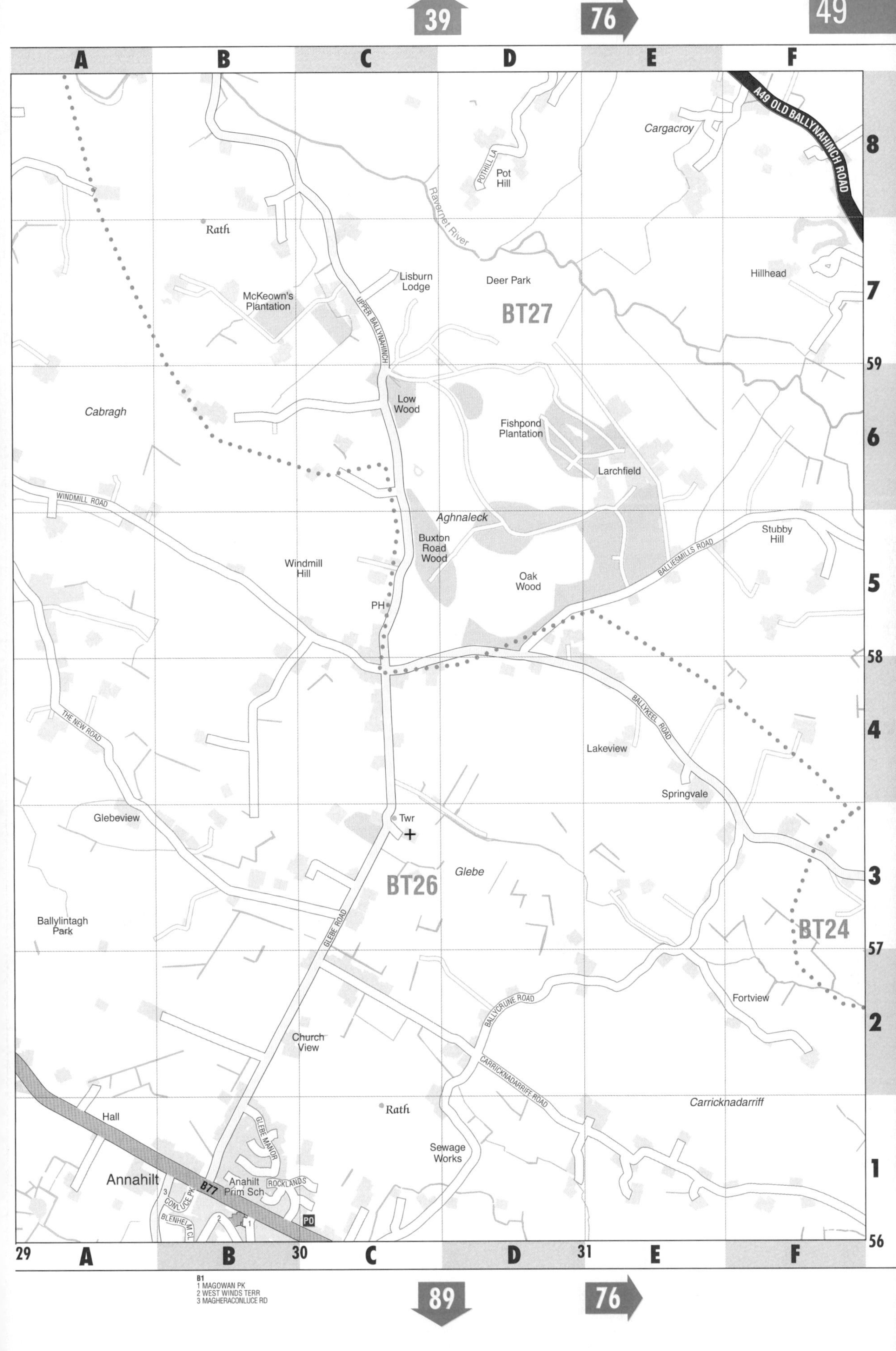
39
76
A
B
C
D
E
F
A49 OLD BALLYNAHINCH ROAD
Cargacroy
POTHILL LA
Pot Hill
Ravernet River
Rath
Lisburn Lodge
Deer Park
Hillhead
McKeown's Plantation
UPPER BALLYNAHINCH
BT27
Cabragh
Low Wood
Fishpond Plantation
Larchfield
WINDMILL ROAD
Aghnaleck
Buxton Road Wood
Stubby Hill
BALLIESMILLS ROAD
Windmill Hill
Oak Wood
PH
THE NEW ROAD
BALLYKEEL ROAD
Lakeview
Springvale
Glebeview
Twr
Glebe
BT26
GLEBE ROAD
Ballylintagh Park
BT24
Fortview
BALLYCRUNE ROAD
Church View
CARRICKNADARRIFE ROAD
Carricknadarriff
Hall
Rath
GLEBE MANOR
Sewage Works
Annahilt
B77
Anahilt Prim Sch
ROCKLANDS
CONLUCE PK
BLENHEIM CL
PO
8
7
59
6
5
58
4
3
57
2
1
56
29
30
31
B1
1 MAGOWAN PK
2 WEST WINDS TERR
3 MAGHERACONLUCE RD
89
76

85
74

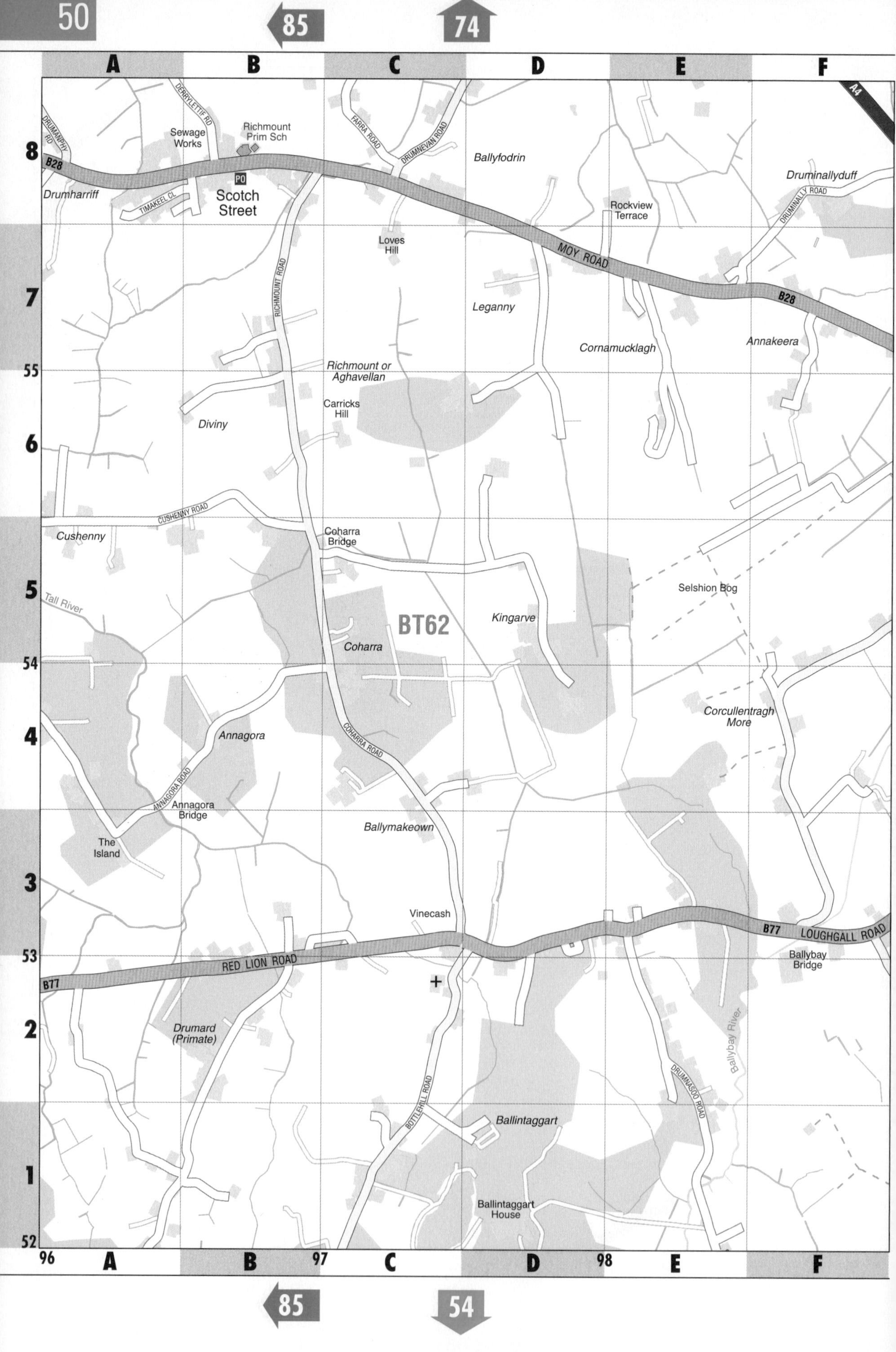
A
B
C
D
E
F
8
7
55
6
5
54
4
3
53
2
1
52
96
97
98
A4
DRUMANPHY RD
DERRYLETTIF RD
Sewage Works
Richmount Prim Sch
PO
FARRA ROAD
DRUMNEVAN ROAD
Ballyfodrin
B28
Drumharriff
TIMAKEEL CL
Scotch Street
Druminallyduff
DRUMINALLY ROAD
Rockview Terrace
Loves Hill
MOY ROAD
RICHMOUNT ROAD
Leganny
B28
Cornamucklagh
Annakeera
Richmount or Aghavellan
Carricks Hill
Diviny
CUSHENNY ROAD
Cushenny
Coharra Bridge
Selshion Bog
Tall River
BT62
Kingarve
Coharra
Corcullentragh More
Annagora
COHARRA ROAD
ANNAGORA ROAD
Annagora Bridge
The Island
Ballymakeown
Vinecash
B77
LOUGHGALL ROAD
RED LION ROAD
Ballybay Bridge
B77
Drumard (Primate)
Ballybay River
DRUMNASOO ROAD
BOTTLEHILL ROAD
Ballintaggart
Ballintaggart House

85
54

74
52

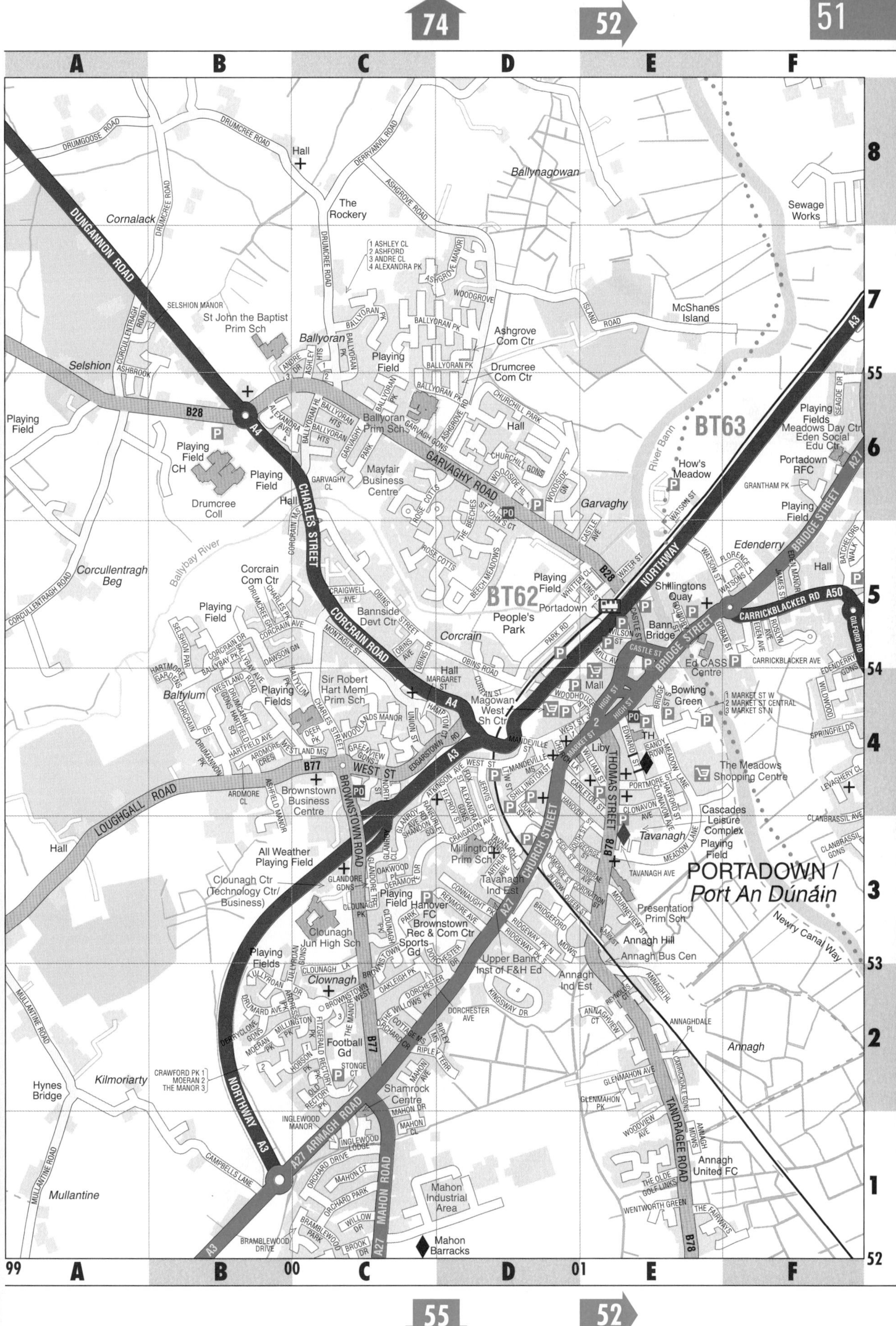
PORTADOWN /
Port An Dúnáin
BT62
BT63
Ballynagowan
Cornalack
Selshion
Corcullentragh Beg
Ballyoran
Garvaghy
Edenderry
Corcrain
Baltylum
Clownagh
Kilmoriarty
Mullantine
Tavanagh
Annagh
McShanes Island
Sewage Works
The Rockery
St John the Baptist Prim Sch
Ashgrove Com Ctr
Drumcree Com Ctr
Ballyoran Prim Sch
Mayfair Business Centre
Drumcree Coll
Corcrain Com Ctr
Bannside Devt Ctr
Sir Robert Hart Meml Prim Sch
Magowan West Sh Ctr
People's Park
Brownstown Business Centre
All Weather Playing Field
Clounagh Ctr (Technology Ctr/ Business)
Clounagh Jun High Sch
Millington Prim Sch
Tavanagh Ind Est
Hanover FC
Brownstown Rec & Com Ctr
Upper Bann Inst of F&H Ed
Annagh Ind Est
Shamrock Centre
Mahon Industrial Area
Mahon Barracks
Annagh United FC
Presentation Prim Sch
Annagh Hill
Annagh Bus Cen
Cascades Leisure Complex
The Meadows Shopping Centre
Ed CASS Centre
Bowling Green
Shillingtons Quay
Bann Bridge
How's Meadow
Portadown RFC
Meadows Day Ctr
Eden Social Edu Ctr
Hynes Bridge
River Bann
Ballybay River
Newry Canal Way
DUNGANNON ROAD
CHARLES STREET
CORCRAIN ROAD
GARVAGHY ROAD
NORTHWAY
BRIDGE STREET
CARRICKBLACKER RD
LOUGHGALL ROAD
WEST ST
BROWNSTOWN ROAD
ARMAGH ROAD
MAHON ROAD
CHURCH STREET
THOMAS STREET
TANDRAGEE ROAD
DRUMCREE ROAD
DRUMGOOSE ROAD
DERRYANVIL ROAD
ASHGROVE ROAD
ISLAND ROAD
OBINS STREET
MULLANTINE ROAD
CAMPBELLS LANE
1 ASHLEY CL
2 ASHFORD
3 ANDRE CL
4 ALEXANDRA PK
1 MARKET ST W
2 MARKET ST CENTRAL
3 MARKET ST N
CRAWFORD PK 1
MOERAN 2
THE MANOR 3
A B C D E F
8 7 6 5 4 3 2 1
55 54 53 52
99 00 01

55
52

51
40

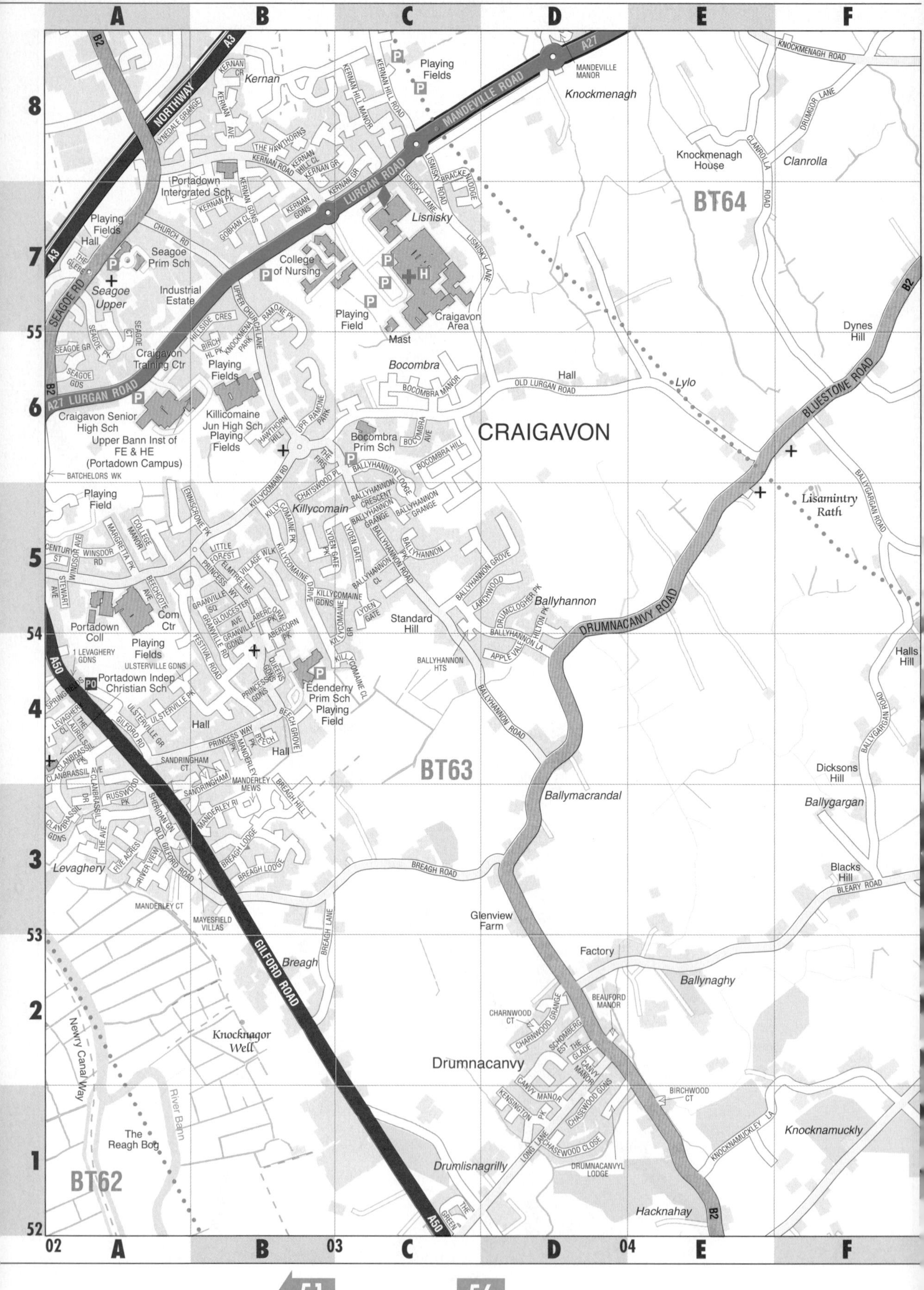
A
B
C
D
E
F
8
7
55
6
5
54
4
3
53
2
1
52
02
03
04
NORTHWAY
A3
B2
A27
MANDEVILLE ROAD
LURGAN ROAD
A27 LURGAN ROAD
Kernan
KERNAN CR
KERNAN AVE
KERNAN HILL MANOR
KERNAN HILL ROAD
LYNEDALE GRANGE
THE HAWTHORNS
KERNAN HILL CL
KERNAN ROAD
KERNAN GR
KERNAN GDNS
KERNAN PK
GOBHAN CL
Playing Fields
MANDEVILLE MANOR
Knockmenagh
KNOCKMENAGH ROAD
DRUMGOR LANE
Knockmenagh House
CLANROLLA ROAD
Clanrolla
BT64
Portadown Intergrated Sch
LISNISKY ROAD
BRACKEN LODGE
LISNISKY LANE
Lisnisky
Playing Fields
Hall
CHURCH RD
THE GLEBE
Seagoe Prim Sch
Seagoe Upper
Industrial Estate
College of Nursing
Craigavon Area
Playing Field
Mast
SEAGOE RD
SEAGOE GR
SEAGOE PK
SEAGOE CT
SEAGOE GDNS
HILLSIDE CRES
BIRCH HL PK
KNOCKMENA PARK
UPPER CHURCH LANE
RAMONE PK
Craigavon Training Ctr
Playing Fields
Bocombra
BOCOMBRA MANOR
OLD LURGAN ROAD
Hall
Lylo
Dynes Hill
BLUESTONE ROAD
Craigavon Senior High Sch
Killicomaine Jun High Sch
Upper Bann Inst of FE & HE (Portadown Campus)
Playing Fields
HAWTHORN HILL
UPR RAMONE PARK
Bocombra Prim Sch
BOCOMBRA AVE
BOCOMBRA HILL
CRAIGAVON
BATCHELORS WK
THE FIRS
CHATSWOOD PL
BALLYHANNON LODGE
BALLYHANNON CRESCENT
BALLYHANNON GRANGE
Killycomain
Lisamintry Rath
BALLYGARGAN ROAD
Playing Field
ENNISCRONE PK
KILLYCOMAIN RD
COLLEGE MANOR
MARGRETTA PK
CENTURY ST
WINDSOR AVE
WINDSOR RD
LITTLE FOREST
ELMTREE MS
VILLAGE WLK
KILLYCOMAINE PK
LYDEN GATE
BALLYHANNON PK
BALLYHANNON GROVE
LARCHWOOD
PRINCESS WY
KILLYCOMAINE DRIVE
BALLYHANNON ROAD
BALLYHANNON CL
Ballyhannon
DRUMACLOGHER PK
HILTON PK
DRUMNACANVY ROAD
STEWART AVE
BEECHCOTE AVE
Com Ctr
Portadown Coll
GRANVILLE SQ
GLOUCESTER AVE
GRANVILLE RD
ABERCORN PK
KILLYCOMAINE GDNS
KILLYCOMAINE GR
Standard Hill
BALLYHANNON LA
APPLE VALE
BALLYHANNON HTS
Halls Hill
1 LEVAGHERY GDNS
Playing Fields
ULSTERVILLE GDNS
FESTIVAL ROAD
QUEENS GDNS
PRINCESS GDNS
KILLYCOMAINE CL
Edenderry Prim Sch
Playing Field
A50
PO
Portadown Indep Christian Sch
SPRINGFIELDS
ULSTERVILLE PK
LEVAGHERY CL
THE LAURELS
ULSTERVILLE GR
GILFORD RD
Hall
BEECH GROVE
BEECH PK
PRINCESS WAY
MANDERLEY PK
Hall
CLANBRASSIL PK
CLANBRASSIL AVE
SANDRINGHAM CT
SANDRINGHAM
MANDERLEY MEWS
BREAGH HILL
BT63
Dicksons Hill
Ballymacrandal
Ballygargan
RUSSWOOD PK
CLANBRASSIL DR
CLANBRASSIL GDNS
THE AVE
FIVE ACRES
RIVER VIEW
OLD GILFORD ROAD
SHERIDAN GN
MANDERLEY RI
BREAGH LODGE
Levaghery
BREAGH ROAD
Blacks Hill
BLEARY ROAD
MANDERLEY CT
MAYESFIELD VILLAS
Glenview Farm
GILFORD ROAD
Breagh
BREAGH LANE
Factory
Ballynaghy
Newry Canal Way
Knocknagor Well
CHARNWOOD CT
CHARNWOOD GRANGE
BEAUFORD MANOR
SCHOMBERG EST
THE GLADE
CANVY MANOR
Drumnacanvy
River Bann
KENSINGTON PK
CANVY MANOR
CHASEWOOD GDNS
BIRCHWOOD CT
The Reagh Bog
LONG LANE
CHASEWOOD CLOSE
KNOCKNAMUCKLEY LA
Knocknamuckly
BT62
Drumlisnagrilly
DRUMNACANVYL LODGE
THE GREEN
Hacknahay

51
56

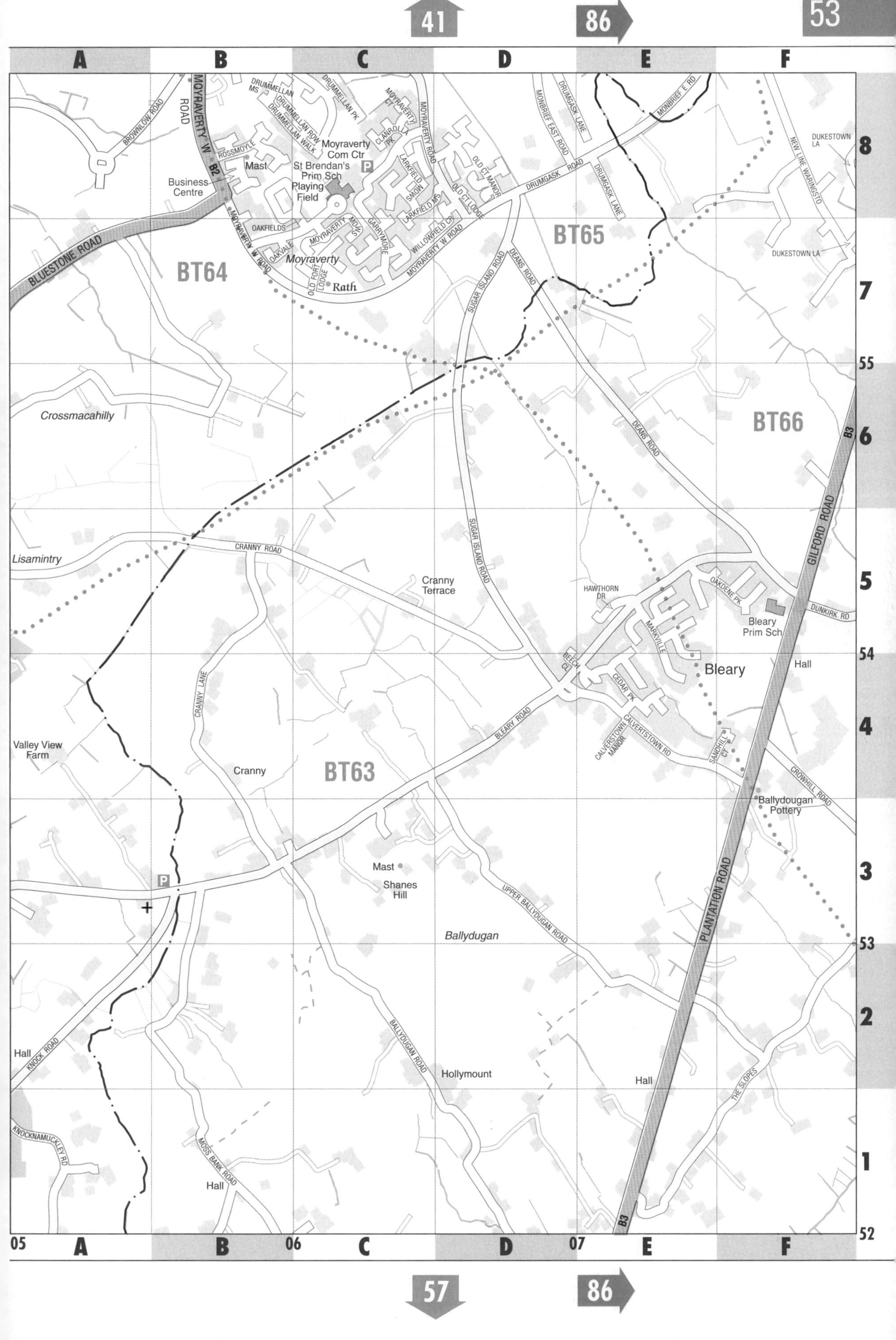
41
86
A
B
C
D
E
F
8
7
55
6
5
54
4
3
53
2
1
52
05
06
07
57
BT64
BT65
BT66
BT63
MOYRAVERTY W ROAD
B2
BLUESTONE ROAD
BROWNLOW ROAD
Business Centre
Mast
ROSSMOYLE
DRUMMELLAN MS
DRUMMELLAN ROW
DRUMMELLAN WALK
DRUMMELLAN PK
Moyraverty Com Ctr
St Brendan's Prim Sch
Playing Field
MOYRAVERTY CT
CLANROLLA PK
MOYRAVERTY ROAD
LARKFIELD MWS
LARKFIELD MS
OLD CT MANOR
OLD CT LODGE
WILLOWFIELD CR
GARRYMORE
MOYRAVERTY
OAKFIELDS
OAKVALE
OLD FORT LODGE
Moyraverty
Rath
DRUMGASK ROAD
DRUMGASK LANE
MONBRIEF EAST ROAD
MONBRIEF E RD
DUKESTOWN LA
NEW LINE WARINGSTOWN
SUGAR ISLAND ROAD
DEANS ROAD
Crossmacahilly
Lisamintry
CRANNY ROAD
Cranny Terrace
HAWTHORN DR
OAKDENE PK
Bleary Prim Sch
DUNKIRK RD
GILFORD ROAD
B3
MARKVILLE
BEECH CL
CEDAR PK
Bleary
Hall
CALVERSTOWN MANOR
CALVERTSTOWN RD
SANDHILL CT
CROWHILL ROAD
Ballydougan Pottery
CRANNY LANE
BLEARY ROAD
Valley View Farm
Cranny
Mast
Shanes Hill
UPPER BALLYDUGAN ROAD
PLANTATION ROAD
Ballydugan
KNOCK ROAD
BALLYDUGAN ROAD
Hollymount
THE SLOPES
KNOCKNAMUCKLEY RD
MOSS BANK ROAD

85
50

A
B
C
D
E
F
8
7
51
6
5
50
4
3
49
2
1
48
96
97
98
Hoops Hill
Bottlehill
DRUMARD ROAD
DRUMNASOO ROAD
BALLINTAGGART ROAD
Drumnasoo
A3
ANNABOE ROAD
BOTTLEHILL ROAD
Clonroot
Highway Gap
VICARAGE ROAD
THE OAKS
DOBBIN ROAD
CLONROOT ROAD
Whitlas Hill
Sewage Works
DERRYHALE LANE
Hall
BROOMHILL
BT62
Drumnahunshin
McBroom's Hill
Sturgeon's Hill
STURGEONS HILL
MULLADRY ROAD
Mulladry
Mulladry Cottage
DERRYHALE ROAD
Derryhale
BROMPTON PK
Rowantrees Hill
Hill Farm
Glenbank
Wilson's Hill
Ballybay River
BT61
King's Hill
Ballybreagh House
TROUGHTON'S HILL
MULLALELISH ROAD
Wheat Field
BALLYBREAGH ROAD
Troughton's Hill
P

85
100

51
56

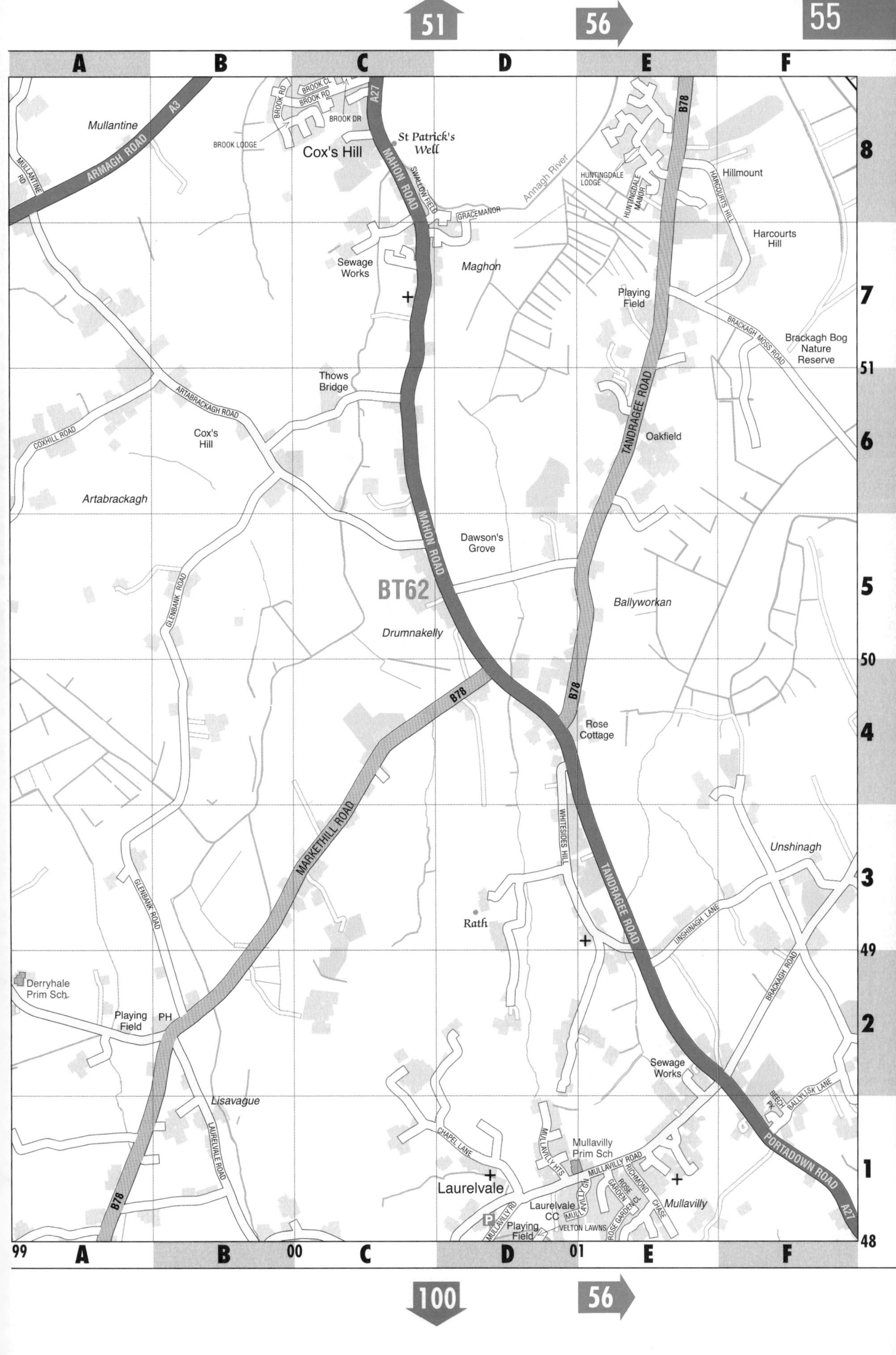
A
B
C
D
E
F
Mullantine
ARMAGH ROAD
A3
MULLANTINE RD
BROOK CL
BROOK RD
BROOK DR
BROOK LODGE
Cox's Hill
A27
St Patrick's Well
MAHON ROAD
SWALLOW FIELD
GRACEMANOR
Annagh River
HUNTINGDALE LODGE
HUNTINGDALE MANOR
B78
HARCOURTS HILL
Hillmount
Harcourts Hill
Sewage Works
Maghon
Playing Field
BRACKAGH MOSS ROAD
Brackagh Bog Nature Reserve
Thows Bridge
ARTABRACKAGH ROAD
COXHILL ROAD
Cox's Hill
TANDRAGEE ROAD
Oakfield
Artabrackagh
Dawson's Grove
MAHON ROAD
GLENBANK ROAD
BT62
Ballyworkan
Drumnakelly
B78
Rose Cottage
MARKETHILL ROAD
WHITESIDES HILL
Unshinagh
GLENBANK ROAD
TANDRAGEE ROAD
Rath
UNSHINAGH LANE
BRACKAGH ROAD
Derryhale Prim Sch
Playing Field
PH
Sewage Works
Lisavague
BEECH PK
BALLYLISK LANE
LAURELVALE ROAD
CHAPEL LANE
MULLAVILLY HTS
Mullavilly Prim Sch
MULLAVILLY ROAD
PORTADOWN ROAD
B78
Laurelvale
RICHMOND
ROSE GARDEN
ROSE GARDEN CL
MULLAVILLY GN
Mullavilly
CHASE
Laurelvale CC
MULLAVILLY RD
P
Playing Field
VELTON LAWNS
A27
8
7
51
6
5
50
4
3
49
2
1
48
99
00
01

100
56

55
52

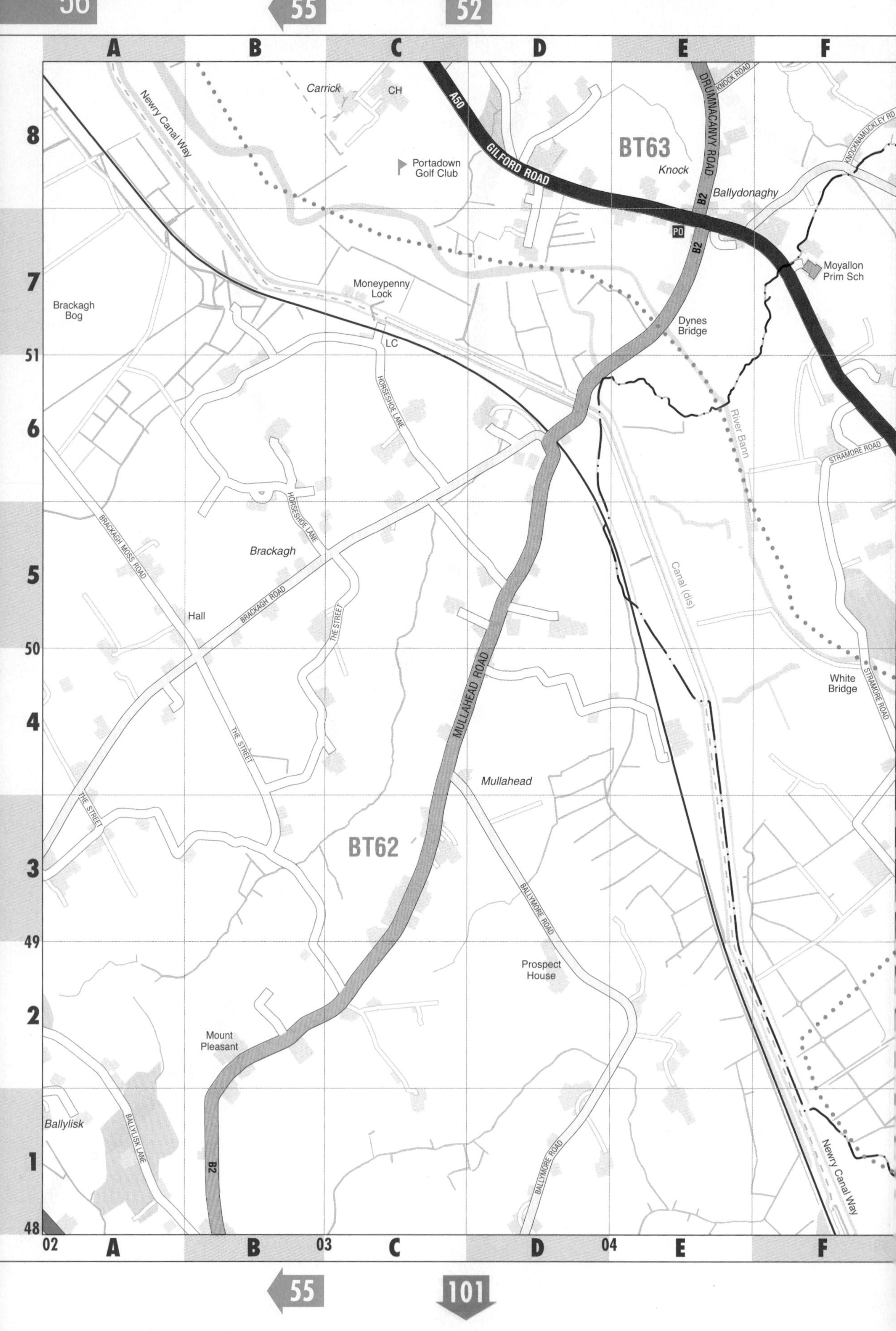
A
B
C
D
E
F
8
7
51
6
5
50
4
3
49
2
1
48
02
03
04
Carrick
CH
Newry Canal Way
A50
GILFORD ROAD
Portadown Golf Club
BT63
Knock
DRUMMACANVY ROAD
KNOCK ROAD
KNOCKNAMUCKLEY RD
Ballydonaghy
B2
PO
Moyallon Prim Sch
Brackagh Bog
Moneypenny Lock
LC
Dynes Bridge
HORSESHOE LANE
River Bann
STRAMORE ROAD
BRACKAGH MOSS ROAD
Brackagh
Canal (dis)
Hall
BRACKAGH ROAD
THE STREET
MULLAHEAD ROAD
White Bridge
Mullahead
BT62
BALLYMORE ROAD
Prospect House
Mount Pleasant
Ballylisk
BALLYLISK LANE
Newry Canal Way

55
101

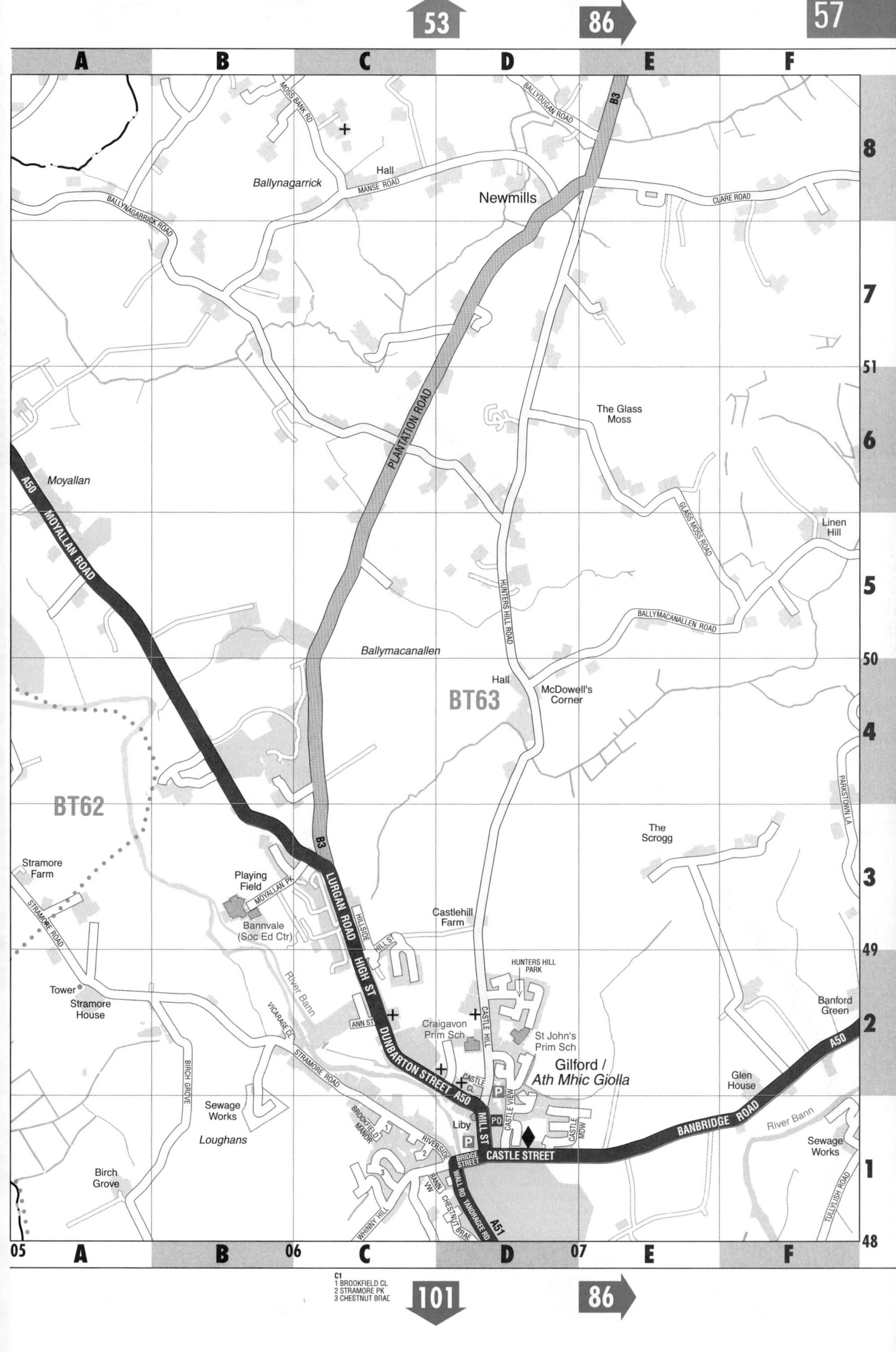
53
86
A
B
C
D
E
F
8
7
51
6
5
50
4
3
49
2
1
48
05
06
07
Ballynagarrick
Hall
MANSE ROAD
Newmills
CLARE ROAD
MOSS BANK RD
BALLYDUGAN ROAD
B3
BALLYNAGARRICK ROAD
PLANTATION ROAD
The Glass Moss
Moyallan
A50
MOYALLAN ROAD
GLASS MOSS ROAD
Linen Hill
HUNTERS HILL ROAD
BALLYMACANALLEN ROAD
Ballymacanallen
Hall
McDowell's Corner
BT63
BT62
PARKSTOWN LA
The Scrogg
Stramore Farm
Playing Field
MOYALLAN PK
LURGAN ROAD
HILLSIDE
Bannvale (Soc Ed Ctr)
STRAMORE ROAD
Castlehill Farm
HILL ST
HIGH ST
HUNTERS HILL PARK
River Bann
Tower
Stramore House
VICARAGE CL
ANN ST
DUNBARTON STREET
Craigavon Prim Sch
CASTLE HILL
St John's Prim Sch
Banford Green
BIRCH GROVE
STRAMORE ROAD
Gilford / Ath Mhic Giolla
Glen House
CASTLE CL
A50
P
PO
CASTLE VIEW
Sewage Works
BROOKFIELD MANOR
Liby
MILL ST
CASTLE MDW
BANBRIDGE ROAD
River Bann
Loughans
RIVERSIDE
BRIDGE STREET
CASTLE STREET
Sewage Works
Birch Grove
BANN VW
WALL RD
TANDRAGEE RD
CHESTNUT BRAE
WHINNY HILL
A51
TULLYLISH ROAD
C1
1 BROOKFIELD CL
2 STRAMORE PK
3 CHESTNUT BRAE

101
86

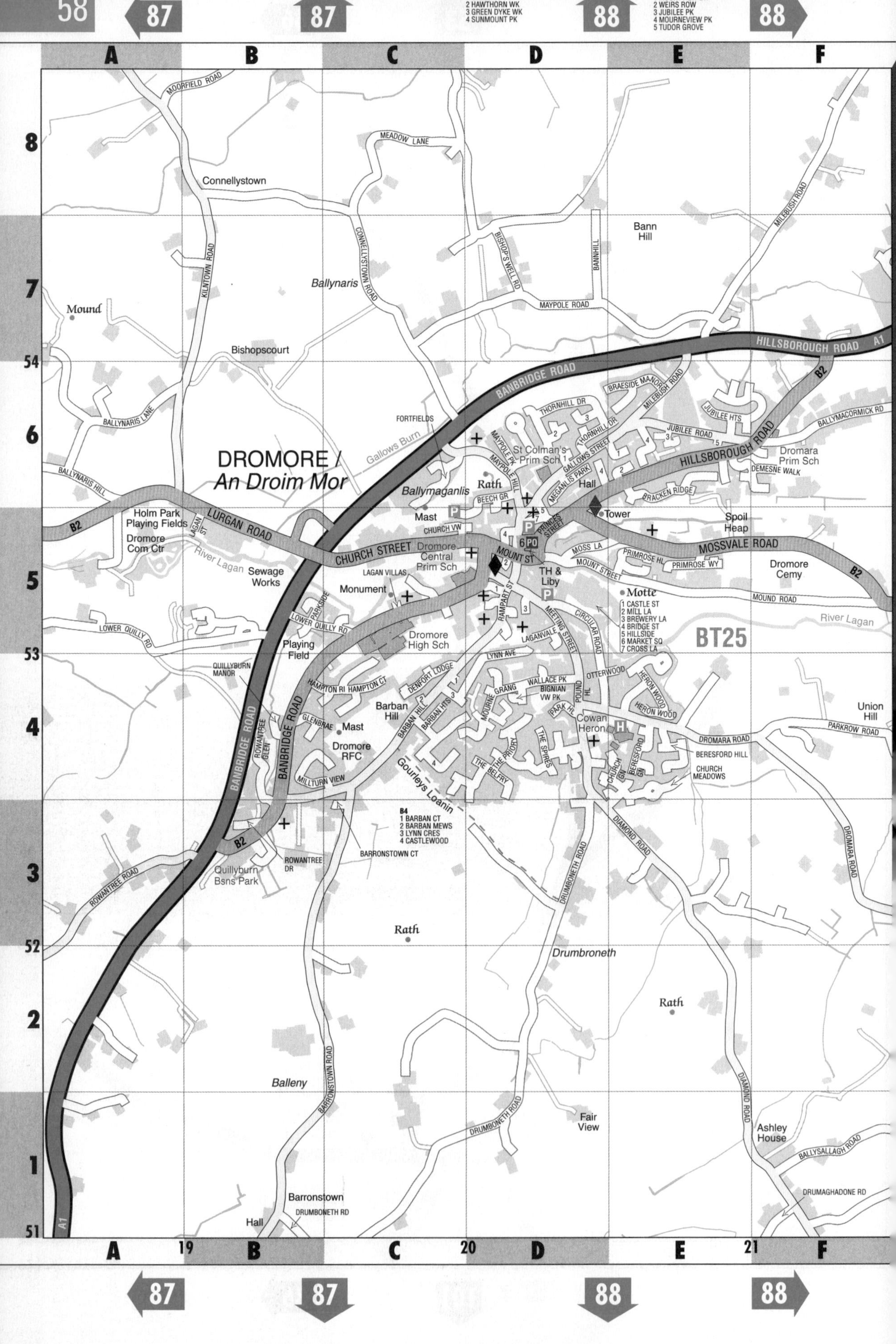
87
87
88
88
D6
1 GALLOWS PL
2 HAWTHORN WK
3 GREEN DYKE WK
4 SUNMOUNT PK
E6
1 MOUNTVIEW DR
2 WEIRS ROW
3 JUBILEE PK
4 MOURNEVIEW PK
5 TUDOR GROVE
A
B
C
D
E
F
8
7
54
6
5
53
4
3
52
2
1
51
19
20
21
MOORFIELD ROAD
MEADOW LANE
Connellystown
KILNTOWN ROAD
CONNELLYSTOWN ROAD
BISHOP'S WELL RD
BANNHILL
Bann Hill
MILEBUSH ROAD
Mound
Ballynaris
MAYPOLE ROAD
HILLSBOROUGH ROAD
A1
Bishopscourt
BANBRIDGE ROAD
BRAESIDE MANOR
MILEBUSH ROAD
B2
THORNHILL DR
JUBILEE HTS
BALLYMACORMICK RD
BALLYNARIS LANE
FORTFIELDS
JUBILEE ROAD
HILLSBOROUGH ROAD
DROMORE /
An Droim Mor
Gallows Burn
MAYPOLE PK
MAYPOLE HILL
St Colman's Prim Sch
GALLOWS STREET
THORNHILL DR
Dromara Prim Sch
DEMESNE WALK
BALLYNARIS HILL
Ballymaganlis
Rath
MEGANLIS PARK
Hall
BRACKEN RIDGE
BEECH GR
Mast
Tower
Spoil Heap
Holm Park Playing Fields
LURGAN ROAD
LAGAN ST
B2
CHURCH VW
PRINCES STREET
PO
Dromore Com Ctr
CHURCH STREET
Dromore Central Prim Sch
MOUNT ST
MOSS LA
PRIMROSE HL
MOSSVALE ROAD
River Lagan
Sewage Works
MOUNT STREET
PRIMROSE WY
Dromore Cemy
B2
LAGAN VILLAS
TH & Liby
Monument
RAMPART ST
Motte
1 CASTLE ST
2 MILL LA
3 BREWERY LA
4 BRIDGE ST
5 HILLSIDE
6 MARKET SQ
7 CROSS LA
MOUND ROAD
LOWER PARKSIDE
MEETING STREET
CIRCULAR ROAD
River Lagan
LOWER QUILLY RD
LOWER QUILLY RD
Dromore High Sch
LAGANVALE
BT25
Playing Field
LYNN AVE
QUILLYBURN MANOR
DENFORT LODGE
OTTERWOOD
HAMPTON RI
HAMPTON CT
WALLACE PK
BIGNIAN VW PK
HERON WOOD
HERON WOOD
Union Hill
BANBRIDGE ROAD
Barban Hill
BARBAN HILL
BARBAN HTS
MOURNE GRANG
POUND HL
PARK HL
Cowan Heron
PARKROW ROAD
ROWANTREE GLEN
GLENBRAE
Mast
DROMARA ROAD
Dromore RFC
THE SPIRES
THE PRIORY
BERESFORD GN
BERESFORD HILL
Gourleys Loanin
THE BELFRY
CHURCH GN
CHURCH MEADOWS
MILLTURN VIEW
B4
1 BARBAN CT
2 BARBAN MEWS
3 LYNN CRES
4 CASTLEWOOD
DIAMOND ROAD
B2
BARRONSTOWN CT
DRUMBONETH ROAD
DROMARA ROAD
ROWANTREE DR
Quillyburn Bsns Park
ROWANTREE ROAD
Rath
Drumbroneth
Rath
Balleny
BARRONSTOWN ROAD
DRUMBONETH ROAD
Fair View
DIAMOND ROAD
Ashley House
BALLYSALLAGH ROAD
DRUMAGHADONE RD
Barronstown
DRUMBONETH RD
Hall
A1

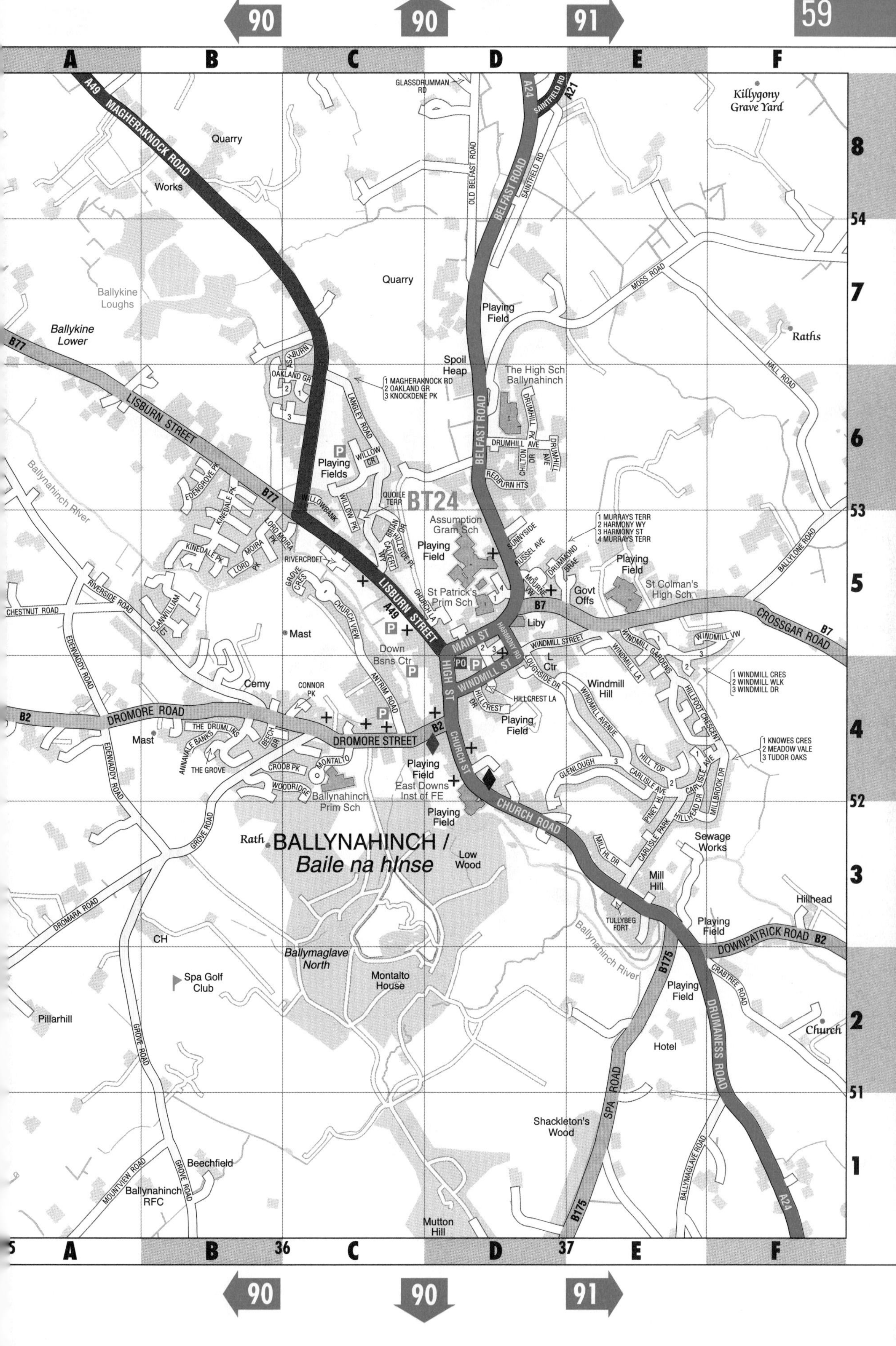

90
90
91
A
B
C
D
E
F
MAGHERAKNOCK ROAD
A49
GLASSDRUMMAN RD
OLD BELFAST ROAD
BELFAST ROAD
A24
SAINTFIELD RD
A21
Killygony Grave Yard
Quarry
Works
Quarry
Ballykine Loughs
Ballykine Lower
Playing Field
MOSS ROAD
Raths
HALL ROAD
B77
LISBURN STREET
ASHBURN
OAKLAND GR
1 MAGHERAKNOCK RD
2 OAKLAND GR
3 KNOCKDENE PK
LANGLEY ROAD
Spoil Heap
The High Sch Ballynahinch
DRUMHILL PK
DRUMHILL AVE
CHILTON DR
REDBURN HTS
Playing Fields
WILLOW CR
WILLOW PK
WILLOWBANK
QUOILE TERR
BT24
Ballynahinch River
EDENGROVE PK
KINEDALE PK
LORD MOIRA PK
Assumption Gram Sch
SUNNYSIDE
RUSSEL AVE
1 MURRAYS TERR
2 HARMONY WY
3 HARMONY ST
4 MURRAYS TERR
DRUMMOND BRAE
Playing Field
St Colman's High Sch
BALLYLOWE ROAD
RIVERCROFT
GROVE CRES
HILLSIDE PL
CALVERT WY
St Patrick's Prim Sch
MOURNE VW
Govt Offs
Liby
RIVERSIDE ROAD
CHESTNUT ROAD
CLANWILLIAM
CHURCH VIEW
CHURCH LA
Mast
MAIN ST
HARMONY RD
B7
CROSSGAR ROAD
WINDMILL STREET
WINDMILL GARDENS
WINDMILL VW
1 WINDMILL CRES
2 WINDMILL WLK
3 WINDMILL DR
EDENVADDY ROAD
Down Bsns Ctr
HIGH ST
PO
WINDMILL ST
LOUGHSIDE DR
L Ctr
Windmill Hill
HILLFOOT CRESCENT
Cemy
CONNOR PK
ANTRIM ROAD
HILLCREST DR
HILLCREST LA
WINDMILL AVENUE
B2
DROMORE ROAD
Mast
THE DRUMLINS
ANNAVALE BANKS
THE GROVE
BEECH GR
DROMORE STREET
CHURCH ST
Playing Field
1 KNOWES CRES
2 MEADOW VALE
3 TUDOR OAKS
CROOB PK
MONTALTO
WOODRIDGE
Ballynahinch Prim Sch
Playing Field
East Downs Inst of FE
GLENLOUGH
HILL TOP
CARLISLE AVE
MILLBROOK DR
PINEY HL
HILLHEAD CR
CHURCH ROAD
Playing Field
GROVE ROAD
Rath
BALLYNAHINCH /
Baile na hInse
Low Wood
MILL HL DR
CARLISLE PARK
Sewage Works
Mill Hill
Hillhead
DROMARA ROAD
TULLYBEG FORT
Playing Field
DOWNPATRICK ROAD
CH
Ballymaglave North
Montalto House
B175
CRABTREE ROAD
Spa Golf Club
Playing Field
Pillarhill
GROVE ROAD
DRUMANESS ROAD
Church
Hotel
SPA ROAD
Shackleton's Wood
Beechfield
MOUNTVIEW ROAD
Ballynahinch RFC
BALLYMAGLAVE ROAD
Mutton Hill
8
54
7
6
53
5
4
52
3
2
51
1
35
36
37

C5
1 St Patrick's Cathedral

D5
1 The Mall Shopping Centre
2 St Malachy's Primary School
3 The Market Place Theatre & Arts Centre
4 St Patrick's Trian Visitor Complex & Armagh Ancestry
5 LITTLE BARRACK ST
6 JENNYS ROW
7 RUSSELL ST

98 98 98

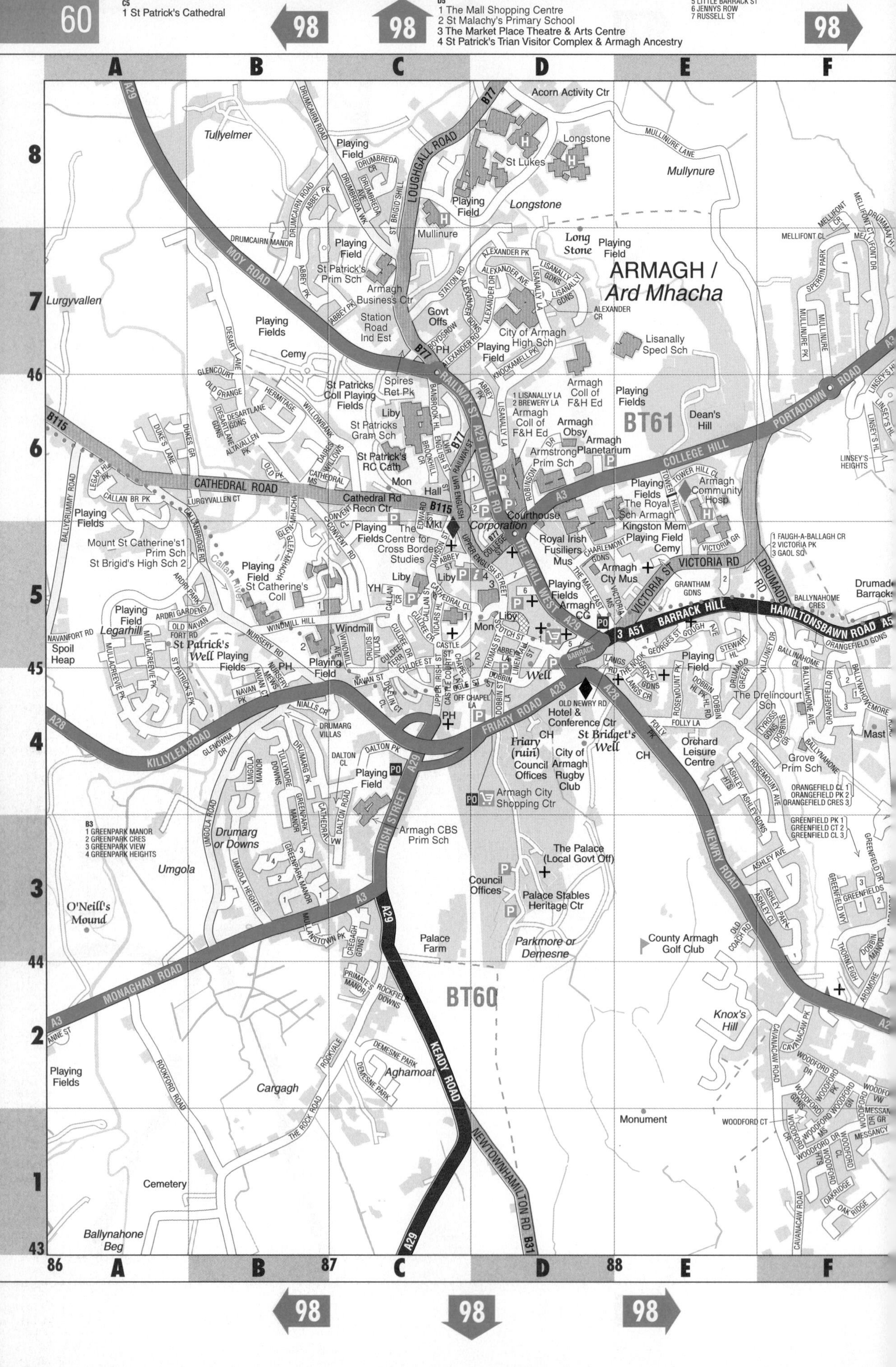

98 98 98

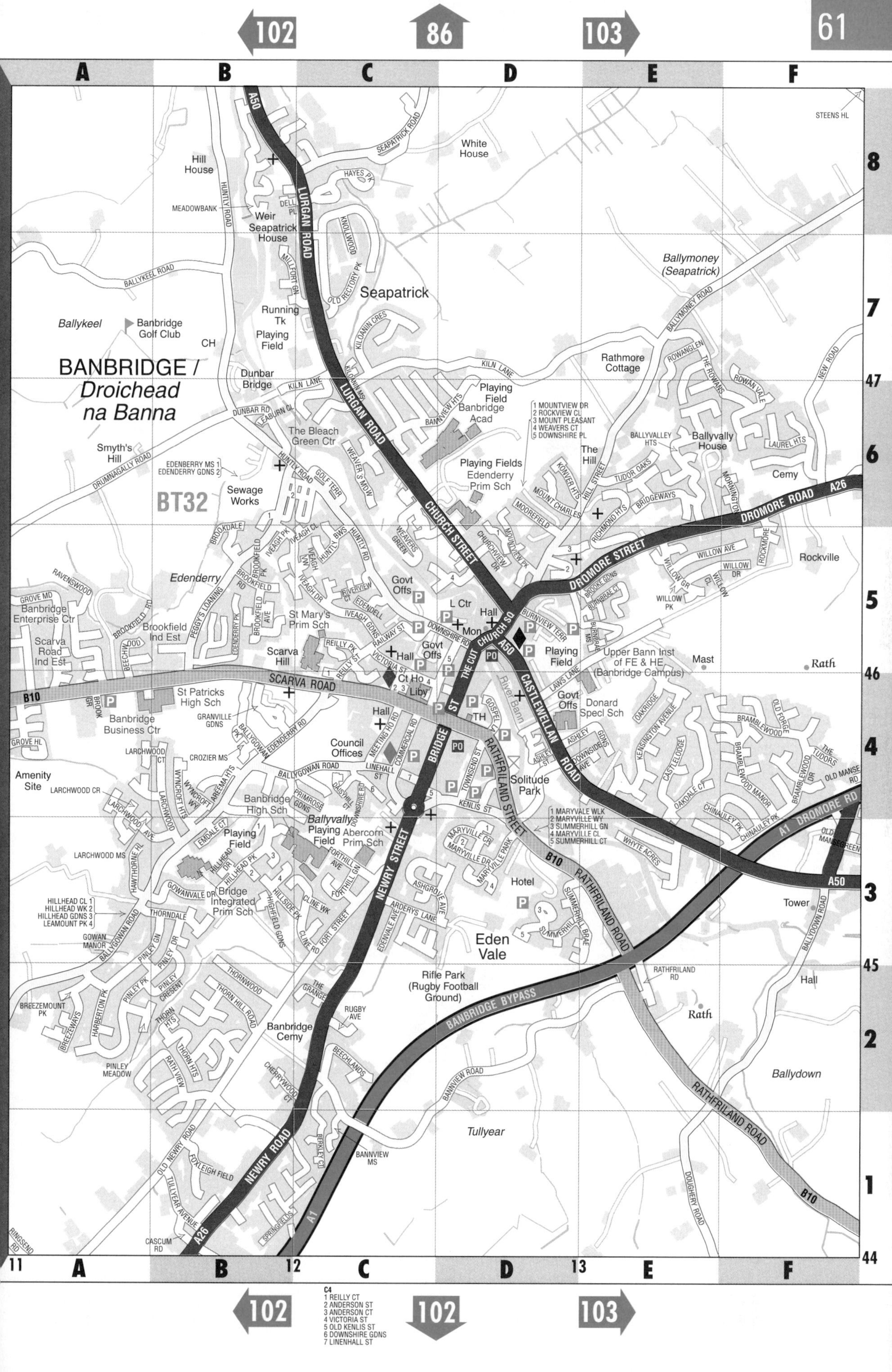
102
86
103
A
B
C
D
E
F
8
7
47
6
5
46
4
3
45
2
1
44
11
12
13
BANBRIDGE /
Droichead
na Banna
BT32
Hill
House
White
House
Weir
Seapatrick
House
Seapatrick
Running
Tk
Playing
Field
Ballykeel
Banbridge
Golf Club
CH
Dunbar
Bridge
Rathmore
Cottage
Ballymoney
(Seapatrick)
Playing
Field
Banbridge
Acad
The Bleach
Green Ctr
Smyth's
Hill
Sewage
Works
Playing Fields
Edenderry
Prim Sch
The
Hill
Ballyvally
House
Cemy
Rockville
Edenderry
Banbridge
Enterprise Ctr
Scarva
Road
Ind Est
Brookfield
Ind Est
St Mary's
Prim Sch
Scarva
Hill
Govt
Offs
L Ctr
Hall
Mon
Playing
Field
Upper Bann Inst
of FE & HE
(Banbridge Campus)
Mast
Rath
Ct Ho
Liby
St Patricks
High Sch
Banbridge
Business Ctr
Donard
Specl Sch
TH
River Bann
Council
Offices
Solitude
Park
Amenity
Site
Banbridge
High Sch
Ballyvally
Playing
Field
Abercorn
Prim Sch
Bridge
Integrated
Prim Sch
Hotel
Tower
Eden
Vale
Rifle Park
(Rugby Football
Ground)
Hall
Banbridge
Cemy
Pinley
Meadow
Ballydown
Tullyear
LURGAN ROAD
CHURCH STREET
DROMORE STREET
DROMORE ROAD
CASTLEWELLAN ROAD
SCARVA ROAD
BRIDGE ST
NEWRY STREET
NEWRY ROAD
RATHFRILAND STREET
RATHFRILAND ROAD
BANBRIDGE BYPASS
A50
A26
A1
B10
1 MOUNTVIEW DR
2 ROCKVIEW CL
3 MOUNT PLEASANT
4 WEAVERS CT
5 DOWNSHIRE PL
1 MARYVALE WLK
2 MARYVILLE WY
3 SUMMERHILL GN
4 MARYVILLE CL
5 SUMMERHILL CT
HILLHEAD CL 1
HILLHEAD WK 2
HILLHEAD GDNS 3
LEAMOUNT PK 4
EDENDERRY MS 1
EDENDERRY GDNS 2
C4
1 REILLY CT
2 ANDERSON ST
3 ANDERSON CT
4 VICTORIA ST
5 OLD KENLIS ST
6 DOWNSHIRE GDNS
7 LINENHALL ST

108

C4
1 MARY STREET / SRÁID MHÚIRE

108

C5
1 CHURCH AVE
2 FOUNTAIN ST / SRÁID AN FHUARÁIN
3 KENNEDY SQ / CEARNÓG UÍ CHINNÉIDE
4 SAUL WAY
5 DE COURCY PL
6 BRITCHES CL

109

109

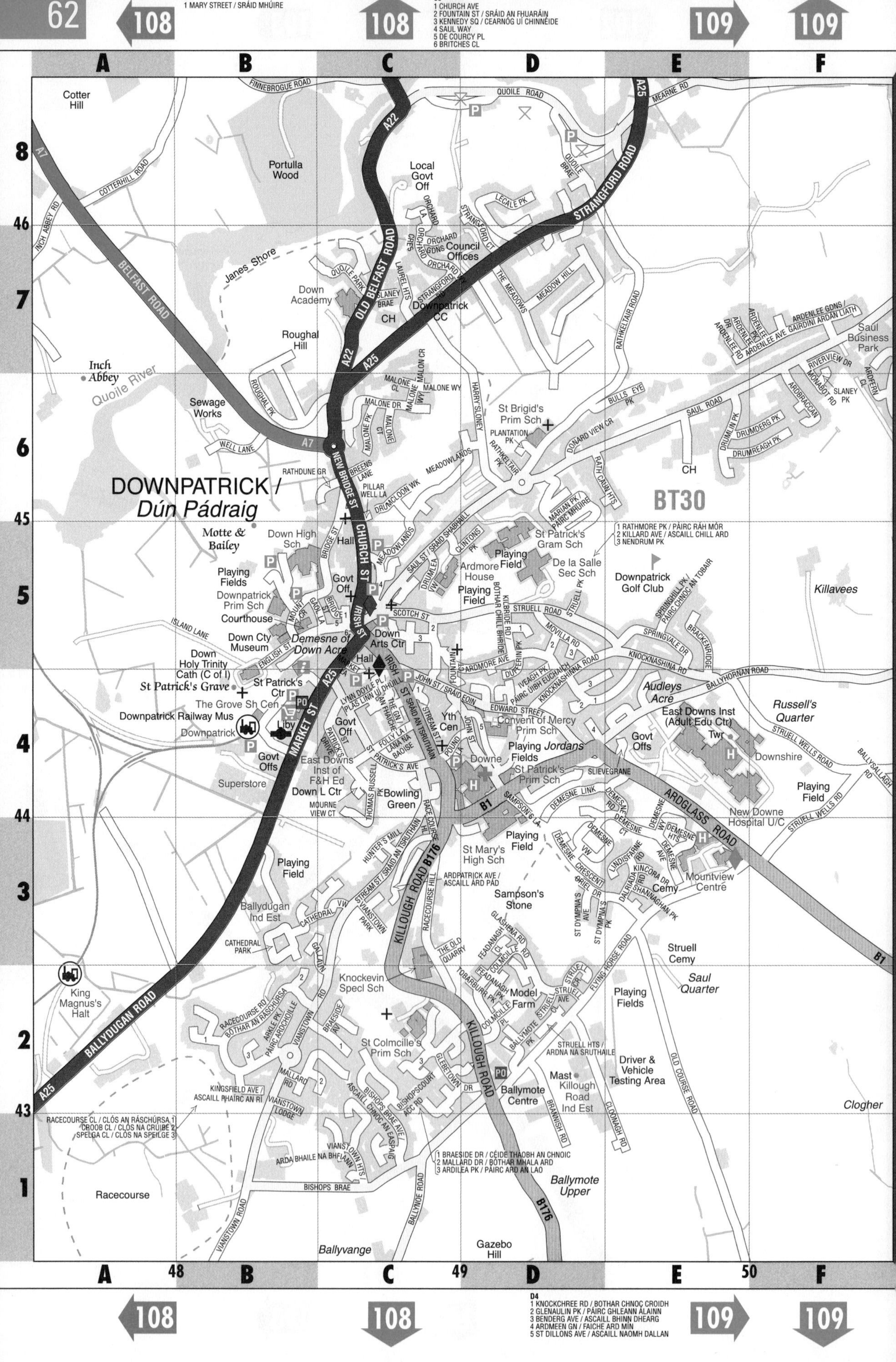

D4
1 KNOCKCHREE RD / BÓTHAR CHNOC CROIDH
2 GLENAULIN PK / PÁIRC GHLEANN ÁLAINN
3 BENDERG AVE / ASCAILL BHINN DHEARG
4 ARDMEEN GN / FAICHE ARD MÍN
5 ST DILLONS AVE / ASCAILL NAOMH DALLAN

108

108

109

109

B5
1 TULLYBRANNIGAN WY
2 TULLYBRANNIGAN AVE
3 TULLYBRANNIGAN BRAE
4 TULLYBRANNIGAN GDNS
5 MOUNTAIN SPRINGS
6 TULLYBRANNIGAN CRES
7 TULLYBRANNIGAN CL
8 TULLYBRANNIGAN BRAE

D5
1 SHIMNA PAR
2 BEVERLEY GDNS
3 ST MARY'S LA
4 CASTLE PL / PLÁS AN CHAISLEÁIN

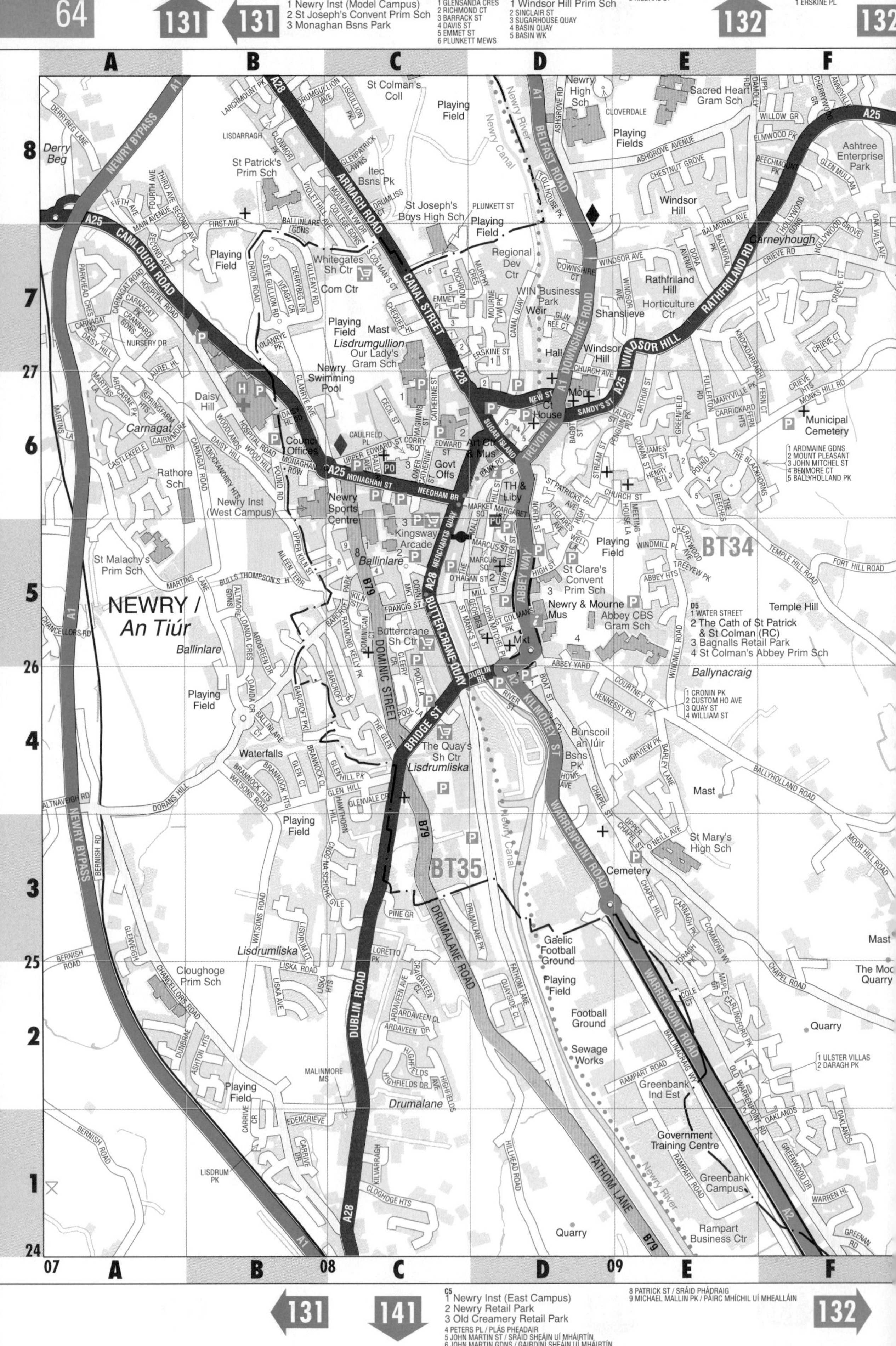

C5
1 Newry Inst (East Campus)
2 Newry Retail Park
3 Old Creamery Retail Park
4 PETERS PL / PLÁS PHEADAIR
5 JOHN MARTIN ST / SRÁID SHEÁIN UÍ MHÁIRTÍN
6 JOHN MARTIN GDNS / GAIRDÍNÍ SHEÁIN UÍ MHÁIRTÍN
7 JAMES CONNOLLY PK / PÁIRC SHÉAMAIS UÍ CHONGHAILE
8 PATRICK ST / SRÁID PHÁDRAIG
9 MICHAEL MALLIN PK / PÁIRC MHÍCHÍL UÍ MHEALLÁIN

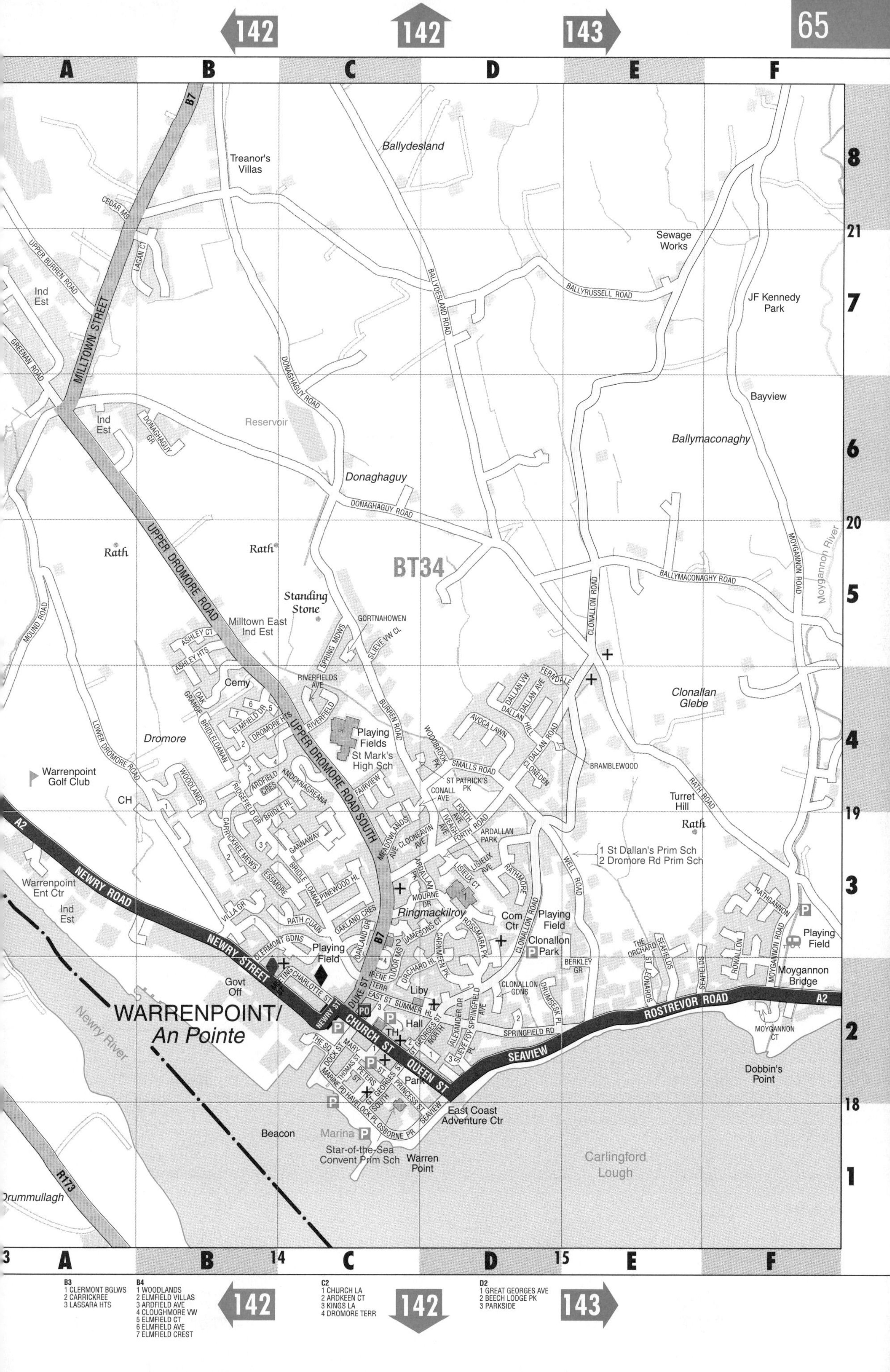
142
142
143
Ballydesland
Treanor's Villas
Sewage Works
JF Kennedy Park
BALLYRUSSELL ROAD
BALLYDESLAND ROAD
CEDAR MS
UPPER BURREN ROAD
LAGAN CT
Ind Est
MILLTOWN STREET
GREENAN ROAD
DONAGHAGUY ROAD
Bayview
Ind Est
DONAGHAGUY GR
Reservoir
Ballymaconaghy
Donaghaguy
DONAGHAGUY ROAD
Rath
Rath
BT34
BALLYMACONAGHY ROAD
MOYGANNON ROAD
Moygannon River
UPPER DROMORE ROAD
Standing Stone
CLONALLON ROAD
MOUND ROAD
Milltown East Ind Est
GORTNAHOWEN
SLIEVE VW CL
ASHLEY CT
ASHLEY HTS
SPRING MDWS
RIVERFIELDS AVE
Cemy
FERNDALE
DALLAN VW
DALLAN AVE
DALLAN HILL
Clonallan Glebe
OAK GRANGE
ELMFIELD DR
DROMORE HTS
RIVERFIELD
UPPER DROMORE ROAD SOUTH
BURREN ROAD
Playing Fields
St Mark's High Sch
AVOCA LAWN
WOODBROOK PK
DALLAN ROAD
LOWER DROMORE ROAD
Dromore
BRIDLELOANAN
SMALLS ROAD
BRAMBLEWOOD
Warrenpoint Golf Club
WOODLANDS
ARDFIELD CRES
KNOCKNAGREENA
FAIRVIEW
ST PATRICK'S PK
CONALL AVE
CLONEDEN
RATH ROAD
Turret Hill
CH
RIDGEFIELD GR
BRIDLE HL
FORTH AVE
FORTH ROAD
A2
CARRICKKREE MEWS
GANNAWAY
MEADOWLANDS
AVE CLOONEAVIN AVE
IVEAGH AVE
ARDALLAN PARK
Rath
LISIEUX AVE
1 St Dallan's Prim Sch
2 Dromore Rd Prim Sch
WELL ROAD
NEWRY ROAD
Warrenpoint Ent Ctr
Ind Est
ESSMORE
BRIDLE LOANAN
PINEWOOD HL
ARDALLAN PK
MOURNE DR
LISIEUX CT
RATHMORE
RATHGANNON
Ringmackilroy
VILLA GR
RATH CUAIN
OAKLAND CRES
JAMESONS CT
ROSSMARA PK
Com Ctr
Playing Field
Clonallan Park
P
Playing Field
NEWRY STREET
CLERMONT GDNS
Playing Field
OAKLAND GR
B7
TUDOR MS
CARNMEEN PK
ORCHARD HL
THE ORCHARD
SEAFIELDS
ST LEONARDS
SEAFIELDS
ROWALLON
MOYGANNON ROAD
Moygannon Bridge
BERKLEY GR
Govt Off
MEETING
CHARLOTTE ST
IRENE TERR
EAST ST
SUMMER HL
Liby
SPRINGFIELD AVE
CLONALLON GDNS
DRUMSESK PL
ROSTREVOR ROAD
A2
WARRENPOINT/
An Pointe
Newry River
NEWRY ST
DUKE ST
PO
CHURCH ST
Hall
ALEXANDER DR
SLIEVE FOY PL
SPRINGFIELD RD
MOYGANNON CT
THE SQ
DOCK ST
MARY ST
THOMAS ST
PETERS ST
GEORGES ST
QUEEN ST
SEAVIEW
Dobbin's Point
MARINE PD
HAVELOCK PL
ST GEORGES SOUTH
PRINCESS ST
Park
SEAVIEW
East Coast Adventure Ctr
Beacon
Marina
OSBORNE PR
Star-of-the-Sea Convent Prim Sch
Warren Point
Carlingford Lough
R173
Drummullagh
A B C D E F
8 7 6 5 4 3 2 1
21 20 19 18
13 14 15
B3
1 CLERMONT BGLWS
2 CARRICKREE
3 LASSARA HTS
B4
1 WOODLANDS
2 ELMFIELD VILLAS
3 ARDFIELD AVE
4 CLOUGHMORE VW
5 ELMFIELD CT
6 ELMFIELD AVE
7 ELMFIELD CREST
C2
1 CHURCH LA
2 ARDKEEN CT
3 KINGS LA
4 DROMORE TERR
D2
1 GREAT GEORGES AVE
2 BEECH LODGE PK
3 PARKSIDE
142
142
143

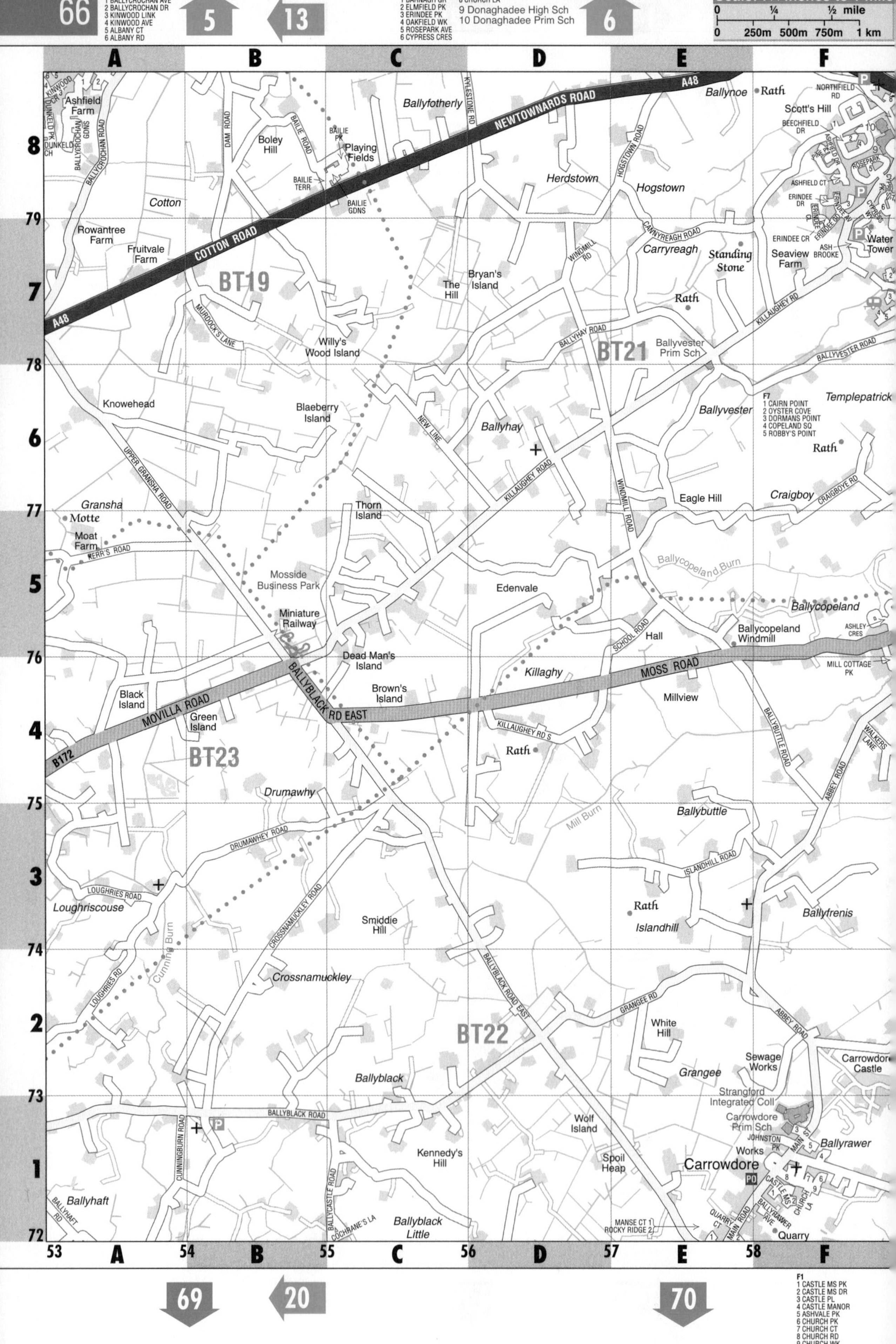
A8
1 BALLYCROCHAN AVE
2 BALLYCROCHAN DR
3 KINWOOD LINK
4 KINWOOD AVE
5 ALBANY CT
6 ALBANY RD
5
13
F8
1 BARNAGH GR
2 ELMFIELD PK
3 ERINDEE PK
4 OAKFIELD WK
5 ROSEPARK AVE
6 CYPRESS CRES
7 CYPRESS CL
8 CHURCH LA
9 Donaghadee High Sch
10 Donaghadee Prim Sch
6
Scale: 1¾ inches to 1 mile
0 ¼ ½ mile
0 250m 500m 750m 1 km
A B C D E F
8
79
7
78
6
77
5
76
4
75
3
74
2
73
1
72
Ashfield Farm
BALLYCROCHAN GDNS
BALLYCROCHAN ROAD
DUNKELD PK
DUNKELD CH
KINWOOD
Rowantree Farm
Fruitvale Farm
Cotton
COTTON ROAD
A48
DAM ROAD
Boley Hill
BAILIE ROAD
BAILIE PK
Playing Fields
BAILIE TERR
BAILIE GDNS
BT19
MURDOCK'S LANE
Willy's Wood Island
Ballyfotherly
KYLESTONE RD
NEWTOWNARDS ROAD
The Hill
Bryan's Island
Herdstown
HOGSTOWN ROAD
Hogstown
WINDMILL RD
CANNYREAGH ROAD
Carryreagh
Standing Stone
Rath
BALLYHAY ROAD
BT21
Ballyvester Prim Sch
Ballynoe
Rath
NORTHFIELD RD
Scott's Hill
BEECHFIELD DR
ASHFIELD DR
PINE PK
ROSEPARK
CYPRESS
ASHFIELD CT
ERINDEE DR
ERINDEE CL
ERINDEE AV
ERINDEE CR
ASH BROOKE
Seaview Farm
Water Tower
KILLAUGHEY RD
BALLYVESTER ROAD
Knowehead
Blaeberry Island
NEW LINE
Ballyhay
Ballyvester
F7
1 CAIRN POINT
2 OYSTER COVE
3 DORMANS POINT
4 COPELAND SQ
5 ROBBY'S POINT
Templepatrick
Rath
UPPER GRANSHA ROAD
KILLAUGHEY ROAD
WINDMILL ROAD
Eagle Hill
Craigboy
CRAIGBOYE RD
Gransha
Motte
Moat Farm
KERR'S ROAD
Thorn Island
Mosside Business Park
Edenvale
Ballycopeland Burn
Ballycopeland
Miniature Railway
SCHOOL ROAD
Hall
Ballycopeland Windmill
ASHLEY CRES
MILL COTTAGE PK
Dead Man's Island
Killaghy
MOSS ROAD
Black Island
Brown's Island
Millview
MOVILLA ROAD
BALLYBLACK RD EAST
Green Island
B172
KILLAUGHEY RD S
Rath
BALLYBUTTLE ROAD
WALKERS LANE
ABBEY ROAD
BT23
Drumawhy
Mill Burn
Ballybuttle
DRUMAWHEY ROAD
ISLANDHILL ROAD
LOUGHRIES ROAD
Loughriscouse
Rath
Islandhill
Ballyfrenis
Cunning Burn
CROSSNAMUCKLEY ROAD
Smiddie Hill
Crossnamuckley
BALLYBLACK ROAD EAST
LOUGHRIES RD
GRANGEE RD
ABBEY ROAD
BT22
White Hill
Sewage Works
Carrowdore Castle
Ballyblack
Grangee
Strangford Integrated Coll
BALLYBLACK ROAD
Carrowdore Prim Sch
Wolf Island
CUNNINGBURN ROAD
Kennedy's Hill
JOHNSTON PK
MAIN ST
Ballyrawer
Works
Spoil Heap
Carrowdore
PO
CASTLE MS
CHURCH LA
Ballyhaft
BALLYHAFT RD
BALLYCASTLE ROAD
COCHRANE'S LA
Ballyblack Little
MANSE CT 1
ROCKY RIDGE 2
QUARRY CT
MAIN ROAD
BALLYRAWER AVE
Quarry
53 A 54 B 55 C 56 D 57 E 58 F
69
20
70
F1
1 CASTLE MS PK
2 CASTLE MS DR
3 CASTLE PL
4 CASTLE MANOR
5 ASHVALE PK
6 CHURCH PK
7 CHURCH CT
8 CHURCH RD
9 CHURCH WK

Scale: 1¾ inches to 1 mile
0 ¼ ½ mile
0 250m 500m 750m 1 km

A7
1 MEETINGHOUSE POINT
2 KINNEGAR ROCKS
3 STELLENBOSCH AVE
4 THE MOORINGS
5 EDGEWATER COVE
6 EDGEWATER BAY
7 SEAHILL RIDGE
8 SEAHILL
9 EDGEWATER
10 NORFOLK AVE
11 GARRET ROCKS
12 SUNNYDALE AVE
13 SHINGLE BAY
14 GARRET RIDGE
15 THE ANCH GRANGE
16 GALLOWAY POINT

A8
1 VICTORIA CRES
2 LESLIE HL CRES
3 EDWARD ST
4 THE GENERAL'S WK
5 VICTORIA MS
6 GLOUCESTER AVE
7 MANOR CT
8 SALTWORKS ST
9 DORMAN'S CT
10 GREENBANK AVE
11 MOUNT ROYAL
12 MEETING HO ST
13 BOW ST
14 TOWN HALL LA
15 HUNTER'S LA
16 SHORE ST
17 NEW ST
18 BRIDGE ST
19 SEAHILL PK
20 SEAHILL VALE
21 MORAY DR
22 NORWYN AVE
23 THE PARADE
24 LESLIE HL
25 MEADOWBANK AVE
26 St Anne's Prim Sch

A5
1 STRAND AVE
2 MILL RD

A4
1 BALLYMACRUISE DR
2 COPELAND AVE
3 WINDMILL GDNS
4 MANSE WY
5 BALLYMACRUISE PK
6 CHURCHILL AVE
7 ABBEY GDNS
8 ABBEY CT
9 BALLYMACRUISE CL
10 MASONIC AVE
11 SEAVIEW AVE
12 MILLBANK RD
13 MILLBANK CT
14 MILLBANK CRES
15 Millisle Prim Sch

70
71

18
24
19

Scale: 1¾ inches to 1 mile

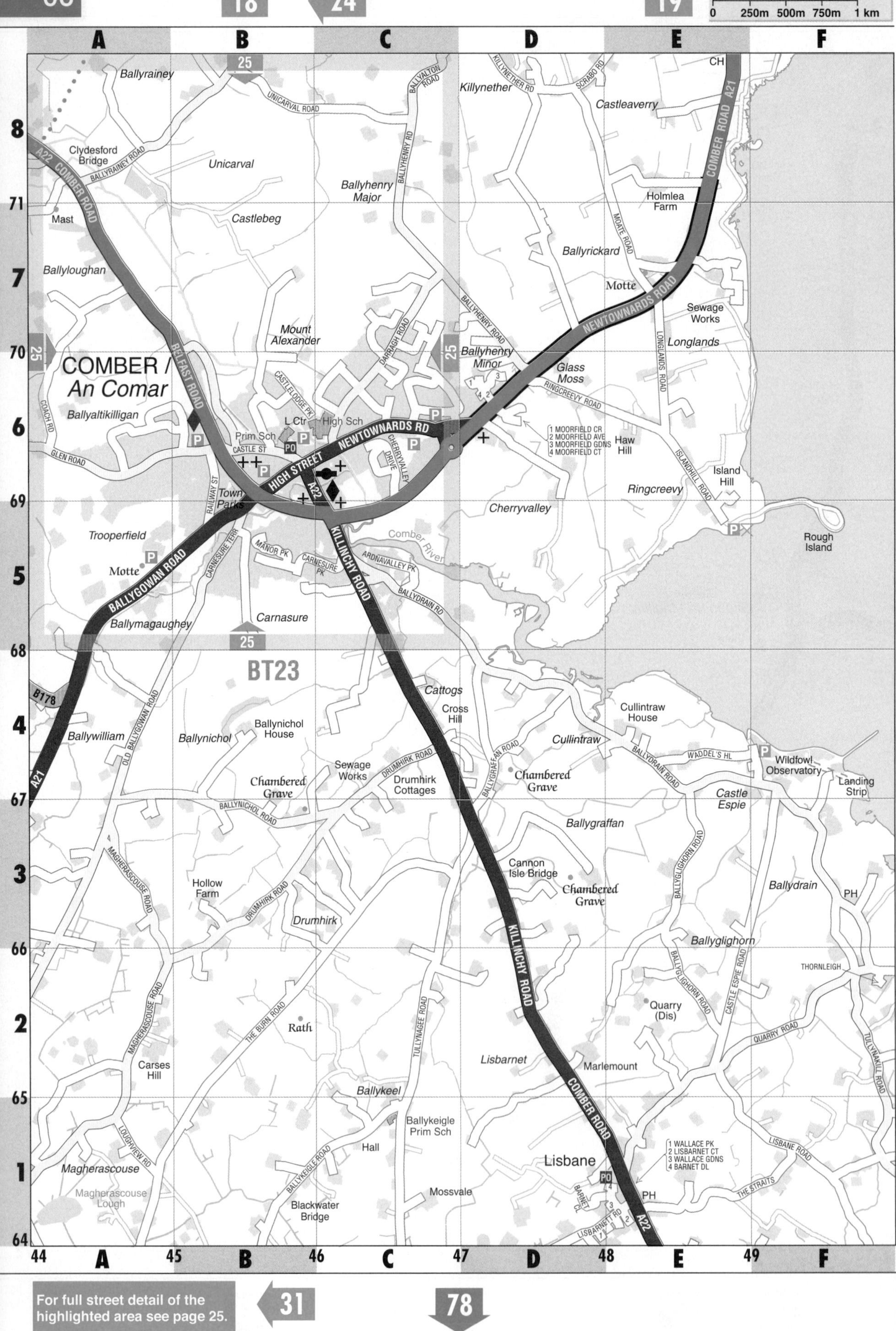

For full street detail of the highlighted area see page 25.
31
78

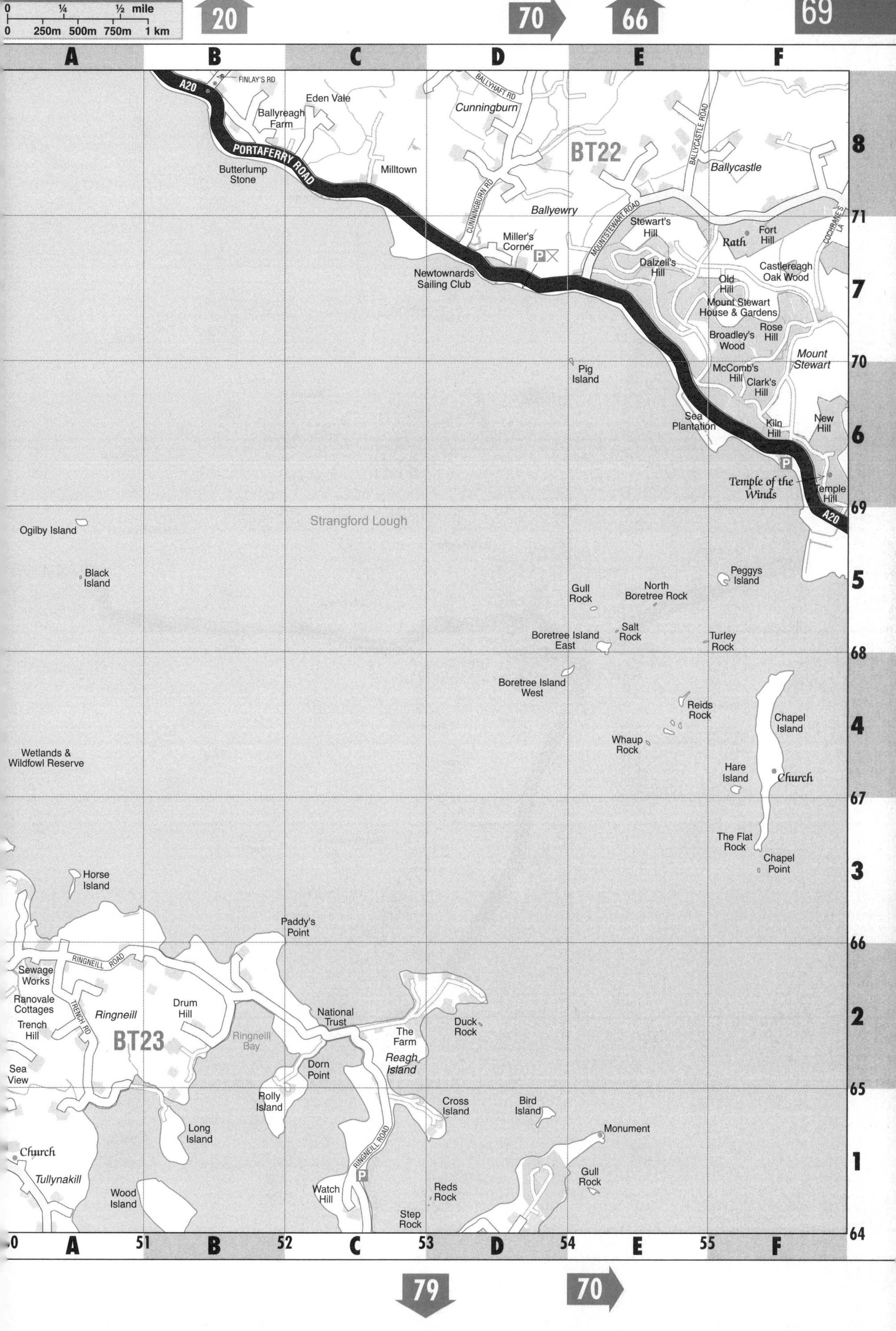
Scale: 1¾ inches to 1 mile
0 ¼ ½ mile
0 250m 500m 750m 1 km
20
70
66
A B C D E F
FINLAY'S RD
A20
Eden Vale
Ballyreagh Farm
BALLYHAFT RD
Cunningburn
BT22
BALLYCASTLE ROAD
Ballycastle
PORTAFERRY ROAD
Butterlump Stone
Milltown
CUNNINGBURN RD
Ballyewry
MOUNTSTEWART ROAD
Stewart's Hill
Rath
Fort Hill
COCHRANE'S LA
Miller's Corner
Dalzell's Hill
Castlereagh Oak Wood
Newtownards Sailing Club
Old Hill
Mount Stewart House & Gardens
Broadley's Wood
Rose Hill
Mount Stewart
Pig Island
McComb's Hill
Clark's Hill
Sea Plantation
Kiln Hill
New Hill
Temple of the Winds
Temple Hill
Ogilby Island
Strangford Lough
Black Island
Peggys Island
Gull Rock
North Boretree Rock
Boretree Island East
Salt Rock
Turley Rock
Boretree Island West
Reids Rock
Chapel Island
Whaup Rock
Wetlands & Wildfowl Reserve
Hare Island
Church
The Flat Rock
Chapel Point
Horse Island
Paddy's Point
RINGNEILL ROAD
Sewage Works
Ranovale Cottages
TRENCH RD
Ringneill
Drum Hill
National Trust
Duck Rock
Trench Hill
BT23
Ringneill Bay
The Farm
Reagh Island
Sea View
Dorn Point
Rolly Island
Cross Island
Bird Island
Long Island
Monument
Church
RINGNEILL ROAD
Gull Rock
Tullynakill
Wood Island
Watch Hill
Reds Rock
Step Rock
8 71 7 70 6 69 5 68 4 67 3 66 2 65 1 64
50 51 52 53 54 55
79
70

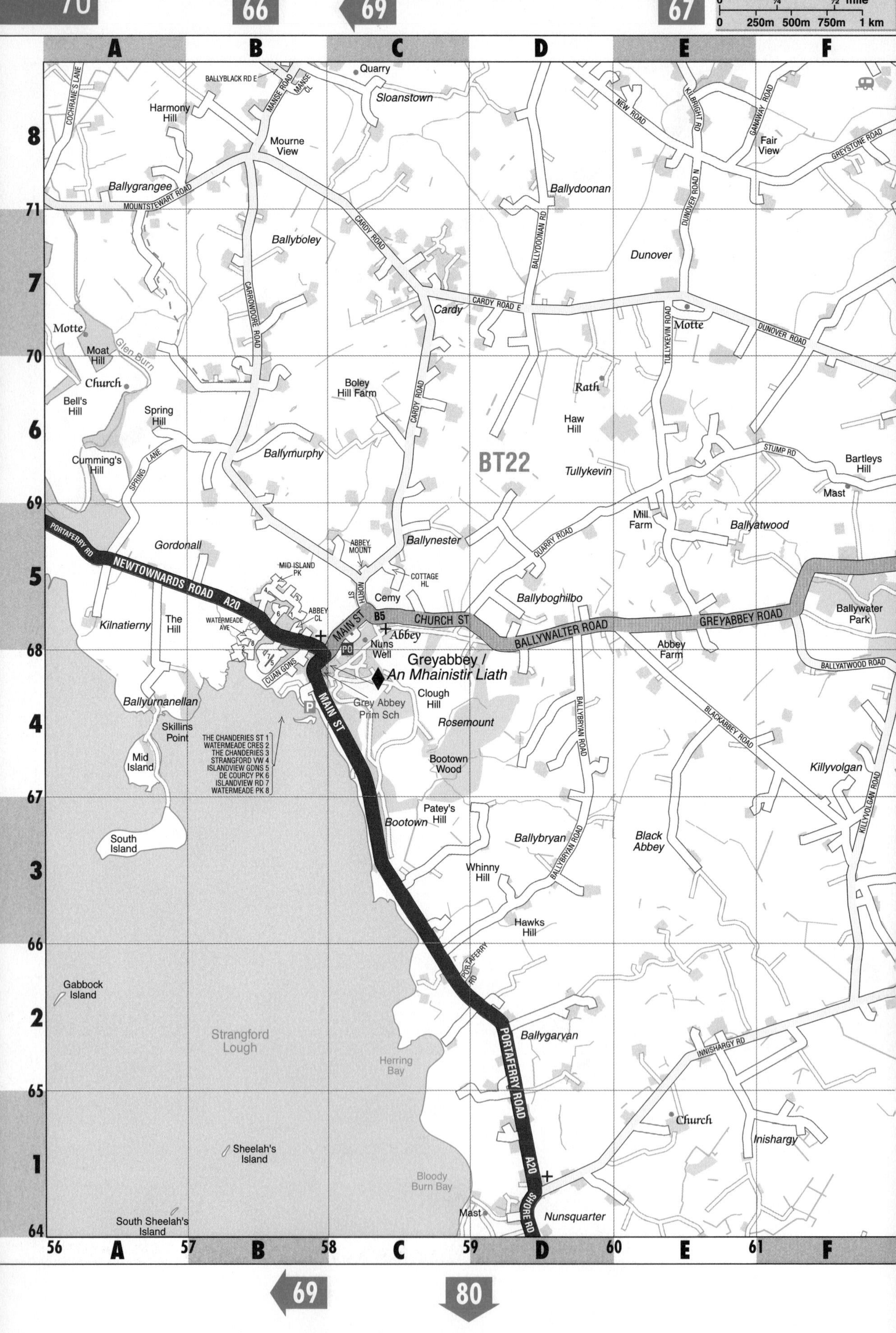
66
69
67
Scale: 1¾ inches to 1 mile
0 ¼ ½ mile
0 250m 500m 750m 1 km
A B C D E F
8 7 6 5 4 3 2 1
71 70 69 68 67 66 65 64
56 57 58 59 60 61
Quarry
Sloanstown
BALLYBLACK RD E
MANSE ROAD
MANSE CL
COCHRANE'S LANE
Harmony Hill
Mourne View
Ballygrangee
MOUNTSTEWART ROAD
NEW ROAD
KILBRIGHT RD
GANAWAY ROAD
Fair View
GREYSTONE ROAD
DUNOVER ROAD N
Ballydoonan
BALLYDOONAN RD
Ballyboley
CARDY ROAD
Dunover
CARROWDORE ROAD
Cardy
CARDY ROAD E
TULLYKEVIN ROAD
Motte
DUNOVER ROAD
Motte
Moat Hill
Glen Burn
Church
Bell's Hill
Rath
Boley Hill Farm
Spring Hill
Haw Hill
Cumming's Hill
SPRING LANE
Ballymurphy
BT22
Tullykevin
STUMP RD
Bartleys Hill
Mast
PORTAFERRY RD
Gordonall
ABBEY MOUNT
Ballynester
Mill Farm
QUARRY ROAD
Ballyatwood
MID ISLAND PK
NEWTOWNARDS ROAD A20
NORTH ST
COTTAGE HL
Cemy
Ballyboghilbo
ABBEY CL
MAIN ST
B5
CHURCH ST
GREYABBEY ROAD
Ballywater Park
Kilnatierny
The Hill
WATERMEADE AVE
PO
Abbey
Nuns Well
BALLYWALTER ROAD
Abbey Farm
Greyabbey / An Mhainistir Liath
BALLYATWOOD ROAD
CUAN GDNS
Clough Hill
Grey Abbey Prim Sch
Ballyurnanellan
P
Rosemount
BALLYBRYAN ROAD
BLACKABBEY ROAD
Skillins Point
THE CHANDERIES ST 1
WATERMEADE CRES 2
THE CHANDERIES 3
STRANGFORD VW 4
ISLANDVIEW GDNS 5
DE COURCY PK 6
ISLANDVIEW RD 7
WATERMEADE PK 8
Mid Island
Bootown Wood
Killyvolgan
KILLYVOLGAN ROAD
Patey's Hill
Bootown
South Island
Ballybryan
BALLYBRYAN ROAD
Black Abbey
Whinny Hill
Hawks Hill
PORTAFERRY RD
Gabbock Island
Strangford Lough
Ballygarvan
PORTAFERRY ROAD
Herring Bay
INNISHARGY RD
Church
Inishargy
Sheelah's Island
A20
Bloody Burn Bay
SHORE RD
Mast
Nunsquarter
South Sheelah's Island

Scale: 1¾ inches to 1 mile
0 ¼ ½ mile
0 250m 500m 750m 1 km

67

A6
1 WESTLAND CT
2 BROOKFIELD DR
3 SALTWATER CL
4 DUNOVER PK
5 STEWART CR
6 DUNLEATH DR
7 WINDYRIDGE CTS
8 FOWLER WY
9 THE SQUARE
10 WESTLAND AVE
11 Ballywalter Prim Sch

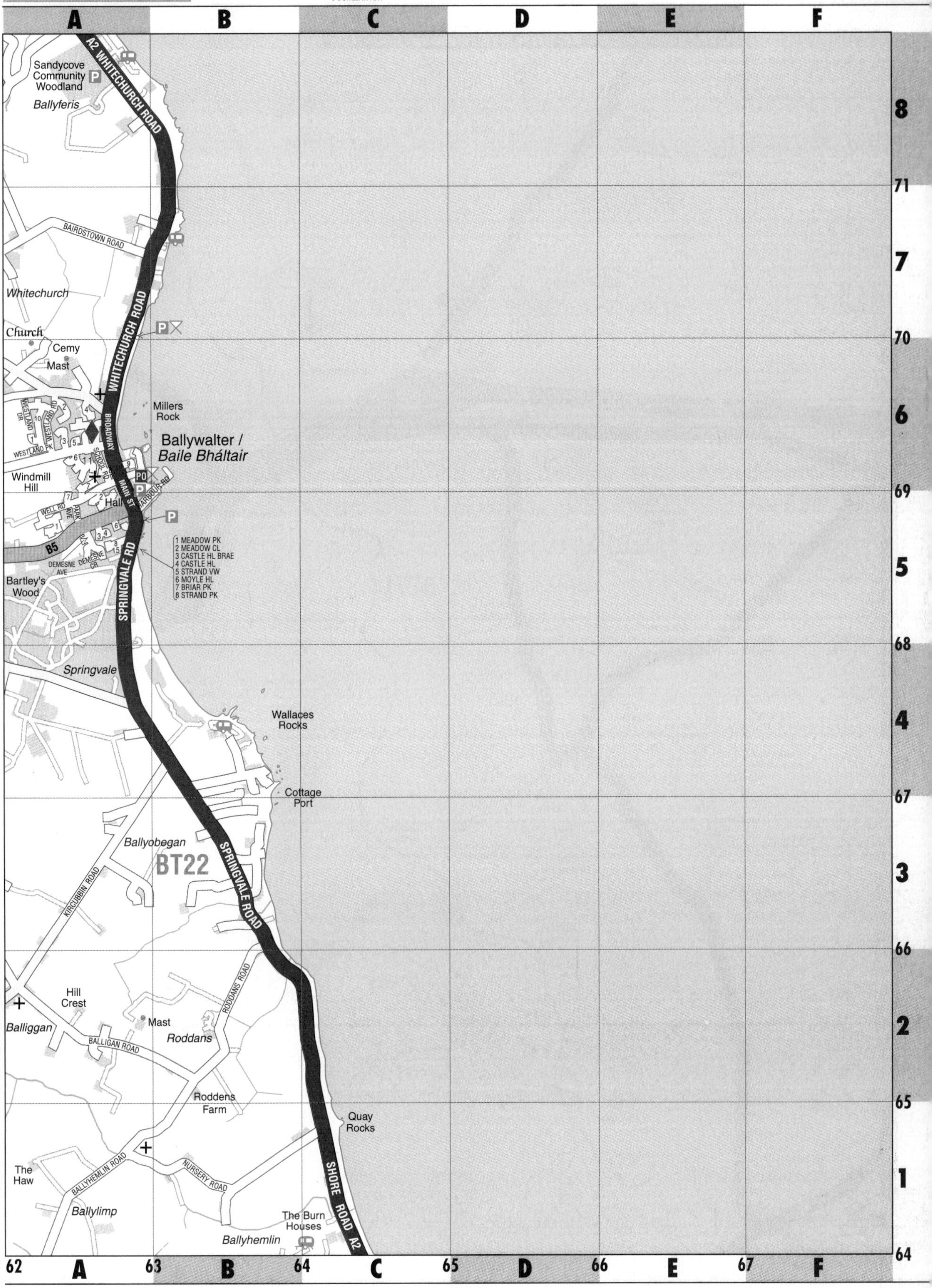

A B C D E F

Sandycove Community Woodland
Ballyferis
A2 WHITECHURCH ROAD
BAIRDSTOWN ROAD
Whitechurch
WHITECHURCH ROAD
Church
Cemy
Mast
Millers Rock
Ballywalter /
Baile Bháltair
WESTLAND DR
WESTLAND AVE
WESTLAND PK
BROADWAY
SCHOOL RD
MAIN ST
HARBOUR RD
PO
Windmill Hill
Hall
WELL RD
PARK AVE
B5
DEMESNE AVE
DEMESNE CR
SPRINGVALE RD

1 MEADOW PK
2 MEADOW CL
3 CASTLE HL BRAE
4 CASTLE HL
5 STRAND VW
6 MOYLE HL
7 BRIAR PK
8 STRAND PK

Bartley's Wood
Springvale
Wallaces Rocks
Cottage Port
Ballyobegan
BT22
SPRINGVALE ROAD
KIRCUBBIN ROAD
RODDANS ROAD
Hill Crest
Balliggan
BALLIGAN ROAD
Mast
Roddans
Roddens Farm
Quay Rocks
The Haw
BALLYHEMLIN ROAD
NURSERY ROAD
Ballylimp
SHORE ROAD A2
The Burn Houses
Ballyhemlin

8 71 7 70 6 69 5 68 4 67 3 66 2 65 1 64

62 A 63 B 64 C 65 D 66 E 67 F

81

Scale: 1¾ inches to 1 mile
0 ¼ ½ mile
0 250m 500m 750m 1 km

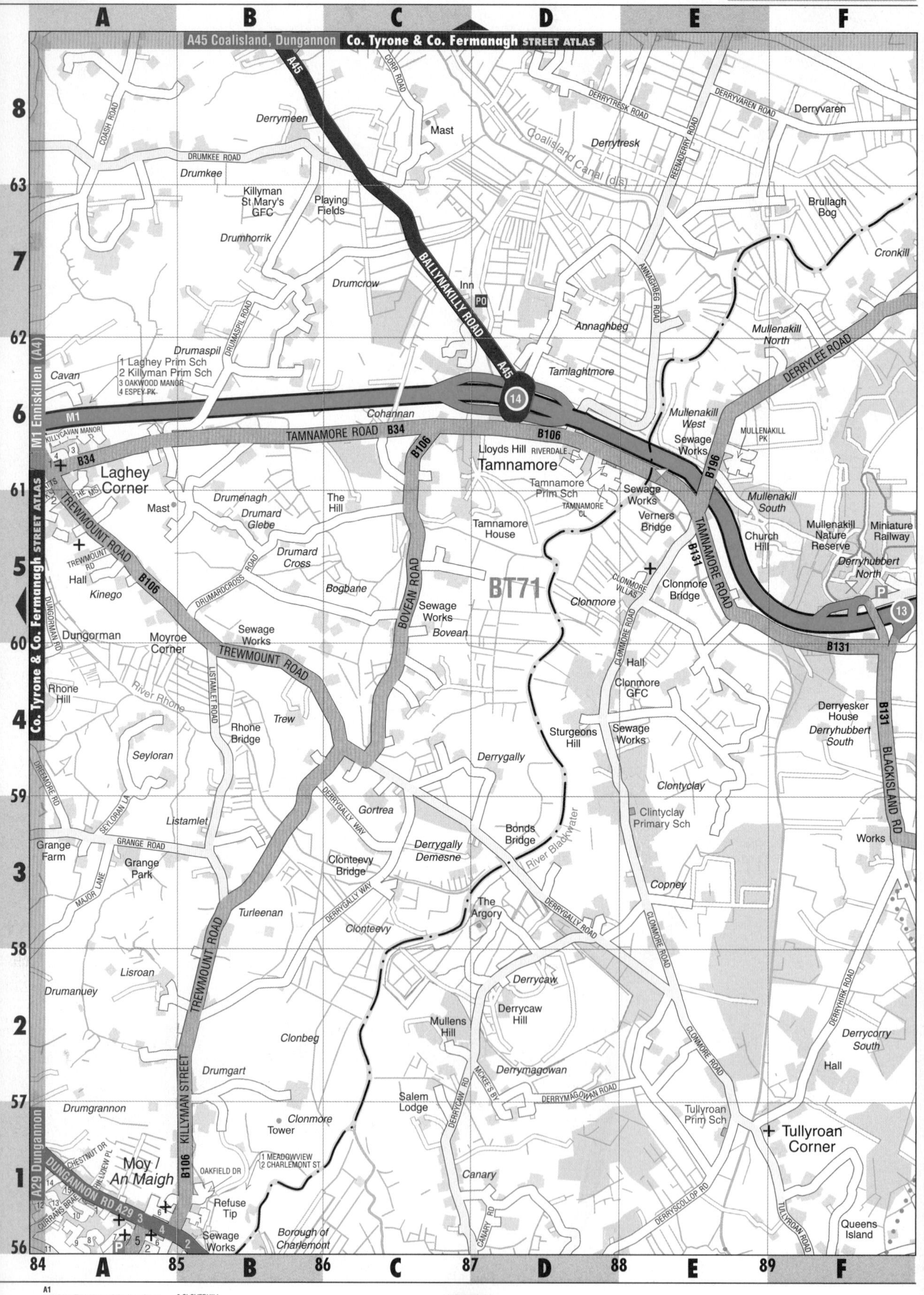

A1
1 Moy Regional Prim Sch
2 St John's Prim Sch
3 DUNGANNON ST
4 THE DIAMOND
5 BENBURB RD
6 THE DIAMOND
7 JOCKEY LA
8 THE HOLLOWS
9 CLOVERHILL
10 ROXBOROUGH PK
11 GORESTOWN RD
12 ARDEAN MANOR
13 ROXBOROUGH HTS
14 RIDGEWOOD AVE
15 HILLSIDE CRES

84

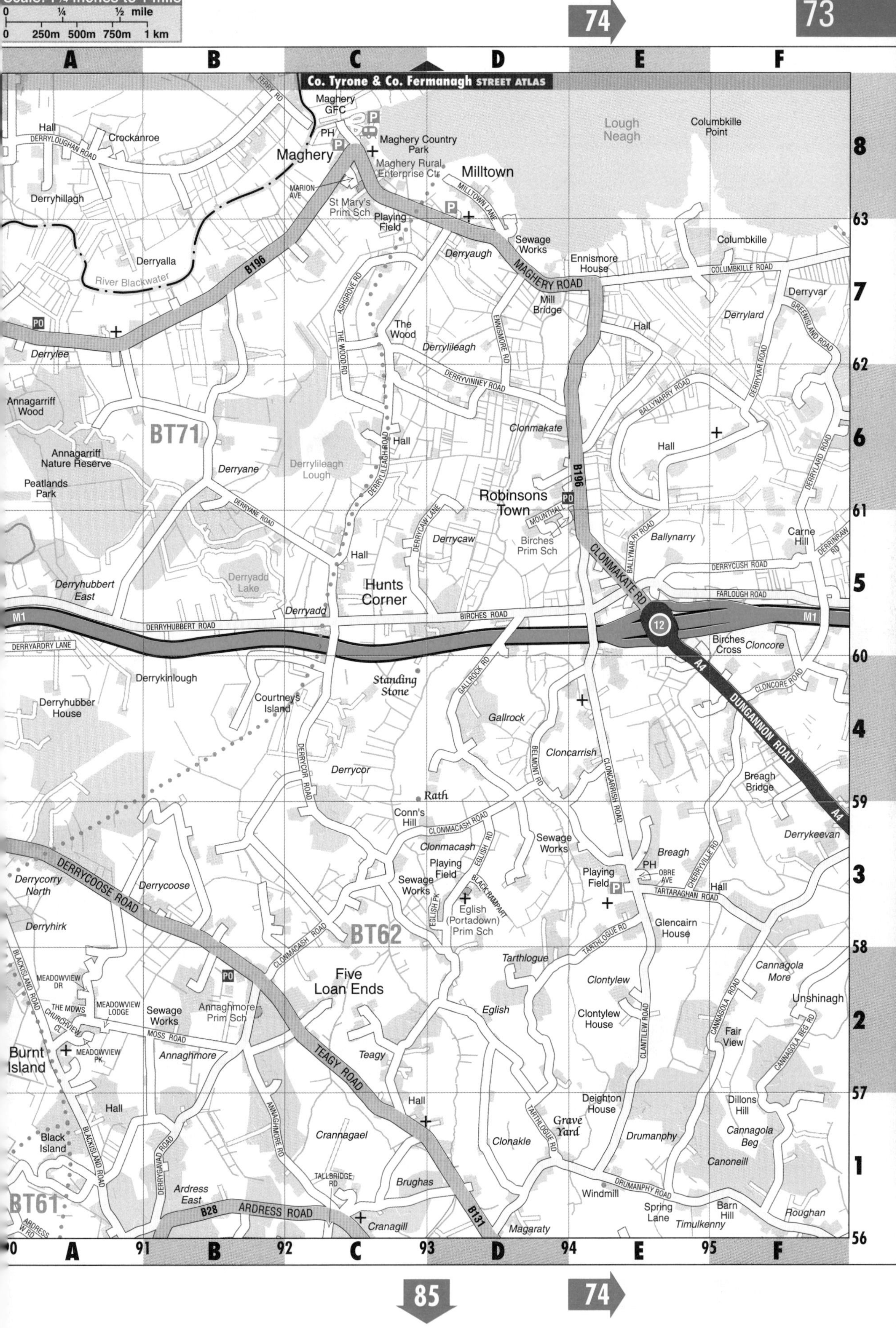
Scale: 1¾ inches to 1 mile
0 ¼ ½ mile
0 250m 500m 750m 1 km
Co. Tyrone & Co. Fermanagh STREET ATLAS
Maghery
Maghery GFC
Maghery Country Park
Maghery Rural Enterprise Ctr
Milltown
Lough Neagh
Columbkille Point
Columbkille
Crockanroe
Derryhillagh
Derryalla
River Blackwater
Derrylee
Annagarriff Wood
Annagarriff Nature Reserve
Peatlands Park
BT71
Derryane
Derrylileagh Lough
Derrylileagh
The Wood
Derryaugh
Ennismore House
Mill Bridge
Sewage Works
St Mary's Prim Sch
Playing Field
Clonmakate
Robinsons Town
Birches Prim Sch
Derrycaw
Hunts Corner
Derryadd
Derryadd Lake
Derryhubbert East
Derrykinlough
Derryhubber House
Courtneys Island
Standing Stone
Gallrock
Cloncarrish
Derrycor
Rath
Conn's Hill
Clonmacash
Ballynarry
Derryvar
Derrylard
Carne Hill
Birches Cross
Cloncore
Breagh Bridge
Derrykeevan
Breagh
Glencairn House
Tarthlogue
Clontylew
Clontylew House
Cannagola More
Unshinagh
Fair View
Dillons Hill
Cannagola Beg
Canoneill
Drumanphy
Grave Yard
Clonakle
Windmill
Spring Lane
Barn Hill
Timulkenny
Roughan
Magaraty
Eglish
Eglish (Portadown) Prim Sch
BT62
Five Loan Ends
Teagy
Crannagael
Brughas
Cranagill
Ardress East
BT61
Annaghmore
Annaghmore Prim Sch
Burnt Island
Black Island
Derrycorry North
Derrycoose
Derryhirk
Hall
PH
MAGHERY ROAD
COLUMBKILLE ROAD
DERRYLOUGHAN ROAD
MARION AVE
MILLTOWN LANE
ASHGROVE RD
THE WOOD RD
DERRYVINNEY ROAD
ENNISMORE RD
DERRYLILEAGH ROAD
DERRYANE ROAD
DERRYCAW LANE
MOUNTHALL
CLONMAKATE RD
BALLYNARRY ROAD
BALLYNARRY RD
DERRYVAR ROAD
GREENISLAND ROAD
DERRYLARD ROAD
DERRINRAW RD
DERRYCUSH ROAD
FARLOUGH ROAD
BIRCHES ROAD
DERRYHUBBERT ROAD
DERRYARDRY LANE
M1
A4
DUNGANNON ROAD
CLONCORE ROAD
GALLROCK RD
BELMONT RD
CLONCARRISH ROAD
DERRYCOR ROAD
CLONMACASH ROAD
EGLISH RD
BLACK RAMPART
EGLISH PK
OBRE AVE
CHERRYVILLE RD
TARTARAGHAN ROAD
TARTHLOGUE RD
CLANTILEW ROAD
CANNAGOLA ROAD
CANNAGOLA BEG RD
DERRYCOOSE ROAD
TEAGY ROAD
B131
B28 ARDRESS ROAD
ARDRESS W RD
TALLBRIDGE RD
TARTHLOGUE ROAD
DRUMANPHY ROAD
ANNAGHMORE RD
DERRYGAVAD ROAD
MOSS ROAD
BLACKISLAND ROAD
MEADOWVIEW DR
THE MDWS
MEADOWVIEW LODGE
CHURCHVIEW CL
MEADOWVIEW PK
B196
FERRY RD
12
A B C D E F
8 7 6 5 4 3 2 1
63 62 61 60 59 58 57 56
90 91 92 93 94 95

74
85
74

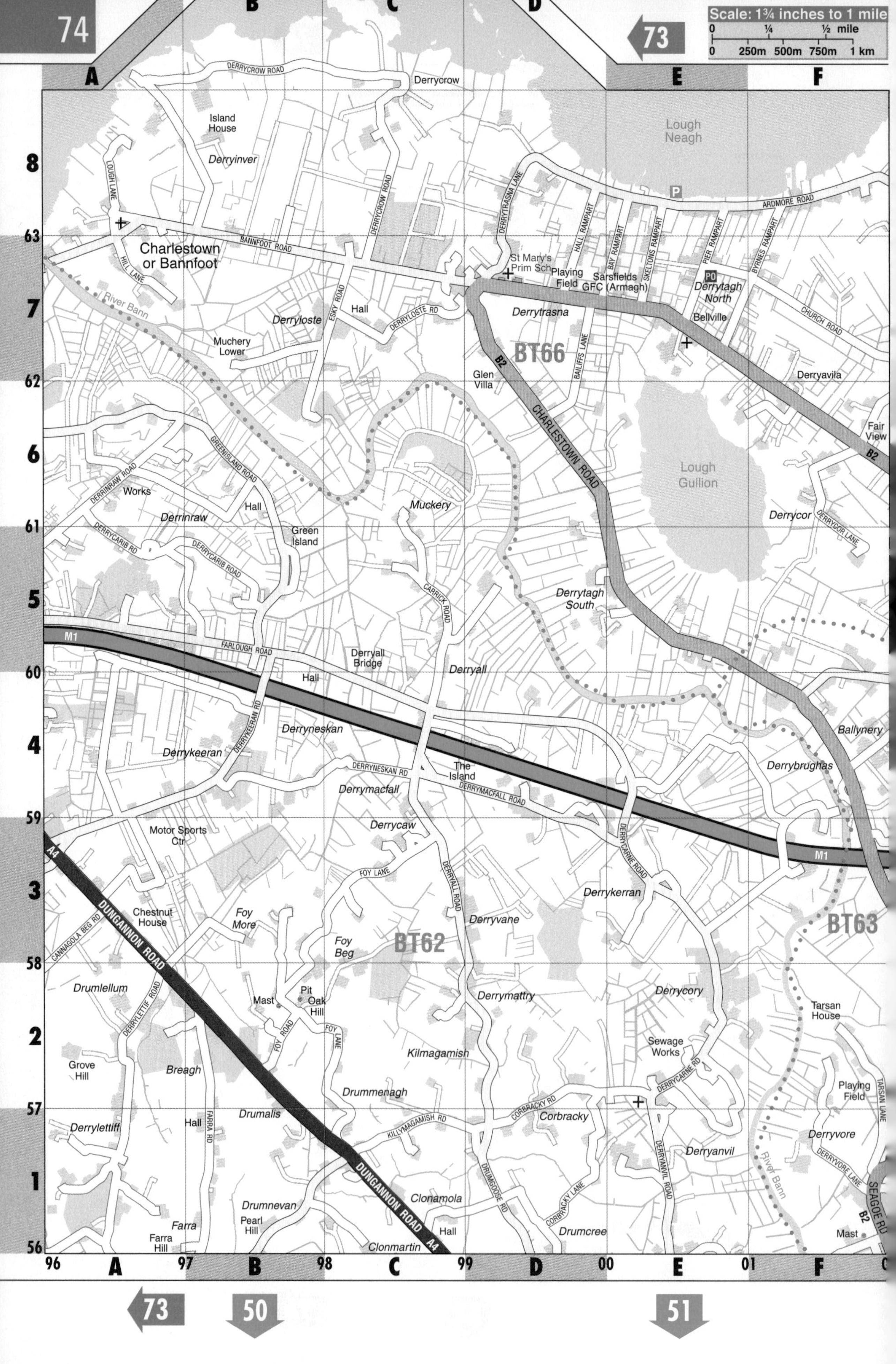
Scale: 1¾ inches to 1 mile
0 ¼ ½ mile
0 250m 500m 750m 1 km
73
Lough Neagh
Derrycrow
DERRYCROW ROAD
Island House
Derryinver
LOUGH LANE
Charlestown or Bannfoot
BANNFOOT ROAD
HILL LANE
River Bann
DERRYCROW ROAD
ESKY ROAD
Hall
Derryloste
DERRYLOSTE RD
Muchery Lower
DERRYTRASNA LANE
St Mary's Prim Sch
Playing Field
Sarsfields GFC (Armagh)
HALL RAMPART
BAY RAMPART
SKELTONS RAMPART
PIER RAMPART
BYRNES RAMPART
ARDMORE ROAD
P
PO
Derrytagh North
Bellville
CHURCH ROAD
Derrytrasna
BT66
BAILIFFS LANE
B2
Glen Villa
CHARLESTOWN ROAD
Derryavila
Fair View
Lough Gullion
GREENISLAND ROAD
DERRINRAW ROAD
Works
Hall
Derrinraw
Muckery
Derrycor
DERRYCOR LANE
DERRYCARIB RD
DERRYCARIB ROAD
Green Island
CARRICK ROAD
Derrytagh South
M1
FARLOUGH ROAD
Derryall Bridge
Hall
Derryall
Derryneskan
DERRYKEERAN RD
Derrykeeran
Ballynery
DERRYNESKAN RD
The Island
Derrymacfall
DERRYMACFALL ROAD
Derrybrughas
Derrycaw
Motor Sports Ctr
A4
DERRYCARNE ROAD
FOY LANE
DERRYALL ROAD
Derrykerran
Chestnut House
DUNGANNON ROAD
CANNAGOLA BEG RD
Foy More
Foy Beg
BT62
Derryvane
BT63
Drumlellum
DERRYLETTIF ROAD
Mast
Pit
Oak Hill
Derrymattry
Derrycory
Tarsan House
FOY ROAD
FOY LANE
Kilmagamish
Sewage Works
Grove Hill
Breagh
DERRYCARNE RD
Playing Field
Drummenagh
TARSAN LANE
CORBRACKY ROAD
Corbracky
Drumalis
Hall
FARRA RD
Derrylettiff
KILLYMAGAMISH RD
DERRYANVIL ROAD
Derryanvil
Derryvore
DERRYVORE LANE
River Bann
DUNGANNON ROAD
DRUMGOOSE RD
CORBRACKY LANE
SEAGOE RD
Drumnevan
Clonamola
Pearl Hill
Farra
Farra Hill
Hall
Drumcree
Mast
Clonmartin
A B C D E F
8 7 6 5 4 3 2 1
63 62 61 60 59 58 57 56
96 97 98 99 00 01
73
50
51

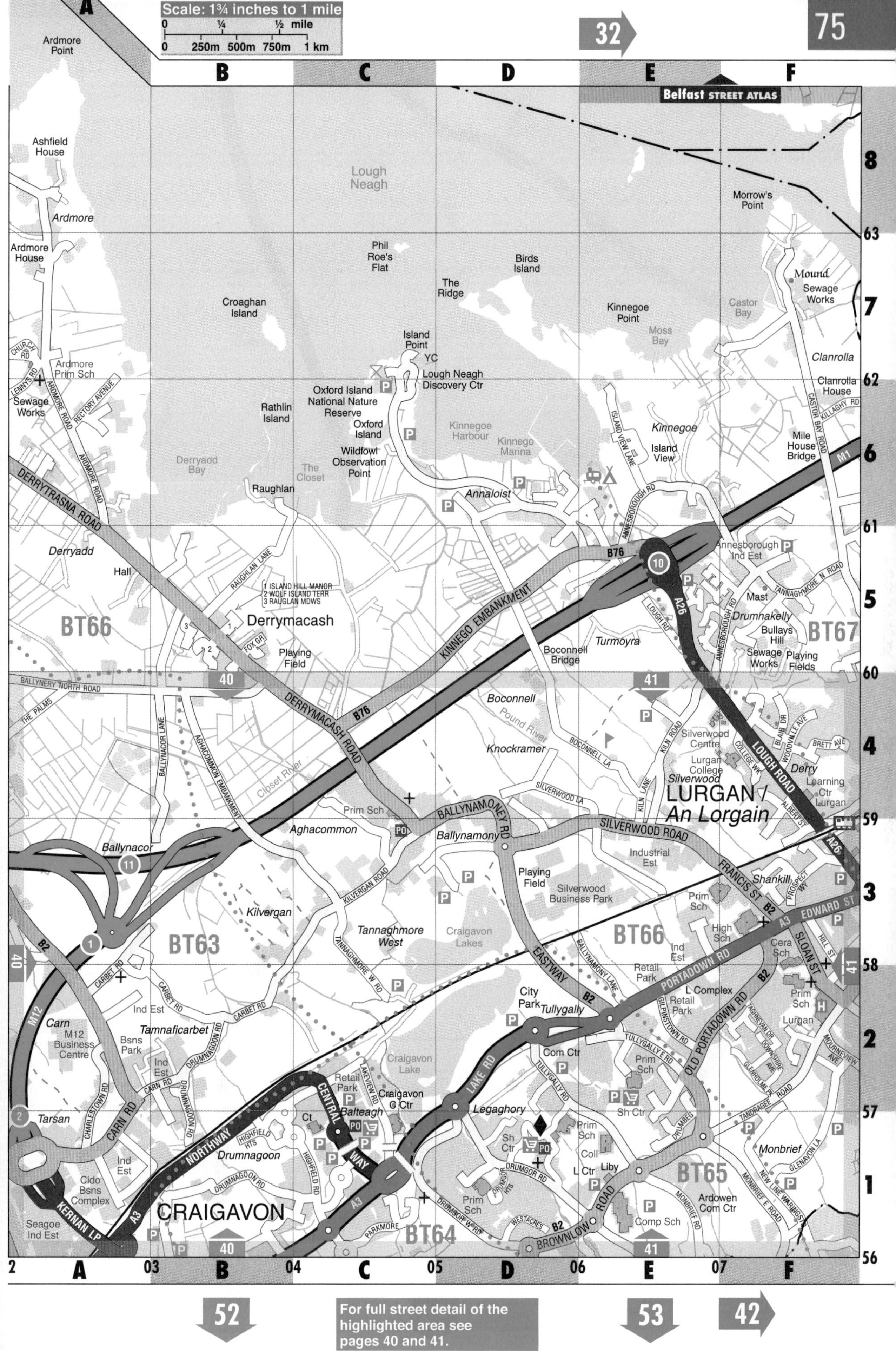

For full street detail of the highlighted area see pages 40 and 41.

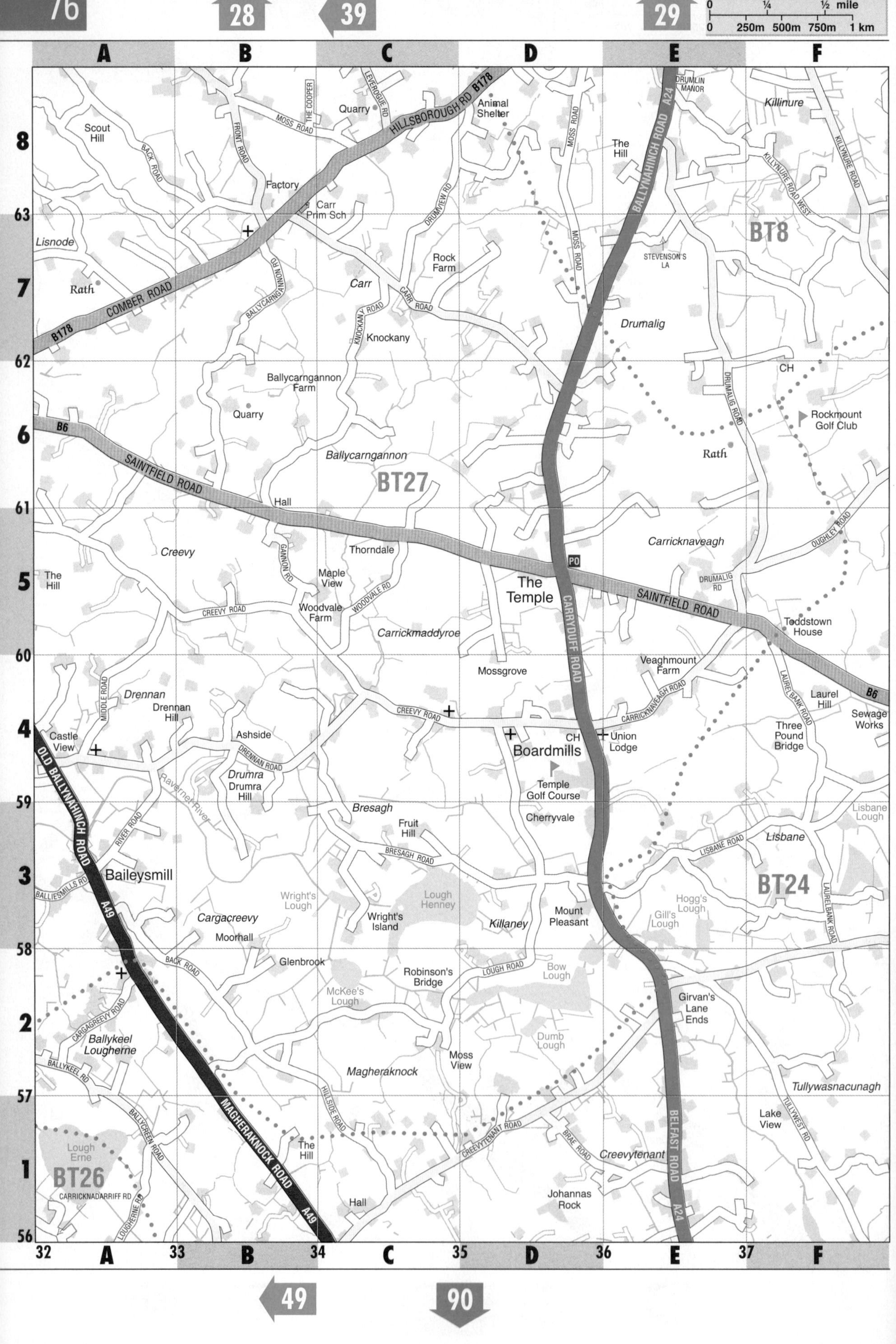
28
39
29
49
90
Scale: 1¾ inches to 1 mile
0 ¼ ½ mile
0 250m 500m 750m 1 km
A B C D E F
8 63 7 62 6 61 5 60 4 59 3 58 2 57 1 56
32 33 34 35 36 37
Scout Hill
Quarry
Animal Shelter
Drumlin Manor
Killinure
The Hill
Factory
Carr Prim Sch
Lisnode
Rath
Rock Farm
Carr
BT8
Stevenson's La
Knockany
Drumalig
Ballycarngannon Farm
Quarry
CH
Rockmount Golf Club
Ballycarngannon
BT27
Rath
Hall
Creevy
Thorndale
Carricknaveagh
The Hill
Maple View
Woodvale Farm
The Temple
PO
Toddstown House
Carrickmaddyroe
Mossgrove
Veaghmount Farm
Laurel Hill
Sewage Works
Drennan
Drennan Hill
Castle View
Ashside
Boardmills
CH
Union Lodge
Three Pound Bridge
Drumra
Drumra Hill
Temple Golf Course
Bresagh
Fruit Hill
Cherryvale
Lisbane Lough
Lisbane
Baileysmill
BT24
Wright's Lough
Lough Henney
Hogg's Lough
Gill's Lough
Cargacreevy
Wright's Island
Killaney
Mount Pleasant
Moorhall
Glenbrook
Robinson's Bridge
Bow Lough
McKee's Lough
Girvan's Lane Ends
Ballykeel Lougherne
Dumb Lough
Moss View
Magheraknock
Tullywasnacunagh
Lake View
The Hill
Creevytenant
Lough Erne
BT26
Hall
Johannas Rock
HILLSBOROUGH RD B178
COMBER ROAD B178
SAINTFIELD ROAD B6
BALLYNAHINCH ROAD A24
CARRYDUFF ROAD
BELFAST ROAD A24
OLD BALLYNAHINCH ROAD
MAGHERAKNOCK ROAD A49
CREEVY ROAD
BRESAGH ROAD
LOUGH ROAD
LISBANE ROAD
CREEVYTENANT ROAD

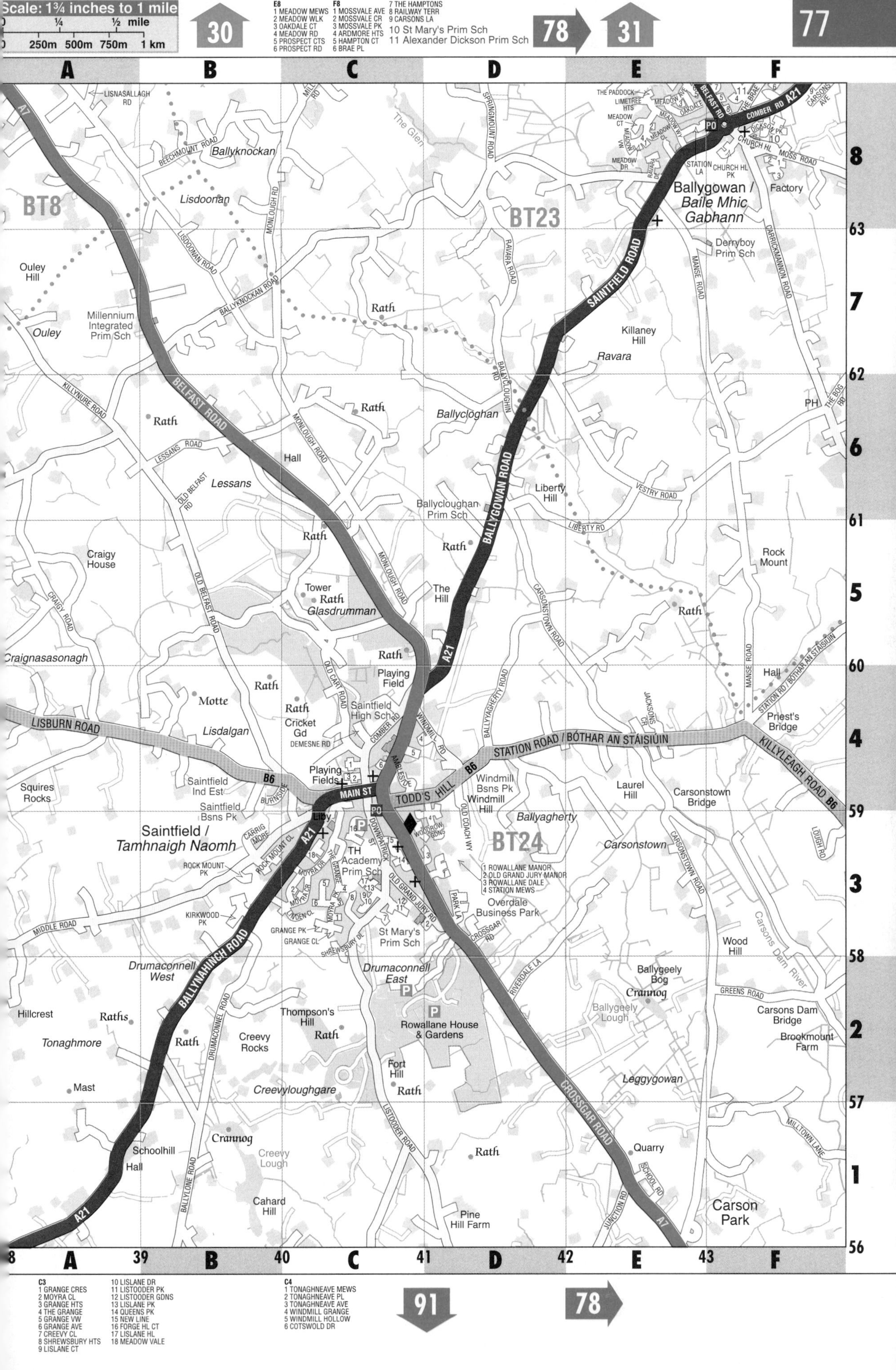

Scale: 1¾ inches to 1 mile
¼
½ mile
250m 500m 750m 1 km
30
E8
1 MEADOW MEWS
2 MEADOW WLK
3 OAKDALE CT
4 MEADOW RD
5 PROSPECT CTS
6 PROSPECT RD
F8
1 MOSSVALE AVE
2 MOSSVALE CR
3 MOSSVALE PK
4 ARDMORE HTS
5 HAMPTON CT
6 BRAE PL
7 THE HAMPTONS
8 RAILWAY TERR
9 CARSONS LA
10 St Mary's Prim Sch
11 Alexander Dickson Prim Sch
78
31
77
A
B
C
D
E
F
LISNASALLAGH RD
MILL RD
The Glen
SPRINGMOUNT ROAD
THE PADDOCK
LIMETREE HTS
MEADOW CT
MEADOW VW
MEADOW DR
BELFAST RD
THE BRAE
COMBER RD
A21
CARSONS AVE
DICKSON PK
CHURCH HL
MOSS ROAD
STATION LA
CHURCH HL PK
Factory
BEECHMOUNT ROAD
Ballyknockan
Lisdoonan
MONLOUGH RD
BT8
BT23
Ballygowan /
Baile Mhic Gabhann
Derryboy Prim Sch
Ouley Hill
LISDOONAN ROAD
BALLYKNOCKAN ROAD
RAVARA ROAD
SAINTFIELD ROAD
MANSE ROAD
CARRICKMANNON ROAD
Millennium Integrated Prim Sch
Ouley
Rath
Killaney Hill
Ravara
BALLYCLOUGHIN RD
KILLYNURE ROAD
BELFAST ROAD
Rath
Ballycloghan
PH
THE BOG RD
LESSANS ROAD
MONLOUGH ROAD
Hall
BALLYGOWAN ROAD
Lessans
OLD BELFAST RD
Liberty Hill
VESTRY ROAD
Ballycloughan Prim Sch
LIBERTY RD
Craigy House
Rath
CARSONSTOWN ROAD
Rock Mount
CRAIGY ROAD
OLD BELFAST ROAD
Tower
Glasdrumman
The Hill
Rath
Craignasasonagh
Playing Field
Hall
MANSE ROAD
STATION RD / BÓTHAR AN STÁISIÚIN
Motte
Saintfield High Sch
OLD CARY ROAD
BALLYAGHERTY ROAD
JACKSONS CR
Priest's Bridge
LISBURN ROAD
Lisdalgan
Cricket Gd
DEMESNE RD
COMBER RD
WINDMILL RD
STATION ROAD / BÓTHAR AN STÁISIÚIN
KILLYLEAGH ROAD
B6
Squires Rocks
Saintfield Ind Est
Playing Fields
AMBLESIDE
TODD'S HILL
Windmill Bsns Pk
Windmill Hill
Laurel Hill
Carsonstown Bridge
Saintfield Bsns Pk
BURNSIDE
MAIN ST
Liby
PO
Ballyagherty
OLD COACH WY
Saintfield /
Tamhnaigh Naomh
CARRIG MORE
ROCK MOUNT CL
TH
Academy Prim Sch
DOWNPATRICK ST
WOODROW GDNS
BT24
Carsonstown
LOUGH RD
ROCK MOUNT PK
MOYRA DR
THE GRANGE
1 ROWALLANE MANOR
2 OLD GRAND JURY MANOR
3 ROWALLANE DALE
4 STATION MEWS
CARSONSTOWN ROAD
MOYRA CR
OLD GRAND JURY RD
PARK LA
Overdale Business Park
KIRKWOOD PK
MIDDLE ROAD
GRANGE PK
GRANGE CL
SHREWSBURY DL
St Mary's Prim Sch
CROSSGAR RD
Carsons Dam River
Wood Hill
Drumaconnell West
BALLYNAHINCH ROAD
Drumaconnell East
RIVERDALE LA
Ballygeely Bog
Crannog
GREENS ROAD
DRUMACONNEL ROAD
Rowallane House & Gardens
Ballygeely Lough
Carsons Dam Bridge
Hillcrest
Raths
Thompson's Hill
Tonaghmore
Creevy Rocks
Brookmount Farm
Fort Hill
Mast
Creevyloughgare
Leggygowan
CROSSGAR ROAD
MILLTOWN LANE
Crannog
Schoolhill
Hall
Creevy Lough
LISTOODER ROAD
Quarry
SCHOOL RD
BALLYLONE ROAD
Cahard Hill
JUNCTION RD
Pine Hill Farm
Carson Park
A7
8
63
7
62
6
61
5
60
4
59
3
58
2
57
1
56
38
39
40
41
42
43
C3
1 GRANGE CRES
2 MOYRA CL
3 GRANGE HTS
4 THE GRANGE
5 GRANGE VW
6 GRANGE AVE
7 CREEVY CL
8 SHREWSBURY HTS
9 LISLANE CT
10 LISLANE DR
11 LISTOODER PK
12 LISTOODER GDNS
13 LISLANE PK
14 QUEENS PK
15 NEW LINE
16 FORGE HL CT
17 LISLANE HL
18 MEADOW VALE
C4
1 TONAGHNEAVE MEWS
2 TONAGHNEAVE PL
3 TONAGHNEAVE AVE
4 WINDMILL GRANGE
5 WINDMILL HOLLOW
6 COTSWOLD DR
91
78

77
68

Scale: 1¾ inches to 1 mile

77
92

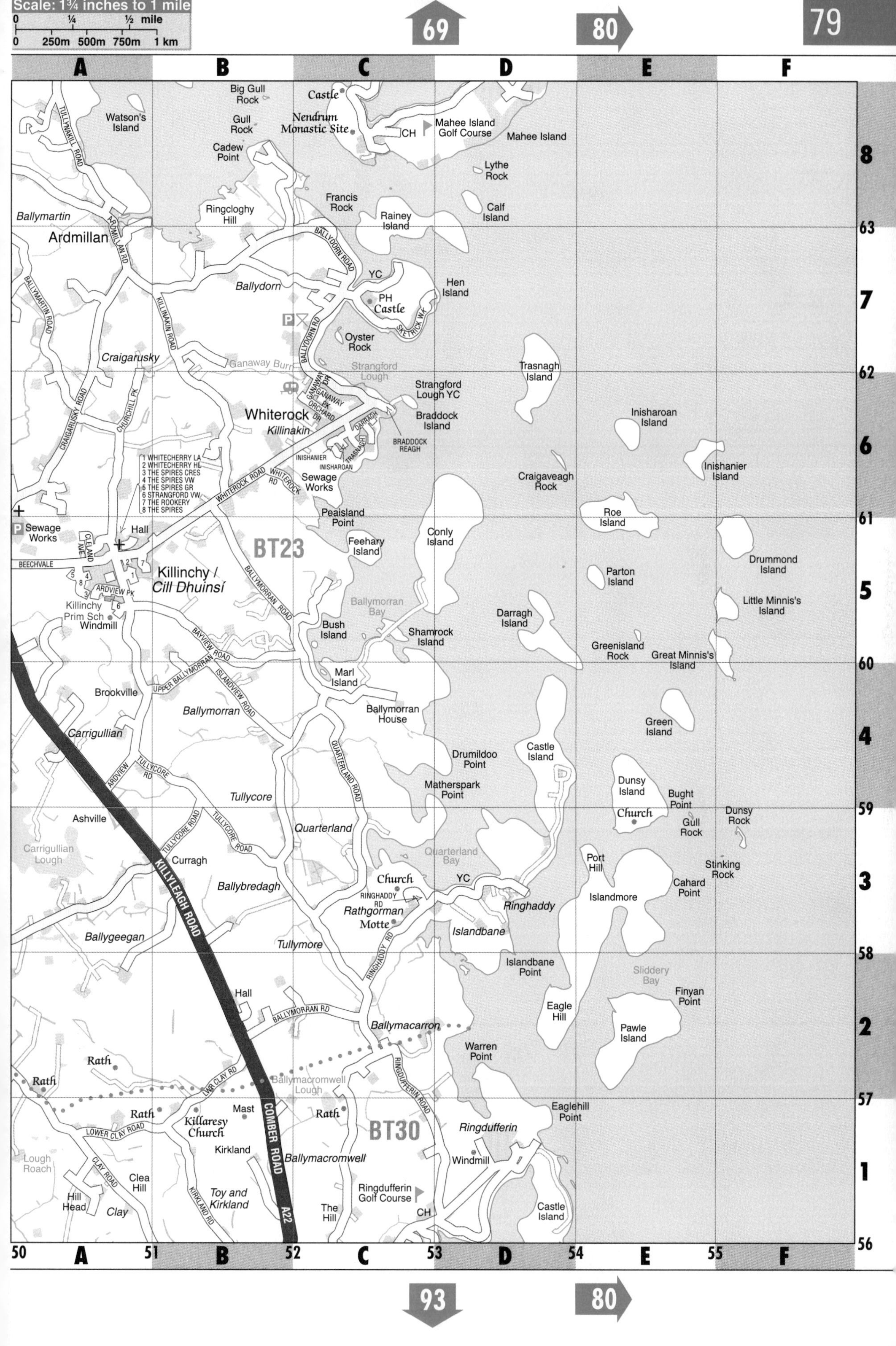
Scale: 1¾ inches to 1 mile
0 ¼ ½ mile
0 250m 500m 750m 1 km
69
80
Ardmillan
Ballymartin
Watson's Island
Big Gull Rock
Gull Rock
Cadew Point
Castle
Nendrum Monastic Site
Mahee Island Golf Course
Mahee Island
Lythe Rock
Calf Island
Francis Rock
Rainey Island
Ringcloghy Hill
Ballydorn
YC
Hen Island
PH
Castle
Oyster Rock
Craigarusky
Ganaway Burn
Strangford Lough
Trasnagh Island
Strangford Lough YC
Braddock Island
Whiterock
Killinakin
Inisharoan Island
Inishanier Island
Craigaveagh Rock
Sewage Works
Peaisland Point
Roe Island
Sewage Works
Hall
Feehary Island
Conly Island
BT23
Drummond Island
Killinchy / Cill Dhuinsí
Parton Island
Little Minnis's Island
Killinchy Prim Sch
Windmill
Ballymorran Bay
Bush Island
Shamrock Island
Darragh Island
Greenisland Rock
Great Minnis's Island
Marl Island
Brookville
Ballymorran House
Ballymorran
Green Island
Carrigullian
Castle Island
Drumildoo Point
Dunsy Island
Bught Point
Matherspark Point
Tullycore
Church
Dunsy Rock
Gull Rock
Ashville
Quarterland
Carrigullian Lough
Quarterland Bay
Port Hill
Stinking Rock
Curragh
Church
YC
Cahard Point
Ballybredagh
Ringhaddy
Islandmore
Rathgorman Motte
Islandbane
Ballygeegan
Tullymore
Islandbane Point
Sliddery Bay
Finyan Point
Eagle Hill
Hall
Ballymacarron
Pawle Island
Warren Point
Rath
Rath
Ballymacromwell Lough
Eaglehill Point
Rath
Mast
Rath
Killaresy Church
BT30
Ringdufferin
Kirkland
Ballymacromwell
Windmill
Lough Roach
Clea Hill
Toy and Kirkland
Ringdufferin Golf Course
Hill Head
Clay
The Hill
CH
Castle Island
TULLYNAKILL ROAD
ARDMILLAN RD
BALLYDORN ROAD
BALLYMARTIN ROAD
KILLINAKIN ROAD
SKETRICK WK
BALLYDORN RD
CRAIGARUSKY ROAD
CHURCHILL PK
GANAWAY DR
GANAWAY PK
ORCHARD DR
DARRAGH
TRASNAGH
BRADDOCK REAGH
INISHANIER
INISHAROAN
1 WHITECHERRY LA
2 WHITECHERRY HL
3 THE SPIRES CRES
4 THE SPIRES VW
5 THE SPIRES GR
6 STRANGFORD VW
7 THE ROOKERY
8 THE SPIRES
WHITEROCK ROAD
WHITEROCK RD
CLELAND AVE
BEECHVALE
ARDVIEW PK
BALLYMORRAN ROAD
BAYVIEW ROAD
UPPER BALLYMORRAN
ISLANDVIEW ROAD
QUARTERLAND ROAD
ARDVIEW
TULLYCORE RD
TULLYCORE ROAD
KILLYLEAGH ROAD
RINGHADDY RD
BALLYMORRAN RD
LWR CLAY RD
RINGDUFFERIN ROAD
LOWER CLAY ROAD
CLAY ROAD
COMBER ROAD
KIRKLAND RD
A22
A B C D E F
8 7 6 5 4 3 2 1
63 62 61 60 59 58 57 56
50 51 52 53 54 55
93
80

79
70

Scale: 1¾ inches to 1 mile
0 ¼ ½ mile
0 250m 500m 750m 1 km
A B C D E F
8 7 6 5 4 3 2 1
63 62 61 60 59 58 57 56
56 57 58 59 60 61
Newtown Rock
Long Skart Rock
Round Skart Rock
Bird Island
Strangford Lough
Marine Nature Reserve
Kircubbin Sailing Club
Kircubbin Bay
Kircubbin / Cill Ghobáin
Monaghan Bank
St Mary's Prim Sch
Sewage Works
A20 SHORE ROAD
THE OLD MILL
MILL HTS
MAIN ST
COOKS BRAE
COOKS COVE
CHURCH AVE
CHURCH WY
BOYD AVE
RODEN ST
RECTORY PK
RECTORY WY
PARSONAGE RD
TUBBER RD
Hall
Cemy
PO
1 ROUND ISLAND PK
2 PARSONAGE CL
3 BIRD ISLAND WK
4 LONG SHEELAH AVE
5 Kircubbin Prim Sch
LONG ISLAND DR
Fish Quarter
Quarry (Dis)
COULTER'S HL
B173
Doctors Bay
Ballycran GAC
CH
MCKENNA RD
Rowreagh
Rowreagh Point
ROWREAGH ROAD
Cairn
Rubane
RUBANE MEWS
NT
Horse Island
Rubane House
Echlinville
BT22
Playing Field
Hare Island
Gransha
GRANSHA ROAD
Blackstaff Bridge
Blackstaff River
Sewage Works
Scady Rocks
Mid Island
Gransha Point
Boyds Rock
Ballycranbeg
The Dorn Nature Reserve
PH
Cookstown
Far Craiglee Rocks
Near Craiglee Rock
LISBANE ROAD
Lisbane
Rath
Ashview House
UPPER BALLYGELAGH ROAD
Ballygelagh
BALLYGELAGH ROAD
Long Island
Castle
Castle Hill
Sleetch Rock
Peeltown
Strife Rock
Dorn Rock
Church
A20
DEERPARK ROAD
Ardkeen
TULLYCROSS ROAD
Dorn Hill
Phersons Island
Round Island
Tullycross
LOUGHDOO ROAD
ABBACY RD
Ballywallon Island
Jocks Islands
Old Mans Head
Ballywaddan
Loughdoo

79
94

Scale: 1¾ inches to 1 mile

0 ¼ ½ mile

0 250m 500m 750m 1 km

71

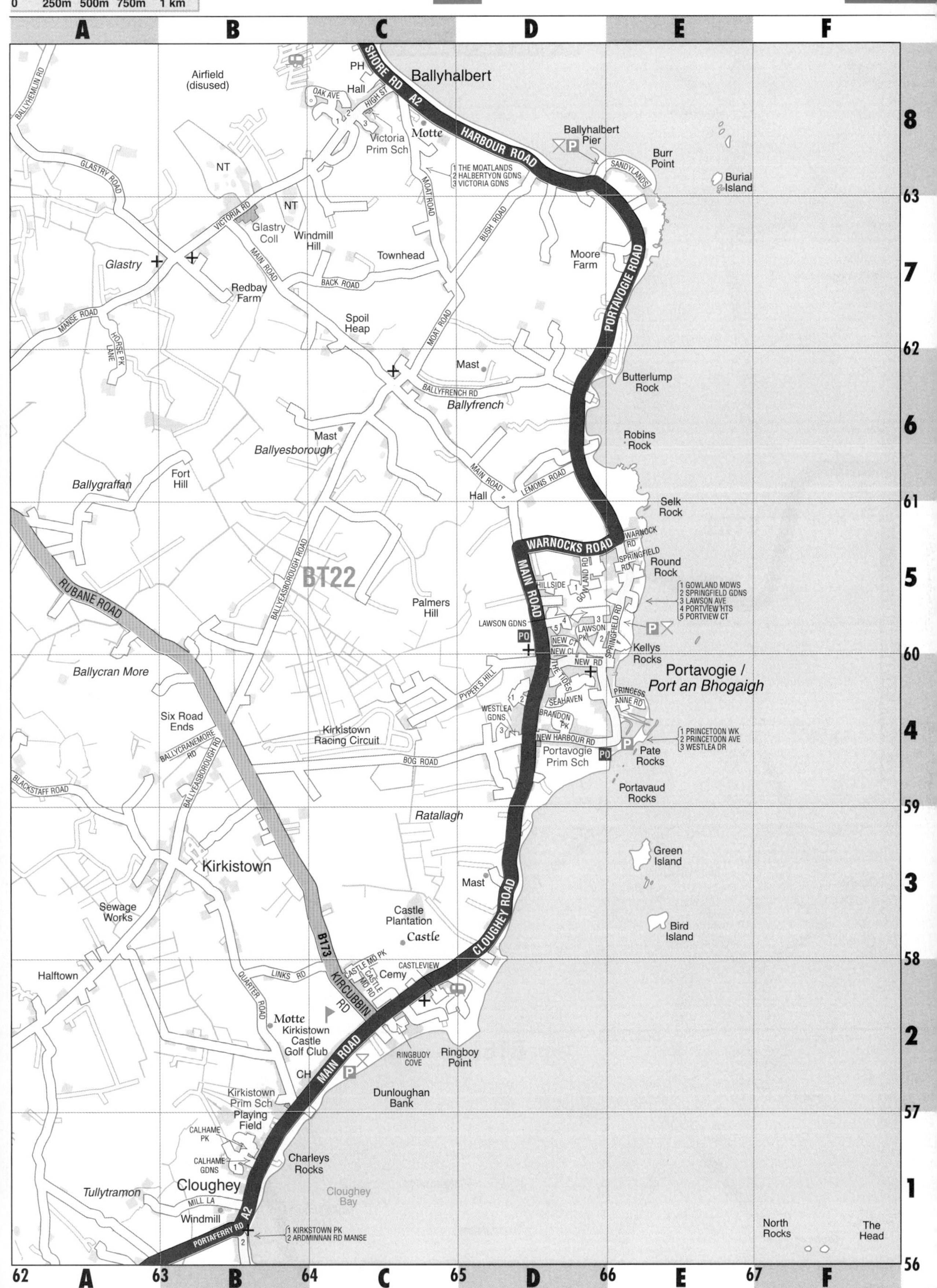

95

Scale: 1¾ inches to 1 mile

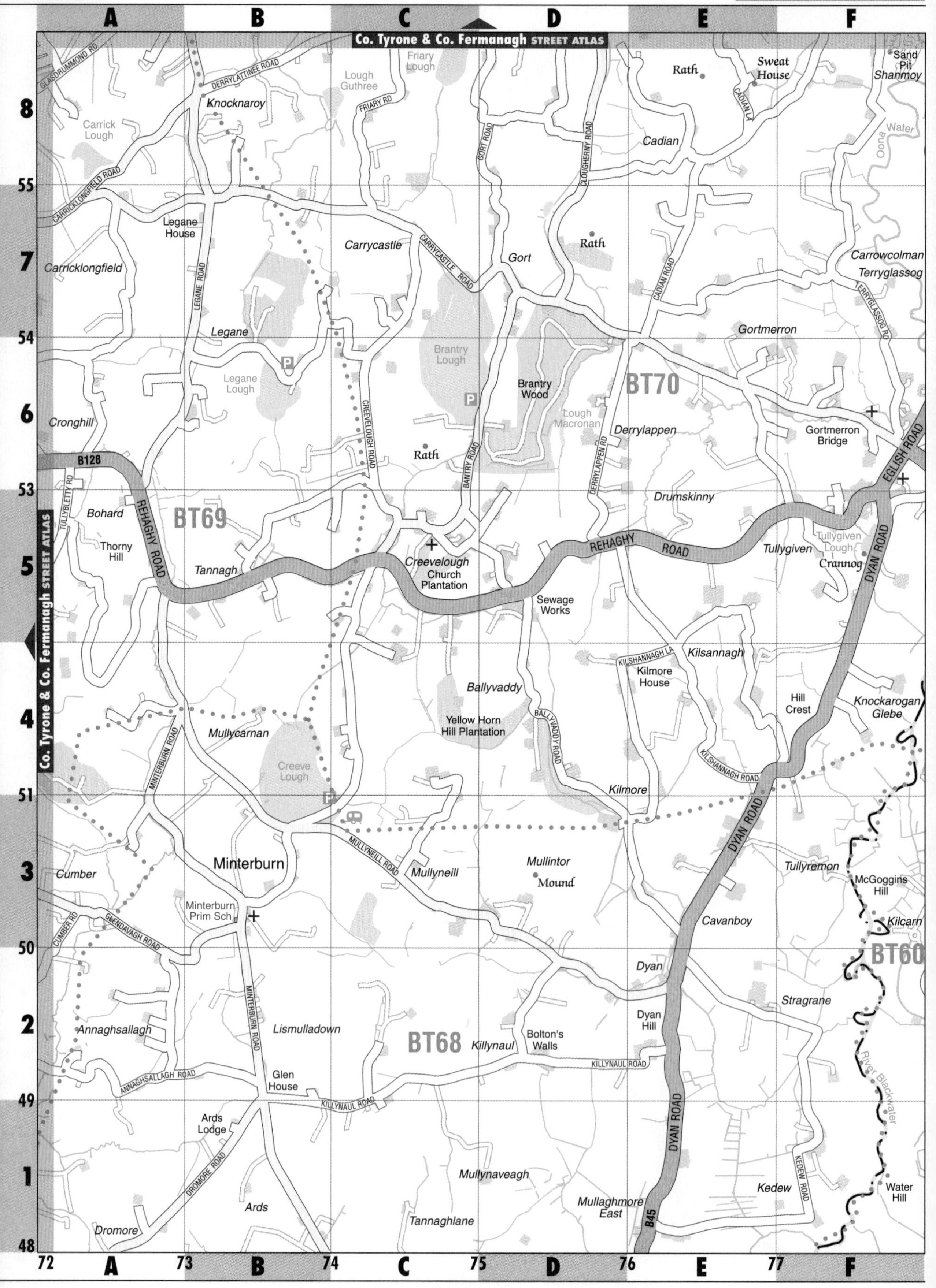

Scale: 1¾ inches to 1 mile

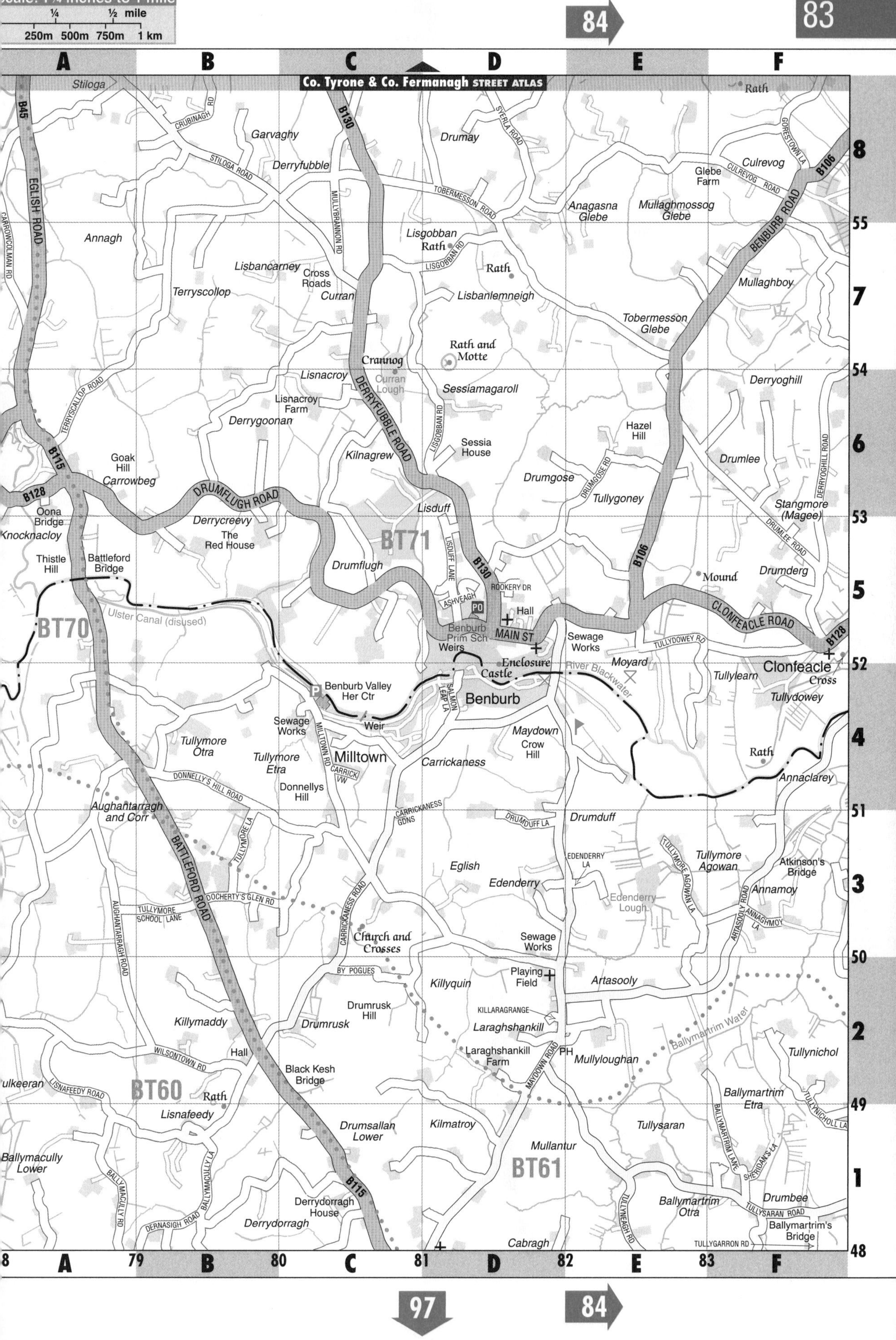

83
72

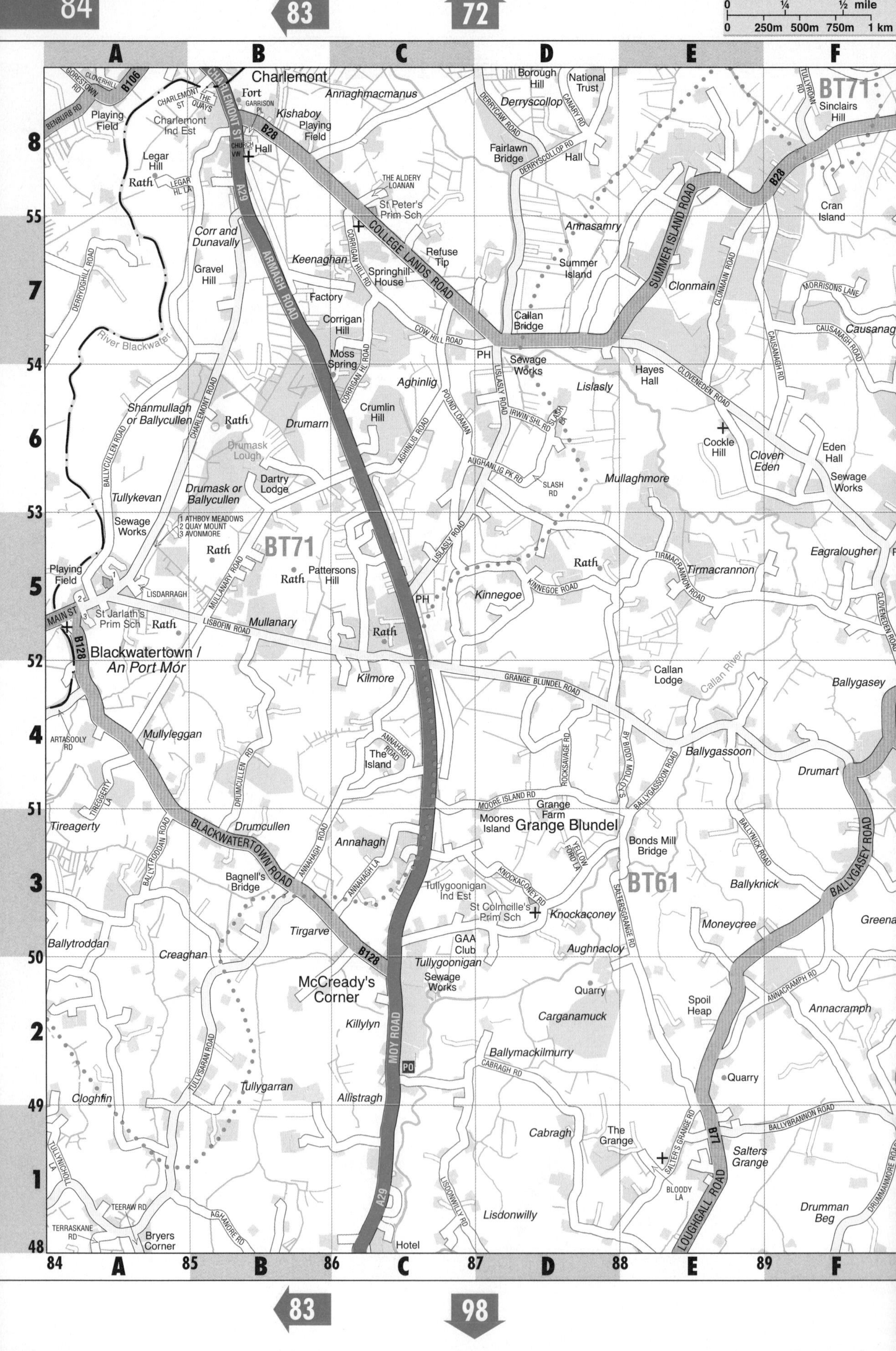
Scale: 1¾ inches to 1 mile
0
¼
½ mile
0
250m
500m
750m
1 km
A
B
C
D
E
F
Charlemont
Fort
Annaghmacmanus
Borough Hill
National Trust
BT71
Sinclairs Hill
Playing Field
Charlemont Ind Est
Kishaboy
Playing Field
Derryscollop
Legar Hill
Rath
Hall
Fairlawn Bridge
Hall
Cran Island
St Peter's Prim Sch
Annasamry
Corr and Dunavally
Gravel Hill
Keenaghan
Refuse Tip
Springhill House
Summer Island
Clonmain
Factory
Corrigan Hill
Callan Bridge
Causanag
River Blackwater
Moss Spring
PH
Sewage Works
Hayes Hall
Aghinlig
Lislasly
Shanmullagh or Ballycullen
Rath
Drumarn
Crumlin Hill
Cockle Hill
Eden Hall
Drumask Lough
Cloven Eden
Sewage Works
Dartry Lodge
Mullaghmore
Tullykevan
Drumask or Ballycullen
Sewage Works
1 ATHBOY MEADOWS
2 QUAY MOUNT
3 AVONMORE
Rath
BT71
Eagralougher
Rath
Playing Field
Rath
Pattersons Hill
Tirmacrannon
Kinnegoe
PH
St Jarlath's Prim Sch
Rath
Mullanary
Rath
Blackwatertown /
An Port Mór
Kilmore
Callan Lodge
Callan River
Ballygasey
Mullyleggan
Ballygassoon
The Island
Drumart
Tireagerty
Drumcullen
Grange Farm
Moores Island
Grange Blundel
Bonds Mill Bridge
Annahagh
Bagnell's Bridge
Tullygoonigan Ind Est
BT61
Ballyknick
St Colmcille's Prim Sch
Knockaconey
Moneycree
Greena
Tirgarve
Ballytroddan
Creaghan
GAA Club
Aughnacloy
Tullygoonigan
McCready's Corner
Sewage Works
Quarry
Spoil Heap
Annacramph
Killylyn
Carganamuck
Ballymackilmurry
Quarry
Tullygarran
Cloghfin
Allistragh
Cabragh
The Grange
Salters Grange
Lisdonwilly
Drumman Beg
Bryers Corner
Hotel
PO
A29
B28
B106
B128
B77
84
85
86
87
88
89

83
98

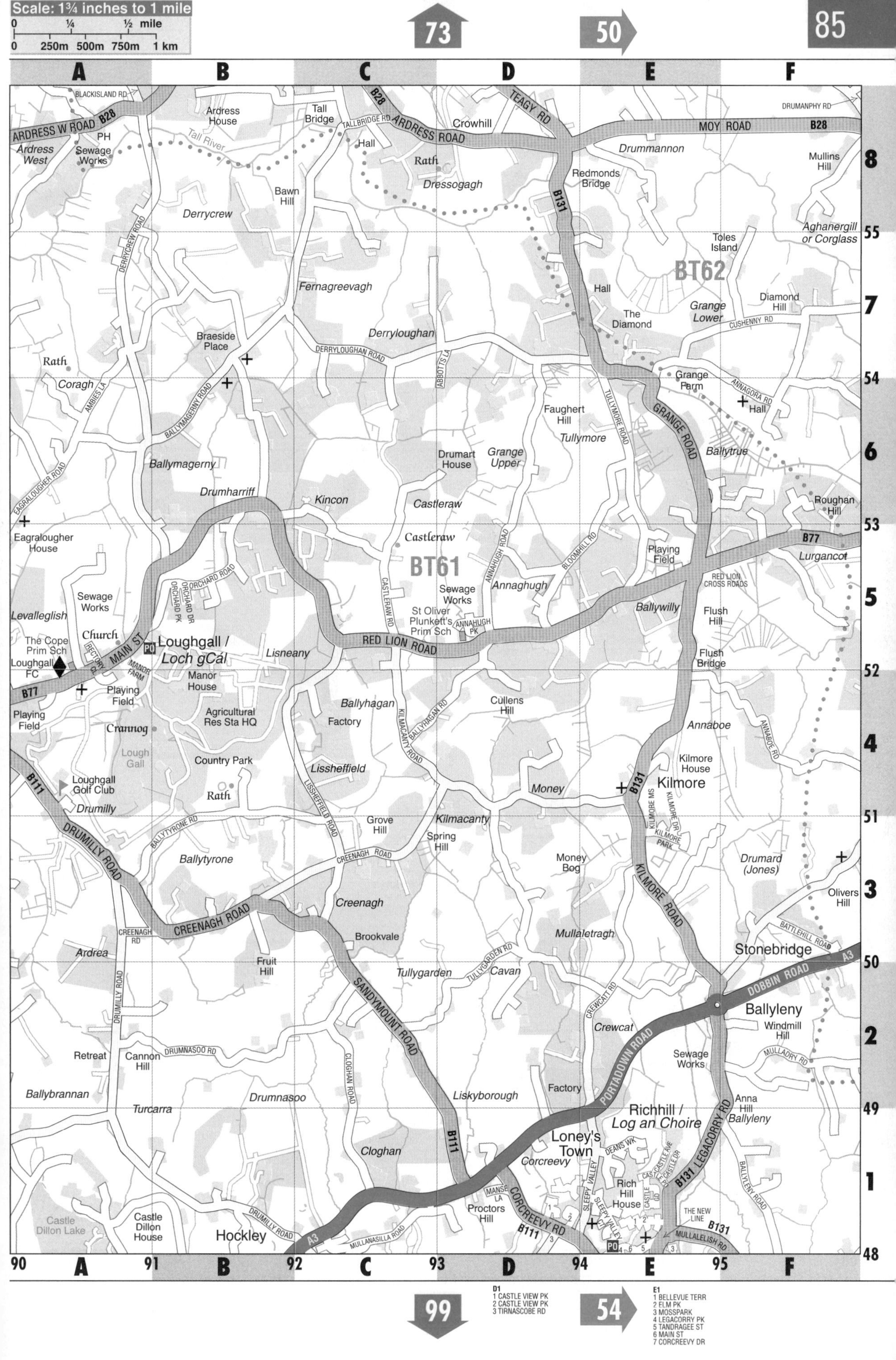
Scale: 1¾ inches to 1 mile
0 ¼ ½ mile
0 250m 500m 750m 1 km
73
50
85
A B C D E F
BLACKISLAND RD
ARDRESS W ROAD B28
PH
Ardress West
Sewage Works
Ardress House
Tall River
Tall Bridge
TALLBRIDGE RD
B28 ARDRESS ROAD
Crowhill
Hall
TEAGY RD
MOY ROAD B28
DRUMANPHY RD
Rath
Dressogagh
Drummannon
Redmonds Bridge
Mullins Hill
8
Bawn Hill
Derrycrew
DERRYCREW ROAD
B131
55
Aghanergill or Corglass
Toles Island
BT62
Fernagreevagh
Hall
The Diamond
Grange Lower
Diamond Hill
CUSHENNY RD
7
Braeside Place
Derryloughan
DERRYLOUGHAN ROAD
ABBOTTS LA
Rath
Coragh
AMBIES LA
BALLYMAGERNY ROAD
Grange Farm
ANNAGORA RD
Hall
54
Faughert Hill
Tullymore
TULLYMORE ROAD
GRANGE ROAD
Drumart House
Grange Upper
Ballytrue
6
Ballymagerny
EAGRALOUGHER ROAD
Drumharriff
Kincon
Castleraw
Roughan Hill
Eagralougher House
Castleraw
BLOOMHILL RD
ANNAHUGH ROAD
Playing Field
B77
53
Lurgancot
BT61
ORCHARD ROAD
ORCHARD PK
ORCHARD DR
Sewage Works
CASTLERAW RD
Sewage Works
Annaghugh
RED LION CROSS ROADS
Levalleglish
Church
St Oliver Plunkett's Prim Sch
ANNAHUGH PK
Ballywilly
Flush Hill
5
The Cope Prim Sch
RECTORY
MAIN ST
PO
Loughgall / Loch gCal
Lisneany
RED LION ROAD
Flush Bridge
Loughgall FC
MANOR FARM
Manor House
52
B77
Playing Field
Playing Field
Agricultural Res Sta HQ
Ballyhagan
Factory
BALLYHAGAN RD
Cullens Hill
Annaboe
ANNABOE RD
Crannog
Lough Gall
Country Park
KILMACANTY ROAD
Lissheffield
Kilmore House
4
B111
Loughgall Golf Club
Drumilly
Rath
Money
B131
Kilmore
KILMORE MS
KILMORE DR
KILMORE PARK
BALLYTYRONE RD
LISSHEFFIELD ROAD
Grove Hill
Kilmacanty
Spring Hill
51
DRUMILLY ROAD
Ballytyrone
CREENAGH ROAD
Money Bog
Drumard (Jones)
Olivers Hill
3
Creenagh
KILMORE ROAD
CREENAGH RD
CREENAGH ROAD
Brookvale
Mullaletragh
BATTLEHILL ROAD
Ardrea
Fruit Hill
TULLYGARDEN RD
Tullygarden
Cavan
Stonebridge
A3
50
SANDYMOUNT ROAD
DRUMILLY ROAD
CREWCATT RD
DOBBIN ROAD
Ballyleny
Crewcat
PORTADOWN ROAD
Windmill Hill
2
Retreat
Cannon Hill
DRUMNASOO RD
CLOGHAN ROAD
Sewage Works
MULLADRY RD
Ballybrannan
Drumnasoo
Liskyborough
Factory
Anna Hill Ballyleny
49
Turcarra
Richhill / Log an Choire
LEGACORRY RD
B111
Loney's Town
Cloghan
DEANS WK
Corcreevy
CASTLE AVE
CASTLE DR
BALLYLENY ROAD
1
SLEEPY VALLEY
Rich Hill House
B131
MANSE LA
CORCREEVY RD
Castle Dillon Lake
Castle Dillon House
Hockley
DRUMILLY ROAD
Proctors Hill
THE NEW LINE
B131
B111
A3
MULLANASILLA ROAD
PO
MULLALELISH RD
48
90 A 91 B 92 C 93 D 94 E 95 F
99
D1
1 CASTLE VIEW PK
2 CASTLE VIEW PK
3 TIRNASCOBE RD
54
E1
1 BELLEVUE TERR
2 ELM PK
3 MOSSPARK
4 LEGACORRY PK
5 TANDRAGEE ST
6 MAIN ST
7 CORCREEVY DR

Scale: 1¾ inches to 1 mile

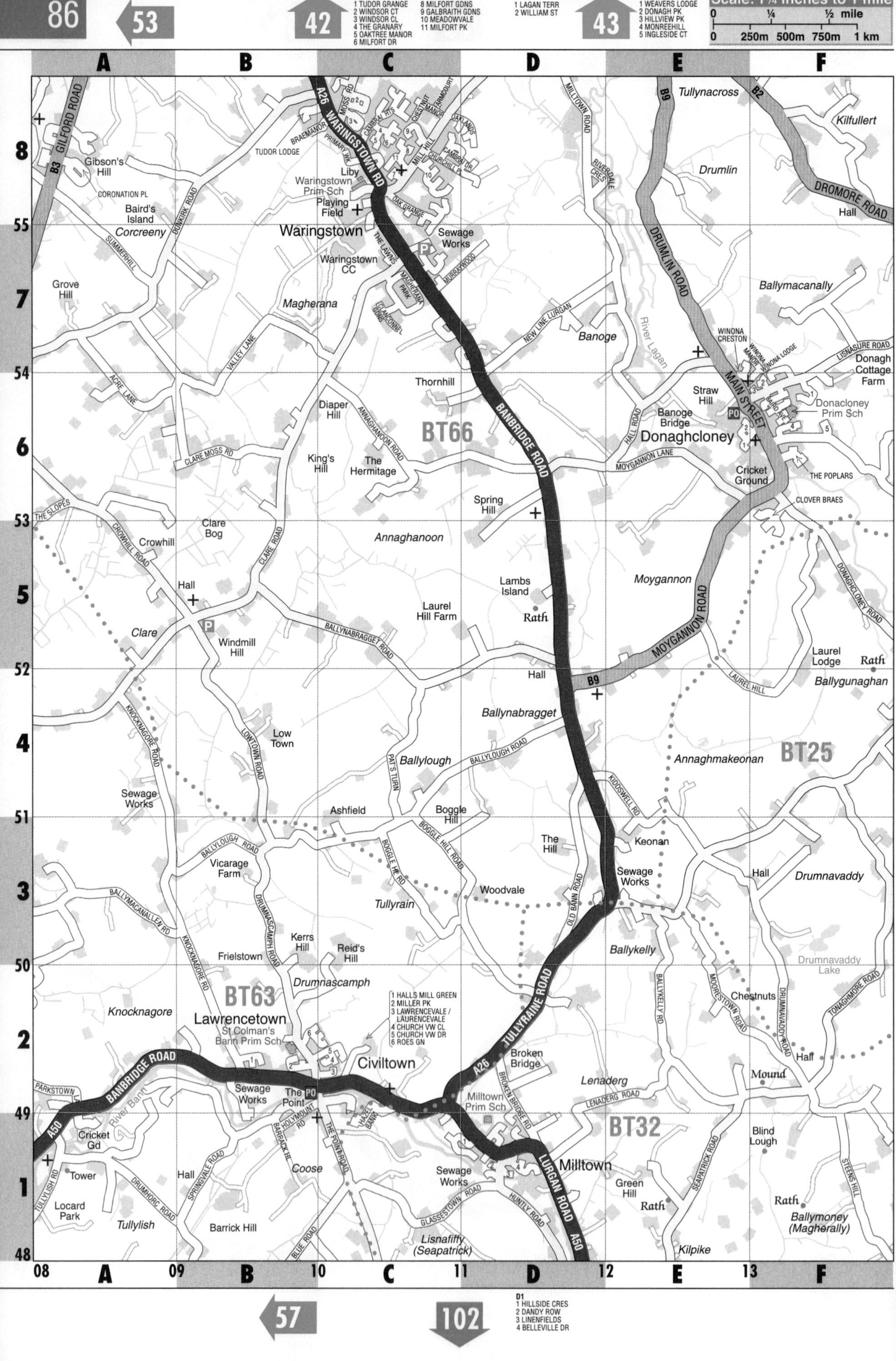

Scale: 1¾ inches to 1 mile
0 ¼ ½ mile
0 250m 500m 750m 1 km

44
45
88

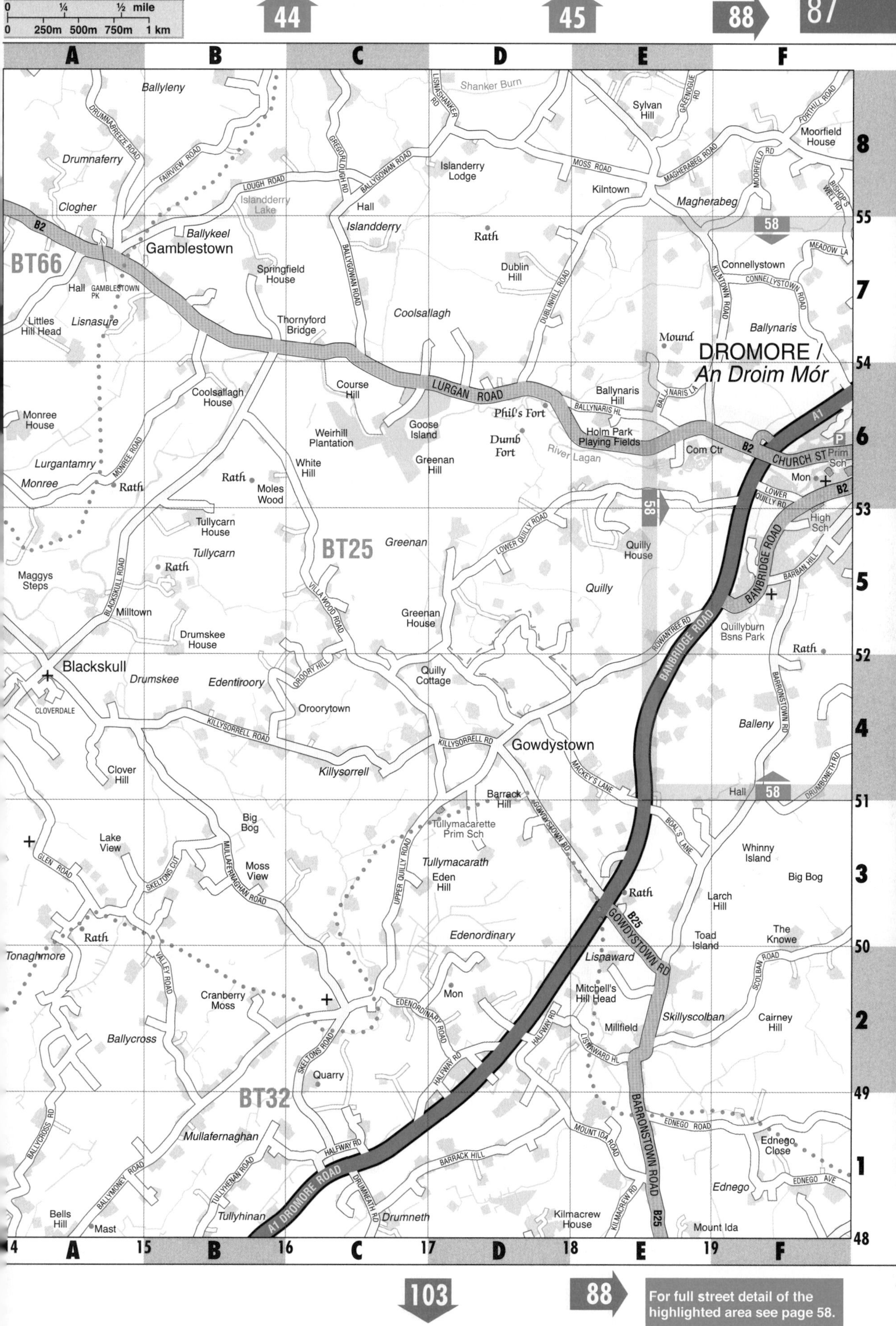

103
88
For full street detail of the highlighted area see page 58.

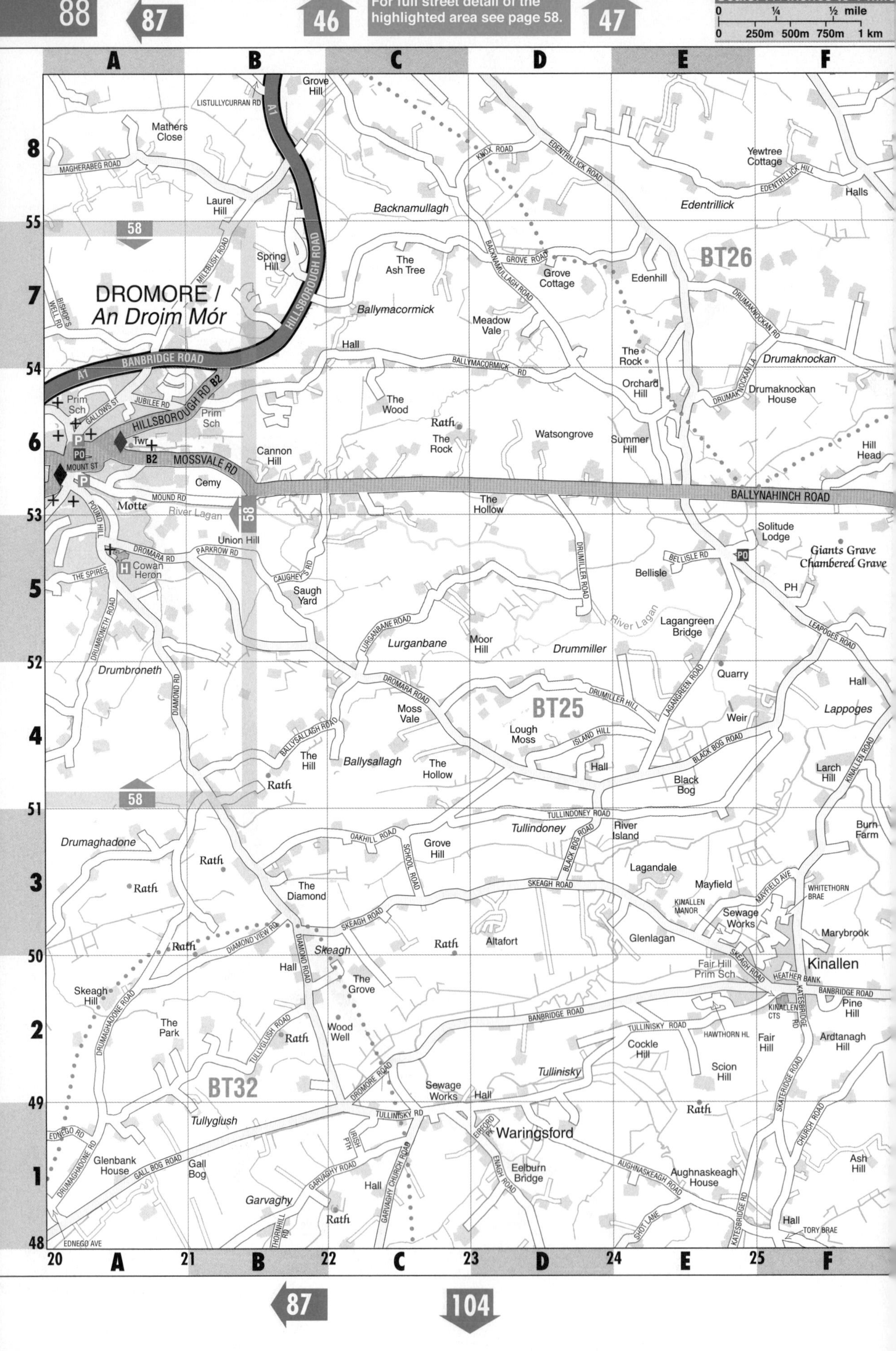
A B C D E F
8
55
7
54
6
53
5
52
4
51
3
50
2
49
1
48
20 21 22 23 24 25
Grove Hill
LISTULLYCURRAN RD
A1
Mathers Close
MAGHERABEG ROAD
KNOX ROAD
EDENTRILLICK ROAD
Yewtree Cottage
EDENTRILLICK HILL
Halls
Laurel Hill
Backnamullagh
Edentrillick
58
MILEBUSH ROAD
Spring Hill
HILLSBOROUGH ROAD
The Ash Tree
GROVE ROAD
BACKNAMULLAGH ROAD
Grove Cottage
Edenhill
BT26
DROMORE /
An Droim Mór
BISHOP'S WELL RD
Ballymacormick
Meadow Vale
DRUMAKNOCKAN RD
The Rock
Drumaknockan
Hall
BANBRIDGE ROAD
BALLYMACORMICK RD
Orchard Hill
DRUMAKNOCKAN LA
Drumaknockan House
Prim Sch
GALLOWS ST
JUBILEE RD
HILLSBOROUGH RD B2
Prim Sch
The Wood
Rath
The Rock
Watsongrove
Summer Hill
Hill Head
Twr
PO
B2
MOSSVALE RD
Cannon Hill
MOUNT ST
Cemy
MOUND RD
The Hollow
BALLYNAHINCH ROAD
Motte
River Lagan
58
Union Hill
Solitude Lodge
POUND HILL
DROMARA RD
PARKROW RD
DRUMILLER ROAD
BELLISLE RD
PO
Giants Grave Chambered Grave
Cowan Heron
THE SPIRES
CAUGHEY'S RD
Bellisle
PH
Saugh Yard
DRUMBONETH ROAD
LURGANBANE ROAD
River Lagan
Lagangreen Bridge
LEAPOGES ROAD
Lurganbane
Moor Hill
Drummiller
Drumbroneth
DIAMOND RD
DROMARA ROAD
Quarry
Hall
DRUMILLER HILL
LAGANGREEN ROAD
Moss Vale
BT25
Lappoges
Weir
Lough Moss
ISLAND HILL
BALLYSALLAGH ROAD
BLACK BOG ROAD
KINALLEN ROAD
The Hill
Ballysallagh
The Hollow
Hall
Larch Hill
Black Bog
Rath
58
TULLINDONEY ROAD
Drumaghadone
Tullindoney
River Island
Burn Farm
OAKHILL ROAD
Grove Hill
BLACK BOG ROAD
Rath
SCHOOL ROAD
Lagandale
Rath
Mayfield
MAYFIELD AVE
WHITETHORN BRAE
The Diamond
SKEAGH ROAD
KINALLEN MANOR
Sewage Works
SKEAGH ROAD
DIAMOND VIEW RD
Marybrook
Rath
Altafort
Glenlagan
Rath
Skeagh
Kinallen
Hall
DIAMOND ROAD
Fair Hill Prim Sch
SKEAGH ROAD
HEATHER BANK
Skeagh Hill
The Grove
BANBRIDGE ROAD
DRUMAGHADONE ROAD
KINALLEN CTS
Pine Hill
BANBRIDGE ROAD
KATESBRIDGE RD
The Park
TULLYGLUSH ROAD
Wood Well
TULLINISKY ROAD
HAWTHORN HL
Rath
Cockle Hill
Fair Hill
Ardtanagh Hill
Tullinisky
Scion Hill
BT32
DROMORE ROAD
Sewage Works
Hall
SKATERIDGE ROAD
TULLINISKY RD
Rath
EDNEGO RD
Tullyglush
IRISH PTH
EIRFORD PK
Waringsford
CHURCH ROAD
Glenbank House
GALL BOG ROAD
Gall Bog
GARVAGHY ROAD
GARVAGHY CHURCH ROAD
Eelburn Bridge
AUGHNASKEAGH ROAD
Aughnaskeagh House
Ash Hill
DRUMAGHADONE ROAD
Garvaghy
Hall
ENAGH ROAD
Rath
THORNHILL RD
SHOT LANE
KATESBRIDGE RD
Hall
TORY BRAE
EDNEGO AVE

Scale: 1¾ inches to 1 mile

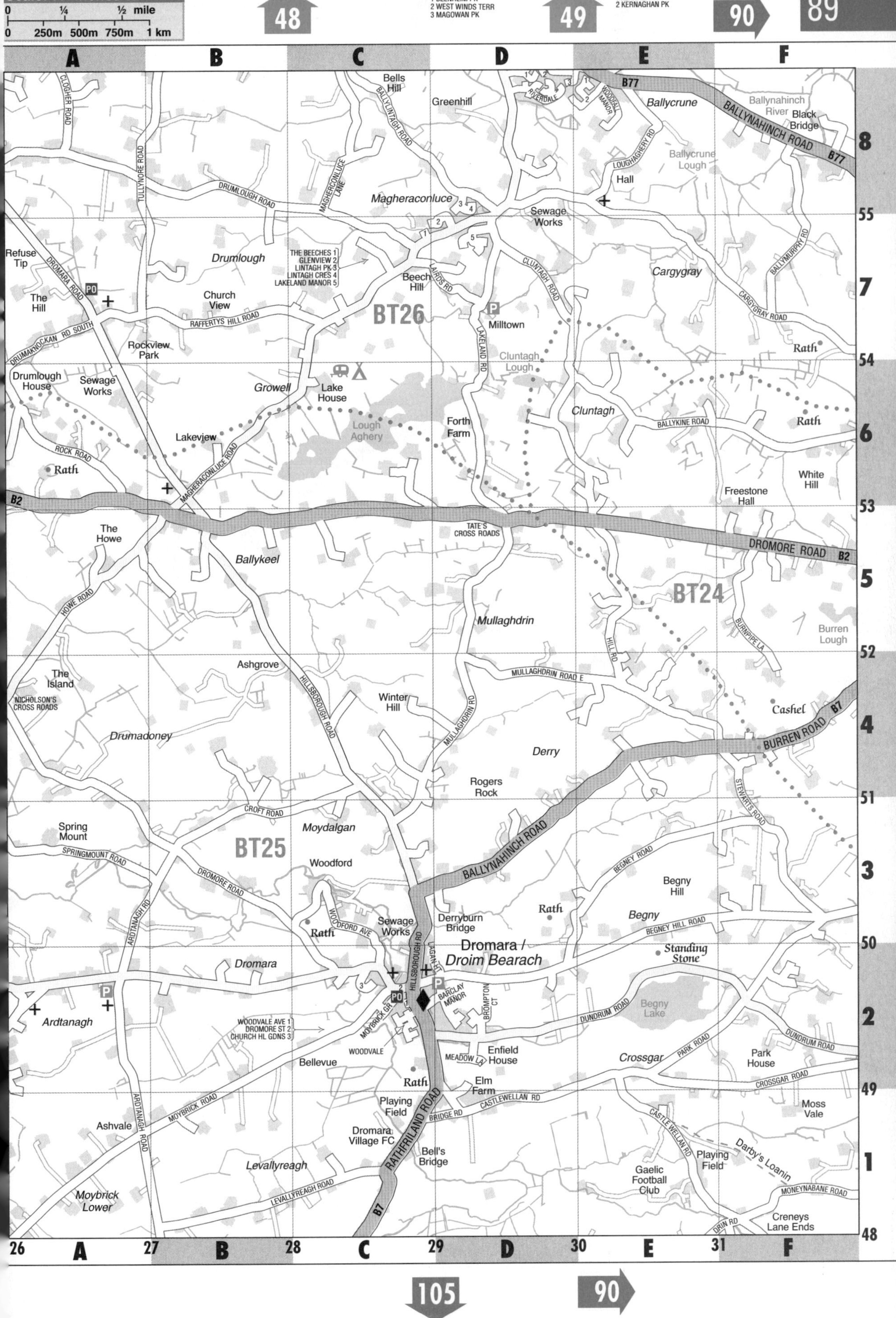

89
76
For full street detail of the highlighted area see page 59.

Scale: 1¾ inches to 1 mile

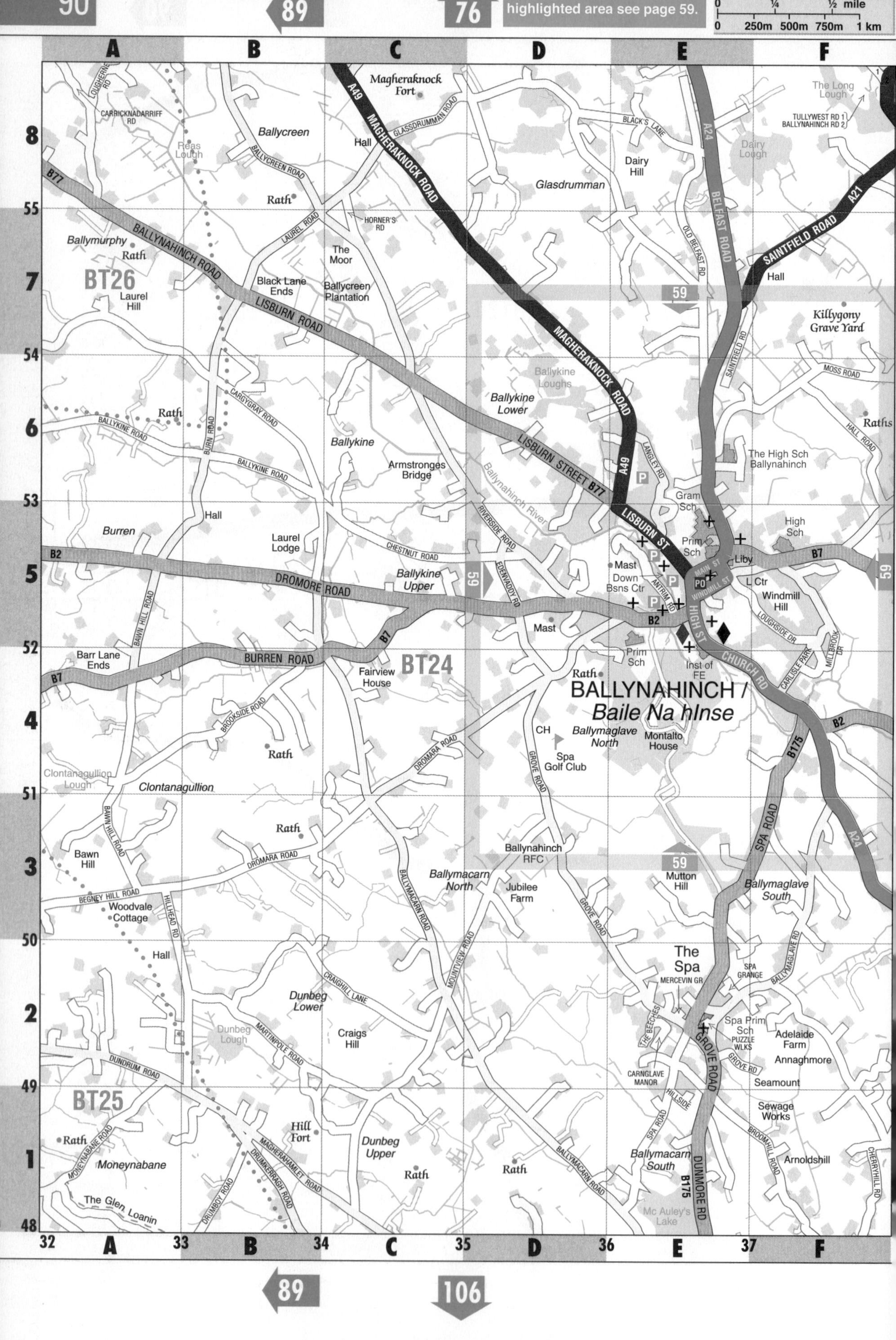

89
106

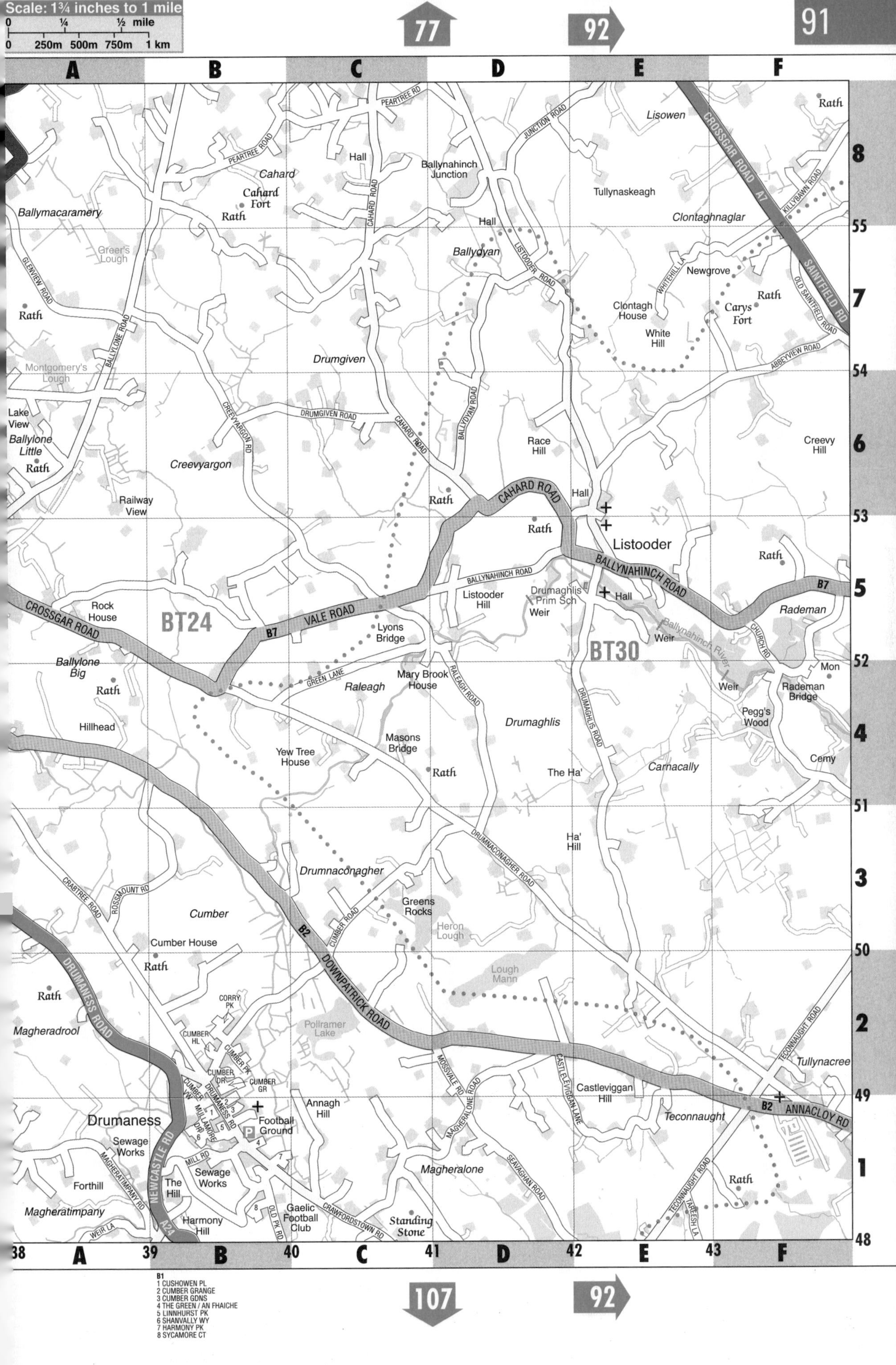

B1
1 CUSHOWEN PL
2 CUMBER GRANGE
3 CUMBER GDNS
4 THE GREEN / AN FHAICHE
5 LINNHURST PK
6 SHANVALLY WY
7 HARMONY PK
8 SYCAMORE CT

Scale: 1¾ inches to 1 mile

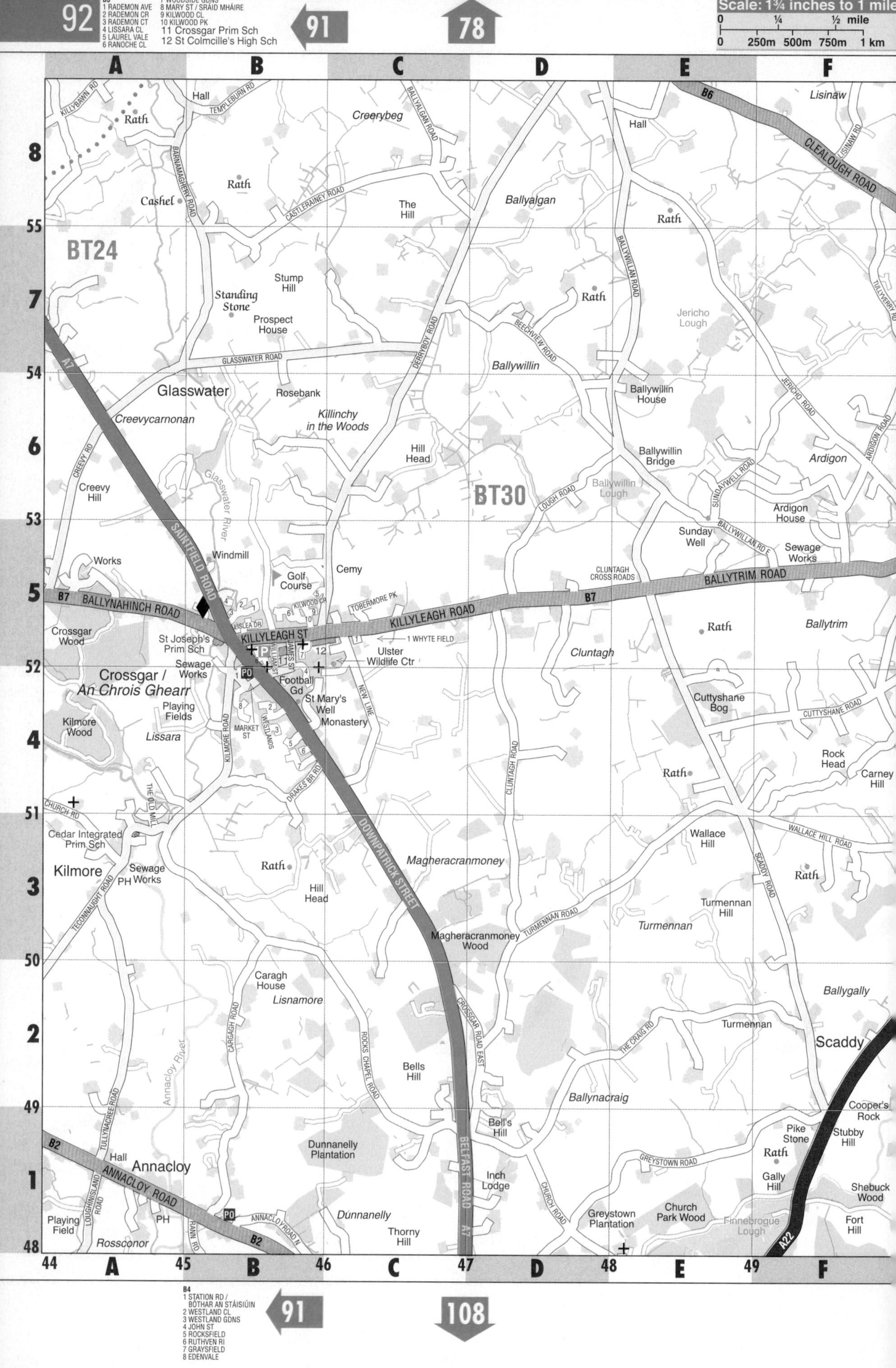

Scale: 1¾ inches to 1 mile

79
94

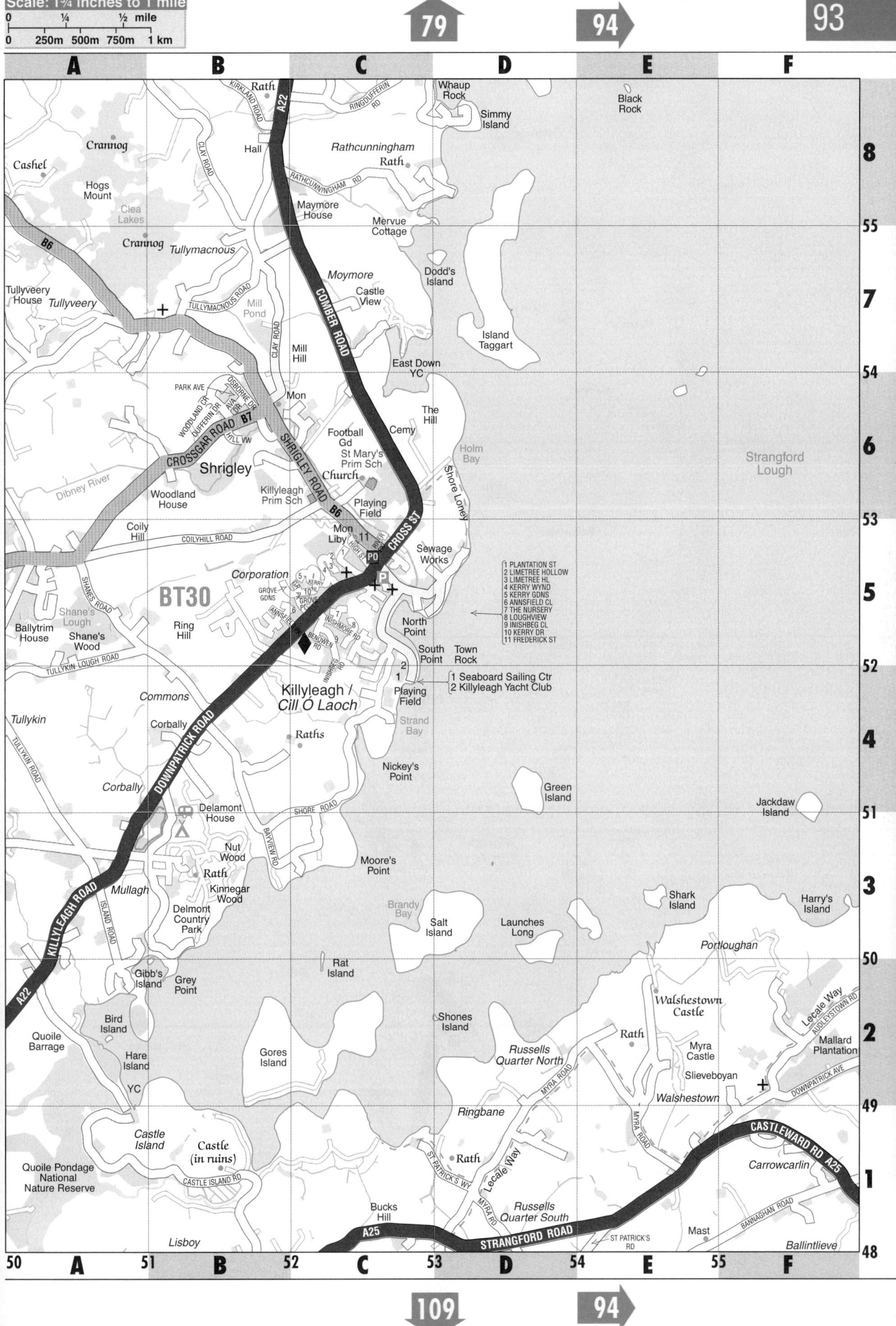

109
94

93
80

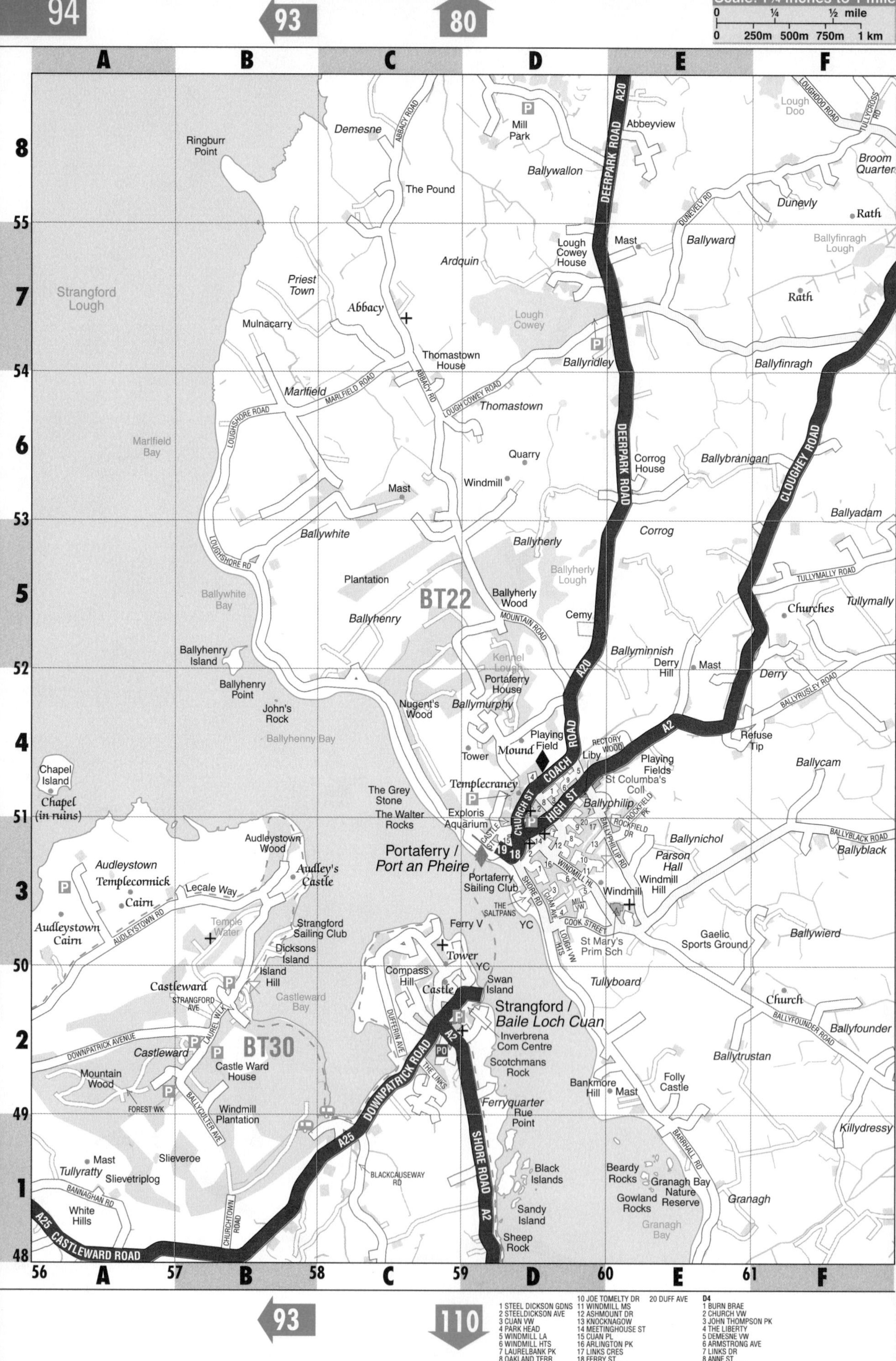

93
110

1 STEEL DICKSON GDNS
2 STEELDICKSON AVE
3 CUAN VW
4 PARK HEAD
5 WINDMILL LA
6 WINDMILL HTS
7 LAURELBANK PK
8 OAKLAND TERR
9 ASHMOUNT PK
10 JOE TOMELTY DR
11 WINDMILL MS
12 ASHMOUNT DR
13 KNOCKNAGOW
14 MEETINGHOUSE ST
15 CUAN PL
16 ARLINGTON PK
17 LINKS CRES
18 FERRY ST
19 THE STRAND
20 DUFF AVE

D4
1 BURN BRAE
2 CHURCH VW
3 JOHN THOMPSON PK
4 THE LIBERTY
5 DEMESNE VW
6 ARMSTRONG AVE
7 LINKS DR
8 ANNE ST
9 MARIAN WY

A
B
C
D
E
F
Mast
Castleboy
PORTAFERRY RD
A2
Broom Hill
Church
Drumardan Quarter
Nun's Bridge
Rath
DRUMARDEN RD
Slanes Point
Slanes Bay
Church
Souterrain
Rath
Drumardan
Slanes
White House
BALLYGALGET ROAD
ARDMINNAN ROAD
Gaelic Sports Ground
Knockdoo
Ballywhollart
Ballyspurge
Upper Ballyspurge
Hems Rock
DRUMARDEN RD
MANSE
Rath
Ardminnan
St Patrick's Prim Sch
Killeavey
Ballygalget
Rath
Moss Side
Raths
ARDMINNAN ROAD
Ballymacnamee
Newcastle
Sewage Works
South Rock Lighthouse
Mount Ross
NEWCASTLE ROAD
Ballygarvigan
BT22
Dooey Hill
Standing Stone
BALLYGARVIGAN ROAD
Dooey
National Trust
Ballyrusley
The Mill Stone
Kearney
Rath
Kearney Farm
Windmill
Knockinelder
KEARNEY ROAD
Rath
Ardgeehan
Knockinelder Bay
Kearney Point
Halftide Rock
Cross Hill
Tullynacrew
Ballymarter
KEARNEY RD
CRAIGARODDAN ROAD
Castle
Quintin Bay
Crab Rock
Tower
QUINTIN BAY RD
Craigaroddan
Bavan Rock
Standing Stone
Carrstown Burn
Rath
Cairn
Millin Bay
Keentagh
MILLINBAY RD
Tara
Tara Fort
Tara
Millin Hill
BALLYQUINTON RD
Tieveshilly
South Bay
8
55
7
54
6
53
5
52
4
51
3
50
2
49
1
48
62
63
64
65
66
67

82

Scale: 1¾ inches to 1 mile

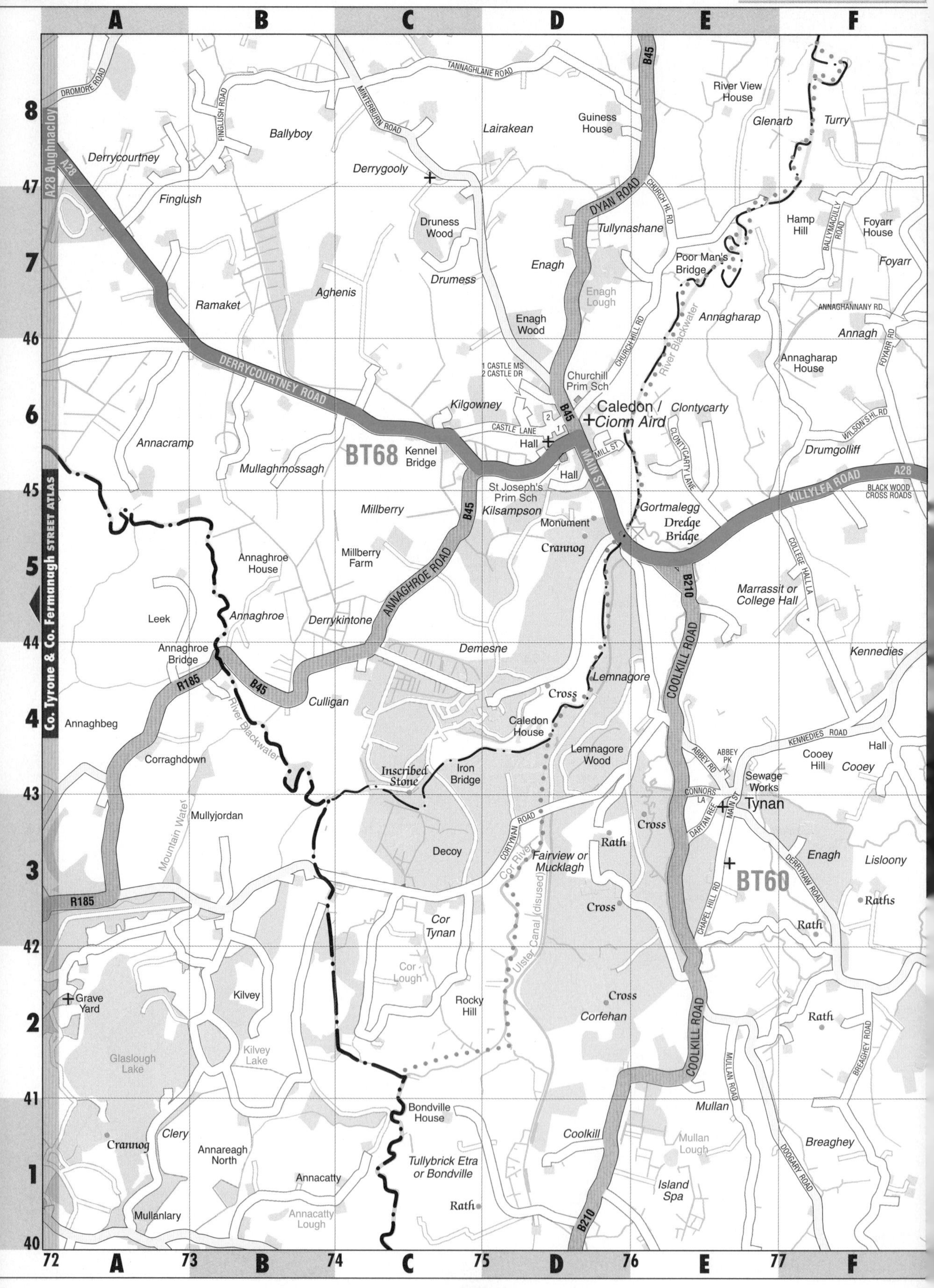

Co. Tyrone & Co. Fermanagh STREET ATLAS

Scale: 1¾ inches to 1 mile

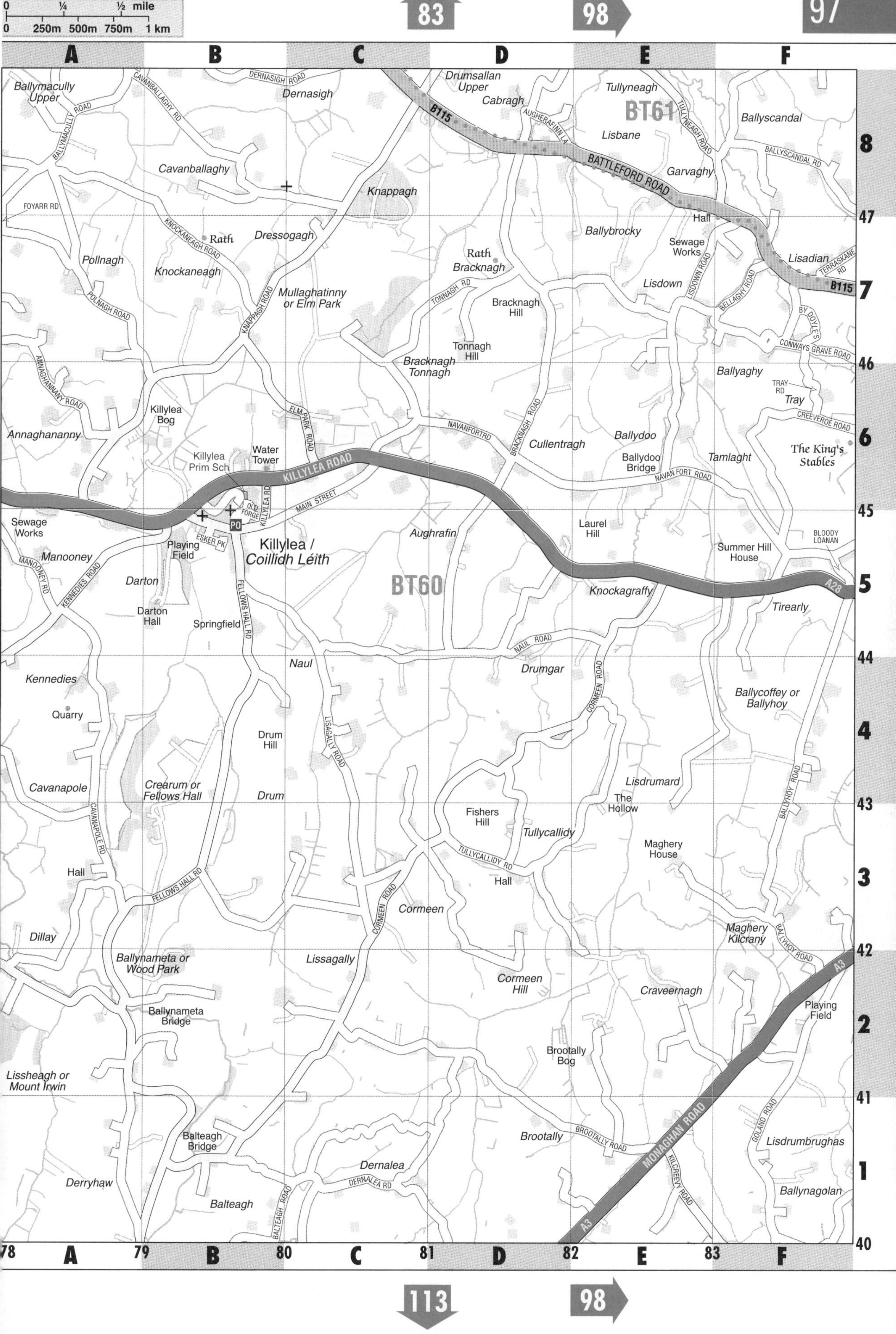

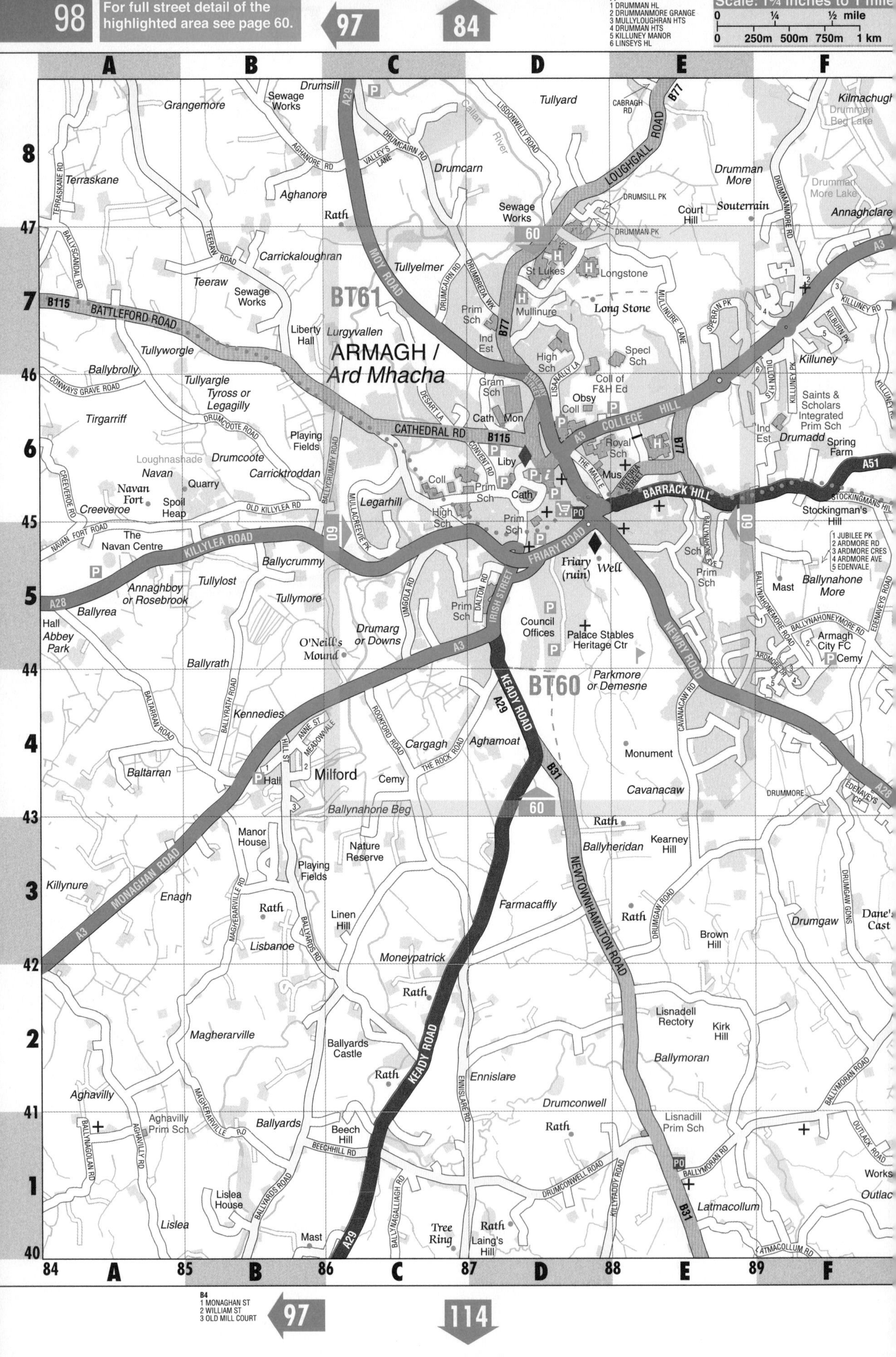
F7
1 DRUMMAN HL
2 DRUMMANMORE GRANGE
3 MULLYLOUGHRAN HTS
4 DRUMMAN HTS
5 KILLUNEY MANOR
6 LINSEYS HL
Scale: 1¾ inches to 1 mile
ARMAGH /
Ard Mhacha
BT61
BT60
Milford
Navan Fort
The Navan Centre
Palace Stables Heritage Ctr
Council Offices
Friary (ruin)
Well
Long Stone
O'Neill's Mound
Ballyards Castle
1 JUBILEE PK
2 ARDMORE RD
3 ARDMORE CRES
4 ARDMORE AVE
5 EDENVALE
B4
1 MONAGHAN ST
2 WILLIAM ST
3 OLD MILL COURT

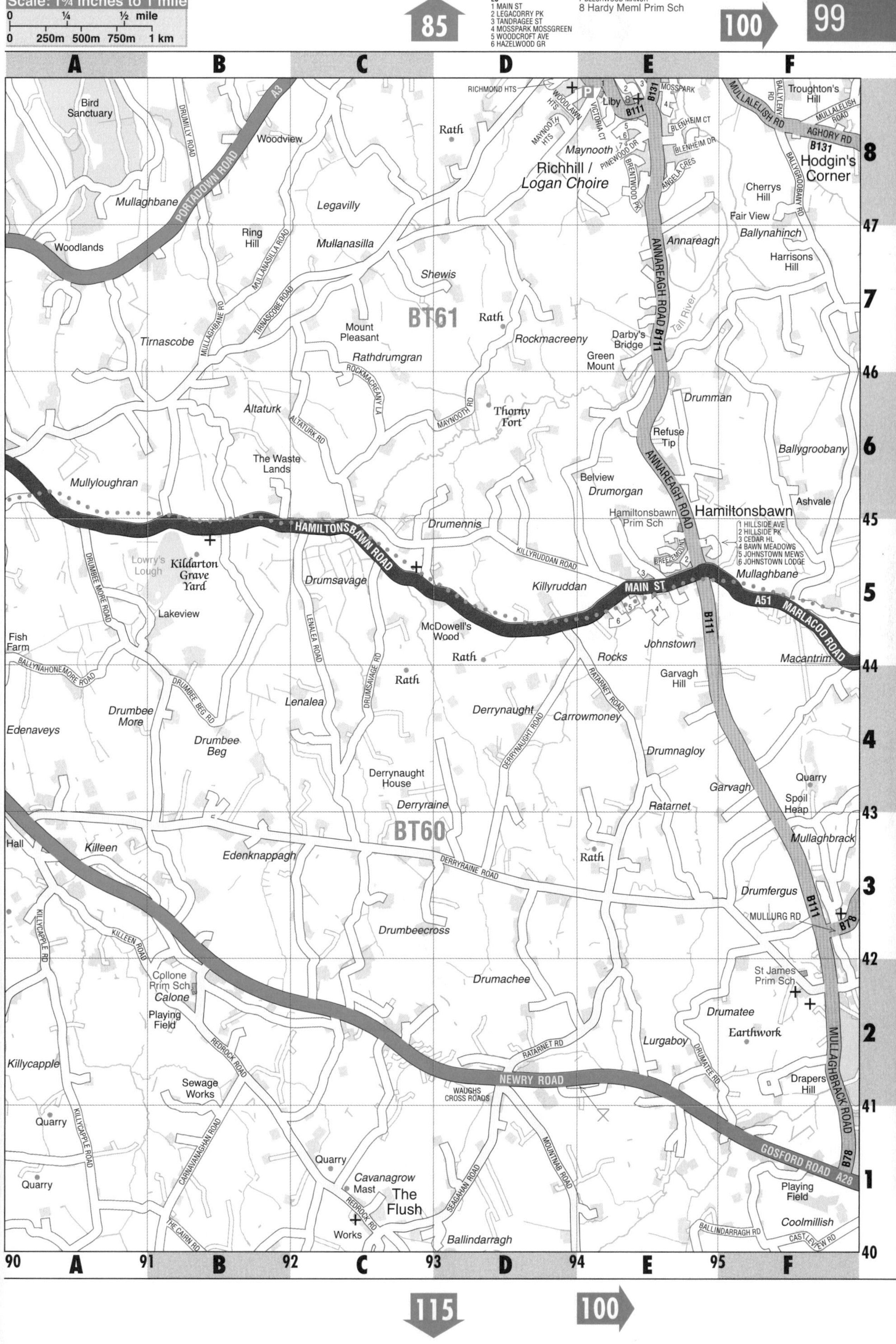

Scale: 1¾ inches to 1 mile
0 ¼ ½ mile
0 250m 500m 750m 1 km
85
E8
1 MAIN ST
2 LEGACORRY PK
3 TANDRAGEE ST
4 MOSSPARK MOSSGREEN
5 WOODCROFT AVE
6 HAZELWOOD GR
7 BEECHWOOD MANOR
8 Hardy Meml Prim Sch
100
99
A
B
C
D
E
F
Bird Sanctuary
DRUMILLY ROAD
A3
PORTADOWN ROAD
Woodview
Mullaghbane
Woodlands
Ring Hill
MULLANASILLA ROAD
Legavilly
Mullanasilla
Rath
RICHMOND HTS
WOODLAWN HTS
MAYNOOTH HTS
VICTORIA CT
Liby
B111
B131
MOSSPARK
BLENHEIM CT
BLENHEIM DR
Maynooth
PINEWOOD DR
BRENTWOOD PK
ANGELA CRES
Richhill / Logan Choire
Troughton's Hill
MULLALELISH RD
BALLYLENY RD
MULLALELISH ROAD
AGHORY RD
Hodgin's Corner
Cherrys Hill
Fair View
BALLYGROOBANY RD
Ballynahinch
Harrisons Hill
Annareagh
ANNAREAGH ROAD
Shewis
TIRNASCOBE ROAD
MULLAGHBANE RD
Tirnascobe
Mount Pleasant
BT61
Rath
Rockmacreeny
Darby's Bridge
Tall River
Green Mount
Rathdrumgran
ROCKMACREEANY LA
Altaturk
ALTATURK RD
MAYNOOTH RD
Thorny Fort
Drumman
Refuse Tip
Ballygroobany
The Waste Lands
Mullyloughran
Belview
Drumorgan
Hamiltonsbawn Prim Sch
Hamiltonsbawn
Ashvale
HAMILTONSBAWN ROAD
Drumennis
1 HILLSIDE AVE
2 HILLSIDE PK
3 CEDAR HL
4 BAWN MEADOWS
5 JOHNSTOWN MEWS
6 JOHNSTOWN LODGE
Lowry's Lough
Kildarton Grave Yard
KILLYRUDDAN ROAD
BREEZEMOUNT
Mullaghbane
Drumsavage
Killyruddan
MAIN ST
A51
MARLACOO ROAD
DRUMBEE MORE ROAD
Lakeview
LENALEA ROAD
McDowell's Wood
Fish Farm
Rath
Johnstown
Rocks
Macantrim
BALLYNAHONEMORE ROAD
DRUMSAVAGE RD
Rath
RATARNET ROAD
Garvagh Hill
DRUMBEE BEG RD
Lenalea
Drumbee More
Derrynaught
DERRYNAUGHT ROAD
Carrowmoney
Edenaveys
Drumbee Beg
Drumnagloy
Quarry
Derrynaught House
Garvagh
Spoil Heap
Derryraine
Ratarnet
BT60
Hall
Killeen
Edenknappagh
Rath
Mullaghbrack
DERRYRAINE ROAD
Drumfergus
MULLURG RD
B78
KILLYCAPPLE RD
KILLEEN ROAD
Drumbeecross
Collone Prim Sch
Calone
Drumachee
St James Prim Sch
Playing Field
Drumatee
Earthwork
REDROCK ROAD
RATARNET RD
Lurgaboy
DRUMATEE RD
MULLAGHBRACK ROAD
Killycapple
Sewage Works
NEWRY ROAD
WAUGHS CROSS ROADS
Drapers Hill
Quarry
KILLYCAPPLE ROAD
CARNAVANAGHAN ROAD
MOUNTNAB ROAD
Quarry
SEAGAHAN ROAD
GOSFORD ROAD
A28
Quarry
Cavanagrow Mast
The Flush
Playing Field
REDROCK RD
Coolmillish
THE CAIRN RD
Works
Ballindarragh
BALLINDARRAGH RD
CASTLEVIEW RD
48
47
7
46
6
45
5
44
4
43
3
42
2
41
1
40
90
91
92
93
94
95
115
100

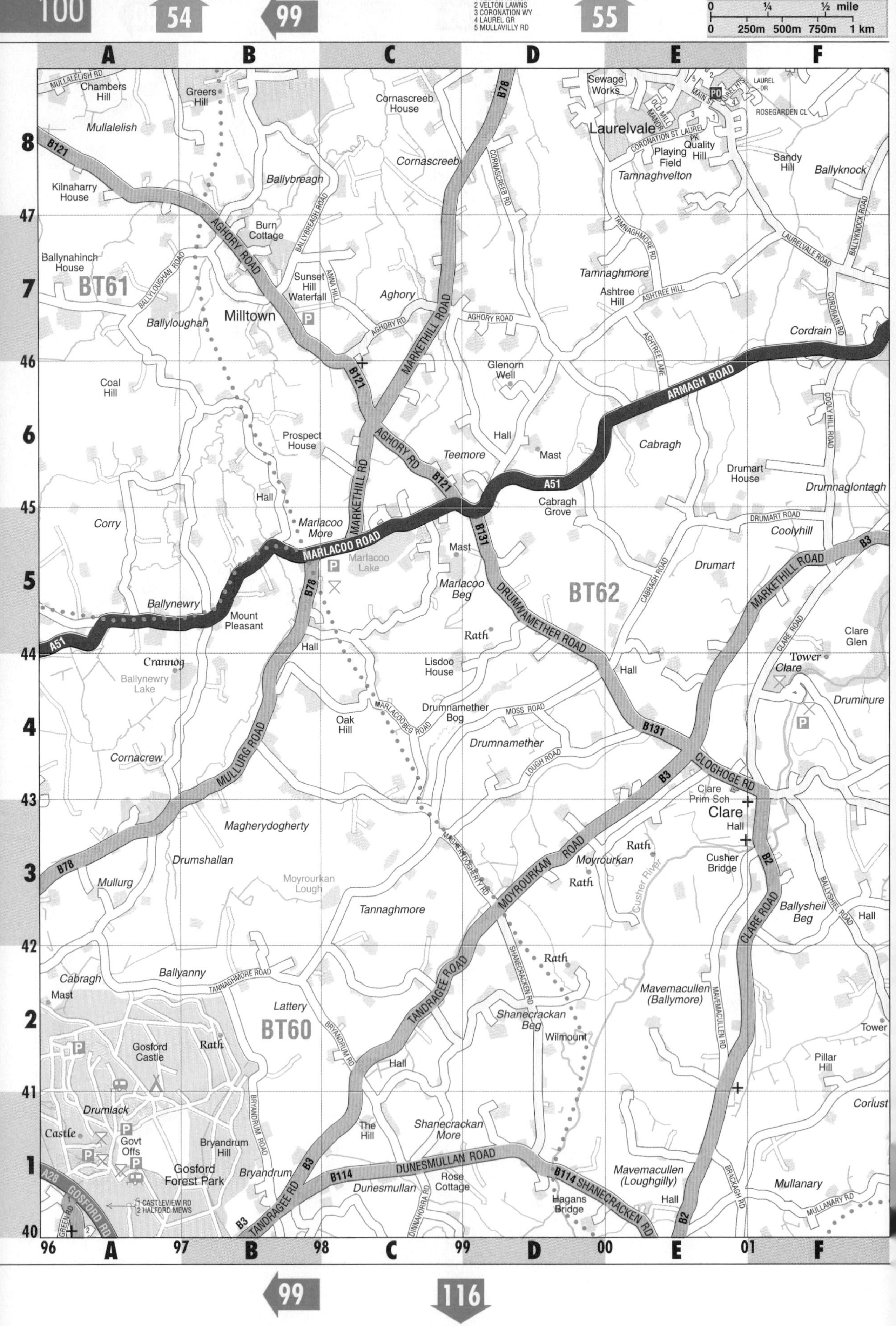
E8
1 VELTON MANOR
2 VELTON LAWNS
3 CORONATION WY
4 LAUREL GR
5 MULLAVILLY RD
Scale: 1¾ inches to 1 mile
0 ¼ ½ mile
0 250m 500m 750m 1 km
A
B
C
D
E
F
8
47
7
46
6
45
5
44
4
43
3
42
2
41
1
40
96
97
98
99
00
01
MULLALELISH RD
Chambers Hill
Greers Hill
Mullalelish
B121
Kilnaharry House
Ballybreagh
BALLYBREAGH ROAD
Burn Cottage
AGHORY ROAD
Ballynahinch House
BT61
BALLYLOUGHAN ROAD
Ballyloughan
Milltown
Sunset Hill Waterfall
ANNA HILL
Aghory
AGHORY RD
Coal Hill
Prospect House
Hall
Corry
Marlacoo More
MARLACOO ROAD
Marlacoo Lake
Ballynewry
Mount Pleasant
A51
Crannog
Ballynewry Lake
Cornacrew
MULLURG ROAD
Hall
Oak Hill
MARLACOO BEG ROAD
Magherydogherty
B78
Drumshallan
Mullurg
Moyrourkan Lough
Tannaghmore
Cabragh
Mast
Ballyanny
TANNAGHMORE ROAD
Lattery
BT60
BRYANDRUM RD
Gosford Castle
Rath
Drumlack
Castle
Govt Offs
Bryandrum Hill
BRYANDRUM ROAD
Gosford Forest Park
Bryandrum
A28
GOSFORD RD
GREEN RD
1 CASTLEVIEW RD
2 HALFORD MEWS
Cornascreeb House
Cornascreeb
B78
CORNASCREEB RD
MARKETHILL ROAD
AGHORY ROAD
Glenorn Well
MARKETHILL RD
AGHORY RD
Teemore
Hall
Mast
Mast
Marlacoo Beg
B131
Rath
Lisdoo House
Drumnamether Bog
MOSS ROAD
Drumnamether
LOUGH ROAD
MAGHERYDOGHERTY RD
MOYROURKAN ROAD
TANDRAGEE ROAD
SHANECRACKAN RD
Rath
Shanecrackan Beg
Wilmount
Hall
The Hill
Shanecrackan More
DUNESMULLAN ROAD
B114
Dunesmullan
DINNAHORRA RD
Rose Cottage
TANDRAGEE RD
B3
Hagans Bridge
B114 SHANECRACKAN RD
Sewage Works
MAIN ST
LAUREL HTS
LAUREL DR
OLD MILL
MANOR
PO
Laurelvale
CORONATION ST
LAUREL PK
Playing Field
Quality Hill
ROSEGARDEN CL
Tamnaghvelton
Sandy Hill
Ballyknock
BALLYKNOCK ROAD
LAURELVALE ROAD
TAMNAGHMORE RD
Tamnaghmore
Ashtree Hill
ASHTREE HILL
ASHTREE LANE
CORDRAIN RD
Cordrain
ARMAGH ROAD
COOLY HILL ROAD
Cabragh
Drumart House
Drumnaglontagh
Cabragh Grove
DRUMART ROAD
Coolyhill
CABRAGH ROAD
Drumart
BT62
DRUMNAMETHER ROAD
MARKETHILL ROAD
CLARE ROAD
Clare Glen
Tower
Clare
Hall
Druminure
B131
CLOGHOGE RD
Clare Prim Sch
Clare
Hall
Rath
Moyrourkan
Rath
Cusher River
Cusher Bridge
B2
CLARE ROAD
Ballysheil Beg
BALLYSHEIL ROAD
Hall
Mavemacullen (Ballymore)
MAVEMACULLEN RD
Tower
Pillar Hill
Corlust
Mavemacullen (Loughgilly)
BRACKAGH RD
Hall
Mullanary
MULLANARY RD

Scale: 1¾ inches to 1 mile

0 ¼ ½ mile

0 250m 500m 750m 1 km

B7
1 RICHMOND GDNS
2 RICHMOND CT
3 RICHMOND GR
4 RICHMOND CL
5 RICHMOND AVE
6 RICHMOND VW
7 BEECHILL CRES
8 EPWORTH CL
9 BALLYBEG PK
10 MOURNEVIEW PK
11 MONTAGU PK
12 MANDEVILLE DR
13 CASTLE MEWS
14 WILLOWFIELD HTS
15 WOODVIEW PK
16 MONTAGUE ST
17 CORNMARKET ST
18 THORNHILL AVE
19 THORNHILL CRES
20 CHURCH ST
21 THE SQUARE

56 102 57 117 102

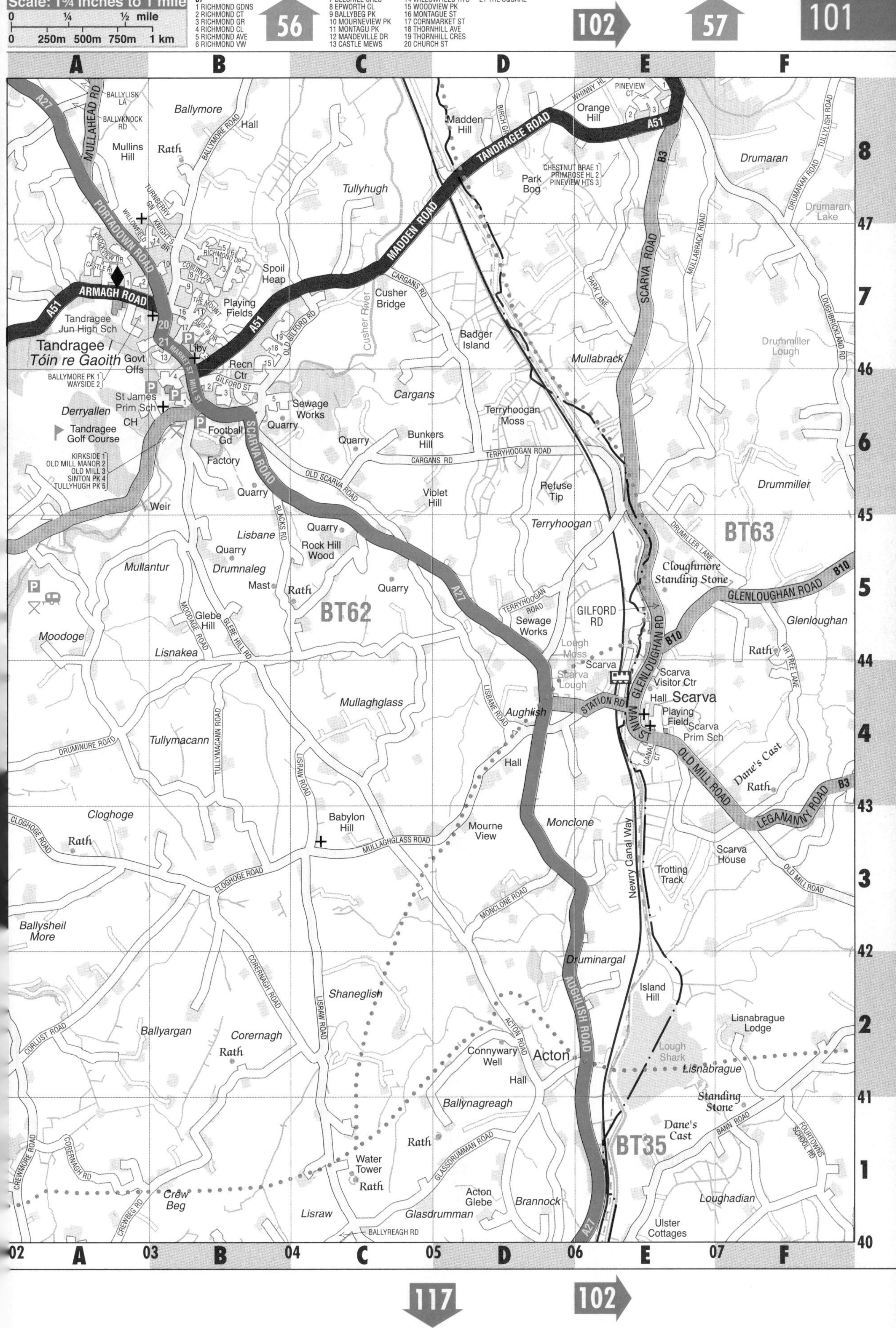

101
86
For full street detail of the highlighted area see page 61.

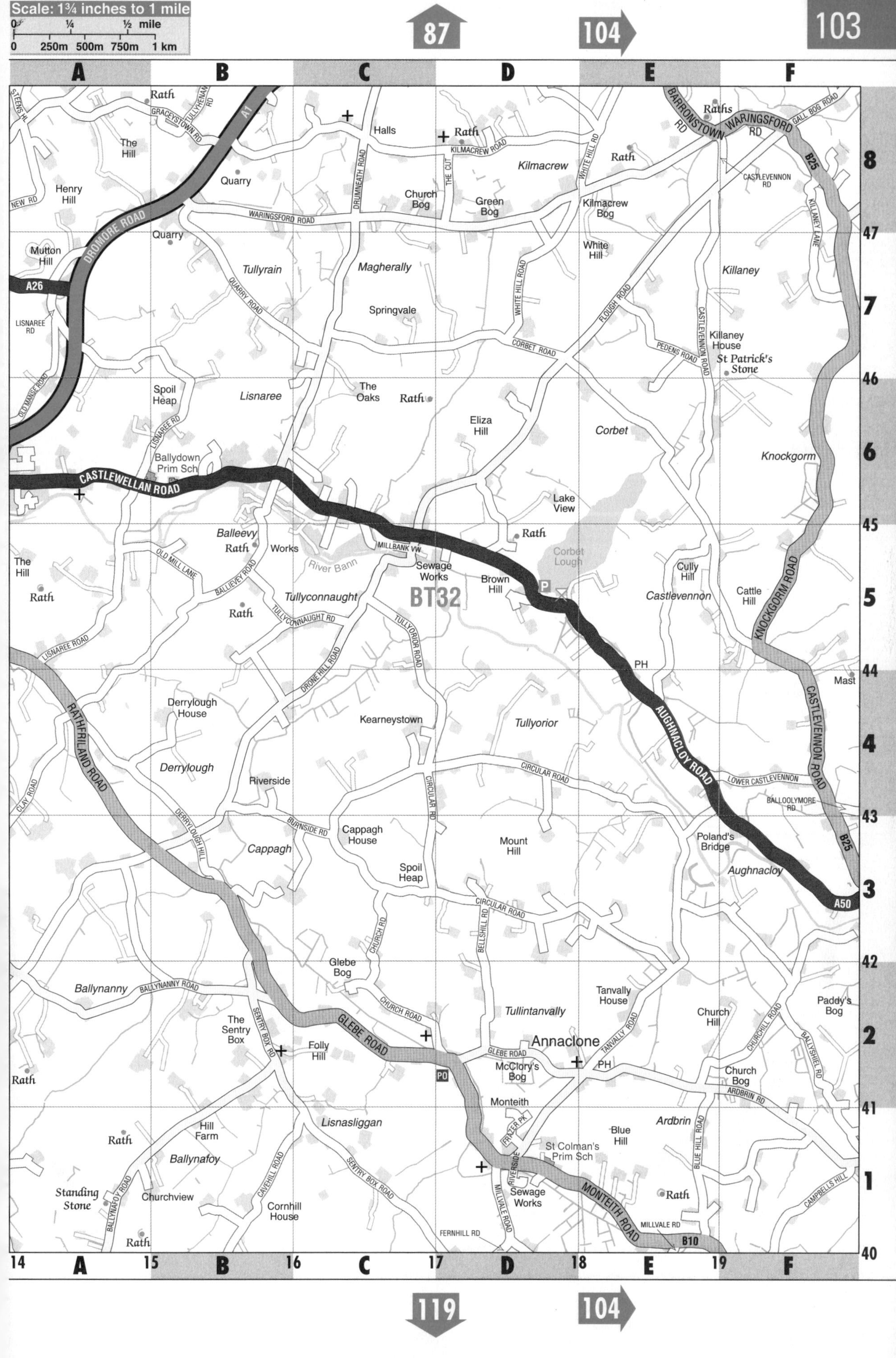
Scale: 1¾ inches to 1 mile
87
104
Halls
Rath
Kilmacrew
Church Bog
Green Bog
Quarry
The Hill
Henry Hill
Mutton Hill
Tullyrain
Magherally
Springvale
Kilmacrew Bog
White Hill
Killaney
Killaney House
St Patrick's Stone
Lisnaree
Spoil Heap
The Oaks
Eliza Hill
Corbet
Knockgorm
Ballydown Prim Sch
CASTLEWELLAN ROAD
Lake View
Corbet Lough
Balleevy
Works
River Bann
Sewage Works
Brown Hill
BT32
Cully Hill
Castlevennon
Cattle Hill
Tullyconnaught
PH
Mast
Derrylough House
Kearneystown
Tullyorior
Derrylough
Riverside
Cappagh House
Cappagh
Mount Hill
Spoil Heap
Poland's Bridge
Aughnacloy
AUGHNACLOY ROAD
RATHFRILAND ROAD
Glebe Bog
Ballynanny
Tanvally House
Tullintanvally
Church Hill
Paddy's Bog
The Sentry Box
Folly Hill
GLEBE ROAD
Annaclone
McClory's Bog
Church Bog
Monteith
Lisnasliggan
Ardbrin
Blue Hill
Hill Farm
Ballynafoy
St Colman's Prim Sch
Standing Stone
Churchview
Cornhill House
Sewage Works
MONTEITH ROAD
119
104

103
88

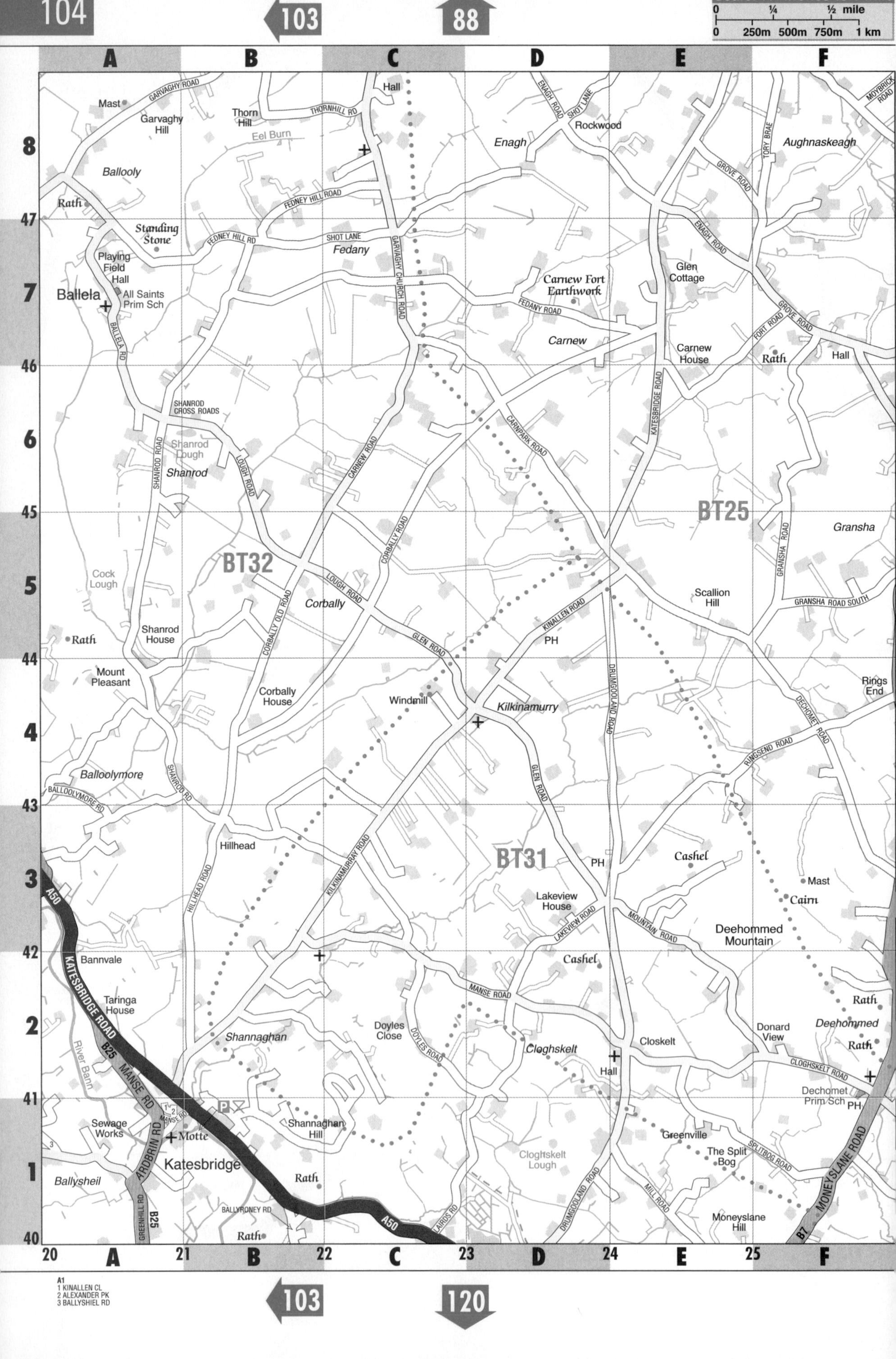

A1
1 KINALLEN CL
2 ALEXANDER PK
3 BALLYSHIEL RD

103
120

Scale: 1¾ inches to 1 mile

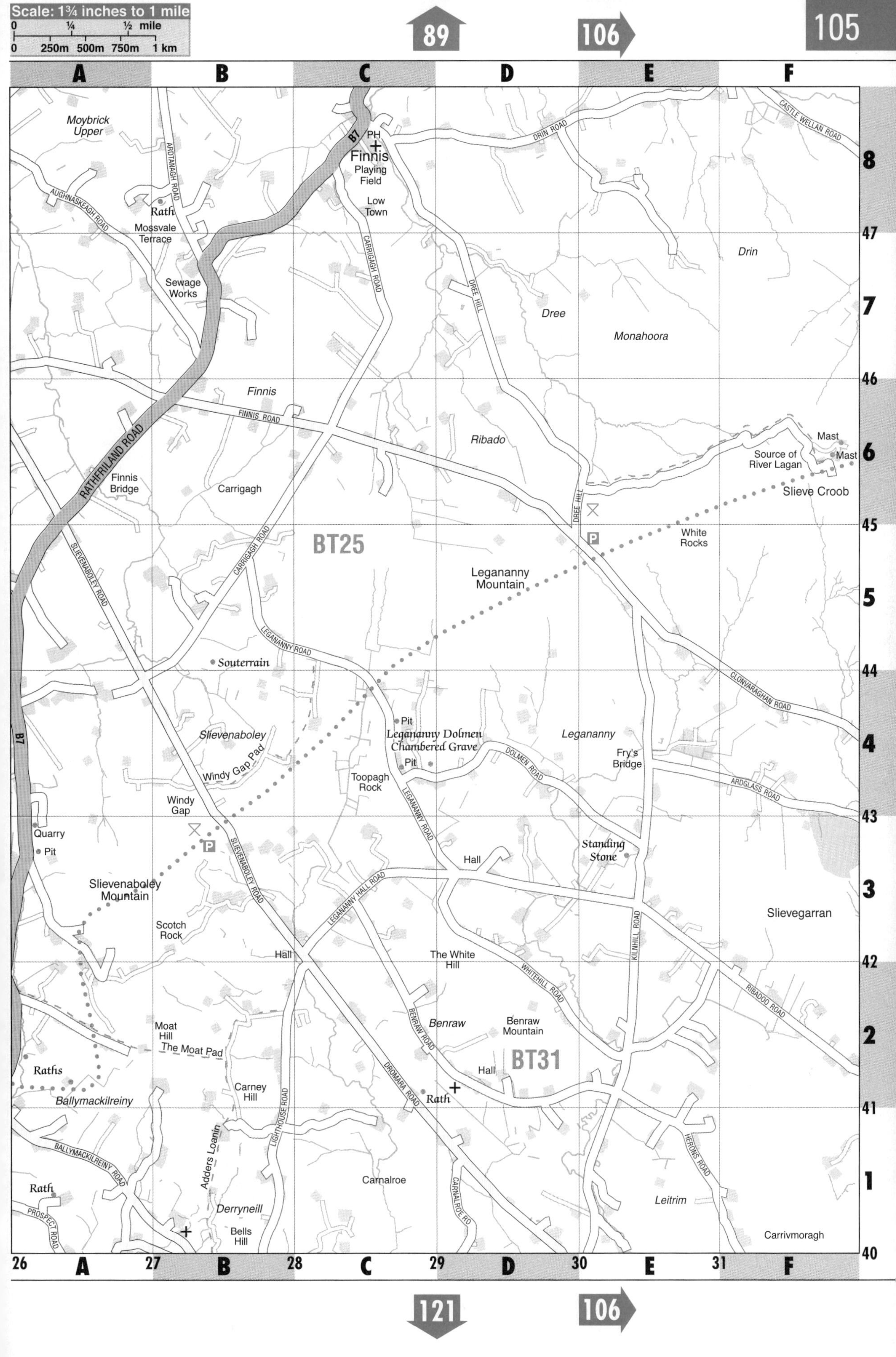

105
90

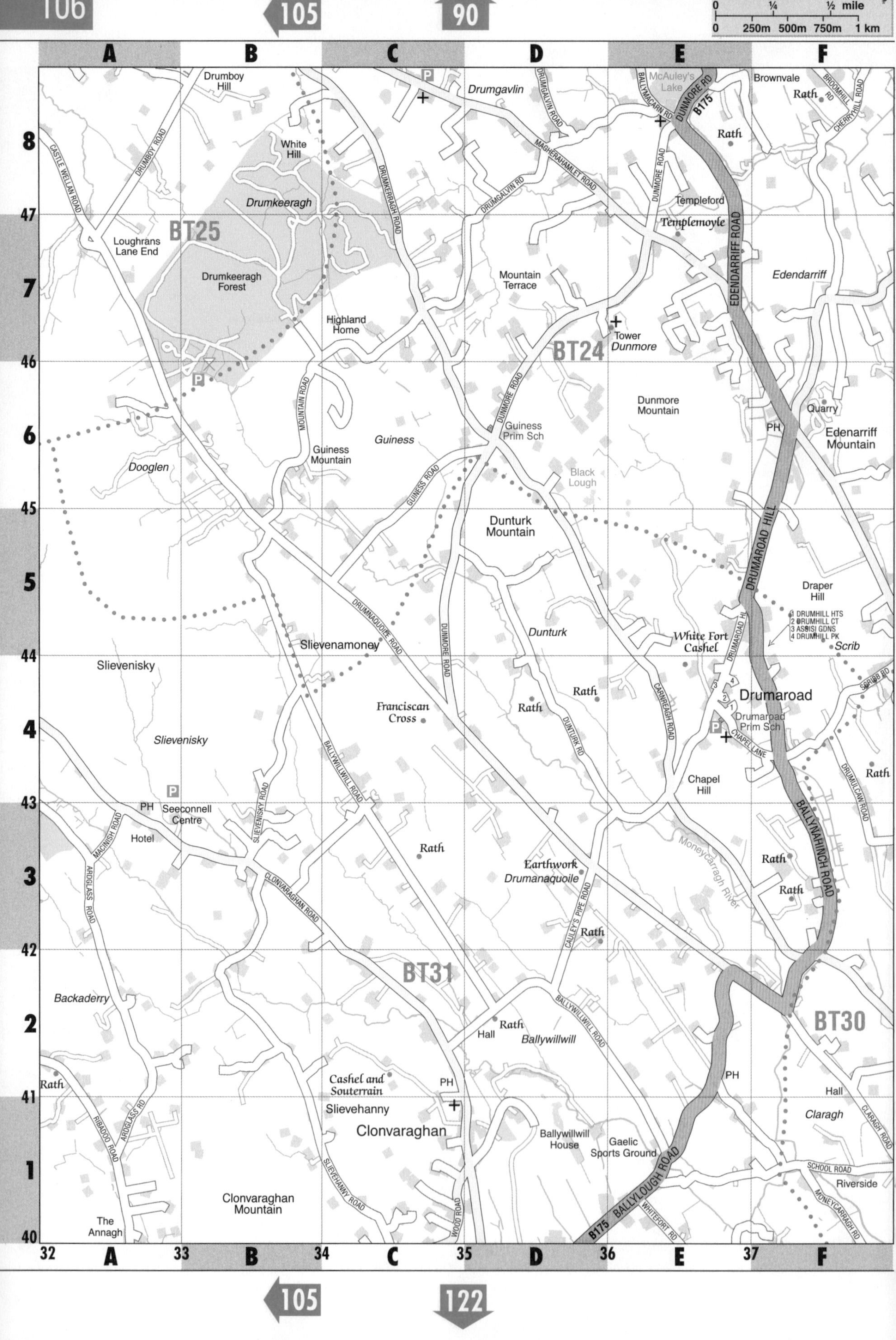

105
122

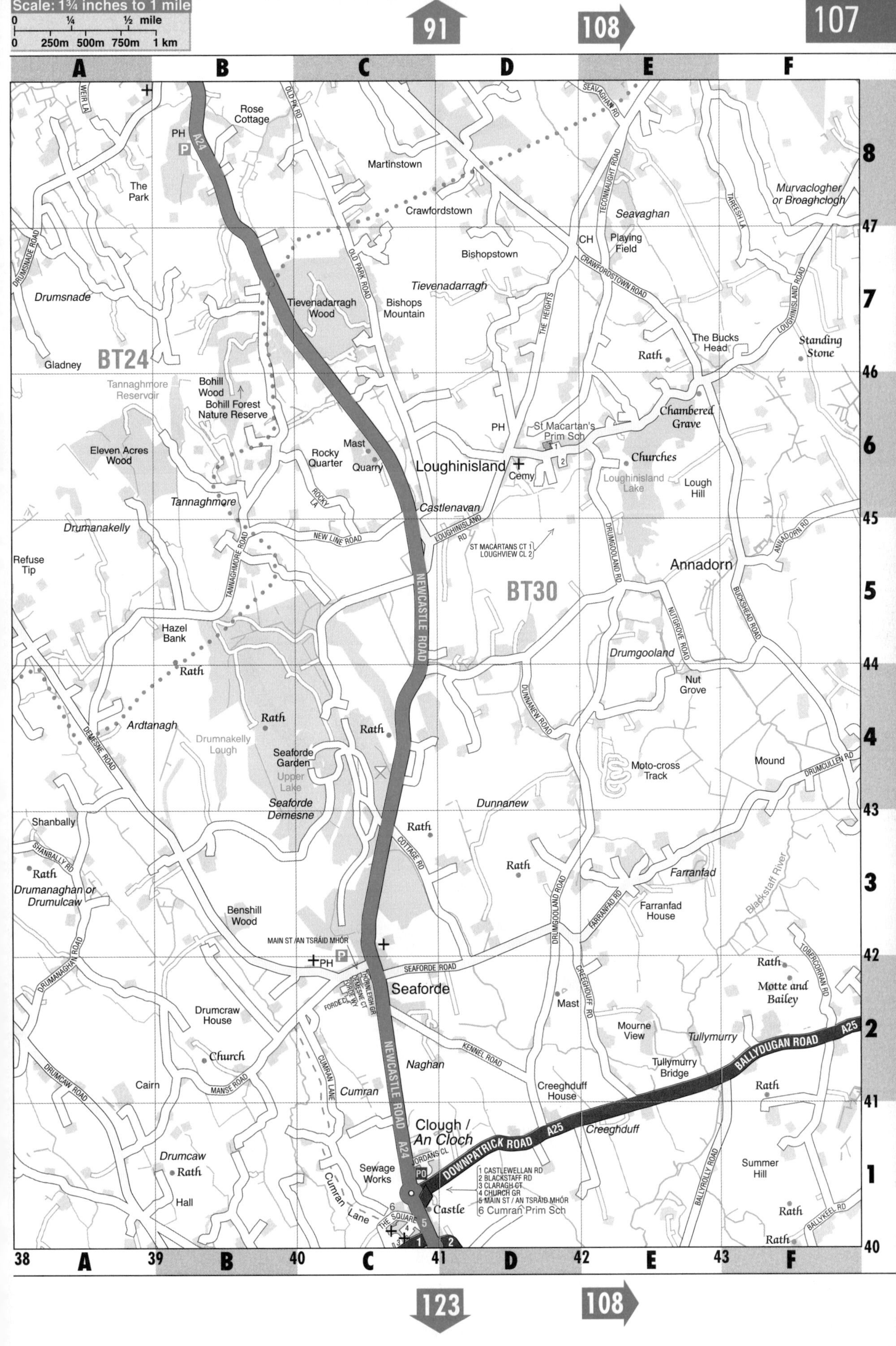
Scale: 1¾ inches to 1 mile
0 ¼ ½ mile
0 250m 500m 750m 1 km
91
108
Rose Cottage
Martinstown
The Park
Crawfordstown
Seavaghan
Murvaclogher or Broaghclogh
Playing Field
Bishopstown
Drumsnade
Tievenadarragh Wood
Bishops Mountain
Tievenadarragh
The Bucks Head
Standing Stone
Gladney
BT24
Tannaghmore Reservoir
Bohill Wood
Bohill Forest Nature Reserve
Chambered Grave
St Macartan's Prim Sch
Eleven Acres Wood
Rocky Quarter
Mast
Quarry
Loughinisland
Cemy
Churches
Loughinisland Lake
Lough Hill
Tannaghmore
Castlenavan
Drumanakelly
Refuse Tip
ST MACARTANS CT 1
LOUGHVIEW CL 2
Annadorn
BT30
Hazel Bank
Drumgooland
Nut Grove
Ardtanagh
Drumnakelly Lough
Seaforde Garden
Upper Lake
Seaforde Demesne
Moto-cross Track
Mound
Dunnanew
Shanbally
Drumanaghan or Drumulcaw
Farranfad
Farranfad House
Benshill Wood
Seaforde
Motte and Bailey
Drumcraw House
Church
Mourne View
Tullymurry
Naghan
Tullymurry Bridge
Cairn
Cumran
Creeghduff House
Clough / An Cloch
Creeghduff
Drumcaw
Sewage Works
Summer Hill
Hall
Castle
1 CASTLEWELLAN RD
2 BLACKSTAFF RD
3 CLARAGH CT
4 CHURCH GR
5 MAIN ST / AN TSRÁID MHÓR
6 Cumran Prim Sch
NEWCASTLE ROAD
DOWNPATRICK ROAD
BALLYDUGAN ROAD
A24
A25
Rath
123
108

For full street detail of the highlighted area see page 62.

Scale: 1¾ inches to 1 mile
0 ¼ ½ mile
0 250m 500m 750m 1 km

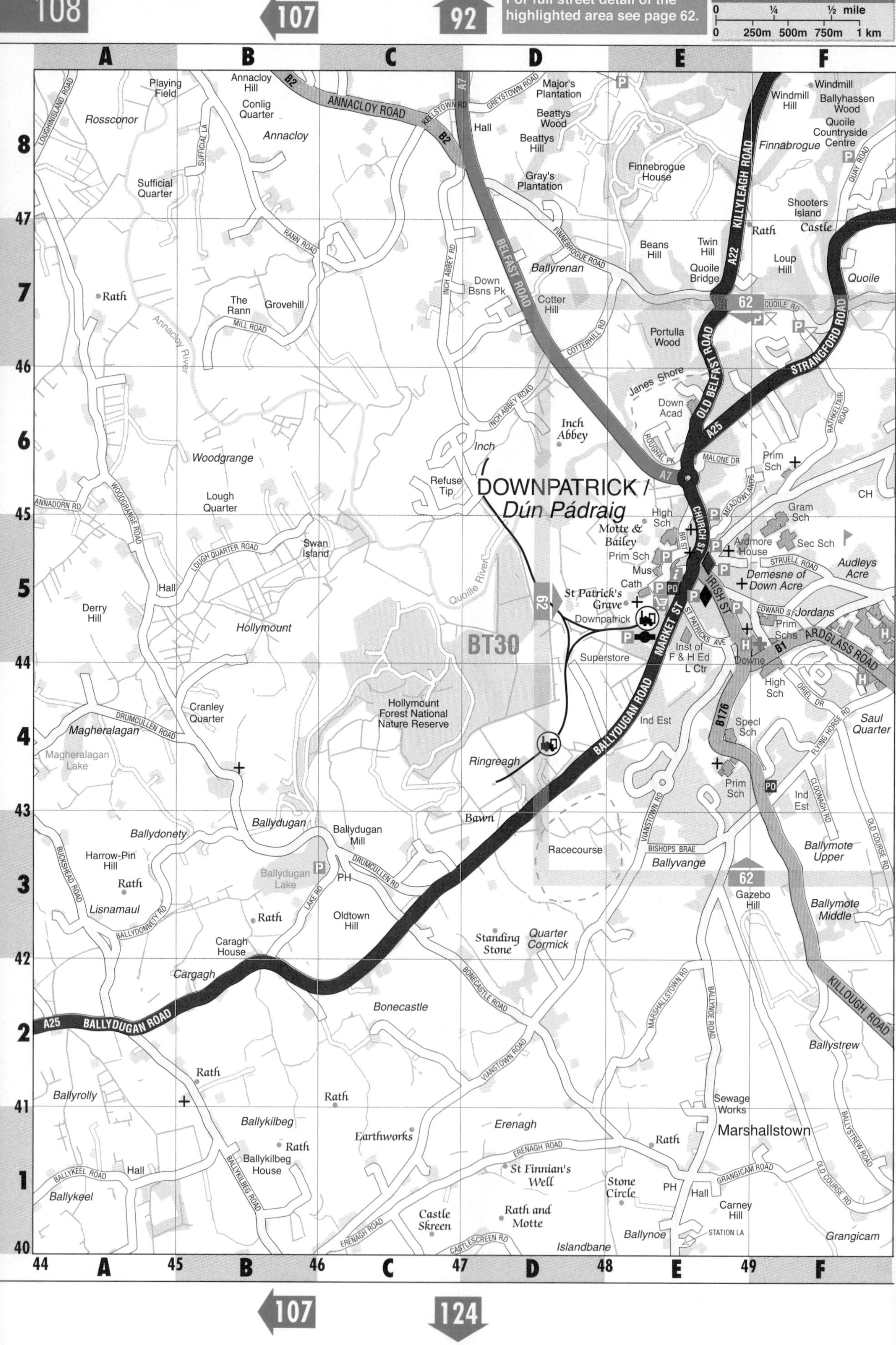

93
110

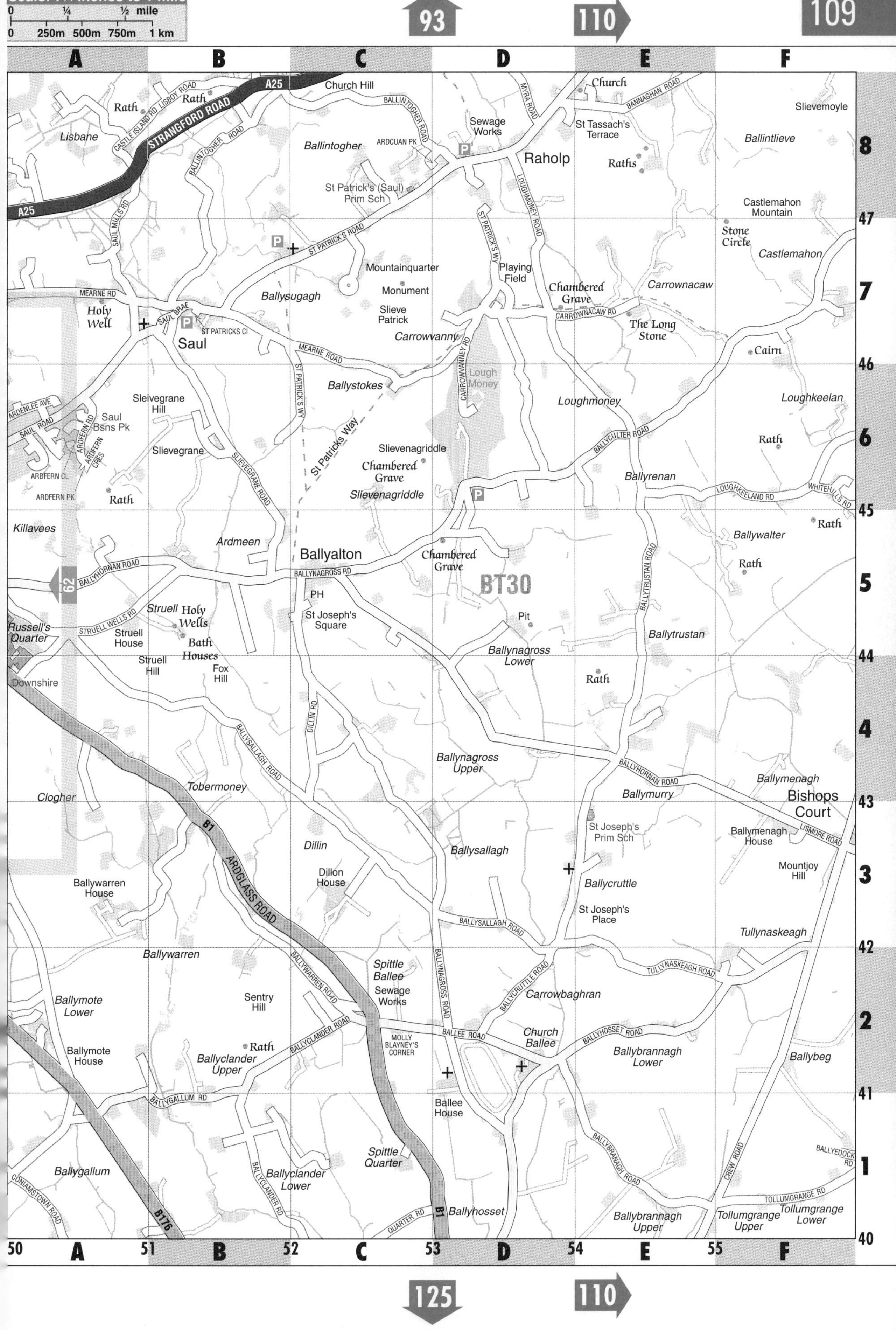

125
110

Scale: 1¾ inches to 1 mile

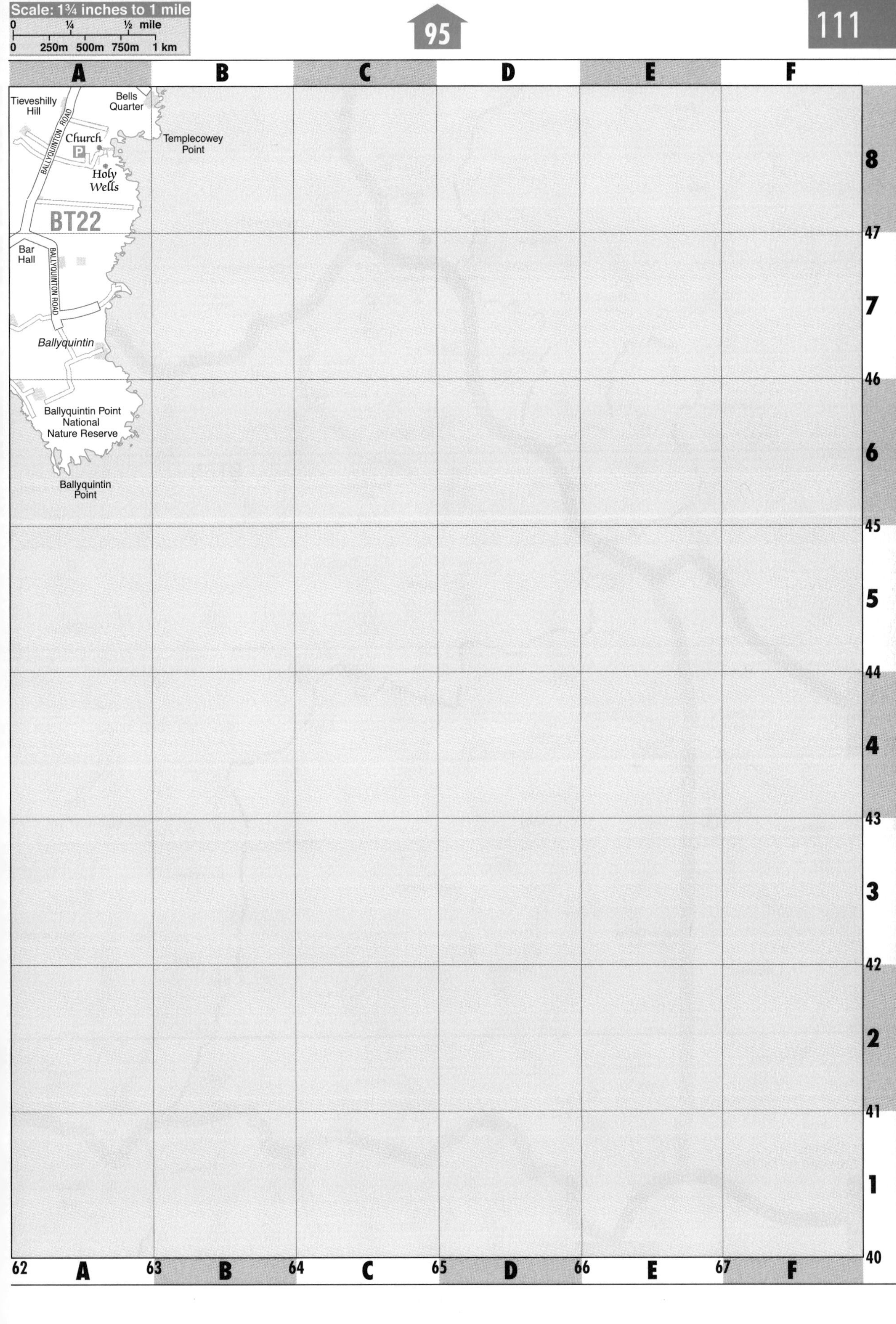
Scale: 1¾ inches to 1 mile
0 ¼ ½ mile
0 250m 500m 750m 1 km
95
A
B
C
D
E
F
Tieveshilly Hill
Bells Quarter
BALLYQUINTON ROAD
Church
P
Templecowey Point
Holy Wells
BT22
Bar Hall
Ballyquintin
Ballyquintin Point National Nature Reserve
Ballyquintin Point
8
47
7
46
6
45
5
44
4
43
3
42
2
41
1
40
62
63
64
65
66
67

96

Scale: 1¾ inches to 1 mile

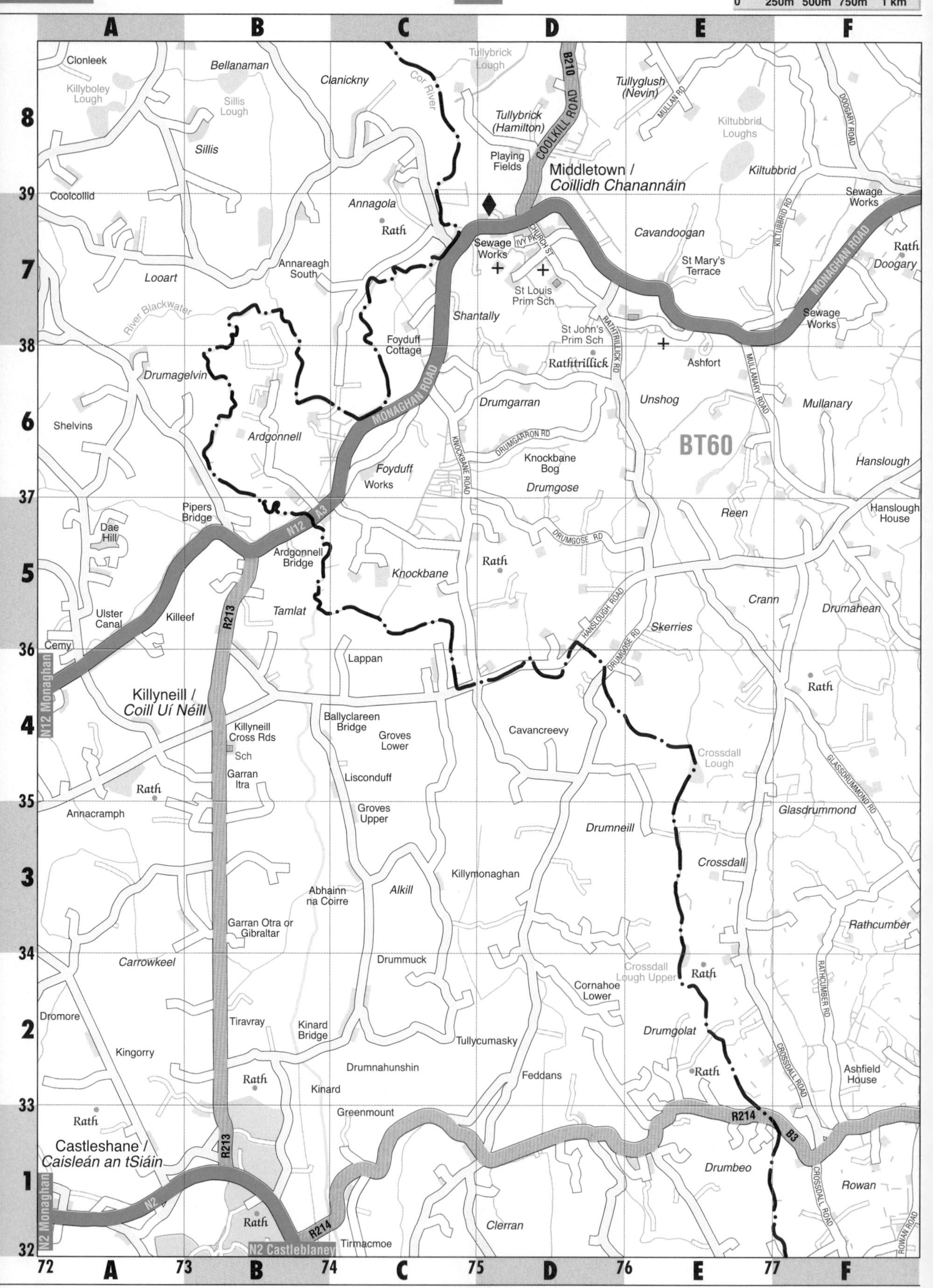

Scale: 1¾ inches to 1 mile

97
114

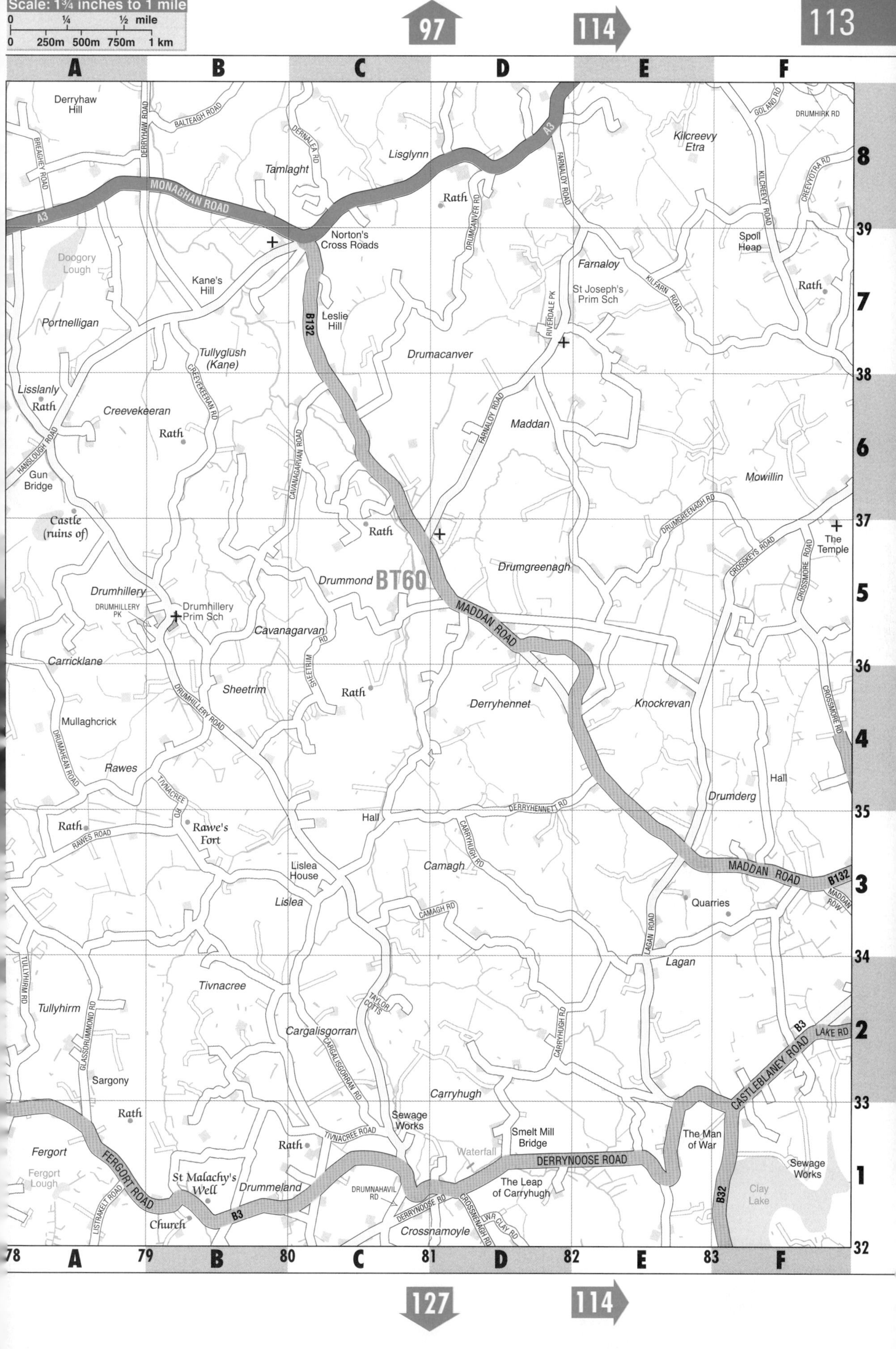

127
114

113

98

Scale: 1¾ inches to 1 mile
0 ¼ ½ mile
0 250m 500m 750m 1 km

1 RATHMOYLE DR
2 RATHMOYLE PK
3 CA RAMOYLE EST
4 GRANEMORE HTS / ARD-NA-GRAINSEACH
5 ANNVALE GDNS

1 CROSSDENED ROW
2 MAKEM PK
3 CARBREY DR
4 CHURCH ST
5 LIR GDNS
6 CARBREY HTS

A3
1 MOUNTVIEW
2 MULLAGHMORE PK
3 MULLAGHMORE AVE
4 CROSSMORE GDNS
5 GLENVIEW GDNS
6 RICHVIEW HTS
7 CHURCH PL
8 MARKET ST
9 RAILWAY CR
10 BRIDGE ST
11 DALTON PK
12 FAIR GREEN PK
13 FAIR GREEN AVE
14 CHURCH ST
15 MADDAN ROAD
16 St Francis of Assisi Prim Sch
17 Keady Prim Sch
18 St Patrick's High Sch

113

128

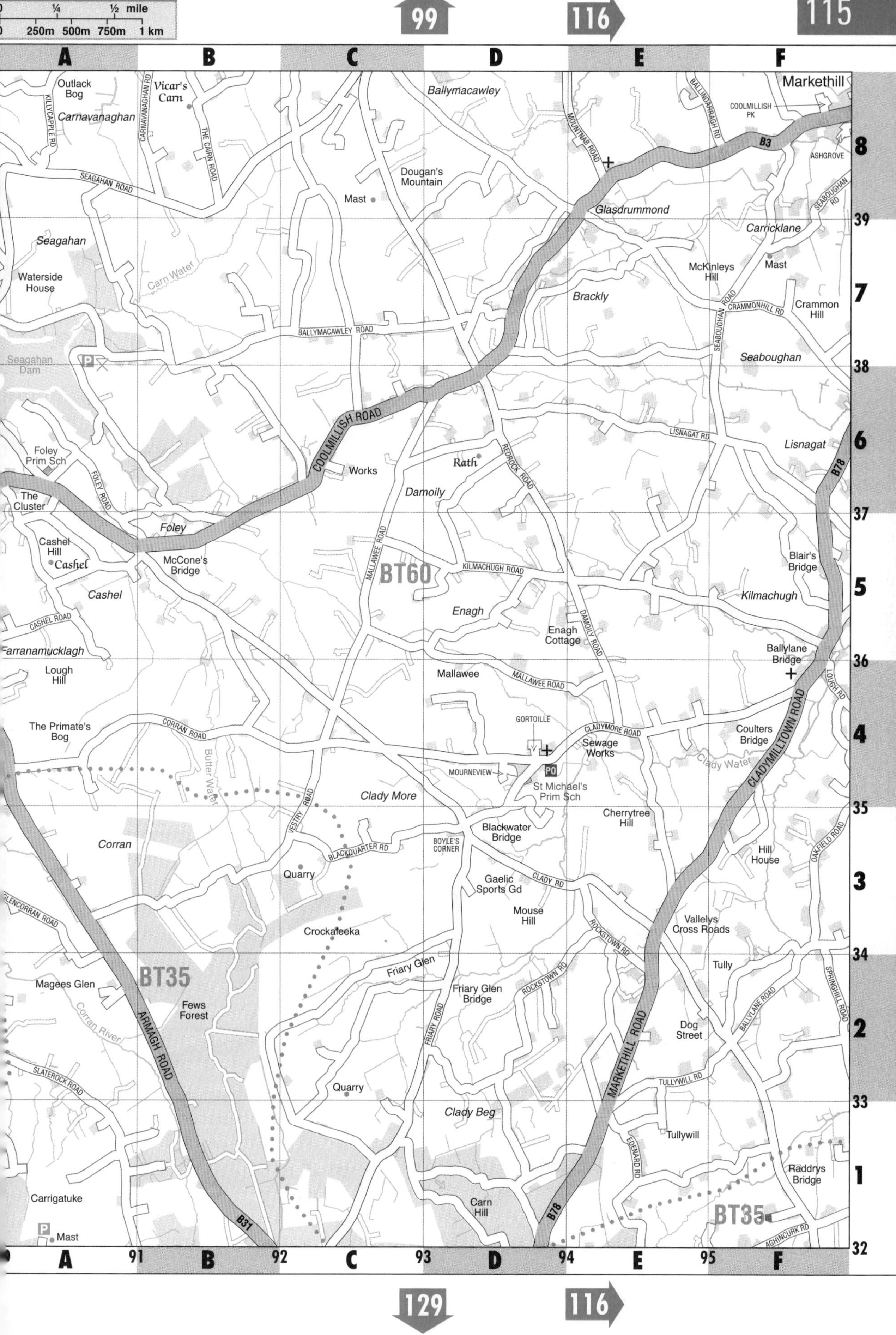
Scale: 1¾ inches to 1 mile
0 ¼ ½ mile
0 250m 500m 750m 1 km
99
116
A B C D E F
Outlack Bog
Vicar's Carn
Carnavanaghan
Ballymacawley
Markethill
COOLMILLISH PK
ASHGROVE
B3
Dougan's Mountain
Mast
Glasdrummond
Seagahan
Carricklane
Waterside House
Carn Water
McKinleys Hill
Mast
Brackly
Crammon Hill
Seaboughan
Seagahan Dam
Lisnagat
Foley Prim Sch
Works
Rath
Damoily
The Cluster
Foley
Cashel Hill
Cashel
McCone's Bridge
BT60
Blair's Bridge
Kilmachugh
Cashel
Enagh
Enagh Cottage
Farranamucklagh
Lough Hill
Mallawee
Ballylane Bridge
The Primate's Bog
GORTOILLE
Sewage Works
Coulters Bridge
Clady Water
Butter Water
MOURNEVIEW
PO
St Michael's Prim Sch
Clady More
Cherrytree Hill
Corran
Blackwater Bridge
BOYLE'S CORNER
Hill House
Quarry
Gaelic Sports Gd
Mouse Hill
Crockafeeka
Vallelys Cross Roads
Tully
BT35
Magees Glen
Friary Glen
Friary Glen Bridge
Fews Forest
Corran River
Dog Street
Quarry
Clady Beg
Tullywill
Raddrys Bridge
Carrigatuke
Carn Hill
BT35
Mast
KILLYCAPPLE RD
CARNAVANAGHAN RD
THE CAIRN ROAD
SEAGAHAN ROAD
MOUNTNAB ROAD
BALLINDARRAGH RD
SEABOUGHAN RD
BALLYMACAWLEY ROAD
SEABOUGHAN ROAD
CRAMMONHILL RD
COOLMILLISH ROAD
LISNAGAT RD
REDROCK ROAD
FOLEY ROAD
B78
MALLAWEE ROAD
KILMACHUGH ROAD
CASHEL ROAD
DAMOILY ROAD
MALLAWEE ROAD
LOUGH RD
CORRAN ROAD
CLADYMORE ROAD
CLADYMILLTOWN ROAD
VESTRY ROAD
BLACKQUARTER RD
CLADY RD
OAKFIELD ROAD
GLENCORRAN ROAD
ROCKSTOWN RD
ROCKSTOWN ROAD
SPRINGHILL ROAD
BALLYLANE ROAD
FRIARY ROAD
MARKETHILL ROAD
ARMAGH ROAD
SLATEROCK ROAD
TULLYWILL RD
EDENARD RD
B31
B78
AGHINCURK RD
8 39 7 38 6 37 5 36 4 35 3 34 2 33 1 32
91 92 93 94 95

A8
1 GOSFORD GDNS
2 KEADY ST
3 ASHLEA BEND
4 DEANSWIFT MS
5 OLD TANDRAGEE RD
6 EDEN CT
7 EDEN RI
8 MOWHAN CT
9 EDENKENNEDY WY
10 EDEN DR
11 COOLMILLISH RD
12 KEADY ST
13 FAIRGREEN RD
14 NEWRY ST
15 Markethill Prim Sch
16 Markethill Bsns Ctr

115
100

Scale: 1¾ inches to 1 mile

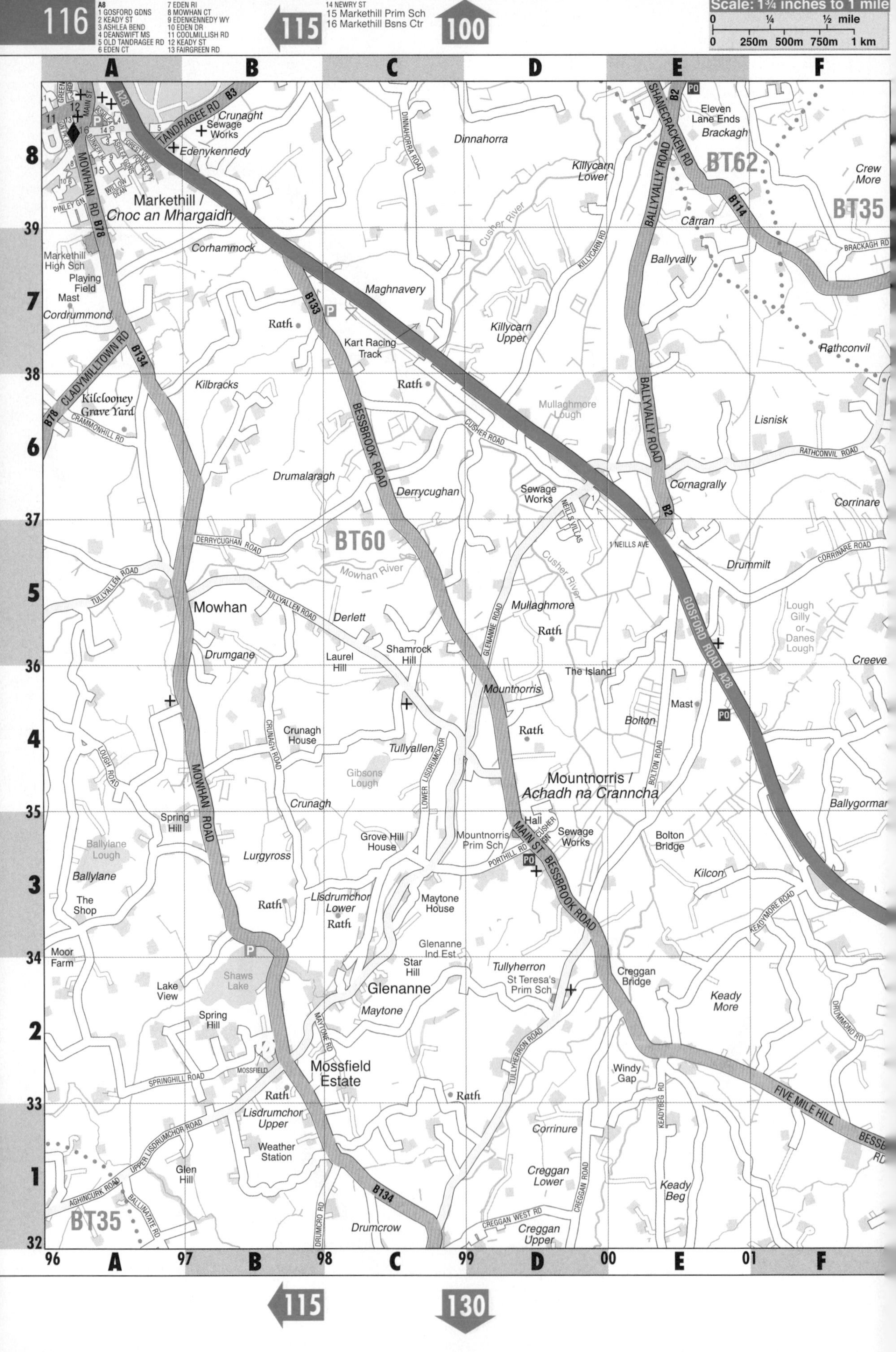

115
130

Scale: 1¾ inches to 1 mile

¼ ½ mile

0 250m 500m 750m 1 km

101 118

D8
1 Poyntzpass Prim Sch

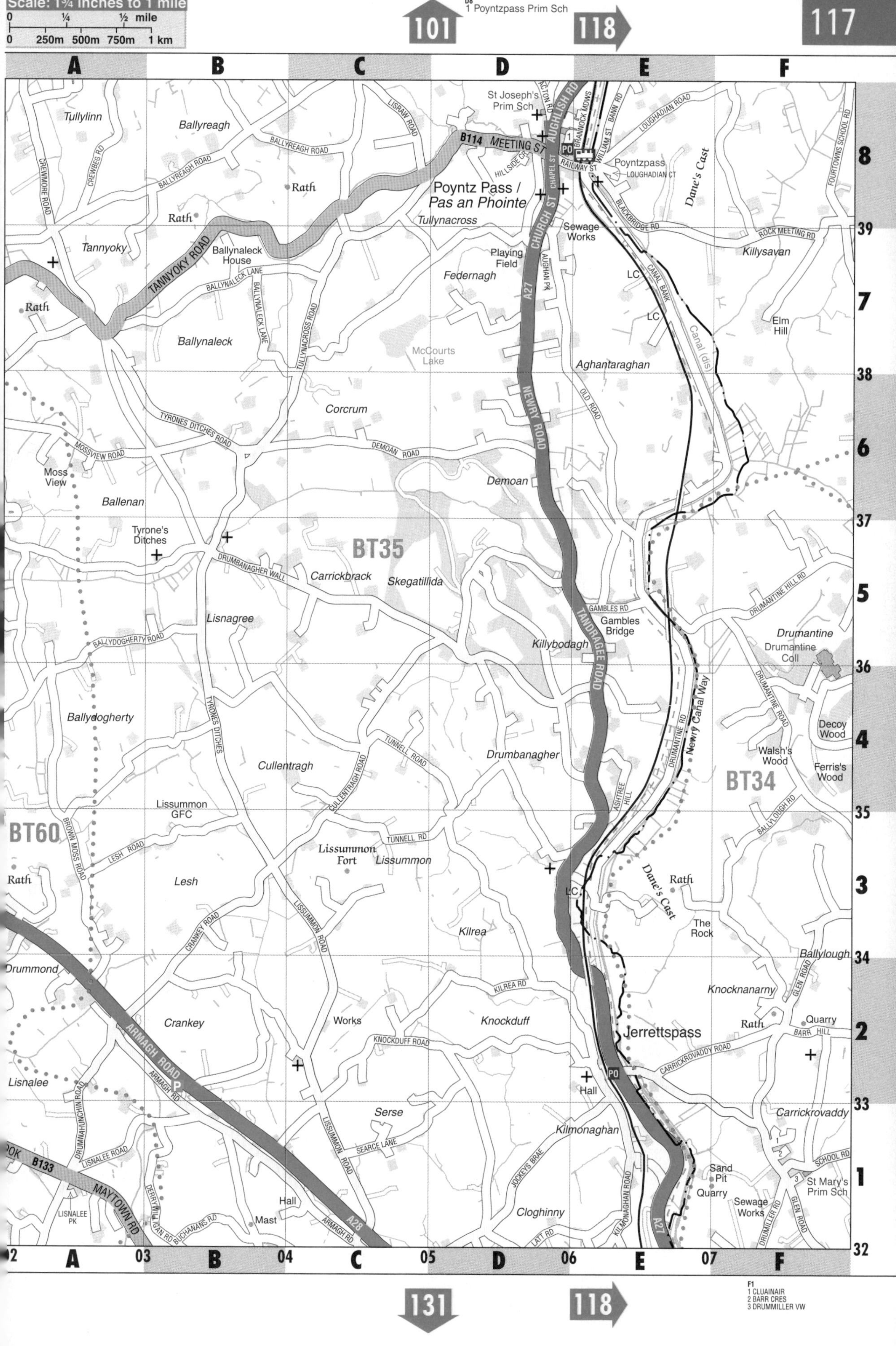

A 03 B 04 C 05 D 06 E 07 F
8 39 7 38 6 37 5 36 4 35 3 34 2 33 1 32

131 118

F1
1 CLUAINAIR
2 BARR CRES
3 DRUMMILLER VW

117
102

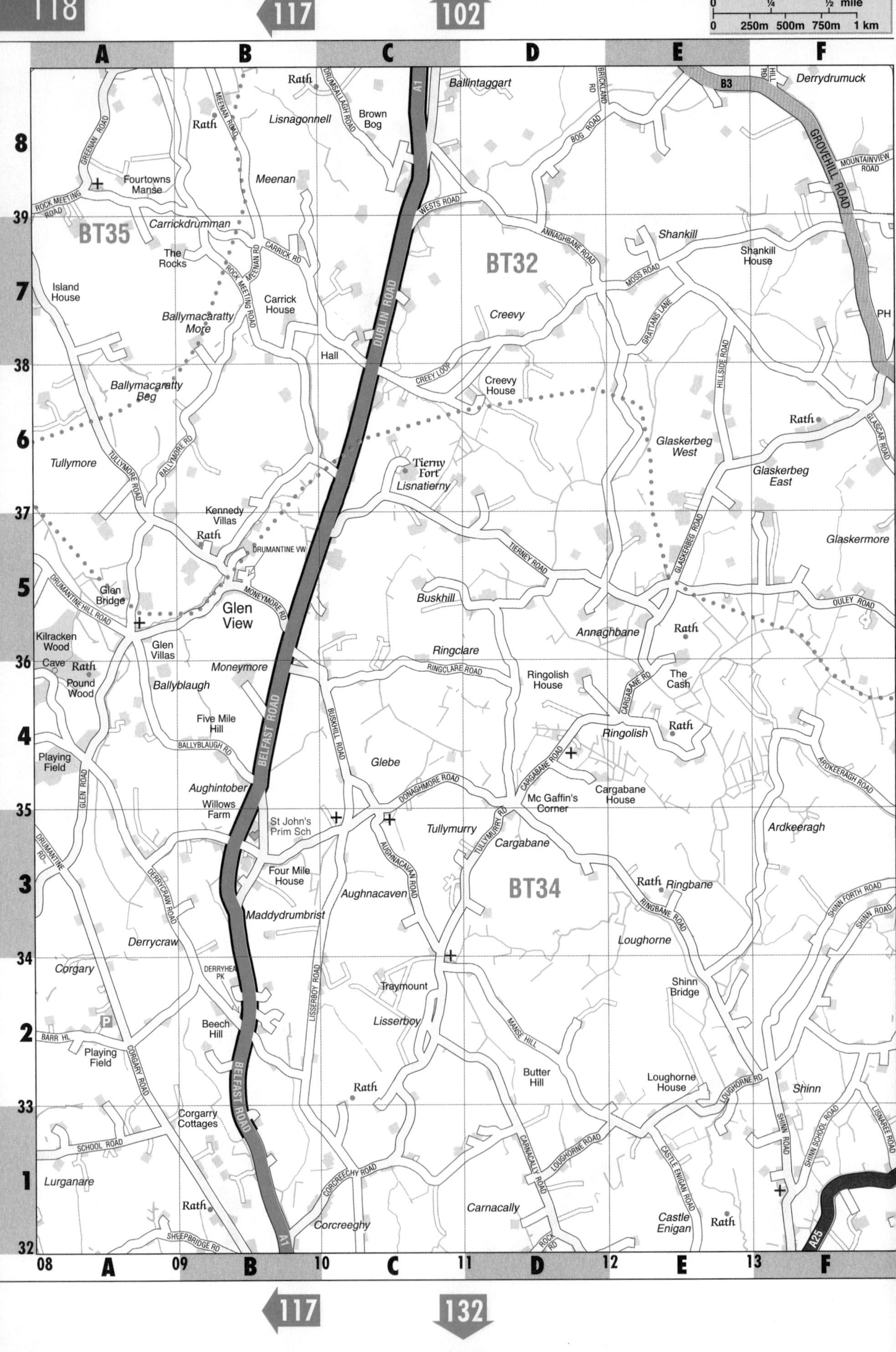

117
132

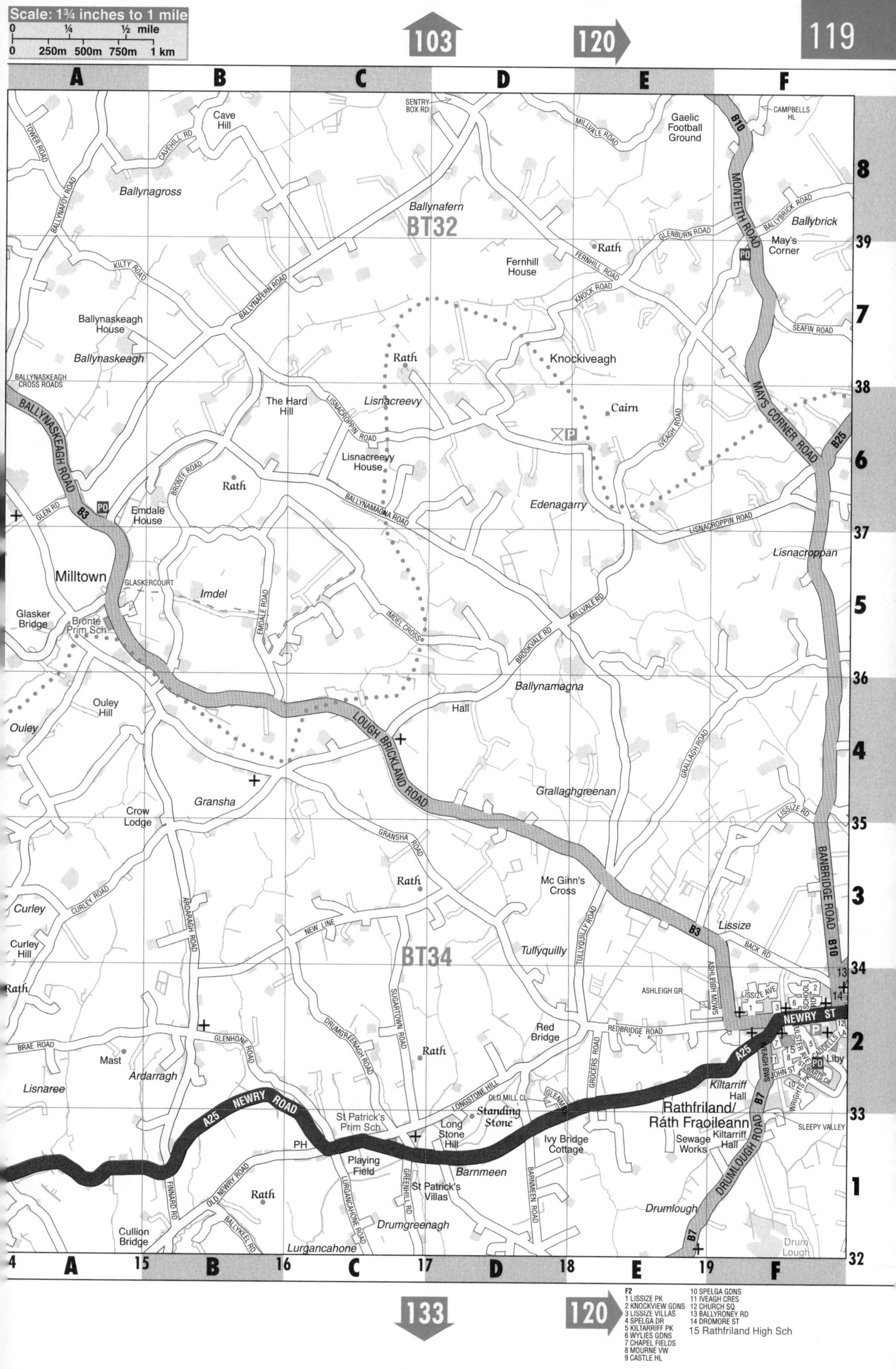

F2
1 LISSIZE PK
2 KNOCKVIEW GDNS
3 LISSIZE VILLAS
4 SPELGA DR
5 KILTARRIFF PK
6 WYLIES GDNS
7 CHAPEL FIELDS
8 MOURNE VW
9 CASTLE HL
10 SPELGA GDNS
11 IVEAGH CRES
12 CHURCH SQ
13 BALLYRONEY RD
14 DROMORE ST
15 Rathfriland High Sch

119
104

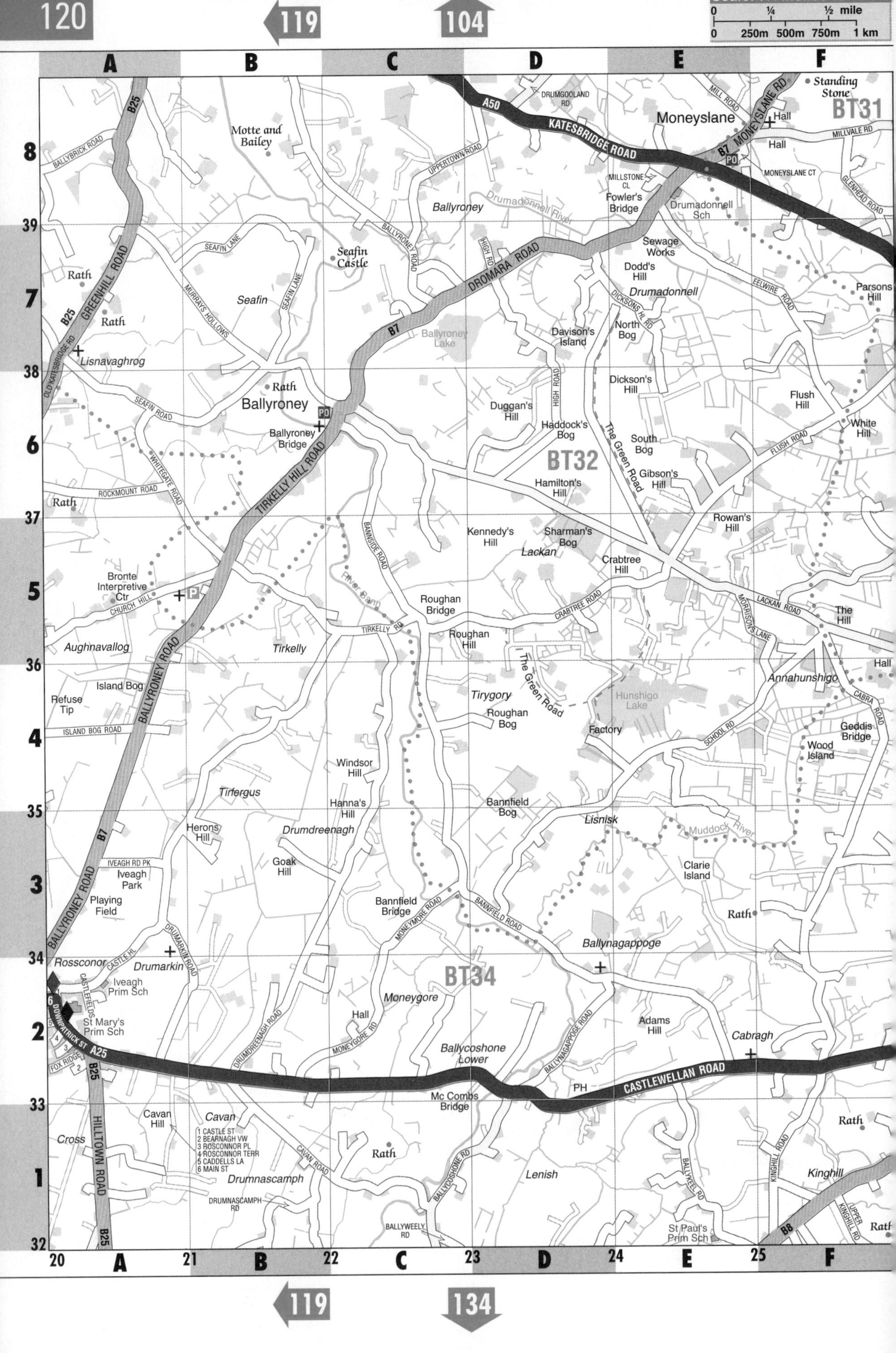

119
134

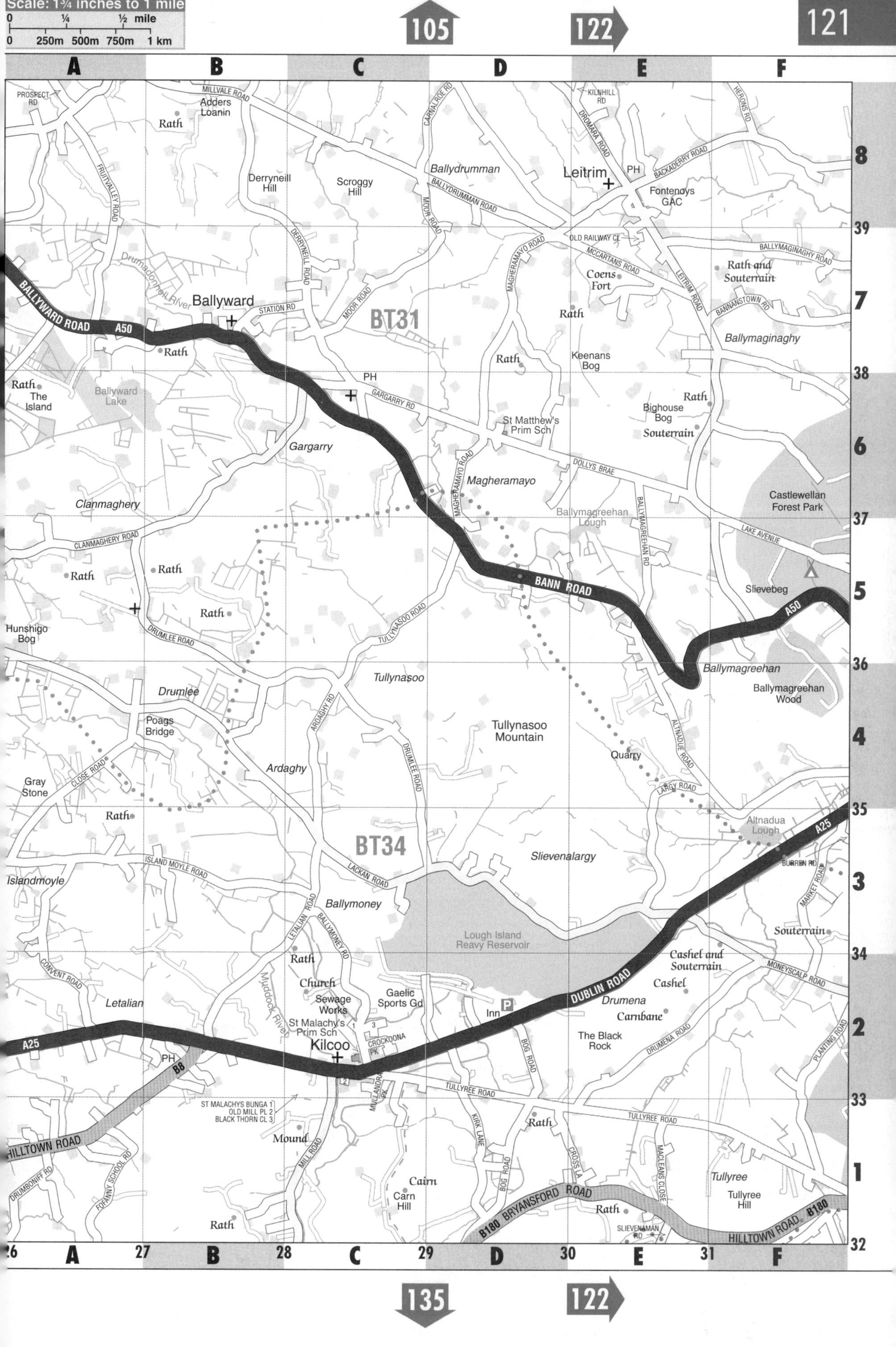
Scale: 1¾ inches to 1 mile
0 ¼ ½ mile
0 250m 500m 750m 1 km
105
122
A B C D E F
PROSPECT RD
MILLVALE ROAD
Adders Loanin
Rath
CARNALROE RD
KILNHILL RD
HERONS RD
DROMARA ROAD
FRUITVALLEY ROAD
Derryneill Hill
Scroggy Hill
Ballydrumman
BALLYDRUMMAN ROAD
MOUR ROAD
Leitrim
PH
BACKADERRY ROAD
Fontenoys GAC
OLD RAILWAY CL
MCCARTANS ROAD
MAGHERAMAYO ROAD
LEITRIM ROAD
BALLYMAGINAGHY ROAD
Rath and Souterrain
Coens Fort
Drumadonnell River
DERRYNEILL ROAD
MOOR ROAD
Ballyward
STATION RD
BT31
BANNANSTOWN RD
Ballymaginaghy
BALLYWARD ROAD
A50
Rath
Keenans Bog
PH
GARGARRY RD
Rath
The Island
Ballyward Lake
Bighouse Bog
Souterrain
St Matthew's Prim Sch
Gargarry
DOLLYS BRAE
Magheramayo
Clanmaghery
Castlewellan Forest Park
Ballymagreehan Lough
BALLYMAGREEHAN RD
LAKE AVENUE
CLANMAGHERY ROAD
BANN ROAD
Slievebeg
Hunshigo Bog
TULLYNASOO ROAD
DRUMLEE ROAD
Tullynasoo
Ballymagreehan
Ballymagreehan Wood
Drumlee
Poags Bridge
ARDAGHY RD
Tullynasoo Mountain
DRUMLEE ROAD
Quarry
ALTNADUE ROAD
CLOSE ROAD
Ardaghy
Gray Stone
LARGY ROAD
Altnadua Lough
A25
BT34
Slievenalargy
BURREN RD
MARKET ROAD
ISLAND MOYLE ROAD
Islandmoyle
LACKAN ROAD
Ballymoney
LETALIAN ROAD
BALLYMONEY RD
Lough Island Reavy Reservoir
Souterrain
Cashel and Souterrain
MONEYSCALP ROAD
CONVENT ROAD
Church
Cashel
Letalian
Muddock River
Sewage Works
Gaelic Sports Gd
DUBLIN ROAD
Drumena
Inn
Carnbane
St Malachy's Prim Sch
The Black Rock
DRUMENA ROAD
PLANTING ROAD
Kilcoo
CROCKOONA PK
B8
MULLANDRA PK
BOG ROAD
TULLYREE ROAD
ST MALACHYS BUNGA 1
OLD MILL PL 2
BLACK THORN CL 3
KIRK LANE
CROSS LA
MACLEANS CLOSE
Mound
HILLTOWN ROAD
MILL ROAD
DRUMBONIFF RD
FOFANNY SCHOOL RD
Cairn
Carn Hill
Tullyree
Tullyree Hill
B180 BRYANSFORD ROAD
B180
SLIEVENAMAN RD
HILLTOWN ROAD
26 27 28 29 30 31 32
39 38 37 36 35 34 33 32
8 7 6 5 4 3 2 1
135
122

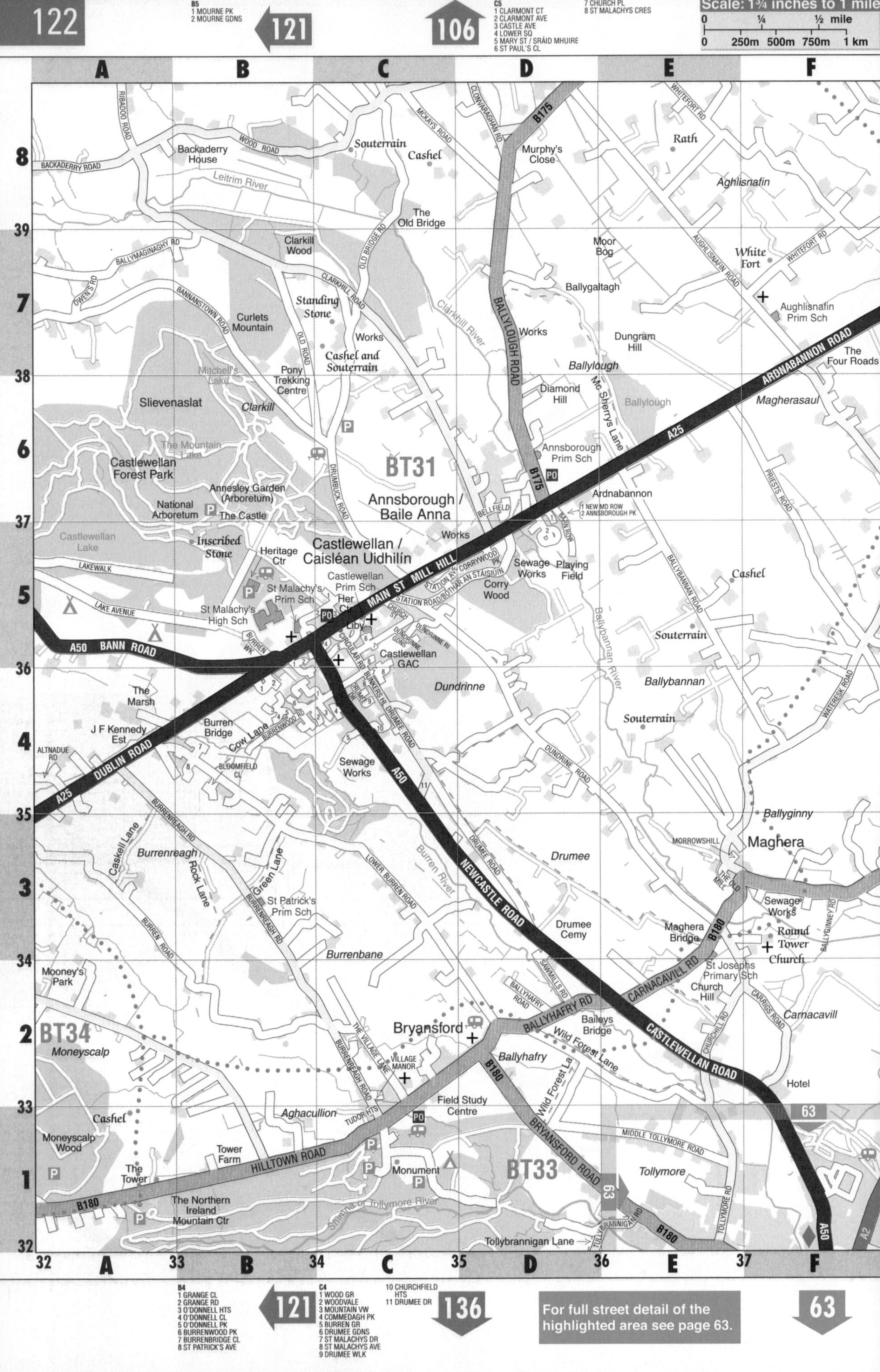

122
B5
1 MOURNE PK
2 MOURNE GDNS
121
106
C5
1 CLARMONT CT
2 CLARMONT AVE
3 CASTLE AVE
4 LOWER SQ
5 MARY ST / SRÁID MHUIRE
6 ST PAUL'S CL
7 CHURCH PL
8 ST MALACHYS CRES
Scale: 1¾ inches to 1 mile
0 ¼ ½ mile
0 250m 500m 750m 1 km
A
B
C
D
E
F
8
39
7
38
6
37
5
36
4
35
3
34
2
33
1
32
RIBADOO ROAD
WOOD ROAD
BACKADERRY ROAD
Backaderry House
Leitrim River
Souterrain
Cashel
MCKAYS ROAD
CLONVARAGHAN RD
B175
Murphy's Close
WHITEFORT RD
Rath
Aghlisnafin
The Old Bridge
OLD BRIDGE RD
Clarkill Wood
BALLYMAGINAGHY RD
Moor Bog
White Fort
WHITEFORT RD
AUGHLISNAFIN ROAD
CLARKHILL ROAD
Ballygaltagh
Aughlisnafin Prim Sch
OWEN'S RD
BANNANSTOWN ROAD
Standing Stone
Curlets Mountain
Clarkhill River
BALLYLOUGH ROAD
Works
Dungram Hill
ARDNABANNON ROAD
The Four Roads
OLD ROAD
Works
Cashel and Souterrain
Mitchell's Lake
Pony Trekking Centre
Ballylough
Diamond Hill
Mc Sherrys Lane
Ballylough
Magherasaul
Slievenaslat
Clarkill
A25
The Mountain Lake
DRUMBUCK ROAD
BT31
Annsborough Prim Sch
PO
Castlewellan Forest Park
PRIESTS ROAD
Annesley Garden (Arboretum)
Annsborough / Baile Anna
Ardnabannon
National Arboretum
The Castle
BELLFIELD
1 NEW MD ROW
2 ANNSBOROUGH PK
BARN ROW
Castlewellan Lake
Inscribed Stone
Works
Castlewellan / Caisleán Uidhilín
Heritage Ctr
MAIN ST MILL HILL
CORRYWOOD PK
Sewage Works
Playing Field
LAKEWALK
STATION AV / ASCAILL AN STÁISIÚIN
Castlewellan Prim Sch
Corry Wood
Cashel
St Malachy's Prim Sch
Her Ctr
STATION ROAD / BÓTHAR AN STÁISIÚIN
Ballybannan River
BALLYBANNAN ROAD
LAKE AVENUE
St Malachy's High Sch
CHURCH ST
Liby
DUNDRINNE RI
Souterrain
BURREN WK
DUNDRINNE GDNS
A50 BANN ROAD
CIRCULAR RD
Castlewellan GAC
Ballybannan
BUNKERS HL
DRUMEE ROAD
Dundrinne
The Marsh
DRUMEE DR
Souterrain
WATERESK ROAD
J F Kennedy Est
Burren Bridge
Cow Lane
BURRENWOOD RD
ALTNADUE RD
DUBLIN ROAD
BLOOMFIELD CL
Sewage Works
A50
DUNDRINE ROAD
A25
Caskell Lane
BURRENREAGH RD
Ballyginny
MORROWSHILL
Maghera
Burrenreagh
Rock Lane
Green Lane
LOWER BURREN ROAD
Burren River
DRUMEE ROAD
Drumee
THE OLD MILL
NEWCASTLE ROAD
Sewage Works
BURREN ROAD
BURRENREAGH RD
St Patrick's Prim Sch
Drumee Cemy
Maghera Bridge
B180
Round Tower Church
BALLYGINNEY RD
Burrenbane
SAWMILLS RD
CARNACAVILL RD
St Josephs Primary Sch
Mooney's Park
BALLYHAFRY ROAD
Church Hill
CARRIGS ROAD
BT34
BALLYHAFRY RD
Baileys Bridge
CASTLEWELLAN ROAD
Carnacavill
Moneyscalp
THE VILLAGE LANE
Bryansford
Wild Forest Lane
CHURCHILL RD
BURRENREAGH ROAD
VILLAGE MANOR
Ballyhafry
B180
Wild Forest La
Hotel
Cashel
Aghacullion
TUDOR HTS
Field Study Centre
63
Moneyscalp Wood
PO
BRYANSFORD ROAD
MIDDLE TOLLYMORE ROAD
Tower Farm
HILLTOWN ROAD
The Tower
Monument
BT33
Tollymore
B180
The Northern Ireland Mountain Ctr
Shimna or Tollymore River
63
TULLYBRANNIGAN RD
B180
TOLLYMORE RD
A50
A2
Tollybrannigan Lane
32
33
34
35
36
37
A
B
C
D
E
F
B4
1 GRANGE CL
2 GRANGE RD
3 O'DONNELL HTS
4 O'DONNELL CL
5 O'DONNELL PK
6 BURRENWOOD PK
7 BURRENBRIDGE CL
8 ST PATRICK'S AVE
121
C4
1 WOOD GR
2 WOODVALE
3 MOUNTAIN VW
4 COMMEDAGH PK
5 BURREN GR
6 DRUMEE GDNS
7 ST MALACHYS DR
8 ST MALACHYS AVE
9 DRUMEE WLK
10 CHURCHFIELD HTS
11 DRUMEE DR
136
For full street detail of the highlighted area see page 63.
63

Scale: 1¾ inches to 1 mile
¼
½ mile
250m 500m 750m 1 km
107
124
A
B
C
D
E
F
Savage's Fort
Moneycarragh River
MONEYCARRAGH RD
DRUMCAW ROAD
CLARAGH ROAD
A25
CASTLEWELLAN ROAD
Knockstickn
THE SQUARE 1
CHURCH CT 2
CLARAGH CT 3
KNOCKSTICKEN ROAD
A2
BT30
Ardilea
Motte
Blackstaff Bridge
BALLYROLLY ROAD
BLACKSTAFF ROAD
TOBERDORAN ROAD
Ardilea Lower
Lismahon Motte
Moneycarragh
Moneycarragh Bridge
Moneycarragh Bridge
Collins Bog
Moneycarragh Hill
DUNDRUM ROAD
ARDILEA RD
Ardilea Bridge
Lecale Way
FORD RD
BAY ROAD
POINT RD
BT31
Rath
Cloghram
COMMONS RD
Hall
TYRELLA RD
PH
Holly Bush
Church Hill
HOLLYBUSH ROAD
DROMARA ROAD
Cloghram Hill
CARRICKINAB ROAD
Ballykinler Middle
Rath
Moneylane
Dundrum Castle
Green Island
Islandnamuck
Commons of Clanmaghery
CASTLE HILL
MONEYLANE ROAD
KILMEGAN ROAD
Gaelic Sports Gd
Black Rock
Dundrum Inner Bay
Ballykinler House
CLANMAGHERY CT
CASTLE HEIGHTS
MC MINNS LA
WARREN CL
Shague Hill
DE COURCEY WY
SHORE ROAD
1 MEADOW HILL
2 CASTLE GLEN
3 CARRIGVALE
4 DE COURCY WY
5 CARRIGARD
6 MURLOUGH VW
7 CASTLE VW
8 BAR VW
9 CHURCH CL
10 MURLOUGH BAY CT
11 MURLOUGH QUAY
12 Sacred Heart Prim Sch
BT33
ROBIN HILL
DELINVILLA LA
MANSE RD
SCHOOL HL
THE QUAY
Tyrella Prim Sch
Ballykinler
SAND LA
CLANMAGHERY GR 1
RING SALLIN GDNS 2
MARIAN PK / PAIRC MHUIRE 3
Cricket Ground
OLD ROAD
MAIN STREET
Dundrum / Dun Droma
Dundrum Bay
Wateresk Hill
Wateresk
B180
NEWCASTLE ROAD
Sewage Works
Downshire Bridge
Ballykinler Upper
BALLYLOUGHLIN ROAD
Dundrum Inner Bay
Murbugh Farm
KEEL POINT
BALLYLOUGHLIN RD
Mountpleasant
Murlough Lower
Chambered Grave
Ballyloughlin
Standing Stone
FLUSH ROAD
Slidderyford Bridge
Murlough National Nature Reserve
Carrigs River
Dunes
DUNDRUM ROAD
Lecale Way
Murlough Upper
63
NEWCASTLE/
An Caisleán Nua
8
39
40
41
42
43
137
124
32
33
34
35
36
37
38
39
1
2
3
4
5
6
7
8

123
108

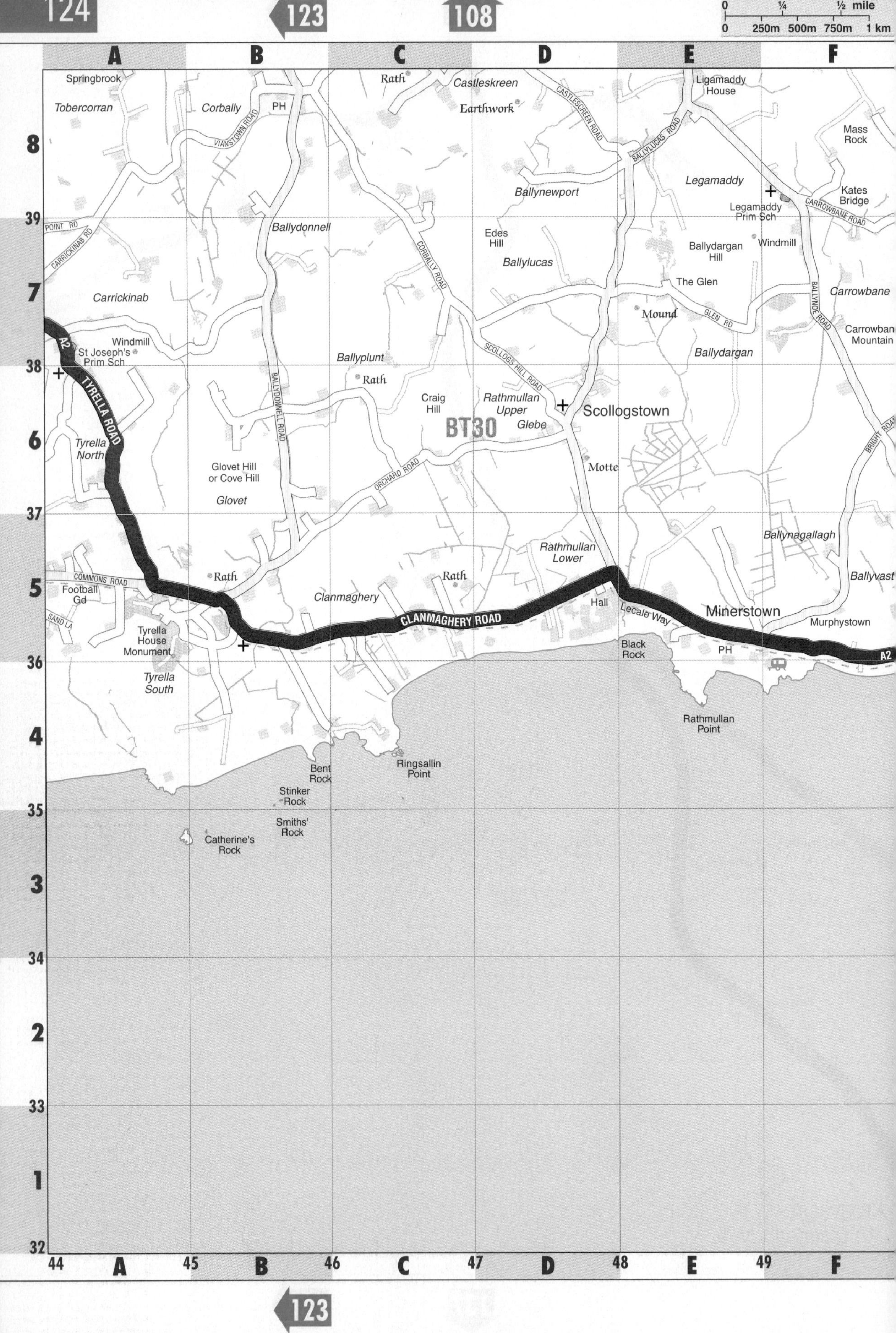
Scale: 1¾ inches to 1 mil
0 ¼ ½ mile
0 250m 500m 750m 1 km
A B C D E F
8 39 7 38 6 37 5 36 4 35 3 34 2 33 1 32
44 45 46 47 48 49
Springbrook
Tobercorran
Corbally
PH
VIANSTOWN ROAD
Rath
Castleskreen
Earthwork
CASTLESCREEN ROAD
Ligamaddy House
BALLYLUCAS ROAD
Mass Rock
Legamaddy
Ballynewport
Legamaddy Prim Sch
Kates Bridge
CARROWBANE ROAD
POINT RD
CARRICKINAB RD
Ballydonnell
CORBALLY ROAD
Edes Hill
Ballylucas
Ballydargan Hill
Windmill
The Glen
Carrowbane
Carrickinab
Mound
GLEN RD
BALLYNOE ROAD
Carrowbane Mountain
A2
Windmill
St Joseph's Prim Sch
Ballyplunt
SCOLLOGS HILL ROAD
Ballydargan
Rath
TYRELLA ROAD
BALLYDONNELL ROAD
Craig Hill
Rathmullan Upper
Scollogstown
BT30
Glebe
Tyrella North
BRIGHT ROAD
Glovet Hill or Cove Hill
ORCHARD ROAD
Motte
Glovet
Ballynagallagh
Rathmullan Lower
COMMONS ROAD
Rath
Rath
Ballyvast
Football Gd
Clanmaghery
Hall
Lecale Way
Minerstown
SAND LA
CLANMAGHERY ROAD
Murphystown
Tyrella House Monument
Black Rock
PH
A2
Tyrella South
Rathmullan Point
Bent Rock
Ringsallin Point
Stinker Rock
Smiths' Rock
Catherine's Rock

123

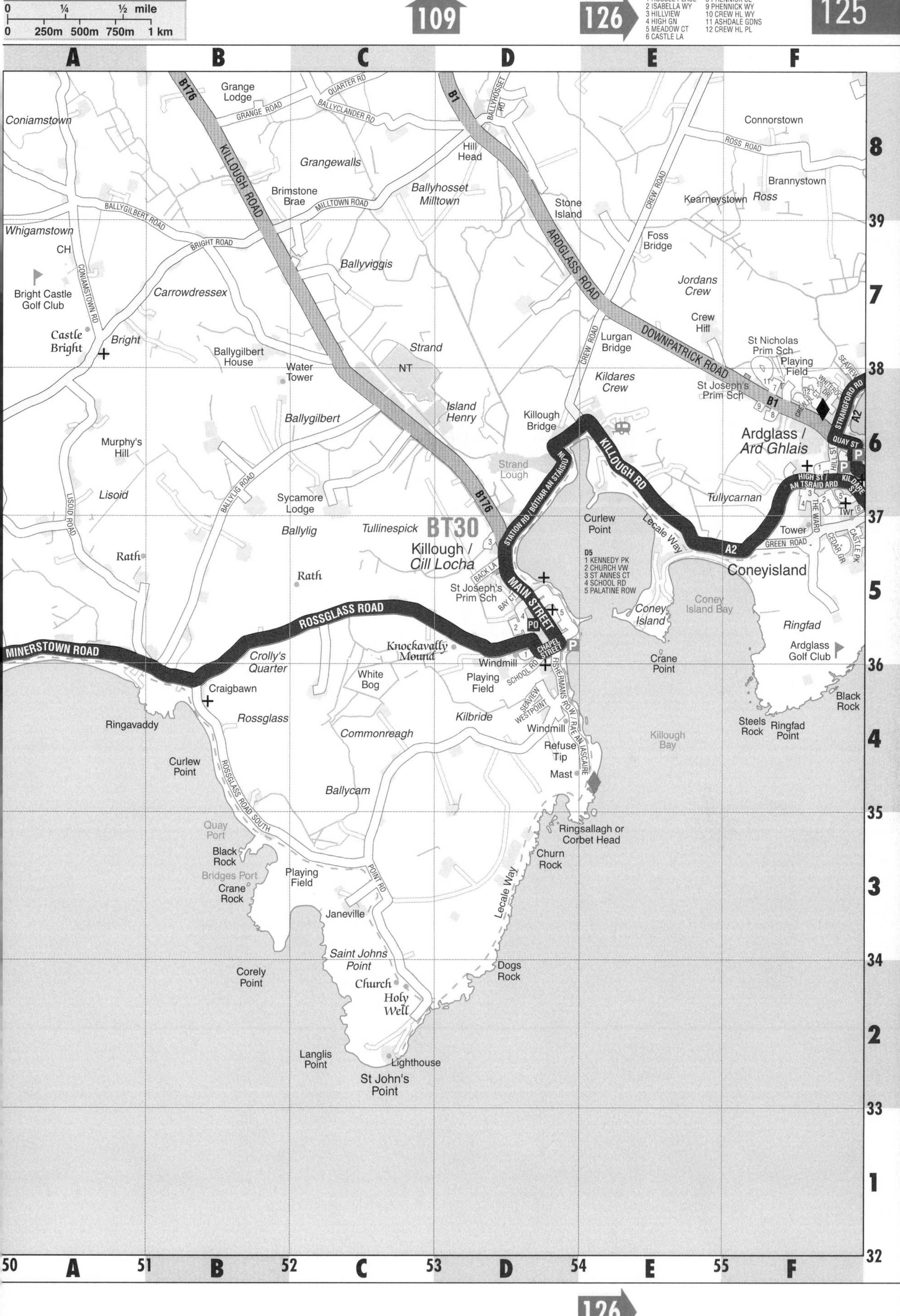
Scale: 1¾ inches to 1 mile
0 ¼ ½ mile
0 250m 500m 750m 1 km
109
126
F6
1 RUSSEL PLACE
2 ISABELLA WY
3 HILLVIEW
4 HIGH GN
5 MEADOW CT
6 CASTLE LA
7 ASHDALE AVE
8 PHENNICK CL
9 PHENNICK WY
10 CREW HL WY
11 ASHDALE GDNS
12 CREW HL PL
A
B
C
D
E
F
Grange Lodge
GRANGE ROAD
QUARTER RD
BALLYCLANDER RD
BALLYHOSSET RD
B176
B1
Coniamstown
Connorstown
ROSS ROAD
KILLOUGH ROAD
Grangewalls
Hill Head
Brimstone Brae
Ballyhosset Milltown
MILLTOWN ROAD
Brannystown
BALLYGILBERT ROAD
Stone Island
CREW ROAD
Kearneystown
Ross
Whigamstown
BRIGHT ROAD
ARDGLASS ROAD
Foss Bridge
CH
Ballyviggis
CONIAMSTOWN RD
Bright Castle Golf Club
Carrowdressex
Jordans Crew
Crew Hill
Castle Bright
Bright
Strand
Lurgan Bridge
DOWNPATRICK ROAD
CREW ROAD
St Nicholas Prim Sch
Playing Field
Ballygilbert House
Water Tower
NT
Kildares Crew
St Joseph's Prim Sch
STRANGFORD RD
SEAVIEW
Island Henry
Ballygilbert
Killough Bridge
Ardglass / Ard Ghlais
A2
QUAY ST
Murphy's Hill
BALLYLIG ROAD
Strand Lough
KILLOUGH RD
STATION RD / BÓTHAR AN STÁISIÚIN
HIGH ST
AN TSRAID ARD
Lisoid
LISOID ROAD
Sycamore Lodge
Tullycarnan
Curlew Point
Lecale Way
Tower
Twr
THE WARD
Ballylig
Tullinespick
BT30
GREEN ROAD
CEDAR GR
CASTLE PK
Rath
Killough / Cill Locha
D5
1 KENNEDY PK
2 CHURCH VW
3 ST ANNES CT
4 SCHOOL RD
5 PALATINE ROW
Coneyisland
Rath
BACK LA
St Joseph's Prim Sch
BAY CT
MAIN STREET
Coney Island
Coney Island Bay
ROSSGLASS ROAD
PO
Ringfad
Knockavally Mound
Ardglass Golf Club
MINERSTOWN ROAD
Crolly's Quarter
CHAPEL STREET
Windmill
Crane Point
White Bog
Playing Field
SCHOOL RD
Craigbawn
SEAVIEW
WESTPOINT
Black Rock
Ringavaddy
Rossglass
Kilbride
FISHERMANS ROW / RAE AN IASCAIRE
Windmill
Steels Rock
Ringfad Point
Commonreagh
Killough Bay
Refuse Tip
Curlew Point
ROSSGLASS ROAD SOUTH
Mast
Ballycam
Quay Port
Ringsallagh or Corbet Head
Black Rock
Churn Rock
Bridges Port
Playing Field
POINT RD
Crane Rock
Lecale Way
Janeville
Saint Johns Point
Dogs Rock
Corely Point
Church
Holy Well
Langlis Point
Lighthouse
St John's Point
8
39
7
38
6
37
5
36
4
35
3
34
2
33
1
32
50
51
52
53
54
55
126

125
110

Scale: 1¾ inches to 1 mile

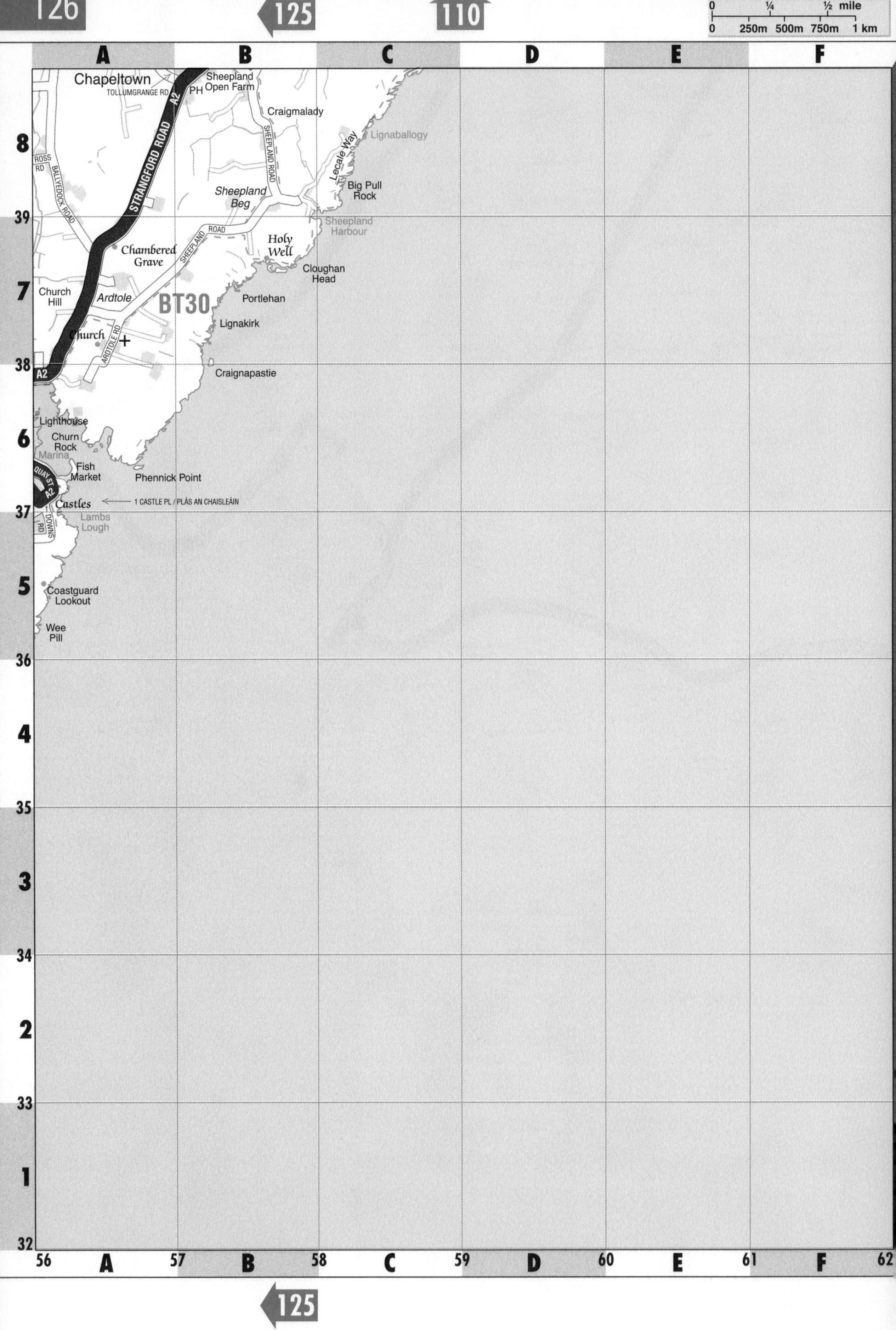

125

113
128

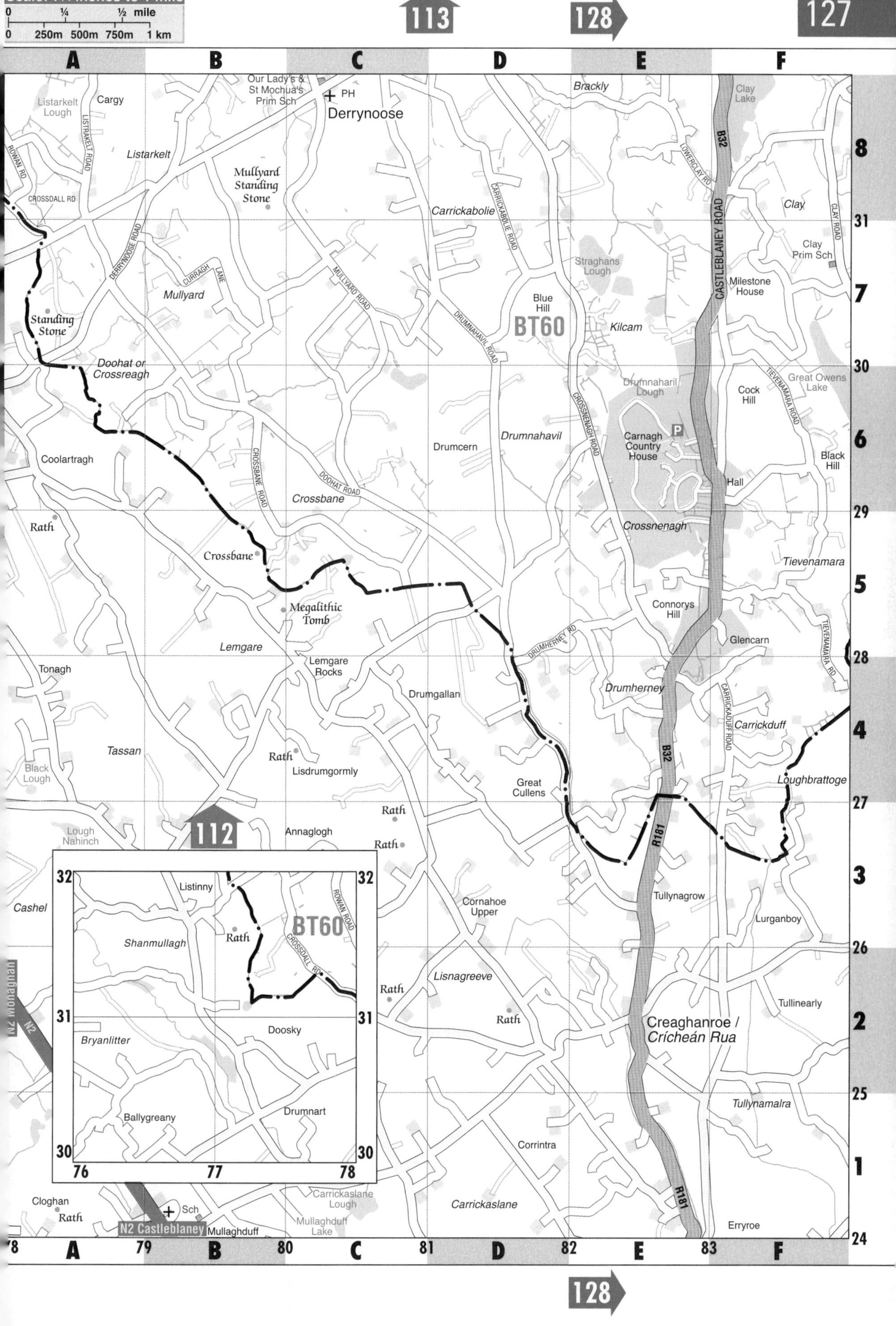
Scale: 1¾ inches to 1 mile
0 ¼ ½ mile
0 250m 500m 750m 1 km
A B C D E F
Our Lady's & St Mochua's Prim Sch
PH
Derrynoose
Brackly
Clay Lake
Listarkelt Lough
Cargy
ROWAN RD
LISTRAKELT ROAD
Listarkelt
CROSSDALL RD
Mullyard Standing Stone
Carrickabolie
CARRICKABOLIE ROAD
LOWERCLAY RD
B32
CASTLEBLANEY ROAD
Clay
CLAY ROAD
Clay Prim Sch
DERRYNOOSE ROAD
CURRAGH LANE
Mullyard
MULLYARD ROAD
Straghans Lough
Milestone House
Blue Hill
BT60
DRUMNAHAVIL ROAD
Kilcam
Standing Stone
Doohat or Crossreagh
Drumnaharil Lough
Cock Hill
TIEVENAMARA ROAD
Great Owens Lake
CROSSNENAGH ROAD
Carnagh Country House
P
Drumnahavil
Drumcern
Coolartragh
CROSSBANE ROAD
DOOHAT ROAD
Black Hill
Hall
Crossbane
Rath
Crossnenagh
Crossbane
Tievenamara
Megalithic Tomb
Connorys Hill
DRUMHERNEY RD
Glencarn
Lemgare
Lemgare Rocks
Tonagh
Drumherney
Drumgallan
CARRICKADUFF ROAD
Carrickduff
Tassan
Rath
Lisdrumgormly
Black Lough
Great Cullens
Loughbrattoge
Rath
112
Lough Nahinch
Annaglogh
Rath
R181
Tullynagrow
Cashel
Listinny
Cornahoe Upper
Lurganboy
Shanmullagh
Rath
BT60
ROWAN ROAD
CROSSDALL RD
Lisnagreeve
Rath
N2 Monaghan
Rath
Tullinearly
Creaghanroe / Crícheán Rua
Bryanlitter
Doosky
Tullynamalra
Ballygreany
Drumnart
Corrintra
76 77 78
32 31 30
Cloghan
Rath
Sch
Carrickaslane Lough
Carrickaslane
Mullaghduff Lake
Erryroe
N2 Castleblaney
Mullaghduff
8 31 7 30 6 29 5 28 4 27 3 26 2 25 1 24
78 79 80 81 82 83

128

127 114

Scale: 1¾ inches to 1 mile

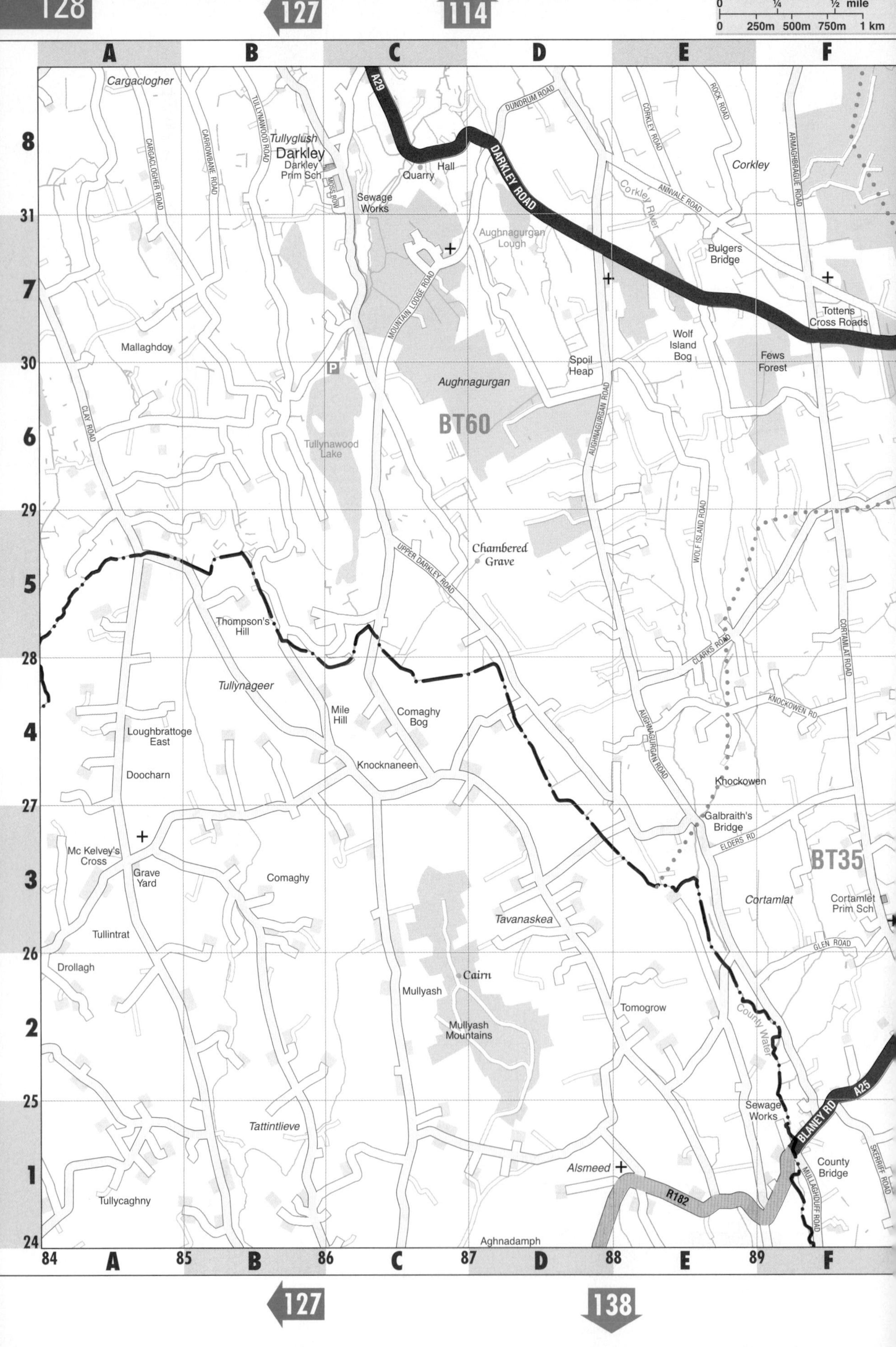

127 138

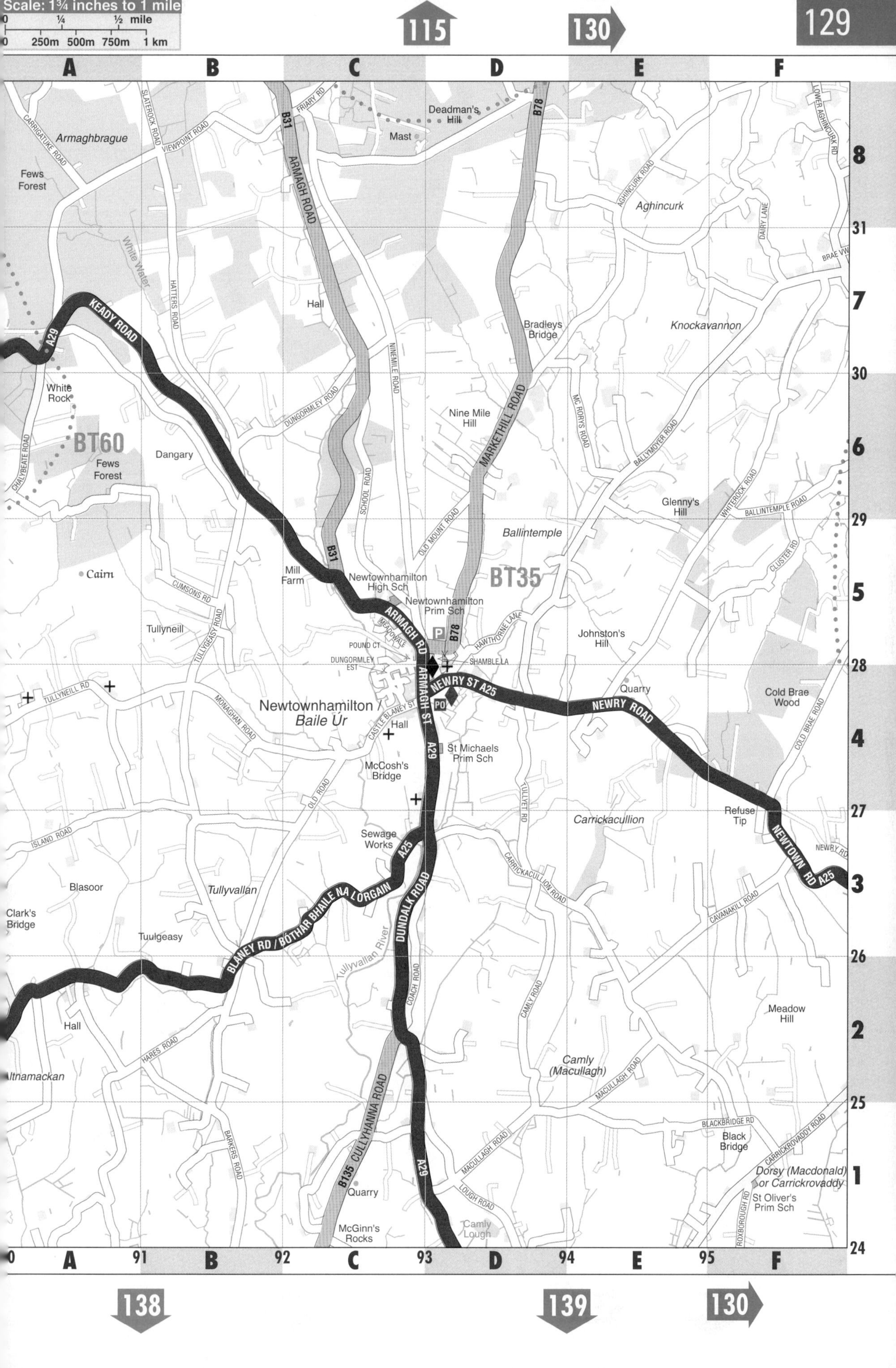
Scale: 1¾ inches to 1 mile
0 ¼ ½ mile
0 250m 500m 750m 1 km
115
130
129
A B C D E F
8 31 7 30 6 29 5 28 4 27 3 26 2 25 1 24
Armaghbrague
Fews Forest
CARRIGATUKE ROAD
SLATEROCK ROAD
VIEWPOINT ROAD
FRIARY RD
B31
Deadman's Hill
Mast
B78
ARMAGH ROAD
LOWER AGHINCURK RD
AGHINCURK ROAD
Aghincurk
DAIRY LANE
BRAE VW
White Water
HATTERS ROAD
Hall
KEADY ROAD
A29
Bradleys Bridge
Knockavannon
White Rock
NINEMILE ROAD
DUNGORMLEY ROAD
Nine Mile Hill
MC RORYS ROAD
BT60
CHALYBEATE ROAD
Fews Forest
Dangary
MARKETHILL ROAD
BALLYMOYER ROAD
SCHOOL ROAD
Glenny's Hill
WHITEROCK ROAD
BALLINTEMPLE ROAD
OLD MOUNT ROAD
Ballintemple
Cairn
Mill Farm
Newtownhamilton High Sch
BT35
CLUSTER RD
CUMSONS RD
Newtownhamilton Prim Sch
Tullyneill
TULLYGEASY ROAD
ARMAGH RD
MEADOWVALE
HAWTHORNE LANE
Johnston's Hill
POUND CT
DUNGORMLEY EST
SHAMBLE LA
TULLYNEILL RD
NEWRY ST A25
Quarry
NEWRY ROAD
Cold Brae Wood
MONAGHAN ROAD
Newtownhamilton / Baile Úr
CASTLE BLANEY ST
PO
Hall
ARMAGH ST
St Michaels Prim Sch
COLD BRAE ROAD
McCosh's Bridge
OLD ROAD
TULLYET RD
ISLAND ROAD
Carrickacullion
Refuse Tip
Sewage Works
NEWRY RD
CARRICKACULLION ROAD
NEWTOWN RD A25
Blasoor
Tullyvallan
BLANEY RD / BOTHAR BHAILE NA LORGAIN
DUNDALK ROAD
Clark's Bridge
CAVANAKILL ROAD
Tuulgeasy
Tullyvallan River
COACH ROAD
CAMLY ROAD
Meadow Hill
Hall
HARES ROAD
Altnamackan
Camly (Macullagh)
MACULLAGH ROAD
CULLYHANNA ROAD
BARKERS ROAD
BLACKBRIDGE RD
Black Bridge
CARRICKROVADDY ROAD
MACULLAGH ROAD
Dorsy (Macdonald) or Carrickrovaddy
B135
Quarry
LOUGH ROAD
St Oliver's Prim Sch
ROXBOROUGH RD
McGinn's Rocks
Camly Lough
90 91 92 93 94 95
138
139
130

129
116

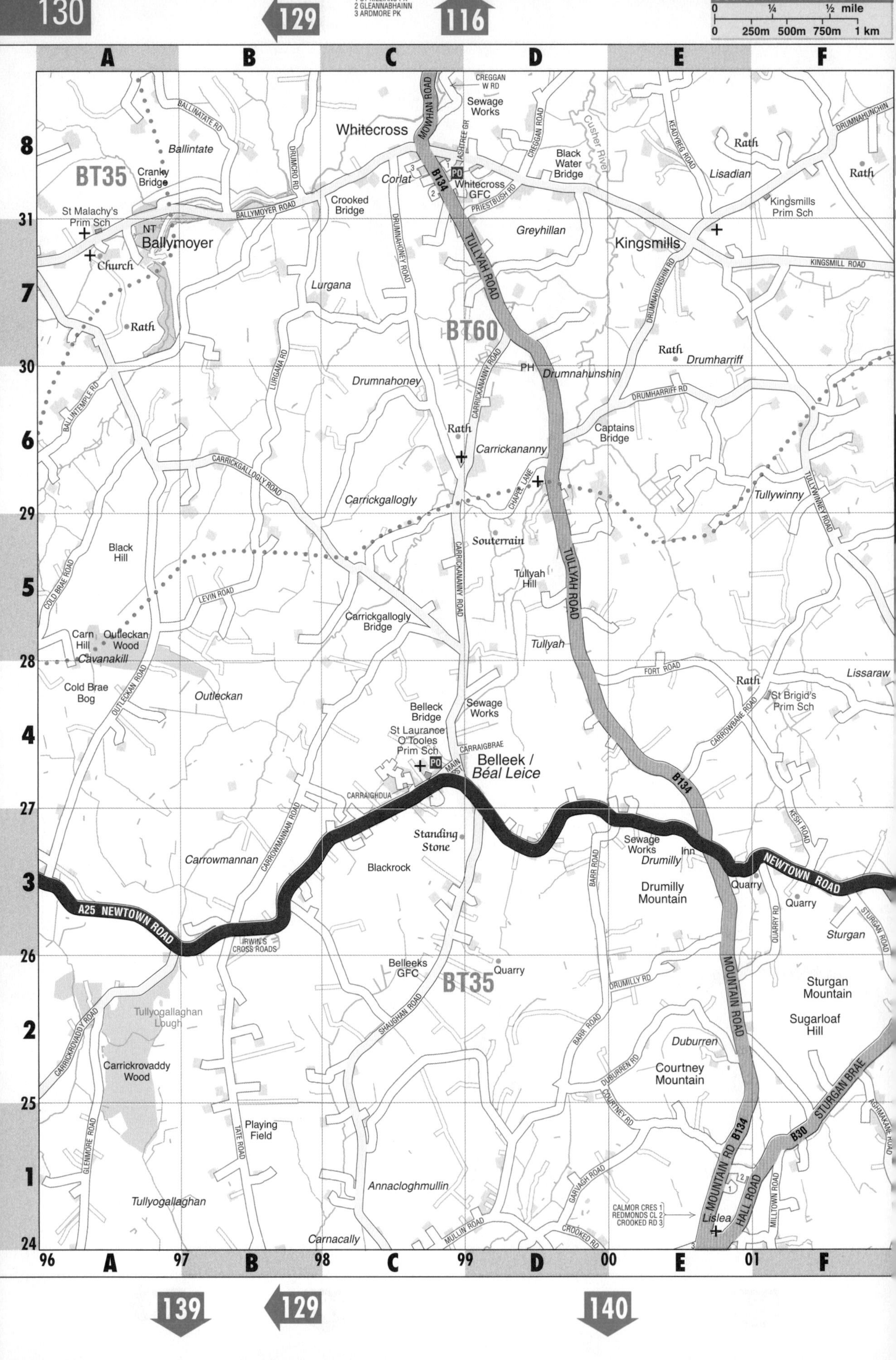

139
129
140

Scale: 1¾ inches to 1 mile
0 ¼ ½ mile
0 250m 500m 750m 1 km

C5
1 CLOUGHAREVEN PK
2 BROOKVILLE CRES
3 CONVENT GDNS
4 BROOKVIEW CL
5 WEAVERS BROOK
6 CAMLOUGH PK
7 DERRYMORE MS
8 CHARLEMONT SQ
9 O'DONAGHUE PK
10 Bessbrook Prim Sch

117

132

F5
1 MEADOWBROOK PK
2 FAIRFIELD HTS
3 LISDRUM AVE
4 LARCHMOUNT PK
5 DRUMGULLION AVE
6 BRACKEN GR
7 SANDY HILL
8 FAIRLAWNS AVE
9 BRACKEN CL

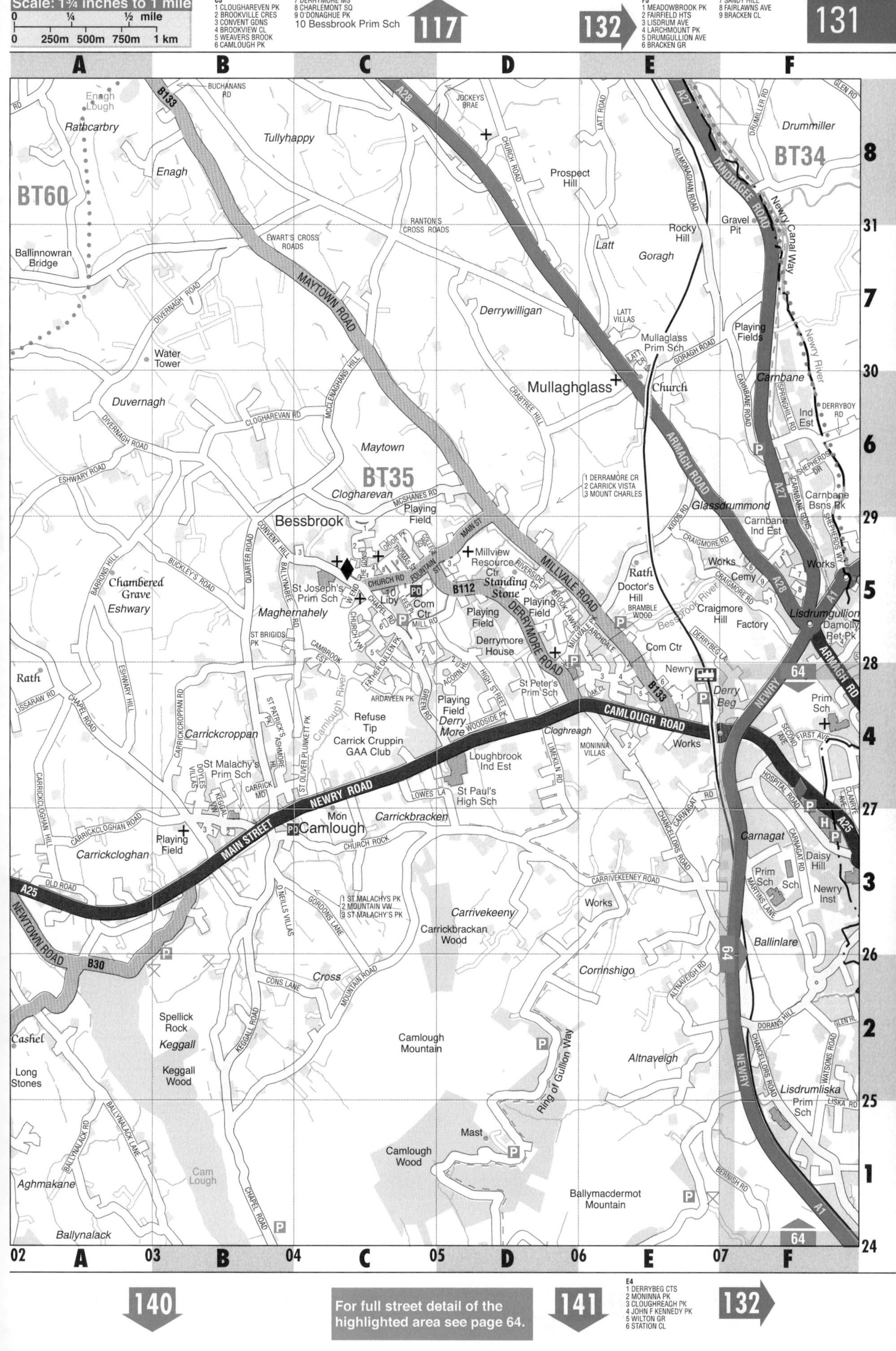

E4
1 DERRYBEG CTS
2 MONINNA PK
3 CLOUGHREAGH PK
4 JOHN F KENNEDY PK
5 WILTON GR
6 STATION CL

140

For full street detail of the highlighted area see page 64.

141

132

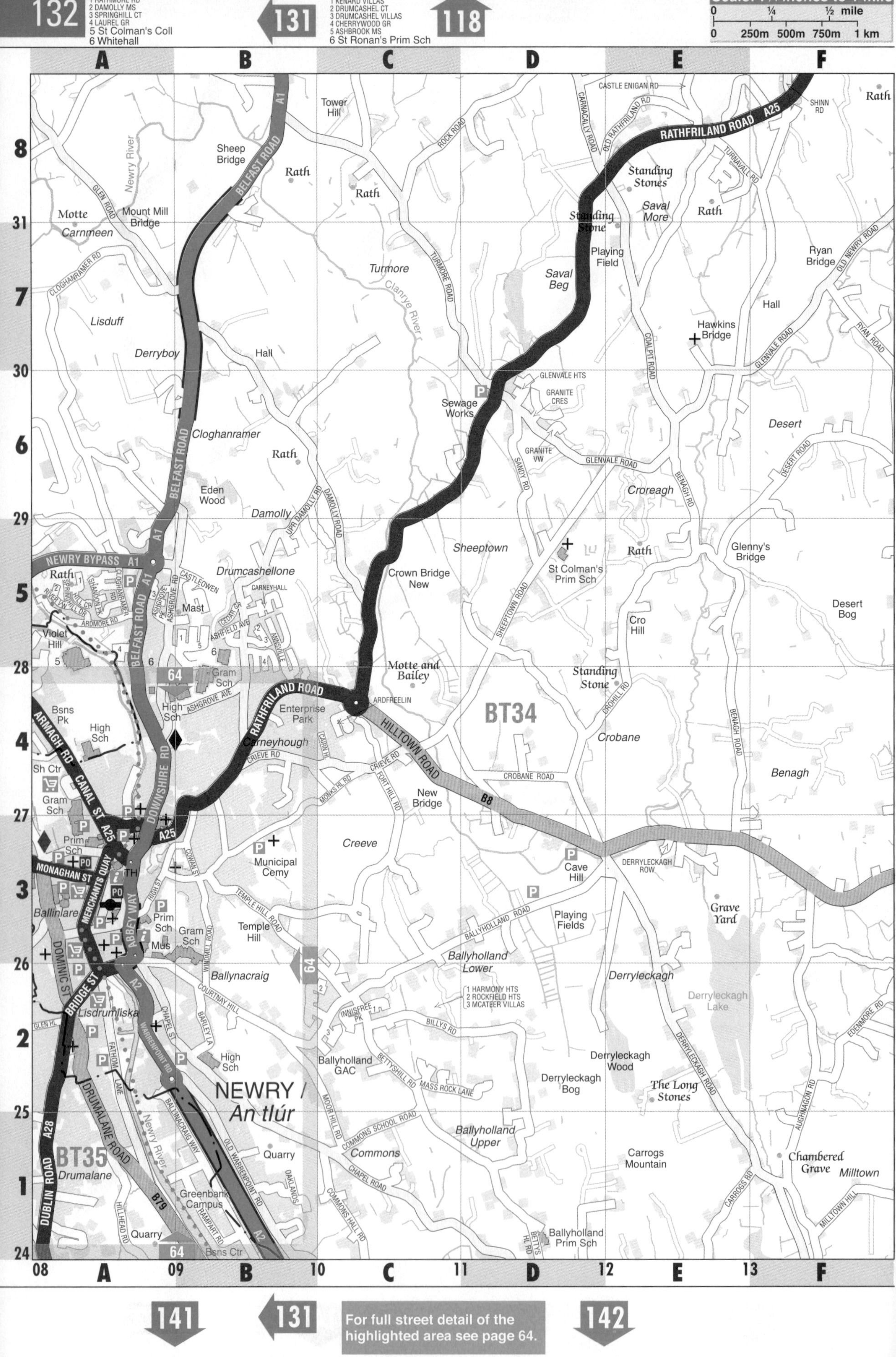
RATHFRILAND ROAD
BELFAST ROAD
Tower Hill
Sheep Bridge
Mount Mill Bridge
Motte
Carnmeen
Turmore
Clanrye River
Standing Stones
Saval More
Saval Beg
Playing Field
Hawkins Bridge
Ryan Bridge
Lisduff
Derryboy
Cloghanramer
Sewage Works
Desert
Eden Wood
Damolly
Croreagh
Sheeptown
Drumcashellone
Crown Bridge New
St Colman's Prim Sch
Glenny's Bridge
Desert Bog
Cro Hill
Violet Hill
Motte and Bailey
Standing Stone
BT34
Enterprise Park
Carneyhough
Crobane
Benagh
New Bridge
HILLTOWN ROAD
Creeve
Municipal Cemy
Cave Hill
Grave Yard
Temple Hill
Ballyholland Lower
Ballynacraig
Derryleckagh
Derryleckagh Lake
Lisdrumliska
Derryleckagh Wood
Derryleckagh Bog
The Long Stones
NEWRY / An tIúr
Ballyholland GAC
Ballyholland Upper
Commons
Carrogs Mountain
Chambered Grave
Milltown
BT35
Drumalane
Quarry
Greenbank Campus
Ballyholland Prim Sch
DUBLIN ROAD
NEWRY BYPASS
ARMAGH RD
CANAL ST
MONAGHAN ST
MERCHANTS QUAY
ABBEY WAY
DOWNSHIRE RD
Ballinlare
1 HARMONY HTS
2 ROCKFIELD HTS
3 MCATEER VILLAS

119
134

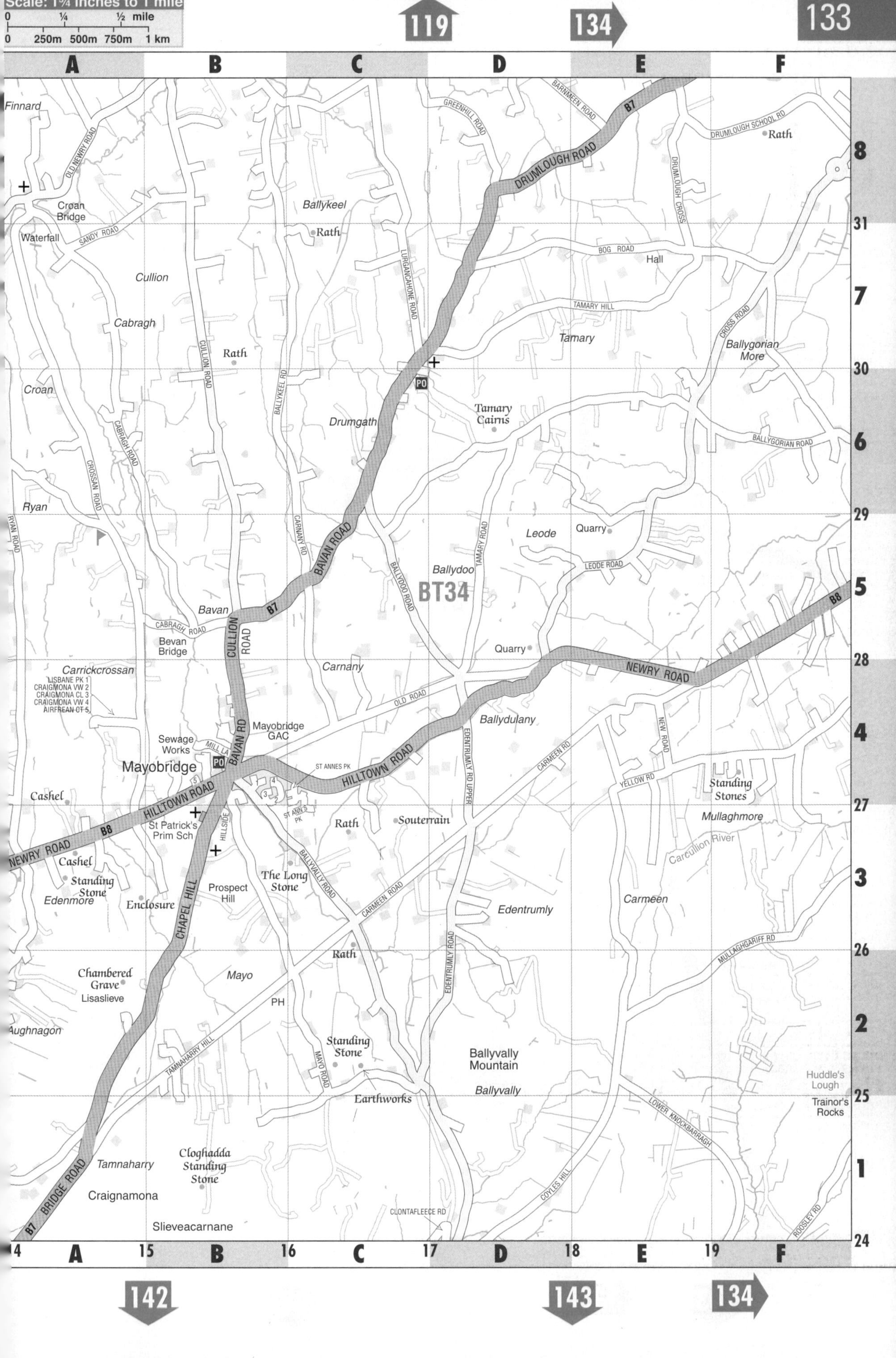

142
143
134

133
120

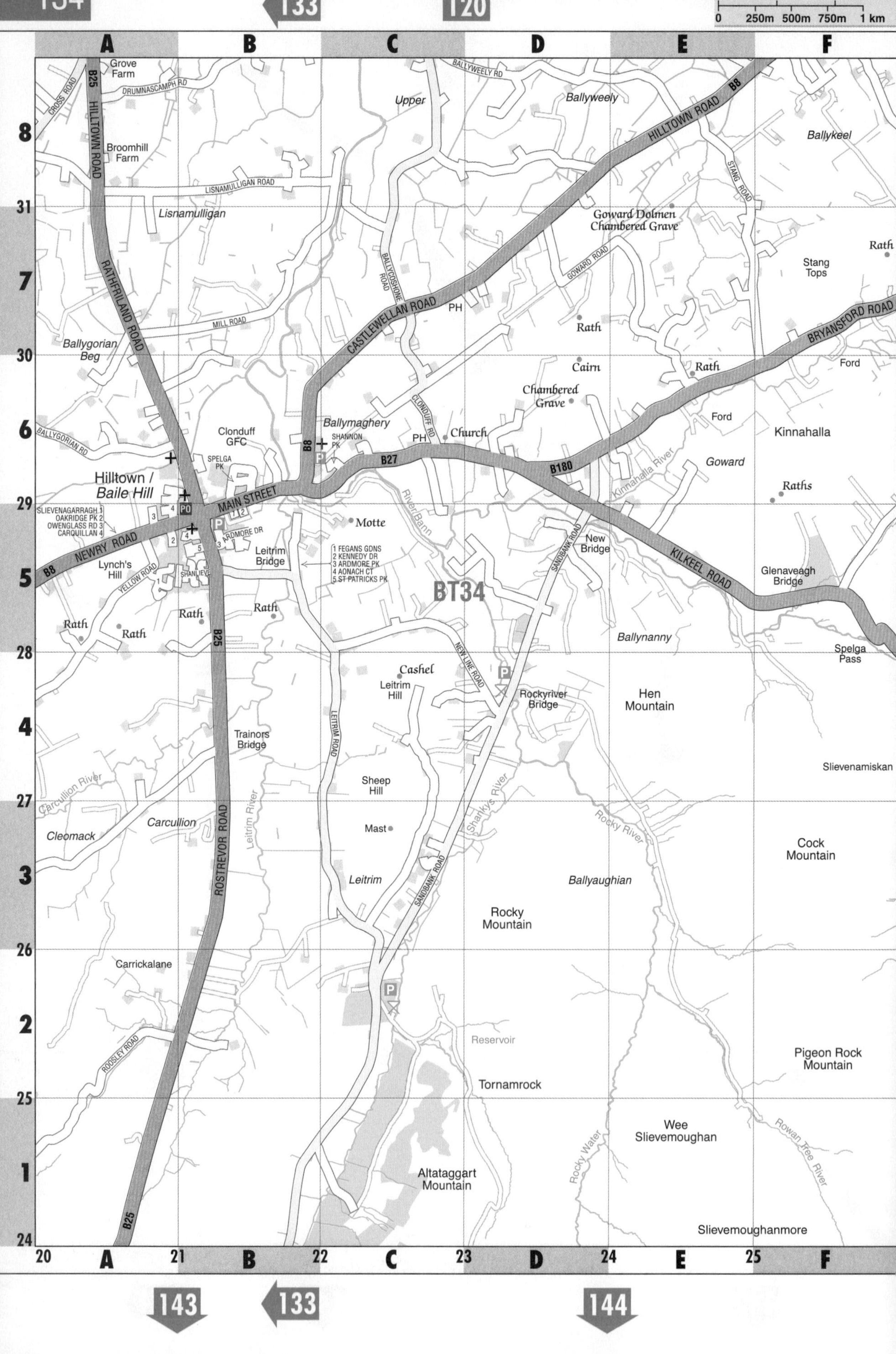

143
133
144

121
136

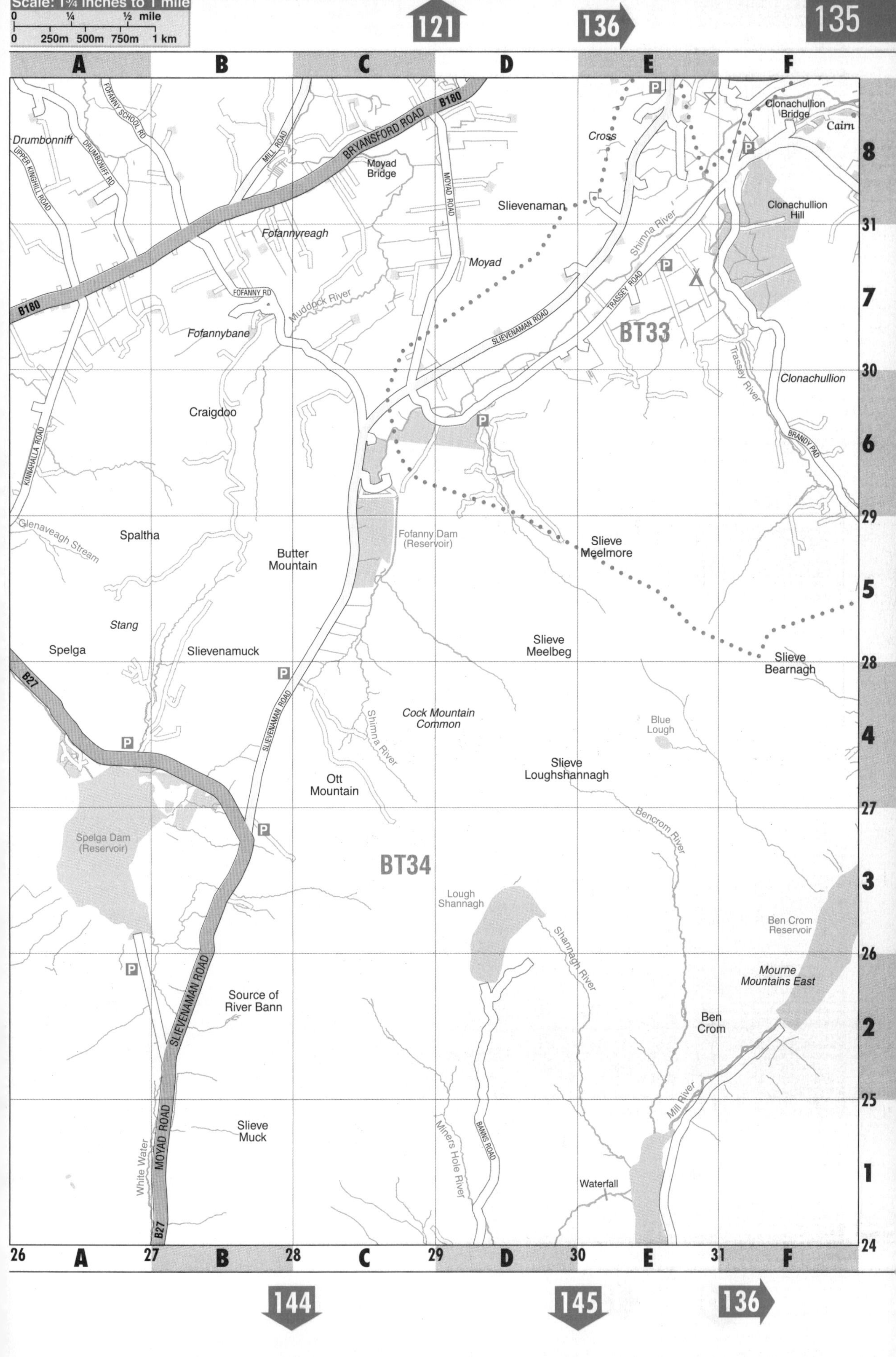

144
145
136

135
122
For full street detail of the highlighted area see page 63.

Scale: 1¾ inches to 1 mile

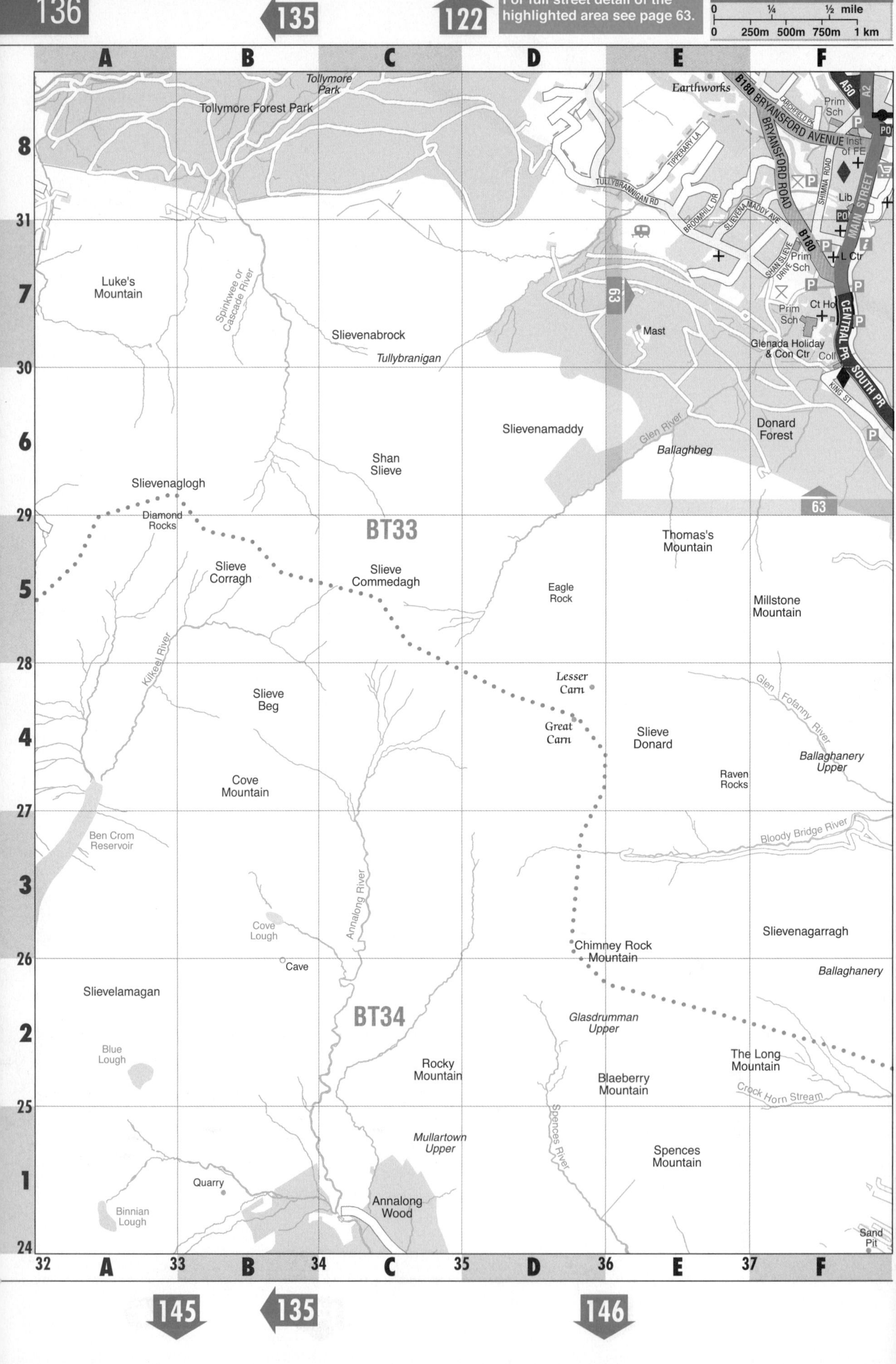

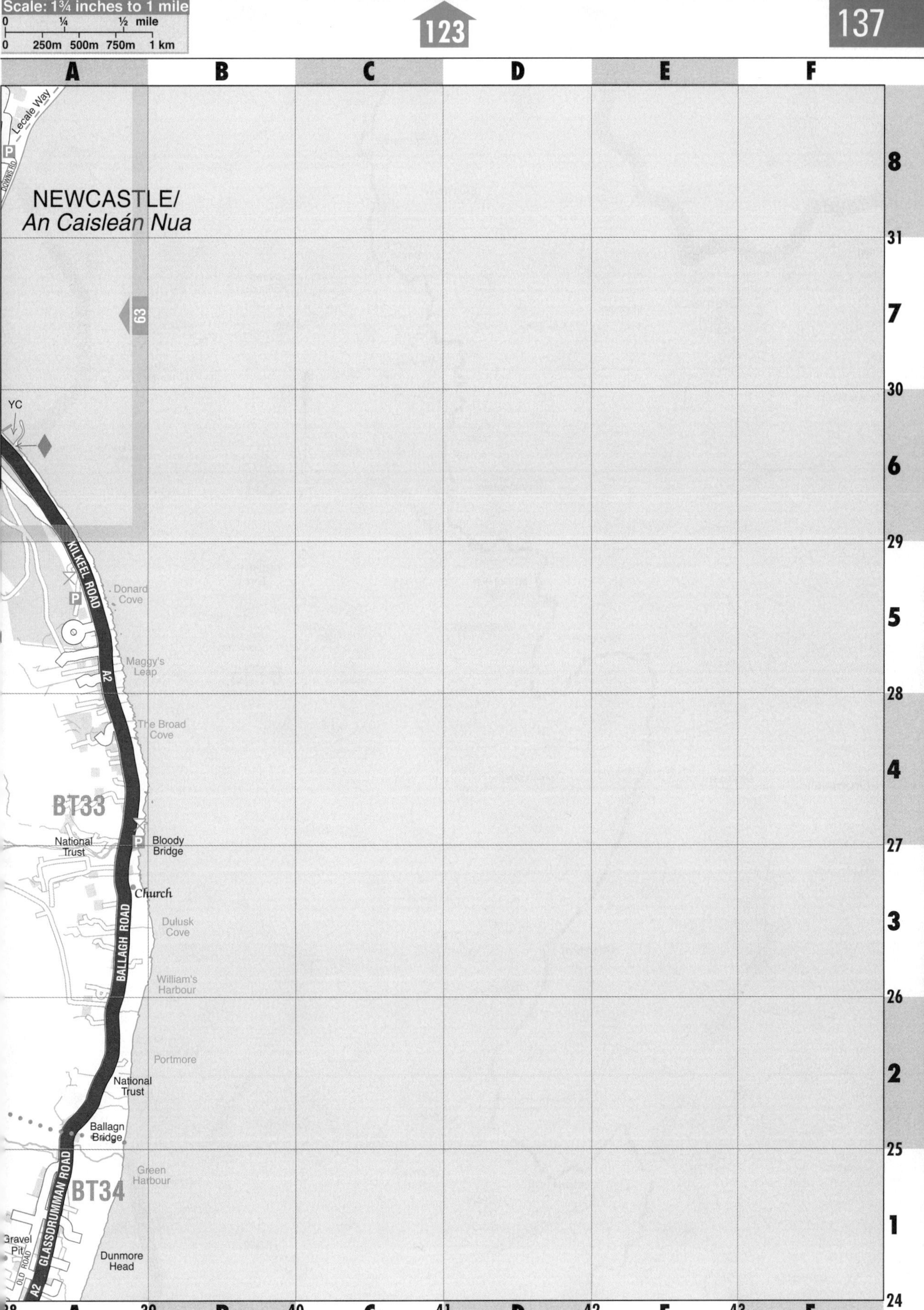
Scale: 1¾ inches to 1 mile
0 ¼ ½ mile
0 250m 500m 750m 1 km
123
A B C D E F
Lecale Way
P
DOWNS RD
NEWCASTLE/
An Caisleán Nua
63
YC
KILKEEL ROAD
P
Donard Cove
Maggy's Leap
A2
The Broad Cove
BT33
P
National Trust
Bloody Bridge
Church
BALLAGH ROAD
Dulusk Cove
William's Harbour
Portmore
National Trust
Ballagh Bridge
GLASSDRUMMAN ROAD
Green Harbour
BT34
Gravel Pit
OLD ROAD
Dunmore Head
A2
8 31 7 30 6 29 5 28 4 27 3 26 2 25 1 24
38 39 40 41 42 43
146

128
129

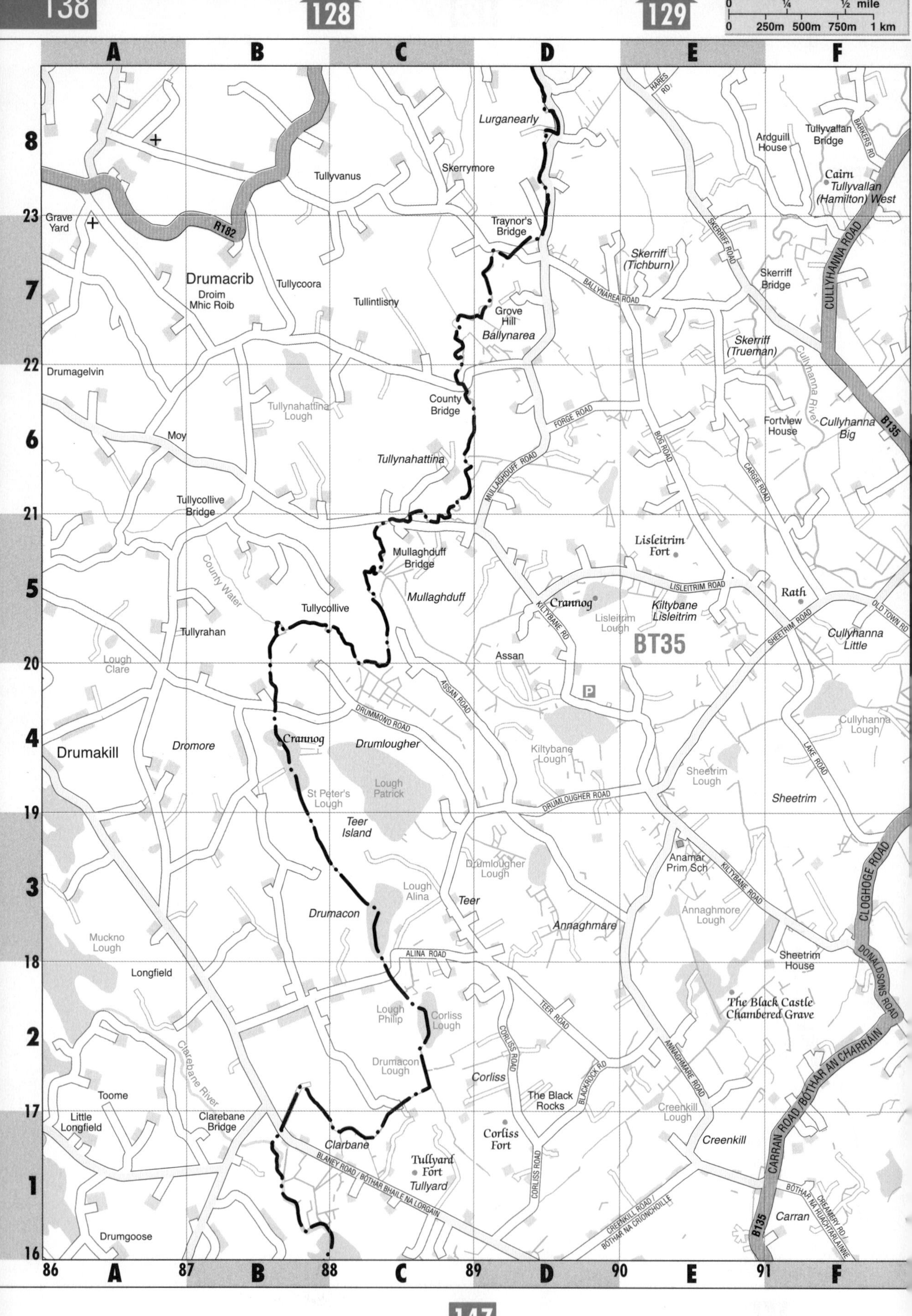
Scale: 1¾ inches to 1 mile
0 ¼ ½ mile
0 250m 500m 750m 1 km
A B C D E F
Lurganearly
Tullyvanus
Skerrymore
Ardguill House
Tullyvallan Bridge
BARKERS RD
HARES RD
Cairn
Tullyvallan (Hamilton) West
Grave Yard
R182
Traynor's Bridge
Drumacrib
Droim Mhic Roib
Tullycoora
Tullintlisny
Skerriff (Tichburn)
SKERRIFF ROAD
BALLYNAREA ROAD
Skerriff Bridge
CULLYHANNA ROAD
Grove Hill
Ballynarea
Skerriff (Trueman)
Drumagelvin
Tullynahattina Lough
County Bridge
FORGE ROAD
BOG ROAD
Cullyhanna River
Fortview House
Cullyhanna Big
B135
Moy
Tullynahattina
MULLAGHDUFF ROAD
CARGIE ROAD
Tullycollive Bridge
County Water
Mullaghduff Bridge
Lisleitrim Fort
LISLEITRIM ROAD
Rath
OLD TOWN RD
Mullaghduff
Tullycollive
Crannog
KILTYBANE RD
Lisleitrim Lough
Kiltybane Lisleitrim
SHEETRIM ROAD
Cullyhanna Little
Tullyrahan
BT35
Lough Clare
Assan
ASSAN ROAD
DRUMMOND ROAD
Cullyhanna Lough
Drumakill
Dromore
Crannog
Drumlougher
Kiltybane Lough
Sheetrim Lough
LAKE ROAD
St Peter's Lough
Lough Patrick
DRUMLOUGHER ROAD
Sheetrim
Teer Island
Anamar Prim Sch
Drumlougher Lough
KILTYBANE ROAD
CLOGHOGE ROAD
Lough Alina
Teer
Muckno Lough
Drumacon
Annaghmare
Annaghmore Lough
ALINA ROAD
Sheetrim House
Longfield
DONALDSONS ROAD
Lough Philip
Corliss Lough
TEER ROAD
The Black Castle Chambered Grave
Clarebane River
CORLISS ROAD
ANNAGHMARE ROAD
Drumacon Lough
CARRAN ROAD/BÓTHAR AN CHARRÁIN
Corliss
BLACKROCK RD
Toome
The Black Rocks
Creenkill Lough
Little Longfield
Clarebane Bridge
Corliss Fort
Creenkill
Clarbane
Tullyard Fort
BLANEY ROAD / BÓTHAR BHAILE NA LORGAIN
Tullyard
CORLISS ROAD
CREENKILL ROAD / BÓTHAR NA CRÍONCHOILLE
BÓTHAR NA HUACHTARLAINNE
CREAMERY RD /
Carran
B135
Drumgoose
86 87 88 89 90 91
8 23 7 22 6 21 5 20 4 19 3 18 2 17 1 16

147

129 140 130

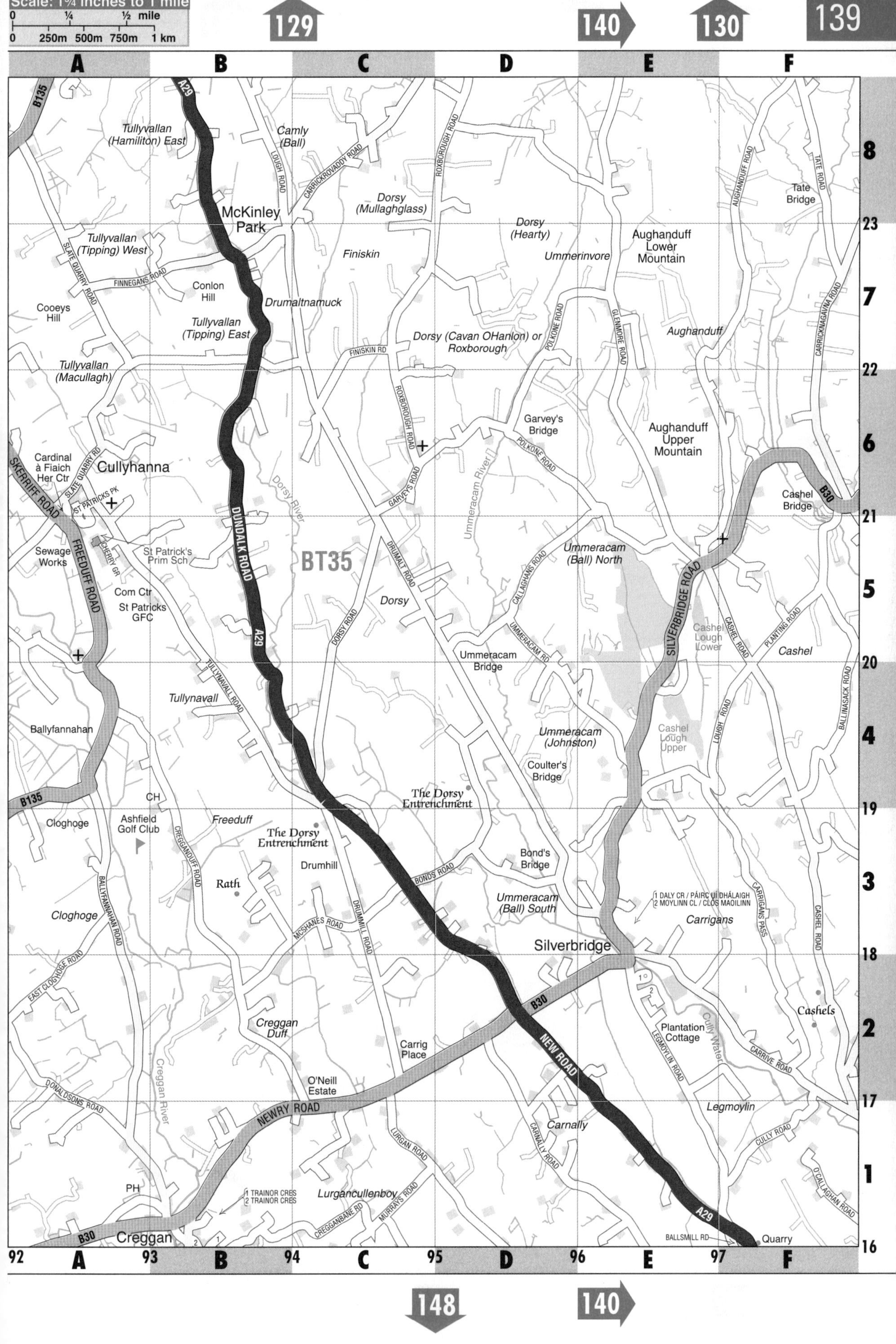

Scale: 1¾ inches to 1 mile
A B C D E F
Tullyvallan (Hamilton) East
Camly (Ball)
McKinley Park
Dorsy (Mullaghglass)
Dorsy (Hearty)
Ummerinvore
Aughanduff Lower Mountain
Tate Bridge
Tullyvallan (Tipping) West
Finiskin
Conlon Hill
Cooeys Hill
Drumaltnamuck
Tullyvallan (Tipping) East
Dorsy (Cavan OHanlon) or Roxborough
Aughanduff
Tullyvallan (Macullagh)
Garvey's Bridge
Aughanduff Upper Mountain
Cardinal à Fiaich Her Ctr
Cullyhanna
Cashel Bridge
BT35
Sewage Works
St Patrick's Prim Sch
Ummeracam (Ball) North
Com Ctr
St Patricks GFC
Dorsy
Cashel Lough Lower
Cashel
Ummeracam Bridge
Tullynavall
Ballyfannahan
Ummeracam (Johnston)
Cashel Lough Upper
Coulter's Bridge
The Dorsy Entrenchment
Cloghoge
Ashfield Golf Club
Freeduff
Drumhill
Bond's Bridge
Rath
Ummeracam (Ball) South
Carrigans
Silverbridge
Plantation Cottage
Cashels
Creggan Duff
Carrig Place
O'Neill Estate
Legmoylin
Carnally
Lurgancullenboy
Creggan
Quarry
PH
CH
1 DALY CR / PÁIRC UÍ DHÁLAIGH
2 MOYLINN CL / CLÓS MAOILINN
1 TRAINOR CRES
2 TRAINOR CRES

Scale: 1¾ inches to 1 mile

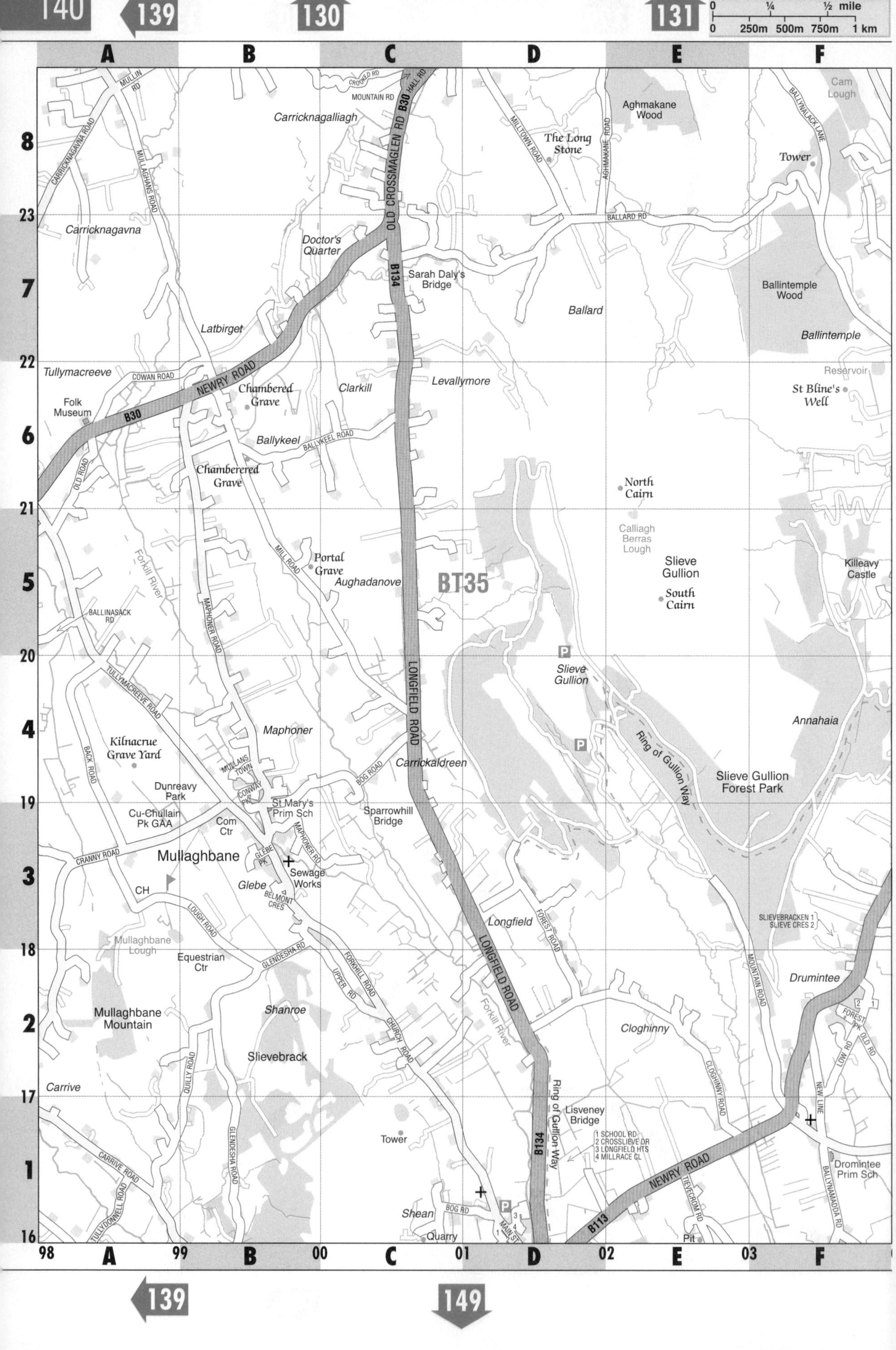

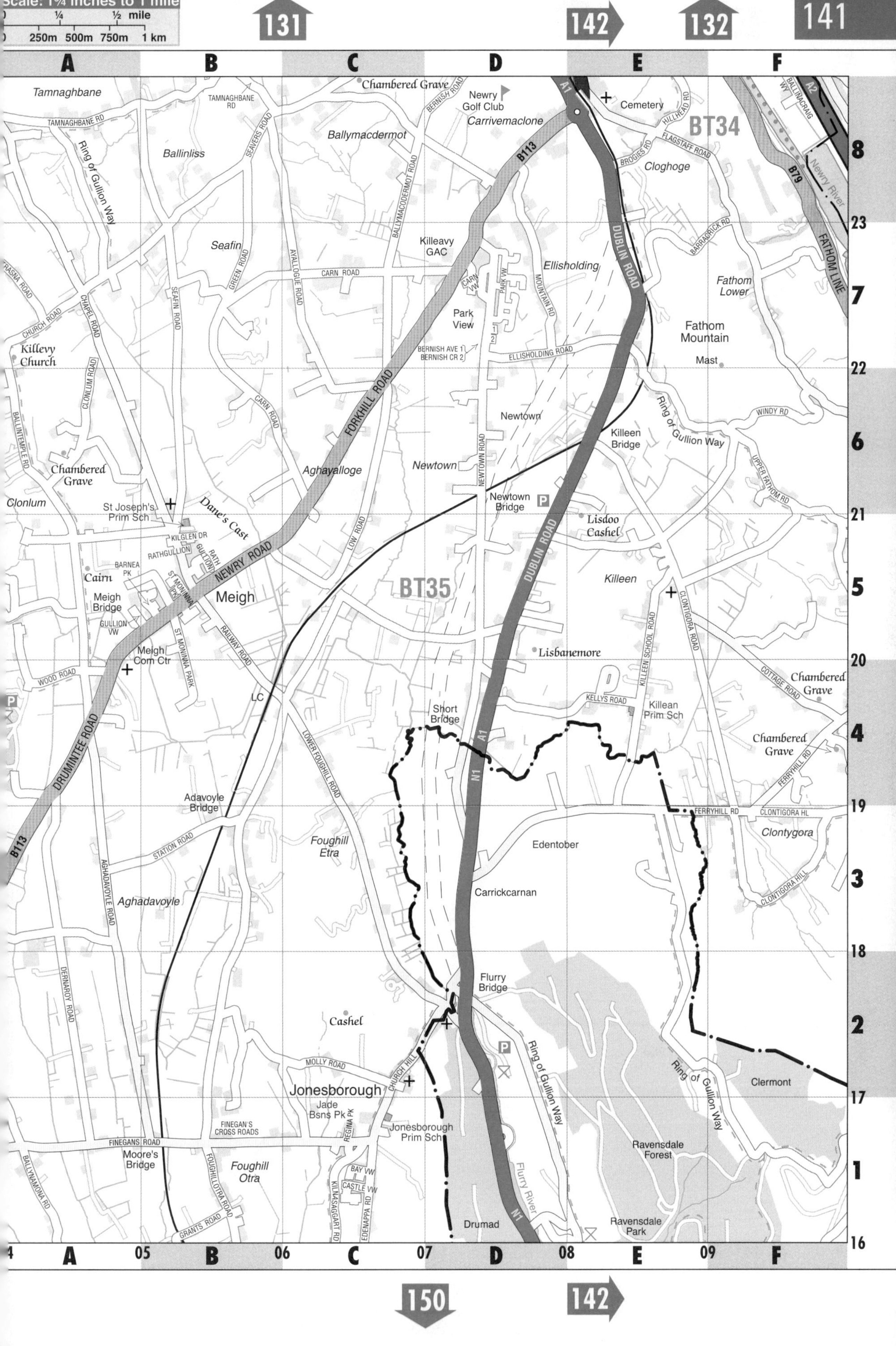
Scale: 1¾ inches to 1 mile
¼ ½ mile
250m 500m 750m 1 km
131
142
132
Tamnaghbane
TAMNAGHBANE RD
Ring of Gullion Way
Ballinliss
Seafin
Chambered Grave
Newry Golf Club
Carrivemaclone
Ballymacdermot
Cemetery
BT34
Cloghoge
Killeavy GAC
Ellisholding
Fathom Lower
Park View
Fathom Mountain
Mast
Killevy Church
CARN ROAD
FORKHILL ROAD
ELLISHOLDING ROAD
Newtown
Killeen Bridge
Aghayalloge
Chambered Grave
Clonlum
St Joseph's Prim Sch
Dane's Cast
Newtown Bridge
Lisdoo Cashel
Cairn
Meigh Bridge
Meigh
NEWRY ROAD
BT35
Killeen
Meigh Com Ctr
Lisbanemore
Chambered Grave
Killean Prim Sch
Short Bridge
DUBLIN ROAD
Chambered Grave
Adavoyle Bridge
DRUMINTEE ROAD
Foughill Etra
Edentober
Clontygora
Aghadavoyle
Carrickcarnan
Flurry Bridge
Cashel
Ring of Gullion Way
Jonesborough
Jade Bsns Pk
Clermont
Jonesborough Prim Sch
Moore's Bridge
Foughill Otra
Ravensdale Forest
Flurry River
Drumad
Ravensdale Park
150
142

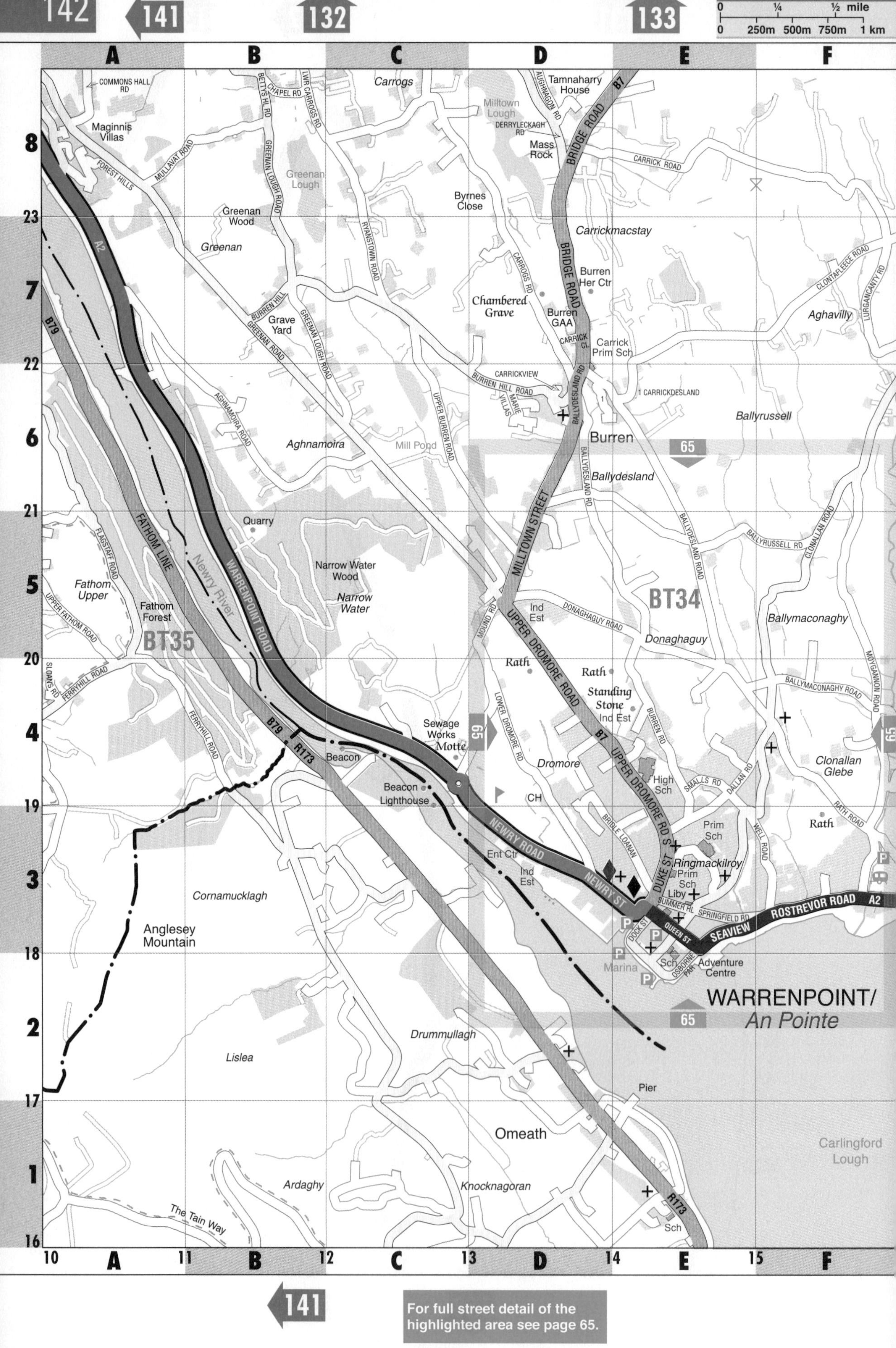

141
For full street detail of the highlighted area see page 65.

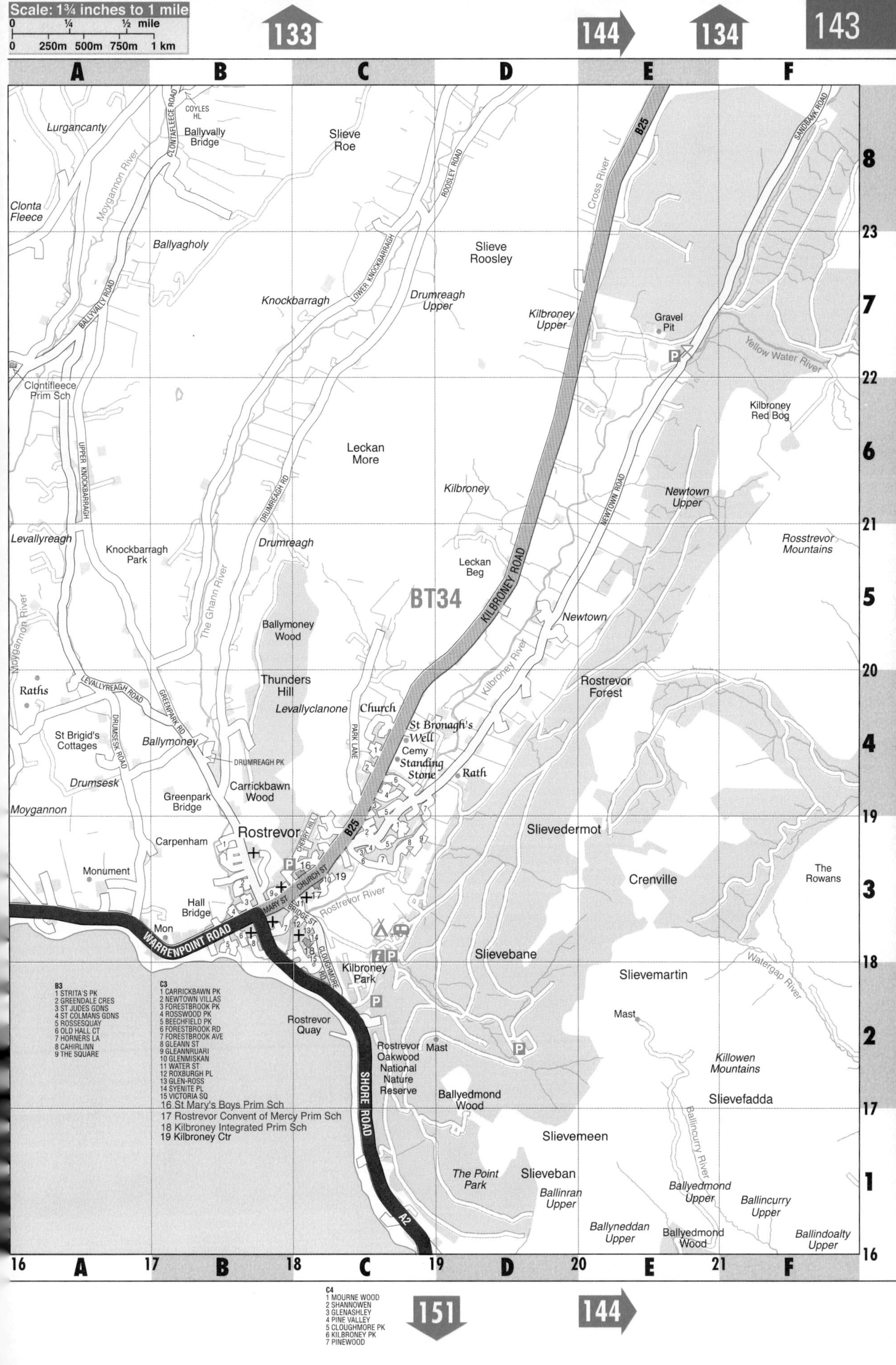
Scale: 1¾ inches to 1 mile
0 ¼ ½ mile
0 250m 500m 750m 1 km
133
144
134
Lurgancanty
Ballyvally Bridge
COYLES HL
CLONTAFLEECE ROAD
Slieve Roe
ROOSLEY ROAD
B25
SANDBANK ROAD
Moygannon River
Clonta Fleece
Cross River
Ballyagholy
Slieve Roosley
LOWER KNOCKBARRAGH
Knockbarragh
Drumreagh Upper
Kilbroney Upper
Gravel Pit
BALLYVALLY ROAD
Yellow Water River
Clontifleece Prim Sch
Kilbroney Red Bog
Leckan More
UPPER KNOCKBARRAGH
Kilbroney
Newtown Upper
NEWTOWN ROAD
DRUMREAGH RD
Levallyreagh
Knockbarragh Park
Drumreagh
Rosstrevor Mountains
Leckan Beg
BT34
KILBRONEY ROAD
The Ghann River
Ballymoney Wood
Newtown
Thunders Hill
Kilbroney River
Raths
LEVALLYREAGH ROAD
Levallyclanone
Church
Rostrevor Forest
GREENPARK RD
St Bronagh's Well
St Brigid's Cottages
DRUMSESK ROAD
Ballymoney
PARK LANE
Cemy
DRUMREAGH PK
Standing Stone
Rath
Drumsesk
Carrickbawn Wood
Greenpark Bridge
Moygannon
Rostrevor
CHERRY HILL
Slievedermot
Carpenham
Monument
CHURCH ST
Crenville
The Rowans
Hall Bridge
MARY ST
Rostrevor River
BRIDGE ST
Mon
WARRENPOINT ROAD
Slievebane
Kilbroney Park
CLOUGHMORE RD
Slievemartin
Watergap River
B3
1 STRITA'S PK
2 GREENDALE CRES
3 ST JUDES GDNS
4 ST COLMANS GDNS
5 ROSSESQUAY
6 OLD HALL CT
7 HORNERS LA
8 CAHIRLINN
9 THE SQUARE
C3
1 CARRICKBAWN PK
2 NEWTOWN VILLAS
3 FORESTBROOK PK
4 ROSSWOOD PK
5 BEECHFIELD PK
6 FORESTBROOK RD
7 FORESTBROOK AVE
8 GLEANN ST
9 GLEANNRUARI
10 GLENMISKAN
11 WATER ST
12 ROXBURGH PL
13 GLEN-ROSS
14 SYENITE PL
15 VICTORIA SQ
16 St Mary's Boys Prim Sch
17 Rostrevor Convent of Mercy Prim Sch
18 Kilbroney Integrated Prim Sch
19 Kilbroney Ctr
Rostrevor Quay
Mast
Rostrevor Oakwood National Nature Reserve
Mast
Killowen Mountains
SHORE ROAD
Ballyedmond Wood
Slievefadda
Slievemeen
Ballincurry River
The Point Park
Slieveban
Ballinran Upper
Ballyedmond Upper
Ballincurry Upper
A2
Ballyneddan Upper
Ballyedmond Wood
Ballindoalty Upper
A B C D E F
8 7 6 5 4 3 2 1
23 22 21 20 19 18 17 16
16 17 18 19 20 21
C4
1 MOURNE WOOD
2 SHANNOWEN
3 GLENASHLEY
4 PINE VALLEY
5 CLOUGHMORE PK
6 KILBRONEY PK
7 PINEWOOD
151
144

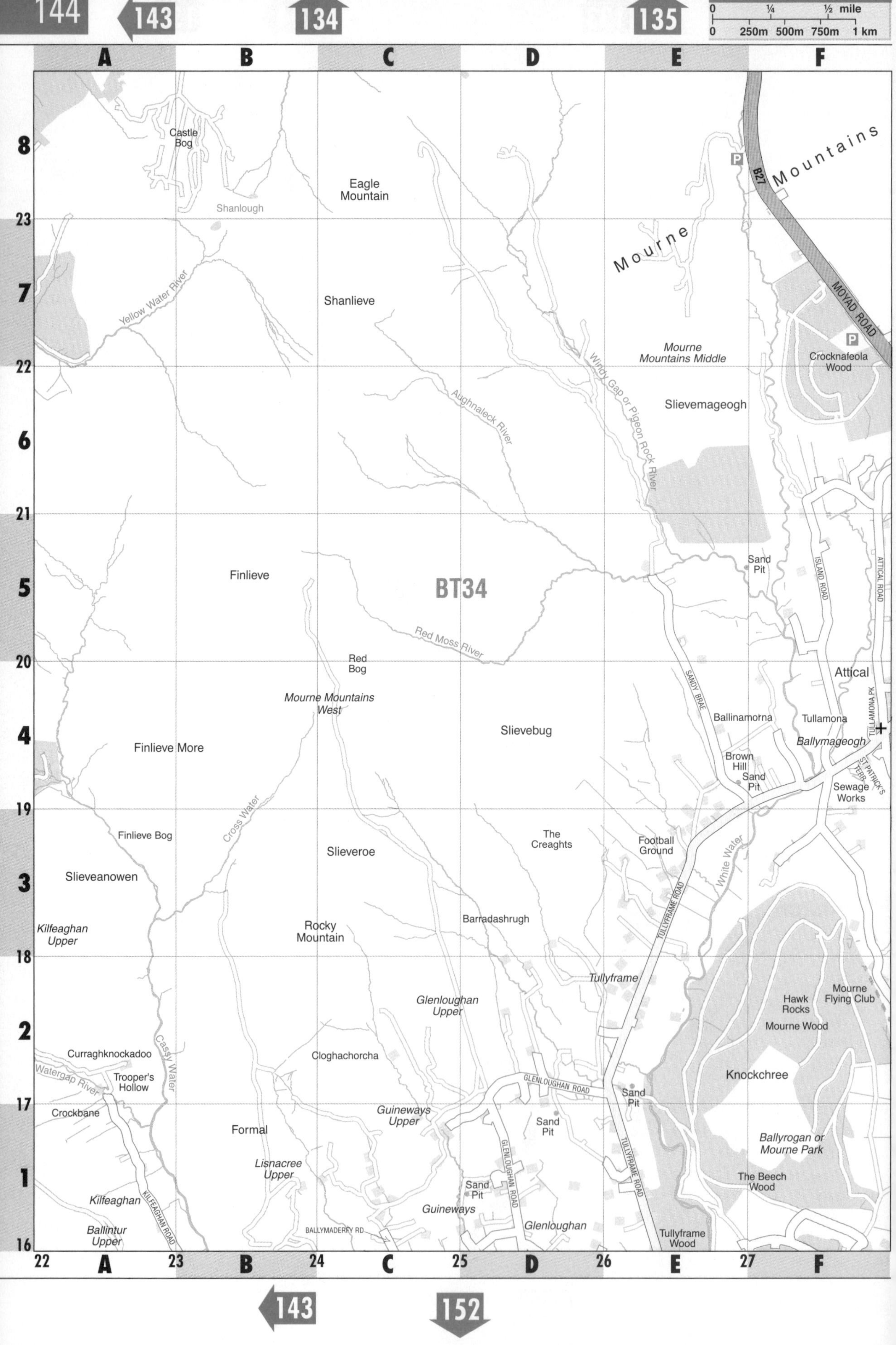
143
134
135
Scale: 1¾ inches to 1 mile
0 ¼ ½ mile
0 250m 500m 750m 1 km
A B C D E F
Castle Bog
Eagle Mountain
Shanlough
Mourne Mountains
B27
Yellow Water River
Shanlieve
MOYAD ROAD
Mourne Mountains Middle
Crocknafeola Wood
Windy Gap or Pigeon Rock River
Aughnaleck River
Slievemageogh
Finlieve
BT34
Sand Pit
ISLAND ROAD
ATTICAL ROAD
Red Moss River
Red Bog
Attical
SANDY BRAE
TULLAMONA PK
Mourne Mountains West
Ballinamorna
Tullamona
Slievebug
Ballymageogh
Finlieve More
Brown Hill
ST PATRICK'S TERR
Sewage Works
Cross Water
Finlieve Bog
The Creaghts
Football Ground
White Water
Slieveroe
Slieveanowen
TULLYFRAME ROAD
Barradashrugh
Kilfeaghan Upper
Rocky Mountain
Tullyframe
Hawk Rocks
Mourne Flying Club
Glenloughan Upper
Mourne Wood
Curraghknockadoo
Cassy Water
Cloghachorcha
Knockchree
Watergap River
Trooper's Hollow
GLENLOUGHAN ROAD
Guineways Upper
Crockbane
Formal
GLENLOUGHAN ROAD
Ballyrogan or Mourne Park
Lisnacree Upper
The Beech Wood
Kilfeaghan
KILFEAGHAN ROAD
Guineways
Glenloughan
Ballintur Upper
BALLYMADERFY RD
Tullyframe Wood
8 23 7 22 6 21 5 20 4 19 3 18 2 17 1 16
22 23 24 25 26 27
143
152

135 146 136

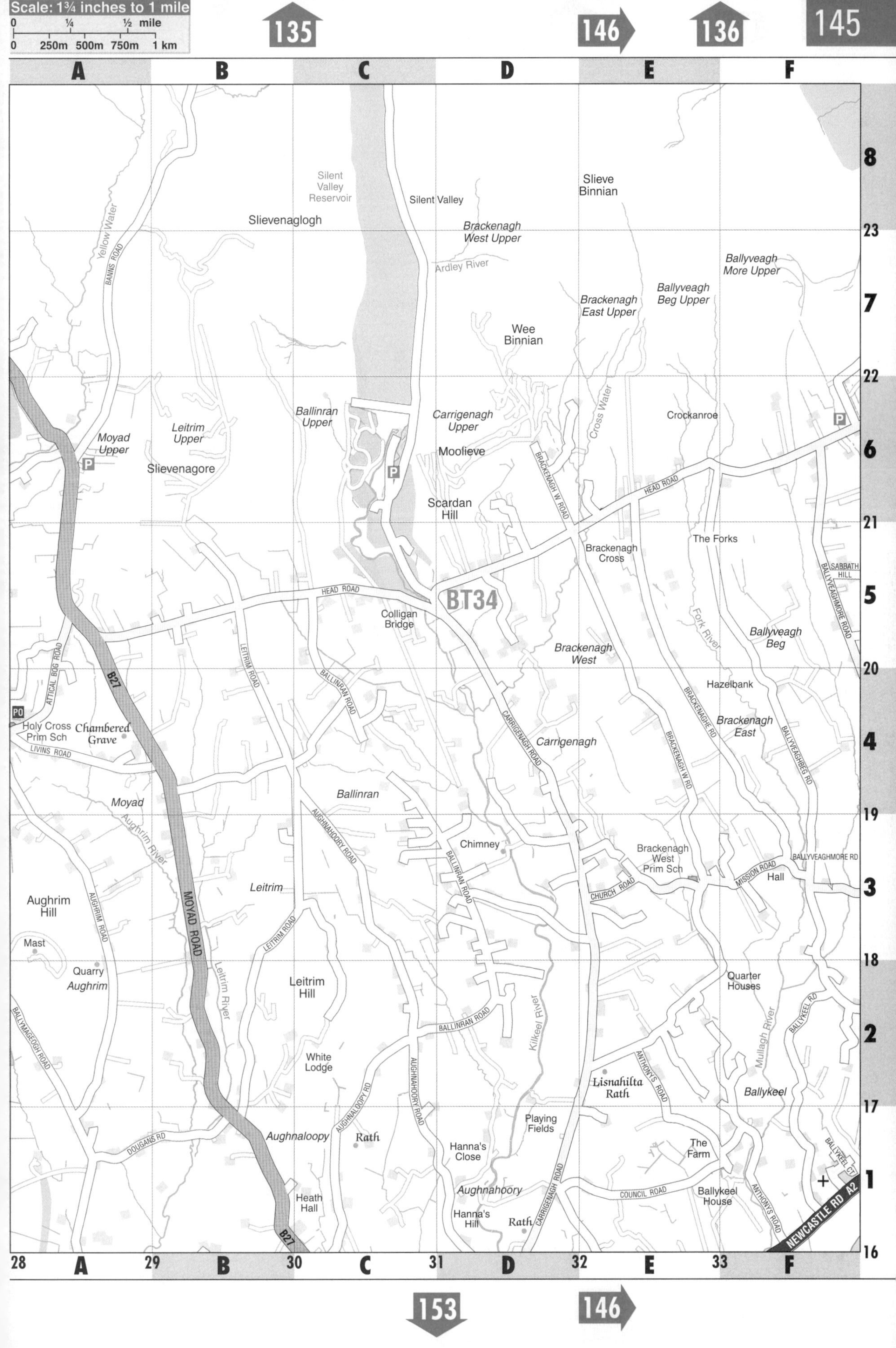
Scale: 1¾ inches to 1 mile
0 ¼ ½ mile
0 250m 500m 750m 1 km
A B C D E F
8 23 7 22 6 21 5 20 4 19 3 18 2 17 1 16
28 29 30 31 32 33
Silent Valley Reservoir
Silent Valley
Slievenaglogh
Slieve Binnian
Brackenagh West Upper
Ardley River
Ballyveagh More Upper
Ballyveagh Beg Upper
Brackenagh East Upper
Wee Binnian
Yellow Water
BANNS ROAD
Ballinran Upper
Carrigenagh Upper
Cross Water
Crockanroe
Moyad Upper
Leitrim Upper
Slievenagore
Moolieve
Scardan Hill
BRACKENAGH W ROAD
HEAD ROAD
Brackenagh Cross
The Forks
SABBATH HILL
BALLYVEAGHMORE ROAD
BT34
Colligan Bridge
Fork River
Ballyveagh Beg
Brackenagh West
ATTICAL BOG ROAD
B27
LEITRIM ROAD
BALLINRAN ROAD
Hazelbank
BRACKENAGHE RD
Brackenagh East
PO
Holy Cross Prim Sch
Chambered Grave
LIVINS ROAD
CARRIGENAGH ROAD
Carrigenagh
BRACKENAGH W RD
BALLYVEAGHBEG RD
Ballinran
Moyad
Aughrim River
AUGHNAHOORY ROAD
Chimney
Brackenagh West Prim Sch
BALLYVEAGHMORE RD
MISSION ROAD
Hall
CHURCH ROAD
Leitrim
Aughrim Hill
AUGHRIM ROAD
MOYAD ROAD
Mast
Quarry
Aughrim
LEITRIM ROAD
Leitrim Hill
Leitrim River
Quarter Houses
Kilkeel River
BALLYKEEL RD
Mullagh River
BALLYMAGEOGH ROAD
BALLINRAN ROAD
White Lodge
ANTHONYS ROAD
Lisnahilta Rath
Ballykeel
DOUGANS RD
AUGHNALOOPY RD
AUGHNAHOORY ROAD
Playing Fields
Aughnaloopy
Rath
Hanna's Close
The Farm
BALLYKEEL CT
Aughnahoory
COUNCIL ROAD
Ballykeel House
ANTHONYS ROAD
Heath Hall
Hanna's Hill
Rath
CARRIGENAGH ROAD
NEWCASTLE RD A2
P

145
136
137

Scale: 1¾ inches to 1 mile

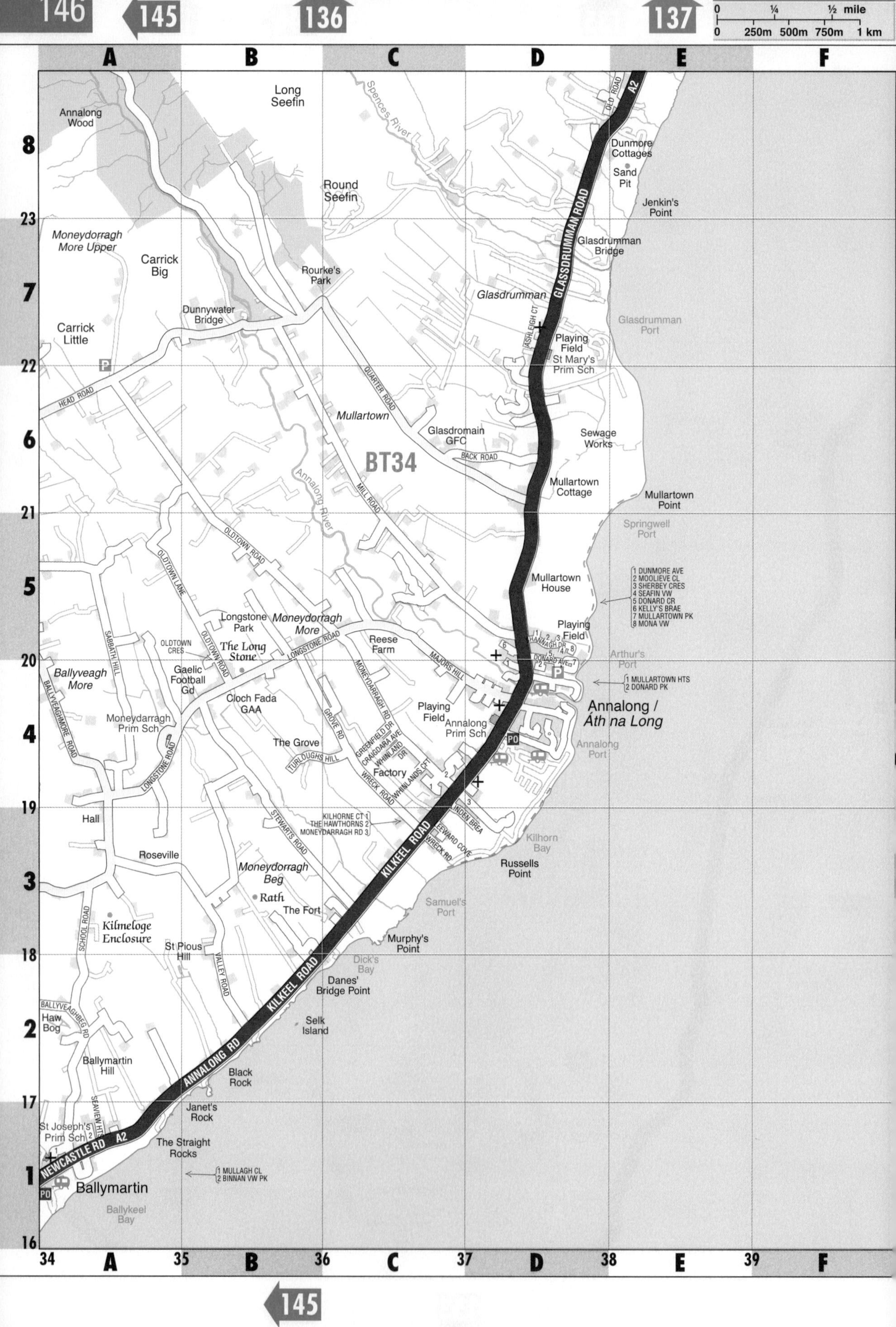

145

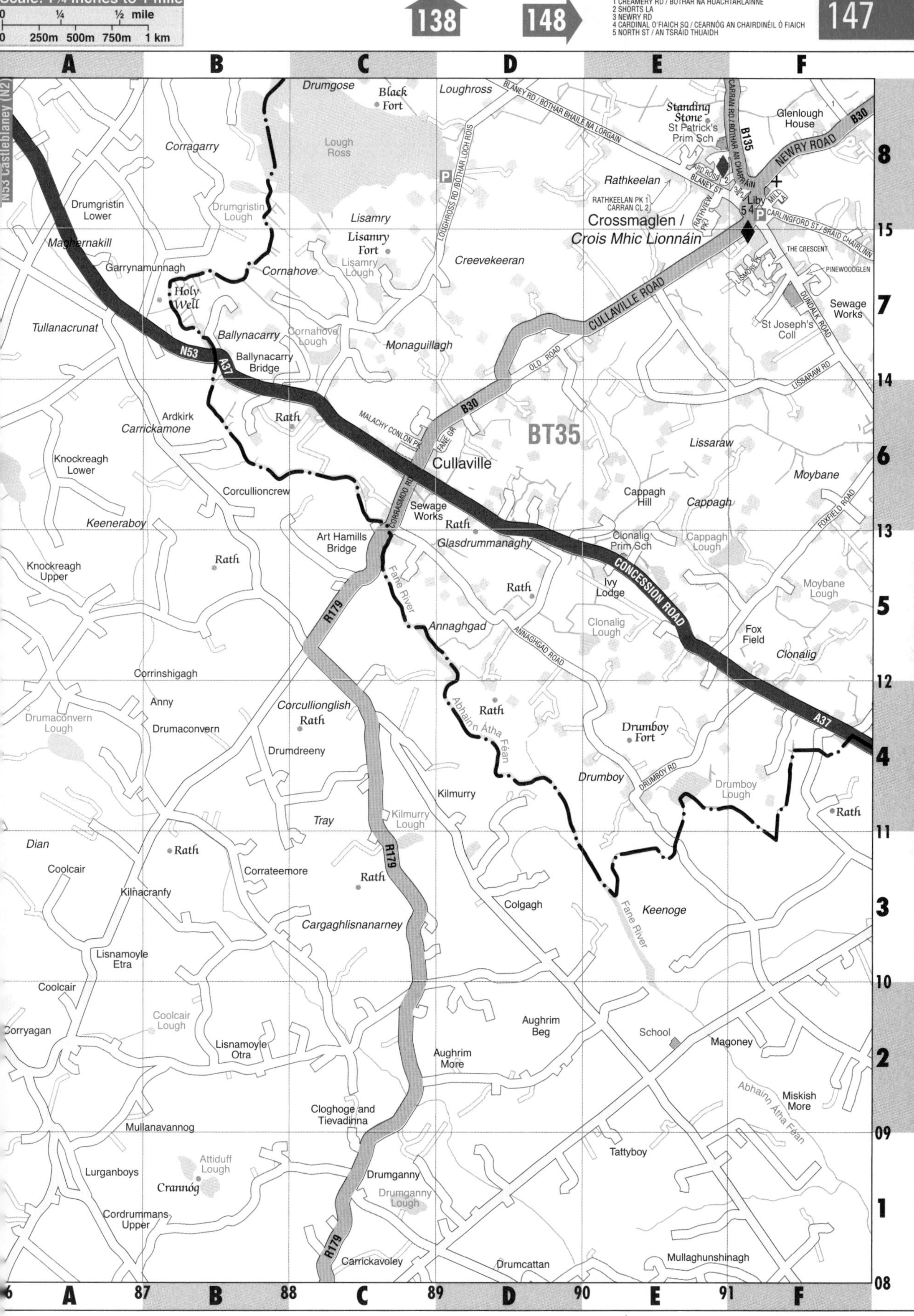
Scale: 1¾ inches to 1 mile
0
¼
½ mile
0
250m
500m
750m
1 km
138
148
F8
1 CREAMERY RD / BÓTHAR NA HUACHTARLAINNE
2 SHORTS LA
3 NEWRY RD
4 CARDINAL O'FIAICH SQ / CEARNÓG AN CHAIRDINÉIL Ó FIAICH
5 NORTH ST / AN TSRÁID THUAIDH
A
B
C
D
E
F
N53 Castleblaney (N2)
Drumgose
Black Fort
Loughross
BLANEY RD / BÓTHAR BHAILE NA LORGAN
Standing Stone
St Patrick's Prim Sch
CARRAN RD / BÓTHAR AN CHARRÁIN
B135
Glenlough House
NEWRY ROAD
B30
8
Corragarry
Lough Ross
LOUGHROSS RD / BÓTHAR LOCH ROIS
Rathkeelan
ARD ROSS
BLANEY ST
RATHKEELAN PK
CARRAN CL
RATHVIEW PK
Liby
MILL LA
Crossmaglen /
Crois Mhic Lionnáin
CARLINGFORD ST / SRÁID CHAIRLINN
THE CRESCENT
PINEWOODGLEN
LISMORE PK
Drumgristin Lower
Drumgristin Lough
Lisamry
Lisamry Fort
Lisamry Lough
15
Maghernakill
Garrynamunnagh
Cornahove
Creevekeeran
CULLAVILLE ROAD
Holy Well
Sewage Works
St Joseph's Coll
DUNDALK ROAD
7
Tullanacrunat
Ballynacarry
Cornahove Lough
Monaguillagh
N53
A37
Ballynacarry Bridge
OLD ROAD
LISSARAW RD
14
Ardkirk
Carrickamone
Rath
MALACHY CONLON PK
FANE GR
B30
BT35
Lissaraw
Knockreagh Lower
Cullaville
6
Moybane
Corcullioncrew
CORRASMOD RD
Cappagh Hill
Cappagh
Sewage Works
Rath
FOXFIELD ROAD
Keeneraboy
Art Hamills Bridge
Glasdrummanaghy
Clonalig Prim Sch
Cappagh Lough
13
Knockreagh Upper
Rath
Fane River
Rath
CONCESSION ROAD
Ivy Lodge
Moybane Lough
5
R179
Annaghgad
ANNAGHGAD ROAD
Clonalig Lough
Fox Field
Clonalig
Corrinshigagh
12
Anny
Corcullionglish
Abhainn Átha Féan
Rath
Drumaconvern Lough
Drumaconvern
Rath
Drumboy Fort
A37
Drumdreeny
4
Drumboy
DRUMBOY RD
Drumboy Lough
Kilmurry
Rath
Tray
Kilmurry Lough
11
Dian
Rath
R179
Coolcair
Corrateemore
Rath
Kilnacranfy
Colgagh
3
Keenoge
Fane River
Cargaghlisnanarney
Lisnamoyle Etra
10
Coolcair
Coolcair Lough
Aughrim Beg
School
Corryagan
Lisnamoyle Otra
Magoney
Aughrim More
2
Abhainn Átha Féan
Miskish More
Cloghoge and Tievadinna
Mullanavannog
09
Tattyboy
Attiduff Lough
Lurganboys
Drumganny
Crannóg
Drumganny Lough
1
Cordrummans Upper
R179
Carrickavoley
Drumcattan
Mullaghunshinagh
08
A
87
B
88
C
89
D
90
E
91
F

B8
1 TRAINOR CRES
2 URCHILL
3 CREGGANBANE RD

147
139

Scale: 1¾ inches to 1 mile
0 ¼ ½ mile
0 250m 500m 750m 1 km

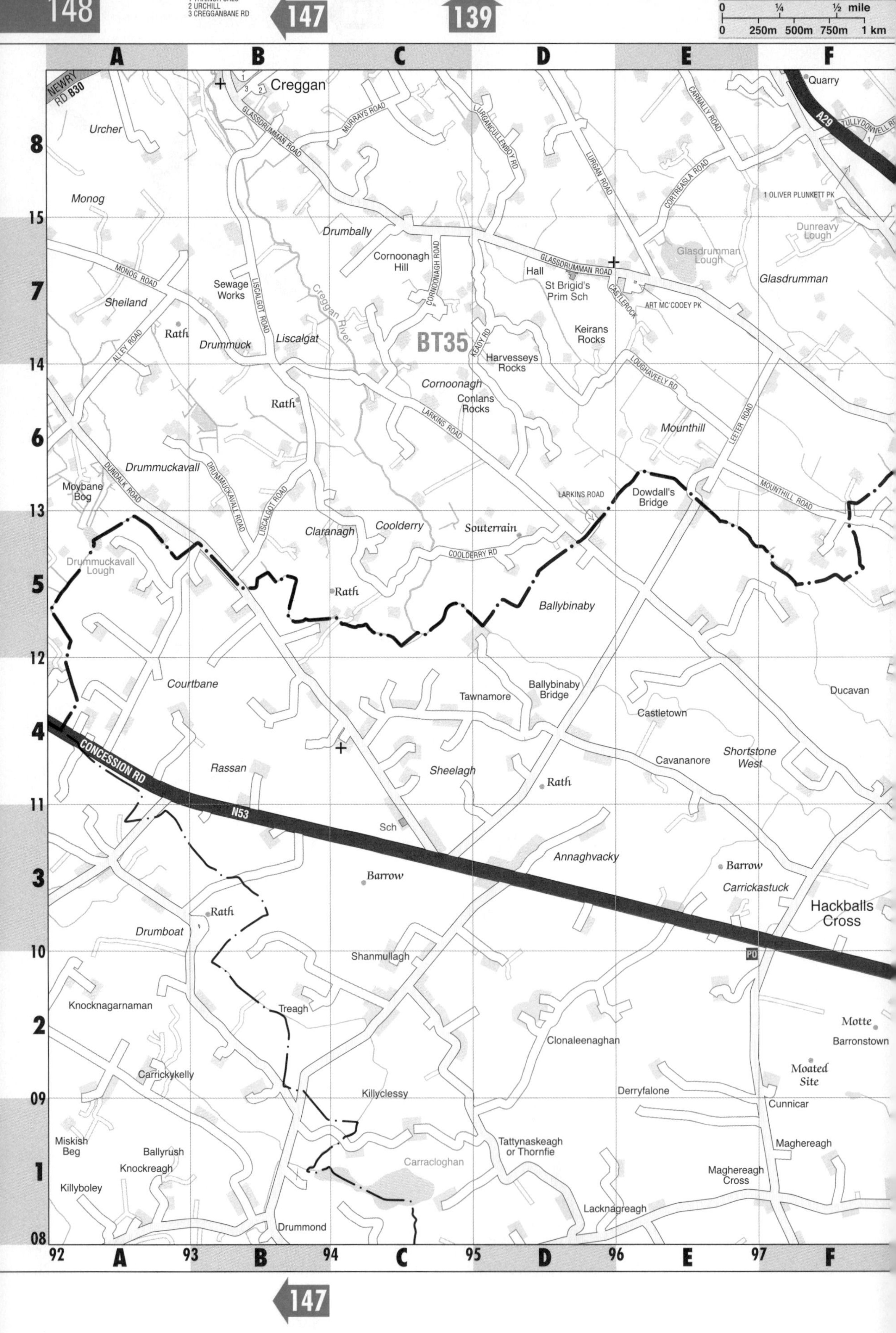

147

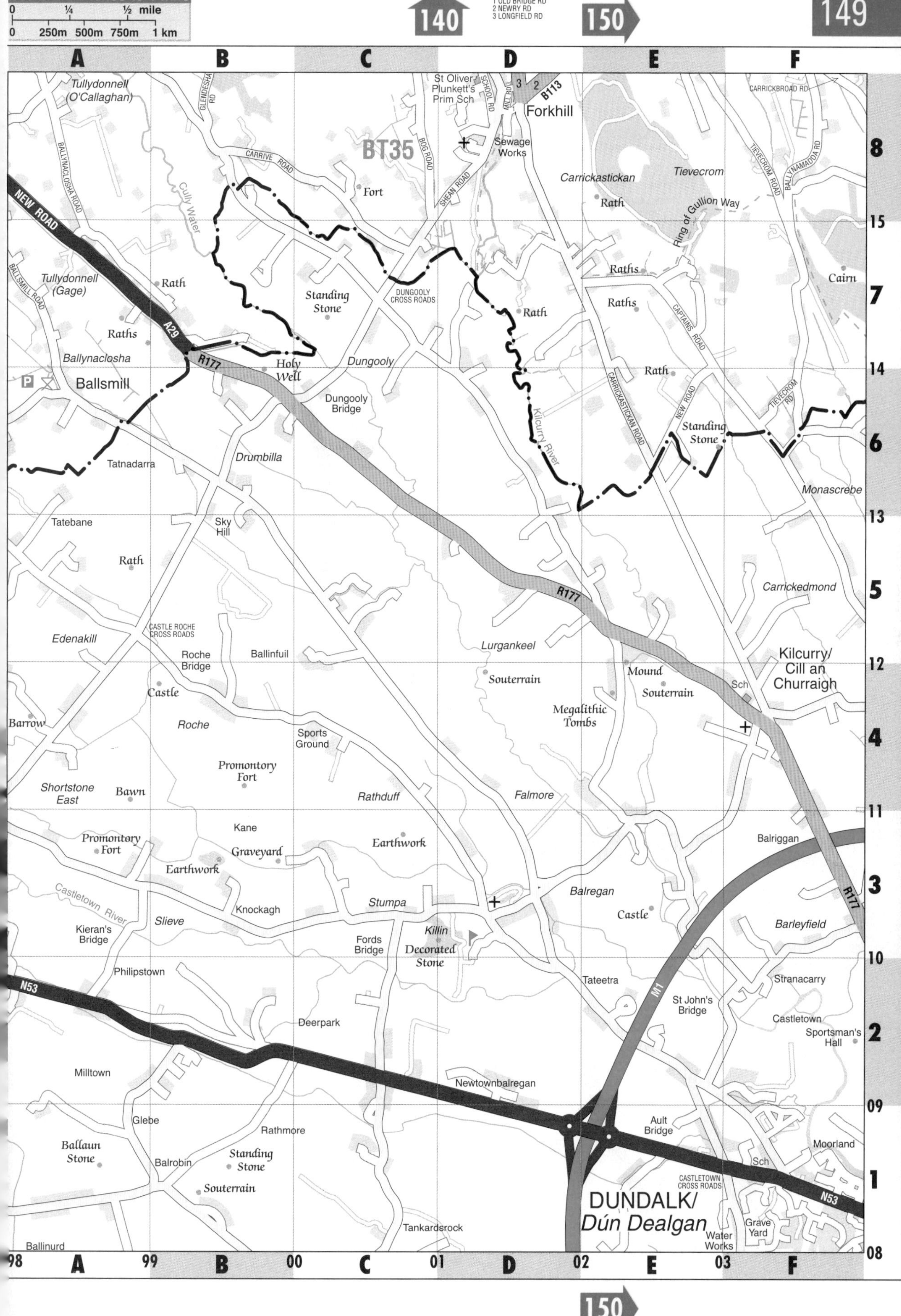
Scale: 1¾ inches to 1 mile
0 ¼ ½ mile
0 250m 500m 750m 1 km
140
D8
1 OLD BRIDGE RD
2 NEWRY RD
3 LONGFIELD RD
150
A
B
C
D
E
F
Tullydonnell
(O'Callaghan)
GLENDESHA RD
St Oliver Plunkett's Prim Sch
SCHOOL RD
MILL RD
B113
Forkhill
CARRICKBROAD RD
BALLYNACLOSHA ROAD
CARRIVE ROAD
BT35
BOG ROAD
Sewage Works
8
NEW ROAD
Cully Water
Fort
SHEAN ROAD
Carrickastickan
Tievecrom
TIEVECROM ROAD
BALLYNAMADDA RD
Rath
Ring of Gullion Way
15
BALLSMILL ROAD
Tullydonnell
(Gage)
Rath
Standing Stone
DUNGOOLY CROSS ROADS
Raths
Raths
CAPTAINS ROAD
Cairn
7
Rath
A29
Raths
Ballynaclosha
R177
Holy Well
Dungooly
Rath
14
Ballsmill
Dungooly Bridge
CARRICKASTICKAN ROAD
NEW ROAD
TIEVECROM RD
Standing Stone
Kilcurry River
6
Tatnadarra
Drumbilla
Monascrebe
Tatebane
Sky Hill
13
Rath
Carrickedmond
R177
5
CASTLE ROCHE CROSS ROADS
Edenakill
Roche Bridge
Ballinfuil
Lurgankeel
Kilcurry/
Cill an
Churraigh
12
Castle
Souterrain
Mound
Sch
Souterrain
Megalithic Tombs
Barrow
Roche
Sports Ground
4
Promontory Fort
Shortstone East
Bawn
Rathduff
Falmore
11
Kane
Balriggan
Promontory Fort
Graveyard
Earthwork
Earthwork
3
Castletown River
Stumpa
Balregan
R177
Slieve
Knockagh
Castle
Kieran's Bridge
Killin
Barleyfield
Fords Bridge
Decorated Stone
10
Philipstown
Tateetra
Stranacarry
N53
M1
St John's Bridge
Castletown
Deerpark
Sportsman's Hall
2
Milltown
Newtownbalregan
09
Glebe
Ault Bridge
Rathmore
Moorland
Ballaun Stone
Standing Stone
Sch
Balrobin
1
CASTLETOWN CROSS ROADS
Souterrain
N53
DUNDALK/
Dún Dealgan
Grave Yard
Tankardsrock
Water Works
Ballinurd
08
98
99
00
01
02
03

149
141

Scale: 1¾ inches to 1 mile
0 ¼ ½ mile
0 250m 500m 750m 1 km

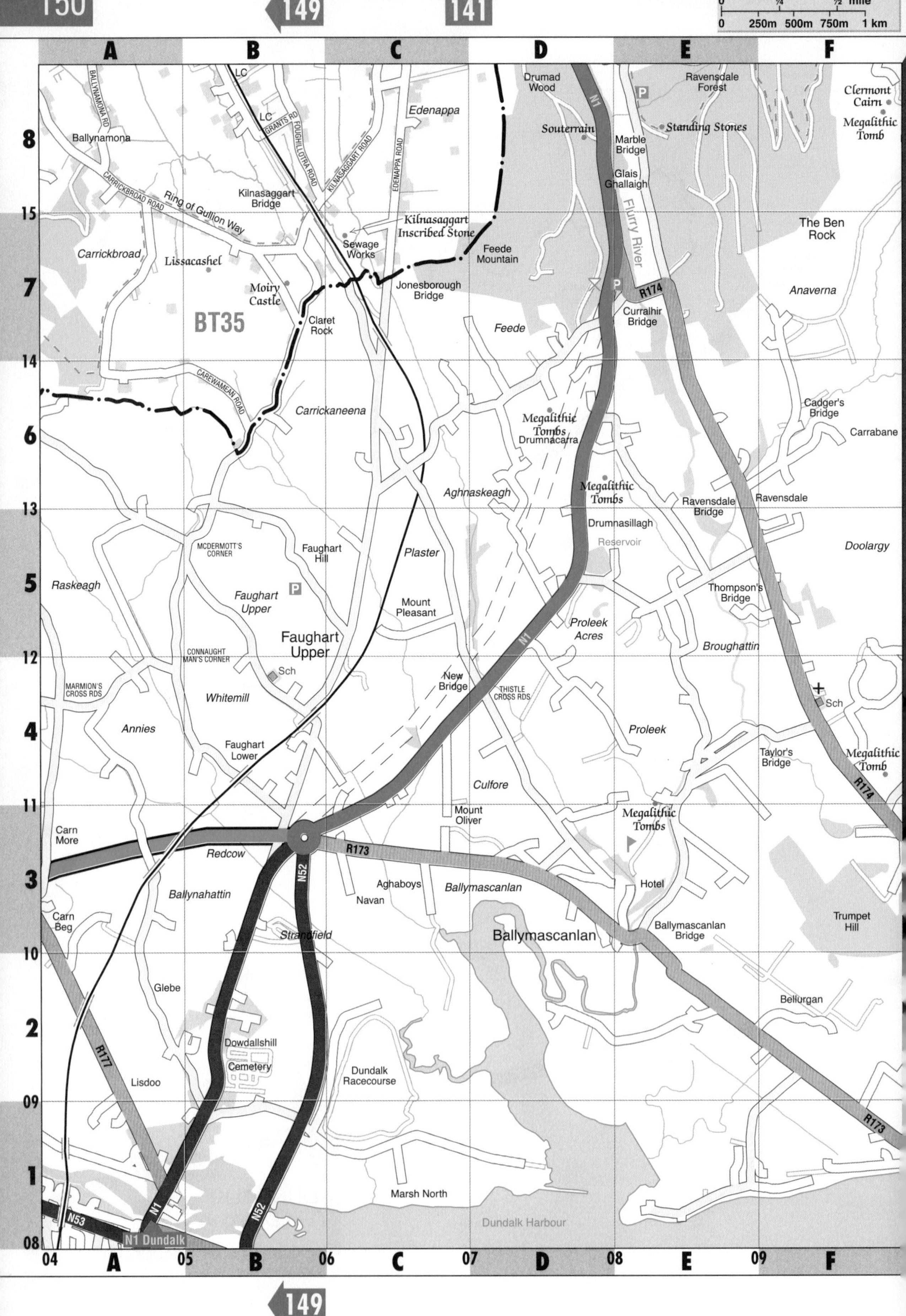

149

Scale: 1¾ inches to 1 mile

143
152

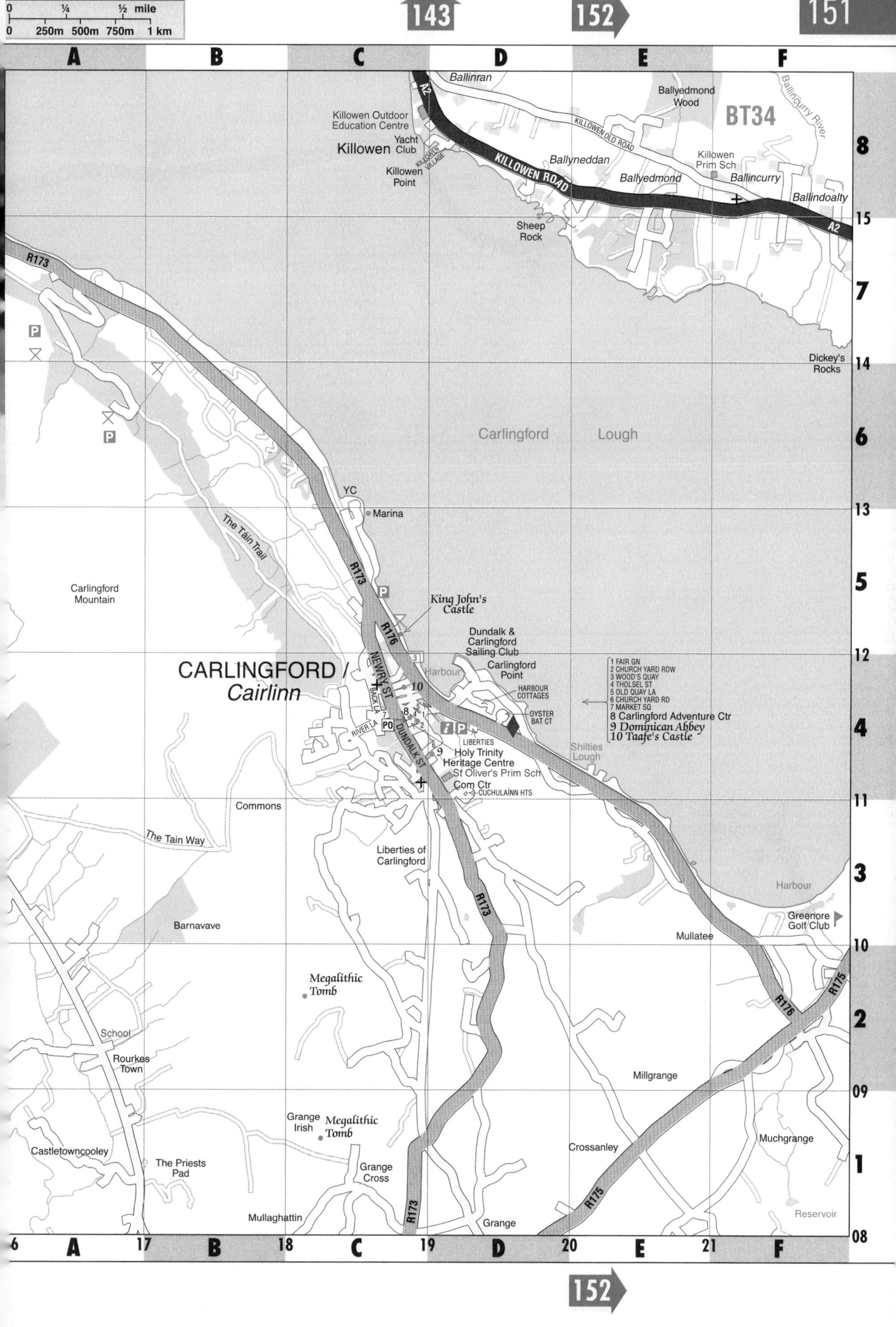

152

151
144
Scale: 1¾ inches to 1 mile

Scale: 1¾ inches to 1 mile

0 ¼ ½ mile

0 250m 500m 750m 1 km

B7
1 SPRINGDALE CR
2 HILLSIDE CL
3 DUNNAMAN PK
4 MOSSVALE PK
5 THE BRAMBLES
6 SPRINGDALE CT

C7
1 CHURCH MDW
2 ROONEY PK
3 THE COVE
4 MEETING HO LA
5 MANOR CT
6 THE ROYAL MS
7 FINLIEVE PL
8 IRVINGTON PK
9 BRIDGE ST
10 THE SQUARE
11 DONARD PL
12 BAYVIEW PK
13 RANDALL HTS
14 SEAVIEW AVE
15 CHURCHVIEW CL
16 SLIEVESHAN PK
17 SPELGA PL
18 MELROSE PK
19 IRVINGTON CL
20 St Colman's Prim Sch
21 Kilkeel Inst of FE
22 Kilkeel Prim Sch

145

E8
1 HAWOOD CR
2 HAWOOD WY
3 SHEEMORE CR
4 COUNCIL RD
5 BLACKFORD MS

D8
1 KILMOREY CR
2 BIGNIAN AVE
3 MOURNEVIEW CL
4 HAZELBANK DR

D7
1 ANCHORAGE CT
2 ANCHORAGE COVE
3 ALEXANDER DR
4 Kilkeel High Sch
5 Nautilus Ctr

C6
1 LANE AT MANSE RD
2 ELEASTAN PK
3 MEADOW LANDS AVE
4 MEADOWLANDS

A B C D E F

8 15 7 14 6 13 5 12 4 11 3 10 2 09 1 08

Drumcro
DRUMCRO ROAD
BALLYMAGEOGH ROAD
AUGHNALOOPY RD
MOYAD RD
MOUNTAIN ROAD
B27
BT34
Aughrim River
A2
MAGOWAN PK
CAHILL PL
Chambered Grave
ROSE VALE
GRANGE MANOR
Mourne District
BENCROM PL
Camphill Community Mourne Grange
MT CARMEL
GROVE HL
Motte
ABBEY PK
FEARON CL
HILLSIDE DR
NEWRY ST
St Louis Gram Sch
Dunnaman
CARN GDNS
L Ctr
GREENCASTLE ST
MUNRO VILLAS
Magheramurphy
Liby
HARBOUR DR
KNOCKCHREE AVE
BALLYARDLE ROAD
BELMONT RD
Ballyardel
SCROGG ROAD
GRAHAMVILLE ESTATE
SHANDON DR
IRVINGTON AVE
NEEDHAM CT
MANSE ROAD
MOURNE ESP
Ben Hill
DERRYOGUE PK
Rath
MCGOLDRICKS VILLAS
KITTYS RD
CORRICK WY
CASEMENT PK
Kilkeel Bay
GREENCASTLE ROAD
DUNNAVAL ROAD
BALLYNAHATTEN RD
Rath
An Riocht GFC
Derryoge
DERRYOGE RD
Dunnaval
Sand Pit Works
Sand Pit
NICHOLSONS ROAD
Derryoge Harbour
Crawfords Point
Ballynahatten
SLATEMILL ROAD
Sand Pit
Nicholsons Point
CROMLECH PK
MILL ROAD
CEDAR HTS
MILLVALE
AUGHNAHOORY RD
Kilkeel River
RIVERSIDE PK
RIVERDALE DR
CARRIGENAGH ROAD
MOURNEVIEW PK
COUNCIL RD
St Columban's Coll
NEWCASTLE ROAD
NEWCASTLE ST
Kilkeel / Cill Chaoil
Sewage Works
ROONEY ROAD
HARBOUR ROAD
Mourne Ind Christian Sch
KILMOREY CT
Mast
Kilkeel Bsns Pk
MOOR ROAD
Sand Pit
Factory
Harbour Master's & Customs House
Kilkeel L Ctr and Swimming Pool
Maghereagh
LEESTONE ROAD
Sewage Works
Mullagh River
WRACK ROAD
PATS ROAD
Ballykeel Bay
Braged Harbour
Sewage Works
Lee Stone Point
Lee Stone Harbour

28 A 29 B 30 C 31 D 32 E 33 F

A3
1 SEVASTAPOL ST / SRÁID SEIBHEÁSTOPOL
2 CLONARD PL / PLÁS CHLUAIN ARD
3 CLONARD HTS / ARDA CHLUAIN ARD
4 CLONARD RI / MALA CHLUAIN ARD
5 CLONARD CRES / CORRÁN CHLUAIN ARD
6 FALLS CT / CÚIRT NA BHFÁL

14

C4
1 ALTON ST / SRÁID LOCH ALTÁIN
2 TYRONE ST / SRÁID THÍR EOGHAIN
3 ARNON ST / SRÁID EARNÁIN
4 KILDARE ST / SRÁID CHILL DARA
5 SHERBROOK TERR
6 SHANKILL TERR

Scale: 7 inches to 1 mile
0 110 yards 220 yards
0 125 m 250 m

14

One-way streets

House numbers
1 59
HIGH ST

14
15

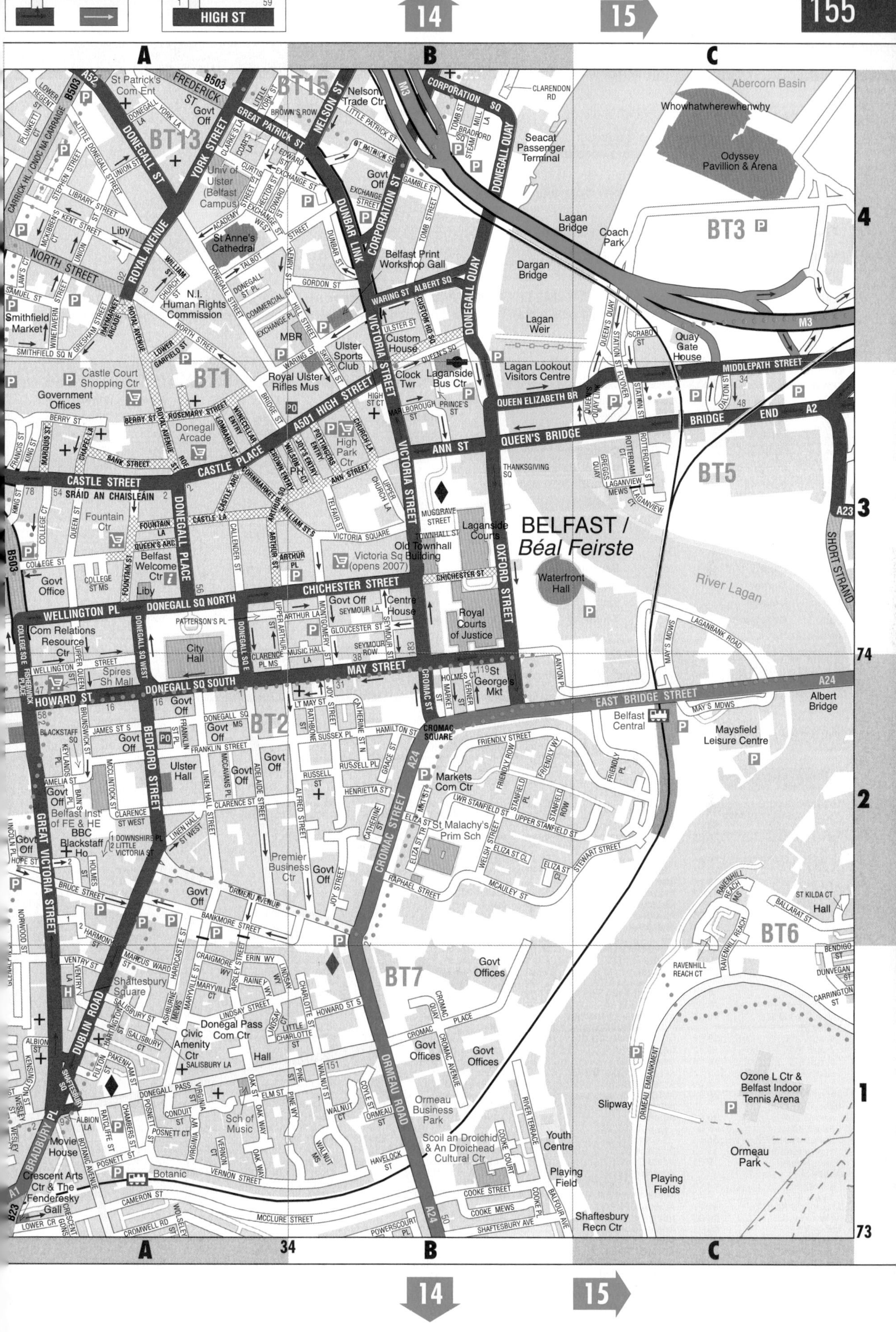

14
15

Index

Place name May be abbreviated on the map

Location number Present when a number indicates the place's position in a crowded area of mapping

Locality, town or village Shown when more than one place has the same name

Postcode district District for the indexed place

Page and grid square Page number and grid reference for the standard mapping

Church La [2] Lisburn BT28.........**26** B1

Cities, towns and villages are listed in CAPITAL LETTERS **Public and commercial buildings** are highlighted in **magenta**
Places of interest are highlighted in **blue** with a star★ **Townlands** are indicated by Ⓣ in the index and *italic* type on the maps

Abbreviations used in the index

Acad	**Academy**	Comm	**Common**	Gd	**Ground**	L	**Leisure**	Prom	**Promenade**
App	**Approach**	Cott	**Cottage**	Gdn	**Garden**	La	**Lane**	Rd	**Road**
Arc	**Arcade**	Cres	**Crescent**	Gn	**Green**	Liby	**Library**	Recn	**Recreation**
Ave	**Avenue**	Cswy	**Causeway**	Gr	**Grove**	Mdw	**Meadow**	Ret	**Retail**
Bglw	**Bungalow**	Ct	**Court**	H	**Hall**	Meml	**Memorial**	Sh	**Shopping**
Bldg	**Building**	Ctr	**Centre**	Ho	**House**	Mkt	**Market**	Sq	**Square**
Bsns, Bus	**Business**	Ctry	**Country**	Hospl	**Hospital**	Mus	**Museum**	St	**Street**
Bvd	**Boulevard**	Cty	**County**	HQ	**Headquarters**	Orch	**Orchard**	Sta	**Station**
Cath	**Cathedral**	Dr	**Drive**	Hts	**Heights**	Pal	**Palace**	Terr	**Terrace**
Cir	**Circus**	Dro	**Drove**	Ind	**Industrial**	Par	**Parade**	TH	**Town Hall**
Cl	**Close**	Ed	**Education**	Inst	**Institute**	Pas	**Passage**	Univ	**University**
Cnr	**Corner**	Emb	**Embankment**	Int	**International**	Pk	**Park**	Wk, Wlk	**Walk**
Coll	**College**	Est	**Estate**	Intc	**Interchange**	Pl	**Place**	Wr	**Water**
Com	**Community**	Ex	**Exhibition**	Junc	**Junction**	Prec	**Precinct**	Yd	**Yard**

Index of towns, villages, townlands, streets, hospitals, industrial estates, railway stations, schools, shopping centres, universities and places of interest

Abb–Alt

A

Abbacy Rd BT22 .... 80 C1
Abbey Christian Brothers Gram Sch BT34 .... 64 E5
Abbey Cl BT22 .... 70 B5
Abbey Ct [8] BT22 .... 67 A4
Abbeydale Ave BT23 .... 20 A6
Abbeydale Dr BT23 .... 20 A6
Abbeydale Pk BT23 .... 20 A6
Abbey Dr BT20 .... 4 A2
Abbey Gdns
Belfast BT5 .... 16 D4
[7] Millisle BT22 .... 67 A4
Abbey Hill Dr BT20 .... 4 A2
Abbey Hts BT34 .... 64 E5
Abbey La BT61 .... 60 D5
Abbey Mews BT23 .... 20 A6
Abbey Mount
Bangor BT20 .... 4 A2
Newtownards BT22 .... 70 C5
Abbey ParkⓉ BT60 .... 98 A5
Abbey Pk
Armagh BT61 .... 60 C7
Bangor BT20 .... 4 A2
Belfast BT5 .... 16 E4
Kilkeel BT34 .... 153 B7
Millisle BT22 .... 67 A4
Abbey Prim Sch BT23 .... 20 B6
Abbey Rd
Armagh BT60 .... 96 E4
Belfast BT5 .... 16 D4
Newtownards BT22 .... 66 F4
Newtownards BT23 .... 19 F5
Abbey Ring BT18 .... 9 C5
Abbey St
Armagh BT61 .... 60 C5
Bangor BT20 .... 4 A3
Abbeyview Rd BT30 .... 91 F7
Abbey Way BT34 .... 64 D5
Abbey Yd BT34 .... 64 D5
Abbot Cl BT23 .... 20 C5
Abbot Cres BT23 .... 20 C5
Abbot Cres Mews BT23 .... 20 B5
Abbot Ct BT23 .... 20 C5
Abbot Dr BT23 .... 20 B4
Abbot Gdns BT23 .... 20 C5
Abbot Gdns Mews BT23 .... 20 C5
Abbot Link BT23 .... 20 B5
Abbot Link Ct BT23 .... 20 B5
Abbot Link Mews BT23 .... 20 B5
Abbot Pk BT23 .... 20 B5
Abbots Cl BT20 .... 4 A1
Abbots Wlk BT20 .... 4 A1
Abbots Wood BT18 .... 9 D5
Abbotts La BT61 .... 85 D6
Abbot View BT23 .... 20 B5
Abbot Wlk BT23 .... 20 B4
Abercorn Dr BT26 .... 47 E7
Abercorn Pk
Hillsborough BT26 .... 47 C8
Portadown BT63 .... 52 B5
Abercorn Prim Sch BT32 .... 61 C3
Abercorn St N BT12 .... 154 A2
Abercorn St [5] BT9 .... 14 C2
Aberdeen St BT13 .... 154 B4
Aberdelghy Golf Course BT27 .... 26 E6
Aberdelghy Gve BT27 .... 26 D5
Abetta Par BT5 .... 15 C4
Abingdon Dr BT12 .... 154 B1
Abyssinia St BT12 .... 154 B2
Academy Prim Sch BT24 .... 77 C3
Academy St BT1 .... 155 A4
ACHADH NA CRANNCHA (MOUNTNORRIS) BT60 .... 116 D4
Acorn Activity Ctr BT61 .... 60 D8
Acorn Hill BT35 .... 131 D4
Acre La BT66 .... 86 A6
Acre McCricketⓉ BT30 .... 110 C7
Acres Rd BT67 .... 43 C4
ACTON BT35 .... 101 D2
Acton Rd BT35 .... 101 D2
Acton St
[11] Belfast BT13 .... 14 A7
Belfast BT13 .... 154 A4
Adam St [16] BT15 .... 14 D8
Adela Gdns BT23 .... 24 C1
Adelaide Ave BT9 .... 21 A8
Adelaide Chase BT9 .... 21 B8
Adelaide Ind Est BT12 .... 14 A1
Adelaide Pk BT9 .... 21 B8
Adelaide St BT2 .... 155 A2
Adelaide Sta BT12 .... 21 A8
Adela Pl BT15 .... 14 C7
Adela St BT15 .... 14 C7
Agars Rd BT28 .... 36 B8
AghacommonⓉ BT66 .... 40 E7
Aghacommon Emb BT66 .... 40 C7
Aghacommon Gr BT66 .... 40 F7
AghacullionⓉ BT33 .... 122 B1
AghadavoyleⓉ BT35 .... 141 B3
Aghadavoyle Rd BT35 .... 141 A3
Aghaderg Rd BT32 .... 102 E3
AghadrumglasnyⓉ BT67 .... 33 D6
AGHAGALLON BT67 .... 32 F8
Aghalee Rd BT67 .... 32 F8
AghamoatⓉ BT60 .... 60 C2
AghandunvarranⓉ BT26 .... 47 A1
Aghanergill or CorglassⓉ BT62 .... 85 F8
AghanoreⓉ BT61 .... 98 B8
Aghanore Rd BT61 .... 84 B1
AghantaraghanⓉ BT35 .... 117 E7
AghavillyⓉ
Armagh BT60 .... 98 A2
Newry BT34 .... 142 F7
Aghavilly Prim Sch BT60 .... 98 A1
Aghavilly Rd BT60 .... 98 A1
AghayallogeⓉ BT35 .... 141 C6
AghenisⓉ BT68 .... 96 C7
AghincurkⓉ BT35 .... 129 E8
Aghincurk Rd BT35 .... 115 F1
AghinligⓉ BT71 .... 84 C6
Aghinlig Rd BT71 .... 84 C6
AghlisnafinⓉ BT31 .... 122 F8
AghmakaneⓉ BT35 .... 131 A1
Aghmakane Rd BT35 .... 130 F2
AghnacloyⓉ BT66 .... 41 F4
AghnaleckⓉ BT27 .... 49 D5
AghnamoiraⓉ BT34 .... 142 B6
Aghnamoira Rd BT34 .... 142 B6
AghnaskeaghⓉ 150 D6
AghnatriskⓉ BT26 .... 36 D1
Aghnatrisk Rd BT26 .... 36 E1
AghoryⓉ BT62 .... 100 C7
Aghory Rd
Armagh BT61 .... 99 F8
Craigavon BT62 .... 100 B7
AghyoghillⓉ BT34 .... 152 B8
Agincourt Ave BT7 .... 14 E1
Agincourt St BT7 .... 14 E2
Agnes Cl BT13 .... 14 B7
Agnes St Ind Est BT13 .... 14 B7
Agnes St BT13 .... 154 B4
Agra St BT7 .... 14 E1
Agriculture & Food Science Centre The BT9 .... 21 C4
Aigburth Pk BT4 .... 15 D6
Aileen Terr BT35 .... 64 B5
Ailesbury Cres BT7 .... 21 E7
Ailesbury Dr BT7 .... 21 E8
Ailesbury Gdns BT7 .... 21 F7
Ailesbury Rd BT7 .... 21 F7
Ailsa Pk BT19 .... 3 B5
Ailsa Rd BT18 .... 1 C2
Ailsbury Gdns BT66 .... 41 E3
Ailsbury Pk BT66 .... 41 E3
Airfrean Ct [5] BT34 .... 133 B4
Airport Rd BT3 .... 8 D1
Airport Rd W BT3 .... 9 A2
Airport Rd W Link BT3 .... 9 A3
Alanbrooke Ave [1] BT27 .... 38 C8
Alanbrooke Cres BT23 .... 20 B6
Alanbrooke Pk Ind Est BT6 .... 15 D1
Alanbrooke Rd BT6 .... 15 D1
Alan Cl BT33 .... 63 B5
Alandale BT19 .... 5 A4
Alandale Mews BT19 .... 5 A4
Alanhill Dr BT67 .... 41 F8
Alanhill Pk BT67 .... 41 F8
Alanwood Pk BT20 .... 4 F5
Albany Ave BT19 .... 5 A1
Albany Cres BT19 .... 5 A1
Albany Ct BT19 .... 5 A1
Albany Pk BT19 .... 5 A1
Albany Pl BT13 .... 154 B4
Albany Rd
[3] Bangor BT19 .... 4 F1
Bangor BT19 .... 13 F8
Albany Sq BT13 .... 154 B4
Albert Ave BT66 .... 41 E6
Albertbridge Rd BT5 .... 15 B5
Albert Ct BT12 .... 154 C3
Albert Dr BT6 .... 22 C8
Albert Sq BT1 .... 155 B4
Albert St
Bangor BT20 .... 4 B5
Belfast BT12 .... 154 B3
Lurgan BT66 .... 41 E7
Albert Terr
Belfast BT12 .... 154 B3
Lurgan BT66 .... 41 F6
Albertville Dr [20] BT14 .... 14 B8
Albion La BT7 .... 155 A1
Albion St BT12 .... 154 C1
Alder Ave BT23 .... 19 B5
Alder Cl
Castlereagh BT5 .... 16 C1
Dunmurry BT17 .... 27 A8
Alder Grange Pk BT23 .... 19 A5
Alder La BT24 .... 78 A2
Aldervale BT65 .... 41 C2
Alderwood Hill BT8 .... 22 A1
Aldery Loanan The BT71 .... 84 C8
Alexander Ave
Armagh BT61 .... 60 D7
Lisburn BT27 .... 38 C8
Alexander Cres BT61 .... 60 D7
Alexander Dickson Prim Sch BT23 .... 77 F8
Alexander Dr
Armagh BT61 .... 60 D7
Kilkeel BT34 .... 153 D7
Warrenpoint BT34 .... 65 D2
Alexander Gdns
Armagh BT61 .... 60 C7
Bangor BT20 .... 3 F1
Alexander Pk
Armagh BT61 .... 60 D7
[2] Banbridge BT32 .... 104 A1
Newtownards BT22 .... 20 E2
Alexander Rd
Armagh BT61 .... 60 C7
Belfast BT6 .... 15 C1
Alexandra Ave BT62 .... 51 B6
Alexandra Cres BT66 .... 41 F5
Alexandra Gdns BT62 .... 51 D4
Alexandra Pk
Holywood BT18 .... 9 D5
Portadown BT62 .... 51 B6
Alexandra Pl BT18 .... 9 D7
Alexandra Rd BT21 .... 6 F2
Alford Pk [2] BT5 .... 16 E3
Alfred Cres BT33 .... 63 B5
Alfred St
[8] Bangor BT20 .... 4 B4
Belfast BT2 .... 155 B2
Alfred Terr BT66 .... 42 F5
Alina Rd BT35 .... 138 C3
AlkillⓉ 112 C3
All Childrens Integrated Prim Sch BT33 .... 63 C3
Allengrove BT67 .... 41 F8
Alley Rd BT35 .... 148 A7
AllistraghⓉ BT61 .... 84 C2
Alloa St [1] BT14 .... 14 B8
All Saints Prim Sch BT32 .... 104 A7
Alpine Rd BT23 .... 19 E6
AlsmeedⓉ 128 D1
AltaturkⓉ BT61 .... 99 B6
Altaturk Rd BT61 .... 99 B6
Altavallen Pk BT61 .... 60 B6
Altcar Ct (Cúirt Allt an Chairthe) [37] BT5 .... 15 A5
Alt Min Ave BT8 .... 22 B3
Altmore Gdns BT35 .... 64 B5

Altmore Rd BT65 41 D1
Altnacreeva Ave BT8 21 C1
Altnacreeva Cl BT8 21 C1
Altnadue Rd BT31 121 E4
Altnamackan Ⓣ BT35 129 A2
Altnaveigh Ⓣ BT35 131 E2
Altnaveigh Rd BT35 64 A4
Altona Rd BT27 38 C7
Altona Rd E BT27 38 C7
Alton St (Sráid Loch Altáin) 1 BT13 154 C4
Alveston Dr BT8 29 E2
Alveston Pk BT8 29 E2
Ambies La BT61 85 A6
Ambleside BT24 77 C4
Ambleside Cres 2 BT20 4 E3
Ambleside Ct BT13 14 A7
Ambleside Dr BT20 4 E3
Ambleside Rd BT20 4 E3
Ambleside St BT13 14 A7
Amelia St BT2 155 A2
Ameracam La BT34 152 D3
Ampere St BT6 15 A2
Anadale Flats BT7 14 E1
Anagasna Glebe Ⓣ BT71 83 E8
Anahilt Prim Sch BT26 49 B1
Anamar Prim Sch BT35 138 E3
Anaverna Ⓣ 150 F7
AN CAISLEÁN NUA (NEWCASTLE) BT33 63 B6
AN CÉIDE (KEADY) BT60 114 B3
Anch Grange The 15 BT21 67 A7
Anchorage Cove BT34 153 D7
Anchorage Ct BT34 153 D7
AN CHROIS GHEARR (CROSSGAR) BT30 92 A4
AN CLOCH (CLOUGH) BT30 107 D1
AN COMAR (COMBER) BT23 25 D1
Anderson Ct
3 Banbridge BT32 61 C4
3 Belfast BT5 15 A5
Anderson's Hill BT23 11 F2
Anderson St 2 BT32 61 C4
Andre Cl BT62 51 C7
Andre Dr BT62 51 B7
Andrews Meml Prim Sch BT23 25 D2
Andrews Shorefield BT19 5 C7
AN DROIM MÓR (DROMORE) BT25 58 B6
An Fhaiche (Green The)
Downpatrick BT30 62 C4
4 Drumaness BT24 91 B1
Angela Cres BT61 99 E8
AN GRIANFORT (GREENORE) BT34 152 A3
AN LORGAIN (LURGAN) BT66 41 E7
AN MAIGH (MOY) BT71 72 A1
AN MHAINISTIR LIATH (GREYABBEY) BT22 70 C4
Annaboe Ⓣ BT61 85 E4
Annaboe Rd
Armagh BT61 85 F4
Craigavon BT62 54 A7
Annaclarey Ⓣ BT71 83 F4
Annacloghmullin Ⓣ BT35 130 C1
ANNACLONE BT32 103 D2
ANNACLOY BT30 92 A1
Annacloy Ⓣ
Downpatrick BT30 108 B8
Hillsborough BT26 36 F1
Annacloy Rd BT30 91 F1
Annacloy Rd N BT30 92 B1
Annacramp Ⓣ BT68 96 A6
Annacramph Ⓣ BT61 84 F2
Annacramph Rd BT61 84 F2
Annadale Ave BT7 21 F6
Annadale Cres BT7 21 D8
Annadale Dr BT7 21 E7
Annadale Emb BT7 14 E1
Annadale Flats BT7 21 E8
Annadale Gdns BT7 21 E8
Annadale Gn BT7 21 E7
Annadale Gr BT7 21 E8
ANNADORN BT30 107 F5
Annadorn Rd BT30 107 F5
Annagh Ⓣ
Armagh BT60 96 F7
Dungannon BT71 83 A7
Portadown BT62 51 F2
Annaghananny Ⓣ BT60 97 A6
Annaghannany Rd BT60 96 F7
Annaghanoon Ⓣ BT66 86 C5
Annaghanoon Rd BT66 86 C6
Annagharap Ⓣ BT60 96 E7
Annaghbane Ⓣ BT34 118 D5
Annaghbane Rd BT32 118 D7
Annaghbeg Ⓣ BT71 72 D7
Annaghbeg Rd BT71 72 E7
Annaghboy or Rosebrook Ⓣ BT60 98 A5
Annagh Bsns Ctr BT62 51 E3
Annaghclare Ⓣ BT61 98 F8
Annaghdale Pl BT62 51 E2
Annagh Dr BT63 40 A2
Annaghdroghal La BT67 32 C6
Annaghgad Ⓣ BT35 147 D5
Annaghgad Rd BT35 147 D5
Annagh Hill BT62 51 E2
Annagh Ind Est BT62 51 D2
Annaghmacmanus Ⓣ BT71 84 C8
Annaghmakeonan Ⓣ BT25 86 E4
Annaghmare Ⓣ BT35 138 D3
Annaghmare Rd BT35 138 E2
Annagh Mdws BT62 51 E1
Annaghmore Ⓣ BT62 73 B2
Annaghmore Prim Sch BT62 73 B2
Annaghmore Rd BT62 73 B1
Annaghmoy La BT71 83 F3
Annaghroe Ⓣ BT68 96 B5
Annaghroe Rd BT68 96 C5
Annaghsallagh Ⓣ BT68 82 A2
Annaghsallagh Rd BT68 82 A2
Annaghugh Ⓣ BT61 85 D5
Annaghvacky Ⓣ 148 D3
Annaghview Ct BT62 51 E2
Annagola Ⓣ 112 C7
Annagora Ⓣ BT62 50 B4
Annagora Rd BT62 50 A3
Annahagh Ⓣ BT71 84 C3
Annahagh La BT71 84 C3
Annahagh Rd BT71 84 B3
Annahaia Ⓣ BT35 140 F4
Anna Hill BT62 100 C7
ANNAHILT BT26 49 A1
Annahugh Pk BT61 85 D5
Annahugh Rd BT61 85 D5
Annahunshigo Ⓣ BT32 120 F4
Annakeera Ⓣ BT62 50 F7
Annalee Ct BT14 14 B8
Annaloist Ⓣ BT66 75 D6
ANNALONG (ÁTH NA LONG) BT34 146 E4
Annalong Prim Sch BT34 146 D4
Annalong Rd BT34 146 B2
Annamoy Ⓣ BT71 83 F3
Annareagh Ⓣ BT61 99 E7
Annareagh Rd BT61 99 E7
Annasamry Ⓣ BT61 84 D7
Annavale Ave BT8 29 D3
Annavale Banks BT24 59 B4
Annavale Dr BT8 29 D3
Annesborough Ind Est BT67 75 F5
Annesborough Rd BT67 41 E8
Annesley Gdn (Arboretum)★ BT31 122 B6
Annesley Hall BT26 37 B1
Annesley St BT15 14 C7
Anne St
Armagh BT60 60 A2
8 Portaferry BT22 94 D4
Anne Way BT23 25 F4
Annies Ⓣ 150 A4
ANNSBOROUGH (BAILE ANNA) BT31 122 C6
Annsborough Pk BT31 122 D5
Annsborough Prim Sch BT31 122 D6
Annsborough St BT13 154 A4
Annsfield Cl 6 BT30 93 C5
Annsfield Pk BT30 93 B5
Ann St
Belfast BT1 155 B3
Gilford BT63 57 C2
Lurgan BT66 41 F4
Newtownards BT23 19 E5
Annsville BT34 64 F8
Annvale Gdns BT60 114 B3
Annvale Hts BT60 114 B3
Annvale Ind Est BT60 114 B3
Annvale Rd
Armagh BT60 114 C1
Keady BT60 114 B2
AN POINTE (WARRENPOINT) BT34 65 B2
AN PORT MÓR (BLACKWATERTOWN) BT71 84 A5
Ansfield BT26 47 D7
Anson Gdns BT23 19 C2
Anthonys Rd BT34 145 F1
Antigua Ct BT14 14 A8
AN TIÚR (NEWRY) BT35 64 A5
Antrim Ct BT67 42 B7
Antrim Rd
Ballynahinch BT24 59 C4
Belfast BT15 14 C8
Lisburn BT28 26 A2
Lurgan BT67 42 A7
Antrim St BT28 26 A2
An Tsráid Ard (High St) BT30 125 F6
An Tsráid Mhór (Main St) 5 BT30 107 C1
An Tsráid Thuaidh (North St) 5 BT35 147 F8
Aonach Ct BT34 134 B5
Apollo Rd BT12 14 A1
Apple Vale BT63 52 D4
Apsley St BT7 155 A1
Aquinas Diocesan Gram Sch BT6 22 A8
Arcadia Leisure Centre BT33 63 D4
Archdale BT35 131 E5
Archdale Dr BT8 21 D2
Archdale Pk BT8 21 D2
Arches Art Gall★ BT4 15 C5
Arches Bsns Ctr BT4 15 C5
Arches The BT30 78 A2
Arda Bhaile na Bhfiann (Vianstown Hts) BT30 62 C1
Arda Chluain Ard (Clonard Hts) 3 BT13 154 A3
Ardaghy Ⓣ
Newry BT34 121 C4
Omeath 142 B1
Ardaghy Rd BT34 121 C4
Ardallan Pk BT34 65 C3
Ardaluin Ct BT33 63 A7
Ardaluin Hts BT33 63 B7
Ardara Ave BT16 17 B3
Ardara Beeches BT23 25 C2
Ardara Elms BT23 25 B2
Ardaragh Rd BT34 119 B3
Ardara Gr BT23 25 B2
Ardara Mews BT16 17 B3
Ardara Oaks BT23 25 C2
Ardara Pines BT23 25 C2
Ardara Wood BT23 25 C2
Ardarragh Ⓣ BT34 119 B2
Ardaveen Ave BT35 64 C2
Ardaveen Cl BT35 64 C2
Ardaveen Dr BT35 64 C2
Ardaveen Pk BT35 131 C4
Ardboe Dr BT66 42 A4
Ardbraccan BT30 62 F6
Ardbrin Ⓣ BT32 103 E1
Ardbrin Rd BT32 103 F2
Ardcarn Dr BT5 16 F4
Ardcarne Pk BT35 64 A6
Ardcarn Gn BT5 16 F4
Ardcarn Pk BT5 16 F4
Ardcarn Way BT5 16 F4
Ardcuan Dr BT23 20 C5
Ardcuan Pk BT30 109 C8
Ardean Manor 12 BT71 72 A1
Ardenlee Ave
Belfast BT6 15 A2
Downpatrick BT30 62 E7
Ardenlee Cl 5 BT6 15 A2
Ardenlee Cres BT6 15 A2
Ardenlee Ct 2 BT6 15 A2
Ardenlee Dr
Belfast BT6 15 B1
Downpatrick BT30 62 E7
Ardenlee Gdns
Belfast BT6 15 B2
Downpatrick BT30 62 F7
Ardenlee Gn BT7 15 A2
Ardenlee Par BT6 15 B1
Ardenlee Pk
3 Belfast BT6 15 A2
Downpatrick BT30 62 E7
Ardenlee Pl BT6 15 A2
Ardenlee Rd BT30 62 E7
Ardenlee Rise 7 BT6 15 A2
Ardenlee St BT6 15 B1
Ardenlee Way 4 BT6 15 A2
Ardenvohr St BT6 15 B3
Ardenwood 8 BT6 15 A2
Arderys La BT32 61 C3
Ardfeelin BT34 132 C4
Ardfern Cl BT30 62 F6
Ardfern Cres BT30 109 A6
Ardfern Rd BT30 109 A6
Ardfield Ave 3 BT34 65 B4
Ardfield Cres BT34 65 B4
Ardgeehan Ⓣ BT22 95 A4
Ardgeehan Gdns BT19 3 D2
ARD GHLAIS (ARDGLASS) BT30 125 F6
ARDGLASS (ARD GHLAIS) BT30 125 F6
Ardglass Golf Club BT30 125 F5
Ardglass Rd
Castlewellan BT31 105 F4
Downpatrick BT30 62 E4
Ardgonnell Ⓣ BT60 112 B6
Ardgowan Dr BT5 15 C3
Ardgowan St BT6 15 B2
Ardgreenan Cres 14 BT4 16 A5
Ardgreenan Dr BT4 16 A5
Ardgreenan Gdns 9 BT4 16 A5
Ardgreenan Mount 2 BT4 16 A5
Ardgreenan Pl 8 BT4 16 A5
Ardgreen Dr BT35 64 B5
Ardigon Ⓣ BT30 92 F6
Ardigon Rd BT30 92 F6
Ardilea Ⓣ BT30 123 D8
Ardilea Lower Ⓣ BT30 123 E8
Ardilea Pk (Páirc Ard an Lao) BT30 62 C2
Ardilea Rd BT30 123 D7
Ardilea St BT14 14 A8
Ardis Ave BT28 26 B4
Ardkeel Pk BT33 63 D7
Ardkeen Ⓣ BT22 80 E1
Ardkeen Ave BT19 3 B5
Ardkeen Cres BT6 15 E1
Ardkeen Ct 2 BT34 65 C2
Ardkeeragh Ⓣ BT34 118 F3
Ardkeeragh Rd BT34 118 F4
Ardlee Ave BT18 9 D6
Ardmaine Gdns BT34 64 E6
Ardmara BT20 4 C6
Ardmeen Ⓣ BT30 109 B5
Ardmeen Gn (Faiche Ard Mín) BT30 62 D4
ARD MHACHA (ARMAGH) BT61 60 E7
ARDMILLAN BT23 79 A7
Ardmillan Cres BT23 19 C3
Ardmillan Gdns BT20 4 D3
Ardmillan Gr BT20 4 D3
Ardmillan Pk BT20 4 D3
Ardmillan Rd BT23 78 F8
Ardminnan Ⓣ BT22 95 B6
Ardminnan Rd BT22 95 B6
Ardminnan Rd Manse BT22 81 B1
Ardmore BT60 60 F2
Ardmore Ⓣ BT66 75 A8
Ardmore Ave
Armagh BT60 98 F4
Ardmore Ave *continued*
Belfast BT7 21 F7
Downpatrick BT30 62 D4
Dundonald BT16 17 E3
Holywood BT18 9 F6
Newtownards BT23 19 F5
Ardmore Cl BT62 51 B4
Ardmore Cres BT62 51 B4
Ardmore Cresent BT60 98 F4
Ardmore Ct BT18 9 F7
Ardmore Dr
Armagh BT60 98 F5
Hilltown BT34 134 B5
Ardmore Gdns BT20 4 A2
Ardmore Grange BT23 31 E1
Ardmore House BT30 62 D5
Ardmore Hts
Ballygowan BT23 31 E1
Holywood BT18 9 F6
Ardmore Manor BT23 31 D1
Ardmore Pk
3 Armagh BT60 130 C8
Hilltown BT34 134 B5
Holywood BT18 9 F7
Ardmore Prim Sch BT66 75 A7
Ardmore Rd
Armagh BT60 98 F5
Craigavon BT66 74 F8
Holywood BT18 9 F6
Newry BT34 132 A5
Ardmore Terr BT18 9 F7
Ardmoulin Ave BT13 154 B3
Ardmoulin Cl BT13 154 B3
Ardmoulin Pl BT12 154 B3
Ardmoulin St BT12 154 B3
Ardmoulin Terr BT12 154 B3
Ardnabannon Rd BT31 122 F6
Ard-na-grainseach (Granemore Hts) BT60 114 B3
Ardnagreena Gdns BT18 9 D4
Ardna na Sruthaile (Struell Hts) BT30 62 D2
Ard-na-ree BT19 5 B7
Ardnavalley Pk BT23 25 E2
Ardnoe Ave BT16 17 C4
Ardowen BT65 41 D2
Ardpatrick Ave (Ascaill Ard Pádraig) BT30 62 C3
Ardpatrick Gdns BT6 15 D1
Ardquin Ⓣ BT22 94 C7
Ardrea Ⓣ BT61 85 A3
Ardress East Ⓣ BT62 73 B1
Ardress House★ BT62 85 B8
Ardress Pk BT62 51 B2
Ardress Rd BT62 73 B1
Ardress West Ⓣ BT61 85 A8
Ardress W Rd BT61 73 A1
Ardri Gdns BT60 60 A5
Ardri Pk BT60 60 A5
Ard Ross BT35 147 E8
Ards Ⓣ BT68 82 B1
Ards Arena BT23 19 D4
Ards Art Centre★ BT23 19 D5
Ards Bsns Ctr BT23 19 D3
Ards Com Hospl BT23 19 C5
Ards Crafts★ BT23 19 D5
Ards FC Sports Club BT23 19 E4
Ards Leisure Centre BT23 19 C6
Ards Sh Ctr BT23 19 C5
Ardtanagh Ⓣ
Downpatrick BT30 107 A4
Dromore BT25 89 A2
Ardtanagh Rd BT25 89 A1
Ardtole Ⓣ BT30 126 A7
Ardtole Rd BT30 126 A7
Ardvanagh Ave BT23 13 A6
Ardvanagh Brae BT23 13 B6
Ardvanagh Cl BT23 13 A6
Ardvanagh Cres BT23 13 A6
Ardvanagh Ct BT23 13 B6
Ardvanagh Dr BT23 13 B6
Ardvanagh Grange BT23 13 B6
Ardvanagh Manor BT23 13 A6
Ardvanagh Mdws BT23 13 B6
Ardvanagh Mews BT23 13 A6
Ardvanagh Pk BT23 13 A6
Ardvanagh Rd BT23 13 A6
Ardvarna Cres BT4 16 A7
Ardvarna Pk BT4 16 A7
Ardview BT23 79 A4
Ardview Pk BT23 79 A5
Areema Hts BT32 61 B4
Argory The★ BT71 72 D3
Argyle Bsns Ctr BT13 154 B4
Argyle Ct BT13 154 A4
Argyle St BT13 154 A4
Ariel St BT13 154 B4
Arindale BT67 35 B7
Arkle Pk (Páirc Ardchoille) BT30 62 B2
Ark Open Farm★ BT23 12 F2
Arlee Mews BT4 9 B2
Arleigh Ct BT19 13 C7
Arlington Pk 16 BT22 94 D3
ARMAGH (ARD MHACHA) BT61 60 E7
Armaghbrague Ⓣ BT35 129 A8
Armaghbrague Rd BT60 114 F2
Armagh Bsns Ctr BT61 60 C7
Armagh CBS Prim Sch BT60 60 C3
Armagh Coll of Further & Higher Ed BT61 60 D6
Armagh Com Hospl BT61 60 E6
Armagh Cty Mus★ BT61 60 E5
Armagh Observatory★ BT61 60 D6
Armagh Rd
Armagh BT60 114 B5
Craigavon BT62 55 A8
Dungannon BT71 84 B7
Newry BT35 115 B2
Portadown BT62 51 C1
Tandragee BT62 101 A7
Armagh St BT35 129 C4
Armitage Cl BT4 15 C6
Armstrong Ave 6 BT22 94 D4
Armstrong Prim Sch BT61 60 D6
Arney Cl BT6 22 B7
Arnon St (Sráid Earnúin) 3 BT13 154 C4
Arran Ct (Cúirt Arann) 4 BT5 15 A5
Arran Pk BT16 17 E4
Arran St (Sráid Arann) 2 BT5 15 A5
Arras Pk BT20 4 C3
Artabrackagh Ⓣ BT62 55 A6
Artabrackagh Rd BT62 55 B6
Artana St BT7 14 E2
Artasooly Ⓣ BT71 83 E2
Artasooly Rd BT71 83 F3
Arthur Ave BT62 51 D3
Arthur La BT1 155 A3
Arthur Pl BT1 155 A3
Arthur Sq BT1 155 A3
Arthur St
Belfast BT1 155 A3
Hillsborough BT26 47 C6
Lurgan BT66 41 F5
Newry BT34 64 E6
Artipinny Rd BT26 46 B7
Art Mc'Cooey Pk BT35 148 E7
Arundel Courts BT12 154 B2
Arundel Wlk BT12 154 B2
Ascaill Ard Pádraig (Ardpatrick Ave) BT30 62 C3
Ascaill Bhinn Dhearg (Benderg Ave) BT30 62 D4
Ascaill Chill Ard (Killard Ave) BT30 62 D5
Ascaill Chnoc An Easpaig (Bishops Brae Ave) BT30 62 C2
Ascaill Naomh Dallan (St Dillons Ave) BT30 62 D4
Ascaill Phairc An Rí (Kingsfield Ave) BT30 62 B2
Ascot Gdns BT5 16 A2
Ascot Mews 1 BT5 16 A2
Ascot Pk
Belfast BT5 16 A2
Newtownards BT23 19 B6
Ashbourne Pk BT27 26 C5
Ashbrook BT62 51 A7
Ashbrook Cres 3 BT4 15 F7
Ash Brooke BT21 66 F7
Ashbrooke Dr BT4 15 F7
Ashbrook Mews 5 BT34 132 B5
Ashburn BT24 59 C6
Ashburne Mews BT7 155 A1
Ashburn Gn BT4 16 A7
Ashbury Ave BT19 4 F1
Ashbury Cres BT19 4 F2
Ashbury Ct BT19 4 F1
Ashbury Gdns BT19 4 F2
Ashbury Gr BT19 4 F1
Ashbury Pk BT19 4 F2
Ashbury Rd BT19 4 F2
Ashcroft Pk
Lisburn BT28 38 A7
Newtownards BT23 20 A7
Ashdale Ave 7 BT30 125 F6
Ashdale Cres BT20 4 C2
Ashdale Gdns 11 BT30 125 F6
Ashdale St BT5 15 C5
Ashdene Grange BT23 25 F1
Ashdene Pk BT66 41 E4
Ashdene Rd BT23 30 E6
Ashes The 9 BT19 13 E8
Ashfield Ave BT34 132 B5
Ashfield Boys High Sch BT4 16 A8
Ashfield Ct BT21 66 F8
Ashfield Dr BT21 66 F8
Ashfield Girls' High Sch BT4 15 F8
Ashfield Golf Club BT35 139 A3
Ashfield Manor BT62 51 B4
Ashford BT62 51 C6
Ashford Ave BT19 4 F3
Ashford Dr BT19 4 F4
Ashford Gn 1 BT4 15 F7
Ashford Grange BT67 32 A1
Ashford Pk BT19 4 F4
Ash Gn BT18 9 D5
Ash Gr BT17 27 A8
Ashgrove
Markethill BT60 115 F8
Newtownards BT23 19 D6
Ashgrove Ave
Banbridge BT32 61 C3
Lurgan BT67 42 A8
Newry BT34 64 E8
Ashgrove Cl BT67 32 A1
Ashgrove Cres BT67 41 F8
Ashgrove Dr
Craigavon BT67 35 A8
Lurgan BT67 41 F8
Ashgrove Gdns BT67 32 A1
Ashgrove Manor BT62 51 C7

Ashgrove Pk
Craigavon BT67 35 A7
Lisburn BT28 38 A7
Lurgan BT67 42 A8
Newry BT34 132 A5
Ashgrove Rd
Dungannon BT71 73 C7
Newry BT34 64 D8
Newry BT34 132 A5
Portadown BT62 51 D6
Ashlea Bend 3 BT60 116 A8
Ashlea Cl BT60 116 A8
Ashlea Gdns BT60 116 A8
Ashlea Pl BT28 38 A7
Ashleigh BT33 63 B6
Ashleigh Cres BT66 42 C4
Ashleigh Ct
6 Belfast BT6 15 A2
Newry BT34 146 D7
Ashleigh Gr BT34 119 E2
Ashleigh Hts BT33 63 B7
Ashleigh Manor BT9 14 B1
Ashleighmeadows BT34 119 F3
Ashley Ave
Armagh BT60 60 E3
Belfast BT9 14 B2
Ashley Cl
Armagh BT60 60 E3
Portadown BT62 51 C7
Ashley Cres BT22 66 F5
Ashley Ct BT34 65 B5
Ashley Dr
Bangor BT20 4 E4
Belfast BT9 14 B2
Ashley Gdns
Armagh BT60 60 E4
Banbridge BT32 61 D4
Bangor BT20 4 F5
Ashley Hts
Armagh BT60 60 E4
Portadown BT62 51 C6
Warrenpoint BT34 65 B4
Ashley Mews BT9 14 B2
Ashley Pk
Armagh BT60 60 F3
Bangor BT20 4 E5
Carryduff BT8 29 E3
Millisle BT22 67 A5
Ashley St BT32 61 D4
Ashmore Hill BT35 131 B4
Ashmore Pl BT13 154 A3
Ashmore St BT13 154 A3
Ashmount Dr 12 BT22 94 D3
Ashmount Gdns BT27 26 D1
Ashmount Gr BT4 16 A7
Ashmount Pk
2 Belfast BT4 15 F7
Lisburn BT27 26 D1
9 Portaferry BT22 94 D3
Ashton Hts BT35 62 B2
Ashtree Ent Pk BT34 64 F8
Ashtree Gr BT60 130 C8
Ashtree Hill
Craigavon BT62 100 E7
Newry BT35 117 E3
Ashtree La BT62 100 E7
Ashvale Dr
Banbridge BT32 102 C3
Hillsborough BT26 47 D7
Ashvale Hts BT26 47 D7
Ashvale Pk
5 Carrowdore BT22 66 F1
Hillsborough BT26 47 D7
Ashveagh BT71 83 D5
Ashwood BT66 41 E5
Aspen BT21 6 E1
Assan Rd BT35 138 C4
Assisi Gdns BT31 106 E4
Assumption Gram Sch
BT24 59 D5
Aston Gdns
Bangor BT19 3 F1
Belfast BT4 16 A5
Astoria Gdns 3 BT5 16 A4
Athboy Mdws BT71 84 A5
ATH MHIC GIOLLA (GILFORD)
BT63 57 D2
ÁTH NA LONG (ANNALONG)
BT34 146 E4
Athol St BT12 154 C2
Atkinson Ave BT62 51 C4
ATTICAL BT34 144 F4
Attical Bog Rd BT34 145 A4
Attical Rd BT34 144 F5
Auburn Pk BT20 3 F1
Audley Ave BT28 26 B4
Audleys AcreⓉ BT30 62 E4
Audley's Castle★ BT30 94 C3
Audleys Cl BT23 20 A5
Audleys Dr BT23 20 A5
Audleys Gdns BT23 20 A5
Audleys Pk BT23 20 A4
AudleystownⓉ BT30 94 A3
Audleystown Cairn★
BT30 94 A3
Audleystown Rd BT30 93 F2
Audleys Way BT23 20 A5
AughadanoveⓉ BT35 140 C5
AughanduffⓉ BT35 139 E7
Aughanduff Rd BT35 139 F8
Aughanlig Pk Rd BT71 84 C6
Aughan Pk BT35 117 D7
Aughantarragh and CorrⓉ
BT60 83 A3
Aughantarragh Rd BT60 83 A3
Augherafinn La BT61 97 D8
AughintoberⓉ BT34 118 B4
AughlishⓉ BT62 101 D4
Aughlish Rd
Craigavon BT63 101 D2
Newry BT35 117 D8
Aughlisnafin Prim Sch
BT31 122 F7
Aughlisnafin Rd BT31 122 E7
Aughnacavan Rd BT34 118 C3
AughnacavenⓉ BT34 118 C3
AughnacloyⓉ
Armagh BT61 84 D3
Banbridge BT32 103 F3
Aughnacloy Rd BT32 103 E4
AughnadarraghⓉ BT24 78 A3
AughnadrummanⓉ BT67 34 E1
AughnafoskerⓉ BT67 44 B8
AughnagonⓉ BT34 133 A2
Aughnagon Rd BT34 132 F1
AughnagurganⓉ BT60 128 D6
Aughnagurgan Rd BT60 128 D6
AughnahooryⓉ BT34 145 D1
Aughnahoory Rd
Kilkeel BT34 153 C8
Newry BT34 145 C2
AughnaloopyⓉ BT34 145 C1
Aughnaloopy Rd
Kilkeel BT34 153 C8
Newry BT34 145 C1
AughnaskeaghⓉ BT25 104 F8
Aughnaskeagh Rd BT25 88 E1
AughnavallogⓉ BT34 120 A5
AughrafinⓉ BT60 97 D5
AughrimⓉ BT34 145 A2
Aughrim Pk BT12 154 C1
Aughrim Rd BT34 145 A3
Auster Pk BT23 19 D1
Austin Dr BT62 101 B7
Austin Pl BT63 40 C2
Ava Ave BT7 14 E1
Ava Cres BT7 21 E8
Ava Dr
Belfast BT7 21 E8
Killyleagh BT30 93 B6
Ava Farm BT19 12 D8
Ava Gdns BT7 21 E8
Ava Hospl BT9 14 B2
Ava Par 2 BT7 14 E1
Ava St
Bangor BT20 3 F2
4 Belfast BT7 14 E1
Belfast BT7 21 E8
Lisburn BT27 38 C8
Avenue Rd BT67 42 B4
Avenue The BT63 52 A3
Aves Leisure Ctr BT67 42 B5
Avoca Lawn BT34 65 D4
Avoca St BT14 14 B8
Avondale Manor BT64 40 E2
Avondale St BT5 15 D4
Avoniel Dr BT5 15 C4
Avoniel Leisure Ctr BT5 15 C4
Avoniel Par BT5 15 C4
Avoniel Prim Sch BT5 15 C4
Avoniel Rd BT5 15 B4
Avonlea Cres BT64 40 D3
Avonlea Gr BT63 40 D3
Avonlea Manor BT63 40 D3
Avonlea Pk BT20 3 F2
Avonmere BT64 40 E3
Avonmore BT71 84 A5
Avonmore Pk BT28 37 F7
Avonorr Dr BT5 15 C4
Avonvale BT4 16 A8
Ayallogue Rd BT35 141 C7
Azamor St BT13 154 A4

B

Bachelors Wlk
Armagh BT60 114 B4
Lisburn BT28 26 A1
BackaderryⓉ BT31 106 A2
Backaderry Rd BT31 121 E8
Back Hill BT19 5 B7
Back La
Downpatrick BT30 125 D5
Newry 151 C4
BacknamullaghⓉ BT25 88 C8
Backnamullagh Rd BT25 46 D1
Back Rd
Lisburn BT27 28 A2
Newry BT34 146 C6
Newry BT35 140 A4
Newtownards BT22 81 C7
Rathfriland BT34 119 F3
Backwood Rd
Craigavon BT67 33 E4
Moira BT67 34 A3
Bagnalls Ret Pk BT34 64 D5
Bagot St BT34 64 D6
BAILE ANNA
(ANNSBOROUGH)
BT31 122 C6
BAILE BHÁLTAIR
(BALLYWALTER) BT22 71 B6
BAILE HILL (HILLTOWN)
BT34 134 A6
BAILE LOCH CUAN
(STRANGFORD) BT30 94 D2
BAILE MHIC GABHANN
(BALLYGOWAN) BT23 77 F8
BAILE NA HINSE
(BALLYNAHINCH) BT24 59 C3
BAILE NUA NA HARDA
(NEWTOWNARDS) BT23 19 E3
BAILE ÚR
(NEWTOWNHAMILTON)
BT35 129 C4
BAILEYSMILL BT27 76 A3
Bailie Gdns BT19 66 C8
Bailie Pk BT19 66 C8
Bailie Rd BT19 66 B8
Bailie Terr BT19 66 B8
Bailiffs La BT66 74 D7
Bain's Pl BT2 155 A2
Baird Ave BT66 86 F6
Bairdstown Rd BT22 71 A7
Balfour Ave BT7 155 B1
Balfour St BT23 19 D6
Balinree Pk BT23 78 F5
Balkan St BT12 154 B3
BallaghaneryⓉ BT33 136 F2
Ballaghanery UpperⓉ
BT33 136 F4
BallaghbegⓉ BT33 63 B1
Ballaghbeg Pk BT33 63 C7
Ballagh Rd BT33 137 A3
Ballagh Bridge★ BT33 137 A2
Ballarat Ct 4 BT6 15 A4
Ballarat St
1 Belfast BT6 15 A4
Belfast BT6 155 C2
BallardⓉ BT35 140 D7
Ballard Rd BT35 140 E7
Ballaun Stone★ 149 A1
BalleerⓉ BT60 114 D7
Ballee Rd BT30 109 D2
BalleevyⓉ BT32 103 B5
BALLELA BT32 104 A7
Ballela Rd BT32 104 A7
BallenanⓉ BT35 117 A6
BallenyⓉ BT25 58 B2
Balliesmills Rd BT27 49 E5
Ballievey Rd BT32 103 B5
Balligan Gdns BT19 3 D1
Balligan Rd BT22 71 A2
BalligganⓉ BT22 71 A2
Ballinacraig Way BT34 64 E2
Ballinahome Cl BT60 60 F5
BallinarryⓉ BT30 110 B5
Ballinasack Rd BT35 139 F4
Ballinatate Rd BT60 116 A1
BallincurryⓉ BT34 151 F8
Ballincurry UpperⓉ
BT34 143 F1
BallindarraghⓉ BT60 99 D1
Ballindarragh Rd BT60 99 E1
BallindoaltyⓉ BT34 151 F8
Ballindoalty UpperⓉ
BT34 143 F1
BallinlareⓉ BT35 64 C5
Ballinlare Ct BT35 64 B4
Ballinlare Gdns BT35 64 B7
BallinlissⓉ BT35 141 B8
BallinranⓉ
Newry BT34 145 C4
Newry BT34 151 D8
Ballinran Rd BT34 145 D3
Ballinran UpperⓉ
Newry BT34 143 D1
Newry BT34 145 C6
BallintaggartⓉ
Banbridge BT32 118 D8
Craigavon BT62 50 D1
Ballintaggart Rd BT62 54 D8
BallintateⓉ BT60 130 B8
BallintempleⓉ
Newry BT35 129 D5
Newry BT35 140 F7
Ballintemple Rd
Armagh BT60 130 A6
Newry BT35 129 F6
Newry BT35 141 A6
BallintineⓉ BT27 38 B6
BallintlieveⓉ
Downpatrick BT30 93 F1
Downpatrick BT30 109 F8
BallintogherⓉ BT30 109 C8
Ballintogher Rd BT30 109 C8
BallinturⓉ BT34 152 A8
Ballintur UpperⓉ BT34 144 A1
BallooⓉ
Bangor BT19 13 B7
Killinchy BT23 78 F5
BALLOO BT23 78 F5
Balloo Ave BT19 13 A8
Balloo Cotts BT19 13 C8
Balloo Cres BT19 13 A8
Balloo Cross Roads BT23 78 F5
Balloo Ct BT19 13 B8
Balloo Dr BT19 13 B8
Balloo Ind Pk BT19 4 B1
Balloo Link BT19 13 A8
Balloo LowerⓉ BT19 5 D6
BalloolyⓉ BT32 104 A8
BalloolymoreⓉ BT32 104 A4
Balloolymore Rd BT32 103 F4
BallooniganⓉ BT67 34 F1
Balloo Pk BT19 4 B1
Balloo Pl BT19 13 B8
Balloo Rd BT19 13 C7
Balloo Ret Pk BT19 13 A8
Balloo S Ind Est BT19 13 A7
Balloo Way BT19 13 B8
Balloo Wlk BT19 13 C8
BALLSMILL BT35 149 A6
Ballsmill Rd BT35 139 E1
BallyadamⓉ BT22 94 F6
BallyaghertyⓉ BT24 77 D3
BallyaghlisⓉ BT27 27 E3
BallyagholyⓉ BT34 143 B7
BallyaghyⓉ BT60 97 F6
BallyalganⓉ BT30 92 D8
Ballyalgan Rd BT30 78 C1
BallyalicockⓉ BT23 20 D5
BallyallolyⓉ BT23 31 D8
Ballyalloly Rd BT23 24 D1
BallyaltikilliganⓉ BT23 25 B4
BALLYALTON BT30 109 C5
BallyaltonⓉ BT23 18 F1
Ballyalton Rd BT23 18 F1
BallyannyⓉ BT60 100 B2
BallyardelⓉ BT34 153 A6
Ballyardle Rd BT34 153 A7
BallyardsⓉ BT60 98 B1
Ballyards Rd BT60 98 B3
BallyarganⓉ BT62 101 B2
BallyatwoodⓉ BT22 70 E5
Ballyatwood Rd BT22 70 F4
BallyaughianⓉ BT34 134 D3
BallybannanⓉ BT31 122 E4
Ballybannan Rd BT31 122 E5
BallybarnesⓉ BT23 18 E8
Ballybarnes Cotts BT23 18 E7
Ballybarnes Rd BT23 11 E2
Ballybay Ave BT62 51 B5
Ballybay Pk BT62 51 B4
BALLYBEEN BT16 17 D4
BallybeenⓉ BT23 31 C6
Ballybeen Pk BT16 17 D4
Ballybeen Rd BT23 31 A7
Ballybeen Sq BT16 17 D4
BallybegⓉ BT30 109 F2
Ballybeg Pk 9 BT62 101 B7
BallybinabyⓉ 148 D5
BallyblackⓉ
Newtownards BT22 66 C2
Newtownards BT22 94 F3
Ballyblack LittleⓉ BT22 66 C1
Ballyblack Rd
Newtownards BT22 20 F2
Newtownards BT22 94 F3
Ballyblack Rd E BT22 66 D2
BallyblaghⓉ BT66 42 B4
BallyblaughⓉ BT34 118 B4
Ballyblaugh Rd BT34 118 B4
BallyboghilboⓉ BT22 70 D5
Ballybog Rd BT17 26 F8
BallyboleyⓉ BT22 70 B7
BallyboyⓉ BT68 96 B8
Ballybranagh Rd BT30 109 E1
BallybraniganⓉ BT22 94 E6
Ballybrannagh LowerⓉ
BT30 109 E2
Ballybrannagh UpperⓉ
BT30 109 E1
BallybrannanⓉ BT61 85 A2
Ballybrannon Rd BT61 84 F1
BallybreaghⓉ BT62 100 B8
Ballybreagh Rd BT62 54 C1
BallybredaghⓉ BT23 79 B3
BallybrickⓉ BT32 119 F8
Ballybrick Rd BT32 119 F8
BallybrockyⓉ BT60 97 E7
BallybrollyⓉ
Armagh BT60 98 A7
Armagh BT60 114 D5
Ballybrone Rd BT60 114 D3
BallybryanⓉ BT22 70 D3
Ballybryan Rd BT22 70 D4
Ballybunden Rd BT23 78 E7
BallybuttleⓉ BT22 66 E3
Ballybuttle Rd BT22 66 F4
Ballycairn Cl BT8 21 D1
Ballycairn Dr BT8 21 C1
BallycamⓉ
Downpatrick BT30 125 C4
Newtownards BT22 94 F4
BallycanalⓉ BT67 34 D3
BallycarnⓉ BT8 28 B5
BallycarngannonⓉ BT27 76 C6
Ballycarngannon Rd BT27 76 B7
BallycastleⓉ BT22 69 F8
Ballycastle Ct 13 BT14 14 B8
Ballycastle Rd BT22 66 C1
Ballyclander LowerⓉ
BT30 109 C1
Ballyclander Rd BT30 109 B1
Ballyclander UpperⓉ
BT30 109 B2
BallycloghanⓉ
Ballynahinch BT24 77 D6
Belfast BT4 16 C6
Ballycloughan Prim Sch
BT24 77 D6
Ballycloughin Rd BT23 77 D7
Ballycoan Rd BT8 28 F5
Ballycoffey or BallyhoyⓉ
BT60 97 F4
BallycopelandⓉ BT22 66 F5
Ballycoshone LowerⓉ
BT34 120 D2
Ballycoshone Rd BT34 120 C1
Ballycotting Cl BT30 110 D6
BallycowanⓉ BT8 28 E6
BALLYCRANBEG BT22 80 F4
Ballycranemore Rd BT22 81 B4
Ballycran GAC BT22 80 F6
Ballycran MoreⓉ BT22 81 A4
BallycreellyⓉ BT23 31 D5
Ballycreely Rd BT23 31 D5
BallycreenⓉ BT24 90 B8
Ballycreen Rd BT24 76 A1
Ballycrochan Ave 1 BT19 66 A8
Ballycrochan Ct BT19 5 A1
Ballycrochan Dr 2 BT19 66 A8
Ballycrochan Gdns BT19 66 A8
Ballycrochan Rd BT19 5 A3
BallycroghanⓉ BT19 5 A1
BallycrossⓉ
Banbridge BT32 87 A2
Ballycross *continued*
Donaghadee BT21 6 B1
Ballycross Rd BT32 87 A1
BallycrummyⓉ BT60 98 B5
Ballycrummy Rd BT60 60 A5
BallycruneⓉ BT26 89 E8
Ballycrune Rd BT26 49 D2
BallycruttleⓉ BT30 109 E3
Ballycruttle Rd BT30 109 D2
BallycullenⓉ BT23 19 A4
Ballycullen Rd BT71 84 A6
BALLYCULTER BT30 110 B8
Ballyculter Ave BT30 94 B2
Ballyculter LowerⓉ
BT30 110 B7
Ballyculter Rd BT30 109 E6
Ballyculter UpperⓉ
BT30 110 B8
BallycultraⓉ BT18 10 C8
BallydarganⓉ BT30 124 E7
BallydaveyⓉ BT18 11 A8
BallydeslandⓉ BT34 65 C8
Ballydesland Rd BT34 65 D7
BallydoghertyⓉ BT35 117 A4
Ballydogherty Rd BT35 117 A5
BallydollaghanⓉ BT8 28 F8
BallydonaghyⓉ BT63 56 E8
BallydonetyⓉ BT30 108 B3
BallydonnellⓉ BT30 124 B7
Ballydonnell Rd BT30 124 B6
Ballydonnety Rd BT30 108 A2
BallydooⓉ
Armagh BT60 97 E6
Newry BT34 133 D5
BallydoonanⓉ BT22 70 D8
Ballydoonan Rd BT22 70 D7
Ballydoo Rd BT34 133 C5
BallydornⓉ BT23 79 B7
Ballydorn Rd BT23 79 C7
Ballydougan Potter★
BT66 53 F3
BallydownⓉ BT32 61 F2
Ballydown Prim Sch
BT32 103 B6
Ballydown Rd BT32 61 F3
BallydrainⓉ BT23 68 F3
Ballydrain Rd
Comber BT23 25 F1
Newtownards BT23 68 E4
BallydrummanⓉ BT31 121 D8
Ballydrumman Rd BT31 121 D8
BallyduganⓉ
Craigavon BT63 53 D3
Downpatrick BT30 108 B3
Ballydugan Ind Est BT30 62 B3
Ballydugan Rd
Craigavon BT63 53 C2
Downpatrick BT30 62 A2
BallydulanyⓉ BT34 133 D4
BallydyanⓉ BT24 91 D7
Ballydyan Rd BT30 91 D6
Ballyeasborough Rd BT22 81 B5
BallyedmondⓉ BT34 151 E8
Ballyedmond UpperⓉ
BT34 143 E1
Ballyedock LowerⓉ
BT30 110 A1
Ballyedock or CarrstownⓉ
BT22 110 E8
Ballyedock Rd BT30 110 A1
Ballyedock UpperⓉ
BT30 110 A1
BallyesboroughⓉ BT22 81 B6
BallyewryⓉ BT22 69 D8
Ballyfannahan Rd BT35 139 A3
BallyferisⓉ BT22 71 A8
Ballyferris Mews 4 BT19 3 D1
Ballyferris Wlk 5 BT19 3 D1
BallyfinraghⓉ BT22 94 F7
BallyfodrinⓉ BT62 50 D8
BallyfotherlyⓉ BT21 66 C8
BallyfounderⓉ BT22 94 F2
Ballyfounder Rd BT22 94 F2
BallyfrenchⓉ BT22 81 D6
Ballyfrench Rd BT22 81 C6
BallyfrenisⓉ BT22 66 F3
BALLYGALGET BT22 95 A6
Ballygalget Rd BT22 95 A7
BallygallumⓉ BT30 109 A1
Ballygallum Rd BT30 109 B1
BallygallyⓉ BT30 92 F2
BallygarganⓉ BT63 52 F3
Ballygargan Rd BT64 52 F6
BallygarvanⓉ BT22 70 D2
BallygarviganⓉ BT22 95 B5
Ballygarvigan Rd BT22 95 A5
BallygaseyⓉ BT61 84 F4
Ballygasey Rd BT61 84 F3
BallygassoonⓉ BT61 84 E4
Ballygassoon Rd BT61 84 E3
BallygeeganⓉ BT23 79 A3
BallygelaghⓉ BT22 80 F2
Ballygelagh Rd BT22 80 F2
BallygilbertⓉ
Bangor BT19 2 D1
Downpatrick BT30 125 C6
Ballygilbert Rd BT30 125 A8
Ballyginney Rd BT33 122 F3
BallyginnyⓉ BT33 122 F3
BallyglighornⓉ BT23 68 E3
Ballyglighorn Rd BT23 68 E2
Ballygorian BegⓉ BT34 134 A7
Ballygorian MoreⓉ
BT34 133 F7
Ballygorian Rd BT34 133 F6
BallygormanⓉ BT60 116 F4
BallygoskinⓉ BT30 78 F2
Ballygoskin Rd BT30 78 F1

- **Ballygowan**
  - Ballygowan BT23 . . . 31 D1
  - Banbridge BT32 . . . 102 C5
  - Belfast BT17 . . . 27 D5
  - Hillsborough BT26 . . . 45 D3
  - Newry BT34 . . . 152 D7
- **BALLYGOWAN (BAILE MHIC GABHANN)** BT23 . . . 77 F8
- **Ballygowan Gdns** BT19 . . . 12 D8
- **Ballygowan Pk** BT32 . . . 61 B4
- **Ballygowan Rd**
  - Ballynahinch BT24 . . . 77 D5
  - Banbridge BT32 . . . 61 A3
  - Belfast BT5 . . . 23 B4
  - Comber BT23 . . . 25 B1
  - Dromara BT25 . . . 45 D2
  - Hillsborough BT26 . . . 46 C5
  - Newtownards BT23 . . . 31 F5
- **Ballygraffan**
  - Newtownards BT22 . . . 81 A6
  - Newtownards BT23 . . . 68 D3
- **Ballygraffan Rd** BT23 . . . 68 D4
- **Ballygrainey**
  - Bangor BT19 . . . 13 E5
  - Holywood BT18 . . . 1 F1
- **Ballygrainey Rd** BT18 . . . 1 G2
- **Ballygrangee** BT22 . . . 70 A8
- **Ballygroobany** BT61 . . . 99 F6
- **Ballygroobany Rd** BT61 . . . 99 F8
- **Ballygrot** BT19 . . . 2 D5
- **Ballygunaghan** BT25 . . . 86 F4
- **Ballyhackamore** BT5 . . . 15 E4
- **BALLYHACKAMORE** BT5 . . . 16 A3
- **Ballyhafry** BT33 . . . 122 D2
- **Ballyhafry Rd** BT31 . . . 122 D2
- **Ballyhaft** BT22 . . . 66 A1
- **Ballyhaft Rd** BT22 . . . 20 F1
- **Ballyhagan** BT61 . . . 85 C4
- **Ballyhagan Rd** BT61 . . . 85 C4
- **BALLYHALBERT** BT22 . . . 81 C8
- **Ballyhalbert Gdns** BT19 . . . 3 C1
- **Ballyhannon** BT63 . . . 52 D5
- **Ballyhannon Cl** BT63 . . . 52 C5
- **Ballyhannon Gr** BT63 . . . 52 C5
- **Ballyhannon Hts** BT63 . . . 52 C4
- **Ballyhannon La** BT63 . . . 52 D4
- **Ballyhannon Lodge** BT63 . 52 C6
- **Ballyhannon Pk** BT63 . . . 52 C5
- **Ballyhannon Rd** BT63 . . . 52 C4
- **Ballyhanwood** BT5 . . . 23 F8
- **Ballyhanwood Rd**
  - Belfast BT5 . . . 16 E1
  - Dundonald BT16 . . . 17 A2
- **Ballyharry** BT23 . . . 20 B7
- **Ballyharry Hts** BT23 . . . 20 A7
- **Ballyharry Pk** BT23 . . . 20 A7
- **Ballyhaskin** BT22 . . . 67 B2
- **Ballyhaskin Rd** BT22 . . . 67 C1
- **Ballyhay** BT21 . . . 66 D6
- **Ballyhay Rd** BT21 . . . 66 D7
- **Ballyhemlin** BT22 . . . 71 B1
- **Ballyhemlin Rd** BT22 . . . 71 A1
- **Ballyhenny** BT23 . . . 20 E8
- **Ballyhenry** BT22 . . . 94 C5
- **Ballyhenry Major** BT23 . 25 E7
- **Ballyhenry Minor** BT23 . 68 D6
- **Ballyhenry Rd**
  - Comber BT23 . . . 68 D7
  - Newtownards BT23 . . . 25 F6
- **Ballyheridan** BT60 . . . 98 E3
- **Ballyherly** BT22 . . . 94 D5
- Ballyholland GAC BT34 . . 132 C2
- **Ballyholland Lower** BT34 . . . 132 D3
- **Ballyholland Pk** BT34 . . . 64 E6
- Ballyholland Prim Sch BT34 . . . 132 D1
- **Ballyholland Rd** BT34 . . . 64 E4
- **Ballyholland Upper** BT34 . . . 132 D1
- **BALLYHOLME** BT19 . . . 5 A6
- **Ballyholme** BT20 . . . 4 E4
- **Ballyholme Espl** BT20 . . . 4 E5
- Ballyholme Prim Sch BT20 . 4 E5
- **Ballyholme Prom** BT20 . . . 4 E5
- **Ballyholme Rd** BT20 . . . 4 C5
- **Ballyhomra** BT26 . . . 48 D8
- **BALLYHORNAN** BT30 . . . 110 C3
- Ballyhornan Activity Ctr* BT30 . . . 110 D2
- **Ballyhornan Rd** BT30 . . . 62 E4
- **Ballyhosset Milltown** BT30 . . . 125 D8
- **Ballyhosset Rd** BT30 . . . 109 E2
- **Ballyhoy Rd** BT60 . . . 97 F3
- **Ballykeel**
  - Banbridge BT32 . . . 61 A7
  - Craigavon BT67 . . . 33 B7
  - Downpatrick BT30 . . . 108 A1
  - Dromore BT25 . . . 87 B7
  - Dromore BT25 . . . 89 B5
  - Holywood BT18 . . . 10 B3
  - Newry BT34 . . . 133 C8
  - Newry BT34 . . . 134 F8
  - Newry BT34 . . . 145 F2
  - Newry BT35 . . . 140 B6
  - Newtownards BT23 . . . 30 D8
  - Newtownards BT23 . . . 68 C2
- **Ballykeel Artifinny** BT26 . . . 46 D5
- **Ballykeel Ct** BT34 . . . 145 F1
- **Ballykeel Edenagonnell (Blaris)** BT26 . . . 48 A7
- **Ballykeel Edenagonnell (Hillsborough)** BT26 . . 48 B4
- **Ballykeel Lougherne** BT24 . . . 76 A2
- **Ballykeel Rd**
  - Ballynahinch BT24 . . . 76 A2
  - Banbridge BT32 . . . 61 A7
  - Craigavon BT67 . . . 33 C7
  - Downpatrick BT30 . . . 107 F1
  - Hillsborough BT26 . . . 49 E4
  - Newry BT34 . . . 119 B1
  - Newry BT34 . . . 145 F2
  - Newry BT35 . . . 140 B6
  - Newtownards BT23 . . . 23 C1
- **Ballykeel Rd S** BT8 . . . 30 C6
- Ballykeigle Prim Sch BT23 . . . 68 C1
- **Ballykeigle Rd** BT23 . . . 68 B1
- **Ballykelly** BT32 . . . 86 E3
- **Ballykelly Rd** BT32 . . . 86 E2
- **Ballykilbeg** BT30 . . . 108 B1
- **Ballykilbeg Rd** BT30 . . . 108 B1
- **Ballykillare** BT19 . . . 3 A4
- **Ballykine** BT24 . . . 90 C6
- **Ballykine Lower** BT24 . . 59 A7
- **Ballykine Rd** BT24 . . . 89 E6
- **Ballykine Upper** BT24 . . 90 C5
- **BALLYKINLER** BT30 . . . 123 F5
- **Ballykinler Middle** BT30 . . . 123 F6
- **Ballykinler Upper** BT30 . . . 123 E4
- **Ballyknick** BT61 . . . 84 E3
- **Ballyknock**
  - Craigavon BT62 . . . 100 F8
  - Craigavon BT67 . . . 45 E7
- **Ballyknockan** BT23 . . . 77 B8
- **Ballyknockan Pk** BT28 . . . 37 D8
- **Ballyknockan Rd** BT24 . . . 77 B7
- **Ballyknock Rd**
  - Craigavon BT62 . . . 100 F7
  - Hillsborough BT26 . . . 45 E4
- **Ballylane** BT60 . . . 116 A3
- **Ballylane Rd** BT60 . . . 115 F2
- **Ballyleidy** BT19 . . . 12 A7
- **Ballylenagh** BT30 . . . 110 A7
- **Ballylenaghan Ave** BT8 . . 22 C1
- **Ballylenaghan Hts** BT8 . . 22 B2
- **Ballylenaghan Pk** 2 BT8 . 22 B1
- **Ballylenaghan Rd** 1 BT8 . 22 B1
- **Ballylenaghan Upper** BT8 . . . 21 F3
- **BALLYLENY** BT61 . . . 85 F2
- **Ballyleny**
  - Craigavon BT66 . . . 87 B8
  - Richhill BT61 . . . 85 F1
- **Ballyleny Rd** BT61 . . . 85 F1
- **BALLYLESSON** BT8 . . . 28 B7
- **Ballylesson Rd**
  - Belfast BT8 . . . 21 B2
  - Lisburn BT27 . . . 27 E4
- **Ballylig** BT30 . . . 125 C5
- **Ballylig Rd** BT30 . . . 125 B6
- **Ballylimp** BT22 . . . 71 A1
- **Ballylintagh** BT26 . . . 48 F2
- **Ballylintagh La** BT26 . . . 48 E1
- **Ballylintagh Rd** BT26 . . . 48 D2
- **Ballylisbredan** BT16 . . . 17 F2
- **Ballylisk** BT62 . . . 56 A1
- **Ballylisk La** BT62 . . . 55 F1
- **Ballylone Big** BT24 . . . 91 A4
- **Ballylone Little** BT24 . . . 91 A6
- **Ballylone Rd** BT24 . . . 59 F5
- **Ballylough**
  - Castlewellan BT31 . . . 122 D7
  - Craigavon BT66 . . . 86 C4
  - Newry BT34 . . . 117 F2
- **Ballyloughan**
  - Armagh BT61 . . . 100 A7
  - Newtownards BT23 . . . 25 A6
- **Ballyloughan Rd** BT61 . . . 100 A7
- **Ballyloughlin** BT33 . . . 123 A3
- **Ballyloughlin Rd** BT33 . . . 123 A3
- **Ballylough Rd**
  - Castlewellan BT31 . . . 106 E1
  - Craigavon BT66 . . . 86 D4
  - Newry BT34 . . . 117 F3
- **Ballylucas** BT30 . . . 124 D7
- **Ballylucas Rd** BT30 . . . 124 E8
- **Ballymacanab** BT60 . . . 114 F6
- **Ballymacanallen** BT63 . . 57 C5
- **Ballymacanallen Rd** BT63. 57 E5
- **Ballymacanally** BT66 . . . 86 F7
- **Ballymacaramery** BT24. 91 A8
- **Ballymacaratty Beg** BT35 . . . 118 A6
- **Ballymacaratty More** BT35 . . . 118 B7
- **Ballymacarn North** BT24 . . . 90 C3
- **Ballymacarn Rd** BT24 . . . 90 D1
- **Ballymacarn South** BT24 . . . 90 E1
- **BALLYMACARRET** BT5 . . . 15 B5
- **Ballymacarret Intake** BT3 . . . 15 B7
- **Ballymacarrett Rd** BT4 . . 15 A5
- Ballymacarrett Recn Ctr BT4 . . . 15 C5
- **Ballymacarrett Walkway** BT4 . . . 15 C5
- **Ballymacarron** BT23 . . . 79 C2
- **Ballymacashen** BT23 . . . 78 C5
- **Ballymacashen Rd** BT23 . . 78 D5
- **Ballymacateer** BT66 . . . 43 A4
- **Ballymacawley** BT60 . . 115 D8
- **Ballymacawley Rd** BT60 . 115 C7
- **Ballymacbredan** BT67 . . 43 B6
- **Ballymacbredan Rd** BT67. 43 B7
- **Ballymacbrennan**
  - Dromore BT25 . . . 44 E3
  - Lisburn BT27 . . . 39 E5
- **Ballymacdermot** BT35. 141 C8
- **Ballymackilmurry** BT61. 84 D2
- **Ballymackilreiny** BT31. 105 A2
- **Ballymackilreiny Rd** BT31 . . . 105 A1
- **Ballymacmaine** BT67 . . . 43 D5
- **Ballymacnab Rd** BT60 . . . 114 F6
- **Ballymacnamee** BT22 . . . 95 A6
- **Ballymacodermot Rd** BT35 . . . 141 C7
- **Ballymaconaghy**
  - Belfast BT6 . . . 15 C2
  - Castlereagh BT6 . . . 22 C6
  - Newry BT34 . . . 65 F6
- **Ballymaconaghy Ms** BT8 . 22 D3
- **Ballymaconaghy Rd**
  - Castlereagh BT8 . . . 22 D3
  - Warrenpoint BT34 . . . 65 E5
- **Ballymaconnell** BT19 . . . 5 B3
- **Ballymaconnell Rd** BT20 . . . 4 F5
- **Ballymaconnell Rd S** BT19. 5 A4
- **Ballymacormick**
  - Bangor BT19 . . . 4 F7
  - Dromore BT25 . . . 88 C7
- **Ballymacormick Ave** BT19. 5 A4
- **Ballymacormick Cres** BT19 . 5 B5
- **Ballymacormick Dr** BT19 . . 5 B5
- **Ballymacormick Gdns** BT19 4 F5
- **Ballymacormick Link** BT19 . 5 B5
- **Ballymacormick Pk** BT19 . . 5 B5
- **Ballymacormick Rd**
  - Bangor BT19 . . . 5 A5
  - Dromara BT25 . . . 58 F6
- **Ballymacrandal** BT63 . . . 52 D3
- **Ballymacreelly** BT23 . . . 78 E4
- **Ballymacreely Rd** BT23 . . . 78 E4
- **Ballymacromwell** BT30. 79 C1
- **Ballymacruise** BT22 . . . 67 A4
- **Ballymacruise Cl** 9 BT22. 67 A4
- **Ballymacruise Dr** 1 BT22 67 A4
- **Ballymacruise Pk** 5 BT22 67 A4
- **Ballymacully La** BT60 . . . 83 B1
- **Ballymacully Lower** BT60 . . . 83 A1
- **Ballymacully Rd** BT60 . . . 83 A1
- **Ballymacully Upper** BT60 . . . 97 A8
- **Ballymadeerfy** BT34 . . . 152 C8
- **Ballymaderfy Rd** BT34 . . . 144 B1
- **Ballymaganlis** BT25 . . . 58 C6
- **Ballymagaraghan** BT67. 44 C6
- **Ballymagart** BT34 . . . 152 F7
- **Ballymagart La** BT34 . . . 152 F7
- **Ballymagaughey** BT23 . . 25 B1
- **Ballymagee** BT20 . . . 4 E2
- Ballymagee Prim Sch BT19 4 F1
- **Ballymageogh** BT34 . . . 144 F4
- **Ballymagerny** BT61 . . . 85 B6
- **Ballymagerny Rd** BT61 . . . 85 B6
- **Ballymaghan**
  - Belfast BT4 . . . 16 B8
  - Holywood BT18 . . . 9 D1
- **Ballymaghery** BT34 . . . 134 C6
- **Ballymagin** BT67 . . . 43 B8
- **Ballymaginaghy** BT31 . 121 F7
- **Ballymaginaghy Rd** BT31 121 F7
- **Ballymagin Rd** BT67 . . . 43 B8
- **Ballymaglaff** BT16 . . . 24 B7
- **Ballymaglaff Rd** BT5 . . . 24 B5
- **Ballymaglave North** BT24 . . . 59 C2
- **Ballymaglave Rd** BT24. . . 59 E1
- **Ballymaglave South** BT24 . . . 90 F3
- **Ballymagreehan**
  - Castlewellan BT31 . . . 121 F4
  - Newtownards BT23 . . . 18 D1
- **Ballymagreehan Rd** BT31 . . . 121 E6
- **Ballymakeonan** BT67 . . . 43 E8
- **Ballymakeown** BT62 . . . 50 C3
- **Ballymalady** BT23 . . . 24 E2
- **Ballymaleddy Rd** BT23 . . . 24 E2
- **Ballymarter** BT22 . . . 95 A3
- **BALLYMARTIN** BT34 . . . 146 A1
- **Ballymartin** BT23 . . . 79 A8
- **Ballymartin Rd** BT23 . . . 79 A7
- **Ballymartrim Etra** BT61 83 F2
- **Ballymartrim La** BT61 . . . 83 F1
- **Ballymartrim Otra** BT61 83 E1
- **BALLYMASCANLAN** . . . 150 D3
- **Ballymascanlan** . . . 150 D3
- **Ballymena Ct** 12 BT14 . . . 14 B8
- **Ballymenagh**
  - Downpatrick BT30 . . . 109 F4
  - Holywood BT18 . . . 10 C6
- **Ballymenoch La** BT18 . . . 10 A7
- **Ballymenoch Pk** BT18 . . . 9 E8
- **Ballymenoch Rd** BT18 . . . 10 A7
- **Ballyminetragh** BT19 . . . 5 E4
- **Ballyminetragh Gdns** 2 BT19 . . . 13 C8
- **Ballyministragh** BT23 . . 78 F7
- **Ballyministragh Rd** BT23 . 78 E6
- **Ballyminnish** BT22 . . . 95 E5
- **Ballymiscaw** BT16 . . . 16 F7
- **Ballymiscaw Rd** BT18 . . . 10 C2
- **Ballymoney**
  - Newry BT34 . . . 121 C3
  - Newtownards BT22 . . . 67 A1
  - Newtownards BT23 . . . 11 A6
  - Rostrevor BT34 . . . 143 B4
- **Ballymoney (Magherally)** BT32 . . . 86 F1
- **Ballymoney Rd**
  - Banbridge BT32 . . . 61 E7
  - Holywood BT18 . . . 2 A1
  - Newry BT34 . . . 121 C3
- **Ballymoney Rd** *continued*
  - Newtownards BT23 . . . 11 A4
- **Ballymoney (Seapatrick)** BT32 . . . 61 E7
- **Ballymoney St** 3 BT14 . . . 14 B8
- **Ballymoran** BT60 . . . 98 E2
- **Ballymoran Rd** BT60 . . . 98 F2
- **Ballymore** BT62 . . . 101 B8
- **Ballymore Pk** BT62 . . . 101 A7
- **Ballymore Rd**
  - Banbridge BT32 . . . 118 A6
  - Craigavon BT62 . . . 56 D1
- **Ballymorran** BT23 . . . 79 B4
- **Ballymorran Rd** BT23 . . . 79 B5
- **Ballymote Lower** BT30 109 A2
- **Ballymote Middle** BT30 . . . 108 F3
- **Ballymote Pk** BT30 . . . 62 D2
- **Ballymote Upper** BT30 . 62 D1
- **BALLYMOYER** BT35 . . . 130 A7
- **Ballymoyer Rd**
  - Armagh BT60 . . . 130 B8
  - Newry BT35 . . . 129 E6
- **Ballymullan**
  - Crawfordsburn BT19 . . . 2 F2
  - Lisburn BT27 . . . 26 E1
  - Lisburn BT27 . . . 39 A8
- **Ballymullan Rd**
  - Crawfordsburn BT19 . . . 2 E3
  - Lisburn BT27 . . . 38 F7
- **Ballymurphy**
  - Hillsborough BT26 . . . 90 A7
  - Newtownards BT22 . . . 70 B6
  - Newtownards BT22 . . . 94 D4
- **Ballymurphy Rd** BT26 . . . 89 F7
- **Ballymurry** BT30 . . . 109 E4
- **Ballynabee Rd** BT35 . . . 131 B5
- **Ballynabragget** BT66 . . . 86 D4
- **Ballynabragget Rd** BT66 . . 86 C5
- **Ballynacarry** BT35 . . . 147 B7
- **Ballynaclosha** BT35 . . . 149 A7
- **Ballynaclosha Rd** BT35 . . 149 A8
- **Ballynacor** BT63 . . . 40 B6
- **Ballynacor La** BT63 . . . 40 C8
- **Ballynacorr Manor** BT63 . . 40 B4
- **Ballynacraig**
  - Downpatrick BT30 . . . 92 D2
  - Newry BT34 . . . 64 E4
- **Ballynadrone** BT67 . . . 43 E6
- **BALLYNAFEIGH** BT6 . . . 22 A8
- **Ballynafern** BT32 . . . 119 D8
- **Ballynafern Rd** BT32 . . . 119 B7
- **Ballynafoy**
  - Banbridge BT32 . . . 103 B1
  - Belfast BT7 . . . 14 F1
- **Ballynafoy Rd** BT32 . . . 103 A1
- **Ballynagallagh** BT30 . . . 124 F5
- **Ballynagalliagh** BT60 . . 114 C8
- **Ballynagalliagh Rd** BT60. . 98 C1
- **Ballynagappoge** BT34 . 120 E3
- **Ballynagappoge Rd** BT34 . . . 120 D2
- **Ballynagarrick**
  - Belfast BT8 . . . 29 A1
  - Craigavon BT63 . . . 57 B8
  - Downpatrick BT30 . . . 110 C5
- **Ballynagarrick Rd**
  - Belfast BT8 . . . 28 F3
  - Craigavon BT63 . . . 57 A8
- **Ballynaghy** BT63 . . . 52 E2
- **Ballynagolan** BT60 . . . 97 F1
- **Ballynagolan Rd** BT60 . . . 98 A1
- **Ballynagowan** BT62 . . . 51 D8
- **Ballynagreagh** BT35 . . . 101 D1
- **Ballynagross** BT32 . . . 119 B8
- **Ballynagross Lower** BT30 . . . 109 D4
- **Ballynagross Rd** BT30 . . . 109 D2
- **Ballynagross Upper** BT30 . . . 109 D4
- **Ballynahatten** BT34 . . . 153 A4
- **Ballynahatten Rd** BT34 . . . 153 A5
- **Ballynahattin** . . . 150 B3
- **Ballynahatty** BT8 . . . 21 A1
- **Ballynahatty Rd** BT8 . . . 21 A1
- **Ballynahinch** BT61 . . . 99 F7
- **BALLYNAHINCH (BAILE NA HINSE)** BT24 . . . 59 C3
- Ballynahinch Prim Sch BT24 . . . 59 C4
- **Ballynahinch Rd**
  - Ballynahinch BT24 . . . 77 B2
  - Belfast BT8 . . . 76 E8
  - Carryduff BT8 . . . 29 D1
  - Castlewellan BT31 . . . 106 F3
  - Downpatrick BT30 . . . 91 D5
  - Dromara BT25 . . . 88 E6
  - Hillsborough BT26 . . . 47 E6
  - Lisburn BT27 . . . 38 D7
- Ballynahinch RFC BT24 . . . 59 B1
- **Ballynahinch St** BT26 . . . 47 C6
- **Ballynahome Cres** BT61 . . 60 F5
- **Ballynahone** BT60 . . . 60 F4
- **Ballynahone Ave** BT60 . . . 60 F5
- **Ballynahone Beg** BT60 . 60 A1
- **Ballynahone More** BT60 98 F5
- **Ballynahoneymore Rd** BT60 . . . 60 F5
- **Ballynakilly Rd** BT71 . . . 72 C7
- **Ballynalack** BT35 . . . 131 A1
- **Ballynalack La** BT35 . . . 131 A1
- **Ballynalack Rd** BT35 . . . 131 A1
- **Ballynalargy** BT67 . . . 35 D8
- **Ballynaleck** BT35 . . . 117 B7
- **Ballynaleck La** BT35 . . . 117 B7
- **Ballynamadda Rd** BT35 . . 140 F1
- **Ballynamagna** BT34 . . . 119 D4
- **Ballynamagna Rd** BT32 . . 119 C6
- **Ballynameta or Wood Park** BT60 . . . 97 B2
- **Ballynamona Rd** BT35 . . . 141 A1
- **Ballynamony** BT66 . . . 41 A6
- **Ballynamony La** BT66 . . . 41 C4
- **Ballynamony Pk** BT66 . . . 41 A7
- **Ballynamony Rd** BT66 . . . 41 A6
- **Ballynanaghten** BT67 . . . 34 C7
- **Ballynanny**
  - Banbridge BT32 . . . 103 A2
  - Newry BT34 . . . 134 E5
- **Ballynanny Rd** BT32 . . . 103 A2
- **Ballynarea** BT35 . . . 138 D7
- **Ballynarea Rd** BT35 . . . 138 D7
- **Ballynaris** BT25 . . . 58 C7
- **Ballynaris Hill** BT25 . . . 58 A6
- **Ballynaris La** BT25 . . . 58 A6
- **Ballynarry** BT62 . . . 73 E5
- **Ballynarry Rd** BT62 . . . 73 E5
- **Ballynaskeagh** BT32 . . . 119 A7
- **Ballynaskeagh Cross Roads** BT32 . . . 119 A7
- **Ballynaskeagh Rd** BT32 . 119 A6
- **Ballynavally** BT8 . . . 21 C2
- **Ballyneddan** BT34 . . . 151 E8
- **Ballyneddan Upper** BT34 . . . 143 E1
- **Ballynery** BT63 . . . 74 F4
- **Ballynery N Rd** BT63 . . . 40 B8
- **Ballynester** BT22 . . . 70 C5
- **Ballynewport** BT30 . . . 124 D8
- **Ballynewry** BT61 . . . 100 A5
- **Ballynichol**
  - Newtownards BT23 . . . 68 B4
  - Portaferry BT22 . . . 94 E3
- **Ballynichol Rd** BT23 . . . 68 B3
- **Ballynick Rd** BT61 . . . 84 E3
- **Ballynoe** BT21 . . . 66 E8
- **Ballynoe Gdns** BT19 . . . 3 C1
- **Ballynoe Rd** BT30 . . . 62 C1
- **Ballynure St** BT14 . . . 14 B8
- **Ballyobegan** BT22 . . . 71 B3
- **Ballyoran**
  - Dundonald BT16 . . . 17 F4
  - Portadown BT62 . . . 51 C7
- Ballyoran Ctr BT16 . . . 17 E4
- **Ballyoran Hill** BT62 . . . 51 C6
- **Ballyoran Hts** BT62 . . . 51 C6
- **Ballyoran La** BT16 . . . 17 E5
- **Ballyoran Pk** BT62 . . . 51 C6
- Ballyoran Prim Sch BT62. 51 C6
- **Ballyorgan** BT30 . . . 110 A4
- **Ballyphilip** BT22 . . . 94 E4
- **Ballyphillip Rd** BT22 . . . 94 D3
- **Ballyplunt** BT30 . . . 124 C7
- **Ballyquintin** BT22 . . . 111 A7
- **Ballyquinton Gdns** BT19 . . . 3 C1
- **Ballyquinton Rd** BT22 . . . 95 A1
- **Ballyrainey** BT23 . . . 25 B8
- **Ballyrainey Rd** BT23 . . . 18 E2
- **Ballyrath** BT60 . . . 98 B5
- **Ballyrath Rd** BT60 . . . 98 B4
- **Ballyrawer** BT22 . . . 66 F1
- **Ballyrawer Ave** BT22 . . . 66 F1
- **Ballyrea** BT60 . . . 98 A5
- **Ballyreagh**
  - Newry BT35 . . . 117 B8
  - Newtownards BT23 . . . 20 C2
- **Ballyreagh Ct** BT23 . . . 20 B4
- **Ballyreagh Pl** BT23 . . . 20 B5
- **Ballyreagh Rd**
  - Newry BT35 . . . 101 C1
  - Newtownards BT23 . . . 20 B4
- **Ballyreagh Way**
  - Newtownards BT23 . . . 20 B4
  - Newtownards BT23 . . . 20 C4
- **Ballyree** BT19 . . . 13 E8
- **Ballyree Dr** BT19 . . . 4 C1
- **Ballyree Gdns** BT19 . . . 13 B8
- **Ballyree Wlk** BT19 . . . 13 B8
- **Ballyregan** BT16 . . . 17 C6
- **Ballyregan Ave** BT16 . . . 17 C5
- **Ballyregan Cres** BT16 . . . 17 C5
- **Ballyregan Pk** BT16 . . . 17 C5
- **Ballyregan Rd**
  - Dundonald BT16 . . . 17 B7
  - Holywood BT18 . . . 10 B1
- **Ballyrenan** BT30 . . . 109 E6
- **Ballyrickard** BT23 . . . 68 D7
- **Ballyridley** BT22 . . . 94 D7
- **Ballyrobert** BT19 . . . 2 A4
- **Ballyrobert Rd** BT19 . . . 2 E3
- **Ballyrogan** BT23 . . . 18 E6
- **Ballyrogan or Mourne Park** BT34 . . . 144 F1
- **Ballyrogan Pk** BT23 . . . 18 C6
- **Ballyrogan Rd** BT23 . . . 18 D5
- **Ballyrolly**
  - Downpatrick BT30 . . . 108 A2
  - Newtownards BT22 . . . 67 A3
- **Ballyrolly Cotts** BT22 . . . 67 A3
- **Ballyrolly Rd** BT30 . . . 107 E1
- **BALLYRONEY** BT32 . . . 120 B6
- **Ballyroney** BT32 . . . 120 C8
- **Ballyroney Rd**
  - Banbridge BT32 . . . 104 B1
  - 13 Rathfriland BT34 . . . 119 F2
- **Ballyrush** BT23 . . . 31 F4
- **Ballyrushboy** BT5 . . . 15 D2
- **Ballyrusley** BT22 . . . 95 A4
- **Ballyrusley Rd** BT22 . . . 94 F4
- **Ballyrussell**
  - Belfast BT16 . . . 24 D6
  - Newry BT34 . . . 142 F6

Ballyrussell Rd
Belfast BT5 24 C6
Newry BT34 65 E7
Newtownards BT23 24 C3
BallysallaghⓉ
Downpatrick BT30 109 D3
Dromore BT25 88 C4
Ballysallagh MajorⓉ
BT23 11 C5
Ballysallagh MinorⓉ
BT19 11 E6
Ballysallagh Rd
Bangor BT19 12 A7
Downpatrick BT30 62 F4
Dromara BT25 58 F1
Dromara BT25 88 B4
Newtownards BT23 11 E5
BallyscandalⓉ BT61 97 F8
Ballyscandal Rd BT61 97 F8
BallysheilⓉ BT32 104 A1
Ballysheil BegⓉ BT62 100 F3
Ballysheil MoreⓉ BT62 101 A3
Ballyshiel Rd
Banbridge BT32 103 F2
Craigavon BT62 100 F3
BALLYSKEAGH BT27 27 A6
Ballyskeagh Dog Track
BT27 27 A6
Ballyskeagh HighⓉ BT23 11 E2
Ballyskeagh LowⓉ BT23 12 B3
Ballyskeagh Rd BT17 27 B6
BallyspurgeⓉ BT22 95 C7
BallystockartⓉ BT23 24 E5
Ballystockart Rd BT23 24 D4
BallystokesⓉ BT30 109 C6
BallystrewⓉ BT30 108 F2
Ballystrew Rd BT30 108 F1
BallysugaghⓉ BT30 109 C7
BallytrimⓉ BT30 92 F5
Ballytrim Rd BT30 92 E5
BallytroddanⓉ BT71 84 A3
Ballytroddan Rd BT71 84 A3
BallytrueⓉ BT61 85 F6
BallytrustanⓉ
Downpatrick BT30 109 E5
Newtownards BT22 94 E2
Ballytrustan Rd BT30 109 E5
BallytyroneⓉ BT61 85 B3
Ballytyrone Rd BT61 85 B3
BallyurnanellanⓉ BT22 70 A4
BallyvaddyⓉ BT70 82 D4
Ballyvaddy Rd BT70 82 D4
Ballyvalley Heights BT32 61 E6
BallyvallyⓉ
Armagh BT60 116 E7
Banbridge BT32 61 C3
Newry BT34 133 D2
Ballyvally Rd
Armagh BT60 116 E7
Mayobridge BT34 133 C3
Newry BT34 143 A7
BallyvangeⓉ
Downpatrick BT30 62 C1
Downpatrick BT30 108 E3
BallyvarleyⓉ BT32 102 B6
BallyvarnetⓉ BT19 12 D7
BallyvastonⓉ BT30 124 F5
Ballyveagh BegⓉ BT34 145 F5
Ballyveaghbeg Rd BT34 145 F4
Ballyveagh Beg UpperⓉ
BT34 145 E7
Ballyveagh MoreⓉ BT34 146 A4
Ballyveaghmore Rd
BT34 145 F5
Ballyveagh More UpperⓉ
BT34 145 F7
BallyvesterⓉ BT21 66 E6
Ballyvester Gr BT19 13 B8
Ballyvester Prim Sch
BT21 66 E7
Ballyvester Rd BT21 66 F7
BallyviggisⓉ BT30 125 C7
BallywaddanⓉ BT22 80 C1
BallywallonⓉ BT22 94 D8
BallywalterⓉ BT30 109 F5
BALLYWALTER (BAILE BHÁLTAIR) BT22 71 B6
Ballywalter Prim Sch 11
BT22 71 A6
Ballywalter Rd BT22 67 C2
BALLYWARD BT31 121 B7
BallywardⓉ BT22 94 E7
Ballyward Rd BT31 121 A7
BallywarrenⓉ BT30 109 B2
Ballywarren Rd BT30 109 C2
BallywatticockⓉ BT23 20 E2
BallyweelyⓉ BT34 134 D8
Ballyweely Rd BT34 120 C1
BallywhiskinⓉ BT22 67 B2
Ballywhiskin Rd BT22 67 C2
BallywhiteⓉ BT22 94 C5
BallywhollartⓉ BT22 95 B7
BallywierdⓉ BT22 94 F3
Ballywillan Rd BT30 92 E7
Ballywillan Rd E BT30 92 E5
BallywilliamⓉ
Donaghadee BT21 6 C3
Newtownards BT23 68 A4
BallywillinⓉ BT30 92 D7
BallywillwillⓉ BT31 106 D2
Ballywillwill Rd BT31 106 D2
BallywillyⓉ BT61 85 E5
BallywoodanⓉ BT30 110 C4
Ballywoodan Rd BT30 110 C4
BallyworfyⓉ BT26 48 D5
Ballyworfy Rd BT26 48 C6
BallyworkanⓉ BT62 55 E5
Ballyyagherty Rd BT24 77 D4
Balmoral Ave
3 Bangor BT19 13 D7
Newry BT34 64 E7
Balmoral Cl 5 BT19 13 D7
Balmoral Cres 7 BT19 13 D7
Balmoral Ct 6 BT19 13 D7
Balmoral Dale 9 BT19 13 D7
Balmoral Dr
4 Bangor BT19 13 D7
Lurgan BT66 42 A2
Balmoral Golf Club BT8 21 F5
Balmoral Pk
6 Bangor BT19 13 D7
Newry BT34 64 E7
Balmoral Sq BT19 13 D7
BalreganⓉ 149 E3
BaltarranⓉ BT60 98 A4
Baltarran Rd BT60 98 A4
BalteaghⓉ
Armagh BT60 97 B1
Craigavon BT64 40 E2
Balteagh Rd
Armagh BT60 97 B1
Craigavon BT64 40 E3
BaltylumⓉ BT62 51 B4
Baltylum Pk BT62 51 B5
Banbridge Acad BT32 61 D6
Banbridge Bsns Ctr BT32 61 A4
Banbridge Bypass BT32 61 D2
BANBRIDGE (DROICHEAD NA BANNA) BT32 61 B6
Banbridge Ent Ctr BT32 61 A5
Banbridge Golf Club BT32 61 B7
Banbridge High Sch BT32 61 B4
Banbridge Leisure Ctr
BT32 61 D5
Banbridge Rd
Banbridge BT32 102 C3
Craigavon BT63 86 A2
Dromara BT25 58 B4
Gilford BT63 57 E1
Lurgan BT66 42 C4
Newry BT34 119 F3
Banbrook Hill BT61 60 C6
Banbury St BT4 15 C6
Bandon Ct 16 BT14 14 B8
Banff Pk BT16 17 D3
Banff Wlk BT16 17 D3
Bangor Abbey BT20 4 A3
Bangor Acad & Sixth Form Coll BT20 4 B3
Bangor Acad & Sixth Form Coll (Clanmorris Campus)
BT19 13 D8
BANGOR (BEANNCHAR)
BT20 4 D3
Bangor Castle Leisure Centre
BT20 4 B3
Bangor Com Hospl BT20 4 B3
Bangor Golf Club BT20 4 D3
Bangor Gram Sch BT20 4 C5
Bangor Rd
Bangor BT19 5 A7
Holywood BT18 1 E2
Bangor Sta BT20 4 A3
Bangor W Sta BT20 3 D3
Baniff BT21 6 E1
Bankmore St BT7 155 A2
Bank Par BT34 64 D6
Banks La BT20 4 F6
Bank St BT1 155 A3
Bannaghan Rd BT30 93 F1
Bannagh Cnr BT6 22 B7
Bannanstown Rd BT31 121 F7
Bann Ct 19 BT14 14 B8
Bannfield Rd BT32 120 D3
Bannfoot Rd BT66 74 B7
Bannhill BT25 58 D7
Bann Rd
Castlewellan BT31 121 D5
Craigavon BT63 102 A2
Newry BT35 101 F1
Bannside Development Centre BT62 51 C5
Bannside Rd BT32 120 C5
Banns Rd BT34 135 D1
Bann St BT62 51 E3
Bann View BT63 57 C1
Bannview Hts BT32 61 C6
Bannview Mews BT32 61 C1
Bannview Rd BT32 61 D2
BanogeⓉ BT66 86 D7
Bantry Rd BT70 82 C6
Bapaume Ave BT6 22 C8
Barban Ct BT25 58 C4
Barban Hill BT25 58 C4
Barban Hts BT25 58 C4
Barban Mews BT25 58 C4
Barbour Ct BT27 38 C8
Barclay Manor BT25 89 D2
Barcroft Pk BT35 64 B4
Barkers Rd BT35 129 B1
BarleyfieldⓉ 149 F3
Barley Hill BT27 26 D2
Barley La BT34 64 E4
Barleywood Mill BT28 26 B8
Barnagh Gr 1 BT21 66 F8
BarnamagheryⓉ BT30 78 B1
Barnamaghery Rd BT30 78 A2
Barnea Pk BT35 141 A5
Barnet Cl BT23 68 D1
Barnet Dale BT23 68 E1
Barnet Rd BT3 14 F8
Barnett's Chase BT5 16 C4
Barnett's Cres BT5 16 C4
Barnett's Ct BT5 16 D4
Barnett's Ct Mews BT5 16 D4
Barnett's Gn BT5 16 C4
Barnett's Lodge BT5 16 D4
Barnett's Rd BT5 16 C4
Barnfield Rd BT28 26 B8
Barn Hill BT21 6 D3
BarnmeenⓉ BT34 119 D1
Barnmeen Rd BT34 119 D1
Barn Oak La BT5 16 D4
Barn Row BT31 122 D6
Baroda Dr 7 BT7 14 E1
Baroda Par 8 BT7 14 E1
Baroda St BT7 14 E1
Baronscourt Ave BT8 29 E4
Baronscourt Cl BT8 29 D4
Baronscourt Dr BT8 29 D4
Baronscourt Gdns BT8 29 E4
Baronscourt Glen BT8 29 D4
Baronscourt Hts BT8 29 E4
Baronscourt La BT8 29 E4
Baronscourt Link BT8 29 D4
Baronscourt Mews BT8 29 D4
Baronscourt Pk BT8 29 D4
Baronscourt Rd BT8 29 D4
Barrack Hill
Armagh BT60 60 E5
Banbridge BT32 87 D1
Craigavon BT63 86 B1
Barrack St
Armagh BT60 60 D5
Belfast BT12 154 C3
3 Newry BT35 64 C7
Barracrick Rd BT35 141 E7
Barr Cres 2 BT34 117 F1
Barrhall Rd BT22 94 E1
Barr Hill BT34 117 F2
Barrington Gdns BT12 154 B1
Barrons Hill BT35 131 A5
Barronstown Ct BT25 58 C3
Barronstown Rd
Banbridge BT32 103 E8
Dromara BT25 58 B1
Barr Rd BT35 130 D2
Barscourt BT27 26 B5
Bar View BT33 123 C5
Basin Quay 4 BT34 64 D6
Basin Wlk 5 BT34 64 D6
Baskin St 7 BT5 15 B5
Batchelors Wlk BT63 51 F5
Bathgate Dr 6 BT4 15 E6
Bath Houses★ BT30 109 B4
Bath La BT33 63 D2
Batley St BT5 15 D4
Battenberg St BT13 154 A4
Battleford Rd BT60 83 B3
Battlehill Rd BT61 85 F3
BavanⓉ BT34 133 B5
Bavan Rd BT34 133 B4
Bawn Hill Rd BT24 90 A3
Bawn La BT30 78 B1
Bawn Mdws BT60 99 E5
Bawnmore Rd BT9 21 B6
Bay Ct BT30 125 D5
Baylands Ct BT20 4 D4
Baylands Fifth Ave BT20 4 C5
Baylands Fourth Ave BT20 4 C4
Baylands Fst Ave BT20 4 C5
Baylands Second Ave BT20 4 D4
Baylands Sixth Ave BT20 4 D5
Baylands Third Ave BT20 4 C4
Bay Rampart BT66 74 E7
Bay Rd BT30 123 E7
Bay View BT35 141 C1
Bayview Ind Pk BT3 8 A3
Bayview Pk 12 BT34 153 C7
Bayview Rd
Bangor BT19 5 A5
Downpatrick BT30 93 B3
Newtownards BT23 79 B5
BBC Blackstaff House★
BT2 155 A2
Beach Ave BT33 63 D5
Beachlea BT22 20 F2
BÉAL FEIRSTE (BELFAST)
BT1 155 C3
BÉAL LEICE (BELLEEK)
BT35 130 C4
BEANNCHAR (BANGOR)
BT20 4 D3
Bearnagh View BT34 120 A2
Beaties Rd BT26 48 B4
Beatrice Ave 7 BT20 4 B4
Beatrice Rd BT20 4 B4
Beauford Manor BT63 52 D2
Beaufort Ave BT8 21 F3
Beaufort Cres BT8 21 F3
Beaufort Gdns BT8 21 F3
Beaufort Gr BT8 21 F3
Beaufort Pk BT8 22 A3
Beaufort Wlk BT23 19 C2
Beauly Dr BT16 17 D3
Beaumont Dr 1 BT19 4 F1
Beaumont Gr BT19 4 E1
Beaumont Hts 2 BT19 4 F1
Beaumount Sq BT66 41 E6
Bedford St BT2 155 A2
Beech Cl BT63 53 D4
Beechcote Ave BT63 52 A5
Beechcroft BT66 42 E5
Beechcroft Pk BT23 20 A6
Beech Ct BT66 41 F5
Beechdene Cres BT23 20 A6
Beech Dr BT23 19 D6
Beech End BT18 9 D5
Beeches The
Ballynahinch BT24 90 E2
Bangor BT19 13 D8
Beeches The *continued*
Castlereagh BT8 21 E2
Hillsborough BT26 89 C7
Killinchy BT23 78 F5
Newry BT34 64 E6
Portadown BT62 51 D5
Beechfield Ave BT19 12 F6
Beechfield Cres BT19 12 F6
Beechfield Ct 35 BT5 15 A5
Beechfield Dr
Bangor BT19 12 F6
Donaghadee BT21 66 F8
Beechfield Pk
Bangor BT19 12 F6
Lisburn BT28 37 C8
5 Rostrevor BT34 143 C3
Beechfield Prim Sch 38
BT5 15 A5
Beechfield St
Belfast BT5 15 A5
34 Belfast BT5 15 A5
Beech Gr
Ballynahinch BT24 59 B4
Dromara BT25 58 D6
Dunmurry BT17 26 F8
Portadown BT63 52 B4
Beechgrove BT27 26 B4
Beechgrove Ave
Castlereagh BT6 22 B5
Craigavon BT67 32 F7
Beechgrove Cres BT6 22 C6
Beechgrove Dr
Castlereagh BT6 22 B6
Craigavon BT67 32 F7
Beechgrove Gdns BT6 22 B6
Beechgrove Pk
Castlereagh BT6 22 B6
Craigavon BT67 32 E8
Beechgrove Rise BT6 22 C6
Beechhill Rd BT60 98 B1
Beechill Ave BT8 22 B2
Beechill Cres 7 BT62 101 B7
Beechill Ct BT8 22 A2
Beechill Gr BT28 26 B8
Beechill Ind Pk BT8 21 F2
Beechill Pk BT8 22 A3
Beechill Pk Ave BT8 22 A2
Beechill Pk E BT8 22 B3
Beechill Pk N BT8 22 B3
Beechill Pk S BT8 22 B2
Beechill Pk W BT8 22 A3
Beechill Rd BT8 21 F3
Beechland Dr BT28 38 A7
Beechlands
Banbridge BT32 61 C2
Belfast BT9 21 C8
Beechlands Pk BT18 2 A4
Beechland Way BT28 38 A7
Beechland Wlk BT28 38 A7
Beechlawn Sch BT26 47 C5
Beech Lodge Pk 2 BT34 65 D2
Beech Mdws BT62 51 D5
Beechmount Pk BT34 64 F8
Beechmount Rd
Belfast BT8 29 E8
Belfast BT8 77 B8
Beechnut Pl 8 BT14 14 B8
Beechpark St 7 BT14 14 B8
Beechpath Lakeside BT66 42 F5
Beech Pk
Belfast BT6 22 D8
Craigavon BT62 55 F1
Lisburn BT27 26 B4
Portadown BT63 52 B4
Beechvale BT23 79 A5
Beechview Rd BT30 92 D7
Beechwood BT32 61 A5
Beechwood Ave
Bangor BT20 3 F2
Moira BT67 34 B2
Beechwood Cres BT67 34 A2
Beechwood Ct
Castlereagh BT8 21 F2
Moira BT67 34 A1
Beechwood Gdns
Bangor BT20 3 F2
Moira BT67 34 B2
Beechwood Gr BT8 21 F2
Beechwood Manor
Dundonald BT16 17 B3
7 Richhill BT61 99 E8
Beechwood Mews BT8 21 F2
Beechwood Pk BT67 34 A1
Beechwood St BT5 15 D4
Beersbridge Rd BT5 15 D4
Begney Hill Rd BT25 89 E3
Begney Rd BT25 89 E3
BegnyⓉ BT25 89 E3
Beit St BT12 154 B1
Belair Ave BT23 18 D7
Bel-air Ave BT19 3 B4
Belair Pk BT23 18 D7
Belfast Airport Conservation Area★ BT3 9 A5
BELFAST (BÉAL FEIRSTE)
BT1 155 C3
Belfast Central Sta BT7 155 C2
Belfast City Hospl BT9 154 C1
Belfast Harbour Ind Est
BT3 8 C4
Belfast Inst of FE & HE
BT1 154 C3
Belfast Lough Reserve★
BT3 8 E4
Belfast Print Workshop Gall★ BT1 155 B4
Belfast Rd
Ballygowan BT23 77 E8
Belfast Rd *continued*
Ballynahinch BT24 59 D6
Bangor BT19 2 D1
Belfast BT8 29 F1
Comber BT23 25 C4
Downpatrick BT30 62 A7
Dundonald BT16 17 F5
Holywood BT18 2 B2
Lisburn BT27 26 C2
Newry BT34 64 D8
Newtownards BT23 18 C7
Newtownards BT23 31 C2
Belfast Royal Acad BT14 14 C8
Belfast Welcome Ctr★
BT1 155 A3
Belfry The BT25 58 D4
Belgrave St BT13 154 B4
Belgravia Ave
Bangor BT19 5 A1
Belfast BT9 14 B2
Belgravia Cres BT19 5 B1
Belgravia Gdns BT19 5 A1
Belgravia Gn BT19 5 A1
Belgravia Pk BT19 5 A1
Belgravia Rd BT19 5 A1
Bellaghy Rd BT60 97 F7
BellanamanⓉ 112 B8
Bell Cl BT13 14 A7
BELLEEK (BÉAL LEICE)
BT35 130 C4
Belleville Dr BT32 86 D1
Bellevue BT20 4 E4
Bellevue Dr BT28 26 A2
Bellevue Pk BT28 26 A2
Bellevue St BT13 154 A4
Bellevue Terr 1 BT61 85 E1
Bellfield BT31 122 D6
Bellisle Rd BT25 88 E5
Bellshill Rd BT32 103 D3
Bells La BT27 26 D6
Bell Twrs BT7 21 F7
BELMONT BT4 16 B5
Belmont Ave
Bangor BT19 3 C2
2 Belfast BT4 15 F5
Belmont Ave W BT4 15 F5
Belmont Church Rd BT4 15 F6
Belmont Cl 1 BT4 15 F5
Belmont Cres
3 Bangor BT19 3 C2
Newry BT35 140 B3
Belmont Ct 3 BT4 15 F6
Belmont Dr
Bangor BT19 3 C2
Belfast BT4 16 A5
Belmont Grange BT4 15 F5
Belmont Mews 11 BT4 15 E6
Belmont Pk
Bangor BT19 3 C2
Belfast BT4 15 F5
Belmont Prim Sch BT4 15 F5
Belmont Rd
Belfast BT4 15 E5
Craigavon BT62 73 D4
Newry BT34 153 A7
Belsize La BT27 26 B4
Belsize Pk BT27 26 B4
Belsize Rd BT27 26 B4
Belvedere Manor
Belfast BT9 21 B8
Lurgan BT67 42 B7
Belvedere Pk BT9 21 D7
Belvedere Rd BT23 19 E6
Belvoir Cl BT8 21 C2
Belvoir Cres
Castlereagh BT8 21 D2
Lisburn BT28 37 F8
Belvoir Dr BT8 21 C2
Belvoir Pk BT28 37 F8
Belvoir Pk Hospl BT8 21 D1
Belvoir Pk Prim Sch BT8 21 D2
Belvoir Rd BT8 21 F3
Belvoir St BT5 15 B5
BenaghⓉ BT34 132 F4
Benagh LowerⓉ BT34 152 E5
Benagh Rd
Newry BT34 132 E4
Newry BT34 152 D6
Benagh UpperⓉ BT34 152 E6
Benagh Upper (Main Portion)Ⓣ BT34 152 D5
BENBURB BT71 83 D4
Benburb Prim Sch BT71 83 D5
Benburb Rd
Dungannon BT71 83 F7
5 Moy BT71 72 A1
Moy BT71 84 A8
Benburb St BT12 154 A1
Benburb Valley Heritage Ctr★ BT71 83 C4
Ben Crom BT66 42 A3
Ben Crom Pk BT33 63 B4
Bencrom Pl BT34 153 C8
Benderg Ave (Ascaill Bhinn Dhearg) BT30 62 D4
Benderg Pk BT30 110 D
Bendigo St BT6 155 C
Benford Dr BT23 20 B
Benford Pk
Lisburn BT27 38 D
Newtownards BT23 20 B
Benmore Ct BT34 64 E
Bennan Pk BT16 17 C
Bennett's Ave 5 BT21 6 F
Bennet Wood BT19 2 D
Benowen Rd BT30 93 C
BenrawⓉ BT31 105 D
Benraw Rd BT31 105 C

Benson St BT28 . . . . 26 A2
Bentham Dr BT12 . . . . . . 154 B1
Bentinck St [7] BT15 . . . . . 14 E8
Bentrim Link Rd BT28 . . . 26 A2
Benvisteen Pk BT28 . . . . . 37 D8
Beresford Gn BT25 . . . . . . 58 E4
Beresford Hill BT25 . . . . . 58 E4
Berkeley Rd BT3 . . . . 14 F7
Berkley Ct
Banbridge BT32 . . . . 61 C1
Castlereagh BT8 . . . . 21 F3
Berkley Gr BT34 . . . . 65 E2
Berkley Sq BT19 . . . . 13 C7
Berkshire Sh Ctr BT23 . . . 20 A7
Berlin St BT13 . . . . 154 A4
Bernagh Gn BT33 . . . . 63 D7
Bernish Ave BT35 . . . . . . 141 D7
Bernish Cres BT35 . . . . . 141 D7
Bernish Rd BT35 . . . . 64 A2
Berry St BT1 . . . . 155 A3
Berwick Hts BT67 . . . . 34 C1
Berwick View BT67 . . . . . . 34 C1
Berwick View Spine Rd
BT67 . . . . 34 D1
BESSBROOK BT35 . . . . 131 C5
Bessbrook Prim Sch [10]
BT35 . . . . 131 C5
Bessbrook Rd BT60 . . . . . 116 C6
Best's Hill BT8 . . . . 21 E1
Best's Hill Ct BT8 . . . . 21 E1
Best's Hill Glen BT8 . . . . . . 21 F1
Best's Hill La BT8 . . . . 21 E1
Best's Hill View BT8 . . . . . . 21 F1
Bethany St [5] BT4 . . . . . . 15 F5
Bettys Hill Rd BT34 . . . . . 132 C2
Beverley Ave BT23 . . . . 19 F8
Beverley Cl BT23 . . . . 20 A8
Beverley Cres BT23 . . . . . . 20 A8
Beverley Ct BT23 . . . . 19 F8
Beverley Dr BT23 . . . . 20 A8
Beverley Gdns
Bangor BT20 . . . . 4 D4
[2] Newcastle BT33 . . . . 63 D5
Beverley Hills BT20 . . . . 4 D3
Beverley Hills Dr BT20 . . . . 4 D4
Beverley Hts BT23 . . . . 19 F8
Beverley Mews BT23 . . . . . 20 A8
Beverley Pk BT23 . . . . 19 F8
Beverley Rd BT23 . . . . 19 F8
Beverley Rise BT23 . . . . . . 20 A8
Beverley Wlk BT23 . . . . 19 F8
Beverly St BT13 . . . . 154 B4
Bexley Dr BT19 . . . . 13 E8
Bexley Gn BT19 . . . . 13 E8
Bexley Hill [1] BT19 . . . . . . 13 E8
Bexley Mdw BT19 . . . . 13 E8
Bexley Parks BT19 . . . . 13 E8
Bexley Rd BT19 . . . . 13 E8
Bignian Ave BT34 . . . . 153 D8
Bignian View Pk BT25 . . . . 58 D4
Billys Rd BT34 . . . . 132 C2
Bingham La [3] BT20 . . . . . . 4 B4
Bingham St E [2] BT20 . . . . . 4 B4
Bingham St S BT20 . . . . 4 B4
Binnan View Pk BT34 . . . 146 A1
Binnian Ave BT23 . . . . 19 F4
Binnian Ct BT23 . . . . 19 F4
Birchdale BT67 . . . . 42 D5
Birch Dr
Bangor BT19 . . . . 12 D8
Holywood BT18 . . . . 9 D7
Birches Prim Sch BT62 . . . 73 D5
Birches Rd BT62 . . . . 73 D5
Birch Gn BT17 . . . . 26 F8
Birch Gr
Craigavon BT63 . . . . 101 D8
Gilford BT63 . . . . 57 B2
Birch Hill Pk BT63 . . . . 52 B6
Birch Pk BT19 . . . . 12 D8
Birchwood Ct BT63 . . . . . . 52 E1
Bird Island Wlk [3] BT22 . . . 80 E7
Bishops Brae BT30 . . . . 62 B1
Bishops Brae Ave (Ascaill Chnoc an Easpaig) BT30 . . 62 C2
BISHOPS COURT BT30 . . . . 109 F3
Bishopscourt Acc Rd
BT30 . . . . 62 C2
Bishops Court Racing Circuit★ BT30 . . . . 110 B3
Bishopscourt Rd BT30 . . . 110 C6
Bishop's Well Rd BT25 . . . 58 D7
Black Abbey BT22 . . . . 70 E3
Blackabbey Rd BT22 . . . . . 70 E4
Black Bog Rd BT25 . . . . 88 E4
Blackbridge Rd
Newry BT35 . . . . 117 E8
Newry BT35 . . . . 129 E1
Black Castle Chambered Grave The★ BT35 . . . . . . 138 F2
Blackcauseway Rd BT30 . . . 94 C1
Blackford Mews [5] BT34 153 E8
Black Fort★ BT35 . . . . 147 C8
Blackhorns The BT34 . . . . . 64 E6
Blackisland Rd
Craigavon BT62 . . . . 73 A2
Dungannon BT71 . . . . 72 F4
Blackquarter Rd BT35 . . . 115 C3
Black Rampart BT62 . . . . . 73 D3
Blackrock Rd BT35 . . . . . . 138 D2
BLACKSKULL BT25 . . . . 87 A4
Blackskull Rd BT25 . . . . 87 A5
Black's La BT24 . . . . 90 E8
Blacks Rd BT62 . . . . 101 B6
Blackstaff Rd
[2] Downpatrick BT30 . . . . 107 D1
Newtownards BT22 . . . . . . 80 F4
Blackstaff Sq BT2 . . . . 155 A2
Black Thorn Cl BT34 . . . . 121 C2
BLACKWATERTOWN (AN PORT MÓR) BT71 . . . . 84 A5
Blackwatertown Rd BT71 . 84 B3
Blackwater Way BT12 . . . 154 B2
Blackwood Cres BT19 . . . . . 2 D5
Black Wood Cross Roads
BT60 . . . . 96 F6
Blackwood St [3] BT7 . . . . . 14 E1
Bladon Ave BT23 . . . . 19 E6
Bladon Ct BT9 . . . . 21 C6
Bladon Dr BT9 . . . . 21 C6
Bladon Pk BT9 . . . . 21 B6
Blair Dr BT66 . . . . 41 E7
Blair Mayne Rd N BT23 . . . 19 B5
Blairmayne Rd S BT23 . . . . 19 B4
Blairmont Rd BT60 . . . . . . 114 C6
Blair Pk
Bangor BT19 . . . . 5 B5
Lurgan BT66 . . . . 41 E8
Blakeley Terr BT12 . . . . . 154 C2
Blanchflower Pk★ BT4 . . . . 9 A1
Blaney Rd
Newry BT35 . . . . 128 F1
Newry BT35 . . . . 129 B2
Newry BT35 . . . . 147 D8
Blaney St
Belfast BT13 . . . . 14 B7
Crossmaglen BT35 . . . . . . 147 E8
Blaris BT27 . . . . 37 D6
Blaris Ind Est BT27 . . . . . . 38 B7
Blaris Old Burial Gd★
BT27 . . . . 37 D6
Blaris Pk BT28 . . . . 37 F7
Blaris Rd BT27 . . . . 37 D6
Bleach Gn Ctr The BT32 . . 61 C6
BLEARY BT66 . . . . 53 E4
Bleary Prim Sch BT66 . . . . 53 F5
Bleary Rd BT63 . . . . 52 F3
Blenheim Cl BT26 . . . . 49 B1
Blenheim Ct BT61 . . . . 99 E8
Blenheim Dr
Belfast BT6 . . . . 15 D1
Carryduff BT8 . . . . 29 D3
Newtownards BT23 . . . . . . 19 C2
Richhill BT61 . . . . 99 E8
Blenheim Pk
Carryduff BT8 . . . . 29 D3
[1] Hillsborough BT26 . . . . . 89 D8
Blenheim Pk S BT8 . . . . . . 29 D3
Blessington Ct BT26 . . . . . . 47 C7
Blondin St BT12 . . . . 154 C1
Bloody Bridge★ BT33 . . . 137 B4
Bloody La BT61 . . . . 84 E1
Bloody Loanan BT60 . . . . . 97 F5
Bloomdale St BT5 . . . . 15 C5
Bloomfield Ave BT5 . . . . . . 15 D4
Bloomfield Cl BT31 . . . . . 122 B4
Bloomfield Collegiate Sch
BT5 . . . . 16 A4
Bloomfield Commercial Ctr
BT5 . . . . 15 C4
Bloomfield Cres [3] BT5 . . 15 C4
Bloomfield Ct [1] BT5 . . . . . 15 C4
Bloomfield Ctr BT19 . . . . . . 4 C1
Bloomfield Dr BT5 . . . . 15 C4
Bloomfield Gdns BT5 . . . . . 15 D3
Bloomfield Link [1] BT19 . . 13 C8
Bloomfield Par BT5 . . . . . . 15 C4
Bloomfield Pk BT5 . . . . 15 D3
Bloomfield Pk W [1] BT5 . . 15 D3
Bloomfield Pl BT20 . . . . 4 B2
Bloomfield Prim Sch
BT19 . . . . 13 C8
Bloomfield Rd
Bangor BT20 . . . . 4 B2
Belfast BT5 . . . . 15 D4
Bloomfield Rd S BT19 . . . . . 4 C1
Bloomfield St [2] BT5 . . . . . 15 C4
Bloomfield Wlk BT19 . . . . . 13 C8
Bloom Hill Rd BT61 . . . . . . 85 D5
Blue Hill Rd BT32 . . . . . . 103 E1
Blue Rd BT63 . . . . 86 B1
Bluestone Rd BT64 . . . . . . 53 A7
Blythefield Prim Sch
BT12 . . . . 154 B1
Blythe St BT12 . . . . 154 C1
Boal's La BT25 . . . . 87 E3
BOARDMILLS BT27 . . . . 76 D4
Boat St BT34 . . . . 64 D4
Bocombra BT63 . . . . 52 C6
Bocombra Ave BT63 . . . . . . 52 C6
Bocombra Hill BT63 . . . . . . 52 C6
Bocombra Manor BT63 . . . 52 C6
Bocombra Prim Sch BT63 52 C6
Boconnel Ct BT66 . . . . 41 D7
Boconnell BT66 . . . . 41 B8
Boconnell La BT66 . . . . 41 C7
Bogbane BT71 . . . . 72 C5
Boggle Hill Rd BT66 . . . . . . 86 C3
Bog Rd
Banbridge BT32 . . . . 118 D8
Forkhill BT35 . . . . 140 C1
Lisburn BT27 . . . . 36 F5
Newry BT34 . . . . 121 D1
Newry BT34 . . . . 133 E7
Newry BT35 . . . . 138 E6
Newtownards BT22 . . . . . . 81 C4
Bog Rd The BT23 . . . . 77 F6
Bohard BT69 . . . . 82 A5
Bolton BT60 . . . . 116 E4
Bolton Rd BT60 . . . . 116 E4
Bombay St BT13 . . . . 154 A3
Bonds Rd BT35 . . . . 139 C3
Bonecastle BT30 . . . . 108 C2
Bonecastle Rd BT30 . . . . . 108 D2
Bootle St BT13 . . . . 14 A7
Bootown
Newtownards BT22 . . . . 70 C3
Bootown *continued*
Newtownards BT23 . . . . . . 20 B4
Boretree Island Pk BT23 . . 19 F7
Borough of Charlemont
BT71 . . . . 72 B1
Botanic Ave BT7 . . . . 155 A1
Botanic Ct BT9 . . . . 14 D1
Botanic Prim Sch BT9 . . . . 14 D1
Botanic Sta BT7 . . . . 155 A1
Bóthar an Charráin (Carran Rd)
Crossmaglen BT35 . . . . . . 147 E8
Newry BT35 . . . . 138 F1
Bóthar an Ráschúrsa (Racecourse Rd) BT30 . . . . 62 B2
Bóthar an Stáisiúin (Station Rd)
Ballynahinch BT24 . . . . 77 F4
Castlewellan BT31 . . . . . . 122 C5
Downpatrick BT30 . . . . . . 125 D5
Saintfield BT24 . . . . 77 D4
Bóthar Bhaile na Lorgain (Blaney Rd) BT35 . . . . . . 129 B2
Bóthar Chill Bhríde (Kilbride Rd) BT30 . . . . 62 D5
Bóthar Chluanaí (Springfield Rd) BT12 . . . . 154 A3
Bóthar Chnoc Croidh (Knockchree Rd) BT30 . . . . 62 D4
Bóthar Loch Rois (Loughross Rd) BT35 . . . . 147 D7
Bóthar Mhala Ard (Mallard Dr) BT30 . . . . 62 C2
Bóthar na Bhfál (Falls Rd)
BT12 . . . . 154 A2
Bóthar na Críonchoille (Creenkill Rd) BT35 . . . . . 138 E1
Bóthar na Huachtarlainne (Creamery Rd)
[1] Crossmaglen BT35 . . . . 147 F8
Newry BT35 . . . . 138 F1
Bóthar Thulach Forde (Mountforde Rd) [23] BT5 . . 15 A5
Bóthar Thulach Phoitinséir (Mountpottinger Rd) [7]
BT5 . . . . 15 A5
Bóthar Tullach Phoitinséir (mountpottinger Rd) [7]
BT5 . . . . 15 A5
Botter Rd BT67 . . . . 45 B7
Bottier BT67 . . . . 45 A6
Bottier Rd BT67 . . . . 45 A8
Bottlehill BT62 . . . . 54 B8
Bottlehill Rd BT62 . . . . 50 C1
Boucher Bsns Ctr BT12 . . . 14 A1
Boulevard The BT7 . . . . 21 E7
Boundary St BT13 . . . . . . 154 C4
Boundary Way BT13 . . . . . 154 C4
Boundary Wlk BT13 . . . . . 154 C4
Bovean BT71 . . . . 72 C5
Bovean Rd BT71 . . . . 72 C5
Bovennett BT32 . . . . 102 B3
Bovennett Hts BT32 . . . . . 102 C3
Bowens Cl BT66 . . . . 42 C3
Bowens La BT66 . . . . 42 C2
Bowens Manor BT66 . . . . . 42 C2
Bowlands Hts BT23 . . . . . . 20 A4
Bowmount Pk BT23 . . . . . . 20 A4
Bowness St [1] BT13 . . . . . 14 A7
Bow St Mall BT28 . . . . 26 A1
Bow St
Donaghadee BT21 . . . . 67 A8
Lisburn BT28 . . . . 26 B1
Bowtown Gr BT23 . . . . 20 A5
Bowtown Rd [2] BT23 . . . . . 19 F4
Boyd Ave BT22 . . . . 80 D7
Boydsrow BT61 . . . . 60 C7
Boyd St BT13 . . . . 154 C4
Boyle's Cnr BT60 . . . . 115 D3
Boyne Bridge BT12 . . . . . . 154 C2
Boyne Ct BT12 . . . . 154 C1
Brackagh
Craigavon BT62 . . . . 56 B5
Craigavon BT62 . . . . 116 E8
Brackagh Moss Rd BT62 . . 55 F7
Brackagh Rd
Craigavon BT62 . . . . 55 F2
Newry BT35 . . . . 116 F7
Brackenagh East BT34 145 F4
Brackenagh East Upper
BT34 . . . . 145 E7
Brackenagh E Rd BT34 . . 145 E4
Brackenagh West
BT34 . . . . 145 E5
Brackenagh West Upper
BT34 . . . . 145 D8
Brackenagh W Prim Sch
BT34 . . . . 145 E3
Brackenagh W Rd BT34 . 145 D6
Bracken Ave BT33 . . . . 63 D7
Bracken Cl [9] BT35 . . . . . 131 F5
Bracken Gr [6] BT35 . . . . . 131 F5
Brackenlodge BT63 . . . . . . 52 C7
Brackenridge BT30 . . . . . . 62 E5
Bracken Ridge BT25 . . . . . 58 E6
Brackenvale Bsns Pk BT8 29 C6
Brackenwood Cres BT8 . . 29 C8
Brackenwood Dr BT8 . . . . 29 C8
Brackly
Armagh BT60 . . . . 115 E7
Armagh BT60 . . . . 127 E8
Bracknagh BT60 . . . . 97 D7
Bracknagh Rd BT60 . . . . . . 97 D6
Bracknagh Tonnagh
BT60 . . . . 97 C6
Bradbury Pl BT7 . . . . 155 A1
Braddock Reagh BT23 . . . . 79 C6
Bradford Ct [4] BT8 . . . . . . 22 A6
Bradford Pl [2] BT8 . . . . . . 22 A6
Bradford Sq BT1 . . . . 155 B4
Brae Gr BT23 . . . . 31 E1
Braehead BT19 . . . . 4 D1
Braemanor BT66 . . . . 86 B8
Braemar Ave
Lurgan BT66 . . . . 42 A2
Newcastle BT33 . . . . 63 D7
Braemar Pk BT20 . . . . 4 C5
Brae Pk BT23 . . . . 31 E1
Brae Pl BT23 . . . . 31 E1
Brae Rd
Ballynahinch BT24 . . . . 76 D1
Newry BT34 . . . . 119 A2
Braeside BT23 . . . . 19 A6
Braeside Ave BT30 . . . . 62 C2
Braeside Cl BT20 . . . . 4 B1
Braeside Dr (Céide Thaobh an Chnoic) BT30 . . . . 62 C2
Braeside Gr BT5 . . . . 16 A1
Braeside Manor BT25 . . . . 58 E6
Brae The
Ballygowan BT23 . . . . 31 E1
Groomsport BT19 . . . . 5 B7
Brae View BT35 . . . . 129 F7
Brague Rd BT32 . . . . 102 F2
Brambles The
Bangor BT19 . . . . 12 E8
Craigavon BT66 . . . . 40 F7
[5] Kilkeel BT34 . . . . 153 B7
Bramblewood
Banbridge BT32 . . . . 61 F4
Craigavon BT67 . . . . 35 A7
Warrenpoint BT34 . . . . 65 E4
Bramble Wood
Newry BT35 . . . . 131 E5
Newtownards BT23 . . . . . . 20 A3
Bramblewood Dr
Banbridge BT32 . . . . 61 F4
Portadown BT62 . . . . 51 B1
Bramblewood Manor
BT32 . . . . 61 F4
Bramblewood Pk BT62 . . . 51 C1
Bramcote St BT5 . . . . 15 D4
Brandon Gr BT19 . . . . 13 D8
Brandon Par BT4 . . . . 15 D6
Brandon Pk BT22 . . . . 81 D4
Brandon Terr BT4 . . . . 15 D6
Brandra St BT4 . . . . 15 D6
Brandy Pad BT33 . . . . 135 F6
BRANIEL BT5 . . . . 16 A1
Braniel BT5 . . . . 23 B8
Braniel Cres BT5 . . . . 16 A1
Braniel Pk BT5 . . . . 16 A1
Braniel Prim Sch BT5 . . . . 16 B1
Braniel Rd BT27 . . . . 27 B1
Braniel Way [7] BT5 . . . . . 16 A1
Brannish Rd BT30 . . . . 62 D2
Brannock BT35 . . . . 101 D1
Brannock Cl BT35 . . . . 64 B4
Brannock Hts BT35 . . . . 64 B4
Brannockmeadows BT35 117 E8
Brassey St BT12 . . . . 154 B2
Breach Cl [12] BT5 . . . . 15 B4
Bread St BT12 . . . . 154 B3
Breagh
Craigavon BT62 . . . . 73 E3
Craigavon BT62 . . . . 74 A2
Portadown BT63 . . . . 52 B2
Breaghey BT60 . . . . 96 F1
Breaghey Rd BT60 . . . . 96 F2
Breagh Hill BT63 . . . . 52 B4
Breagh La BT63 . . . . 52 B2
Breagh Lodge BT63 . . . . . . 52 B3
Breagh Rd
Craigavon BT63 . . . . 40 A1
Portadown BT63 . . . . 52 C3
Brecken Ridge BT21 . . . . 6 E1
Breda Ave BT8 . . . . 22 A4
Breda Cres BT8 . . . . 22 A4
Breda Dr BT8 . . . . 22 B4
Breda Gdns BT8 . . . . 22 A4
Breda Par BT8 . . . . 22 A4
Breda Pk BT8 . . . . 22 A4
Breda Rd BT8 . . . . 22 A4
Breda Terr BT8 . . . . 22 A3
Breens La BT30 . . . . 62 C6
Breezemount BT61 . . . . 99 E5
Breezemount Ave BT23 . . . 13 B5
Breezemount Cl BT23 . . . . 13 B6
Breezemount Gr BT23 . . . . 13 A5
Breezemount Pk
Banbridge BT32 . . . . 61 A2
Newtownards BT23 . . . . . . 13 B5
Breezemount Rise BT23 . . 13 A5
Breezeways BT32 . . . . 61 A2
Brenda St BT5 . . . . 15 C3
Brentwood Pk
Castlereagh BT5 . . . . 15 F1
Richhill BT61 . . . . 99 E8
Brentwood Way BT23 . . . . 20 A6
Brerton Cres BT8 . . . . 21 E2
Brerton Gr BT8 . . . . 21 E2
Bresagh BT27 . . . . 76 C3
Bresagh Rd BT27 . . . . 76 C3
Brett Ave BT67 . . . . 41 F8
Brett Dr BT67 . . . . 41 F7
Brett Gr BT67 . . . . 41 F7
Brett Pk BT67 . . . . 41 F7
Brett Wood BT67 . . . . 41 F8
Brewery La
Armagh BT61 . . . . 60 D6
Dromara BT25 . . . . 58 D5
Newtownards BT23 . . . . . . 19 D5
Brian Dr BT24 . . . . 59 C5
Brianville Ave BT19 . . . . 5 A3
Brianville Dr [2] BT19 . . . . . 4 F3
Brianville Pk BT19 . . . . 5 A3
Briar Hill BT8 . . . . 22 C3
Briar Hill Cl [5] BT8 . . . . . . 22 C3
Briar Pk BT22 . . . . 71 A5
Briarwood Dr BT19 . . . . 4 F1
Briarwood Pk
Bangor BT19 . . . . 4 F1
Belfast BT5 . . . . 16 D2
Briarwood Rd BT19 . . . . 5 A1
Brickland BT32 . . . . 102 D1
Brickland Rd BT32 . . . . . . 102 D1
Bridge End BT5 . . . . 155 C3
Bridge End Sta BT3 . . . . . . 15 A6
Bridgeford Mdws BT62 . . . 51 D3
Bridge Integrated Prim Sch
BT32 . . . . 61 B3
Bridge Rd
Craigavon BT67 . . . . 33 B5
Craigavon BT67 . . . . 35 C1
Dromara BT25 . . . . 89 C1
Helen's Bay BT19 . . . . 2 D5
Newry BT34 . . . . 133 A1
Bridge St Link BT23 . . . . . . 25 E3
Bridge St S BT62 . . . . 51 E4
Bridge St
Banbridge BT32 . . . . 61 C4
Belfast BT1 . . . . 155 A3
Comber BT23 . . . . 25 D3
Donaghadee BT21 . . . . 67 A8
Downpatrick BT30 . . . . 62 C5
Dromara BT25 . . . . 58 D5
Gilford BT63 . . . . 57 D1
[10] Keady BT60 . . . . 114 A3
[9] Kilkeel BT34 . . . . 153 C7
Lisburn BT27 . . . . 26 D3
Newry BT35 . . . . 64 C4
Portadown BT62 . . . . 51 E4
Rostrevor BT34 . . . . 143 B3
Bridgeways BT32 . . . . 61 E6
Bridle Hill BT34 . . . . 65 B3
Bridleloanan BT34 . . . . 65 B4
Bridle Loanan BT34 . . . . . . 65 C3
Briggs The [11] BT19 . . . . . . 5 B7
Bright BT30 . . . . 125 A7
Bright Castle Golf Club
BT30 . . . . 125 A7
Bright Rd BT30 . . . . 124 F6
Bright St [21] BT5 . . . . 15 B5
Bristol Pk BT23 . . . . 19 D2
Bristow Dr BT5 . . . . 16 E2
Britannic Dr BT12 . . . . . . 154 C1
Britannic Pk BT12 . . . . . . 154 C1
Britannic Terr BT12 . . . . . 154 C1
Britches Cl [6] BT30 . . . . . . 62 C5
Broadway
Ballywalter BT22 . . . . 71 A6
Bangor BT20 . . . . 4 C4
Belfast BT12 . . . . 14 A2
Broadway Ind Est BT12 . . 154 A1
Broadway Par BT12 . . . . . . 14 A2
Brodick Way BT16 . . . . 17 E4
Brogies Rd BT35 . . . . 141 E8
Broken Bridge Rd BT32 . . . 86 D2
Bromley St BT13 . . . . 14 A7
Brompton Ct BT25 . . . . 89 D2
Brompton Pk BT62 . . . . 54 F4
Brompton Rd BT20 . . . . 3 E5
Bronte Prim Sch BT32 . . . 119 A5
Bronte Rd BT32 . . . . 119 B6
Brook Cl BT62 . . . . 55 C8
Brookdale BT32 . . . . 61 B5
Brook Dr BT62 . . . . 51 C1
Brooke Gdns BT32 . . . . 61 E5
Brookehill BT66 . . . . 42 A4
Brookfield Ave BT32 . . . . . . 61 B5
Brookfield Cl [1] BT63 . . . . . 57 C1
Brookfield Dr [2] BT22 . . . . 71 A6
Brookfield Ind Est BT32 . . 61 B5
Brookfield Manor BT63 . . . 57 C1
Brookfield Pk BT32 . . . . . . 61 B5
Brookfield Rd BT32 . . . . . . 61 B5
Brookfield Sch BT27 . . . . . 37 B3
Brookfield Specl Sch
BT67 . . . . 35 B4
Brook Gr BT32 . . . . 61 A4
Brookhill Cres BT61 . . . . . . 60 C6
Brook La BT19 . . . . 12 F7
Brooklands BT20 . . . . 4 F4
Brooklands Ave BT16 . . . . . 17 D4
Brooklands Cres BT16 . . . . 17 D5
Brooklands Dr
Dundonald BT16 . . . . 17 D4
Newtownards BT23 . . . . . . 19 B4
Brooklands Gdns BT16 . . . 17 D4
Brooklands Manor BT20 . . . 4 F4
Brooklands Pk
Dundonald BT16 . . . . 17 D4
Newtownards BT23 . . . . . . 19 B5
Brooklands Prim Sch
BT16 . . . . 17 E5
Brooklands Rd
Dundonald BT16 . . . . 17 D4
Newtownards BT23 . . . . . . 19 B4
Brookland St BT9 . . . . 21 A8
Brook Lawns BT35 . . . . . . 131 D5
Brook Lodge BT62 . . . . 55 B8
Brooklyn Ave BT20 . . . . 4 E4
Brooklyn Pk BT20 . . . . 4 E5
Brookmount St BT13 . . . . 154 A4
Brook Rd BT62 . . . . 55 C8
Brookside Rd BT24 . . . . 90 B4
Brook St BT18 . . . . 9 E7
Brookvale Ave BT19 . . . . . . 13 E7
Brookvale Cres [4] BT19 . . . 13 E7
Brookvale Pk [6] BT19 . . . . 13 E7
Brookvale Rd BT34 . . . . . . 119 D5

Brookvale Rise 1 BT28 .. 26 A1
Brookview BT19 .... 13 C6
Brookview Cl 4 BT35 ... 131 C5
Brookville Cres 2 BT35 . 131 C5
Broomhill BT62 .... 54 B5
Broomhill Cl
Belfast BT9 .... 21 B6
Newtownards BT23 .... 20 C6
Broomhill Ct BT9 .... 21 B6
Broomhill Dr BT33 .... 63 B4
Broomhill Gdns BT33 ...... 63 B4
Broomhill Gr BT66 .... 42 A3
Broomhill Pk
Bangor BT20 .... 4 E4
Belfast BT9 .... 21 B6
Newtownards BT23 .... 20 C6
Broomhill Pk Central BT9 21 C6
Broomhill Rd BT24 .... 90 E1
Broom Quarter BT22 ... 94 F8
Brootally BT60 .... 97 D1
Brootally Rd BT60 .... 97 E1
Brougham St BT15 .... 14 E8
Broughan BT60 .... 114 D8
Broughattin 150 E5
Broughmore BT28 ...... 36 A5
Broughton Gdns BT7 ...... 15 A1
Broughton Pk BT7 .... 15 A1
Brownlee Prim Sch BT27 . 26 B2
Brownlow Integrated Coll
BT65 .... 41 C2
Brownlow Rd BT65 .... 41 B1
Brownlow St BT23 .... 25 C3
Brownlow Terr BT67 ...... 41 F6
Brown Moss Rd BT60 .... 117 A3
Brown's Brae BT18 .... 10 B6
Brown's Pk BT18 .... 9 F8
Brown's Row BT1 .... 155 A4
Browns Sq BT13 .... 154 C4
Brown St BT13 .... 154 C4
Brownstown Bsns Ctr
BT62 .... 51 C4
Brownstown Pk BT62 ...... 51 C2
Brownstown Rd BT62 ..... 51 C4
Brownstown Recn & Com Ctr
BT62 .... 51 D3
Brownstown W BT62 ...... 51 C2
Bruce Ave BT23 .... 25 E3
Bruce St BT2 .... 155 A2
Brucevale Ct 2 BT14 ..... 14 C8
Brucevale Pk BT14 .... 14 C8
Brughas BT62 .... 73 C1
Brunswick Ave BT20 .... 3 F4
Brunswick Pk BT20 .... 3 E3
Brunswick Rd BT20 .... 3 F3
Brunswick St BT2 .... 155 A2
Brussels St 8 BT13 .... 14 A7
Bryandrum BT60 .... 100 B1
Bryandrum Rd BT60 ..... 100 B1
Bryansburn La BT20 .... 3 F4
Bryansburn Rd BT20 .... 3 D4
BRYANSFORD BT33 ...... 122 C2
Bryansford Ave BT33 ..... 63 C6
Bryansford Cliff BT20 ..... 3 D3
Bryansford Gdns BT33 .... 63 D5
Bryansford Mdw BT20 ..... 3 D3
Bryansford Pl
23 Belfast BT6 .... 15 A3
Newcastle BT33 .... 63 C4
Bryansford Rd
Newcastle BT33 .... 63 A7
Newry BT34 .... 121 D1
Bryansglen BT20 .... 3 D4
Bryansglen Ave BT20 ...... 3 D4
Bryansglen Cres BT20 ...... 3 E4
Bryansglen Pk BT20 .... 3 D4
Bryansglen W BT19 .... 3 D4
Bryansmore Pk BT33 ..... 63 B7
Bryson Ct (Cúirt uí Bhríosáin) 26 BT5 .... 15 A5
Bryson Gdns (Garraithe uí Bhríosáin) 29 BT5 .... 15 A5
Bryson St BT5 .... 15 A5
Bthar an Stáisiúin (Station Rd) 1 BT30 .... 92 B4
Buchanans Rd BT35 ...... 117 B1
Buckley's Rd BT35 .... 131 B5
Buckshead Rd BT30 ..... 107 F5
Bulgers Bridge Rd BT60 . 114 E3
Bulls Eye Pk BT30 .... 62 E6
Bulls Thompson's Hill
BT35 .... 64 B5
Bunker Hill BT60 .... 116 A8
Bunkers Hill BT31 .... 122 C4
Bunscoil an Iœir BT34 .... 64 D4
Burmah St BT7 .... 14 E1
Burnaby Ct BT12 .... 154 B2
Burnaby Pk BT12 .... 154 B2
Burnaby Pl BT12 .... 154 B2
Burnaby Way BT12 .... 154 B2
Burnaby Wlk BT12 .... 154 B2
Burn Brae 1 BT22 .... 94 D4
Burnbrae Ave BT62 .... 51 D3
Burnbrae Ct BT32 .... 61 E5
Burnbrae Mews BT32 ..... 61 E5
Burnpipe La BT24 .... 89 F5
Burn Rd BT24 .... 90 B6
Burn Rd The BT23 .... 68 B2
Burnreagh Ct BT23 .... 20 B4
Burnreagh Dr BT23 .... 20 B4
Burnreagh Pk BT23 .... 20 B4
Burnside
Craigavon BT65 .... 41 A2
Saintfield BT24 .... 77 B4
Burnside Ave BT8 .... 22 B3
Burnside Pk
Castlereagh BT8 .... 22 B3
Crawfordsburn BT19 .... 2 E2
Burnside Rd BT32 .... 103 B3
BURNT ISLAND BT71 ...... 73 A2
Burntollet Way BT6 .... 22 B8
Burnview Dr BT8 .... 29 D5
Burnview Terr BT32 .... 61 D5
Burren BT24 .... 90 A5
Burrenbane BT31 ...... 122 C3
Burrenbridge Cl 7 BT31 122 B4
Burren Cl BT66 .... 42 A3
Burrendale Pk Cl BT33 ... 63 D7
Burrendale Pk Rd BT33 ... 63 D7
Burren Gaa BT34 .... 142 D7
Burren Gr BT31 .... 122 C4
Burren Her Ctr* BT34 ... 142 D7
Burren Hill BT34 .... 142 B7
Burren Hill Rd BT34 ..... 142 D6
Burren Pk BT33 .... 63 D6
Burren Rd
Ballynahinch BT24 .... 89 F4
Castlewellan BT31 ...... 122 A3
Newry BT34 .... 121 F3
Warrenpoint BT34 .... 65 C4
Burrenreagh BT31 ..... 122 A3
Burrenreagh Rd BT31 ... 122 B3
Burrenview Way BT33 .... 63 C7
Burren Way BT6 .... 22 B8
Burren Wlk BT31 .... 122 B5
Burrenwood Pk 6 BT31 . 122 B4
Burrenwood Rd BT31 ... 122 B4
Burton Ave BT16 .... 17 C4
Burton Dr BT16 .... 17 C4
Bushfield Rd BT67 .... 35 F7
Bush Rd BT22 .... 81 D7
Buskhill BT34 .... 118 C5
Buskhill Rd BT34 .... 118 C4
Bute Pk BT16 .... 17 D4
Butter Crane Quay BT34 .. 64 C5
Buttercrane Sh Ctr BT35 . 64 C5
By Biddy Molloy's BT61 ... 84 E4
By Doyle's BT60 .... 97 F7
By Mckee's BT71 .... 72 D2
By Pogues BT61 .... 83 C2
Byrnes Rampart BT66 .... 74 F7
Byron Pl Mews BT18 .... 9 C7

C

Cabin Hill Gdns BT5 ...... 16 C4
Cabin Hill Mews BT5 ...... 16 C4
Cabin Hill Pk BT5 .... 16 B4
Cabin Hill Prep Sch BT4 .. 16 B5
Cabragh
Armagh BT60 .... 100 A2
Armagh BT61 .... 83 D1
Armagh BT61 .... 84 D1
Armagh BT61 .... 97 D8
Craigavon BT62 .... 100 E6
Hillsborough BT26 .... 49 A6
Newry BT34 .... 120 E2
Newry BT34 .... 133 A7
Cabragh Rd
Armagh BT61 .... 84 D2
Craigavon BT62 .... 100 E5
Newry BT34 .... 133 A6
Cabra Rd
Hillsborough BT26 .... 38 F1
Newry BT34 .... 120 F4
Caddells La BT34 .... 119 F2
Cadger Rd BT8 .... 29 F4
Cadian BT70 .... 82 E8
Cadian La BT70 .... 82 E8
Cadian Rd BT70 .... 82 E7
Cadogan Pk BT9 .... 21 B8
Cadogan St BT7 .... 14 E2
Cafolla Gdns BT66 .... 41 E6
Cahard BT24 .... 91 B8
Cahard Fort* BT24 .... 91 B8
Cahard Rd BT24 .... 91 C6
Cahill Pl BT34 .... 153 A8
Cahirlinn 8 BT34 .... 143 B3
CAIRLINN
(CARLINGFORD) 151 C4
Cairnburn Ave BT4 .... 16 B8
Cairnburn Cres BT4 .... 16 B7
Cairnburn Dr BT4 .... 16 B7
Cairnburn Gdns BT4 ...... 16 B7
Cairnburn Grange BT4 ... 16 A7
Cairnburn Pk BT4 .... 16 B7
Cairnburn Rd BT4 .... 16 A7
Cairndore Ave BT23 .... 20 B6
Cairndore Cl BT23 .... 20 B5
Cairndore Cres BT23 ..... 20 B6
Cairndore Gdns BT23 ..... 20 B6
Cairndore Grange BT23 .. 20 B6
Cairndore Pk BT23 .... 20 B6
Cairndore Rd BT23 .... 20 B6
Cairndore Vale BT23 ...... 20 B6
Cairndore Way BT23 ...... 20 B6
Cairndore Wlk BT23 .... 20 B7
Cairn Hill BT34 .... 64 F7
Cairnmore Dr BT35 .... 64 A6
Cairn Point BT21 .... 66 F7
Cairn Rd The BT60 .... 99 B1
CAIRNSHILL BT8 .... 22 C2
Cairnshill Ave BT8 .... 22 B2
Cairnshill Cl BT8 .... 22 C3
Cairnshill Cres BT8 .... 22 B2
Cairnshill Ct 3 BT8 .... 22 B1
Cairnshill Dr BT8 .... 22 B3
Cairnshill Gdns BT8 ...... 22 B3
Cairnshill Gn BT8 .... 22 B3
Cairnshill Pk BT8 .... 22 B3
Cairnshill Prim Sch BT8 .. 22 B3
Cairnshill Rd BT8 .... 22 B2
Cairnsmore Ave BT16 .... 17 D4
Cairns St BT12 .... 154 A2
Cairns The BT4 .... 16 A6
Cairnsville Pk BT19 .... 5 A3
Cairnsville Rd BT19 .... 5 A3
Cairo St BT7 .... 14 E2
CAISLEÁN AN TSIÁIN
(CASTLESHANE) 112 A1
CAISLEÁN UIDHILÍN
(CASTLEWELLAN)
BT31 .... 122 C5
CALEDON (CIONN AIRD)
BT68 .... 96 D6
Calhame Gdns BT22 .... 81 B1
Calhame Pk BT22 .... 81 B1
California Cl BT13 ...... 154 C4
Callaghans Rd BT35 ..... 139 D5
Callan Bridge Pk BT60 ... 60 A6
Callanbridge Rd BT61 .... 60 A6
Callan Cres BT61 .... 60 C5
Callan St BT61 .... 60 C5
Callan Way BT6 .... 22 B8
Callender St BT1 .... 155 A3
Calmor Cres BT35 .... 130 E1
Calone BT60 .... 99 B2
Calverstown Manor BT63 . 53 E4
Calvertstown Rd BT63 .... 53 E4
Calvert Way BT24 .... 59 C5
Calvin St BT5 .... 15 B4
Camagh BT60 .... 113 D3
Camagh Rd BT60 .... 113 C3
Cambourne Cres BT23 ... 19 E2
Cambourne Mews BT23 .. 19 D2
Cambourne Pk
Belfast BT9 .... 21 A4
Newtownards BT23 .... 19 D2
Cambourne Rd BT23 ...... 19 D2
Cambourne View BT23 .... 19 E2
Cambrai Dr BT66 .... 86 C8
Cambrai Hts BT66 .... 86 C8
Cambrai St BT13 .... 14 A8
Cambridge Ave BT66 ...... 41 E8
Cambridge St 8 BT15 .... 14 E8
Cambrook Est BT35 ...... 131 C5
Camden St BT9 .... 14 C2
Cameronian Dr BT5 .... 15 E2
Cameron St BT7 .... 155 A1
CAMLOUGH BT35 .... 131 C3
Camlough Pk 6 BT35 ... 131 C5
Camlough Pl BT6 .... 22 E8
Camlough Rd BT35 .... 64 A7
Camly (Ball) BT35 ..... 139 B8
Camly (Macullagh)
BT35 .... 129 E2
Camly Rd BT35 .... 129 D2
Campbell Cl BT28 .... 36 E6
Campbell Coll BT4 .... 16 C6
Campbell Ct
6 Belfast BT4 .... 16 A5
Lisburn BT28 .... 36 E6
Campbell Pk Ave 1 BT4 .. 16 A5
Campbells Hill BT32 ..... 103 F1
Campbells La BT62 .... 51 B1
Campbell Wlk BT67 .... 42 A7
Camross Pk 3 BT9 .... 14 C2
Canada St 2 BT6 .... 15 A3
Canal Bank BT35 .... 117 E7
Canal Ct BT63 .... 101 E4
Canal Quay BT35 .... 64 D7
Canal Row 1 BT23 .... 19 E4
Canal St
Lisburn BT27 .... 26 C1
Newry BT35 .... 64 C7
Canary BT71 .... 72 D1
Canary Rd BT71 .... 72 D1
Canberra Gdns
Dundonald BT16 .... 17 C5
Newtownards BT23 .... 19 D1
Canberra Pk BT16 .... 17 C5
Candahar St BT7 .... 14 E1
Canmore Cl BT13 .... 154 A3
Canmore Ct BT13 .... 154 A4
Canmore St BT13 .... 154 A4
Cannagola Beg BT62 ... 73 F1
Cannagola Beg Rd BT62 .. 73 F2
Cannagola More BT62 .. 73 F2
Cannagola Rd BT62 .... 73 F2
Canning Pl 9 BT15 .... 14 E8
Canning's Ct BT13 .... 154 B4
Cannyreagh Rd BT21 ..... 66 E7
Canoneill BT62 .... 73 F1
Canton Ct BT6 .... 15 B4
Canvy Manor BT63 .... 52 D2
Cappagh
Banbridge BT32 .... 103 B3
Newry BT35 .... 147 E6
Cappagh Gdns BT6 .... 22 B8
Captains Rd BT35 .... 149 E7
Caramoyle Est BT60 ..... 114 B3
Carbet Rd BT63 .... 40 C4
Carbrey Dr BT60 .... 114 A2
Carbrey Hts BT60 .... 114 A2
Carcullion BT34 .... 134 A3
Cardinal á Fiaich Heritage Ctr* BT35 .... 139 A6
Cardinal O'Fiaich Sq (Cearng an Chairdinéil Fiaich) 4
BT35 .... 147 F8
Cardy BT22 .... 70 C7
Cardy Cl BT19 .... 3 E2
Cardy Rd BT22 .... 70 C6
Cardy Rd E BT22 .... 70 D7
Carewamean Rd BT35 ... 150 B6
Carew St BT4 .... 15 C5
Cargabane BT34 .... 118 D3
Cargabane Rd BT34 ...... 118 D4
Cargaclogher BT60 .... 128 A8
Cargaclogher Rd BT60 .. 114 A1
Cargacreevy BT27 ...... 76 B3
Cargacroy BT27 .... 49 E8
Cargagh
Armagh BT60 .... 60 B2
Downpatrick BT30 .... 108 B2
Downpatrick BT30 .... 110 B6
Cargaghlisnanarney .. 147 C3
Cargagh Rd BT30 .... 92 B2
Cargagreevy Rd BT24 .... 76 A2
Cargalisgorran BT60 .. 113 C2
Cargalisgorran Rd BT60 . 113 C2
Carganamuck BT61 ..... 84 D2
Cargans BT62 .... 101 C6
Cargans Rd BT62 .... 101 C7
Cargie Rd BT35 .... 138 E6
Cargill St BT13 .... 154 C4
Cargoes Cres BT19 .... 2 F3
Cargygray BT26 .... 89 E7
Cargygray Rd
Ballynahinch BT24 .... 90 B6
Hillsborough BT26 .... 89 F7
Cariff Ct BT30 .... 110 D6
Carleton St BT62 .... 51 D4
CARLINGFORD
(CAIRLINN) 151 C4
Carlingford Pk BT34 ...... 64 E2
Carlingford St
Belfast BT6 .... 15 B3
Crossmaglen BT35 ...... 147 F8
Carlisle Ave BT24 .... 59 E4
Carlisle Par BT15 .... 14 D7
Carlisle Pk BT24 .... 59 E3
Carlisle Rd BT15 .... 14 D7
Carlisle Terr BT15 .... 14 D7
Carlow St BT13 .... 154 B4
Carlston Ave BT18 .... 10 A7
Carlton Hills BT8 .... 29 D4
Carlton Hts BT19 .... 4 F1
Carlton Pk BT19 .... 4 F1
Carmeen BT34 .... 133 E3
Carmeen Gdns BT23 ...... 19 C3
Carmeen Rd BT34 .... 133 C3
Carmel St BT7 .... 14 D2
Carmen La BT20 .... 3 E2
Carn BT63 .... 40 B4
Carnacally
Downpatrick BT30 .... 91 E4
Newry BT34 .... 118 D1
Newry BT35 .... 130 C1
Carnacally Rd BT34 ...... 118 D1
Carnacavill BT33 .... 122 F2
Carnacavill Rd BT31 ..... 122 E2
Carnagat BT35 .... 64 A6
Carnagat Pk BT35 .... 64 A7
Carnagat Rd BT35 .... 64 B6
Carnagh Pk BT34 .... 64 E3
Carnalbanagh East
BT67 .... 34 C2
Carnalbanagh West
BT67 .... 34 B2
Carnalea BT19 .... 3 C5
Carnalea Ave BT19 .... 3 B4
Carnalea Dr BT19 .... 3 B4
Carnalea Glen BT19 .... 3 B4
Carnalea Golf Club BT19 .. 3 D5
Carnalea Pk BT19 .... 3 B4
Carnalea Pl 3 BT15 .... 14 E8
Carnalea Sta BT19 .... 3 C5
Carnally BT35 .... 139 D1
Carnally Rd BT35 .... 139 D1
Carnalroe Rd BT31 ...... 105 D1
Carnamena Ave BT6 .... 22 D8
Carnamena Gdns 1 BT6 . 22 D8
Carnamena Pk 2 BT6 .... 22 D8
Carnamuck BT5 .... 15 F1
Carnan St BT13 .... 154 A4
Carnany BT34 .... 133 C4
Carnany Rd BT34 .... 133 C5
Carnasure BT23 .... 25 D1
Carnathen La BT21 .... 6 F1
Carnavanaghan BT60 .. 115 A8
Carnavanaghan Rd BT60 . 99 B1
Carnbane
Lisburn BT27 .... 37 E2
Newry BT35 .... 131 F6
Carnbane Bsns Pk BT35 . 131 F6
Carnbane Gdns BT35 ..... 131 F6
Carnbane Ind Est BT35 .. 131 F5
Carnbane Rd
Lisburn BT27 .... 37 E2
Newry BT35 .... 131 F6
Carnbrae Ave BT8 .... 22 C3
Carnbrae Pk BT8 .... 22 C3
Carn Bsns Pk BT63 .... 40 B3
Carncaver Rd
1 Belfast BT6 .... 15 E1
Belfast BT6 .... 22 E8
Carnegie Bsns Ctr BT12 . 154 C1
Carnegie St BT66 .... 42 A5
Carn End BT18 .... 9 D5
Carnesure Ave BT23 ...... 25 C2
Carnesure Dr BT23 .... 25 C2
Carnesure Gdns BT23 .... 25 C2
Carnesure Hts BT23 .... 25 D2
Carnesure Manor BT23 ... 25 D2
Carnesure Pk BT23 .... 25 D2
Carnesure Rd BT23 .... 25 C2
Carnesure Terr BT23 ...... 25 C2
Carnew BT25 .... 104 D7
Carnew Fort Earthwork*
BT25 .... 104 D7
Carnew Rd BT32 .... 104 C6
Carney Cres BT6 .... 22 E8
Carneyhall BT34 .... 132 B5
Carney Hill BT18 .... 1 H2
Carney Hill BT22 .... 67 A1
Carneyhough BT34 .... 64 F7
Carnforth St BT5 .... 15 B5
Carn Gdns BT34 .... 153 B7
Carnglave Manor BT24 ... 90 E2
Carn Ind Est BT63 .... 40 B2
Carnlougherin BT67 ..... 35 E5
Carnlougherin Rd BT67 .. 35 E5
Carnmeen BT34 .... 132 A7
Carnmeen Pk BT34 .... 65 D3
Carnpark Rd BT25 .... 104 D6
Carn Rd
Craigavon BT63 .... 40 C3
Newry BT35 .... 141 B6
Carnreagh BT64 .... 40 D1
Carnreagh BT26 .... 47 E8
Carnreagh Ave BT26 ...... 47 E7
Carnreagh Rd
Castlewellan BT31 ...... 106 E4
Hillsborough BT26 .... 47 D7
Carn View BT35 .... 141 D7
Carolan Rd BT7 .... 21 F7
Carolhill Dr
Bangor BT20 .... 4 F5
Belfast BT4 .... 15 F7
Carolhill Gdns BT4 .... 15 F7
Carolhill Pk
Bangor BT20 .... 4 F5
Belfast BT4 .... 15 F7
Carolina St BT13 .... 154 A4
Caroline Ave BT66 .... 41 E7
Caroline Gdns BT19 .... 5 A5
Carolsteen Ave BT19 .... 2 E4
Carolsteen Dr BT19 .... 2 E5
Carolsteen Gdns BT19 ..... 2 E5
Carolsteen Pk BT19 .... 2 E5
Carquillan BT34 .... 134 A5
Carr BT27 .... 76 C7
Carraigbrae BT35 .... 130 C4
Carraighdua BT35 .... 130 C4
Carran
Craigavon BT62 .... 116 E8
Crossmaglen BT35 ...... 138 F1
Carran Cl BT35 .... 147 E8
Carran Rd (Bóthar an Charráin)
Crossmaglen BT35 ...... 147 E8
Newry BT35 .... 138 F1
Carriage Mews BT19 .... 2 D5
Carrick BT63 .... 56 B8
Carrickabolie BT60 .... 127 D8
Carrickabolie Rd BT60 .. 127 D8
Carrickacullion BT35 .. 129 E3
Carrickacullion Rd BT35 129 D3
Carrickaduff Rd BT60 ... 127 F4
Carrickaldreen BT35 .. 140 C4
Carrickaloughran BT61 . 98 B7
Carrickamone 147 B6
Carrickananny BT60 .. 130 D6
Carrickananny Rd BT60 . 130 D6
Carrickaneena 150 C6
Carrickaness BT71 ..... 83 D4
Carrickaness Gdns BT71 .. 83 C3
Carrickaness Rd BT61 .... 83 C3
Carrickard BT34 .... 64 E6
Carrickaslane 127 D1
Carrickastickan BT35 . 149 E8
Carrickastickan Rd BT35 149 E6
Carrickastuck 148 E3
Carrickbawn Pk 1 BT34 . 143 C3
Carrickblacker Ave BT63 . 51 F5
Carrickblacker Rd BT63 .. 51 F5
Carrickbrack BT35 ..... 117 C5
Carrickbracken BT35 .. 131 C3
Carrickbroad BT35 ..... 150 A7
Carrickbroad Rd BT35 ... 149 F8
Carrick Cl BT34 .... 142 D7
Carrickcloghan BT35 .. 131 A3
Carrickcloghan Hill
BT35 .... 131 A4
Carrickcloghan Rd BT35 . 131 A3
Carrickcroppan BT35 .. 131 B4
Carrickcroppan Rd BT35 131 B4
Carrickcrossan BT34 .. 133 A4
Carrick Cruppin GAA Club
BT35 .... 131 C4
Carrickdale Gdns BT62 ... 51 E2
Carrickdesland BT34 .... 142 E6
Carrick Dr BT66 .... 42 C4
Carrick Dr Mews BT66 .... 42 C4
Carrickdrumman BT35 118 B7
Carrickduff BT60 .... 127 F4
Carrickedmond 149 F5
Carrickgallogly BT60 .. 130 C6
Carrickgallogly Rd BT60 . 130 B6
Carrick Hill (Cnoc na Carraige) BT13 .... 155 A4
Carrickinab BT30 ...... 124 A7
Carrickinab Rd BT30 .... 123 E6
Carricklane
Armagh BT60 .... 113 A4
Armagh BT60 .... 115 F7
Carricklongfield BT69 .. 82 A7
Carricklongfield Rd BT69 . 82 A7
Carrickmacstay BT34 .. 142 E7
Carrickmaddyroe BT27 . 76 C5
Carrickmannan BT23 ... 78 A6
Carrickmannin Gdns 1
BT19 .... 3 D1
Carrickmannon Prim Sch
BT23 .... 78 A6
Carrickmannon Rd BT23 .. 77 F8
Carrick Mdw BT35 .... 131 B4
Carricknadarriff BT26 .. 49 F1
Carricknadarriff Rd BT26 . 49 D2
Carricknagalliagh
BT35 .... 140 B8
Carricknagavna BT35 . 140 A7
Carricknagavna Rd BT35 139 F7
Carricknaveagh BT27 .. 76 E5
Carricknaveagh Rd BT27 . 76 E4

Carrick Prim Sch
Lurgan BT66 41 F4
Newry BT34 142 D7
Carrick Rd
Banbridge BT32 118 B7
Craigavon BT62 74 C5
Newry BT34 142 E8
Carrickree 2 BT34 65 B3
Carrickree Mews BT34 65 B3
Carrickrovaddy BT34 117 F1
Carrickrovaddy Rd
Newry BT34 117 E2
Newry BT35 129 F1
Carricktroddan BT60 98 B6
Carrickvale BT66 41 E4
Carrickvale Ave BT66 41 E4
Carrickview BT34 142 D6
Carrick View BT71 83 C4
Carrick Vista 2 BT35 131 D5
Carrigagh Rd BT25 105 B5
Carrigans BT35 139 E3
Carrigans Pass BT35 139 F3
Carrigard BT33 123 C5
Carrigart BT65 41 C3
Carrigart Manor BT65 41 C4
Carrigatuke Rd
Armagh BT60 114 F2
Newry BT35 129 A8
Carrigbeg Ave 1 BT23 19 F4
Carrig Dene BT19 2 C6
Carrigenagh BT34 145 D4
Carrigenagh Rd
Kilkeel BT34 153 D8
Newry BT34 145 D1
Carrigenagh Upper
BT34 145 D6
Carrig More BT24 77 B3
Carrigs Rd BT33 122 F2
Carrigullian BT23 79 A4
Carrigvale BT33 123 C5
Carrington St BT6 155 C1
Carrintaggart BT30 110 A8
Carrisbrook Gdns BT27 26 B6
Carrive BT35 140 A2
Carrive Cres BT35 64 B1
Carrive Dr BT35 64 B1
Carrivekeeney Rd BT35 131 E3
Carrivekeeny BT35 131 D3
Carrivemaclone BT35 141 D8
Carrive Rd BT35 139 F2
Carrogs BT34 142 C8
Carrogs Rd BT34 132 E1
Carrowbaghran BT30 109 E2
Carrowbane BT30 124 F7
Carrowbane Rd
Armagh BT60 114 B1
Downpatrick BT30 124 F8
Newry BT35 130 E4
Carrowbeg BT71 83 A6
Carrowcarlin BT30 93 F1
Carrowcolman BT70 82 F7
Carrowcolman Rd BT70 83 A8
CARROWDORE BT22 66 E1
Carrowdore Gdns BT19 3 D2
Carrowdore Prim Sch
BT22 66 E1
Carrowdore Rd BT22 70 B7
Carrowdressex BT30 125 B7
Carrowkeel 112 A2
Carrowmannan BT35 130 B3
Carrowmannan Rd BT35 130 B3
Carrowmoney BT60 99 E4
Carrownacaw BT30 109 E7
Carrownacaw Rd BT30 109 E7
Carrowreagh BT16 17 E6
Carrowreagh Bsns Pk
BT16 17 E5
Carrowreagh Gdns BT16 17 E4
Carrowreagh Pk BT16 17 E4
Carrowreagh Rd
Belfast BT16 10 F1
Dundonald BT16 17 F6
Carrowvanney Rd BT30 109 D6
Carrowvanny BT30 109 D7
Carr Prim Sch BT27 76 C8
Carr Rd BT27 76 C7
Carrycastle BT70 82 C7
Carrycastle Rd BT70 82 C7
Carryduff Bsns Pk BT8 29 E3
CARRYDUFF (CEATHRÚ AODHA DHUIBH) BT8 29 C3
Carryduff Prim Sch BT8 29 E3
Carryduff Rd BT27 76 D5
Carryduff Sh Ctr The BT8 29 D2
Carryhugh BT60 113 D2
Carryhugh Rd BT60 113 D3
Carryreagh BT21 66 E7
Carshaulton Rd BT21 6 F1
CARSON PARK BT24 77 F1
Carsons Ave BT23 31 F1
Carsons Ct BT23 31 F1
Carsons La 9 BT23 77 F8
Carsons Mews BT23 31 F1
Carsons Rd BT23 31 F1
Carsonstown BT24 77 E3
Carsonstown Rd BT24 77 D5
Carys Fort★ BT30 91 F7
Casaeldona Cres BT6 22 F8
Casaeldona Dr 1 BT6 22 F8
Casaeldona Gdns BT6 22 E8
Casaeldona Pk BT6 22 E8
Casaeldona Rise BT6 22 F8
Cascades Leisure Complex
BT62 51 F4
Cascum Rd BT32 61 B1
Casement Pk BT34 153 C6
Cashel
Armagh BT60 115 A5
Cashel *continued*
Creaghanroe 127 A3
Newry BT35 139 F5
Cashel Rd
Armagh BT60 115 A5
Newry BT35 139 F3
Caskum BT32 102 E3
Castle Arc BT1 155 A3
Castle Ave
3 Castlewellan BT31 122 C5
Moira BT67 34 B2
Portadown BT62 51 E5
Richhill BT61 85 E1
Castleaverry BT23 68 E8
Castlebeg BT23 25 C6
Castleblaney Rd
Armagh BT60 113 F1
Keady BT60 114 A2
Castle Blaney St BT35 129 C4
Castleboy BT22 95 A8
Castleboy Ave BT8 21 E3
Castle Bright★ BT30 125 A7
Castle Campus BT20 4 B3
Castle Cl BT63 57 D2
Castlecoole Lodge BT8 21 E3
Castlecoole Pk BT8 21 E2
Castlecoole Wlk BT8 21 E3
Castle Court Sh Ctr BT1 155 A3
Castle Ct
Armagh BT60 60 C4
Castlereagh BT6 22 F8
Castledillon Rd BT8 21 E2
Castle Dr
Caledon BT68 96 D6
Richhill BT61 85 E1
Castle Enigan BT34 118 E1
Castle Enigan Rd BT34 118 E1
Castle Espie BT23 68 E4
Castle Espie Rd BT23 68 E2
Castlefields BT34 120 A2
Castle Gdns BT61 85 E1
Castle Gdns Prim Sch
BT23 20 A4
Castle Glen BT33 123 B5
Castle Grange BT5 23 A8
Castle Hill
Ballywalter BT22 71 A5
Comber BT23 25 E5
Dundrum BT33 123 C6
Gilford BT63 57 D2
9 Rathfriland BT34 119 F2
Castle Hill Ave BT23 25 E5
Castle Hill Brae BT22 71 A5
Castle Hill Cres BT23 25 E5
Castlehill Dr BT4 16 C6
Castle Hill Farm BT5 23 A8
Castle Hill Hts BT23 25 E5
Castlehill Manor BT4 16 C6
Castlehill Pk BT4 16 C5
Castle Hill Pk BT23 25 E5
Castlehill Pk W BT4 16 C5
Castlehill Rd BT4 16 C5
Castle Hill View BT23 25 E5
Castle Hts BT33 123 B5
Castlehume Gdns BT8 21 E2
Castle Island BT30 93 B1
Castle Island Dr BT23 19 F7
Castle Island Rd BT30 93 B1
Castlekaria Manor BT4 16 D6
Castlekeele BT35 64 A6
Castle La
6 Ardglass BT30 125 F6
Belfast BT1 155 A3
Caledon BT68 96 D6
Lurgan BT67 42 A5
Castleleviggan La BT24 91 D2
Castlelodge BT32 61 E4
Castlelodge Pk BT23 25 D4
Castlemahon BT30 109 F7
Castle Manor 4 BT22 66 F1
Castle Mdw Pk BT22 81 C2
Castle Mdw Rd BT22 81 C2
Castle Mdws
Carrowdore BT22 66 F1
Gilford BT63 57 D1
Castle Mdws Dr 2 BT22 66 F1
Castle Mdws Pk 1 BT22 66 F1
Castle Mews
Caledon BT68 96 D6
Castlereagh BT6 22 F8
13 Tandragee BT62 101 B7
Castlemore Ave BT6 22 E7
Castlemore Pk BT6 22 E7
Castlenavan BT30 107 D6
Castleorr Manor BT4 16 C6
Castleowen BT34 132 B5
Castle Par BT61 85 E1
Castle Pk BT30 125 F5
Castle Pk Ave BT20 4 A3
Castle Pk Rd BT20 4 B3
Castle Pl
Belfast BT1 155 A3
3 Carrowdore BT22 66 F1
Newtownards BT23 19 E5
1 Ardglass BT30 126 A6
4 Newcastle BT33 63 D5
Castlerагh Ind Est BT6 15 E1
Castlerainey Rd BT30 92 B8
Castleraw BT61 85 D6
Castleraw Rd BT61 85 C5
CASTLEREAGH BT6 15 D1
Castlereagh BT6 22 E7
Castlereagh Coll of Further Ed BT6 15 C1
Castlereagh Ind Est BT6 15 C1
Castlereagh Par BT5 15 C3
Castlereagh Pl BT5 15 A4
Castlereagh Rd BT6 15 D2
Castle Rise BT62 101 A7
Castlerobin Rd BT8 21 E3
Castle Roche Cross Roads 149 B5
Castlerock BT35 148 D7
Castlescreen Rd BT30 124 D8
CASTLESHANE (CAISLEÁN AN TSIÁIN) 112 A1
Castleskreen BT30 124 D8
Castle St
Armagh BT61 60 C5
Bangor BT20 4 B4
Belfast BT1 155 A3
Comber BT23 25 C3
1 Donaghadee BT21 6 F1
Dromara BT25 58 D5
Gilford BT63 57 D1
Lisburn BT27 26 B1
Newtownards BT23 19 E4
Portadown BT62 51 E5
Portaferry BT22 94 D3
Rathfriland BT34 120 A2
Castletown Cross Roads 149 E1
Castlevennon BT32 103 E5
Castlevennon Rd BT32 103 E7
Castleview
Newry BT35 141 C1
Newtownards BT22 81 C2
Castle View
Dundrum BT33 123 C5
Gilford BT63 57 D1
Castle View Pk 2 BT61 85 D1
Castleview Rd
Belfast BT5 16 D4
Markethill BT60 99 F1
Castleview Terr 3 BT4 15 F5
Castlevue Gdns BT67 34 B2
Castlevue Pk BT67 34 B2
Castleward BT30 94 A2
Castle Ward House★
BT30 94 B2
Castleward Pk BT8 21 E3
Castleward Rd BT30 93 F1
CASTLEWELLAN (CAISLEÁN UIDHILÍN) BT31 122 C5
Castlewellan GAC BT31 122 C5
Castlewellan Prim Sch
BT31 122 C5
Castlewellan Rd
Banbridge BT32 61 D4
Castlewellan BT31 122 E2
1 Downpatrick BT30 107 C1
Dromara BT25 89 D1
Newcastle BT33 63 D7
Newry BT34 120 E2
Castle Wellan Rd BT25 89 E1
Castlewood BT25 58 C4
Castor Bay Rd
Craigavon BT67 75 F6
Lurgan BT67 32 A1
Catalina Gdns BT23 19 C2
Cathedral Cl BT61 60 C5
Cathedral Mews BT61 60 B6
Cathedral Pk BT30 62 B3
Cathedral Rd BT61 60 B6
Cathedral Rd Recn Ctr
BT61 60 C6
Cathedral View
Armagh BT60 60 B4
Downpatrick BT30 62 B3
Catherine St N BT2 155 B2
Catherine St
Belfast BT2 155 B2
Newry BT35 64 C6
Catherwoods Fort★ BT8 30 B8
Cath of St Patrick & St Colman (RC) The BT34 64 D5
Cattogs BT23 68 C4
Caughey's Rd BT25 88 B5
Cauley's Pipe Rd BT31 106 D3
Caulfield Pl BT35 64 C6
Causanagh BT61 84 F7
Causanagh Rd BT61 84 F7
Causeway Rd BT33 63 C4
Cavan
Armagh BT61 85 D2
Dungannon BT71 72 A6
Newry BT34 120 B1
Cavanacaw Pk BT60 60 F2
Cavanacaw Rd BT60 60 F1
Cavanagarvan BT60 113 C5
Cavanagarvan Rd BT60 113 C6
Cavanagrow BT60 99 C1
Cavanakill BT35 130 A4
Cavanakill Rd BT35 129 F3
Cavanapole BT60 97 A4
Cavanapole Rd BT60 97 A3
Cavanballaghy BT60 97 B8
Cavanballaghy Rd BT60 97 A8
Cavanboy BT68 82 E3
Cavandoogan BT60 112 E7
Cavan Rd BT34 120 B1
Cavehill Rd BT32 103 B1
Cavendish Sq BT12 154 A2
Cavendish St BT12 154 A2
Cawnpore St BT13 154 C4
Cayman Ave BT19 13 D7
Cayman Dr BT19 13 D7
Ceara Specl Sch BT66 41 F5
Cearng an Chairdinéil Fiaich (Cardinal O'fiaich Sq) 4 BT35 147 F8
Cearng uí Chinnéide (Kennedy Sq) 3 BT30 62 C5
CEATHRÚ AODHA DHUIBH (CARRYDUFF) BT8 29 C3
Cecil St
Newry BT35 64 C6
Portadown BT62 51 D3
Cedar Dr BT23 19 D6
Cedar Gr
Ardglass BT30 125 F5
Bangor BT20 3 F4
Belfast BT4 9 B2
Newry BT34 132 B5
Cedar Hill BT61 99 E5
Cedar Hts BT34 153 C7
Cedarhurst Ct BT8 22 A2
Cedarhurst Rd BT8 21 F2
Cedarhurst Rise BT8 21 F3
Cedar Integrated Prim Sch
BT30 92 A3
Cedar La BT18 1 E3
Cedar Mews BT34 65 A8
Cedar Mount BT20 3 F4
Cedar Pk BT63 53 E4
Cedars The 8 BT19 13 E8
Céide Chlann Aodha Buí (Clandeboye Dr) 31 BT5 15 A4
Céide Thaobh an Chnoic (Braeside Dr) BT30 62 C2
Céide Thulach Forde (Mountforde Dr) 16 BT5 15 A5
Central Ave BT20 4 A4
Central Prom BT33 63 D3
Central St 12 BT20 4 A4
Central Way BT64 40 E3
Centre House BT1 155 B3
Century St BT63 52 A5
Chadolly St 14 BT4 15 B5
Chadwick St BT9 14 A1
Chalybeate Rd BT60 129 A6
Chamberlain St 19 BT5 15 B5
Chambers St BT7 155 A1
Chancellors Rd BT35 64 A2
Chanderies St The BT22 70 B5
Chanderies The BT22 70 B5
Chandlers Ct BT16 17 B2
Channel Commercial Pk
BT3 15 B8
Channing St BT5 15 C3
Chapel Fields 7 BT34 119 F2
Chapel Hill
Lisburn BT28 26 A1
Newry BT34 64 E3
Chapel Hill Rd BT60 96 E3
Chapel Island Pk BT23 19 F6
Chapel La
Armagh BT61 60 C5
Belfast BT1 155 A3
Castlewellan BT31 106 E4
Craigavon BT62 55 D1
Newry BT35 130 D6
Chapel Rd
Bessbrook BT35 131 C5
Newry BT34 64 F2
Chapel St
Downpatrick BT30 125 D5
Newry BT34 64 D4
CHAPELTOWN BT30 126 A8
CHARLEMONT BT71 84 B8
Charlemont Gdns BT61 60 D5
Charlemont Ind Est BT71 84 A8
Charlemont Rd BT71 84 B6
Charlemont Sq 8 BT35 131 C5
Charlemont St BT71 72 B1
Charles Baron Lodge
BT66 42 C4
Charles Mount BT20 4 E3
Charles Pk BT62 51 B5
Charles Pl 4 BT23 19 F5
Charles St S BT12 154 C2
Charles St
Lurgan BT66 41 F6
Portadown BT62 51 C4
Charleston Road Ind Est
BT63 40 B4
Charlestown Dr BT63 40 B4
Charlestown New Rd
BT63 40 B3
CHARLESTOWN OR BANNFOOT BT66 74 A7
Charlestown Rd BT63 40 A2
Charleville Ave 1 BT9 21 A8
Charleville St BT13 14 B7
Charley Memorial Prim Sch
BT17 27 C7
Charlotte St
Belfast BT7 155 B1
Warrenpoint BT34 65 C2
Charnwood Ct BT63 52 D2
Charnwood Grange BT63 52 D2
Charters Ave 2 BT5 16 D2
Chartwell Pk BT8 22 B3
Chase The BT21 6 C4
Chasewood Cl BT63 52 D1
Chasewood Gdns BT63 52 D1
Chater St BT4 15 C5
Chatswood Pl BT63 52 B5
Chatsworth BT19 13 E7
Chatsworth St BT5 15 B4
Chelsea St BT4 15 C6
Cheltenham Gdns BT6 22 A7
Cheltenham Pk BT6 22 A7
Chemical St (Sráid na Gceimiceán) 15 BT5 15 A5
Chequer Hill BT35 64 C7
Cherry Gr BT35 139 A5
Cherryhill BT9 21 C8
Cherry Hill BT34 143 C3
Cherryhill Ave BT16 17 B5
Cherryhill Cres BT16 17 C5
Cherryhill Dr BT16 17 B5
Cherryhill Gdns BT16 17 B5
Cherryhill Pk BT16 17 B5
Cherryhill Rd
Ballynahinch BT24 90 F1
Dundonald BT16 17 C5
Cherrymount Pk BT20 4 E3
Cherry Tree BT5 16 C2
Cherrytree Wlk BT66 41 E6
Cherry Tree Wlk BT5 16 B3
Cherry Vale BT28 38 A7
Cherryvalley BT5 16 B3
Cherryvalley BT23 68 D5
Cherryvalley Dr BT23 25 E3
Cherryvalley Gdns BT5 16 C3
Cherryvalley Gn BT5 16 B3
Cherryvalley Pk BT5 16 B3
Cherryvalley Pk W BT5 16 C2
Cherryville Pk BT66 42 B3
Cherryville Rd BT62 73 E3
Cherryville St BT6 15 A3
Cherrywood Ave BT34 64 E5
Cherrywood Ct BT32 61 C2
Cherrywood Gr BT34 64 F8
Chesham Cres BT6 15 B2
Chesham Dr BT6 15 A2
Chesham Gdns 2 BT6 15 B2
Chesham Gr BT6 15 A2
Chesham Par BT6 15 A2
Chesham Pk BT6 15 A2
Chesham Terr 1 BT6 15 B2
Chester Ave BT20 3 F2
Chesterbrook Cres BT23 20 A6
Chesterfield Pk BT6 22 A6
Chester Pk BT20 3 F2
Chestnut BT66 86 C8
Chestnut Brae 3 BT63 57 C1
Chestnut Dr BT71 72 A1
Chestnut Gr
Craigavon BT66 40 F7
Newry BT34 64 E8
Chestnut Hill BT27 26 C8
Chestnut Hill Rd BT67 34 C6
Chestnut Hollow BT27 26 C8
Chestnut Lodge BT27 28 B2
Chestnut Rd BT24 59 A5
Cheviot Ave BT4 15 D5
Cheviot St BT4 15 D5
Chichester St BT1 155 B3
Childhaven Conference Ctr
BT21 67 A5
Chilton Dr BT24 59 D6
Chimera Wood BT19 2 E5
Chinauley Pk BT32 61 F3
Chippendale Ave BT20 4 E4
Chippendale Dr BT20 4 F3
Chippendale Glen BT20 4 E3
Chippendale Pk BT20 4 E3
Chippendale Vale BT20 4 E3
Chlorine Gdns BT9 14 C1
Chobham St BT5 15 D5
Christ Church Cath BT27 26 B1
Christian Pl BT12 154 B3
Christine Ave 3 BT20 4 E3
Church Ave
Bangor BT20 3 F2
Carryduff BT8 29 D3
1 Downpatrick BT30 62 C5
Dundrum BT33 123 C5
Holywood BT18 9 E7
Kircubbin BT22 80 D7
Newry BT34 64 D7
Church Ballee BT30 109 D2
Church Cl BT33 123 C5
Church Cres BT20 3 F2
Church Ct
7 Carrowdore BT22 66 F1
Downpatrick BT30 123 C8
Holywood BT18 9 E6
Church Dr
Banbridge BT32 102 C3
Bangor BT20 3 F2
Churchfield Hts 10 BT31 122 C4
Church Glen BT28 26 C8
Church Gn
Dromara BT25 58 E4
Dundonald BT16 17 B4
Holywood BT18 9 D7
Church Gr
4 Downpatrick BT30 107 C1
Kircubbin BT22 80 D7
Church Hill
Ballygowan BT23 77 F8
Dunmurry BT27 26 E6
Holywood BT18 9 D7
Newry BT34 120 A5
Newry BT35 141 C2
Church Hill Gdns BT25 89 C2
Church Hill Pk BT23 77 F8
Church Hill Rd BT68 96 E8
Churchill Ave
Lurgan BT66 42 C5
6 Millisle BT22 67 A4
Churchill Cres BT20 4 F4
Churchill Gdns BT62 51 D6
Churchill Pk
Bangor BT20 4 F4
Newtownards BT23 79 A6
Portadown BT62 51 D6
Churchill Pl BT66 86 C8
Churchill Prim Sch BT68 96 D6
Churchill Rd
Banbridge BT32 103 F2
Newcastle BT33 122 E2
Churchill St BT15 14 C7
Church La
Ballynahinch BT24 59 C5

Church La *continued*
Belfast BT1 . . . . . 155 B3
Carrowdore BT22 . . . . . 66 F1
8 Donaghadee BT21 . . . . . 66 F8
2 Lisburn BT28 . . . . . 26 B1
Lisburn BT28 . . . . . 36 B6
Portadown BT62 . . . . . 51 D4
1 Warrenpoint BT34 . . . . . 65 C2
Churchland Cl BT4 . . . . . 9 B2
Church Lodge BT23 . . . . . 30 F6
Church Mdw 1 BT34 . . . . . 153 C7
Church Mdws BT25 . . . . . 58 E4
Church Mews BT16 . . . . . 17 B4
Church Pk 6 BT22 . . . . . 66 F1
Church Pl
7 Castlewellan BT31 . . . . . 122 C5
Keady BT60 . . . . . 114 A3
Church Pl N BT67 . . . . . 42 A6
Church Quarter BT16 . . . . . 17 B4
Church Rd
Ballynahinch BT24 . . . . . 59 D3
Banbridge BT32 . . . . . 103 C2
Belfast BT8 . . . . . 22 A5
Bessbrook BT35 . . . . . 131 C5
8 Carrowdore BT22 . . . . . 66 F1
Carryduff BT8 . . . . . 29 D2
Castlereagh BT6 . . . . . 22 F7
Craigavon BT66 . . . . . 74 F7
Downpatrick BT30 . . . . . 91 F5
Dromara BT25 . . . . . 88 F1
Dundonald BT16 . . . . . 17 B4
Helen's Bay BT19 . . . . . 2 D6
Holywood BT18 . . . . . 9 F6
Moneyreagh BT23 . . . . . 30 F6
Newry BT34 . . . . . 145 E3
Newry BT35 . . . . . 131 D8
Newtownards BT23 . . . . . 78 C8
Portadown BT63 . . . . . 52 A7
Church Rock BT35 . . . . . 131 C7
Church Sq
Banbridge BT32 . . . . . 61 D5
12 Rathfriland BT34 . . . . . 119 F2
Church St
Armagh BT60 . . . . . 112 D7
Ballynahinch BT24 . . . . . 59 D4
Banbridge BT32 . . . . . 61 C6
Bangor BT20 . . . . . 3 F2
Belfast BT1 . . . . . 155 A4
Castlewellan BT31 . . . . . 122 C5
Downpatrick BT30 . . . . . 62 C5
Dromara BT25 . . . . . 58 C5
Keady BT60 . . . . . 114 A3
Newry BT34 . . . . . 64 D6
Newtownards BT22 . . . . . 70 C5
Newtownards BT23 . . . . . 19 C5
Portadown BT62 . . . . . 51 D3
Portaferry BT22 . . . . . 94 D3
Rostrevor BT34 . . . . . 143 C3
20 Tandragee BT62 . . . . . 101 B7
Warrenpoint BT34 . . . . . 65 C2
Churchtown Rd BT30 . . . . . 94 B1
Church View
Ballynahinch BT24 . . . . . 59 C5
Bessbrook BT35 . . . . . 131 C5
Downpatrick BT30 . . . . . 125 D5
Dromara BT25 . . . . . 58 C5
Holywood BT18 . . . . . 9 D6
Moy BT71 . . . . . 84 B8
2 Portaferry BT22 . . . . . 94 D4
Churchview Cl
Craigavon BT62 . . . . . 73 A2
15 Kilkeel BT34 . . . . . 153 C7
Church View Cl BT63 . . . . . 86 C2
Churchview Dr BT32 . . . . . 61 D5
Church View Dr BT63 . . . . . 86 C2
Church View Mews BT18 . . . . . 9 D7
Church Way BT22 . . . . . 80 D7
Church Wlk
9 Carrowdore BT22 . . . . . 66 F1
Lurgan BT67 . . . . . 42 A6
Church Wynd BT5 . . . . . 16 D1
Church Yard Rd 151 D4
Church Yard Row 151 C4
Cicero Gdns BT6 . . . . . 15 D2
Cido Bsns Complex
Craigavon BT63 . . . . . 40 B2
Lurgan BT66 . . . . . 41 F6
CILL AN CHURRAIGH (KILCURRY) 149 F5
CILL CHAOIL (KILKEEL) BT34 . . . . . 153 D7
CILL DHUINSÍ (KILLINCHY) BT23 . . . . . 79 B5
CILL GHOBÁIN (KIRCUBBIN) BT22 . . . . . 80 D7
CILL LOCHA (KILLOUGH) BT30 . . . . . 125 D5
CILL Ó LAOCH (KILLYLEAGH) BT30 . . . . . 93 C4
CIONN AIRD (CALEDON) BT68 . . . . . 96 D6
Circular Rd
Banbridge BT32 . . . . . 103 C4
Belfast BT4 . . . . . 15 F7
Castlewellan BT31 . . . . . 122 C5
Dromara BT25 . . . . . 58 D5
Newtownards BT23 . . . . . 19 C4
Circular Rd E BT18 . . . . . 1 C2
Circular Rd W BT18 . . . . . 1 C2
City Bsns Pk BT17 . . . . . 26 E8
City Hospital Sta BT12 . . . . . 154 C1
Citylink Bsns Pk BT12 . . . . . 154 C3
City of Armagh High Sch BT61 . . . . . 60 D7
City Way BT12 . . . . . 154 C1
CIVILTOWN BT63 . . . . . 86 C2
Clady Beg BT60 . . . . . 115 D1
Cladymilltown Rd BT60 . . . . . 115 F4
Clady More BT60 . . . . . 115 C4
Cladymore Rd BT60 . . . . . 115 E4
Clady Rd BT60 . . . . . 115 D3
Clanbrassil Ave BT63 . . . . . 51 F3
Clanbrassil Ct BT18 . . . . . 1 C2
Clanbrassil Dr BT63 . . . . . 52 A3
Clanbrassil Gdns BT63 . . . . . 51 F3
Clanbrassil Gr BT66 . . . . . 40 F6
Clanbrassil Pk BT63 . . . . . 52 A4
Clanbrassil Rd BT18 . . . . . 1 B1
Clanbrassil Terr BT18 . . . . . 1 B1
Clanconnel Gdns BT66 . . . . . 86 C7
Clandeboye Bsns Pk BT19 . . . . . 12 F8
Clandeboye Cl BT19 . . . . . 3 D1
Clandeboye Dr
6 Bangor BT19 . . . . . 3 D1
31 Belfast BT5 . . . . . 15 A4
Clandeboye Gdns (Gairdíní Chlann Aodha Buí) 30 BT5 . . . . . 15 A5
Clandeboye Golf Club BT23 . . . . . 12 F4
Clandeboye Pl BT20 . . . . . 3 F2
Clandeboye Prim Sch BT20 . . . . . 3 F2
Clandeboye Rd
Bangor BT19 . . . . . 12 D8
3 Bangor BT20 . . . . . 3 E1
Clandeboye Ret Pk BT19 . . . . . 3 E1
Clandeboye St BT5 . . . . . 15 B4
Clandeboye Way BT19 . . . . . 3 E1
Clanickny 112 C8
Clankilvoragh BT67 . . . . . 42 D8
Clanmaghery
Castlewellan BT31 . . . . . 121 A6
Downpatrick BT30 . . . . . 124 C5
Clanmaghery Ct BT30 . . . . . 123 F5
Clanmaghery Gr BT30 . . . . . 123 F5
Clanmaghery Rd
Castlewellan BT31 . . . . . 121 A5
Downpatrick BT30 . . . . . 124 C5
Clanmorris Ave BT20 . . . . . 4 A1
Clanmorris St BT15 . . . . . 14 E8
Clanrolla
Craigavon BT64 . . . . . 52 F8
Craigavon BT67 . . . . . 75 F7
Clanrolla Pk BT65 . . . . . 53 C8
Clanrolla Rd BT64 . . . . . 52 E8
Clanroy Par BT4 . . . . . 15 E5
Clanrye Ave BT35 . . . . . 64 B6
Clantilew Rd BT62 . . . . . 73 E2
Clanwilliam Ct BT24 . . . . . 59 B5
Clara Ave BT5 . . . . . 15 D4
Clara Cres Lower 2 BT5 . . . . . 15 D4
Clara Cres Upper 3 BT5 . . . . . 15 D4
Claragh BT30 . . . . . 106 F1
Claragh Ct
3 Downpatrick BT30 . . . . . 107 C1
Downpatrick BT30 . . . . . 123 C8
Claragh Rd BT30 . . . . . 106 F1
Claranagh BT35 . . . . . 148 B5
Clara Pk BT5 . . . . . 15 F3
Clara Rd BT5 . . . . . 15 F3
Clara St
Belfast BT5 . . . . . 15 B3
Lurgan BT67 . . . . . 41 F6
Clara Way BT5 . . . . . 15 F3
Clarawood Cres BT5 . . . . . 15 F3
Clarawood Dr BT5 . . . . . 15 F2
Clarawood Gr BT5 . . . . . 15 F2
Clarawood Pk BT5 . . . . . 15 F2
Clarawood Sch BT5 . . . . . 15 F3
Clarbane BT35 . . . . . 138 C1
CLARE BT62 . . . . . 100 E3
Clare
Craigavon BT62 . . . . . 100 F4
Craigavon BT66 . . . . . 86 A5
Moira BT67 . . . . . 34 D1
Clarehill Cotts BT18 . . . . . 9 C4
Clarehill La BT18 . . . . . 9 C4
Clarehill Mews BT18 . . . . . 9 C6
Clarehill Rd
Craigavon BT67 . . . . . 44 E5
Moira BT67 . . . . . 34 D1
Claremont Ave BT67 . . . . . 34 C1
Claremont Cres BT67 . . . . . 34 C1
Claremont Ct BT67 . . . . . 34 C1
Claremont Dr BT67 . . . . . 34 C1
Claremont Mews 2 BT9 . . . . . 14 C2
Claremont Pk BT67 . . . . . 34 C1
Claremont St 4 BT9 . . . . . 14 C2
Clare Moss Rd BT66 . . . . . 86 B6
Clarence Pl Mews BT1 . . . . . 155 A2
Clarence St W BT2 . . . . . 155 A2
Clarence St BT2 . . . . . 155 A2
Clarendon Ave BT5 . . . . . 15 D3
Clarendon Dock★ BT1 . . . . . 14 F7
Clarendon Pk BT67 . . . . . 43 E6
Clarendon Rd BT1 . . . . . 155 B4
Clare Prim Sch BT62 . . . . . 100 E4
Clare Rd
Craigavon BT62 . . . . . 100 F5
Craigavon BT63 . . . . . 57 E8
Craigavon BT66 . . . . . 86 B5
Clarke's La BT1 . . . . . 155 A4
Clarkhill Rd BT31 . . . . . 122 C7
Clarkill
Castlewellan BT31 . . . . . 122 B6
Newry BT35 . . . . . 140 C6
Clarks La BT23 . . . . . 25 B4
Clarks Rd BT60 . . . . . 128 E4
Clarmont Ave 2 BT31 . . . . . 122 C5
Clarmont Ct 1 BT31 . . . . . 122 C5
Clay
Armagh BT60 . . . . . 127 F8
Banbridge BT32 . . . . . 102 F3
Clay *continued*
Downpatrick BT30 . . . . . 79 A1
Clay Prim Sch BT60 . . . . . 127 F7
Clay Rd
Armagh BT60 . . . . . 127 F8
Banbridge BT32 . . . . . 103 A4
Downpatrick BT30 . . . . . 78 F2
Keady BT60 . . . . . 114 A2
Killyleagh BT30 . . . . . 93 B7
Clealough Rd BT30 . . . . . 78 D1
Cleaver Ave BT9 . . . . . 21 B8
Cleaver Ct BT9 . . . . . 21 B8
Cleaver Gdns BT9 . . . . . 21 C7
Cleaver Pk BT9 . . . . . 21 B7
Cleery Cres BT35 . . . . . 64 C5
Cleland Ave BT23 . . . . . 79 A5
Cleland Pk 3 BT20 . . . . . 4 A1
Cleland Pk Central BT20 . . . . . 3 F1
Cleland Pk N BT20 . . . . . 3 F1
Cleland Pk S BT19 . . . . . 12 F8
Clementine Dr BT12 . . . . . 154 C1
Clementine Gdns BT12 . . . . . 154 C1
Clementine Pk BT12 . . . . . 154 C1
Cleomack BT34 . . . . . 134 A3
Clermont Bglws 1 BT34 . . . . . 65 B3
Clermont Cairn★ 150 F8
Clermont Gdns BT34 . . . . . 65 B2
Clerran 112 D1
Clery 96 A1
Clevely Pk BT8 . . . . . 22 B3
Cliftonpark Ave BT14 . . . . . 14 B8
Clifton Pk Ct 1 BT14 . . . . . 14 C8
Clifton Rd BT20 . . . . . 4 C5
Clifton Sch BT19 . . . . . 3 B1
Clifton St BT13 . . . . . 14 C7
Cliftonville Rd 10 BT14 . . . . . 14 C8
Cline Rd BT32 . . . . . 61 C3
Cline Wlk BT32 . . . . . 61 C3
Clintons Pk BT30 . . . . . 62 C5
Clintyclay Prim Sch BT71 . . . . . 72 E3
Cliveden Cres BT8 . . . . . 22 C4
Cloch Fada GAA BT34 . . . . . 146 B4
Cloghadda Standing Stone★ BT34 . . . . . 133 B1
Cloghan BT61 . . . . . 85 C1
Cloghan Cres BT5 . . . . . 16 E4
Cloghan Gdns BT5 . . . . . 16 E4
Cloghan Pk BT5 . . . . . 16 E4
Cloghanramer BT34 . . . . . 132 B6
Cloghanramer Rd BT34 . . . . . 132 A5
Cloghan Rd BT61 . . . . . 85 C2
Clogharevan BT35 . . . . . 131 C6
Clogharevan Rd BT35 . . . . . 131 B6
Clogher
Craigavon BT66 . . . . . 87 A8
Downpatrick BT30 . . . . . 62 F2
Hillsborough BT26 . . . . . 47 E1
Lisburn BT27 . . . . . 39 B5
Clogher Rd
Hillsborough BT26 . . . . . 47 F2
Lisburn BT27 . . . . . 39 A5
Cloghfin BT61 . . . . . 84 A2
Cloghinny
Newry BT35 . . . . . 117 D1
Newry BT35 . . . . . 140 E2
Cloghinny Rd BT35 . . . . . 140 E2
Cloghoge
Craigavon BT62 . . . . . 101 A3
Newry BT35 . . . . . 139 A3
Newry BT35 . . . . . 141 E8
Cloghoge Hts BT35 . . . . . 64 C1
Cloghoge Rd
Craigavon BT62 . . . . . 100 E4
Newry BT35 . . . . . 138 F3
Cloghram BT33 . . . . . 123 C7
Cloghreagh BT35 . . . . . 131 E4
Cloghskelt BT31 . . . . . 104 D2
Cloghskelt Rd BT31 . . . . . 104 F2
Cloghy BT30 . . . . . 110 C8
Cloister Ave BT19 . . . . . 12 D8
Clonachullion BT33 . . . . . 135 F6
Clonakle BT62 . . . . . 73 D1
Clonalig BT35 . . . . . 147 F5
Clonalig Prim Sch BT35 . . . . . 147 E5
Clonallan Glebe BT34 . . . . . 65 E4
Clonallon Ct BT4 . . . . . 15 F6
Clonallon Gdns
Belfast BT4 . . . . . 15 F6
Warrenpoint BT34 . . . . . 65 D2
Clonallon Pk BT4 . . . . . 15 F6
Clonallon Rd BT34 . . . . . 65 E5
Clonallon Sq 4 BT4 . . . . . 15 F6
Clonamola BT62 . . . . . 74 C1
Clonard Cres (Corrán Chluain Ard) 5 BT13 . . . . . 154 A3
Clonard Ct BT13 . . . . . 154 A3
Clonard Gdns BT13 . . . . . 154 A3
Clonard Hts (Arda Chluain Ard) 3 BT13 . . . . . 154 A3
Clonard Monastry BT13 . . . . . 154 A3
Clonard Pl (Plás Chluain Ard) 2 BT13 . . . . . 154 A3
Clonard Rise (Mala Chluain Ard) 4 BT13 . . . . . 154 A3
Clonard St BT13 . . . . . 154 A3
Clonaver Cres N BT4 . . . . . 15 F7
Clonaver Cres S BT4 . . . . . 15 F6
Clonaver Dr BT4 . . . . . 15 F6
Clonaver Pk BT4 . . . . . 15 F7
Clonavon Ave BT62 . . . . . 51 E4
Clonbeg BT71 . . . . . 72 B2
Cloncarrish BT62 . . . . . 73 E4
Cloncarrish Rd BT62 . . . . . 73 E4
Cloncore BT62 . . . . . 73 F5
Cloncore Rd BT62 . . . . . 73 F4
Clonduff Dr BT6 . . . . . 15 E1
Clonduff Rd BT34 . . . . . 134 C6
Cloneden BT34 . . . . . 65 D4
Clonevin Pk BT28 . . . . . 26 A2
Clonfaddan Cres BT12 . . . . . 154 C3
Clonfaddan St BT12 . . . . . 154 C3
CLONFEACLE BT71 . . . . . 83 F4
Clonfeacle Rd BT71 . . . . . 83 F5
Clonlee Dr BT4 . . . . . 15 E5
Clonlum BT35 . . . . . 141 A6
Clonlum Rd BT35 . . . . . 141 A6
Clonmacash BT62 . . . . . 73 D3
Clonmacash Rd BT62 . . . . . 73 D3
Clonmain BT61 . . . . . 84 E7
Clonmain Rd BT61 . . . . . 84 E7
Clonmakate BT62 . . . . . 73 D6
Clonmakate Rd BT62 . . . . . 73 E5
Clonmartin BT62 . . . . . 74 C1
Clonmeen BT65 . . . . . 41 B1
Clonmore
Dungannon BT71 . . . . . 72 B1
Dungannon BT71 . . . . . 72 D5
Clonmore Manor BT27 . . . . . 26 C5
Clonmore Pk BT35 . . . . . 64 B8
Clonmore Rd BT71 . . . . . 72 E3
Clonmore Villas BT71 . . . . . 72 E5
Clonroot BT62 . . . . . 54 A7
Clonroot Rd BT62 . . . . . 54 B6
Clonta Fleece BT34 . . . . . 143 A8
Clontafleece Rd BT34 . . . . . 133 C1
Clontaghnaglar BT24 . . . . . 91 E8
Clontanagullion BT24 . . . . . 90 A4
Clontara Pk BT27 . . . . . 26 B6
Clonteevy BT71 . . . . . 72 C3
Clontifleece Prim Sch BT34 . . . . . 143 A6
Clontigora Hill BT35 . . . . . 141 F3
Clontigora Rd BT35 . . . . . 141 E5
Clontonacally Rd BT6 . . . . . 22 F1
Clontonakelly BT8 . . . . . 30 A6
Clontycarty BT60 . . . . . 96 E6
Clontycarty La BT60 . . . . . 96 E6
Clontyclay BT71 . . . . . 72 E4
Clontygora BT35 . . . . . 141 F3
Clontylew BT62 . . . . . 73 E2
CLONVARAGHAN BT31 . . . . . 106 C1
Clonvaraghan Rd BT31 . . . . . 105 F4
Cloonagh Rd BT30 . . . . . 62 E2
Clooneavin Ave BT34 . . . . . 65 C3
Cloreen Pk BT9 . . . . . 14 C1
Clós an Ráschúrsa (Racecourse Cl) BT30 . . . . . 62 B2
Close Rd BT34 . . . . . 121 A4
Close The
Dundonald BT16 . . . . . 17 D2
Holywood BT18 . . . . . 9 F8
Lisburn BT27 . . . . . 38 C8
Newcastle BT33 . . . . . 63 B7
Clós Maoilinn (Moylinn Cl) BT35 . . . . . 139 E2
Clós na Crúibe (Croob Cl) BT30 . . . . . 62 B2
Clós na Speilge (Spelga Cl) BT30 . . . . . 62 B2
Clós na Trá (Strand Cl) 9 BT5 . . . . . 15 A5
CLOUGH (AN CLOCH) BT30 . . . . . 107 D1
Clougharevan Pk 1 BT35 . . . . . 131 C5
Clougherny Rd BT70 . . . . . 82 D7
CLOUGHEY BT22 . . . . . 81 B1
Cloughey Rd BT22 . . . . . 81 D3
Cloughmore Pk 5 BT34 . . . . . 143 C4
Cloughmore Rd BT34 . . . . . 143 C3
Cloughmore Standing Stone★ BT63 . . . . . 101 E5
Cloughmore View 4 BT34 . . . . . 65 B4
Cloughoge Prim Sch BT35 . . . . . 64 B2
Cloughreagh Pk 3 BT35 . . . . . 131 E4
Clounagh Ctr (Technology Centre (Business) BT62 . . . . . 51 B3
Clounagh Jun High Sch BT62 . . . . . 51 C3
Clounagh La BT62 . . . . . 51 C2
Clounagh Pk BT62 . . . . . 51 C3
Cloven Eden BT61 . . . . . 84 F6
Cloveneden Rd BT61 . . . . . 84 F5
Clover Braes BT66 . . . . . 86 F6
Cloverdale
Dromara BT25 . . . . . 87 A4
Newry BT34 . . . . . 64 E8
Cloverhill
9 Moy BT71 . . . . . 72 A1
Moy BT71 . . . . . 84 A8
Cloverhill Ave
Bangor BT19 . . . . . 4 E1
Lisburn BT27 . . . . . 38 C8
Cloverhill Cl 1 BT19 . . . . . 4 E1
Cloverhill Cres BT23 . . . . . 20 C6
Cloverhill Ct 3 BT19 . . . . . 4 E1
Cloverhill Gdns
Bangor BT19 . . . . . 4 E1
Belfast BT4 . . . . . 16 D6
Cloverhill Glen 4 BT19 . . . . . 4 E1
Cloverhill Gn 2 BT19 . . . . . 4 E1
Cloverhill Gr BT19 . . . . . 4 E1
Cloverhill Pk
Bangor BT19 . . . . . 4 E1
Belfast BT4 . . . . . 16 D7
Newtownards BT23 . . . . . 20 C6
Cloverhill Vale BT19 . . . . . 4 E1
Cloverhill Wlk 5 BT19 . . . . . 4 E1
Clover La BT67 . . . . . 35 A8
Clownagh BT62 . . . . . 51 C2
Cluainair 1 BT34 . . . . . 117 F1
Cluan Pl BT5 . . . . . 15 A4
Clundara BT66 . . . . . 40 E7
Cluntagh
Ballynahinch BT24 . . . . . 89 E6
Downpatrick BT30 . . . . . 92 D5
Cluntagh Cross Roads BT30 . . . . . 92 E5
Cluntagh Rd
Downpatrick BT30 . . . . . 92 D4
Hillsborough BT26 . . . . . 89 D7
Cluster Rd BT35 . . . . . 129 F5
Clyde Ct (Cúirt Chluaidh) 1 BT5 . . . . . 15 A5
CNOC AN MHARGAIDH (MARKETHILL) BT60 . . . . . 115 F8
Cnoc na Carraige (Carrick Hill) BT13 . . . . . 155 A4
Cnoc na Sceiche Gile BT35 . . . . . 64 C3
Coachmans Rise BT26 . . . . . 37 B1
Coachmans Way BT26 . . . . . 37 B1
Coach Rd
Newry BT35 . . . . . 129 C2
Newtownards BT23 . . . . . 25 A4
Portaferry BT22 . . . . . 94 D4
Coalpit Rd BT34 . . . . . 132 E7
Coar's La BT1 . . . . . 155 A4
Coash Rd BT71 . . . . . 72 A8
Coast Guard Ave BT19 . . . . . 2 B6
Coast Guard La BT19 . . . . . 5 F7
Coburg St BT6 . . . . . 15 A3
Coburn Dr BT62 . . . . . 101 B7
Cochrane's La BT22 . . . . . 69 F7
Cochron Rd BT35 . . . . . 64 C7
Cockhill Rd BT27 . . . . . 36 B2
Cock Mountain Common BT34 . . . . . 135 D4
Coens Fort★ BT31 . . . . . 121 E7
Cohannan BT71 . . . . . 72 C6
Coharra BT62 . . . . . 50 C5
Coharra Rd BT62 . . . . . 50 C4
COILLIDH CHANANNÁIN (MIDDLETOWN) BT60 . . . . . 112 D8
COILLIDH LÉITH (KILLYLEA) BT60 . . . . . 97 B5
COILL UÍ NÉILL (KILLYNEILL) 112 A4
Coilyhill Rd BT30 . . . . . 93 B5
Colane Mdws BT67 . . . . . 32 E7
Colane Rd BT67 . . . . . 32 E7
Colban Cres BT66 . . . . . 42 A4
Colby Pk BT8 . . . . . 22 B4
Colchester St BT12 . . . . . 154 B1
Cold Brae Rd
Armagh BT60 . . . . . 130 A5
Newry BT35 . . . . . 129 F4
Cole Ct BT34 . . . . . 64 E2
Coleman Dr BT66 . . . . . 40 C8
Coleman Pk BT66 . . . . . 40 C8
Colenso Ct BT9 . . . . . 14 D1
Colenso Par BT9 . . . . . 14 D1
Coleshill Gdns BT8 . . . . . 21 E3
College Ave
Bangor BT20 . . . . . 4 C5
Belfast BT12 . . . . . 154 C3
College Cl BT66 . . . . . 41 E7
College Ct BT1 . . . . . 155 A3
College Dr BT7 . . . . . 21 E7
College Gdns
Belfast BT9 . . . . . 14 C2
Newry BT35 . . . . . 64 C8
College Gn BT7 . . . . . 14 D2
College Gr BT66 . . . . . 41 E7
College Hall La BT60 . . . . . 96 F5
College Hill BT61 . . . . . 60 E6
College Lands Rd BT71 . . . . . 84 C7
College Manor BT63 . . . . . 52 A5
College Mews BT66 . . . . . 41 E8
College of Nursing BT63 . . . . . 52 B7
College Pk BT7 . . . . . 14 D2
College Pk Ave BT7 . . . . . 14 D2
College Pk E BT7 . . . . . 14 D2
College Pl N BT12 . . . . . 154 C3
College St Mews BT1 . . . . . 155 A3
College Sq BT35 . . . . . 131 C5
College Sq E BT1 . . . . . 155 A3
College Sq N BT12 . . . . . 154 C3
College St
Armagh BT61 . . . . . 60 D5
Belfast BT12 . . . . . 155 A3
College Wlk BT66 . . . . . 41 E7
Colligan St BT13 . . . . . 154 A2
Collingwood Ave
Belfast BT7 . . . . . 14 E2
Lurgan BT66 . . . . . 41 E3
Collingwood Dr BT66 . . . . . 41 F3
Collingwood Rd 11 BT7 . . . . . 14 E1
Collone Prim Sch BT60 . . . . . 99 B2
Colmcille Pl BT30 . . . . . 62 D2
Colmcille Rd BT30 . . . . . 62 D2
Columbkille Rd BT62 . . . . . 73 F7
Colvil St BT4 . . . . . 15 D6
COMBER (AN COMAR) BT23 . . . . . 25 D1
Comber Ct (Cúirt an Chomair) 25 BT5 . . . . . 15 A5
Comber Gdns (Garraithe an Chomair) 28 BT5 . . . . . 15 A5
Comber High Sch BT23 . . . . . 25 E4
Comber Leisure Ctr BT23 . . . . . 25 D3
Combermere BT26 . . . . . 47 E7
Combermere St BT2 . . . . . 154 C1
Comber Prim Sch BT23 . . . . . 25 D3
Comber Rd
Ballygowan BT23 . . . . . 31 E1
Belfast BT16 . . . . . 24 F8
Carryduff BT8 . . . . . 29 E3
Downpatrick BT30 . . . . . 93 C7
Dundonald BT16 . . . . . 17 D2
Hillsborough BT26 . . . . . 47 F6

Comber Rd *continued*
Lisburn BT27 . . . 39 C2
Newtownards BT23 . . . 19 D1
Saintfield BT24 . . . 77 C4
Comber Rd Ind Est BT23 . 19 E3
Commedagh Pk
4 Castlewellan BT31 . . . 122 C4
Newcastle BT33 . . . 63 B3
Commercial Ct BT1 . . . 155 A4
Commercial Rd BT32 . . . 61 C4
Commonreagh BT30 . . 125 C4
Commons
Downpatrick BT30 . . . 93 B4
Newry BT34 . . . 132 C1
Commons Brae BT8 . . . 22 A3
Commons Hall Rd BT34 . 132 C1
Commons of Clanmaghery
BT30 . . . 123 F6
Commons Rd BT30 . . . 123 E7
Commons Sch Rd BT34 . 132 C1
Commons Way BT34 . . . 64 E3
Conall Ave BT34 . . . 65 D4
Concession Rd
Hackballs Cross . . . 148 A4
Newry BT35 . . . 147 E5
Conduit St BT7 . . . 155 A1
CONEYISLAND BT30 . . . 125 F5
Coney Island BT30 . . . 125 E5
Coniamstown BT30 . . . 125 A8
Coniamstown Rd BT30 . . 109 A1
Coniston Cl 2 BT13 . . . 14 A7
Coniston Dr 1 BT20 . . . 4 E3
Coniston Rd BT20 . . . 4 E3
CONLIG BT23 . . . 12 F4
Conlig Prim Sch BT23 . . . 12 F4
Conluce Pk BT26 . . . 49 B1
Connaught Man's Cnr . . 150 B5
Connaught Pk
Lurgan BT66 . . . 42 B2
Portadown BT62 . . . 51 D3
Connaught St BT12 . . . 154 B1
Connellystown Rd BT25 . . 58 C7
Connor Pk BT24 . . . 59 C4
Connors La BT60 . . . 96 E3
Connsbank Rd BT3 . . . 15 C7
Connsbrook Ave BT4 . . . 15 D6
Connsbrook Dr BT4 . . . 15 D6
Connsbrook Pk BT4 . . . 15 D7
Connswater Gr 3 BT4 . . . 15 C6
Connswater Ind Est BT5 . . 15 C4
Connswater Link BT4 . . . 15 C5
Connswater Mews 2 BT4 15 C6
Connswater Ret Pk BT5 . . 15 C5
Connswater Sh Ctr BT5 . . 15 C4
Connswater St BT4 . . . 15 C5
Conor Pk BT66 . . . 41 E4
Cons La BT35 . . . 131 B2
Constance St 1 BT5 . . . 15 B4
Convent Cl BT61 . . . 60 B5
Convent Gdns 3 BT35 . . 131 C5
Convent Hill BT35 . . . 131 B5
Convention Ct BT4 . . . 15 B5
Convent of Mercy Prim Sch
BT30 . . . 62 D4
Convent Rd
Armagh BT61 . . . 60 B5
Newry BT34 . . . 121 A2
Conway Ct BT13 . . . 154 A4
Conway Ind Est BT13 . . . 154 A3
Conway La BT17 . . . 26 E8
Conway Link BT13 . . . 154 A3
Conway Pk BT35 . . . 140 B4
Conways Grave Rd BT60 . . 97 F7
Conway Sq BT13 . . . 154 A3
Conway St
Belfast BT13 . . . 154 A4
1 Lisburn BT27 . . . 26 B2
Conway Wlk BT13 . . . 154 A4
Cooey BT60 . . . 96 F4
Cooke Ct BT7 . . . 155 B1
Cooke Mews BT7 . . . 155 B1
Cooke Pl BT7 . . . 155 B1
Cooke St BT7 . . . 155 B1
Cooks Brae BT22 . . . 80 D7
Cooks Cove BT22 . . . 80 D7
Cook St BT22 . . . 94 D3
Cookstown BT22 . . . 80 E3
Coolderry BT35 . . . 148 C5
Coolderry Rd BT35 . . . 148 C5
Cooleen Ave BT23 . . . 20 C6
Cooleen Gdns BT19 . . . 2 F3
Coolfin St BT12 . . . 154 B1
Coolkill BT60 . . . 96 D1
Coolkill Rd BT60 . . . 96 E2
Coolmillish BT60 . . . 99 F1
Coolmillish Pk BT60 . . . 115 F8
Coolmillish Rd
Armagh BT60 . . . 115 C6
Markethill BT60 . . . 116 A8
Coolnacran BT32 . . . 102 C4
Coolnacran Rd BT32 . . . 102 C4
Coolnadrena BT66 . . . 41 D4
Coolpark Ave BT8 . . . 22 B4
Coolraven Pk BT19 . . . 3 C2
Coolsallagh BT25 . . . 87 C7
Coolsara Pk BT28 . . . 26 A2
Coolyhill BT62 . . . 100 F5
Cooly Hill Rd BT62 . . . 100 F6
Cooneen Way BT6 . . . 22 B8
Cooper The BT27 . . . 28 E1
Coose BT63 . . . 86 B1
Cootehall Pk BT19 . . . 2 F3
Cootehall Rd BT19 . . . 2 F2
Copeland Ave
Comber BT23 . . . 25 F4
2 Millisle BT22 . . . 67 A4
Copeland Cres BT23 . . . 25 F4
Copeland Dr BT23 . . . 25 F4
Copeland Island Bird
Observatory★ BT21 . . . 7 D7
Copeland Link BT23 . . . 25 F3
Copeland Pk BT23 . . . 25 F4
Copeland Rd BT23 . . . 25 F4
Copeland Sq BT21 . . . 66 F7
Cope Prim Sch The BT61 . 85 A5
Copney BT71 . . . 72 E3
Copperfield Ct BT67 . . . 35 A8
Copperfields BT67 . . . 35 A8
Coppice Way BT23 . . . 20 A4
Coragh BT61 . . . 85 A6
Corbally
Banbridge BT32 . . . 104 C5
Downpatrick BT30 . . . 93 A4
Downpatrick BT30 . . . 110 A4
Downpatrick BT30 . . . 124 B8
Corbally Old Rd BT32 . . . 104 B5
Corbally Rd
Banbridge BT32 . . . 104 C5
Downpatrick BT30 . . . 124 C7
Corbet BT32 . . . 103 E6
Corbet Rd BT32 . . . 103 D7
Corbracky BT62 . . . 74 D1
Corbracky La BT62 . . . 74 D1
Corbracky Rd BT62 . . . 74 D1
Corby Dr BT66 . . . 42 B2
Corcrain BT62 . . . 51 D5
Corcrain Ave BT62 . . . 51 B5
Corcrain Dr BT62 . . . 51 B4
Corcrain Mews BT62 . . . 51 C5
Corcrain Rd BT62 . . . 51 C5
Corcreaghan BT34 . . . 152 E7
Corcreaghan Rd BT34 . . . 152 E6
Corcreechy Rd BT34 . . . 118 C1
Corcreeghy BT34 . . . 118 C1
Corcreeny
Craigavon BT66 . . . 86 A7
Hillsborough BT26 . . . 46 B5
Corcreeny Rd BT26 . . . 46 C5
Corcreevy BT61 . . . 85 D1
Corcreevy Dr 7 BT61 . . . 85 E1
Corcreevy Rd BT61 . . . 85 D1
Corcrum BT35 . . . 117 C6
Corcullentragh Beg
BT62 . . . 51 A5
Corcullentragh More
BT62 . . . 50 E4
Corcullentragh Rd BT62 . . 51 A5
Corcullionglish . . . 147 C4
Cordrain BT62 . . . 100 F7
Cordrain Rd BT62 . . . 100 F7
Corernagh BT62 . . . 101 B2
Corernagh Rd BT62 . . . 101 B2
Corfehan BT60 . . . 96 D2
Corgary BT34 . . . 118 A2
Corgary Rd BT34 . . . 118 A2
Corhammock BT60 . . . 116 B7
Corkley BT60 . . . 128 E8
Corkley Rd BT60 . . . 114 D1
Corlat BT60 . . . 130 C8
Corliss BT35 . . . 138 D2
Corliss Fort★ BT35 . . . 138 D1
Corliss Rd BT35 . . . 138 D2
Corlust BT62 . . . 100 F1
Corlust Rd BT62 . . . 101 A2
Cormeen BT60 . . . 97 C3
Cormeen Hill BT60 . . . 97 D2
Cormeen Rd BT60 . . . 97 C3
Cormorant Pk BT5 . . . 23 A8
Cornacrew BT60 . . . 100 A4
Cornagrally BT60 . . . 116 E6
Cornahove BT35 . . . 147 B7
Cornakinnegar BT67 . . . 32 C2
Cornakinnegar Rd BT67 . . 32 C5
Cornalack BT62 . . . 51 A8
Cornamucklagh
Craigavon BT62 . . . 50 E7
Omeath . . . 142 B3
Cornascreeb BT62 . . . 100 C8
Cornascreeb Rd BT62 . . . 100 D8
Cornmarket BT1 . . . 155 A3
Cornmarket St 17 BT62 . . 101 B7
Corn Mkt BT35 . . . 64 C5
Cornoonagh BT35 . . . 148 C6
Cornoonagh Rd BT35 . . . 148 C7
Cornreany BT66 . . . 42 A1
Coronation Ave BT23 . . . 12 F4
Coronation Cres BT23 . . . 25 E4
Coronation Gdn BT27 . . . 37 B4
Coronation Pk
Bangor BT19 . . . 3 B2
Dundonald BT16 . . . 17 B2
Coronation Pl BT66 . . . 86 A8
Coronation St
Craigavon BT62 . . . 100 E8
Portadown BT62 . . . 51 D3
Coronation Way 3 BT62 100 E8
Corporation
Armagh BT61 . . . 60 D5
Killyleagh BT30 . . . 93 B5
Corporation North
BT23 . . . 19 E5
Corporation South
BT23 . . . 19 D3
Corporation Sq BT15 . . . 155 B4
Corporation St BT1 . . . 155 B4
Corragarry . . . 147 B8
Corran BT35 . . . 115 A3
Corrán Chluain Ard (Clonard
Cres) 5 BT13 . . . 154 A3
Corr and Dunavally
BT71 . . . 84 B7
Corran Rd BT60 . . . 115 B4
Corrasmoo Rd BT35 . . . 147 C6
Corrick Way BT34 . . . 153 C6
Corrigan Hill Rd BT71 . . . 84 C6
Corrigs Ave BT33 . . . 63 E8
Corrinare BT60 . . . 116 F6
Corrinare Rd BT60 . . . 116 F5
Corrinshigo BT35 . . . 131 E2
Corrinure BT60 . . . 116 D1
Corrog BT22 . . . 94 E5
Corr Rd BT71 . . . 72 C8
Corry BT60 . . . 100 A5
Corry Link BT3 . . . 14 F7
Corry Pk BT24 . . . 91 B2
Corry Pl BT15 . . . 14 F7
Corry Rd BT3 . . . 14 F7
Corry Sq BT35 . . . 64 C6
Corry St BT23 . . . 19 C6
Corrywood Pk BT31 . . . 122 D5
Cortamlat BT35 . . . 128 F3
Cortamlat Rd BT35 . . . 128 F5
Cortamlet Prim Sch
BT35 . . . 128 F3
Cortreasla Rd BT35 . . . 148 E8
Cor Tynan BT68 . . . 96 C3
Cortynan Rd BT68 . . . 96 D3
Corvalley Ct BT19 . . . 3 D4
Cosgrave Hts 17 BT15 . . . 14 D8
Cosgrave St 19 BT15 . . . 14 D8
Cotswold Ave BT8 . . . 22 B3
Cotswold Dr
Bangor BT20 . . . 4 F4
6 Saintfield BT24 . . . 77 C4
Cotswold Gdns BT20 . . . 4 F4
Cottage Ave BT67 . . . 42 F6
Cottage Grange BT67 . . . 42 F6
Cottagehill BT67 . . . 42 F6
Cottage Hill BT22 . . . 70 C5
Cottage Mews BT62 . . . 51 C2
Cottage Rd
Craigavon BT67 . . . 42 E7
Downpatrick BT30 . . . 107 C3
Newry BT35 . . . 141 F4
Cottage Wlk BT67 . . . 42 D7
Cotterhill Rd BT30 . . . 62 A8
Cotton BT19 . . . 66 A8
Cotton Rd BT19 . . . 13 F4
Coulson Ave BT28 . . . 38 B8
Coulter's Hill BT22 . . . 80 F7
Council Rd
Kilkeel BT34 . . . 153 E8
Newry BT34 . . . 145 E1
County Armagh Golf Club
BT60 . . . 60 E3
Courtbane . . . 148 B4
Court House★ BT21 . . . 6 E3
Courtney Ave BT66 . . . 41 F7
Courtney Hill BT34 . . . 64 E4
Courtney Rd BT35 . . . 130 D2
Courtrai St BT13 . . . 14 A7
Court Sq BT23 . . . 19 E4
Court St BT23 . . . 19 E4
Courtyard Mansions BT23 13 A6
Courtyard The
Bangor BT19 . . . 2 F5
Newcastle BT33 . . . 63 B7
Cove Ave BT19 . . . 5 C7
Cove Cres BT19 . . . 5 C7
Cove Hill BT19 . . . 5 C7
Cove Hollow BT19 . . . 5 C7
Cove La BT19 . . . 5 C7
Cove The 3 BT34 . . . 153 C7
Cowan Heron Hospl BT25 58 D4
Cowan Rd BT35 . . . 140 A6
Cowan St BT34 . . . 64 E6
Cow Hill Rd BT71 . . . 84 C7
Coxhill Rd BT62 . . . 55 A6
COX'S HILL BT62 . . . 55 C8
Coyles Hill BT34 . . . 133 D1
Coyle's La BT19 . . . 2 B3
Coyle St BT7 . . . 155 B1
Crabtree Hill BT35 . . . 131 D6
Crabtree Rd
Ballynahinch BT24 . . . 59 F2
Banbridge BT32 . . . 120 D5
Craigantlet Rd BT23 . . . 11 B3
Craigaroddan BT22 . . . 95 A3
Craigaroddan Rd BT22 . . . 95 A3
Craigarusky BT23 . . . 79 A7
Craigarusky Rd
Killinchy BT23 . . . 78 F5
Newtownards BT23 . . . 79 A6
CRAIGAVAD BT18 . . . 1 E3
Craigaveen Cl BT35 . . . 64 C3
CRAIGAVON BT64 . . . 40 D1
Craigavon Area Hospl
BT63 . . . 52 C7
Craigavon Ave BT62 . . . 51 D3
Craigavon Commercial Area
BT64 . . . 40 D2
Craigavon Food Pk BT63 . 40 B2
Craigavon Prim Sch BT63 57 D2
Craigavon Senior High Sch
BT63 . . . 52 A6
Craigboy BT21 . . . 66 F6
Craigboye Rd BT21 . . . 66 F6
Craigboy Pk BT19 . . . 3 D1
Craig Cres BT28 . . . 37 F8
Craigdara Ave BT34 . . . 146 C4
Craigdarragh Pk BT18 . . . 2 A4
Craigdarragh Pk E BT18 . . . 2 A4
Craigdarragh Rd BT19 . . . 2 B4
Craig Gdns 3 BT28 . . . 37 F8
Craighill La BT24 . . . 90 C2
Craiglee Way BT23 . . . 19 C3
Craigleith Dr BT16 . . . 17 D4
Craigmona Close 3
BT34 . . . 133 B4
Craigmona View
2 Mayobridge BT34 . . . 133 B4
4 Mayobridge BT34 . . . 133 B4
Craigmore Rd BT35 . . . 131 E5
Craigmore Way BT7 . . . 155 A1
Craignasasonagh BT24 . 77 A5
Craignish Cres BT16 . . . 17 C4
Craignish Ct BT16 . . . 17 C4
Craigogantlet BT23 . . . 11 A3
Craigowen Pk BT19 . . . 2 A4
Craigowen Rd BT19 . . . 2 A4
Craig Rd The BT30 . . . 92 E2
Craigtara BT18 . . . 9 D6
Craigwell Ave BT62 . . . 51 C5
Craigy Rd BT24 . . . 77 A5
Crammonhill Rd BT60 . . . 115 F7
Cranagh BT21 . . . 6 C4
Cranagill BT62 . . . 73 C1
Cranfield BT34 . . . 152 F3
Cranfield Rd BT34 . . . 152 F3
Crankey BT35 . . . 117 B2
Crankey Rd BT35 . . . 117 B3
Cranley Ave BT19 . . . 4 E1
Cranley Dr BT19 . . . 4 E1
Cranley Gdns 7 BT19 . . . 4 E1
Cranley Gn 2 BT19 . . . 13 E8
Cranley Gr BT19 . . . 4 E1
Cranley Hill BT19 . . . 4 E1
Cranley Mews 6 BT19 . . . 4 E1
Cranley Pk BT19 . . . 4 E1
Cranley Rd BT19 . . . 4 E1
Cranmore Ave
Belfast BT9 . . . 21 A7
Newtownards BT23 . . . 19 F5
Cranmore Gdns BT9 . . . 21 A7
Cranmore Pk BT9 . . . 21 A7
Crann BT60 . . . 112 E5
Crannagael BT62 . . . 73 C1
Crannard Gdns BT35 . . . 64 A7
Cranny La BT63 . . . 53 B4
Cranny Rd
Craigavon BT63 . . . 53 B5
Newry BT35 . . . 140 A3
Craveernagh BT60 . . . 97 E2
Craven St BT13 . . . 154 B4
Crawford Pk
Castlereagh BT5 . . . 22 F7
Portadown BT62 . . . 51 C2
CRAWFORDSBURN BT19 . . . 2 E3
Crawfordsburn Cl BT19 . . . 3 C4
Crawfordsburn Ctry Pk★
BT19 . . . 2 C6
Crawfordsburn Pk
Bangor BT20 . . . 3 D3
Newtownards BT23 . . . 19 B8
Crawfordsburn Prim Sch
BT19 . . . 2 F3
Crawfordsburn Rd
Bangor BT19 . . . 3 B4
Newtownards BT23 . . . 12 B4
Crawfordsburn Way BT23 19 B8
Crawfordsburn Wood BT19 3 A4
Crawfordstown Rd
Downpatrick BT30 . . . 107 E7
Drumaness BT24 . . . 91 C1
Creaghan BT71 . . . 84 A3
CREAGHANROE (CRÍCHEÁN
RUA) . . . 127 E2
Creamery Rd (Bóthar na
Huachtarlainne) BT35 . . . 138 F1
Crearum or Fellows Hall
BT60 . . . 97 B4
Creeghduff BT30 . . . 107 E1
Creeghduff Rd BT30 . . . 107 D2
Creenagh
Armagh BT61 . . . 85 C3
Craigavon BT67 . . . 35 C3
Creenagh Rd BT61 . . . 85 C3
Creenkill BT35 . . . 138 E1
Creenkill Rd (Bóthar na
Críonchoille) BT35 . . . 138 E1
Creerybeg BT30 . . . 92 C8
Creeve
Armagh BT60 . . . 116 F5
Newry BT34 . . . 132 C3
Creevekeeran
Armagh BT60 . . . 113 A6
Newry BT35 . . . 147 D7
Creevekeeran Rd BT60 . . 113 B7
Creevelough BT70 . . . 82 C5
Creevelough Rd BT70 . . . 82 C6
Creeveroe BT60 . . . 98 A6
Creeveroe Rd BT60 . . . 97 F6
Creevy
Banbridge BT32 . . . 118 D7
Lisburn BT27 . . . 76 B5
Creevyargon BT24 . . . 91 B6
Creevyargon Rd BT24 . . . 91 B6
Creevy Ave BT5 . . . 16 B1
Creevybeg BT30 . . . 78 C1
Creevycarnonan BT30 . . 92 A6
Creevy Cl 7 BT24 . . . 77 C3
Creevyloughgare BT24 . 77 C2
Creevyotra Rd BT60 . . . 113 F8
Creevy Rd
Downpatrick BT30 . . . 92 A6
Lisburn BT27 . . . 39 E2
Lisburn BT27 . . . 76 C4
Creevytenant BT24 . . . 76 E1
Creevytenant Rd BT24 . . . 76 D1
Creevy Way BT5 . . . 16 B1
Creey Loop BT32 . . . 118 C6
CREGAGH BT6 . . . 22 B8
Cregagh BT6 . . . 22 D7
Cregagh Ct BT6 . . . 15 B1
Cregagh Gdns BT60 . . . 60 C3
Cregagh Pk BT6 . . . 22 C7
Cregagh Pk E BT6 . . . 22 D7
Cregagh Prim Sch BT6 . . . 22 B8
Cregagh Rd BT6 . . . 15 B1
Cregagh St BT6 . . . 15 B2
CREGGAN BT35 . . . 139 B1
Cregganbane Rd BT35 . . . 139 C1
Creggan Duff BT35 . . . 139 B2
Creggandulf Rd BT35 . . . 139 B3
Creggan Lower BT60 . . 116 D1
Creggan Rd BT60 . . . 116 D1
Creggan Upper BT60 . . 116 D1
Creggan W Rd BT60 . . . 116 D1
Creighton's Gn BT18 . . . 10 C6
Crescent Arts Ctr & The
Fenderesky Gall★ BT7 . 155 A1
Crescent Gdns BT7 . . . 155 A1
Crescent Gr BT23 . . . 25 E4
Crescent Mews BT23 . . . 25 E4
Crescent The
Ballygowan BT23 . . . 31 D1
Carryduff BT8 . . . 29 D3
Crossmaglen BT35 . . . 147 F7
Holywood BT18 . . . 9 D7
Cresent Gr BT23 . . . 25 E4
Crevenish Wlk BT8 . . . 21 E3
Crew Beg BT35 . . . 101 B1
Crewbeg Rd BT35 . . . 101 A1
Crewcat BT61 . . . 85 E2
Crewcatt Rd BT61 . . . 85 E2
Crew Hill Ct BT30 . . . 125 F6
Crew Hill Pl 12 BT30 . . . 125 F6
Crew Hill Way 10 BT30 . . 125 F6
Crew More BT35 . . . 116 F8
Crewmore Rd
Craigavon BT62 . . . 101 A1
Newry BT35 . . . 117 A8
Crew Rd BT30 . . . 109 F1
CRÍCHEÁN RUA
(CREAGHANROE) . . . 127 E2
Cricklewood Cres BT9 . . . 21 D7
Cricklewood Pk BT9 . . . 21 D6
Crieve Ct BT34 . . . 64 F7
Crieve Hts BT34 . . . 64 F6
Crieve Rd BT34 . . . 64 F7
Crimea Cl BT13 . . . 14 B7
Crimea Ct BT13 . . . 154 B4
Crimea St BT13 . . . 154 B4
Croan BT34 . . . 133 A6
Crobane BT34 . . . 132 E4
Crobane Rd BT34 . . . 132 D4
Crochan Ct BT19 . . . 13 C6
Crockoona Pk BT34 . . . 121 C2
Crocus St BT12 . . . 154 A2
Croft Cl BT18 . . . 9 F7
Croft Gdns BT18 . . . 9 F7
Croft Hill BT8 . . . 22 C2
Croft House Ct BT5 . . . 16 E3
Croft Manor BT18 . . . 9 F7
Croft Mdws BT18 . . . 9 F7
Crofton Glen BT18 . . . 9 E7
Croft Pk BT18 . . . 9 F7
Croft Rd
Dromara BT25 . . . 89 B3
Holywood BT18 . . . 9 F7
Croft Rise BT18 . . . 9 F7
Croft St BT20 . . . 3 F3
Crohill Rd BT34 . . . 132 E4
CROIS MHIC LIONNÁIN
(CROSSMAGLEN) BT35 . . 147 E8
Crolly's Quarter BT30 . 125 B5
Cromac Ave BT7 . . . 155 B1
Cromac Pl BT7 . . . 155 B1
Cromac Quay BT7 . . . 155 B1
Cromac Sq BT2 . . . 155 B2
Cromac St BT1 . . . 155 B2
Cromarty Pl 1 BT16 . . . 17 D3
Crombeg Ct BT26 . . . 47 E6
Crombeg Mews BT26 . . . 47 E7
CROMGHLINN
(HILLSBOROUGH) BT26 . . 47 D7
Cromlech Pk BT34 . . . 153 C8
Cromlyn Pk BT26 . . . 47 D6
Crommelin Pl BT28 . . . 38 B8
Cromwell Cl 2 BT27 . . . 26 D1
Cromwells Highway 1
BT27 . . . 26 D1
Cronghill BT69 . . . 82 A6
Cronin Pk BT34 . . . 64 D4
Cronkill BT71 . . . 72 F7
Cronstown BT23 . . . 20 C7
Cronstown Cottage Ave 2
BT23 . . . 20 B7
Cronstown Cottage Cres 1
BT23 . . . 20 B7
Cronstown Cottage Gr
BT23 . . . 20 B7
Cronstown Cottage Pk
BT23 . . . 20 B7
Cronstown Rd BT23 . . . 20 A7
Croob Cl (Clós na Crúibe)
BT30 . . . 62 B2
Croob Pk BT24 . . . 59 B4
Crooked Rd BT35 . . . 130 D1
Croreagh BT34 . . . 132 E6
Crosby St
Bangor BT20 . . . 4 B5
Belfast BT13 . . . 154 B4
Cross
Newry BT34 . . . 135 E8
Newry BT35 . . . 131 C2
Rathfriland BT34 . . . 120 A1
Crossan BT27 . . . 39 D3
Crossan Rd
Lisburn BT27 . . . 39 C1
Newry BT34 . . . 133 A6
Crossan Wlk BT28 . . . 37 E8
Crossbane BT60 . . . 127 C6
Crossbane Rd BT60 . . . 127 B6
Crossdall BT60 . . . 112 E3
Crossdall Rd BT60 . . . 112 F1
Crossdened Row BT60 . . 114 A2

Crossgar BT25 . . . . 89 E2
CROSSGAR (AN CHROIS GHEARR) BT30 . . . . 92 A4
Crossgar Golf Course BT30 . . . . 92 B5
Crossgar Prim Sch 11 BT30 . . . . 92 B5
Crossgar Rd
Ballynahinch BT24 . . . . 59 F5
Downpatrick BT30 . . . . 93 B6
Dromara BT25 . . . . 89 F2
Saintfield BT24 . . . . 77 D3
Crossgar Rd E BT30 . . . . . . 92 C2
Crosskeys Rd BT60 . . . . . 113 F5
Cross La
Dromara BT25 . . . . 58 D5
Lisburn BT28 . . . . 36 E8
Newry BT34 . . . . 121 E1
Crossland Ct BT13 . . . . . 154 A4
Crossland St BT13 . . . . . 154 A4
Crosslieve Dr BT35 . . . . . 140 D1
Crossmacahilly BT64 . . . 53 A6
CROSSMAGLEN (CROIS MHIC LIONNÁIN) BT35 . . . . . . 147 E8
Crossmore BT60 . . . . . . 114 A4
Crossmore Gdns 4 BT60 . . . . 114 A3
Crossmore Gn BT60 . . . . . 114 A4
Crossmore Rd
Armagh BT60 . . . . 113 F5
Downpatrick BT30 . . . . 110 A1
Keady BT60 . . . . 114 A4
CROSSNACREEVY BT5 . . . . . 23 C3
Crossnamoyle BT60 . . . 113 D1
Crossnamuckley BT22 . . 66 B2
Crossnamuckley Rd BT22. 66 B3
Crossnenagh BT60 . . . . 127 E5
Crossnenagh Rd BT60 . . . 113 D1
Cross Par BT7 . . . . 14 F1
Cross Rd BT34 . . . . 133 F7
Cross St BT30 . . . . 93 C5
Crowhill Rd BT66 . . . . 53 F4
Crown Entry BT1 . . . . 155 A3
Crowston Ct BT19 . . . . 13 C7
Croziermews BT32 . . . . . . 61 B4
Crozier Pk BT66 . . . . 41 D3
Crubinagh Rd BT71 . . . . . 83 B8
Crumlin Rd BT13 . . . . 14 A8
Crunagh BT60 . . . . 116 B4
Crunagh Rd BT60 . . . . 116 B4
Crunaght BT60 . . . . 116 B8
Crystal St BT5 . . . . 15 D4
Ctr for Cross Border Studies The BT61 . . . . 60 C5
Cuan Ave BT22 . . . . 94 D3
Cuan Gdns BT22 . . . . 70 B4
CUAN HÉILIN (HELEN'S BAY) BT19 . . . . 2 E6
Cuan Pl
Newtownards BT23 . . . . 19 B4
15 Portaferry BT22 . . . . 94 D3
Cuan View 3 BT22 . . . . 94 D3
Cuba Wlk BT4 . . . . 15 B5
Cu-Chullain Pk GAA BT35 . . . . 140 A3
Cúirt Allt an Chairthe (Altcar Ct) 37 BT5 . . . . 15 A5
Cúirt an Chomair (Comber Ct) 25 BT5 . . . . 15 A5
Cúirt Andarsan (anderson Ct) 3 BT5 . . . . 15 A5
Cúirt Arann (Arran Ct) 4 BT5 . . . . 15 A5
Cúirt Bholcáin (Vulcan Ct) 12 BT5 . . . . 15 A5
Cúirt Chluaidh (Clyde Ct) 1 BT5 . . . . 15 A5
Cúirt Maidrid (Madrid Ct) 6 BT5 . . . . 15 A5
Cúirt Mhaigh Rath (Moira Ct) 5 BT5 . . . . 15 A5
Cúirt na Bhfáll (Falls Ct) 6 BT13 . . . . 154 A3
Cúirt Naoimh Maitiú (St Matthew's Ct) 22 BT5 . . . . 15 A5
Cúirt Phluincéid (Plunkett Ct) BT13 . . . . 155 A4
Cúirt Suí Forde (Seaforde Ct) 20 BT5 . . . . 15 A5
Cúirt Thulach Forde (Mountforde Ct) 18 BT5 . . 15 A5
Cúirt uí Bhríosáin (Bryson Ct) 26 BT5 . . . . 15 A5
Culcavey Bridge BT26 . . . . 37 B1
Culcavey Rd BT26 . . . . 37 B2
CULCAVY BT26 . . . . 37 C1
Culcavy Rd BT26 . . . . 47 B8
Culdee Cres BT61 . . . . 60 C5
Culdee Dr BT61 . . . . 60 C5
Culdee St BT61 . . . . 60 C4
Culdee Terrace BT61 . . . . . 60 C5
Culfore 150 D4
Culkeeran BT60 . . . . 83 A2
CULLAVILLE BT35 . . . . 147 C6
Cullaville Rd BT35 . . . . . . 147 E7
Cullentragh
Armagh BT60 . . . . 97 D6
Newry BT35 . . . . 117 B4
Cullentragh Rd BT35 . . . . 117 C3
Culligan BT68 . . . . 96 B4
Cullingtree Rd BT12 . . . . 154 B2
Cullintraw BT23 . . . . 68 D4
Cullion BT34 . . . . 133 B7
Cullion Rd BT34 . . . . 133 B7
Culloden Est & Spa* BT18 1 D2
CULLYHANNA BT35 . . . . . 139 A6
Cullyhanna Big BT35 . . 138 F6
Cullyhanna Little BT35 138 F5
Cullyhanna Rd BT35 . . . . . 129 C1
Cully Rd BT35 . . . . 139 F1
Culmore Ave BT23 . . . . 19 F5
Culrevog BT71 . . . . 83 F8
Culrevog Rd BT71 . . . . 83 F8
Culross Dr BT16 . . . . 17 D3
CULTRA BT18 . . . . 1 D1
Cultra Ave BT18 . . . . 1 C1
Cultra Pk BT18 . . . . 1 C1
Cultra St 10 BT15 . . . . 14 E8
Cultra Sta BT18 . . . . 1 D1
Cultra Sta Rd BT18 . . . . 1 D1
Cultra Terr BT18 . . . . 1 C1
Cumber
Aughnacloy BT69 . . . . 82 A3
Ballynahinch BT24 . . . . 91 B3
Cumber Dr BT24 . . . . 91 B2
Cumber Gdns 3 BT24 . . . . 91 B1
Cumber Gr BT24 . . . . 91 B2
Cumber Grange 2 BT24 . . 91 B1
Cumber Hill BT24 . . . . 91 B2
Cumberland Ave BT16 . . . . 17 A4
Cumberland Cl BT16 . . . . . 17 A4
Cumberland Ct BT16 . . . . . 17 A4
Cumberland Dr BT16 . . . . . 17 A4
Cumberland La BT16 . . . . . 17 A4
Cumberland Mews BT16 . . 17 A4
Cumberland Pk BT16 . . . . . 17 A4
Cumberland Rd BT16 . . . . . 17 A4
Cumberland St BT13 . . . . 154 B4
Cumberland Wlk BT13 . . 154 B4
Cumber Pk BT24 . . . . 91 B2
Cumber Rd
Aughnacloy BT69 . . . . 82 A3
Ballynahinch BT24 . . . . 91 C3
Cumber View BT24 . . . . . . 91 B2
Cumran BT30 . . . . 107 C2
Cumran La BT30 . . . . 107 C2
Cumran Prim Sch BT30 . 107 C1
Cumsons Rd BT35 . . . . . . 129 B5
Cunningburn BT22 . . . . . 69 D8
Cunningburn Rd BT22 . . . . 66 A1
Cupar St Lower BT13 . . . 154 A3
Cupar Way BT13 . . . . 154 A3
Curlew Cres BT23 . . . . 20 A3
Curley BT34 . . . . 119 A3
Curley Rd BT34 . . . . 119 A3
Curly's Fort* BT23 . . . . 78 B5
Curragh La BT60 . . . . 127 B7
Curran BT71 . . . . 83 C7
Currans Brae BT71 . . . . . . 72 A1
Curran St BT62 . . . . 51 D4
Curtis St BT1 . . . . 155 A4
Curzon St BT7 . . . . 14 E2
Cushenny BT62 . . . . 50 A5
Cushenny Rd BT62 . . . . . . 50 A5
Cusher Gn BT60 . . . . 116 D3
Cusher Rd BT60 . . . . 116 C6
Cushowen Pl 1 BT24 . . . . 91 B1
Cussick St BT9 . . . . 14 B1
Custom House Ave BT34 . . 64 D4
Custom House Sq BT1 . . . 155 B4
Cut The BT32 . . . . 61 D4
Cuttles Cl BT23 . . . . 25 C1
Cuttles Ct BT23 . . . . 25 C1
Cuttles Gn BT23 . . . . 25 C1
Cuttles Rd BT23 . . . . 25 C1
Cuttles Ridge BT23 . . . . 25 C1
Cuttles Rise BT23 . . . . 25 C1
Cutts The BT17 . . . . 26 D8
Cuttyshane Rd BT30 . . . . . 92 F4
Cypress Cl
7 Donaghadee BT21 . . . . . 67 A8
Dunmurry BT17 . . . . 27 A8
Cypress Cres 6 BT21 . . . . 66 F8
Cypress Gdns BT66 . . . . . . 41 E6
Cypress Pk BT21 . . . . 66 F8
Cypress Way BT21 . . . . 66 F8
Cyprus Ave BT5 . . . . 15 E4
Cyprus Gdns BT5 . . . . 15 E4
Cyprus Pk BT5 . . . . 15 E4

D

Dagger Rd BT28 . . . . 36 D8
Daires Willows BT61 . . . . . 60 B6
Dairy La BT35 . . . . 129 F7
Daisyfield St BT13 . . . . 14 B7
Daisy Hill BT35 . . . . 64 B6
Daisyhill Ct BT32 . . . . 61 C4
Daisy Hill Gdns BT35 . . . . . 64 B6
Daisy Hill Hospl BT35 . . . . 64 B6
Dakota Ave BT23 . . . . 19 C2
Dalboyne Gdns BT28 . . . . . 26 B3
Dalboyne Pk BT28 . . . . 26 B3
Dalchoolin BT18 . . . . 1 D2
Dalkeith Gdns 2 BT16 . . . 17 D3
Dallan Ave BT34 . . . . 65 D4
Dallan Hill BT34 . . . . 65 D4
Dallan Rd BT34 . . . . 65 D4
Dallan View BT34 . . . . 65 D4
Dalriada Rd BT30 . . . . 62 E3
Dalry Pk BT5 . . . . 16 E3
Dalton Cl BT60 . . . . 60 C4
Dalton Cres BT23 . . . . 25 B3
Dalton Dr BT23 . . . . 25 B3
Dalton Glade BT23 . . . . 25 B3
Dalton Glen BT23 . . . . 25 B3
Dalton Pk
Armagh BT60 . . . . 60 C4
Comber BT23 . . . . 25 B3
11 Keady BT60 . . . . 114 A3
Dalton Rd BT60 . . . . 60 C3
Dalton St BT5 . . . . 155 C3
Dalton Way BT23 . . . . 25 B3
Dalwhinney Rd BT18 . . . . . 10 A8
Daly Cres (Páirc uí Dhálaigh) BT35 . . . . 139 E2
Damascus St BT7 . . . . 14 E2
Damhead Rd BT67 . . . . 35 E5
Damhill Rd BT67 . . . . 33 A1
Damoily BT60 . . . . 115 D6
Damoily Rd BT60 . . . . 115 E5
Damolly BT34 . . . . 132 B6
Damolly Mdws 2 BT34 . . 132 A5
Damolly Rd BT34 . . . . 132 C6
Damolly Ret Pk BT35 . . . . 131 F5
Dam Rd BT19 . . . . 5 C1
Dandy Row BT32 . . . . 86 D1
Dane's Cast* BT60 . . . . . 114 D7
Danesfort
Belfast BT9 . . . . 21 C7
Moira BT67 . . . . 33 F1
Danns Row 3 BT6 . . . . . . 15 A4
Danube St BT13 . . . . 14 A7
Daphne St BT12 . . . . 154 B1
Daragh Pk BT34 . . . . 64 F2
Dargan Cres BT3 . . . . 8 A4
Dargan Dr BT3 . . . . 8 A3
Dargan Ind Pk BT3 . . . . 8 A3
Dargan Rd BT3 . . . . 8 A4
Darkley BT60 . . . . 114 C1
DARKLEY BT60 . . . . 128 B8
Darkley Prim Sch BT60 . . 128 B8
Darkley Rd BT60 . . . . 114 B1
Darling Ave BT66 . . . . 42 A4
Darragh BT23 . . . . 79 C6
Darragh Cres BT23 . . . . 25 E4
DARRAGH CROSS BT30 . . . . 78 B3
Darragh Gdns BT23 . . . . . . 25 E4
Darragh Rd
Comber BT23 . . . . 25 F5
Downpatrick BT30 . . . . 78 B3
Darragh's La BT23 . . . . 19 C5
Darragh Terr BT23 . . . . 25 E4
Dartan Ree BT60 . . . . 96 E3
Darton BT60 . . . . 97 A5
Davarr Ave BT16 . . . . 17 D4
David St BT13 . . . . 154 A3
Davis St
Keady BT60 . . . . 114 A2
4 Newry BT35 . . . . 64 C7
Davitts Gac BT13 . . . . 154 A3
Dawson Gn BT62 . . . . 51 B5
Dawson St
Armagh BT61 . . . . 60 C5
15 Belfast BT15 . . . . 14 D8
Dayton St BT13 . . . . 154 C4
Deanfield BT19 . . . . 5 A2
Deans Rd BT66 . . . . 53 E6
Deanswift Mews 4 BT60 . . . . 116 A8
Deans Wlk
Lurgan BT66 . . . . 41 F6
Richhill BT61 . . . . 85 E1
Deanwood Cres BT23 . . . . 20 C6
Dechomet Prim Sch BT31 . . . . 104 F2
Dechomet Rd BT25 . . . . . 104 F4
De Courcey Way BT33 . . . 123 B5
De Courcy Pk BT22 . . . . . . 70 B5
De Courcy Pl 5 BT30 . . . . 62 C5
De Courcy Way BT33 . . . . 123 C5
Deehommed BT31 . . . . 104 F2
Deeny Dr BT67 . . . . 42 A8
Deerpark Rd BT22 . . . . 80 E1
Deer Pk BT62 . . . . 51 C4
Dee St BT4 . . . . 15 B5
Dehra Gr BT4 . . . . 15 E6
Delacherois Ave BT27 . . . . 26 D2
Delamont Pk BT6 . . . . 22 E7
De la Salle Sec Sch BT30. 62 D5
Delaware St 7 BT6 . . . . . . 15 A3
Delgany Ave BT8 . . . . 22 C3
Delhi Par BT7 . . . . 14 E1
Delhi St BT7 . . . . 14 E1
Delinvilla La BT33 . . . . . . 123 C5
Dellmount Ave BT20 . . . . . . 4 D2
Dellmount Ct BT20 . . . . 4 D2
Dellmount Dr BT20 . . . . 4 D2
Dellmount Pk BT20 . . . . 4 D2
Dellmount Rd BT20 . . . . 4 D2
Dell Pl BT32 . . . . 61 B8
Demesne
Caledon BT68 . . . . 96 D4
Lurgan BT67 . . . . 42 B6
Newtownards BT22 . . . . 94 C8
Demesne Ave
Ballywalter BT22 . . . . 71 A5
Bangor BT20 . . . . 4 C2
Downpatrick BT30 . . . . 62 E3
Holywood BT18 . . . . 9 E6
Lurgan BT66 . . . . 42 C5
Demesne Cl BT18 . . . . 9 E6
Demesne Cres
Ballywalter BT22 . . . . 71 A5
Downpatrick BT30 . . . . 62 D3
Demesne Ct BT30 . . . . 62 E3
Demesne Gate BT18 . . . . 9 E6
Demesne Gr
Holywood BT18 . . . . 9 E6
Moira BT67 . . . . 34 C2
Demesne Hts BT30 . . . . 62 E3
Demesne Link BT30 . . . . . . 62 D4
Demesne Manor BT18 . . . . . 9 E6
Demesne of Down Acre BT30 . . . . 62 C5
Demesne Pk
Armagh BT60 . . . . 60 C2
Holywood BT18 . . . . 9 E6
Demesne Rd
Ballynahinch BT24 . . . . 107 A4
Demesne Rd *continued*
Downpatrick BT30 . . . . 62 E4
Holywood BT18 . . . . 9 E5
Saintfield BT24 . . . . 77 C4
Demesne View
Downpatrick BT30 . . . . 62 D3
5 Portaferry BT22 . . . . 94 D4
Demesne Wlk BT25 . . . . . . 58 F6
Demiville Ave BT27 . . . . . . 37 A5
Demoan BT35 . . . . 117 D6
Demoan Rd BT35 . . . . 117 C6
Denevale Pk BT19 . . . . 5 A5
Denfort Lodge BT25 . . . . . . 58 C4
Denise Cres BT19 . . . . 2 E5
Denmark St BT13 . . . . 154 C4
Dennet End BT6 . . . . 22 B8
Denorrton Pk BT4 . . . . 15 E7
Depot Rd BT3 . . . . 8 F1
Dept of Veterinary Sciences Queen's Univ Belfast BT16 . . . . 16 F6
Deramore Ave
Belfast BT7 . . . . 21 E8
Moira BT67 . . . . 34 A2
Deramore Cl 1 BT67 . . . . . 34 A2
Deramore Cres 2 BT67 . . 34 A2
Deramore Ct BT9 . . . . 21 C5
Deramore Dr
Belfast BT9 . . . . 21 B6
Lurgan BT67 . . . . 42 A8
3 Moira BT67 . . . . 34 A2
Portadown BT62 . . . . 51 C3
Deramore Gdns BT7 . . . . . 21 E7
Deramore Pk
Belfast BT9 . . . . 21 B6
4 Moira BT67 . . . . 34 A2
Deramore Pk S BT9 . . . . . . 21 B5
Deramore St BT7 . . . . 21 F8
Derlett BT60 . . . . 116 C5
Derlett St 5 BT7 . . . . 14 E1
Dermott Ave BT23 . . . . 25 F4
Dermott Cres BT23 . . . . 25 F5
Dermott Dr BT23 . . . . 25 F4
Dermott Gdns BT23 . . . . . . 25 F4
Dermott Gn BT23 . . . . 25 F4
Dermott Pk BT23 . . . . 25 F4
Dermott Rd BT23 . . . . 25 E5
Dermott Wlk BT23 . . . . 25 F4
Dernalea BT60 . . . . 97 C1
Dernalea Rd BT60 . . . . 97 C1
Dernaroy Rd BT35 . . . . . . 141 A2
Dernasigh BT60 . . . . 97 C8
Dernasigh Rd BT60 . . . . . . 83 B1
Derramore Cres 1 BT35 131 D5
Derriaghy CC BT17 . . . . . . 26 E7
Derriaghy Prim Sch BT28 26 B8
Derriaghy Rd BT28 . . . . . . 26 A8
Derriaghy Sta BT17 . . . . . . 26 E8
Derrinraw BT62 . . . . 74 A6
Derrinraw Rd BT62 . . . . . . 73 F5
Derry
Dromore BT25 . . . . 89 D4
Lurgan BT67 . . . . 41 F7
Newtownards BT22 . . . . 94 F4
Derryadd
Craigavon BT66 . . . . 75 A5
Dungannon BT71 . . . . 73 C5
DERRYAGHY BT27 . . . . 26 C8
Derryall BT62 . . . . 74 D4
Derryallen BT62 . . . . . . 101 A6
Derryall Rd BT62 . . . . 74 C3
Derryane BT71 . . . . 73 B6
Derryane Rd BT71 . . . . 73 B6
Derryanvil BT62 . . . . 74 E1
Derryanvil Rd
Craigavon BT62 . . . . 74 E1
Portadown BT62 . . . . 51 C8
Derryardry La BT71 . . . . . . 73 A5
Derryaugh BT62 . . . . 73 D7
Derry Beg BT35 . . . . 64 A8
Derrybeg Cotts 1 BT35 . 131 E4
Derrybeg Dr BT35 . . . . 64 B7
Derrybeg La BT35 . . . . 64 A8
DERRYBOY BT30 . . . . 78 D1
Derryboy BT34 . . . . 132 A7
Derryboye Rd BT30 . . . . . . 78 F2
Derryboy Prim Sch
Downpatrick BT30 . . . . 78 D1
Newtownards BT23 . . . . 77 F7
Derryboy Rd
Downpatrick BT30 . . . . 78 D1
Newry BT34 . . . . 131 F6
Derrybrughas BT62 . . . . . 74 F4
Derrycarib Rd BT62 . . . . . . 74 A6
Derrycarne Rd BT62 . . . . . . 74 E2
Derrycaw
Craigavon BT62 . . . . 73 D5
Craigavon BT62 . . . . 74 C3
Dungannon BT71 . . . . 72 D2
Derrycaw La BT62 . . . . 73 C5
Derrycaw Rd BT71 . . . . 72 C1
Derryclone Gdns BT62 . . . . 51 B2
Derrycoose BT62 . . . . 73 B3
Derrycoose Rd BT62 . . . . . 73 A3
Derrycor
Craigavon BT62 . . . . 73 C4
Craigavon BT66 . . . . 74 F6
Derrycor La BT66 . . . . 74 F6
Derrycor Rd BT62 . . . . 73 C4
Derrycorry North BT62 . 73 A3
Derrycorry South BT71. 72 F2
Derrycory BT62 . . . . 74 E2
Derrycourtney BT68 . . . . . 96 A8
Derrycourtney Rd BT68 . . . 96 B6
Derrycraw BT34 . . . . 118 A3
Derrycraw Rd BT34 . . . . . 118 A3
Derrycreevy BT71 . . . . . . 83 B5
Derrycrew BT61 . . . . 85 B8
Derrycrew Rd BT61 . . . . . . 85 A7
Derrycrow Rd BT66 . . . . . . 74 C8
Derrycughan BT60 . . . . 116 C6
Derrycughan Rd BT60 . . . . 116 B5
Derrycush Rd BT62 . . . . 73 F5
Derrydorragh BT60 . . . . . 83 B1
Derrydrummult BT67 . . . 34 E3
Derrydrumuck BT32 . . . 118 F8
Derryfubble BT71 . . . . . . 83 C8
Derryfubble Rd BT71 . . . . . 83 C6
Derrygally BT71 . . . . 72 D4
Derrygally Demesne BT71 . . . . 72 C3
Derrygally Rd BT71 . . . . . . 72 D3
Derrygally Way BT71 . . . . . 72 B4
Derrygavad Rd BT62 . . . . . 73 B1
Derrygooly BT68 . . . . 96 C8
Derrygoonan BT71 . . . . . . 83 B6
Derryhale BT62 . . . . 54 E4
Derryhale La BT62 . . . . 54 E5
Derryhale Prim Sch BT62. 55 A2
Derryhale Rd BT62 . . . . 54 F4
Derryhaw BT60 . . . . 97 A1
Derryhaw Rd BT60 . . . . 96 F3
Derryhea Pk BT34 . . . . . . 118 B2
Derryhennet BT60 . . . . . 113 D4
Derryhennett Rd BT60 . . . 113 D3
Derryhirk BT62 . . . . 73 A3
Derryhirk Rd
Craigavon BT67 . . . . 32 D8
Dungannon BT71 . . . . 72 F2
Derryhubbert East BT71 . . . . 73 A5
Derryhubbert North BT71 . . . . 72 F5
Derryhubbert Rd BT71 . . . 73 B5
Derryhubbert South BT71 . . . . 72 F4
Derryinver BT66 . . . . 74 B8
Derrykeeran BT62 . . . . . . 74 B4
Derrykeeran Rd BT62 . . . . 74 B4
Derrykeevan BT62 . . . . . 73 F3
Derrykerran BT62 . . . . . . 74 E3
Derrykintone BT68 . . . . . 96 C5
Derrylappen BT70 . . . . . . 82 E6
Derrylappen Rd BT70 . . . . 82 D5
Derrylard BT62 . . . . 73 F7
Derrylard Rd BT62 . . . . 73 F6
Derrylattinee Rd BT70 . . . . 82 B8
Derryleckagh BT34 . . . . 132 E2
Derryleckagh Rd BT34 . . 132 E2
Derryleckagh Row BT34. 132 E3
Derrylee BT71 . . . . 73 A7
Derrylee Rd BT71 . . . . 72 F6
Derrylettiff BT62 . . . . 74 A1
Derrylettif Rd BT62 . . . . . . 50 A8
Derrylileagh BT62 . . . . . . 73 D7
Derrylileagh Rd BT62 . . . . 73 C6
Derrylisnahavil BT67 . . . 42 D7
Derry Lodge Manor BT66. 41 F7
Derryloste BT66 . . . . 74 B7
Derryloste Rd BT66 . . . . . . 74 C7
Derrylough BT32 . . . . . . 103 B4
Derryloughan BT61 . . . . . 85 C7
Derryloughan Rd
Armagh BT61 . . . . 85 C7
Dungannon BT71 . . . . 73 A8
Derrylough Hill BT32 . . . . 103 B4
DERRYMACASH BT66 . . . . . 75 B5
Derrymacash Rd BT66 . . . . 40 E7
Derrymacfall BT62 . . . . . 74 C4
Derrymacfall Rd BT62 . . . . 74 C4
Derrymagowan BT71 . . . 72 D2
Derrymagowan Rd BT71 . . 72 D2
Derrymattry BT62 . . . . . . 74 D2
Derrymeen BT71 . . . . 72 B8
Derry More BT35 . . . . . . 131 D4
Derrymore Mdws 7 BT35 . . . . 131 C5
Derrymore Rd BT35 . . . . . 131 D5
Derrynahone Rd BT67 . . . . 35 F4
Derrynaseer BT67 . . . . . . 32 F7
Derrynaught BT60 . . . . . . 99 D4
Derrynaught Rd BT60 . . . . 99 D4
Derryneill BT31 . . . . 105 B1
Derryneill Rd BT31 . . . . . . 121 C7
Derryneskan BT62 . . . . . . 74 B4
Derryneskan Rd BT62 . . . . 74 C4
Derrynisk BT67 . . . . 35 C6
DERRYNOOSE BT60 . . . . . . 127 C8
Derrynoose Rd BT60 . . . . 113 C1
Derryoge BT34 . . . . 153 B5
Derryoge Rd BT34 . . . . . . 153 B5
Derryoghill BT71 . . . . 83 F6
Derryoghill Rd BT71 . . . . . . 83 F6
Derryogue Pk BT34 . . . . . 153 B6
Derryraine BT60 . . . . 99 C4
Derryraine Rd BT60 . . . . . . 99 D3
Derryscollop BT71 . . . . . . 84 D8
Derryscollop Rd BT71 . . . . 72 E1
Derry St BT67 . . . . 41 F7
Derrytagh North BT66 . . 74 E7
Derrytagh South BT66 . . 74 D5
Derrytrasna BT66 . . . . . . 74 D7
Derrytrasna La BT66 . . . . . 74 D8
Derrytrasna Rd BT66 . . . . . 40 C8
Derrytresk BT71 . . . . 72 D8
Derrytresk Rd BT71 . . . . . . 72 D8
Derryvane BT62 . . . . 74 D3
Derryvaren Rd BT71 . . . . . 72 E8
Derryvar Rd BT62 . . . . 73 F6
Derryvinney Rd BT62 . . . . . 73 D6
Derryvolgie Ave BT9 . . . . . 14 B1
Derryvolgie Mews 5 BT9 14 B1
Derryvolgie Pk BT27 . . . . . 26 C5
Derryvore BT63 . . . . 74 F1
Derryvore La BT63 . . . . 74 F1
Derrywilligan BT35 . . . . 131 D7

Derrywilligan Rd BT60 .. 117 B1
Derwent Dr BT20 .... 3 E2
Derwent St 13 BT4 .... 15 B5
Desart La BT61 .... 60 B7
Desartlane Gdns BT61.... 60 B6
Desert BT34 .... 132 F6
Desert Rd BT34 .... 132 F6
Desmond Ave BT67 ...... 42 A8
Devenish Ct BT13 .... 154 A3
Devlin's Fort BT60..... 114 C3
Devon Dr BT4........... 15 D6
Devon Par BT4.......... 15 D6
Devonshire Cl BT12 ..... 154 B2
Devonshire Pl BT12 ..... 154 C2
Devonshire Way BT12 ... 154 B2
Dewey St
12 Belfast BT13.......... 14 A7
Belfast BT13 .... 154 A4
De Wind Dr BT23 .... 25 E3
Diamond Rd BT25........ 58 E2
Diamond The
4 Moy BT71............. 72 A1
6 Moy BT71............. 72 A1
Diamond View Rd BT32 .. 88 B3
Dian 147 A3
Dickson Cty Prim Sch
BT66.................. 42 A3
Dicksonia Dr BT23 .... 19 D6
Dickson Pk BT23......... 77 F8
Dicksons Hill Rd BT32... 120 E7
Dill Ave
Lisburn BT27 .... 38 C8
Lurgan BT66 .... 41 F6
Dillay BT60 .... 97 A3
Dillin BT30 .... 109 C3
Dillin Rd BT30 .... 109 C4
Dillon Hts BT61 .... 98 F7
Dill Rd BT6 .... 15 C1
Dinnahorra BT60....... 116 D8
Dinnahorra Rd BT60 .... 100 C1
Distillery Ct BT12 ...... 154 B2
Distillery St BT12 ...... 154 B2
Distillery Wlk BT12...... 154 B2
Divernagh Rd BT35 ..... 131 B7
Diviny BT62............ 50 B6
Divis Ct BT12 .... 154 C3
Divismore Cres BT8...... 21 F1
Divis St BT13 .... 154 B3
Dixon Ave BT20 .... 4 F4
Dixon Pk BT19 .... 5 A4
Dixon Rd BT19 .... 5 A4
Dobbin Hill Pk BT60...... 60 E4
Dobbin Hill Rd BT60...... 60 E4
Dobbin Manor BT60...... 60 F3
Dobbin Rd
Armagh BT61............ 85 F2
Craigavon BT62 .... 54 D6
Dobbin St La BT60 ...... 60 D4
Dobbins Gr BT60........ 60 F4
Dobbin St BT61 .... 60 D4
Docherty's Glen Rd BT61 . 83 B3
Dock St
Belfast BT15 .... 14 E7
Warrenpoint BT34....... 65 C2
Doctor's Quarter BT35 140 C7
Dog Kennel La BT28...... 26 A3
DOLLINGSTOWN BT66..... 42 F4
Dollys Brae BT31........ 121 E6
Dolmen Rd BT31........ 105 D4
DOMHNACH DAOI
(DONAGHADEE) BT21.... 67 A8
Dominican Abbey 151 D4
Dominican Ct BT35 ...... 64 C5
Dominic St BT35 .... 64 C5
Donacloney Prim Sch
BT66.................. 86 F6
DONAGHADEE (DOMHNACH
DAOI) BT21............. 67 A8
Donaghadee Golf Club
BT21..................... 6 E2
Donaghadee High Sch 9
BT21................... 66 F8
Donaghadee Prim Sch 10
BT21................... 66 F8
Donaghadee Rd
Bangor BT20 .... 4 C4
Donaghadee BT21........ 67 A6
Groomsport BT19 .... 5 B7
Newtownards BT23....... 13 C2
Donaghadee RFC BT21.... 6 D1
Donaghaguy BT34 ..... 65 C6
Donaghaguy Gr BT34..... 65 B6
Donaghaguy Rd BT34 .... 65 C7
DONAGHCLONEY BT66 .... 86 E6
Donaghcloney Rd BT25... 86 F5
Donaghmore Rd BT34... 118 C4
Donagh Pk 2 BT66 ...... 86 F6
Donagreagh BT67 .... 32 E1
Donaldsons Rd BT35 .... 138 F3
Donard Ave
Annalong BT34 .... 146 D5
Bangor BT20 .... 3 F3
Newtownards BT23....... 19 C4
Donard Cres BT34...... 146 D5
Donard Gdns BT66....... 42 A4
Donard Pk BT34 .... 146 D4
Donard Pl
11 Kilkeel BT34......... 153 C7
Newcastle BT33.......... 63 D5
Donard Specl Sch BT32 .. 61 E4
Donard St
Belfast BT6 .... 15 A3
Newcastle BT33.......... 63 D6
Donard View Cres BT30 .. 62 D6
Donard View Rd BT32 ... 102 B3
Donegall Arc BT1........ 155 A3
Donegall Ave BT12...... 154 B1
Donegall Gdns BT12 ..... 14 A2
Donegall La BT1 .... 155 A4
Donegall Par BT12....... 14 A2
Donegall Pass BT7...... 155 A1
Donegall Pl BT1 .... 155 A3
Donegall Quay BT1 ..... 155 B4
Donegall Rd BT12....... 154 A1
Donegall Rd Prim Sch
BT12.................. 154 A1
Donegall St Pl BT1...... 155 A4
Donegall Sq E BT1 ...... 155 A3
Donegall Sq Mews BT2.. 155 A2
Donegall Sq N BT1...... 155 A3
Donegall Sq S BT1...... 155 A2
Donegall Sq W BT1 ..... 155 A3
Donegall St BT1 .... 155 A4
Donnelly Gdns BT67...... 42 A8
Donnelly's Hill Rd BT71 .. 83 B4
Donnybrook St BT9 ...... 14 B1
Donore Ct BT15.......... 14 C8
Donovan Par BT6 .... 15 D2
Dooey BT22 .... 95 C5
Doogary BT60 .... 112 F7
Doogary Rd BT60 .... 96 F1
Dooghary BT32 .... 102 F4
Dooglen BT24 .... 106 A6
Doohat or Crossreagh
BT60 .... 127 A6
Doohat Rd BT60 .... 127 C6
Doolargy 150 F5
Doon Pk BT8 .... 29 E2
Dora Ave BT34........... 64 E7
Dorans Hill BT35 .... 64 A4
Dorchester Ave BT62...... 51 D2
Dorchester Dr BT62...... 51 C3
Dorchester Pk
Belfast BT9 .... 21 A4
Portadown BT62 .... 51 C2
Dorchester St BT12 .... 154 B1
Dorman's Ct BT21........ 67 A8
Dormans Point BT21 ..... 66 F7
Dorothy Ave BT20.......... 4 E3
Dorsy BT35 .... 139 C5
Dorsy (Cavan OHanlon) or
Roxborough BT35 ... 139 D7
Dorsy Entrenchment The
BT35.................. 139 C3
Dorsy (Hearty) BT35 .. 139 D7
Dorsy (Macdonald) or
Carrickrovaddy BT35 129 F1
Dorsy (Mullaghglass)
BT35 .... 139 C8
Dorsy Rd BT35.......... 139 C5
Dorwood Pk BT23........ 19 E6
Dougans Rd BT34 .... 145 A1
Dougher BT67 .... 41 F8
Doughery Rd BT32 .... 61 E1
Douglas Ct BT4 .... 15 E5
Dover Pl BT13 .... 154 B4
Dover St BT13 .... 154 C4
Dover Wlk BT13.......... 154 C4
Down Acad BT30.......... 62 B7
Down Arts Ctr BT30 .... 62 C5
Down Bsns Ctr BT24 ..... 59 C5
Down Bsns Pk BT30...... 62 @8
Down Cty Mus BT30.... 62 B5
Downe Hospl BT30....... 62 D4
Downey House Pre & Prep
Sch BT6................ 15 A1
Down High Sch BT30..... 62 B5
Downhill Ave
Bangor BT19 .... 3 B4
Castlereagh BT8 .... 21 D2
Downhill Wlk 5 BT8...... 21 D2
Down Holy Trinity Cath (C of
I) BT30................. 62 B5
Downing St BT13 .... 154 B4
Down Leisure Ctr BT30... 62 B4
Downpatrick Ave BT30 ... 93 F2
Downpatrick Cc BT30 .... 62 C4
DOWNPATRICK (DÚN
PÁDRAIG) BT30......... 62 B6
Downpatrick Golf Club
BT30.................... 62 E5
Downpatrick Prim Sch
BT30.................... 62 B5
Downpatrick Racecourse
BT30.................... 62 A1
Downpatrick Railway Mus
BT30.................... 62 B4
Downpatrick Rd
Ballynahinch BT24........ 59 F2
Downpatrick BT30........ 93 B4
Downpatrick BT30....... 107 D1
Downpatrick BT30....... 125 E7
Downpatrick St
6 Belfast BT4 .... 15 C6
Crossgar BT30........... 92 C3
Rathfriland BT34 .... 120 A2
Saintfield BT24 .... 77 C3
Downpatrick Sta BT30 ... 62 B4
Down Royal BT28 .... 36 D6
Downshire Ave BT66 ..... 41 E3
Downshire Cres BT26 .... 47 E7
Downshire Ct BT34....... 64 D7
Downshire Gdns
6 Banbridge BT32 .... 61 C4
Hillsborough BT26........ 47 E7
Downshire Hospl BT30... 62 F4
Downshire La BT20 .... 3 E5
Downshire Mews BT18 ..... 9 D6
Downshire Par 1 BT6.... 22 C8
Downshire Pk BT26 ...... 47 E7
Downshire Pk Central 1
BT6 .... 22 C7
Downshire Pk E BT6 ..... 22 C8
Downshire Pk N BT6 ..... 22 C7
Downshire Pk S
Belfast BT6 .... 22 C7
Downshire Pk S *continued*
Hillsborough BT26........ 47 E7
Downshire Pl
Banbridge BT32.......... 61 D5
Belfast BT2 .... 155 A2
Holywood BT18 .... 9 D6
Downshire Prim Sch
BT26.................... 47 D7
Downshire Rd
Banbridge BT32.......... 61 C3
Bangor BT20 .... 3 F5
Belfast BT6 .... 22 C7
Holywood BT18 .... 9 D6
Newry BT34............. 64 D6
Downside Ave BT32 ...... 61 D4
Downs Rd
Ardglass BT30.......... 126 A5
Newcastle BT33.......... 63 D5
Dows Rd BT8 .... 28 B4
Doyles Rd BT31 .... 104 C2
Doyles Villas BT35 ...... 131 B4
Drakes Bridge Rd BT30... 92 B4
Dredge Bridge BT60.... 96 E5
Dree BT25............ 105 D7
Dree Hill BT25.......... 105 D7
Dreemore Rd BT71....... 72 A4
Drelincourt Sch The BT60 60 F4
Drelin Ct Cl BT61 .... 60 C4
Drennan BT27 .... 76 A4
Drennan Rd BT27 .... 76 B4
Dressogagh
Armagh BT60............ 97 B7
Craigavon BT62.......... 85 D8
Drin BT25 .... 105 F7
Drinnahilly Pk BT33...... 63 B4
Drin Rd BT25 .... 89 E1
Drive The BT9 .... 21 C6
Driving Range BT27...... 26 F6
DROICHEAD NA BANNA
(BANBRIDGE) BT32...... 61 B6
DROIM BEARACH
(DROMARA) BT25 .... 89 D2
Dromara BT25 .... 89 B2
DROMARA (DROIM
BEARACH) BT25......... 89 D2
Dromara Pk BT28 .... 37 E8
Dromara Prim Sch BT25.. 58 F6
Dromara Rd
Ballynahinch BT24........ 59 A3
Banbridge BT32......... 120 D7
Castlewellan BT31....... 105 C2
Dromara BT25 .... 58 F3
Dundrum BT33.......... 123 C5
Hillsborough BT26........ 89 A7
Newcastle BT33......... 123 B6
Dromara St BT7 .... 14 E2
Dromena Gdns BT23 ..... 19 C4
Dromintee Prim Sch
BT35................... 140 F1
Dromore
Caledon BT68 .... 82 A1
Drumakil 138 B4
Warrenpoint BT34........ 65 B4
DROMORE (AN DROIM MÓR)
BT25 .... 58 B6
Dromorebrague BT32 . 102 F2
Dromore Central Prim Sch
BT25.................... 58 C5
Dromore High Sch BT25.. 58 C5
Dromore Hts BT34 .... 65 B4
Dromore Rd
Ballynahinch BT24........ 59 A4
Banbridge BT32.......... 61 F6
Banbridge BT32.......... 88 C2
Caledon BT68 .... 82 B1
Craigavon BT66.......... 42 E4
Dromara BT25........... 89 B3
Hillsborough BT26........ 46 F2
Dromore Rd Prim Sch
BT34.................... 65 C3
Dromore St
Ballynahinch BT24........ 59 C4
Banbridge BT32.......... 61 D5
Belfast BT6 .... 15 B2
Dromara BT25........... 89 C2
14 Rathfriland BT34 .... 119 F2
Dromore Terr 4 BT34.... 65 C2
Drone Hill Rd BT32...... 103 C4
Druids Villas BT61 .... 60 C5
Drum BT60 .... 97 B4
Drumacanver BT60.... 113 D7
Drumachee BT60 .... 99 D2
Drumacon 138 C3
Drumaconnell East
BT24 .... 77 C2
Drumaconnell West
BT24 .... 77 B2
Drumaconnell Rd BT24 ... 77 B2
DRUMACRIB 138 B7
Drumadd BT61......... 98 F6
Drumadd Gn BT60 .... 60 E4
Drumadd Rd BT61 .... 60 F5
Drumadoney BT25 ..... 89 A4
Drumadonnell BT32... 120 E7
Drumadonnell Sch BT32. 120 E8
Drumadoon Dr BT16 ..... 17 D4
Drumadoon Pk BT16 ..... 17 D3
Drumagelvin 112 A6
Drumaghadone BT25... 88 A3
Drumaghadone Rd
Banbridge BT32.......... 88 A2
Dromara BT25........... 58 F1
Drumaghlis BT30 ...... 91 D4
Drumaghlis Prim Sch
BT30.................... 91 D5
Drumaghlis Rd BT30 ..... 91 E4
Drumahean BT60 ..... 112 F5
Drumahean Rd BT60 .... 113 A4
DRUMAKILL 138 A4
Drumaknockan BT26... 88 F7
Drumaknockan La BT26 .. 88 E6
Drumaknockan Rd BT26.. 88 E7
Drumaknockan Rd S
BT26 .... 89 A6
Drumalane BT35 ...... 64 C2
Drumalane Pk BT35...... 64 C3
Drumalane Rd BT35...... 64 C3
Drumalaragh BT60.... 116 B6
Drumalig BT8.......... 76 E7
Drumalig Rd BT8 .... 76 E6
Drumalis BT62 .... 74 B1
Drumaltnamuck BT35 . 139 C7
Drumalt Rd BT35........ 139 C5
Drumanaghan or
Drumulcaw BT30 .... 107 A3
Drumanaghan Rd BT30.. 107 A2
Drumanakelly BT24 ... 107 A5
Drumanaquoile BT31.. 106 D3
DRUMANESS BT24 .... 91 A1
Drumaness Rd BT24...... 59 F2
Drumannon Pk BT62 ..... 51 B4
Drumanphy BT62 ...... 73 E1
Drumanphy Rd BT62 ..... 50 A8
Drumantine BT34 .... 117 F5
Drumantine Coll BT34... 117 F5
Drumantine Hill Rd BT34 117 F5
Drumantine Rd BT34 .... 117 F4
Drumantine View BT34.. 118 B5
Drumanuey BT71 ...... 72 A2
Drumaran BT63....... 101 F8
Drumaran Rd BT63....... 101 F8
Drumardan BT22....... 95 B7
Drumardan Quarter
BT22 .... 95 A8
Drumard Ave BT62....... 51 B2
Drumard Cross BT71... 72 B5
Drumardcross Rd BT71... 72 B5
Drumarden Rd BT22 ..... 95 A7
Drumard Glebe BT71... 72 B5
Drumard (Jones) BT61 . 85 F3
Drumard (Primate)
BT62 .... 50 B2
Drumard Rd BT62 .... 54 A8
Drumarg or Downs
BT60 .... 60 B3
Drumarg Pk BT60........ 60 B4
Drumarg Villas BT60 ..... 60 B4
Drumarkin BT34 ...... 120 A2
Drumarkin Rd BT34 ..... 120 A3
Drumarn BT71 .... 84 B6
DRUMAROAD BT31....... 106 E4
Drumaroad Hill BT31.... 106 E4
Drumaroad Prim Sch
BT31................... 106 F4
Drumart
Armagh BT61............ 84 F4
Craigavon BT62......... 100 E5
Drumart Dr BT8.......... 21 E2
Drumart Gdns BT8....... 21 E2
Drumart Rd BT62 .... 100 F5
Drumart Sq BT8 .... 21 E2
Drumart Wlk 4 BT8 ..... 21 D2
Drumask or Ballycullen
BT71 .... 84 B6
Drumaspil BT71......... 72 B6
Drumaspil Rd BT71 ...... 72 B6
Drumatee BT60 .... 99 F2
Drumatee Rd BT60....... 99 E2
Drumatihugh (Blaris)
BT26 .... 46 F7
Drumatihugh
(Hillsborough)
BT26 .... 46 F5
Drumawhey Gdns BT19.... 3 D1
Drumawhey Rd BT23 ..... 66 B3
Drumawhy BT23 .... 66 B4
Drumay BT71 .... 83 D8
Drumbally BT35....... 148 C7
Drumbanagher BT35 .. 117 D4
Drumbanagher Wall
BT35 .... 117 B5
Drumbane BT67 .... 34 B4
Drumbane Rd BT67 ...... 33 F6
Drumbee BT61.......... 83 F1
Drumbee Beg BT60 ..... 99 B4
Drumbee Beg Rd BT60 ... 99 B4
Drumbeecross BT60 ... 99 C3
Drumbee More BT60... 99 A4
Drumbee More Rd BT60.. 99 A5
DRUMBEG BT17 .... 27 D6
Drumbeg BT65........... 41 D2
Drumbeg Ct BT28........ 37 F7
Drumbeg Dr BT28........ 37 E8
Drumbeg Rd BT17 .... 27 D5
Drumbeo 112 E1
Drumbilla 149 B6
DRUMBO BT27 .... 28 A3
Drumboat 148 A3
Drumboneth Rd BT25 .... 58 D1
Drumboniff Rd BT34 .... 121 A1
Drumbonniff BT34 .... 135 A8
Drumbo Prim Sch BT27 .. 28 A2
Drumbo Rd BT27......... 27 E3
Drumboy BT35......... 147 E4
Drumboy Fort BT35 ... 147 E4
Drumboy Rd
Dromara BT25........... 90 B1
Newry BT35............ 147 E4
Drumbreda Ave BT61 ..... 60 C8
Drumbreda Cres BT61.... 60 C8
Drumbreda Wlk BT61 .... 60 C8
Drumbroneth BT25..... 58 D2
Drumbuck Rd BT31 ..... 122 C6
Drumcairn Cl BT8........ 21 C1
Drumcairn Manor BT61 .. 60 B7
Drumcairn Rd BT61 ...... 60 B7
Drumcanver Rd BT60.... 113 D7
Drumcarn BT61......... 98 C8
Drumcarn Gdns BT62 .... 51 B4
Drumcashel Ct 2 BT34.. 132 B5
Drumcashellone BT34. 132 B5
Drumcashel Villas 3
BT34 .... 132 B5
Drumcaw BT30 .... 107 B1
Drumcaw Rd BT30 ...... 107 A2
Drumclogher Pk BT63.... 52 D5
Drumcloon Wlk BT30.... 62 C6
Drumconwell BT60..... 98 D2
Drumconwell Rd BT60 ... 98 D1
Drumcoote BT60....... 98 B6
Drumcoote Rd BT60...... 98 B6
Drumcree BT62........ 74 D1
Drumcree Coll BT62 ..... 51 B6
Drumcree Gr BT62....... 51 B5
Drumcree Rd BT62....... 51 B8
Drumcro BT34 .... 153 B8
Drumcro Rd
Armagh BT60........... 116 B1
Newry BT34............ 153 B8
Drumcrow
Armagh BT60........... 116 C1
Dungannon BT71......... 72 C7
Drumcullen BT71 ...... 84 B3
Drumcullen Rd
Downpatrick BT30....... 107 F4
Dungannon BT71......... 84 B4
Drumderg
Armagh BT60........... 113 F4
Dungannon BT71......... 83 F5
Drumderg Pk BT30....... 62 E6
Drumdreenagh BT34.. 120 B3
Drumdreenagh Rd BT34. 120 B2
Drumduff BT71 .... 83 E3
Drumduff La BT71 .... 83 D3
Drumee BT31.......... 122 D3
Drumee Dr BT31 .... 122 C4
Drumee Gdns 6 BT31... 122 C4
Drumee Rd BT31........ 122 D3
Drumee Wlk 9 BT31.... 122 C4
Drumena BT34........ 121 E2
Drumenagh BT71 ...... 72 B5
Drumena Rd BT34....... 121 E2
Drumennis BT61 .... 99 D5
Drumess BT68 .... 96 C7
Drumfad BT22 .... 67 A2
Drumfad Rd BT22 .... 67 B2
Drumfergus BT60 ...... 99 F3
Drumflugh BT71 .... 83 C5
Drumflugh Rd BT71 ...... 83 B6
Drumgalvin Rd BT24 .... 106 D8
Drumgane BT60 ...... 116 B5
Drumgar BT60 .... 97 D4
Drumgarran BT60.... 112 D6
Drumgarron Rd BT60.... 112 D6
Drumgart BT71 .... 72 B2
Drumgask BT65.......... 41 D1
Drumgask La BT65 ...... 41 D1
Drumgaskroad BT65 ..... 53 D8
Drumgath BT34....... 133 C6
Drumgavlin BT24 .... 106 D8
Drumgaw BT60 .... 98 F3
Drumgaw Gdns BT60..... 98 F3
Drumgaw Rd BT60 ...... 98 E3
Drumgiven BT24 .... 91 C7
Drumgiven Rd BT24...... 91 C6
Drumglass BT65 .... 41 B3
Drumglass Ave BT20 ...... 3 F1
Drumglass Pk BT20 .... 3 F1
Drumgolat 112 E2
Drumgolliff BT60 ...... 96 F6
Drumgooland BT30 ... 107 E5
Drumgooland Rd
Banbridge BT32......... 104 D1
Castlewellan BT31....... 104 D4
Downpatrick BT30....... 107 D3
Drumgoose Rd BT62 ..... 51 A8
Drumgor BT65 .... 41 A1
Drumgor Hts BT65 .... 41 A1
Drumgor La BT64 .... 41 A1
Drumgor Pk BT65........ 41 A1
Drumgor Prim Sch BT65 . 41 A1
Drumgor Rd BT65........ 41 B2
Drumgor W Rd BT65 ..... 41 A2
Drumgose
Armagh BT60........... 112 D6
Dungannon BT71......... 83 D6
Newry BT35............ 147 C8
Drumgose Rd
Armagh BT60........... 112 D5
Dungannon BT71......... 83 E6
Drumgrannon BT71 .... 72 A1
Drumgreenagh
Armagh BT60........... 113 D5
Newry BT34............ 119 C1
Drumgreenagh Rd
Armagh BT60........... 113 E5
Newry BT34............ 119 C2
Drumgullion Ave BT35 ... 64 B8
Drumharriff
Armagh BT60........... 130 E7
Armagh BT61............ 85 B6
Craigavon BT62.......... 50 A8
Drumharriff Rd BT60 ... 130 E6
Drumherney BT60..... 127 E4
Drumherney Rd BT60 ... 127 D4
Drumhill Ave BT24 ...... 59 D6
Drumhill Ct BT31 ...... 106 E4
Drumhillery BT60 .... 113 A5
Drumhillery Pk BT60.... 113 A5
Drumhillery Prim Sch
BT60................... 113 B5

Drumhillery Rd BT60 . . . . 113 B4
Drumhill Hts BT31 . . . . . . 106 E4
Drumhill Pk
Ballynahinch BT24 . . . . 59 D6
Castlewellan BT31 . . . . 106 E4
Drumhirk
Armagh BT60 . . . . 114 A7
Newtownards BT23 . . . . 13 C2
Newtownards BT23 . . . . 68 B3
Drumhirk Ave BT23 . . . . . . 13 B1
Drumhirk Dr BT19 . . . . 3 D1
Drumhirk Pl BT19 . . . . 3 D1
Drumhirk Rd
Armagh BT60 . . . . 113 F8
Newtownards BT23 . . . . 68 B3
Drumhirk Way BT23 . . . . . . 13 B3
Drumhorc BT63 . . . . 102 B8
Drumhorc Rd BT63 . . . . 86 A1
Drumhorrik BT71 . . . . . . 72 B7
Drumiller Hill BT25 . . . . . . 88 D4
Drumiller La BT63 . . . . . . 101 E5
Drumiller Rd
Dromara BT25 . . . . 88 D5
Newry BT34 . . . . 117 F1
Drumilly
Armagh BT61 . . . . 85 A4
Newry BT35 . . . . 130 E3
Drumilly Rd
Armagh BT61 . . . . 85 B1
Newry BT35 . . . . 130 E2
Druminallyduff BT62 . . . 50 F8
Druminally Rd BT62 . . . . . . 50 F8
Druminargal BT63 . . . . 101 E2
Drumindoney BT34 . . . 152 F8
Drumintee BT35 . . . . . . 140 F2
Drumintee Rd BT35 . . . . . 141 A4
Druminure BT62 . . . . . . 100 F4
Druminure Rd BT62 . . . . . 101 A4
Drumkee BT71 . . . . 72 B8
Drumkeen Ct BT8 . . . . 22 A6
Drumkeen Manor 1 BT8 . 22 A6
Drumkeen Ret Pk BT8 . . . . 22 A6
Drumkeeragh BT25 . . . 106 B8
Drumkee Rd BT71 . . . . 72 B8
Drumkerragh Rd BT24 . . . 90 B1
Drumlack BT60 . . . . 100 A1
Drumlea View BT30 . . . . . . 62 C5
Drumlee
Castlewellan BT31 . . . . 121 B4
Dungannon BT71 . . . . 83 F6
Drumlee Rd
Castlewellan BT31 . . . . 121 B5
Dungannon BT71 . . . . 83 F5
Newry BT34 . . . . 121 C4
Drumlellum BT62 . . . . . . 74 A2
Drumlin BT66 . . . . 86 E8
Drumlin Dr BT66 . . . . 41 E4
Drumlin Manor BT8 . . . . . . 76 E8
Drumlin Pk BT30 . . . . 62 E6
Drumlin Rd BT66 . . . . 43 C1
Drumlin Rise BT23 . . . . 20 A4
Drumlins The BT24 . . . . 59 B4
Drumlisnagrilly BT63 . . . 52 C1
Drumliss Ct BT35 . . . . 64 C8
Drumlough
Hillsborough BT26 . . . . 89 B7
Newry BT34 . . . . 119 E1
Drumlough Cross BT34 . . 133 E8
Drumlougher BT35 . . . . 138 C4
Drumlougher Rd BT35 . . . 138 D4
Drumlough Gdns BT28 . . . 37 D8
Drumlough Rd
Hillsborough BT26 . . . . 89 B8
Newry BT34 . . . . 119 F1
Drumlough School Rd
BT34 . . . . 133 F8
Drumman BT61 . . . . 99 E6
Drumman Beg BT61 . . . . 84 F1
Drumman Hill 1 BT61 . . . 98 F7
Drumman Hts BT61 . . . . . . 60 F8
Drummanlane BT34 . . . 152 D7
Drummanmore BT34 . . 152 F6
Drumman More BT61 . . . 98 E8
Drummanmore Grange 2
BT61 . . . . 98 F7
Drummanmore Rd
Armagh BT61 . . . . 84 F1
Newry BT34 . . . . 152 E7
Drummannon BT62 . . . . 85 E8
Drummeland BT60 . . . . 113 B1
Drummellan Ct BT65 . . . . . 41 B1
Drummellan Gdns BT65 . . 41 C1
Drummellan Mews BT65 . 53 B8
Drummellan Pk BT65 . . . . . 53 C8
Drummellan Row BT65 . . . 53 B8
Drummellan Wlk BT65 . . . 53 B8
Drummenagh BT62 . . . . 74 C2
Drummiller
Craigavon BT63 . . . . 101 F6
Dromore BT25 . . . . 88 D5
Newry BT34 . . . . 131 F8
Drummiller View 3
BT34 . . . . 117 F1
Drummill Rd BT35 . . . . . . 139 C3
Drummilt BT60 . . . . 116 E5
Drummond
Armagh BT60 . . . . 113 C5
Armagh BT60 . . . . 117 A2
Drummond Brae BT24 . . . . 59 D5
Drummond Pk 3 BT23 . . . 19 F5
Drummond Rd
Armagh BT60 . . . . 116 F2
Newry BT35 . . . . 138 C4
Drummore BT60 . . . . 98 F4
Drummuck BT35 . . . . . . 148 B7
Drummuckavall BT35 . 148 A6
Drummuckavall Rd BT35 148 B6
Drummullagh
Omeath 142 C2
Warrenpoint 65 A1
Drumnabreeze BT66 . . . 44 B2
Drumnabreeze Rd BT67 . . 44 A2
DRUMNACANVY BT63 . . . . . 52 D2
Drumnacanvyl Lodge
BT63 . . . . 52 D1
Drumnacanvy Rd
Craigavon BT63 . . . . 56 E8
Portadown BT63 . . . . 52 D4
Drumnaconagher BT24. 91 C3
Drumnaconagher Rd
BT30 . . . . 91 D3
Drumnaferry BT66 . . . . . 87 A8
Drumnagally BT32 . . . . 102 C7
Drumnagally Rd
Banbridge BT32 . . . . 61 A6
Craigavon BT63 . . . . 102 B7
Drumnaglontagh BT62 100 F6
Drumnagloy BT60 . . . . . . 99 E4
Drumnagoon BT63 . . . . . 40 C2
Drumnagoon Rd BT63 . . . . 40 C3
Drumnahare BT32 . . . . 102 D3
Drumnahavil BT60 . . . . 127 D6
Drumnahavil Rd BT60 . . . 113 C1
Drumnahoney BT60 . . . 130 C6
Drumnahoney Rd BT60 . . 130 C8
Drumnahunchin Rd
BT60 . . . . 117 A1
Drumnahunshin
Armagh BT60 . . . . 130 D6
Craigavon BT62 . . . . 54 A5
Drumnakelly
Craigavon BT62 . . . . 55 C5
Craigavon BT67 . . . . 75 F5
Drumnaleg BT62 . . . . . . 101 B5
Drumnamether BT62 . . 100 D4
Drumnamether Rd BT62 100 D5
Drumnamoe BT67 . . . . . . 42 B8
Drumnamoe Ave BT67 . . . . 42 A8
Drumnamoe Gdns BT67 . . 42 B7
Drumnaquoile Rd BT24 . . 106 C5
Drumnascamph
Craigavon BT63 . . . . 86 C2
Newry BT34 . . . . 120 B1
Drumnascamph Rd
Craigavon BT63 . . . . 86 B3
Newry BT34 . . . . 120 B1
Drumnasoo
Armagh BT61 . . . . 85 B2
Craigavon BT62 . . . . 54 E7
Drumnasoo Rd
Armagh BT61 . . . . 85 B2
Craigavon BT62 . . . . 50 E2
Drumnavaddy BT25 . . . . 86 F3
Drumnavaddy Rd BT25 . . . 86 F2
Drumneath Rd BT32 . . . . . . 87 C1
Drumneill 112 D3
Drumneth BT32 . . . . 87 C1
Drumnevan BT62 . . . . . . 74 B1
Drumnevan Rd BT62 . . . . . 50 C8
Drumnykerne BT67 . . . . 32 F1
Drumo and Drumcro
BT67 . . . . 43 E5
Drumorgan BT61 . . . . 99 E6
Drumra BT27 . . . . 76 B4
Drumragh End BT6 . . . . . . 22 B8
Drumreagh
Newry BT34 . . . . 143 B5
Newtownards BT23 . . . . 78 C6
Drumreagh Pk
Downpatrick BT30 . . . . 62 E6
Rostrevor BT34 . . . . 143 B4
Drumreagh Rd
Newry BT34 . . . . 143 B6
Newtownards BT23 . . . . 78 B5
Drumreagh Upper
BT34 . . . . 143 D7
Drumroe Rd BT30 . . . . 110 B7
Drumrusk BT61 . . . . 83 C2
Drumsallagh BT35 . . . . 102 A1
Drumsallagh Rd BT32 . . . 102 B1
Drumsallan Lower
BT61 . . . . 83 C1
Drumsallan Upper
BT61 . . . . 97 D8
Drumsavage BT60 . . . . . . 99 C5
Drumsavage Rd BT60 . . . . 99 C4
Drumsesk BT34 . . . . 143 A4
Drumsesk Pl BT34 . . . . 65 D2
Drumsesk Rd BT34 . . . . . . 143 A4
Drumshallan BT60 . . . . 100 B3
Drumsill
Armagh BT61 . . . . 98 B8
Lisburn BT28 . . . . 36 C8
Drumsill Pk BT61 . . . . 98 E8
Drumskee BT25 . . . . 87 B4
Drumskinny BT70 . . . . . . 82 E5
Drumsnade BT24 . . . . . . 107 A7
Drumsnade Rd BT24 . . . . 107 A7
Drumulcaw Rd BT30 . . . . 106 F4
Drumview Rd BT27 . . . . . . 76 C7
Dublin Bridge BT34 . . . . . . 64 C4
Dublinhill Rd BT25 . . . . . . 87 D7
Dublin Rd
Banbridge BT32 . . . . 102 C2
Belfast BT2 . . . . 155 A1
Castlewellan BT31 . . . . 122 A4
Newry BT34 . . . . 121 E2
Newry BT35 . . . . 64 C2
Dublin St 8 BT6 . . . . 15 A3
Duburren BT35 . . . . 130 E2
Duburren Rd BT35 . . . . . . 130 D2
Dudley St BT7 . . . . 14 E2
Duff Ave 20 BT22 . . . . 94 D3
Dufferin Ave
9 Bangor BT20 . . . . 4 A4
Strangford BT30 . . . . 94 C2
Dufferin Dr BT30 . . . . 93 B6
Dufferin Hospl BT9 . . . . 14 B2
Dufferin Pk BT30 . . . . 62 D4
Dufferin Rd BT3 . . . . 14 F8
Dufferin Terr BT20 . . . . 4 F5
Dufferin Villas BT20 . . . . 4 F5
Dukes Gr BT61 . . . . 60 A6
Duke's La BT61 . . . . 60 A6
Duke St
33 Belfast BT5 . . . . 15 A5
Portadown BT62 . . . . 51 D4
Warrenpoint BT34 . . . . 65 C2
Dukestown La BT66 . . . . . . 41 F1
Dullisk Way BT23 . . . . 25 E4
Dumb Fort* BT25 . . . . 87 D6
Dunarott Pk BT21 . . . . 6 E3
Dunbar Link BT1 . . . . 155 B4
Dunbar Rd BT32 . . . . 61 B6
Dunbar St BT1 . . . . 155 B4
Dunbarton St BT63 . . . . 57 C2
Dunbeg Gdns BT26 . . . . 47 D7
Dunbeg Lower BT24 . . . . 90 B2
Dunbeg Pk BT26 . . . . 47 D6
Dunbeg Upper BT24 . . . . 90 C1
Dunbrae BT35 . . . . 64 A2
Duncairn Ave 4 BT15 . . . . 14 C8
Duncairn Bsns Pk BT15 . . 14 D8
Duncairn Gdns BT15 . . . . . 14 D8
Duncairn Par BT15 . . . . 14 D7
Duncans Rd BT28 . . . . 26 A4
Duncrue St BT15 . . . . 14 E8
DUNDALK (DÚN
DEALGAN) 149 E1
Dundalk Racecourse* . . 150 C2
Dundalk Rd
Crossmaglen BT35 . . . . . . 147 F7
Newry BT35 . . . . 129 C3
Dundalk St 151 C4
DÚN DEALGAN
(DUNDALK) 149 E1
Dundee St BT13 . . . . 154 B4
Dundela Ave BT4 . . . . 15 E5
Dundela Cl BT4 . . . . 15 E5
Dundela Cres BT4 . . . . 15 E5
Dundela Flats BT4 . . . . 15 E5
Dundela Gdns BT4 . . . . 15 E5
Dundela Inf Sch BT4 . . . . . 15 E5
Dundela Pk BT4 . . . . 15 D5
Dundela St BT4 . . . . 15 E5
Dundela View BT4 . . . . 15 E5
DÚN DÓNAILL (DUNDONALD)
BT16 . . . . 17 E3
DUNDONALD (DÚN DÓNAILL)
BT16 . . . . 17 E3
Dundonald Ent Pk BT16 . . 17 E5
Dundonald High Sch
BT16 . . . . 17 D5
Dundonald Hts BT16 . . . . . 17 A3
Dundonald International Ice
Bowl BT5 . . . . 16 F3
Dundonald Prim Sch
BT16 . . . . 17 C4
Dundrine Rd BT31 . . . . . . 122 D4
Dundrinne BT31 . . . . . . 122 D4
Dundrinne Gdns BT31 . . . 122 C5
Dundrinne Rise BT31 . . . . 122 C5
Dundrod Ct BT28 . . . . 37 E8
Dundrod Rd BT28 . . . . 37 E8
Dundrod Wlk BT28 . . . . 37 F8
DUN DROMA (DUNDRUM)
BT33 . . . . 123 C5
Dundrum BT60 . . . . 114 D3
Dundrum Castle* BT33 . 123 C6
DUNDRUM (DUN DROMA)
BT33 . . . . 123 C5
Dundrum Rd
Armagh BT60 . . . . 114 C6
Dromara BT25 . . . . 89 E2
Newcastle BT33 . . . . 63 D7
Duneight BT27 . . . . 38 E4
Dunesmullan BT60 . . . . 100 C1
Dunesmullan Rd BT60 . . . 100 C1
Dunevely Rd BT22 . . . . 94 E7
Dunevly BT22 . . . . 94 F8
Dungannon Rd
Craigavon BT62 . . . . 73 F4
Moy BT71 . . . . 72 A1
Portadown BT62 . . . . 51 A8
Dungannon St 3 BT71 . . . 72 A1
Dungooly 149 C7
Dungooly Cross Roads . 149 C7
Dungorman Rd BT71 . . . . . 72 A5
Dungormley Est BT35 . . . 129 C5
Dungormley Rd BT35 . . . . 129 C6
Dungoyne Pk BT16 . . . . . . 17 D4
Dunkeld Ave BT19 . . . . 13 F8
Dunkeld Chase BT19 . . . . . 13 F8
Dunkeld Cl BT19 . . . . 13 F8
Dunkeld Cres BT19 . . . . . . 13 F8
Dunkeld Ct BT19 . . . . 13 F8
Dunkeld Dr BT19 . . . . 13 F8
Dunkeld Gdns 3 BT19 . . . 13 F8
Dunkeld Gr BT19 . . . . 13 F8
Dunkeld Pk BT19 . . . . 13 F8
Dunkeld Rd BT19 . . . . 13 F8
Dunkirk Rd BT66 . . . . 53 F5
Dunlady BT16 . . . . 17 D8
Dunlady Ct BT16 . . . . 17 D5
Dunlady Manor BT16 . . . . . 17 C6
Dunlady Rd
Belfast BT16 . . . . 10 E1
Dundonald BT16 . . . . 17 D6
Dunlarg BT60 . . . . 114 B4
Dunlarg Rd BT60 . . . . 114 A5
Dunleady Pk BT16 . . . . 17 C5
Dunleath Dr 6 BT22 . . . . . 71 A6
Dunlewey St BT13 . . . . . . 154 A3
Dunlop Commercial Est
BT19 . . . . 13 B8
Dunluce Ave BT9 . . . . 14 B2
Dunmore BT24 . . . . 106 E7
Dunmore Ave BT34 . . . . . 146 D5
Dunmore Rd BT24 . . . . 90 E1
Dunmurry High Sch BT17 26 F7
Dunmurry Ind Est BT17 . . . 26 D8
Dunnaman BT34 . . . . . . 153 A7
Dunnaman Pk 3 BT34 . . 153 B7
Dunnanelly BT30 . . . . 92 C1
Dunnanew BT30 . . . . 107 D4
Dunnanew Rd BT30 . . . . . 107 D4
Dunnaval BT34 . . . . 153 A5
Dunnaval Rd BT34 . . . . . . 153 A6
Dunnywater Bridge
BT34 . . . . 146 B7
Dunover BT22 . . . . 70 E7
Dunover Pk 4 BT22 . . . . . 71 A6
Dunover Rd BT22 . . . . 70 F7
Dunover Rd N BT22 . . . . . . 70 E7
DÚN PÁDRAIG
(DOWNPATRICK) BT30 . . . 62 B6
Dunraven Ave BT5 . . . . 15 D3
Dunraven Cres 3 BT5 . . . . 15 D3
Dunraven Ct BT5 . . . . 15 D4
Dunraven Dr 4 BT5 . . . . . . 15 D3
Dunraven Gdns BT5 . . . . . . 15 D3
Dunraven Par BT5 . . . . 15 D3
Dunraven Pk BT5 . . . . 15 D3
Dunreavy Pk BT35 . . . . . . 140 A4
Dunseverick Ave BT8 . . . . . 21 E2
Dunsfort BT30 . . . . 110 A2
Dunsy Way BT23 . . . . 25 E4
Dunturk BT31 . . . . 106 D5
Dunturk Rd BT31 . . . . 106 D4
Dunure Pk BT16 . . . . 17 C4
Dunvegan St BT6 . . . . 155 C1
Dunville Pk BT12 . . . . 154 A2
Dunville St BT13 . . . . 154 A2
Dunwellan Pk BT33 . . . . . . 63 D6
Dunygarton Rd BT27 . . . . . 36 B4
Durham Ct BT12 . . . . 154 C3
Durham St BT12 . . . . 154 C3
Duvernagh BT35 . . . . . . 131 A6
Dyan BT68 . . . . 82 E2
Dyan Rd
Caledon BT68 . . . . 82 E3
Dungannon BT70 . . . . 82 F5

E

Eachlann na Trá (Strand
Mews) 11 BT5 . . . . 15 A5
Eagle Terr BT27 . . . . 26 C2
Eagralougher BT61 . . . . 84 F5
Eagralougher Rd BT61 . . . 85 A6
Ean Hill BT18 . . . . 9 D6
Earl Cl BT15 . . . . 14 D7
Earl Haig Cres 3 BT6 . . . . 15 B2
Earl Haig Pk BT6 . . . . 15 B2
Earl's Court The 4 BT4 . . 15 F5
Earlsfort BT67 . . . . 34 A1
Earlswood Dr BT23 . . . . . . 20 B7
Earlswood Gr BT4 . . . . 15 F5
Earlswood Pk BT4 . . . . 15 F5
Earlswood Rd BT4 . . . . 15 F5
Eastbank Rd BT8 . . . . 29 D4
East Belfast Enterprise Pk 4
BT4 . . . . 15 C5
East Belfast Fc BT4 . . . . . . 15 F8
East Bread St BT5 . . . . 15 C5
East Bridge St BT7 . . . . . 155 C2
East Circular Rd BT19 . . . . . 4 E3
East Cloghoge Rd BT35 . . 139 A2
East Downs Inst of FE
Ballynahinch BT24 . . . . 59 C4
Downpatrick BT30 . . . . 62 C4
East Downs Inst of FE
(Newcastle Campus)
BT33 . . . . 63 D6
East Down View BT27 . . . . 26 D2
Eastleigh Dale BT4 . . . . 15 F5
Eastleigh Dr BT4 . . . . 15 F5
East Link BT18 . . . . 9 D5
East Link Rd BT16 . . . . 17 A3
East Mount BT23 . . . . 20 A4
East St
Donaghadee BT21 . . . . 6 F1
Newtownards BT23 . . . . 19 E5
Warrenpoint BT34 . . . . 65 C2
East Twin Rd BT3 . . . . 8 C1
Eastway BT65 . . . . 41 B5
East Way BT20 . . . . 4 B1
Eblana St BT7 . . . . 14 D2
Ebor Dr BT12 . . . . 14 A2
Ebor Par BT12 . . . . 14 A2
Ebor St BT12 . . . . 154 A1
Ebrington Gdns BT4 . . . . . . 15 E5
Eccles St BT13 . . . . 14 A7
Echlinville BT22 . . . . 80 F5
Edenagarry BT34 . . . . . . 119 D6
Edenakill 149 A5
Edenappa BT35 . . . . 150 C8
Edenappa Rd BT35 . . . . . . 141 C1
Edenard Rd BT60 . . . . 115 E1
Eden Ave BT63 . . . . 51 F5
Edenaveys BT60 . . . . 99 A4
Edenaveys Cres BT60 . . . . 98 F4
Edenaveys Rd BT60 . . . . . . 98 F5
Edenballycoggill BT66 . . 43 B3
Edenberry Mews BT32 . . . 61 B6
Edenbrook Cl 13 BT13 . . . . 14 A7
Edenbrooke Prim Sch
BT13 . . . . 14 A8
Edencrieve BT35 . . . . 64 B1
Eden Ct 6 BT60 . . . . 116 A8
Edendarriff BT24 . . . . . . 106 F7
Edendarriff Rd BT24 . . . . 106 E7
Edendell BT32 . . . . 61 C5
Edenderry
Banbridge BT32 . . . . 61 B5
Banbridge BT32 . . . . 102 A4
Belfast BT8 . . . . 28 A8
Dungannon BT71 . . . . 83 D3
Portadown BT63 . . . . 51 F5
Edenderry Cl BT13 . . . . 14 A7
Edenderry Gdns
Banbridge BT32 . . . . 61 B6
Portadown BT63 . . . . 51 F4
Edenderry Ind Est BT13 . . 14 A7
Edenderry La BT71 . . . . 83 E3
Edenderry Pk BT32 . . . . 61 B5
Edenderry Prim Sch
Banbridge BT32 . . . . 61 D6
Portadown BT63 . . . . 52 B4
Edenderry Rd
Banbridge BT32 . . . . 61 B4
Belfast BT8 . . . . 21 A1
Craigavon BT63 . . . . 102 A3
Edenderry St 7 BT13 . . . . 14 A7
Eden Dr BT60 . . . . 116 A8
Edengrove Pk BT24 . . . . . . 59 B6
Edenkennedy Way 9
BT60 . . . . 116 A8
Edenknappagh BT60 . . . . 99 B3
Eden Manor BT63 . . . . 51 F5
Edenmore
Craigavon BT66 . . . . 44 B4
Newry BT34 . . . . 133 A3
Edenmore Rd BT34 . . . . . . 132 F2
Edenordinary BT32 . . . . . 87 D3
Edenordinary Rd BT32 . . . 87 C2
Eden Rd BT5 . . . . 23 F6
Eden Rise 7 BT60 . . . . . . 116 A8
Edenslate BT23 . . . . 31 B2
Edenticullo BT26 . . . . 48 A4
Edenticullo Rd BT26 . . . . . 47 F2
Edentiroory BT25 . . . . . . 87 B4
Edentrillick BT26 . . . . 88 E8
Edentrillick Hill BT26 . . . . . 88 F8
Edentrillick Rd BT26 . . . . . 46 F1
Edentrumly BT34 . . . . . . 133 D3
Edentrumly Rd BT34 . . . . 133 D2
Edentrumly Rd Upper
BT34 . . . . 133 D4
Edenvaddy Rd BT24 . . . . . 59 A4
Edenvale
Armagh BT60 . . . . 98 F4
8 Crossgar BT30 . . . . 92 B4
EDEN VALE BT32 . . . . 61 D3
Edenvale Ave BT32 . . . . 61 C3
Edenvale Cres
Belfast BT4 . . . . 15 E6
Newtownards BT23 . . . . 20 C6
Edenvale Ct 1 BT4 . . . . . . 15 F6
Edenvale Dr 9 BT4 . . . . . . 15 E6
Edenvale Gdns 3 BT4 . . . . 15 E6
Edenvale Gr 2 BT4 . . . . . . 15 F6
Edenvale Pk 7 BT4 . . . . . . 15 E6
Edenview Cres BT67 . . . . . 34 F7
Edenview Gdns BT67 . . . . . 34 F7
Edenview Way BT67 . . . . . . 34 F7
Edenykennedy BT60 . . . 116 B8
Edgar Ave BT8 . . . . 29 E3
Edgar Rd BT8 . . . . 29 E3
Edgar Road Ind Est BT8 . . 29 E4
Edgar St BT5 . . . . 15 A5
Edgarstown Rd BT62 . . . . . 51 C4
Edgecumbe Dr BT4 . . . . . . 15 F6
Edgecumbe Gdns BT4 . . . . 15 F6
Edgecumbe Pk BT4 . . . . . . 15 F6
Edgecumbe View BT4 . . . . 15 E6
Edgehill Coll BT9 . . . . 21 C8
Edgehill Pk BT27 . . . . 38 B7
Edgewater
9 Donaghadee BT21 . . . . . 67 A7
Lisburn BT27 . . . . 38 B8
Edgewater Bay 6 BT21 . . 67 A7
Edgewater Bsns Pk BT3 . . . 8 A4
Edgewater Cove 5 BT21 . 67 A7
Edgewater Rd BT3 . . . . 8 B4
Edinburgh Ave BT18 . . . . . . 9 E6
Edinburgh Mews 2 BT9 . . 14 B1
Edinburgh St BT9 . . . . 14 A1
Edith Helen Rd BT23 . . . . . 19 F5
Edith St 2 BT5 . . . . 15 B4
Edlingham St BT15 . . . . 14 D8
Edmund Rice Prim Sch
BT15 . . . . 14 C7
Ednego BT32 . . . . 87 F1
Ednego Ave BT32 . . . . 87 F1
Ednego Rd
Banbridge BT32 . . . . 87 E1
Dromara BT25 . . . . 88 A1
Edward St
Armagh BT61 . . . . 60 C6
Belfast BT1 . . . . 155 A4
Donaghadee BT21 . . . . 67 A8
Downpatrick BT30 . . . . 62 D4
Lurgan BT66 . . . . 41 F5
Newry BT35 . . . . 64 C6
Portadown BT62 . . . . 51 E4
Edwina St BT13 . . . . 154 A4
Eelwire Rd BT32 . . . . 120 F7
Egeria St BT12 . . . . 154 B1
EGLANTINE BT27 . . . . 37 C3
Eglantine Ave BT9 . . . . 14 B1
Eglantine Ct BT27 . . . . 37 E4
Eglantine Gdns BT9 . . . . . . 14 C1
Eglantine Pk BT26 . . . . 37 B2
Eglantine Pl BT9 . . . . 14 C1
Eglantine Rd BT27 . . . . 37 E4

Eglish
Craigavon BT62 73 D2
Dungannon BT71 83 D3
Eglish Pk BT62 73 D3
Eglish (Portadown) Prim Sch BT62 73 D3
Eglish Rd
Craigavon BT62 73 D3
Dungannon BT70 82 F6
Egmont Gdns BT12 154 B1
Eileen Gdns BT9 21 B8
Eirford Pk BT25 88 D1
Elaine St BT9 14 D1
Elders Rd BT35 128 E3
Eleastan Pk BT34 153 C6
Elesington Ct BT6 15 C1
Elgin St BT7 14 E1
Elizabeth Gdns BT23 25 E4
Elizabeth Rd BT18 9 F6
Elizabeth Terr BT63 40 B3
Eliza Cl BT33 63 B7
Eliza St BT2 155 B2
Eliza Street Cl BT7 155 B2
Eliza Street Terr BT7 155 B2
Ellington Ave BT66 41 E6
Ellisholding BT35 141 E7
Ellisholding Rd BT35 141 D7
Elm Cnr 1 BT17 26 F8
Elm Dr BT23 19 D7
Elmfield Ave 6 BT34 65 B4
Elmfield Crest 7 BT34 65 B4
Elmfield Ct 5 BT34 65 B4
Elmfield Dr BT34 65 B4
Elmfield Pk 2 BT21 66 F8
Elmfield Villas 2 BT34 65 B4
Elmgrove Pk BT33 63 C6
Elmgrove Prim Sch BT5 15 D3
Elmhurst BT67 43 E6
Elm Pk 2 BT61 85 E1
Elm Pk Rd BT60 97 C6
Elm St BT7 155 A1
Elms The BT19 13 D8
Elmtree Mews BT63 52 B5
Elmwood Ave BT9 14 C2
Elmwood Dr
Bangor BT20 3 F2
Lisburn BT28 38 A8
Elmwood House Bsns Ctr BT9 14 B2
Elmwood Mews BT9 14 C2
Elmwood Pk
Lisburn BT27 26 C3
Newry BT34 64 E8
Elmwood Terr BT66 41 E6
Elsinore Ave BT19 3 B5
Elsmere Hts BT5 16 E1
Elsmere Manor BT5 16 E2
Elsmere Pk BT5 16 E2
Emdale Ct BT32 61 B3
Emdale Rd BT32 119 B5
Emerald St 3 BT6 15 A3
Emmet Pl BT35 64 C7
Emmet St 5 BT35 64 C7
Empire Dr BT12 154 A1
Empire Par BT12 154 A1
Empire St BT12 154 A1
Enagh
Armagh BT60 96 F3
Armagh BT60 98 A3
Armagh BT60 115 D5
Caledon BT68 96 D7
Dromore BT25 104 D8
Newry BT35 131 B8
Enagh Rd BT25 88 D1
English St BT30 62 B5
Enid Dr BT5 15 F4
Enid Par BT5 15 F4
Enler Dr BT23 25 D4
Enler Gdns BT23 25 D4
Enler Pk
Comber BT23 25 D4
Dundonald BT16 17 D3
Enler Pk Central BT16 17 C3
Enler Pk E BT16 17 D3
Enler Pk W BT16 17 C3
Ennis Cl BT67 42 A8
Enniscrone Pk BT63 52 A5
Ennis Gn BT67 42 B8
Enniskeen BT65 41 A2
Ennislare BT60 98 D2
Ennislare Rd BT60 98 C2
Ennismore Rd BT62 73 D7
Ennis Tarry BT67 42 B8
Ensbury Dr BT19 5 A1
Enterprise Ct BT19 13 A7
Enterprise Rd BT19 13 A6
Epworth Cl 8 BT62 101 B7
Epworth St BT5 15 B4
Erenagh BT30 108 D1
Erenagh Rd BT30 108 D1
Erindee Ave BT21 66 F8
Erindee Cl BT21 66 F8
Erindee Cres BT21 66 F7
Erindee Dr BT21 66 F8
Erindee Gdns BT21 66 F7
Erindee Pk 3 BT21 66 F8
Erin Way BT7 155 A1
Erskine Pl 1 BT35 64 D7
Erskine St
8 Belfast BT5 15 B5
Newry BT35 64 D7
Eshwary BT35 131 A5
Eshwary Hill BT35 131 A4
Eshwary Rd BT35 131 A6
Esker Pk BT60 97 B5
Esky Dr BT63 40 C3
Esky Rd BT66 74 C7
Espey Pk 4 BT71 72 A6
Espie Way 2 BT6 15 E1
Espl The BT18 9 D7
Essex Gr BT7 14 E2
Essmore BT34 65 B3
Estate Rd BT23 12 A6
Ethel St BT9 14 A1
Eureka Dr BT12 154 C1
Euston Par BT6 15 B3
Euston St Prim Sch 9 BT6 15 B3
Euston St BT6 15 B3
Euterpe St BT12 154 B1
Evelyn Ave BT5 15 D4
Eversleigh St 24 BT6 15 A3
Everton Dr BT6 22 C7
Ewart's Cross Roads BT35 131 B7
Exchange Pl BT1 155 A4
Exchange St W BT1 155 A4
Exchange St BT1 155 B4
Excise Wlk BT12 154 B2

F

Factory St BT5 15 C4
Faiche Ard Mín (Ardmeen Gn) BT30 62 D4
Fairfax Ct BT14 14 A8
Fairfield BT27 26 C4
Fairfield Ave BT20 4 C2
Fairfield Ct BT23 20 B4
Fairfield Glen BT20 4 C3
Fairfield Hts 2 BT35 131 F5
Fairfield Pk BT20 4 C2
Fairfield Pl BT23 20 B4
Fairfield Rd BT20 4 D2
Fairfield Way BT23 20 B4
Fair Gn 151 C4
Fair Green Ave 13 BT60 114 A3
Fair Green Pk 12 BT60 114 A3
Fairgreen Rd BT60 116 A8
Fair Hill Prim Sch BT25 88 E2
Fairlawns Ave 8 BT35 131 F5
Fairley Dr BT66 41 F3
Fair Rd BT34 152 D4
Fairtree Hill BT27 26 C5
Fairview BT34 65 C4
Fairview or Mucklagh BT60 96 D3
Fairview Pk BT17 26 D8
Fairview Rd BT66 44 D1
Fairview St BT13 14 C7
Fairway Gdns BT5 16 B1
Fairways The
Downpatrick BT30 110 B2
Newcastle BT33 63 E7
Portadown BT62 51 E1
Falcon Ave BT23 19 D7
Falcon Dr BT23 19 E7
Falcon Hts BT23 19 D8
Falcon Pk BT23 19 D7
Falcon Rd BT12 14 A1
Falcon Way BT23 19 D7
Falls Ct (Cúirt na Bhfáll) 6 BT13 154 A3
Falls Leisure Ctr BT13 154 B3
Falls Rd (Bóthar na Bhfál) BT12 154 A2
Falmore 149 D4
Fane Gr BT35 147 D6
Fane St Prim Sch BT9 14 B2
Fane St BT9 14 B2
Farlough Rd BT62 73 F5
Farmacaffly BT60 98 D3
Farmcourt BT66 86 C8
Farm Gr BT20 3 D2
Farmhill La BT18 1 B1
Farmhill Rd BT18 1 B1
Farmhurst Gn BT5 16 C1
Farmhurst Way BT5 16 C1
Farnaloy BT60 113 E7
Farnaloy Rd BT60 113 D6
Farnham Pk BT20 3 F4
Farnham Rd BT20 3 F4
Farnham St BT7 14 E2
Farnley BT33 63 B4
Farra BT62 74 A1
Farranamucklagh BT60 115 A5
Farranfad BT30 107 E3
Farranfad Rd BT30 107 E3
Farra Rd BT62 50 C8
Fashoda St BT5 15 C3
Father Cullen Pk BT35 131 C4
Fathom La BT35 64 D2
Fathom Line BT35 141 F7
Fathom Lower BT35 141 F7
Fathom Upper BT35 142 A5
Faugh-a-ballagh Cres BT60 60 E5
FAUGHART UPPER 150 B5
Faulkner Rd BT20 3 E1
Feadanagh Cl BT30 62 D3
Feadanagh Pk BT30 62 D2
Fearon Cl BT34 153 B7
Fedany BT32 104 C7
Fedany Rd BT25 104 D7
Federation St BT6 15 A2
Federnagh BT35 117 D7
Fedney Hill Rd BT32 104 B8
Feede 150 D7
Fegans Gdns BT34 134 B5
Fellows Hall Rd BT60 97 B3
Felt St BT12 154 C1
Feney BT67 44 B7
Feney Rd BT67 44 C7
Fergort BT60 113 A1
Fergort Rd BT60 113 A1
Ferguson Dr 4 BT4 15 E6
Fernagreevagh BT61 85 C7
Fernbank Cl BT19 4 E2
Fernbank Dr BT19 4 E2
Fernbank Gdns BT19 4 E2
Fernbank Hts BT19 4 E2
Fernbank Pk BT19 4 E2
Fernbank Rd BT19 4 E2
Fern Ct BT34 64 F6
Ferndale
Lurgan BT66 41 F3
Warrenpoint BT34 65 D4
Ferndale Ave BT27 38 D8
Ferndale Ct 4 BT9 21 A8
Ferndale St 7 BT9 21 A8
Ferndene Ave BT16 17 C2
Ferndene Gdns BT16 17 C2
Ferndene Pk BT16 17 C2
Ferndene Rd BT16 17 C2
Fern Gr
Bangor BT19 3 C1
Craigavon BT67 32 E7
Ferngrove Ave BT67 32 E7
Ferngrove Cres BT67 32 E7
Ferngrove Dr BT67 32 E8
Ferngrove Manor BT67 32 F7
Ferngrove Pk BT67 32 E7
Fernhill Rd BT32 103 D1
Fern Hts BT34 64 E6
Fernlea Pk BT19 4 E2
Fernmore Ave BT19 4 F3
Fernmore Pk BT19 4 F3
Fernmore Rd BT19 4 F3
Fernvale St BT4 15 E7
Fernwood St BT7 21 E8
Ferryhill Rd BT35 141 E3
Ferryquarter BT30 94 D2
Ferry Rd BT71 73 B8
Ferry St 18 BT22 94 D3
Festival Rd BT63 52 B4
Festival Sq BT66 42 C4
Fifth Ave BT35 64 A8
Fifth St BT13 154 A4
Filbin Cres BT67 42 A7
Finchley Dr 2 BT4 16 B8
Finchley Gdns 1 BT4 16 B8
Finchley Pk BT4 16 B8
Finchley Vale BT4 16 B8
Finegan's Cross Rd BT35 141 B1
Finegans Rd BT35 141 A1
Fingals Ct BT13 154 C3
Finglush BT68 96 A7
Finglush Rd BT68 96 B8
Finiskin BT35 139 C7
Finiskin Rd BT35 139 C7
Finlays Rd BT22 20 D1
Finlay's Rd BT22 69 B8
Finlieve Pl 7 BT34 153 C7
Finmore Ct BT4 15 B5
Finnabrogue BT30 108 F8
Finnard BT34 133 A8
Finnard Rd BT34 119 B1
Finnebrogue Rd BT30 62 B8
Finnegans Rd BT35 139 A7
Finnis BT25 105 B6
FINNIS BT25 105 C8
Finnis Rd BT25 105 B6
Finn Sq BT13 154 C3
Finsbury Ave BT8 22 C2
Finsbury Cres BT8 22 C2
Finsbury Dr BT8 22 C2
Finsbury Pk BT8 22 B2
Finsbury St BT6 15 B1
Finvoy St BT5 15 D5
Fir Dr BT23 19 D7
Firmount Cres BT18 9 D3
First Ave BT35 64 B7
Firs The
Lisburn BT28 36 D6
Portadown BT63 52 B6
First St BT13 154 A3
Fir Tree La BT63 101 F5
Fishermans Row (Rae an Lascaire) BT30 125 D5
Fisherwick Pl BT12 155 A2
Fish Quarter BT22 80 E7
Fitzgerald Pk BT62 51 C2
Fitzjames Pk BT23 19 C6
Fitzroy Ave BT7 14 E2
Fitzroy St BT62 51 D4
Fitzwilliam Ave BT7 21 F8
Fitzwilliam St BT9 14 C2
Five Acres BT63 52 A3
FIVE LOAN ENDS BT62 73 C2
Five Mile Hill BT60 116 F2
Flagship Sh Ctr BT20 4 B4
Flagstaff Rd BT35 141 E8
Flax St BT14 14 A8
Fleetwood St BT15 14 C7
Flora St BT5 15 C4
Florence Ct
Belfast BT13 14 C7
Portadown BT63 51 E5
Florence Pl BT13 14 C7
Florence Sq BT13 14 C7
Florenceville Ave BT7 21 F7
Florenceville Dr BT7 21 F8
Florida Ct BT23 78 D7
Florida Dr BT6 15 A3
Florida Rd BT23 78 C5
Florida St 5 BT6 15 A3
Florwnce Ct BT27 37 B4
Flough Rd BT32 103 E7
Flush Dr BT6 22 A7
Flush Gdns BT6 22 A8
Flush Gn BT6 22 A7
Flush Park Ind Est BT28 37 C8
Flush Pk
Belfast BT6 22 A7
Lisburn BT28 37 C8
Flush Pl BT67 42 B4
Flush Rd
Banbridge BT32 120 F6
Newcastle BT33 123 A3
Flying Horse Rd BT30 62 D2
Fofannybane BT34 135 B7
Fofanny Rd BT34 135 B7
Fofannyreagh BT34 135 C7
Fofanny Sch Rd BT34 121 A1
Foley BT60 115 B5
Foley Prim Sch BT60 115 A6
Foley Rd BT60 115 A6
Folk Mus★ BT35 140 A6
Folly La
Armagh BT60 60 E4
Downpatrick BT30 62 C4
Folly Pk BT60 60 E4
Fontenoys GAC BT31 121 E8
Forde Cl BT30 107 C2
Forde Way BT30 107 C2
Ford Rd BT30 123 E7
Forestbrook Ave 7 BT34 143 C3
Forestbrook Pk 3 BT34 143 C3
Forestbrook Rd 6 BT34 143 C3
Forest Glade BT67 42 B7
Forest Gr BT8 21 E2
Forest Hill
Belfast BT9 21 B5
Newtownards BT23 13 A5
Forest Hills BT34 142 A8
Forest Pk
Markethill BT60 116 A8
Newry BT35 140 F2
Forest Rd BT35 140 D3
Forestside Sh Ctr BT8 22 A5
Forest View BT60 116 A8
Forest Wlk BT30 94 A2
Forge Hill Ct 16 BT24 77 C3
Forge Integrated Prim Sch BT7 21 F7
Forge Rd BT35 138 D6
FORKHILL BT35 149 D8
Forkhill Rd BT35 140 C2
Forster Green Hospl
Castlereagh BT8 22 A5
Lisburn BT27 39 A5
Forster St BT13 14 B7
Fortfield Pl BT15 14 D8
Fortfields BT25 58 C6
Forth Ave BT34 65 D3
Fort Hill
Dundonald BT16 17 B3
Lisburn BT28 26 B2
Forthill Ave BT32 61 C3
Forthill Cl BT19 3 C2
Fort Hill Coll BT27 26 D2
Forthill Gn BT32 61 C3
Forthill Par BT19 3 C3
Forthill Prim Sch BT27 26 C2
Forthill Rd BT25 46 A1
Fort Hill Rd BT34 64 F5
Forth Rd BT34 65 D3
Fort Rd
Belfast BT8 28 C7
Dromara BT25 104 F7
Dundonald BT16 17 B2
Helen's Bay BT19 2 C6
Newry BT35 130 E4
Fort St BT32 61 C3
Fort The BT19 2 D7
Fortuna St BT12 154 B1
Fortwilliam Ind Est BT3 8 A3
Foster Pl BT67 42 B4
Foughill Etra BT35 141 C3
Foughill Otra BT35 141 B1
Foughillotra Rd BT35 141 B1
Foundry St BT62 51 E5
Fountain Ct BT30 62 C5
Fountain Ctr BT1 155 A3
Fountain La BT1 155 A3
Fountain St
Belfast BT1 155 A3
Bessbrook BT35 131 C5
2 Downpatrick BT30 62 C5
Fountainville Ave 6 BT9 14 C2
Fourth Ave BT35 64 A8
Fourtowns Sch Rd BT35 101 F1
FOUR WINDS BT8 22 D4
Four Winds Ave BT8 22 C4
Four Winds Dr BT8 22 C4
Four Winds Pk BT8 22 C4
Four Winds Sh Ctr BT8 22 C4
Fowler Way 8 BT22 71 A6
Foxfield Rd BT35 147 F6
Foxglove St 6 BT5 15 C4
Fox Gr BT66 75 B5
Foxleigh Fields BT32 61 B1
Fox Ridge BT34 120 A2
Fox's Glen BT67 32 A1
Fox's Hill BT67 32 A1
Fox St BT62 51 D4
Foyarr BT60 96 F7
Foyarr Rd BT60 96 F6
Foy Beg BT62 74 C3
Foyduff BT60 112 C6
Foy La BT62 74 C3
Foyle Ct BT14 14 B8
Foy More BT62 74 B3
Foy Rd BT62 74 B2
Frances St BT23 19 E5
Franciscan Cross★ BT31 106 C4
Francis St
Belfast BT1 155 A3
Lurgan BT66 41 E6
Francis St *continued*
Newry BT35 64 C5
Frankhill Dr BT8 29 D3
Frankhill Pk BT8 29 D3
Franklin St Pl BT2 155 A2
Franklin St BT2 155 A2
Franklyn Dr BT66 42 A2
Franklyn Pk BT66 42 B2
Frank St 15 BT5 15 B4
Fraser Pass BT4 15 A5
Frasier St BT3 15 A6
Frazer Pk BT32 103 D1
Frederick Pl BT23 19 C5
Frederick St
Belfast BT1 155 A4
Killyleagh BT30 93 C5
Newtownards BT23 19 D5
Freeduff BT35 139 B3
Freeduff Rd BT35 139 A5
Free Presbyterian Church & Christian Sch BT19 12 D8
Frenchpark St BT12 14 A2
Frenchwood Pk BT18 1 D3
Frensham Rd BT23 19 B6
Friary Rd
Armagh BT60 60 D4
Dungannon BT70 82 C8
Newry BT35 129 C8
Friendly Pl BT7 155 C2
Friendly Row BT7 155 B2
Friendly St BT7 155 B2
Friendly Way BT7 155 B2
Friends Sch BT28 26 B3
Frome St 13 BT4 15 B5
Front Rd BT27 28 B2
Fruithill Pk BT20 4 E4
Fruitvalley Rd BT31 121 A8
Fullerton Rd BT34 64 E6
Fulton St BT7 155 A1
Furlong Ave BT66 41 F7

G

GAA Club BT61 84 C3
Gables The BT8 22 B2
Gaffikin St BT12 154 C1
Gairdíní Ardán Liath (Ardenlee Gdns) BT30 62 F7
Gairdíní Bholcáinin (Vvulcan Gdns) 13 BT5 15 A5
Gairdíní Chlann Aodha Buí (Clandeboye Gdns) 30 BT5 15 A5
Gairdíní Sheáin uí Mháirtín (John Martin Gdns) 6 BT35 64 C5
Gairloch Pk BT18 10 A8
Galbraith Gdns 9 BT66 86 C8
Gallaun BT30 62 B3
Galla Way BT23 19 C7
Gall Bog Rd BT32 88 A1
Galloway Point 16 BT21 67 A7
Gallows Pl 1 BT25 58 D6
Gallows St BT25 58 D6
Gallrock BT62 73 D4
Gallrock Rd BT62 73 D4
Galwally
Belfast BT7 21 F6
Castlereagh BT8 22 B5
Galwally Ave BT8 21 E5
Galwally Mews BT8 21 F5
Galwally Pk BT8 22 A6
Galway Ct BT16 17 A4
Galway Dr BT16 17 A4
Galway Pk BT16 17 A4
Galway St BT12 154 C3
Gambles Rd BT35 117 E5
Gamble St BT1 155 B4
GAMBLESTOWN BT25 87 B7
Gamblestown Pk BT66 87 A7
Ganaway BT22 67 C1
Ganaway Ave BT19 3 D1
Ganaway Dr BT23 79 C6
Ganaway Pk BT23 79 C6
Ganaway Rd BT22 67 C1
Ganaway Wlk 7 BT19 3 D1
Gannaway BT34 65 C3
Gannon Rd BT27 76 B5
Gaol La BT30 62 B5
Gaol Sq BT60 60 E5
Gardeners Rd BT27 39 A3
Gardens The BT35 131 C5
Gardiner Pl BT13 154 C4
Gardiner St BT13 154 C4
Gargarry BT31 121 C6
Gargarry Rd BT31 121 C6
Garland Ave
Castlereagh BT8 22 C4
Lurgan BT66 41 E6
Garland Cres
Castlereagh BT8 22 C5
Lurgan BT66 41 E7
Garland Ct BT66 41 E7
Garland Dr BT66 41 E7
Garland Gn BT8 22 D4
Garland Hill BT8 22 C4
Garland Hts BT66 41 E7
Garland Mews BT66 41 E7
Garland Pk BT8 22 C5
Garmoyle St BT15 14 E7
Garnerville Dr
2 Belfast BT4 9 A1
Belfast BT4 16 A8
Garnerville Gdns BT4 9 A1

Garnerville Pk BT4 . . . . 9 A1
Garnerville Rd BT4 . . . . 9 A1
Garraithe an Chomair
(Comber Gdns) 28 BT5 . . . 15 A5
Garraithe Suí Forde
(Seaforde Gdns) 19 BT5 . . 15 A5
Garraithe Thulach Forde
(Mountforde Gdns) 17
BT5 . . . . 15 A5
Garraithe uí Bhríosáin
(Bryson Gdns) 29 BT5 . . . 15 A5
Garranard Manor BT4 . . . 16 A7
Garranard Pk BT4 . . . . 16 A7
Garret Ridge 14 BT21 . . . 67 A7
Garret Rocks 11 BT21 . . . 67 A7
Garrison Pl BT71 . . . . 84 B8
Garrymore BT65 . . . . 53 C7
Gartross BT66 . . . . 44 C5
Garvagh BT60 . . . . 99 F4
Garvagh Gdns BT62 . . . . 51 C6
Garvagh Rd BT35 . . . . 130 D1
Garvaghy
Armagh BT61 . . . . 97 E8
Banbridge BT32 . . . . 88 B1
Dungannon BT71 . . . . 83 B8
Portadown BT62 . . . . 51 E6
Garvaghy Church Rd
BT32 . . . . 88 C1
Garvaghy Cl BT62 . . . . 51 C6
Garvaghy Pk BT62 . . . . 51 C6
Garvaghy Rd
Banbridge BT32 . . . . 88 B1
Portadown BT62 . . . . 51 C6
Garveys Rd BT35 . . . . 139 C6
Gavin Pk BT20 . . . . 4 E3
Gawn St BT4 . . . . 15 C5
Geary Rd BT5 . . . . 16 D2
Geddis Ave BT66 . . . . 42 A3
General's Walk The BT21 . 67 A8
General Transport Galleries & X2 Experience★ BT18 . . 1 D2
Geneva Gdns BT9 . . . . 21 D7
Genoa St BT12 . . . . 154 B2
Geoffrey St 5 BT13 . . . . 14 A7
George Best Belfast City Airport BT3 . . . . 8 E2
Georges La BT34 . . . . 64 D5
Georges St
Armagh BT60 . . . . 60 E5
Newtownards BT23 . . . . 19 E4
George St
Lurgan BT66 . . . . 41 F4
Portadown BT62 . . . . 51 D3
Ghent Pl BT13 . . . . 14 A7
Giants Grave Chambered Grave★ BT25 . . . . 88 F5
Giants Ring Earthwork & Chambered Grave★
BT8 . . . . 28 A8
Giants Ring Rd BT8 . . . . 21 B1
Gibson Park Ave BT6 . . . . 15 B2
Gibson Park Dr BT6 . . . . 15 C2
Gibson Park Gdns BT6 . . . 15 B2
Gibsons Gn BT19 . . . . 13 C7
Gibsons La BT19 . . . . 13 C7
Gibson's La BT23 . . . . 13 C6
Gibson St BT12 . . . . 154 B2
Gilbert Cres BT20 . . . . 4 E4
Gilbourne Ct BT5 . . . . 16 C2
GILFORD (ATH MHIC GIOLLA)
BT63 . . . . 57 D2
Gilford Rd
Craigavon BT66 . . . . 53 F5
Lurgan BT66 . . . . 42 B3
Portadown BT63 . . . . 51 F5
Gilford St BT62 . . . . 101 B6
Gilnahirk BT5 . . . . 23 E7
Gilnahirk Ave BT5 . . . . 16 C2
Gilnahirk Cres BT5 . . . . 16 C2
Gilnahirk Dr BT5 . . . . 16 C2
Gilnahirk Golf Club BT5 . . 23 E7
Gilnahirk Pk BT5 . . . . 16 C2
Gilnahirk Prim Sch BT5 . . 16 D2
Gilnahirk Rd
10 Belfast BT4 . . . . 16 A5
Belfast BT5 . . . . 23 E8
4 Castlereagh BT5 . . . . 16 A1
Gilnahirk Rd W BT5 . . . . 23 E8
Gilnahirk Rise BT5 . . . . 16 C2
Gilnahirk Wlk BT5 . . . . 16 C2
Gilphins Manor BT66 . . . . 41 D4
Gilpin Cres BT66 . . . . 42 F5
Gilpin Pk BT66 . . . . 42 F5
Gilpins Mews BT66 . . . . 41 D3
Gilpinstown Rd BT65 . . . . 41 D3
Gipsy St BT7 . . . . 21 F8
Glade The BT63 . . . . 52 D2
Glandore Gdns BT62 . . . . 51 C3
Glandore Terr BT62 . . . . 51 C3
Glanroy Ave BT62 . . . . 51 C3
Glanroy Cl BT62 . . . . 51 C3
Glascar Rd BT32 . . . . 118 F6
Glasdrumman
Ballynahinch BT24 . . . . 77 C5
Ballynahinch BT24 . . . . 90 D8
Newry BT34 . . . . 146 D7
Newry BT35 . . . . 101 D1
Newry BT35 . . . . 148 F7
Glasdrummanaghy
BT35 . . . . 147 D5
Glasdrumman Upper
BT34 . . . . 136 D2
Glasdrummond
Armagh BT60 . . . . 112 F3
Armagh BT60 . . . . 115 E8
Glasdrummond Rd BT69 . . 82 A8
Glashena Rd BT30 . . . . 62 D3
Glaskerbeg East BT32 . . 118 F6
Glaskerbeg Rd BT32 . . . 118 E5
Glaskerbeg West BT32 118 E6
Glaskercourt BT32 . . . . 119 A5
Glaskermore BT32 . . . . 118 F5
Glassdrumman Rd
Ballynahinch BT24 . . . . 59 C8
Newcastle BT33 . . . . 137 A5
Newry BT34 . . . . 137 A1
Newry BT35 . . . . 101 D1
Newry BT35 . . . . 148 D7
Glassdrummond BT35 . 131 F6
Glassdrummond Rd
BT60 . . . . 112 F4
Glassestown Rd BT32 . . . 86 C1
Glass Moss BT23 . . . . 68 D6
Glass Moss Rd BT63 . . . . 57 E6
Glass Moss The BT63 . . . . 57 E6
GLASSWATER BT30 . . . . 92 A6
Glasswater Rd BT30 . . . . 92 B7
Glastry BT22 . . . . 81 A7
Glastry Coll BT22 . . . . 81 B7
Glastry Gdns BT19 . . . . 3 D1
Glastry Rd BT22 . . . . 81 A8
Gleannabhainn 2 BT60 . 130 C8
Gleann Ruari 9 BT34 . . . 143 C3
Gleann St 8 BT34 . . . . 143 C3
Glebe
Downpatrick BT30 . . . . 110 C6
Downpatrick BT30 . . . . 124 D6
Hillsborough BT26 . . . . 49 D3
Newry BT34 . . . . 118 C4
Newry BT35 . . . . 140 B3
Glebe Ave BT67 . . . . 34 B1
Glebe Cres BT67 . . . . 34 B1
Glebe Gdns BT67 . . . . 34 B1
Glebe Hill Rd BT62 . . . . 101 B5
Glebe Manor BT26 . . . . 49 B1
Glebe Pk
Moira BT67 . . . . 34 B1
Newry BT35 . . . . 140 B3
Glebe Rd
Banbridge BT32 . . . . 103 D2
Downpatrick BT30 . . . . 110 C6
Hillsborough BT26 . . . . 49 C3
Glebe The BT63 . . . . 52 A7
Glebetown Dr BT30 . . . . 62 C2
Glebe Way BT67 . . . . 34 B1
Glebe Wlk BT28 . . . . 37 F8
Glenaan Ct BT20 . . . . 4 C2
Glenaan Pk BT20 . . . . 4 C2
Glenada Holiday & Conference Ctr BT33 . . . . 63 C3
Glenallen St BT5 . . . . 15 B5
Glenalpin St BT2 . . . . 155 A1
GLENANNE BT60 . . . . 116 C2
Glenanne Ind Est BT60 . . 116 C3
Glenanne Rd BT60 . . . . 116 D5
Glen Annesley Ave BT19 . . 13 C7
Glen Annesley Dr BT19 . . 13 C7
Glen Annesley Gdns BT19 13 C7
Glen Annesley Mews
BT19 . . . . 13 C7
Glen Annesley Pk BT19 . . 13 C7
Glen Annesley Rd BT19 . . 13 C7
Glenarb BT68 . . . . 96 E8
Glenard Rd BT23 . . . . 19 D6
Glenariff Dr BT23 . . . . 25 B3
Glenariff Pk BT20 . . . . 4 C2
Glenashley 3 BT34 . . . . 143 C4
Glenaulin Pk (Páirc Ghleann Álainn) BT30 . . . . 62 D4
Glenavon Cres BT66 . . . . 42 A3
Glenavon La BT66 . . . . 41 F2
Glenavy Gdns BT28 . . . . 37 E8
Glenavy Rd BT67 . . . . 34 E6
Glenbank Rd BT62 . . . . 55 A3
Glenbeigh Dr BT8 . . . . 22 B4
Glenbrae BT25 . . . . 58 B4
Glen Brae BT18 . . . . 9 F5
Glenbrook Ave BT5 . . . . 15 D4
Glenbrook Cottages 3
BT66 . . . . 41 F3
Glenbrook Rd BT23 . . . . 19 D6
Glenburn Pk BT20 . . . . 4 E5
Glenburn Rd
Banbridge BT32 . . . . 119 E7
Newtownards BT23 . . . . 19 D7
Glen Cl BT67 . . . . 35 B7
Glencorran Rd BT35 . . . . 115 A3
Glencourt BT61 . . . . 60 B6
GLENCRAIG BT18 . . . . 1 H3
Glencraig Curative Sch
BT18 . . . . 1 G4
Glencraig Integrated Prim Sch BT18 . . . . 2 A4
Glencraig Pk BT18 . . . . 1 G3
Glencregagh Ct BT6 . . . . 22 B5
Glencregagh Dr BT6 . . . . 22 B5
Glencregagh Pk BT6 . . . . 22 B5
Glencregagh Rd BT8 . . . . 22 B5
Glen Cres BT67 . . . . 35 A7
Glencroft BT67 . . . . 43 C6
Glencroft Ave BT23 . . . . 25 A3
Glencroft Dr BT23 . . . . 25 A3
Glen Ct
Lisburn BT27 . . . . 38 B2
Newry BT35 . . . . 64 B4
Glendale Ave BT20 . . . . 4 C2
Glendale Ave E BT8 . . . . 22 B4
Glendale Ave N BT8 . . . . 22 B4
Glendale Ave S BT8 . . . . 22 B4
Glendale Ave W BT8 . . . . 22 B4
Glendale Pk BT8 . . . . 22 A4
Glendarragh BT4 . . . . 9 B2
Glendarragh Mews BT4 . . . 9 B2
Glendavagh Rd BT69 . . . . 82 A3
Glendesha Rd BT35 . . . . 140 B1
Glendhu Gr 1 BT4 . . . . 9 A1
Glendhu Manor BT4 . . . . 9 A1
Glendhu Pk BT4 . . . . 9 B1
Glendowan Way 1 BT19 . 13 D8
Glendower St BT6 . . . . 15 B2
Glendun Pk BT20 . . . . 4 C2
Gleneagles Gdns 3 BT16 . 17 D3
Glen Ebor Hts BT4 . . . . 9 C1
Glen Ebor Pk BT4 . . . . 16 B8
Glenfarne St BT13 . . . . 14 B7
Glenfield Rd BT66 . . . . 41 F4
Glenford Rd BT23 . . . . 19 C6
Glenford Rd Ind Est BT23 . 19 C6
Glenford Way BT23 . . . . 19 C6
Glengall St BT12 . . . . 154 C2
Glenganagh Pk 7 BT19 . . . 5 B7
Glenganagh View 6 BT19 . . 5 B7
Glenhead Rd BT31 . . . . 120 F8
Glen Hill BT35 . . . . 64 C4
Glenhill Pk BT35 . . . . 64 C4
Glenholm Ave BT8 . . . . 22 B4
Glenholm Cres BT8 . . . . 22 B4
Glenholm Dr BT8 . . . . 22 B4
Glenholme Ave BT66 . . . . 41 E3
Glenholme Pk BT66 . . . . 41 E3
Glenholm Pk BT8 . . . . 22 B4
Glenhone Rd BT34 . . . . 119 B2
Glenhoy Dr BT5 . . . . 15 D3
Glenhugh Cres BT8 . . . . 22 A2
Glenhugh Pk BT8 . . . . 22 A2
Glenlea Gr BT4 . . . . 9 B1
Glenlea Pk BT4 . . . . 9 B1
Glenloch Gdns BT4 . . . . 9 B1
Glenlola Collegiate Sch
BT20 . . . . 4 B2
Glenlough BT24 . . . . 59 D4
Glenloughan
Craigavon BT63 . . . . 101 F5
Newry BT34 . . . . 144 D1
Glenloughan Rd
Banbridge BT32 . . . . 102 A5
Craigavon BT63 . . . . 101 F5
Newry BT34 . . . . 144 D2
Glenloughan Upper
BT34 . . . . 144 C2
Glenluce Dr BT4 . . . . 9 B1
Glenluce Gn BT4 . . . . 9 B1
Glenluce Wlk BT4 . . . . 9 A1
Glenlyon Pk★ BT18 . . . . 9 F6
Glenmachan Ave BT4 . . . 16 C7
Glenmachan Dr BT4 . . . . 16 C8
Glenmachan Gr BT4 . . . . 16 C7
Glenmachan Mews BT4 . . 16 C8
Glenmachan Pk BT4 . . . . 9 C1
Glenmachan Rd BT4 . . . . 9 B1
Glenmachan St BT12 . . . . 14 A2
Glenmahon Ave BT62 . . . . 51 E2
Glenmahon Pk BT62 . . . . 51 E2
Glen-mhachna BT61 . . . . 60 B5
Glenmill BT34 . . . . 119 D2
Glenmillan Dr BT4 . . . . 16 B8
Glenmillan Pk BT4 . . . . 16 B8
Glenmiskan 10 BT34 . . . 143 C3
Glenmore Activity Ctr★
BT27 . . . . 26 D4
Glenmore Dr BT27 . . . . 26 D4
Glenmore Rd BT35 . . . . 130 A1
Glenmore St BT5 . . . . 15 B5
Glenmore Wlk BT27 . . . . 26 D4
Glenmount Ave BT23 . . . . 19 C6
Glenmount Dr BT23 . . . . 19 C7
Glenmount Mews BT23 . . . 19 C7
Glenmount Pk BT23 . . . . 19 C7
Glen Mullan BT34 . . . . 64 F8
Glennor Cres BT8 . . . . 29 C2
Glennor Cres E BT8 . . . . 29 C2
Glennor Cres W BT8 . . . . 29 C2
Glenowna Dr BT60 . . . . 60 B4
Glenpark St BT14 . . . . 14 A8
Glenpatrick Lawns BT35 . . 64 C8
Glen Pk
Bangor BT20 . . . . 3 E4
Comber BT23 . . . . 25 B2
Glenravel St BT15 . . . . 14 D7
Glen Rd
Banbridge BT32 . . . . 104 C5
Bangor BT20 . . . . 3 E4
Belfast BT4 . . . . 16 D8
Castlereagh BT5 . . . . 15 F1
Castlewellan BT31 . . . . 104 D4
Comber BT23 . . . . 25 B3
Craigavon BT67 . . . . 35 C7
Downpatrick BT30 . . . . 124 E7
Dromara BT25 . . . . 87 A3
Hillsborough BT26 . . . . 46 E4
Holywood BT18 . . . . 1 D2
Keady BT60 . . . . 114 A3
Lisburn BT27 . . . . 27 D1
Newry BT34 . . . . 117 F1
Newtownards BT23 . . . . 24 E3
Glen Rise BT5 . . . . 16 A1
Glenroe Meghaberry
BT67 . . . . 35 B7
Glenrosa St BT15 . . . . 14 D8
Glen-ross 13 BT34 . . . . 143 C3
Glensanda Crescent 1
BT35 . . . . 64 C7
Glenshane Ave BT66 . . . . 42 C2
Glenshane Cl BT66 . . . . 42 C3
Glensharragh Gdns BT6 . . 22 D8
Glensharragh Pk 3 BT6 . . 22 D8
Glenshesk Pk BT20 . . . . 4 C2
Glenside
Castlereagh BT6 . . . . 22 C7
Comber BT23 . . . . 25 B3
Glenside Ave BT27 . . . . 28 A3
Glenside Pk BT27 . . . . 28 A3
Glen The
Craigavon BT67 . . . . 32 E7
Newry BT35 . . . . 64 C4
Glentoran Pl 14 BT6 . . . . 15 A4
Glenvale Cres BT35 . . . . 64 C4
Glenvale Hts BT34 . . . . 132 D6
Glenvale Rd BT34 . . . . 132 F7
Glenvarlock St BT5 . . . . 15 C3
Glenveigh BT35 . . . . 64 A3
Glenview
Comber BT23 . . . . 25 B3
Craigavon BT67 . . . . 35 B7
Hillsborough BT26 . . . . 89 D7
Glen View BT19 . . . . 5 A4
GLEN VIEW BT34 . . . . 118 B5
Glenview Ave
Castlereagh BT5 . . . . 23 A8
Holywood BT18 . . . . 9 F6
Glenview Cres BT5 . . . . 22 F8
Glenview Dr
Castlereagh BT5 . . . . 23 A8
Lurgan BT66 . . . . 42 C3
Glenview Gdns
Castlereagh BT5 . . . . 16 A1
5 Keady BT60 . . . . 114 A3
Glenview Hts BT5 . . . . 23 A8
Glenview Ind Est BT23 . . . 30 F6
Glenview Pk
Bangor BT19 . . . . 3 D4
1 Castlereagh BT5 . . . . 15 F1
Lurgan BT66 . . . . 42 C3
Newtownards BT23 . . . . 19 D7
Glenview Rd
Ballynahinch BT24 . . . . 91 A7
Holywood BT18 . . . . 9 F6
Glenview St BT14 . . . . 14 A8
Glenwherry Pl 6 BT6 . . . . 15 A4
Glenwood Copse BT17 . . . 26 E7
Glenwood Pk BT17 . . . . 26 E7
Glenwood Pl BT13 . . . . 154 A4
Glenwood Prim Sch
BT13 . . . . 154 A4
Glenwood Row BT17 . . . . 26 F8
Glenwood St BT13 . . . . 154 A4
Glin Ree Ct BT34 . . . . 64 D7
Gloucester Ave
Donaghadee BT21 . . . . 67 A8
Portadown BT63 . . . . 52 B5
Gloucester Ct BT26 . . . . 47 D7
Gloucester Pk BT26 . . . . 47 D7
Gloucester St BT1 . . . . 155 B3
Glovet BT30 . . . . 124 B6
Glrncairn BT27 . . . . 38 B2
Goban St BT63 . . . . 51 E5
Gobhan Cl BT63 . . . . 52 B7
Godfrey Ave BT20 . . . . 4 D5
Goland Rd BT60 . . . . 97 F1
Golf Lks Cres BT33 . . . . 63 D6
Golf Lks Dr BT33 . . . . 63 D6
Golf Lks Rd BT33 . . . . 63 E6
Golf Lks View BT33 . . . . 63 E7
Golf Rd BT19 . . . . 2 D5
Golf Terr BT32 . . . . 61 C6
Goragh BT35 . . . . 131 E7
Goragh Rd BT35 . . . . 131 E7
Gordonall BT22 . . . . 70 A5
Gordon's Fort★ BT60 . . . 114 C3
Gordons La BT35 . . . . 131 C3
Gordon St BT1 . . . . 155 B4
Gorestown La BT71 . . . . 83 F8
Gorestown Rd
11 Moy BT71 . . . . 72 A1
Moy BT71 . . . . 84 A8
Gorse Hill BT23 . . . . 30 E6
Gorse Hill Cl BT23 . . . . 30 F6
Gorse Hill Glen BT23 . . . . 30 E6
Gorse Hill Rd BT23 . . . . 30 E6
Gorse Hill Rise BT23 . . . . 30 E6
Gort BT70 . . . . 82 D7
Gortgrib BT5 . . . . 16 D2
Gortgrib Dr BT5 . . . . 16 D2
Gortin Dr BT5 . . . . 16 D3
Gortin Pk BT5 . . . . 16 C3
Gortland Ave 3 BT5 . . . . 16 D2
Gortland Pk BT5 . . . . 16 D2
Gortlands Mews 1 BT5 . . 16 D2
Gortmalegg BT60 . . . . 96 E5
Gortmerron BT70 . . . . 82 E7
Gortnacor BT67 . . . . 35 F3
Gortnacor Lower BT67 . . 35 F3
Gortnacor Upper BT67 . . 35 F5
Gortnahowen BT34 . . . . 65 C5
Gortnamony BT67 . . . . 33 F1
Gortoille BT60 . . . . 115 D4
Gort Rd BT70 . . . . 82 D8
Gortrea BT71 . . . . 72 C3
Gorvenors Ridge Pk BT26 47 E7
Gosford Gdns 1 BT60 . . . 116 A8
Gosford Rd
Armagh BT60 . . . . 99 F1
Markethill BT60 . . . . 100 A1
Gospel La BT32 . . . . 61 D4
Gosselin Ave BT66 . . . . 41 E8
Gosselin Dr BT66 . . . . 41 E8
Gosselin Pk BT66 . . . . 41 E8
Gotha St BT6 . . . . 15 A3
Gough Ave BT60 . . . . 60 E5
Govan Dr 1 BT5 . . . . 16 E3
Governor's Bridge BT9 . . . 21 D8
Governors Gate BT26 . . . . 47 E6
Governors Rd
3 Lisburn BT28 . . . . 26 A1
Lisburn BT28 . . . . 38 A8
Gowan Hts BT27 . . . . 27 C6
Gowan Manor BT32 . . . . 61 A3
Gowanvale Dr BT32 . . . . 61 B3
Goward BT34 . . . . 134 E6
Goward Dolmen Chambered Grave★ BT34 . . . . 134 E7
Goward Rd BT34 . . . . 134 D7
GOWDYSTOWN BT25 . . . . 87 D4
Gowdystown Rd BT32 . . . 87 D3
Gowland Mdw BT22 . . . . 81 D5
Gowland Rd BT22 . . . . 81 D5
Grace Ave BT5 . . . . 15 D4
Gracefield Lodge BT67 . . . 42 F6
Grace Hill BT16 . . . . 17 C3
Gracemanor BT62 . . . . 55 D8
Gracemount Pk BT8 . . . . 22 B2
Grace St BT2 . . . . 155 B2
Gracey Dr BT66 . . . . 42 A3
Graceystown Rd BT32 . . . 103 B8
Graffan Gdns BT23 . . . . 25 E4
Graham Ct 2 BT67 . . . . 34 C2
Graham Gdns
Belfast BT6 . . . . 15 C1
Lisburn BT28 . . . . 26 B1
Graham House Hospl BT8 22 B1
Graham Ind Pk BT3 . . . . 8 B3
Grahamsbridge Pk BT16 . . 17 C4
Grahamsbridge Rd BT16 . . 17 C3
Graham St 3 BT27 . . . . 26 C1
Grahamville Est BT34 . . . 153 B6
Grallaghgreenan BT34 119 E4
Grallagh Rd BT34 . . . . 119 E4
Grampian Ave BT4 . . . . 15 D5
Granagh BT22 . . . . 94 E1
Granary The
Ballygowan BT23 . . . . 31 E1
4 Waringstown BT66 . . . . 86 C8
Grandmere Pk BT20 . . . . 4 E4
Grand Opera House★
BT12 . . . . 154 C2
Grand Par BT5 . . . . 15 D2
Grand Prix Gr BT16 . . . . 17 B4
Grand Prix Pk BT16 . . . . 17 B3
Grand St BT27 . . . . 26 D3
Granemore BT60 . . . . 114 E2
Granemore Hts (Ard-na-grainseach) BT60 . . . . 114 B3
Granemore Rd BT60 . . . . 114 D3
Grange BT34 . . . . 152 F4
Grange Ave
Bangor BT20 . . . . 3 E3
6 Saintfield BT24 . . . . 77 C3
GRANGE BLUNDEL BT61 . . 84 D3
Grange Blundel Rd BT61 . 84 D4
Grange Cl
1 Castlewellan BT31 . . . . 122 B4
Saintfield BT24 . . . . 77 C3
Grange Cres
Bangor BT20 . . . . 3 E3
1 Saintfield BT24 . . . . 77 C3
Grangee BT22 . . . . 66 E2
Grangee Rd BT22 . . . . 66 E2
Grange Hts 3 BT24 . . . . 77 C3
Grange Lower BT62 . . . . 85 E7
Grange Manor BT34 . . . . 153 B8
Grangemore BT61 . . . . 98 B8
Grange Pk
Bangor BT20 . . . . 3 E3
Saintfield BT24 . . . . 77 B3
Grange Pk Prim Sch BT20 . . 3 E3
Grange Prim Sch BT34 . . 152 F4
Grange Rd
Armagh BT61 . . . . 85 E6
Bangor BT20 . . . . 3 E3
2 Castlewellan BT31 . . . . 122 B4
Downpatrick BT30 . . . . 125 B8
Dungannon BT71 . . . . 72 A3
Newry BT34 . . . . 152 E4
Grange The
Banbridge BT32 . . . . 61 C2
Belfast BT4 . . . . 16 C7
4 Saintfield BT24 . . . . 77 C3
Grange Upper BT61 . . . . 85 D6
Grange View 5 BT24 . . . . 77 C3
Grangeville Pk BT23 . . . . 20 C5
Grangewalls BT30 . . . . 125 C8
Grangewood Ave BT16 . . . 17 C6
Grangewood Cres BT16 . . . 17 C6
Grangewood Dr BT16 . . . . 17 C5
Grangewood Glen BT16 . . 17 C6
Grangewood Gr BT16 . . . . 17 C6
Grangewood Hill BT16 . . . 17 C6
Grangewood Hts BT16 . . . 17 B5
Grangewood La BT16 . . . . 17 C6
Grangewood Manor BT16 17 B6
Grangewood Par BT16 . . . 17 C6
Grangewood Pk BT16 . . . . 17 B5
Grangewood Rd BT16 . . . . 17 C6
Grangewood Terr BT16 . . . 17 B6
Grangicam Rd BT30 . . . . 108 E1
Granite Cres BT34 . . . . 132 D6
Granite View BT34 . . . . 132 D6
Gransha
Bangor BT19 . . . . 66 A6
Dromore BT25 . . . . 104 F5
Newry BT34 . . . . 119 B4
Newtownards BT22 . . . . 80 E5
Newtownards BT23 . . . . 24 B2
Gransha Cl
Newtownards BT23 . . . . 19 F4
Newtownards BT23 . . . . 24 D2
Gransha La BT16 . . . . 17 B2
Gransha Pk BT20 . . . . 4 D2
Gransha Rd
Bangor BT19 . . . . 4 D1
Belfast BT5 . . . . 24 B6
Dromara BT25 . . . . 104 F5
Dundonald BT16 . . . . 17 B1
Newry BT34 . . . . 119 C3
Newtownards BT23 . . . . 23 E2
Gransha Rd S
Bangor BT19 . . . . 13 F3

Gransha Rd S *continued*
Dromara BT25 . . . . 104 F5
Gransha Wlk BT16 . . . . 17 B3
Grantham Gdns BT61. . . . . 60 E5
Grantham Pk BT63 . . . . 51 F6
Granton Pk BT5. . . . . 16 E3
Grants Rd BT35 . . . . 141 B1
Granville Dr BT26 . . . . 47 E7
Granville Gdns
Banbridge BT32. . . . . 61 B4
Portadown BT63 . . . . 52 B4
Granville Hts BT26 . . . . 47 E7
Granville Pl BT12 . . . . 154 B2
Granville Rd BT63. . . . . 52 B5
Granville Sq BT63. . . . . 52 B5
Grattans La BT32 . . . . 118 E7
Grattan St BT67. . . . . 42 A6
Gravelhill Rd BT28 . . . . 36 D6
Graysfield 7 BT30. . . . . . . 92 B4
Gray's Hill BT20. . . . . 4 A4
Gray's La BT18. . . . . 9 D7
Grays Pk BT18 . . . . 2 A3
Gray's Pk BT8 . . . . 21 D2
Gray's Pk Ave BT8 . . . . 21 D2
Grays Pk Dr BT8 . . . . 21 D2
Grays Pk Gdns 3 BT8 . . . . 21 D2
Great Georges Ave 1
BT34 . . . . 65 D2
Great Georges St N BT34 . 65 C2
Great Georges St S BT34 . 65 C1
Great George's St BT15 . . 14 D7
Great Northern Mall
BT12. . . . . 154 C2
Great Northern St BT9 . . . 14 A1
Great Patrick St BT1 . . . . 155 B4
Great Victoria St BT2 . . . 155 A2
Great Victoria Street Sta
BT12. . . . . 154 C2
Green Acres BT19. . . . . 13 D7
Greenan
Armagh BT61. . . . . 84 F3
Banbridge BT32. . . . . 102 C2
Dromore BT25. . . . . 87 C5
Newry BT34. . . . . 142 B7
Greenan Ct BT32. . . . . 102 C3
Greenan Dr BT32 . . . . 102 C3
Greenan Lough Rd BT34. 142 B7
Greenan Rd
Banbridge BT32. . . . . 102 B1
Newry BT34. . . . . 64 F1
Newry BT35. . . . . 118 A8
Greenavon Mews BT27 . . . 38 C8
Greenbank BT27 . . . . 26 B5
Greenbank Ave BT21 . . . . . 67 A8
Greenbank Campus BT34. 64 E1
Greenbank Ind Est BT34. . 64 E2
Greenburn Way BT27. . . . . . 26 C7
Greencastle BT34 . . . . . 152 D4
Green Castle★ BT34 . . . . 152 C4
Greencastle Pier Rd
BT34 . . . . 152 D4
Greencastle Rd BT34. . . . 153 B6
Greencastle St BT34 . . . . 153 C7
Green Cres BT5. . . . . 16 A4
Greendale Cres 2 BT34 . 143 B3
Green Dyke Wlk 3 BT25 . 58 D6
Greenfield Cl BT60. . . . . . . 60 F3
Greenfield Ct BT60. . . . . . . 60 F3
Greenfield Dr
Annalong BT34 . . . . 146 C4
Armagh BT60. . . . . 60 F3
Greenfield Pk
Armagh BT60. . . . . 60 F3
Newry BT34. . . . . 64 E6
Greenfields BT60 . . . . 60 F3
Greenfield Way BT60. . . . . . 60 F3
Green Gables BT23. . . . . . . 13 B6
Greengraves BT23 . . . . . 18 C4
Greengraves Rd BT16 . . . . . 17 F3
Greenhill Pk
Lurgan BT66 . . . . 41 F3
Newcastle BT33. . . . . 63 B4
Greenhill Rd
Banbridge BT32. . . . . 104 A1
Newry BT34. . . . . 119 C1
Green Island Pk BT23 . . . . 19 F7
Greenisland Rd BT62. . . . . 73 F7
Green La
Bangor BT19 . . . . 13 A6
Downpatrick BT30. . . . . 91 C4
Lisburn BT27 . . . . 26 E5
Millisle BT21 . . . . 67 A5
Greenland Dr BT19. . . . . 4 F5
Greenland Drive Link BT19 . 4 F5
Greenland St BT13 . . . . . . 154 C4
Greenlea Cres BT23. . . . . . 20 B4
Greenlea Dr BT23. . . . . 20 B4
Greenlea Gdns 1 BT5. . . . 16 A1
Greenlea Pk BT23. . . . . 20 B4
Green Mount 3 BT5 . . . . . 16 A1
Greenmount Ave BT20 . . . . . 3 F3
Greenmount Gdns BT27 . . 38 C8
Greenmount Pk BT27 . . . . 38 C8
Greenmount Pl 13 BT15 . . 14 D8
Greenoge BT25 . . . . 45 D1
Greenogue Rd BT25. . . . . . 45 E1
GREENORE (AN GRIANFORT)
BT34 . . . . 152 A3
Greenore Golf Club 151 F3
Greenore St BT6. . . . . 15 B3
Greenpark Cres 2 BT60. . 60 B3
Greenpark Hts 4 BT60 . . . 60 B3
Greenpark Manor 1
BT60 . . . . 60 B3
Greenpark Rd BT34 . . . . . 143 B4
Greenspark View 3 BT60 . 60 B3
Green Pastures BT8. . . . . . 29 C1
Green Pk Ave BT60. . . . . . 116 A8

Green Rd
Ardglass BT30. . . . . 125 F5
Belfast BT5 . . . . 16 A4
Bessbrook BT35 . . . . 131 C4
Lisburn BT27. . . . . 38 E2
Markethill BT60. . . . . 100 A1
Millisle BT21 . . . . 67 A5
Newry BT35. . . . . 141 B7
Newtownards BT23. . . . . . . 13 C5
Greenridge Pk BT19. . . . . . . 5 A5
Green Side BT20. . . . . 4 B1
Greens Rd BT24. . . . . 77 F2
Green The
Bangor BT20 . . . . 4 A1
Craigavon BT63 . . . . 52 C1
Holywood BT18 . . . . 9 C5
Kircubbin BT22 . . . . 80 D7
Newtownards BT23. . . . . . . 12 F5
Downpatrick BT30. . . . . 62 C4
4 Drumaness BT24 . . . . . . 91 B1
Green Vale BT27. . . . . 27 B5
Greenview Gdns BT62. . . . 51 C4
Greenville Ave 1 BT5. . . . 15 D4
Greenville Rd BT5. . . . . 15 C4
Greenville St BT5 . . . . 15 C4
Greenway
Belfast BT6 . . . . 22 C8
Newtownards BT23. . . . . . . 13 A5
Greenway Ind Est BT23. . . 13 A6
Greenwell Pl BT23 . . . . 19 E4
Greenwell St BT23 . . . . 19 E4
Greenwood BT27 . . . . 38 C8
Greenwood Ave
Belfast BT4 . . . . 16 A5
Newtownards BT23. . . . . . . 19 D7
Greenwood Dr BT34. . . . . . 64 F1
Greenwood Glen BT8 . . . . 21 F1
Greenwood Hill BT8. . . . . . 21 F1
Greenwood Pk 4 BT4. . . . 16 A5
Greenwood Prim Sch BT4 16 A5
Greer Pk Ave BT8 . . . . 21 E1
Greer Pk Dr BT8 . . . . 21 F1
Greer Pk Hts BT8 . . . . 21 F1
Gregg St Mews BT27 . . . . . 26 C1
Greggs Quay BT5 . . . . 155 C3
Gregg St BT27 . . . . 26 C1
Gregorlough BT25 . . . . . 44 E1
Gregorlough Rd BT25 . . . . 44 E1
Gregstown BT23 . . . . 20 A3
Gregstown Pk BT23 . . . . . . 20 B3
Gresham St BT1 . . . . 155 A4
GREYABBEY (AN MHAINISTIR
LIATH) BT22. . . . . 70 C4
Grey Abbey Prim Sch
BT22. . . . . 70 C4
Greyabbey Rd BT22 . . . . . . 70 E5
Greycastle Manor BT6. . . . 22 F7
Greyhillan BT60. . . . . . . 130 D7
Grey Point BT19 . . . . 2 D7
Grey Point Fort★ BT19 . . . . 2 D7
Greystone Rd BT22. . . . . . . 67 D1
Greystown Rd BT30 . . . . . . 92 E1
Grillagh Wy BT6 . . . . 22 B8
Grocers Rd BT34. . . . . 119 E2
Groomsport Bypass BT19. . 5 A6
Groomsport House Rd
BT19 . . . . 5 C7
Groomsport Integrated Prim
Sch BT19. . . . . 5 B7
GROOMSPORT (PORT AN
GHIOLLA GHRUAMA)
BT19 . . . . 5 A8
Groomsport Rd BT20. . . . . . 4 E5
Groomsport St BT14 . . . . . . 14 B8
Grosvenor Ct BT12 . . . . . . 154 B2
Grosvenor Gram Sch BT5 15 E2
Grosvenor Rd BT12 . . . . . 154 C2
Grosvenor Recn Ctr
BT12. . . . . 154 B2
Grove Cres BT24. . . . . 59 C5
Grovefield Pl 9 BT6 . . . . . 15 A4
Grovefield St 17 BT6 . . . . . 15 A4
Grove Gdns
Armagh BT60. . . . . 60 E5
Killyleagh BT30 . . . . 93 B5
Grove Hill
Banbridge BT32. . . . . 61 A4
Kilkeel BT34. . . . . 153 B7
Grove Hill Gdns BT20. . . . . . 4 E4
Grovehill Rd
Banbridge BT32. . . . . 102 E1
Craigavon BT67 . . . . 44 F7
Grove Mdw BT32. . . . . 61 A5
Grove Pk
Bangor BT20 . . . . 4 D4
Hillsborough BT26. . . . . 37 B1
Killyleagh BT30 . . . . 93 C5
Grove Pl BT30 . . . . 93 C5
Grove Prim Sch BT60 . . . . 60 F4
Grove Rd
Ballynahinch BT24. . . . . 59 B1
Ballynahinch BT24. . . . . 90 E2
Dromara BT25. . . . . 88 D7
Newry BT34. . . . . 146 C4
Grove St E BT5 . . . . 15 C3
Grove Sh Ctr The BT30 . . . 62 B4
Grove St BT27 . . . . 26 D2
Grove The
Ballynahinch BT24. . . . . 59 B4
Holywood BT18 . . . . 9 D5
Lisburn BT27 . . . . 38 E4
Grove Tree N BT12. . . . . . 154 B3
Grove Tree S BT12 . . . . . . 154 B2
Growell BT26 . . . . 89 B6
Guiness BT24. . . . . 106 C6
Guiness Prim Sch BT24 . 106 D6
Guiness Rd BT24. . . . . 106 C6
Guineways BT34 . . . . . . 144 C1

Guineways Upper
BT34 . . . . 144 C1
Gulf La BT26. . . . . 46 D4
Gulf Rd BT26 . . . . 46 D5
Gullion View BT35 . . . . . . 141 A5
Gwyneth Pk BT19 . . . . 3 B5

H

HACKBALLS CROSS. 148 F3
Hacknahay BT63 . . . . 52 E1
Haddington Gdns BT6. . . . 15 B1
Haig St BT5. . . . . 15 B4
Halbertyon Gdns BT22 . . . 81 C8
Halcombe St 20 BT6. . . . . . 15 A4
Half Acre La BT23. . . . . 19 C5
Halford Mews BT60 . . . . . 100 A1
Halfpenny Gate Rd BT67. . 35 C3
Halftown Rd BT27. . . . . 37 A5
Halfway Rd BT32. . . . . 87 D2
Halliday's Rd 9 BT15 . . . . 14 C8
Hall Rampart BT66. . . . . . . 74 D7
Hall Rd
Ballynahinch BT24. . . . . 59 F7
Craigavon BT66. . . . . 86 E6
Newry BT35. . . . . 130 E1
Halls Mill Gn BT63 . . . . 86 B2
Halstein Dr BT5. . . . . 15 F4
Hambleden BT27. . . . . 27 B6
Hamel Dr BT6 . . . . 22 C8
Hamill St BT12. . . . . 154 C3
Hamilton Gdns BT66 . . . . . 42 B4
Hamilton Harty Ct BT26 . . 47 C7
Hamilton Rd
Bangor BT20 . . . . 4 B4
Belfast BT3 . . . . 15 B7
HAMILTONSBAWN BT61 . . . 99 F6
Hamiltonsbawn Prim Sch
BT61. . . . . 99 E6
Hamiltonsbawn Rd BT60 . 60 F5
Hamilton St
Belfast BT2 . . . . 155 B2
Lurgan BT66 . . . . 42 B4
Hamilton Villas BT20. . . . . . . 4 E5
Hamlets The BT4 . . . . 16 B5
Hammond Farm BT67 . . . . 35 A7
Hammond Rd BT28. . . . . . . 34 F8
Hampden Gr BT23 . . . . 19 C2
Hampton Coll 6 BT9 . . . . 14 C1
Hampton Ct
5 Ballygowan BT23 . . . . . . 77 F8
Dromara BT25. . . . . 58 C4
Holywood BT18 . . . . 9 F6
Portadown BT62 . . . . 51 C4
Hampton Dr
10 Bangor BT19 . . . . 13 D7
Belfast BT7 . . . . 21 E8
Hampton Gdns BT19 . . . . . 13 D7
Hampton Gr 1 BT7 . . . . . . 21 E8
Hampton La 5 BT19 . . . . . 13 E7
Hampton Manor BT7. . . . . 21 F6
Hampton Manor Dr BT7. . 21 E6
Hampton Mews 12 BT19. . 13 D7
Hampton Par BT7. . . . . 21 E8
Hampton Pk
Bangor BT19 . . . . 13 D7
Belfast BT7 . . . . 21 F6
Hampton Pl 2 BT7 . . . . . . 21 E8
Hampton Rise BT25 . . . . . . 58 B4
Hamptons The BT23. . . . . . 31 E1
Hampton Strand 3 BT7. . . 21 E8
Hancock St BT27. . . . . 26 C1
Hanna St 4 BT15. . . . . 14 E8
Hannay's Hill BT19. . . . . 5 C2
Hannon Dr BT66 . . . . 42 A3
Hanover Chase BT19 . . . . . . 4 D2
Hanover Cres BT19. . . . . 4 E1
Hanover Ct BT19. . . . . 4 D1
Hanover Dale BT19. . . . . 4 D2
Hanover FC BT62 . . . . 51 C3
Hanover Glen BT19 . . . . 4 E1
Hanover Gr 11 BT19. . . . . . . 4 E1
Hanover Hill BT19. . . . . 4 D2
Hanover Rd BT19 . . . . 4 D1
Hanover Sq 8 BT19. . . . . . . 4 E1
Hanover St BT62 . . . . 51 D4
Hanslough BT60 . . . . . . 112 F6
Hanslough Rd BT60 . . . . . 112 D5
Hanwood Ave BT16 . . . . . . 17 A3
Hanwood Cotts BT16. . . . . 17 B3
Hanwood Ct BT16. . . . . 17 B3
Hanwood Dr BT16. . . . . 17 A3
Hanwood Farm BT16. . . . . 17 A3
Hanwood Hts BT16. . . . . . . 17 A3
Hanwood Pk BT16 . . . . 17 A3
Harberton Pk BT32. . . . . . . 61 A2
Harbour Dr BT34. . . . . 153 C7
Harbour Rd
Ballywalter BT22. . . . . 71 A5
Groomsport BT19 . . . . 5 B7
Kilkeel BT34. . . . . 153 C7
Newtownards BT22. . . . . . . 81 D8
Harcourts Hill BT62 . . . . . . 55 E8
Hardcastle St BT7. . . . . . . 155 A1
Hardford Link BT23 . . . . . . 19 C5
Hardford Mews BT23. . . . . 19 C5
Hardinge Pl 3 BT15 . . . . . 14 D8
Harding Meml Prim Sch
BT6. . . . . 15 B2
Hardy Meml Prim Sch 8
BT61. . . . . 99 E8
Harehills Dr BT20 . . . . 3 E1
Hares Rd BT35. . . . . 129 B2
Harford St BT62 . . . . 51 E4
Harkness Par BT4. . . . . 15 C6
Harland Dr BT4 . . . . 15 A5
Harland Pk BT4. . . . . 15 D5

Harland Tech Pk BT3. . . . . 15 B6
Harland & Wolff Shipyard
BT3. . . . . 15 B7
Harleston St BT9. . . . . 21 D7
Harmony Dr BT27. . . . . 26 C4
Harmony Hill BT27. . . . . . . 26 C3
Harmony Hill Prim Sch
BT27. . . . . 26 C4
Harmony Hts 1 BT34 . . . 132 C2
Harmony Pk 7 BT24 . . . . . 91 B1
Harmony Rd BT24. . . . . 59 D5
Harmony St
Ballynahinch BT24. . . . . 59 D5
Belfast BT2 . . . . 155 A2
Harmony Way BT24 . . . . . . 59 D5
Harper Pk BT19. . . . . 3 C2
Harper St (Sráid Harper) 24
BT5 . . . . 15 A5
Harrow St 10 BT7 . . . . 14 E1
Harrybrook St BT13 . . . . . . 14 B7
Harry'sloney BT30 . . . . 62 D6
Harry's Rd BT26 . . . . 37 C2
Harryville Pk BT27 . . . . 38 B7
Hartfield Ave BT62. . . . . . . 51 B4
Hartfield Sq BT62. . . . . 51 B4
Hartington St BT7. . . . . . . 155 A1
Hart Meml Prim Sch
BT62. . . . . 51 C4
Hartmore Gdns BT62. . . . . 51 B4
Hartwell Pl 11 BT15 . . . . . 14 D8
Harvey Ct 3 BT5. . . . . 15 B5
Harwich Mews BT26 . . . . . 47 C8
Hatfield St BT7 . . . . 14 E2
Hatters Rd BT35 . . . . 129 B7
Hatton Dr BT6 . . . . 15 B3
Havelock Pl BT34 . . . . 65 C2
Havelock St BT7 . . . . 155 B1
Hawe Ct BT19. . . . . 5 B1
Hawe Pk BT19 . . . . 5 A1
Hawe Rd BT19 . . . . 5 C1
Hawood Cres 1 BT34 . . . . 153 E8
Hawood Way 2 BT34 . . . . 153 E8
Hawthorn Ave BT66 . . . . . . 41 E6
Hawthorn Bsns Ctr BT12 . 21 A8
Hawthorn Cl BT23. . . . . 20 B5
Hawthornden Dr BT4. . . . . 16 B6
Hawthornden Gdns 1
BT4 . . . . 16 B6
Hawthornden Pk BT4 . . . . 16 B5
Hawthornden Rd BT4 . . . . 16 B5
Hawthornden Way BT4. . . 16 B6
Hawthorn Dr BT63 . . . . 53 E5
Hawthorne Ct BT20 . . . . 3 E2
Hawthorne Dr BT20 . . . . 3 F2
Hawthorne Hill BT32 . . . . . 61 A3
Hawthorne La
Lisburn BT28 . . . . 26 A3
Newry BT35. . . . . 129 D5
Hawthorn Hil BT23. . . . . . . 20 B5
Hawthorn Hill
Dromara BT25. . . . . 88 E2
Newry BT35. . . . . 64 C3
Portadown BT63 . . . . 52 B6
Hawthorn Manor BT8 . . . . 29 C2
Hawthorn Ridge BT21. . . . . . 6 E1
Hawthorn St BT12. . . . . . . 154 A2
Hawthorns The BT63 . . . . . 52 B8
Hawthorn Wlk 2 BT25 . . . 58 D6
Hayes Pk BT32. . . . . 61 C8
Haymarket Arc BT1 . . . . . 155 A4
Haypark Ave BT7 . . . . 21 E7
Haypark Gdns BT7 . . . . 21 E7
Haywood Ave BT7. . . . . 21 E8
Haywood Dr BT7. . . . . 14 E1
Hazel Ave BT17 . . . . 26 F8
Hazel Bank BT32. . . . . 86 C1
Hazelbank Dr BT34. . . . . . 153 D8
Hazelbrook Ave 1 BT20. . . . 3 F2
Hazeldene Ave BT20 . . . . . . 4 C4
Hazeldene Dr BT20. . . . . 4 C4
Hazeldene Gdns BT20 . . . . . 4 C4
Hazeldene Pk BT20 . . . . 4 C4
Hazelfield St BT13 . . . . 14 B7
Hazelgrove Ave BT67. . . . . 42 D5
Hazelview BT19. . . . . 13 C6
Hazelwood Dr BT23 . . . . . . 20 B6
Hazelwood Gr 6 BT61 . . . 99 E8
Headington Ave BT66 . . . . . 41 E6
Headington Dr BT66 . . . . . 41 E6
Headington Mews BT66 . . 41 E6
Head Rd BT34 . . . . 145 C5
Heather Bank BT25 . . . . . . 88 F2
Heatherbell St BT5. . . . . . . 15 C4
Heathermount Cres BT23. 25 B3
Heathermount Pk BT23. . . 25 B2
Heathers Cl BT67 . . . . 43 D6
Heatherstone Rd BT19 . . . . 5 A5
Hector St BT1 . . . . 155 A4
Hedingham BT67 . . . . 34 A3
Heichbrae Airt (Tullyard
Way) BT6 . . . . 22 E8
Heights The BT30. . . . . 107 D7
HELEN'S BAY (CUAN HÉILIN)
BT19 . . . . 2 E6
Helen's Bay Golf Club BT19 2 E6
Helen's Bay Sta BT19 . . . . . 2 D5
Helens Lea BT5. . . . . 16 D2
Helensview Cres BT23. . . . 19 C8
Helensview Dr BT23. . . . . . 19 C8
Helensview Pk BT23 . . . . . 19 C8
Helgor Pk BT4. . . . . 15 F7
Helgor Pk Mews BT4. . . . . 15 F7
Hemp St BT4 . . . . 15 C5
Henalta Wood 8 BT19. . . . 12 F7
Henderson Ave
Bangor BT19 . . . . 3 C2
Newtownards BT23. . . . . . . 12 F4
Henderson Ct BT4 . . . . 9 B2

Henderson Dr BT19 . . . . 3 C2
Henderson Pk BT19. . . . . 3 C2
Henderson Rd BT19. . . . . 3 B3
Henley Hall BT26 . . . . 46 A8
Hennessy Pk BT34 . . . . 64 D4
Henrietta St BT2. . . . . 155 B2
Henry Pl BT15 . . . . 14 C7
Henry St
Belfast BT1 . . . . 155 A4
Newry BT34. . . . . 64 E6
Herbert St BT14. . . . . 14 A8
Herdman Channel Rd BT3 . 8 A2
Herdstown BT21 . . . . 66 D8
Hermitage
Armagh BT61. . . . . 60 B6
Hillsborough BT26. . . . . 37 B1
Moira BT67 . . . . 34 B2
Hermitage The BT17 . . . . . 27 C6
Heron Cres BT23. . . . . 20 B6
Heron Lodge BT23 . . . . 20 B5
Heron Pk BT23. . . . . 20 B6
Heron Rd BT3 . . . . 8 E3
Heron Ridge BT23 . . . . 20 B6
Herons Rd BT31 . . . . 105 E1
Heron View BT3 . . . . 8 F4
Heron Wood BT25 . . . . 58 E4
Hertford Cres BT28 . . . . . . 37 D8
Hertford Sq BT28 . . . . 37 E8
Hewitt Par BT5 . . . . 15 F4
Hickory Ave BT23 . . . . 19 D6
High Bangor Rd
Bangor BT19 . . . . 5 E2
Donaghadee BT21. . . . . 6 C1
Highfield Gdns BT32 . . . . . 61 B3
Highfield Gr BT64. . . . . 40 E2
Highfield Hts BT64. . . . . . . 40 D2
Highfield Manor BT64. . . . 40 D2
Highfield N Rd BT64 . . . . . 40 D2
Highfield Pk BT64. . . . . 40 D2
Highfield Rd BT64. . . . . 40 D2
Highfields BT35. . . . . 64 C2
Highfields Ave BT35. . . . . . 64 C2
Highfields Dr BT35. . . . . . . 64 C2
High Gn 4 BT30 . . . . 125 F6
Highgrove BT27. . . . . 38 B2
High Pk Ctr BT1 . . . . 155 B3
High Rd BT32. . . . . 120 D7
High Sch Ballynahinch The
BT24. . . . . 59 D6
High St
Ballynahinch BT24. . . . . 59 D4
Bangor BT20 . . . . 4 B4
Belfast BT1 . . . . 155 B3
Bessbrook BT35 . . . . 131 D4
Comber BT23. . . . . 25 D3
Donaghadee BT21. . . . . 67 A8
Gilford BT63 . . . . 57 C2
Holywood BT18 . . . . 9 D6
Keady BT60 . . . . 114 A2
Killyleagh BT30 . . . . 93 C5
Lurgan BT67 . . . . 42 A5
Newry BT34. . . . . 64 D5
Newtownards BT22. . . . . . . 81 C8
Newtownards BT23. . . . . . . 19 D5
Portadown BT62 . . . . 51 E4
Portaferry BT22. . . . . 94 D3
Ardglass BT30. . . . . 125 F6
High Street Ct
Belfast BT1 . . . . 155 B3
Comber BT23. . . . . 25 D3
High Street Gr BT23. . . . . . 25 D3
High Street Mall BT62. . . . 51 E4
High Street Manor BT23. . 25 D3
High Street Sh Arc BT67 . 42 A5
Hilden BT27 . . . . 26 D3
Hilden Brewery★ BT27 . . . 26 D3
Hilden Cres BT27 . . . . 26 D2
Hilden Ct BT27. . . . . 26 D3
Hilden Integrated Prim Sch
BT27. . . . . 26 E3
Hilden Rd BT27 . . . . 26 E4
Hilden Sta BT27 . . . . 26 D4
Hillburn Pk BT6. . . . . 22 D8
Hillcourt BT26 . . . . 47 C7
Hill Cres BT34. . . . . 132 A5
Hillcrest BT20 . . . . 4 A1
Hillcrest Ave BT23 . . . . 19 E6
Hillcrest Cres BT65 . . . . . . 41 C1
Hillcrest Dr BT24 . . . . 59 D4
Hillcrest Gdns BT5 . . . . 15 E4
Hillcrest La BT24. . . . . 59 D4
Hillcrest Manor BT65. . . . . 41 B1
Hillcrest Wlk BT20 . . . . 4 A1
Hillfoot
Groomsport BT19 . . . . 5 A7
Newtownards BT23. . . . . . . 19 B5
Hillfoot Cres BT24 . . . . 59 E4
Hillfoot St BT4. . . . . 15 D6
Hill Gn BT8. . . . . 22 B2
HILLHALL BT27. . . . . 26 F1
Hillhall BT27. . . . . 27 C2
Hillhall Cl 5 BT27 . . . . 26 D1
Hillhall Gdns BT27 . . . . 26 D1
Hillhall Pk BT27. . . . . 26 D1
Hillhall Prim Sch BT27 . . . 27 B1
Hillhall Rd BT27 . . . . 26 E1
Hillhead Cl BT32. . . . . 61 B3
Hillhead Cres BT24. . . . . . . 59 E3
Hillhead Dr BT32. . . . . 61 B3
Hillhead Gdns BT32 . . . . . . 61 B3
Hillhead Pk BT32 . . . . 61 B3
Hillhead Rd
Ballynahinch BT24. . . . . 90 A3
Banbridge BT32. . . . . 104 B3
Belfast BT16 . . . . 24 E7

Hillhead Rd *continued*
Newry BT35 **64** D1
Hillhead Wlk BT32 **61** B3
Hill La BT66 **74** A7
Hillman Cl 8 BT15 **14** D8
Hillman St 9 BT15 **14** D8
Hillmount Dr BT23 **30** F7
Hill Rd
Banbridge BT32 **102** F1
Dromara BT25 **89** E5
Hill St Mews BT18 **9** D7
Hills Ave BT4 **15** D6
Hillsborough BT26 **47** C8
Hillsborough Bypass
Hillsborough BT26 **46** E2
Lisburn BT27 **37** E3
HILLSBOROUGH (CROMGHLINN) BT26 **47** D7
Hillsborough Dr BT6 **15** C3
Hillsborough Fort★ BT26 **47** D6
Hillsborough Gdns BT6 **15** C3
Hillsborough Old Rd BT27 **38** C7
Hillsborough Par BT6 **15** C2
Hillsborough Rd
Belfast BT8 **29** B1
Craigavon BT67 **35** A2
Dromara BT25 **58** E6
Dromara BT25 **89** C2
Hillsborough BT26 **37** E1
Lisburn BT27 **76** C8
Moira BT67 **34** D2
Newtownards BT23 **31** C8
Hillsbrough Rd 2 BT28 **26** A1
Hillside
Ballynahinch BT24 **90** E1
Dromara BT25 **58** D5
Gilford BT63 **57** C3
Mayobridge BT34 **133** B3
Newtownards BT23 **19** D7
Portavogie BT22 **81** D5
Hillside Ave BT61 **99** E5
Hillside Cl 2 BT34 **153** B7
Hillside Cres
Banbridge BT32 **86** D1
Belfast BT9 **21** C6
15 Moy BT71 **72** A1
Newry BT35 **117** D8
Portadown BT63 **52** B6
Hillside Dr
Belfast BT9 **21** C6
Kilkeel BT34 **153** B7
Hillside Gdns
Bangor BT19 **5** A4
Belfast BT9 **21** C6
Hillside Pk
Armagh BT61 **99** E5
Banbridge BT32 **61** B3
Bangor BT19 **5** A4
Belfast BT9 **21** C6
Comber BT23 **25** D3
Hillside Pl BT24 **59** C5
Hillside Rd
Banbridge BT32 **118** E6
Lisburn BT27 **76** C2
Hillside Terr BT26 **37** B2
Hill St
Ardglass BT30 **125** F6
Armagh BT60 **98** B4
Banbridge BT32 **61** E6
Belfast BT1 **155** B4
Gilford BT63 **57** C2
Lisburn BT28 **26** B1
Lurgan BT66 **41** F5
Newry BT34 **64** D6
Hill The BT19 **5** B7
Hill Top BT24 **59** E4
HILLTOWN (BAILE HILL) BT34 **134** A6
Hilltown Rd
Mayobridge BT34 **133** C4
Newcastle BT33 **122** B1
Newry BT34 **121** F1
Rathfriland BT34 **120** A1
Hillview 3 BT30 **125** F6
Hill View BT30 **93** B6
Hillview Ave
Belfast BT5 **15** F4
Lisburn BT27 **26** C5
Hillview Ct 6 BT14 **14** B8
Hillview Ent Pk BT14 **14** B8
Hillview Gdns BT27 **26** C6
Hillview Pk
3 Craigavon BT66 **86** F6
Lisburn BT27 **26** C5
Hillview Pl
Holywood BT18 **9** E6
Moy BT71 **72** A1
Hillview Rd BT14 **14** B8
Hillview Ret Pk BT14 **14** A8
Hilton Pk BT63 **52** D4
Hindsdale Pk BT6 **22** C7
Hobson Pk BT62 **51** C2
HOCKLEY BT61 **85** B1
HODGIN'S CORNER BT61 **99** F8
Hogarth St BT15 **14** D8
Hogstown BT21 **66** E8
Hogstown Rd BT21 **66** E8
Holborn Ave BT20 **4** B5
Holborn Hall BT27 **38** E7
Holland Cres BT5 **15** F4
Holland Dr BT5 **15** F4
Holland Gdns BT5 **15** F4
Holland Pk BT5 **15** F4
Hollows The
Lurgan BT66 **42** A2
Hollows The *continued*
8 Moy BT71 **72** A1
Hollybush Rd BT33 **123** A6
Hollycroft Ave BT5 **15** D4
Hollygate Ave BT8 **29** D3
Hollygate Pk BT8 **29** D3
Hollymount BT30 **108** B5
Hollymount BT17 **26** F8
Hollymount Ave BT23 **19** F7
Hollymount Cres BT23 **19** F7
Hollymount Forest National Nature Reserve★ BT30 **108** C4
Hollymount Gdns 6 BT23 **19** F7
Hollymount Pk 7 BT23 **19** F7
Hollymount Rd BT23 **19** F7
Hollypark Rd BT30 **78** F3
Hollywood Gdns BT34 **64** F7
Hollywood Gr BT34 **64** F7
Holmes Ct BT2 **155** B2
Holmes St BT2 **155** A2
Holy Cross Prim Sch BT34 **145** A4
Holyhill BT67 **42** E5
Holymount Rd BT63 **86** B1
Holyrood BT9 **21** C8
Holy Rosary Prim Sch BT7 **21** E8
Holy Trinity Heritage Ctr★ **151** D4
HOLYWOOD BT18 **9** E7
Holywood Bypass BT18 **9** D7
Holywood Golf Club BT18 **9** E5
Holywood Prim Sch BT18 **9** E7
Holywood Rd
Belfast BT4 **9** A1
Newtownards BT23 **11** A1
Holywood Rudolf Steiner Sch
The BT18 **10** A7
Holywood Sta BT18 **9** C7
Home Ave BT34 **64** D4
Hoophill Pk BT66 **42** A5
Hopedene Ct BT4 **15** F5
Hopedene Mews BT4 **15** E5
Hope St BT12 **154** C2
Hopewell Ave BT13 **14** B7
Hopewell Cres Link BT13 **14** C7
Hopewell Pl BT13 **14** B7
Hopewell Sq BT13 **14** C7
Hornbeam Rd BT17 **26** F7
Hornby Cres 23 BT4 **15** B5
Hornby Par 22 BT5 **15** B5
Hornby St 17 BT4 **15** B5
Horners La 7 BT34 **143** B3
Horner's Rd BT24 **90** C7
Horse Pk La BT22 **81** A7
Horseshoe La BT62 **56** B6
Horticulture Ctr BT34 **64** E7
Hospital Rd
Belfast BT8 **28** D8
Castlereagh BT8 **21** E1
Newry BT35 **64** A7
Houston Ct BT5 **15** F4
Houston Dr BT5 **15** E2
Houston Gdns BT5 **15** E2
Houston Pk
Belfast BT5 **15** D2
Lurgan BT66 **42** A3
Houston Rd BT6 **23** C3
Howard Pl BT28 **26** A1
Howard St S BT7 **155** B1
Howard St BT12 **155** A2
Howe Rd BT25 **89** A5
Howe St BT13 **14** A7
Hughes Ct BT6 **22** B8
Hugh St BT9 **21** A8
Huguenot Dr BT27 **26** D2
Hulls La BT28 **37** B8
Humber Ct BT4 **15** B6
Hunter Pk BT12 **154** C1
Hunters Hill Pk BT63 **57** D2
Hunters Hill Rd BT63 **57** D5
Hunter's La BT21 **67** A8
Hunter's Mill BT30 **62** C3
Hunters Wlk BT33 **63** D6
Huntingdale Lodge BT62 **55** E8
Huntingdale Manor BT62 **55** E8
Huntly Bglws BT32 **61** C5
Huntly Rd
Banbridge BT32 **61** C5
Seapatrick BT32 **61** B8
HUNTS CORNER BT62 **73** C5
Hunt St BT4 **15** C5
Huss Ct BT13 **154** B4
Huss Row BT13 **154** B4
Hutchinson St BT12 **154** C2
Hyndford St BT5 **15** C4

I

Ilex Ave BT23 **19** D6
Ilford Ave BT6 **23** C3
Ilford Cres BT6 **23** C3
Ilford Dr BT6 **23** C3
Ilford Pk BT6 **23** B3
Ilford Rd BT6 **23** C3
Imdel BT32 **119** B5
Imdel Cross BT32 **119** C5
Imperial Dr BT6 **15** A2
Imperial St BT6 **15** A3
Ina St BT4 **15** B6
Inch BT30 **108** D6
Inch Abbey★ BT30 **62** A7
Inch Abbey Rd BT30 **62** A7
Inchmarlo BT9 **21** A7
Inchmarnock Dr BT16 **17** D4
India St BT7 **14** D2
Ingledene Pk BT23 **20** A7
Ingleside Ct 5 BT66 **86** F6
Inglewood BT67 **32** B1
Inglewood Ct BT4 **15** E7
Inglewood Lodge BT62 **51** C1
Inglewood Manor BT62 **51** C1
Inisfree Pk BT23 **19** B6
Inishanier BT23 **79** C6
Inishargie Gdns BT19 **3** C1
Inishargy BT22 **70** F1
Insharoan BT23 **79** C6
Inisharon Ct BT23 **19** F4
Inishbeg Cl 9 BT30 **93** C5
Inishbeg Rd BT30 **93** C5
Inishmore Rd BT30 **93** C5
Inisloughlin BT67 **35** B2
Innisbrook Gdns BT19 **3** D3
Innisfayle Ave BT19 **3** C3
Innisfayle Cres BT19 **3** C3
Innisfayle Dr BT19 **3** C3
Innisfayle Pk BT19 **3** C3
Innisfree Pk BT34 **132** C2
Innis Gdns BT28 **26** B4
Innishargy Rd BT22 **70** E2
Innisloughlin Rd BT67 **35** C2
Innotec Dr BT19 **13** A7
Inn Rd BT67 **42** F5
Institution Pl BT12 **154** C3
Inverary Ave BT4 **15** E8
Inverary Dr BT4 **15** E8
Inver Ct BT4 **15** F7
Invergarry Ave BT18 **10** A8
Invergourie Rd BT18 **10** A8
Inverleith Dr BT4 **15** E8
Invernook Dr BT4 **15** E8
Invernook Pk BT4 **15** E8
Inver Pk BT18 **9** E5
Inverwood Ct BT4 **15** E7
Inverwood Gdns BT4 **15** F7
Irene Terr BT34 **65** C2
Ireton St BT7 **14** D2
Irish Path BT32 **88** C1
Irish St
Armagh BT60 **60** C3
Downpatrick BT30 **62** C4
Irvine Cres BT19 **13** E8
Irvine Pk BT19 **13** E8
Irvington Ave BT34 **153** C6
Irvington Cl 19 BT34 **153** C7
Irvington Pk 8 BT34 **153** C7
Irwin Ave
Belfast BT4 **15** D5
Lurgan BT66 **42** C3
Irwin Cres
Belfast BT4 **15** E5
Lurgan BT66 **42** C4
Irwin Dr
Belfast BT4 **15** D5
Lurgan BT66 **42** C3
Irwin Gdns BT66 **42** C3
Irwin's Cross Roads BT35 **130** B3
Irwin's Hill Rd BT71 **84** D6
Isabella Way 2 BT30 **125** F6
Iskymeadow BT60 **114** B6
Iskymeadow Rd BT60 **114** B6
Islandbane BT23 **79** D3
Island Bog Rd BT34 **120** A4
Island Civic Ctr Arts Centre★ BT27 **26** C1
Islandderry BT25 **87** C7
Island Henry BT30 **125** D6
Islandhill BT22 **66** E3
Island Hill BT25 **88** D4
Islandhill Dr 5 BT23 **19** F7
Island Hill Manor BT66 **75** B5
Islandhill Pk BT23 **19** F7
Islandhill Rd
Newtownards BT22 **66** E3
Newtownards BT23 **68** E6
Island La BT30 **62** A5
Islandmore Ave BT23 **19** F7
Islandmoyle BT34 **121** A3
Island Moyle Rd BT34 **121** B3
Island Rd
Downpatrick BT30 **93** A3
Newry BT34 **144** F5
Newry BT35 **129** A3
Portadown BT62 **51** E7
Island Spa BT60 **96** E1
Island St BT4 **15** B6
Islandview Gdns BT22 **70** B4
Island View La BT67 **75** E6
Islandview Rd
Newtownards BT22 **70** B4
Newtownards BT23 **79** B4
Islay Gdns BT16 **17** C4
Isle McCricket BT30 **110** C7
Isoline St BT5 **15** C3
Isthmus St BT6 **15** B4
Itec Bsns Pk BT35 **64** C8
Ivanhoe Ave BT8 **29** D5
Ivan St BT28 **38** B8
Iveagh Ave BT34 **65** D3
Iveagh Bglws BT34 **119** F2
Iveagh Cl BT32 **61** B5
Iveagh Cres
Newry BT35 **64** B7
11 Rathfriland BT34 **119** F2
Iveagh Dr BT32 **61** C5
Iveagh Gdns BT32 **61** C5
Iveagh Pk
Banbridge BT32 **61** B5
Downpatrick BT30 **62** D4
Iveagh Prim Sch BT34 **120** A2
Iveagh Rd BT32 **119** E6
Iveagh Rd Pk BT34 **120** A3
Iveagh View BT32 **61** C5
Iverna Cl BT12 **154** B1
Iverna St BT12 **154** B1
Ivyhill Ave BT19 **5** A5
Ivyhill Cres BT19 **5** B5
Ivyhill Dr BT19 **5** A5
Ivyhill Pk BT19 **5** A4
Ivy Pk BT60 **112** D7

J

Jacksons Cres BT24 **77** E4
Jacksons Rd BT18 **9** C5
Jade Bsns Pk BT35 **141** C1
Jaffa St BT13 **14** B7
James Connolly Pk (Páirc Shéamais Uí Chonghaile) 7 BT35 **64** C5
James Mount BT20 **4** E3
Jamesons Ct BT34 **65** C3
Jameson St BT7 **21** F8
James St S BT2 **155** A2
James St
Crossgar BT30 **92** B5
Lurgan BT66 **41** F5
Newry BT34 **64** E6
Newtownards BT23 **19** D5
Portadown BT63 **51** F5
Jellicoe Dr BT18 **9** E6
Jennys Row 6 BT61 **60** D5
Jericho Rd BT30 **92** F6
JERRETTSPASS BT34 **117** E2
Jersey Ave BT27 **26** B4
Jersey Pl 6 BT13 **14** A7
Jerusalem St BT7 **14** E2
Jervis St BT62 **51** D4
J F Kennedy Est BT31 **122** A4
Jocelyn Ave BT6 **15** B3
Jocelyn Gdns BT6 **15** B3
Jocelyn St BT6 **15** A3
Jockey La 7 BT71 **72** A1
Jockeys Brae BT35 **117** D1
Joe Tomelty Dr 10 BT22 **94** D3
John F Kennedy Pk 4 BT35 **131** E4
John Martin Gdns (Gairdíní Sheáin uí Mháirtín) 6 BT35 **64** C5
John Martin St (Sráid Sheáin uí Mháirtín) 5 BT35 **64** C5
John Mitchel Pl BT34 **64** D5
John Mitchel St BT34 **64** E6
John St Ct BT23 **19** C4
John St E BT23 **19** D4
John St La BT23 **19** D4
John St
Belfast BT12 **154** C3
4 Crossgar BT30 **92** B4
Downpatrick BT30 **62** D4
Newtownards BT23 **19** C4
Rathfriland BT34 **119** F2
Johnston Ct BT5 **16** B4
Johnstone Rd BT12 **154** A2
Johnston Pk
Carrowdore BT22 **66** F1
Dundonald BT16 **17** B2
Johnstown BT60 **99** E5
Johnstown Lodge BT60 **99** E5
Johnstown Mews BT60 **99** E5
John St (Sráid Eoin) BT30 **62** C4
John Thompson Pk 3 BT22 **94** D4
Jonesboro Pk BT5 **15** C3
JONESBOROUGH BT35 **141** C2
Jonesborough Prim Sch BT35 **141** C1
Jordan Ave BT20 **4** C2
Jordans BT30 **62** D4
Jordans Cl BT30 **107** C1
Jordans Crew BT30 **125** E7
Joy's Entry BT1 **155** B3
Joy St BT2 **155** B2
Jubilee Ave BT28 **37** F8
Jubilee Cotts BT19 **3** C1
Jubilee Ct 8 BT19 **3** C2
Jubilee Dr BT19 **3** C1
Jubilee Hts BT25 **58** E6
Jubilee Pk
Armagh BT60 **98** F5
3 Dromara BT25 **58** E6
Jubilee Pl
Bangor BT19 **3** C1
1 Lisburn BT28 **37** F8
Jubilee Rd
Belfast BT9 **14** B2
Dromara BT25 **58** E6
Newtownards BT23 **19** C3
Judes Cres BT23 **19** C6
Jude St BT12 **154** B3
Julia St BT4 **15** B5
Junction Rd BT24 **77** E1
Junction Row BT62 **51** D3
Juniper Ave BT23 **19** D6

K

Kalmia Ave BT23 **19** D6
Karrington Hts BT16 **17** C2
Kashmir Rd BT13 **154** A3
KATESBRIDGE BT32 **104** B1
Katesbridge Rd
Banbridge BT32 **104** A2
Dromara BT25 **88** E1
Kathleen Ave BT19 **2** D5
Kathleen Ct 9 BT5 **15** B5
Kathleen Dr
Helen's Bay BT19 **2** D5
Kathleen Dr *continued*
Newtownards BT23 **24** F7
KEADY (AN CÉIDE) BT60 **114** B3
Keady Beg BT60 **116** E1
Keadybeg Rd BT60 **116** E1
Keady Bsns Ctr BT60 **114** B3
Keady More BT60 **116** E2
Keadymore Rd BT60 **116** F3
Keady Prim Sch 17 BT60 **114** A3
Keady Rd
Armagh BT60 **60** C2
Newry BT35 **129** A7
Newry BT35 **148** D7
Keady St 2 BT60 **116** A8
KEARNEY BT22 **95** C4
Kearney Mews BT19 **3** D1
Kearney Rd BT22 **95** B3
Keatley St 5 BT5 **15** B5
Kedew BT68 **82** E1
Kedew Rd BT68 **82** F1
Keel Pk BT23 **30** E7
Keel Point BT33 **123** D4
Keelstown Rd BT30 **108** C8
Keenaghan BT71 **84** B7
Keeneraboy **147** A6
Keenoge **147** E3
Keentagh BT22 **95** A2
Keggall BT35 **131** B2
Keggall Rd BT35 **131** B2
Keggal View BT35 **131** B4
Kelly Gdns BT67 **42** B7
Kelly's Brae BT34 **146** D5
Kellys Rd BT35 **141** E4
Kempe Stones Rd BT23 **18** D4
Kenard Villas 1 BT34 **132** B5
Kenbaan Ct 5 BT5 **15** B4
Kenbaan St 6 BT5 **15** B4
Kenbrooke Cres BT19 **5** A5
Kendal Cres BT23 **20** A5
Kendal Pk BT23 **20** A5
Kendal St BT13 **154** B4
Kenlis St BT32 **61** D4
Kenmare Pk BT12 **154** C2
Kennedies
Armagh BT60 **96** F4
Armagh BT60 **97** A4
Armagh BT60 **98** B4
Kennedies Rd BT60 **96** F4
Kennedy Dr
Hilltown BT34 **134** B5
Lisburn BT27 **26** B5
Kennedy Pk BT30 **125** D5
Kennedy Sq (Cearng uí Chinnéide) 3 BT30 **62** C5
Kennel Bridge BT4 **16** B8
Kennel La 2 BT23 **19** E5
Kennel Rd BT30 **107** D2
Kensington Ave
Banbridge BT32 **61** E4
Belfast BT5 **15** D4
Kensington Cl BT27 **38** C7
Kensington Ct
Belfast BT5 **16** B3
Craigavon BT66 **42** F5
Kensington Dr BT5 **16** C3
Kensington Gate BT5 **16** B3
Kensington Gdns
Belfast BT5 **16** B2
Hillsborough BT26 **47** C8
Kensington Gdns S BT5 **16** B2
Kensington Gdns W BT5 **16** B2
Kensington Manor
Belfast BT5 **16** C2
Craigavon BT66 **42** F5
Kensington Pk
Bangor BT20 **3** E4
Belfast BT5 **16** B2
Craigavon BT63 **52** D1
Lisburn BT27 **38** C8
Newtownards BT23 **20** B7
Kensington Rd BT5 **16** B2
Kensington St BT2 **155** A1
Kent St BT1 **155** A4
Kenway Dr BT33 **63** C5
Kernaghan Ct 1 BT26 **89** E8
Kernaghan Pk 2 BT26 **89** E8
Kernan
Craigavon BT63 **102** A7
Portadown BT63 **52** B8
Kernan Ave BT63 **52** B8
Kernan Cres BT63 **52** B8
Kernan Gdns BT63 **52** B7
Kernan Gr BT63 **52** B7
Kernan Hill BT64 **40** C1
Kernan Hill Cl BT63 **52** B8
Kernanhill Manor BT63 **52** C8
Kernan Hill Rd BT63 **52** C8
Kernan Loop BT63 **40** A1
Kernan Lough Rd BT63 **102** B7
Kernan Pk BT63 **52** B7
Kernan Rd
Craigavon BT63 **102** A6
Portadown BT63 **52** B8
Kerries Glen BT23 **78** F6
Kerrsland Cres 3 BT5 **15** F4
Kerrsland Dr 1 BT5 **15** F4
Kerrsland Mews BT5 **15** F4
Kerrsland Par 2 BT5 **15** F4
Kerr's Rd BT23 **13** F2
Kerry Dr 10 BT30 **93** C5
Kerry Gdns 5 BT30 **93** C5
Kerry Hill BT30 **93** C5
Kerrymount Ave BT8 **22** B3
Kerry Wynd 4 BT30 **93** C5
Kesh Rd
Lisburn BT27 **36** E2
Newry BT35 **130** F3
Kestrel Pk BT23 **13** A5

Keswick St BT13 14 A7
Kew Gdns BT8 22 B2
Keylands Pl BT2 155 A2
Kidds Rd BT35 131 E5
Kiddswell Rd BT66 86 E4
Kilberry Pk BT16 17 E4
Kilbourne Pk BT19 3 B5
Kilbracks BT60 116 B6
Kilbride BT30 125 D4
Kilbride Rd (Bthar Chill Bhríde) BT30 62 D5
Kilbright BT22 67 B1
Kilbright Rd BT22 67 A2
Kilbright Rd N BT22 67 A1
Kilbroney BT34 143 D6
Kilbroney Bend BT6 22 C8
Kilbroney Integrated Prim Sch 18 BT34 143 C3
Kilbroney Pk 6 BT34 143 C4
Kilbroney Rd BT34 143 D5
Kilbroney Upper BT34 143 D7
Kilburn Pk BT61 98 F7
Kilburn St BT12 154 B1
Kilcam BT60 127 E7
Kilcarn BT60 82 F3
Kilcarn Rd BT23 78 B5
Kilclief BT30 110 D6
Kilclief Gdns BT19 3 D1
Kilclief Rd BT30 110 D5
Kilclooney Cemy* BT60 116 A6
Kilcon BT60 116 E3
KILCOO BT34 121 C2
Kilcooley Prim Sch BT19 3 D1
Kilcooley Sq BT19 3 D1
Kilcreevy Etra BT60 113 E8
Kilcreevy Rd BT60 97 E1
KILCURRY (CILL AN CHURRAIGH) 149 F5
Kildares Crew BT30 125 E6
Kildare St
Ardglass BT30 125 F6
6 Newry BT34 64 D6
4 Belfast BT13 154 C4
Kildarton Cemy* BT60 99 B5
Kileen (Dundonald) BT4 16 D7
Kilfarn Rd BT60 113 E7
Kilfeaghan BT34 144 A1
Kilfeaghan Rd BT34 144 A1
Kilfeaghan Upper BT34 144 A3
Kilfullert BT66 86 F8
Kilglen Dr BT35 141 B5
Kilgowney BT68 96 C6
Kilhorne Ct BT34 146 C4
Kilhorne Gdns BT5 16 B3
Kilkeel Bsns Pk BT34 153 D8
KILKEEL (CILL CHAOIL) BT34 153 D7
Kilkeel Golf Club BT34 152 F8
Kilkeel High Sch BT34 153 D7
Kilkeel Inst of FE 21 BT34 153 C7
Kilkeel Leisure Ctr & Swimming Pool BT34 153 D6
Kilkeel Prim Sch 22 BT34 153 C7
Kilkeel Rd
Newcastle BT33 63 E1
Newry BT34 134 E5
Newry BT34 146 C3
Kilkinamurry Rd BT31 104 C3
Kilkinamurry BT31 104 D4
Killagan Bend BT6 22 B8
Killaghy
Craigavon BT67 32 B4
Newtownards BT22 66 D4
Killaghy Rd BT67 32 A4
Killaire Ave BT19 3 B5
Killaire Cl BT19 3 B5
Killaire Ct BT19 3 B4
Killaire Pk BT19 3 B4
Killaire Rd BT19 3 B5
Killaney
Banbridge BT32 103 F7
Lisburn BT27 76 D3
Killaney Ave BT28 37 F8
Killaney La BT32 103 F8
Killaragrange BT71 83 D2
Killard Ave (Ascaill Chill Ard) BT30 62 D5
Killard House Sch BT23 19 E6
Killard Lower BT30 110 E4
Killard Rd BT30 110 D4
Killard Sq BT30 110 C2
Killard Upper BT30 110 D3
Killaresy Church* BT30 79 B1
Killarn BT23 18 B7
Killarn Cl BT6 15 E1
Killaughey Rd BT21 66 D6
Killaughey Rd S BT22 66 D4
Killavees BT30 62 F5
Killeaton Prim Sch BT35 141 E4
Killeaton Cres BT17 26 D8
Killeaton Pk BT17 26 D7
Killeaton Pl BT17 26 D7
Killeavy GAC BT35 141 D7
Killeavy Rd BT35 64 B7
Killeen
Armagh BT60 99 A3
Newry BT35 141 E5
Killeen Ave BT19 3 C3
Killeen Cl 2 BT19 3 C2
Killeen Dr BT19 3 C2
Killeen (Holywood) BT4 16 D7
Killeen Pk BT19 3 C2
Killeen Rd BT60 99 A3
Killeen Sch Rd BT35 141 E4
Killen St BT12 154 C3
Killevy Church* BT35 141 A7
Killicomaine Jun High Sch BT63 52 B6
Killin 149 C3
Killinakin BT23 79 B6
Killinakin Rd BT23 79 B7
KILLINCHY (CILL DHUINSÍ) BT23 79 B5
Killinchy in the Woods BT30 92 C6
Killinchy Prim Sch BT23 79 A5
Killinchy Rd
Comber BT23 25 E2
Newtownards BT23 68 D3
Killinchy St BT23 25 D3
Killiney Crest 5 BT61 98 F7
Killinure BT8 76 F8
KILLOUGH (CILL LOCHA) BT30 125 D5
Killough Gdns BT66 41 E4
Killough Rd
Ardglass BT30 125 E6
Downpatrick BT30 62 D2
Killough Rd Ind Est BT30 62 D2
KILLOWEN BT34 151 C8
Killowen Mountains BT34 143 F2
Killowen Old Rd BT34 151 E8
Killowen Outdoor Ed Ctr BT34 151 C8
Killowen Rd BT34 143 C1
Killowen St BT6 15 B3
Killowen Village BT34 151 D8
Killuney BT61 98 F7
Killuney Dr BT60 60 F4
Killuney Pk BT61 98 F6
Killuney Rd BT61 98 F7
Killybawn Rd BT24 78 A1
Killybodagh BT35 117 D5
Killycapple BT60 99 A2
Killycapple Rd BT60 99 A1
Killycarn Lower BT60 116 D8
Killycarn Rd BT60 116 D7
Killycarn Upper BT60 116 D7
Killycavan Manor BT71 72 A6
Killycomain BT63 52 B5
Killycomaine Cl BT63 52 C4
Killycomaine Dr BT63 52 B5
Killycomaine Gdns BT63 52 B5
Killycomaine Gr BT63 52 B4
Killycomaine Pk BT63 52 B5
Killycomain Rd BT63 52 B5
Killydressy BT22 94 F1
Killyfaddy BT60 114 E7
Killyfaddy Rd BT60 98 E1
Killyfaddy Rd E BT60 114 E6
Killygony Cemy* BT24 59 F8
KILLYLEA (COILLIDH LÉITH) BT60 97 B5
KILLYLEAGH (CILL Ó LAOCH) BT30 93 C4
Killyleagh Prim Sch BT30 93 B6
Killyleagh Rd
Crossgar BT30 92 C5
Downpatrick BT30 93 A3
Newtownards BT23 79 B3
Killyleagh St BT30 92 B5
Killylea Prim Sch BT60 97 B6
Killylea Rd BT60 60 A4
Killylyn BT61 84 C2
Killymaddy BT60 83 B2
Killymagamish Rd BT62 74 C1
Killyman Prim Sch 2 BT71 72 A5
Killyman St BT71 72 B1
Killynaul BT68 82 D2
Killynaul Rd BT68 82 D2
KILLYNEILL (COILL UÍ NÉILL) 112 A4
Killynether BT23 68 D8
Killynether Gdns BT8 21 C2
Killynether Rd BT23 18 F3
Killynure BT60 98 A3
Killynure Ave BT8 29 E1
Killynure Cl 3 BT8 29 E2
Killynure Cres BT8 29 E3
Killynure Gdns BT8 29 D2
Killynure Pk 2 BT8 29 E2
Killynure Rd
Ballynahinch BT24 77 A6
Belfast BT8 76 F8
Carryduff BT8 29 E1
Killynure Rd W BT8 76 F8
Killynure Way 1 BT8 29 E2
Killyquin BT71 83 D2
Killyreavy BT60 114 A5
Killyreavy Rd BT60 114 A6
Killyruddan BT61 99 D5
Killyruddan Rd BT61 99 D5
Killysavan BT35 117 F7
Killysorrell BT25 87 C4
Killysorrell Rd BT25 87 B4
Killyvolgan BT22 70 F4
Killyvolgan Rd BT22 70 F3
Kilmacanty BT61 85 D3
Kilmacanty Rd BT61 85 C4
Kilmachugh
Armagh BT60 115 F5
Armagh BT61 98 F8
Kilmachugh Rd BT60 115 D5
Kilmacrew BT32 103 D8
Kilmacrew Rd BT32 87 E1
Kilmagamish BT62 74 C2
Kilmaine Ave BT19 4 F3
Kilmaine Dr BT19 4 F3
Kilmaine Prim Sch BT19 4 F2
Kilmaine Rd BT19 4 F3
Kilmaine St BT67 42 A7
Kilmakee BT17 26 F8
Kilmakee Activity Ctr 4 BT17 26 F8
Kilmakee Pk BT5 16 D2
Kilmatroy BT61 83 D1
Kilmegan Rd BT33 123 A5
Kilmeloge Enclosure* BT34 146 A3
Kilminioge BT67 33 D3
Kilmonaghan BT35 117 E1
Kilmonaghan Rd BT35 117 E1
Kilmood and Ballybunden BT23 78 E6
Kilmood Rd BT23 78 D7
KILMORE BT61 85 E4
Kilmore
Craigavon BT67 32 E5
Dungannon BT70 82 D4
Dungannon BT71 84 C4
Kilmore Cl BT13 154 A3
Kilmore Dr BT61 85 E4
Kilmore Hill Rd BT67 32 C5
Kilmore Mews BT61 85 E3
Kilmore Pk
Armagh BT61 85 E3
Moira BT67 34 B2
Kilmore Rd
Armagh BT61 85 E3
Craigavon BT67 32 F2
Crossgar BT30 92 B4
Lurgan BT67 42 D7
Kilmore Sq BT13 154 A3
Kilmorey Cres BT34 153 D8
Kilmorey Ct BT34 153 D8
Kilmorey St BT34 64 D4
Kilmoriarty BT62 51 A2
Kilmory Gdns BT5 16 E3
Kilmuir Ave BT16 17 C3
Kilnacrue Cemy* BT35 140 A4
Kilnagrew BT71 83 C6
Kilnasaggart Inscribed Stone* BT35 150 C7
Kilnasaggart Rd BT35 141 C1
Kilnatierny BT22 70 A5
Kilnhill Rd BT31 105 E3
Kiln La
Banbridge BT32 61 D7
Lurgan BT66 41 C7
Kiln Lodge BT66 41 D7
Kiln Rd BT66 41 D7
Kiln St BT35 64 C5
Kilntown Rd BT25 45 B1
Kiloanin Cres BT32 61 C7
Kiloanin Mews BT32 61 C7
Kilpike BT32 86 E1
Kilrea BT35 117 D3
Kilrea Rd BT35 117 D2
Kilsampson BT68 96 D5
Kilsannagh BT70 82 E4
Kilshannagh La BT70 82 D4
Kilshannagh Rd BT70 82 E4
Kiltarriff BT34 119 F2
Kiltarriff Pk 5 BT34 119 F2
Kiltonga Leisure Ctr BT23 19 A6
Kiltubbrid BT60 112 E8
Kiltubbrid Rd BT60 112 F7
Kiltybane Lisleitrim BT35 138 E5
Kiltybane Rd BT35 138 D5
Kilty Rd BT32 119 A7
Kilvarragh BT35 64 C1
Kilvergan BT66 40 D5
Kilvergan Hts BT66 40 F6
Kilvergan Rd BT66 40 E7
Kilvoragh Pk BT67 32 B1
Kilwarlin Ave BT26 47 C7
Kilwarlin Cres
Castlereagh BT8 21 C2
Hillsborough BT26 47 C7
Kilwarlin Pk BT26 47 D6
Kilwarlin Rd BT26 45 F6
Kilwarlin Way BT26 47 D6
Kilwarlin Wlk BT8 21 C2
Kilwilke Gdns BT67 42 A8
Kilwilke Rd BT67 42 A7
Kilwood Cl 9 BT30 92 B5
Kilwood Cres BT30 92 B5
Kilwood Pk BT30 92 B5
Kimberley Dr BT7 21 E8
Kimberley St
6 Belfast BT7 14 E1
Belfast BT7 21 E8
Kimona Dr BT4 15 D6
Kimona St BT4 15 D6
KINALLEN BT25 88 F2
Kinallen Cl 1 BT32 104 A1
Kinallen Cotts BT25 88 F2
Kinallen Ct BT7 14 E2
Kinallen Manor BT25 88 E3
Kinallen Rd
Castlewellan BT31 104 D5
Dromara BT25 88 F4
Kinallen St BT7 14 E2
Kincon BT61 85 C6
Kincora Ave BT4 15 F5
Kincora Dr BT30 62 E3
Kinedale Pk BT24 59 B5
Kinedar Cres BT4 16 A5
Kinego BT71 72 A5
Kinelowen St BT60 114 A3
Kingarve BT62 50 D5
Kinghill BT34 120 F1
Kinghill Ave BT33 63 B5
Kinghill Cl BT33 63 B5
Kinghill Dr BT33 63 A5
Kinghill Rd BT34 120 F1
King John's Castle* 151 D5
King Magnus's Halt BT30 62 A2
King St Mews BT12 154 C3
Kingsberry Pk BT6 22 A7
Kings Brae BT5 16 C3
King's Bridge BT9 21 D8
Kingschase BT27 36 D4
Kingscourt Ave 6 BT6 15 B3
Kingscourt Cres 4 BT6 15 B3
King's Cres BT5 16 B3
Kingsdale Pk BT5 16 C3
Kingsden Pk BT5 16 A3
King's Dr BT5 16 B3
Kingsfield Ave (Ascaill Phairc an Rí) BT30 62 B2
Kingsfort Lodge BT67 34 A1
Kings La 3 BT34 65 C2
Kingsland Dr BT5 16 D3
Kingsland Pk BT5 16 D3
Kingsland Sch BT20 4 C6
Kingsley Ct BT4 15 F5
Kings Link BT5 16 D3
Kings Manor BT5 16 B3
Kingsmere Ave BT19 4 E1
Kingsmere Pk 9 BT19 4 E1
Kingsmill Rd BT60 130 F7
KINGSMILLS BT60 130 E7
Kingsmills Prim Sch BT60 130 F8
Kings Park Mews BT67 42 B5
King's Park Prim Sch BT67 42 B5
King's Pk BT5 16 B3
King's Rd BT5 15 F4
Kings Square Sh Ctr BT5 16 C3
King's Stables The* BT60 97 F6
King St
Bangor BT20 4 A4
Belfast BT12 155 A3
Lurgan BT67 42 B4
Newcastle BT33 63 D3
Portadown BT62 51 E5
King's Vale 4 BT5 16 A4
Kingsway BT17 26 E8
Kingsway Arc BT35 64 C5
Kingsway Ave BT5 16 C3
Kingsway Cl BT5 16 C3
Kingsway Dr
Belfast BT5 16 C3
Lurgan BT66 42 B3
Portadown BT62 51 D2
Kingsway Gdns BT5 16 C3
Kingsway Pk BT5 16 D3
Kingswood Pk BT5 16 D3
Kingswood St BT5 15 B4
Kinnahalla Rd BT34 135 A6
Kinnaird Cl 6 BT14 14 C8
Kinnaird Pl 8 BT14 14 C8
Kinnaird St 5 BT15 14 C8
Kinnaird Terr 7 BT14 14 C8
Kinnegar Ave BT19 9 C7
Kinnegar Cl BT20 9 C7
Kinnegar Ct BT18 9 C6
Kinnegar Dr BT18 9 C6
Kinnegar Rd BT21 9 C7
Kinnegar Rocks 2 BT21 67 A7
Kinnegoe
Armagh BT61 84 D5
Craigavon BT67 75 E6
Kinnego Emb BT66 40 E8
Kinnegoe Rd BT61 84 D5
Kinross Ave BT5 16 E3
Kintyre Ave BT18 10 A8
Kinwood Ave 4 BT19 66 A8
Kinwood Cl 5 BT19 4 F1
Kinwood Cres BT19 66 A8
Kinwood Ct BT19 13 F8
Kinwood Dr BT19 4 F1
Kinwood Gdns BT19 4 F1
Kinwood Grange BT19 13 F8
Kinwood Link 3 BT19 66 A8
Kinwood Pk 4 BT19 4 F1
Kipkaren Pk BT23 20 A7
Kircassock BT66 43 F1
KIRCUBBIN (CILL GHOBÁIN) BT22 80 D7
Kircubbin Gdns BT19 3 D1
Kircubbin Prim Sch BT22 80 E7
Kircubbin Rd BT22 71 A3
KIRKISTOWN BT22 81 B3
Kirkistown Ave BT8 21 C2
Kirkistown Castle Golf Club BT22 81 B2
Kirkistown Prim Sch BT22 81 B2
Kirkistown Racing Circuit BT22 81 C4
Kirk La BT34 121 D1
Kirkland Rd BT30 79 B1
Kirkliston Dr BT5 15 E4
Kirkliston Gdns BT5 15 F4
Kirkliston Pk BT5 15 E4
Kirkmichael Pk BT18 10 A7
Kirkside BT62 101 B6
Kirkstown Pk BT22 81 B1
Kirkwood Pk BT24 77 B3
Kirkwood's Pk BT28 26 A5
Kirkwoods Rd BT28 26 B5
Kishaboy BT71 84 B8
Kitchener Dr BT12 154 A1
Kitchen Hill BT66 41 F5
Kittys Rd BT34 153 C6
Klondyke St BT13 14 B7
Knappagh BT60 97 C8
Knappagh Rd BT60 97 B7
Knightsbridge BT66 43 A4
Knight's Bridge BT62 101 B8
Knightsbridge Ct BT19 5 A2
Knightsbridge Manor BT9 21 D6
Knightsbridge Mews BT9 21 C6
Knightsbridge Pk BT9 21 C6
Knock
Belfast BT5 16 A4
Craigavon BT63 56 E8
Knockaconey BT61 84 D3
Knockaconey Rd BT61 84 D3
Knockagraffy BT60 97 E5
Knockamell Pk BT61 60 D6
Knockaneagh BT60 97 B7
Knockaneagh Rd BT60 97 B7
Knockanoney Hts BT35 64 B6
Knockany Rd BT27 76 C7
Knockarogan Glebe BT70 82 F4
Knockashane Mdws BT66 42 D2
Knockavally Mound* BT30 125 C5
Knockavannon BT35 129 E7
Knockbane BT60 112 C5
Knockbane Rd BT60 112 C6
Knockbarragh BT34 143 C7
Knockbracken Cres BT8 29 D5
Knockbracken Dr BT8 29 D6
Knockbracken Healthcare Pk BT8 29 A8
Knockbracken Manor BT8 22 C2
Knockbracken Pk BT6 22 A6
Knockbracken Rd BT6 23 C2
Knockbracken Rd S BT8 22 E1
Knockbreckan BT8 29 D8
Knockbreda Dr BT6 22 A6
Knockbreda Gdns BT6 22 A6
Knockbreda High Sch BT6 22 B6
Knockbreda Pk BT6 22 A6
Knockbreda Prim Sch BT6 22 A6
Knockbreda Rd BT6 22 A7
Knockburn Pk BT5 16 C4
Knockcastle Pk BT5 16 A3
Knockchree Ave BT34 153 C7
Knockchree Rd (Bothar Chnoc Croidh) BT30 62 D4
Knockdarragh BT34 64 E7
Knockdarragh Pk BT4 16 B7
Knockdene BT20 4 C1
Knockdene Gate 1 BT5 16 B4
Knockdene Pk
Ballynahinch BT24 59 C6
Belfast BT5 16 B4
Knockdene Pk N BT5 16 B4
Knockdene Pk S BT5 16 B4
Knockduff BT35 117 D2
Knockduff Rd BT35 117 C2
Knock Eden Cres BT6 22 A8
Knock Eden Dr BT6 22 A7
Knock Eden Gr BT6 22 A8
Knock Eden Par BT6 22 A8
Knockeden Pk 2 BT21 6 F1
Knock Eden Pk BT6 22 A7
Knockevin Specl Sch BT30 62 C2
Knock Gn BT5 16 A2
Knock Golf Club BT16 16 F5
Knockgorm BT32 103 F6
Knockgorm Rd BT32 103 F5
Knock Gr BT5 15 F2
Knockhill Pk BT5 16 A4
Knockinelder BT22 95 B4
Knockland Pk BT5 16 D4
Knock Link 6 BT5 16 A2
Knocklofty Ct 11 BT4 16 A5
Knocklofty Pk BT4 16 B5
Knockmarloch Pk BT4 16 C7
Knockmenagh BT64 52 D8
Knockmenagh Pk BT64 53 B8
Knockmenagh Rd BT64 40 E1
Knockmenapark BT63 52 B6
Knockmore Bsns Ctr BT28 37 C8
Knockmore Ind Est BT28 37 B8
Knockmore Pk BT20 3 E4
Knockmore Prim Sch 2 BT28 37 D8
Knockmore Rd BT28 37 C8
Knockmore Sq BT28 37 E8
Knockmount Gdns 2 BT5 16 A2
Knockmount Pk BT5 16 A2
Knocknacloy BT70 83 A5
Knocknagoney BT18 9 C2
Knocknagoney Ave BT4 9 B1
Knocknagoney Dale BT4 9 A1
Knocknagoney Dr BT4 9 B1
Knocknagoney Gdns BT4 9 B2
Knocknagoney Gn 3 BT4 9 B1
Knocknagoney Gr 2 BT4 9 B1
Knocknagoney Pk BT4 9 A2
Knocknagoney Prim Sch BT4 9 A1
Knocknagoney Rd BT4 9 A2
Knocknagoney Way 1 BT4 9 B1
Knocknagoran 142 D1
Knocknagore BT63 86 A2
Knocknagore Rd BT63 86 A4
Knocknagor Well* BT63 52 B2
Knocknagow 13 BT22 94 D3
Knocknagreana BT34 65 C4
Knocknamuckley La BT63 52 E1
Knocknamuckley Rd BT63 53 A1
Knocknamuckly BT63 52 F1
Knocknanarny BT34 117 F2
Knocknaroy BT70 82 B8

Knocknashane BT66 . . . 42 C2
Knocknashina Rd BT30 . . . 62 E5
Knocknashinna Rd BT30 . . 62 D4
Knock Nature Wlk BT5 . . . 16 B3
Knockowen Rd BT35 . . . . 128 F4
Knockramer BT66 . . . . . 41 B8
Knockramer Mdws BT66 . 41 B7
Knock Rd
Banbridge BT32 . . . . 119 E7
Belfast BT5 . . . . 16 A2
Castlereagh BT5 . . . . 15 F1
Craigavon BT63 . . . . 53 A2
Knockrevan BT60 . . . . . 113 E4
Knockshee BT66 . . . . 42 A3
Knocksticken BT30 . . . . 123 C8
Knocksticken Rd BT30 . . 123 C8
Knocktern Gdns BT4 . . . . . 16 B5
Knockvale Gr BT5 . . . . 16 A3
Knockvale Pk BT5 . . . . 16 A3
Knockview Dr BT62 . . . . . 101 A7
Knockview Gdns 2
BT34 . . . . 119 F2
Knock Way 5 BT5 . . . . 16 A2
Knockwood Cres BT5 . . . . 15 F3
Knockwood Dr 3 BT5 . . . . 16 A2
Knockwood Pk BT5 . . . . . . 15 F2
Knollwood BT32 . . . . 61 C8
Knowes Cres BT24 . . . . 59 E4
Knowes The BT23 . . . . 13 A5
Knox Rd BT25 . . . . 88 D8
Knox's Hill BT60 . . . . 60 E2
Knox's La BT21 . . . . 67 A7
Konver Hts BT32 . . . . 61 D6
Korona Pk BT23 . . . . 19 B6
Kyle Ave BT66 . . . . 42 A3
Kyle St BT4 . . . . 15 D6
Kylestone Rd
Bangor BT19 . . . . 5 E6
Donaghadee BT21 . . . . 66 C8

L

Laburnum Cl BT23 . . . . 25 F3
Laburnum Cres BT23 . . . . . 25 F3
Laburnum Ct
2 Belfast BT5 . . . . 15 D5
Comber BT23 . . . . 25 F3
Laburnum Dr BT23 . . . . 25 F3
Laburnum Gdns BT23 . . . . 25 F3
Laburnum Gr BT23 . . . . 25 F3
Laburnum La 11 BT4 . . . . . 15 C5
Laburnum Pk BT23 . . . . 25 F3
Laburnum Pl BT23 . . . . 25 F3
Laburnum Rise BT23 . . . . . 25 F3
Laburnum St 12 BT5 . . . . . 15 C5
Laburnum Way BT23 . . . . . 25 F3
Lackan BT32 . . . . 120 D5
Lackan Rd
Banbridge BT32 . . . . 120 F5
Newry BT34 . . . . 121 C3
Ladas Dr BT6 . . . . 15 C1
Ladas Way BT6 . . . . 15 C1
Ladas Wlk BT6 . . . . 15 C1
Ladymar Gr BT12 . . . . 154 B3
Ladymar Pk BT12 . . . . 154 B2
Lady St BT12 . . . . 154 B3
Lagan BT60 . . . . 113 E2
Laganbank Rd
Belfast BT1 . . . . 155 C3
Lisburn BT28 . . . . 26 B1
Lagan Coll BT8 . . . . 22 D5
Lagan Ct BT34 . . . . 65 B7
Lagangreen Rd BT25 . . . . . 88 E4
Lagan Hts BT25 . . . . 89 C3
Lagan Lookout Visitors Ctr★
BT1 . . . . 155 B3
Lagan Rd BT60 . . . . 113 E3
Lagan St BT25 . . . . 58 B5
Lagan Terr 1 BT66 . . . . . . 86 E6
Laganvale
Dromara BT25 . . . . 58 D5
Lisburn BT28 . . . . 36 E6
3 Moira BT67 . . . . 44 A8
Laganvale Ct BT9 . . . . 21 D6
Laganvale Manor BT9 . . . . 21 D6
Laganvale Mews BT67 . . . . 44 A8
Laganvale St BT9 . . . . 21 D7
Lagan Valley Hospl BT28 . . 38 B8
Laganvalley Hts BT8 . . . . . 28 B7
Lagan Valley Regional Pk★
BT28 . . . . 38 A6
Lagan Valley Regional Pk Offices & NI RSPB HQ
BT8 . . . . 21 D4
Laganview BT28 . . . . 38 B8
Laganview Ct BT5 . . . . 155 C3
Laganview Golf Ctr BT27 . 26 F6
Laganview Mews BT5 . . . 155 C3
Lagan Villas BT25 . . . . 58 C5
Laganville Pk BT28 . . . . 37 C8
Lagan Wlk BT28 . . . . 37 F7
LAGHEY CORNER BT71 . . . . 72 A6
Laghey Prim Sch 1 BT71 72 A6
Lagnagoppoge BT30 . . 110 C7
LAING'S HILL BT60 . . . . 98 D1
Lairakean BT68 . . . . 96 D8
Lairds Rd
Banbridge BT32 . . . . 104 C1
Hillsborough BT26 . . . . 89 C7
Lake Ave BT31 . . . . 121 F5
Lakeland Manor BT26 . . . . 89 D7
Lakeland Rd BT26 . . . . 89 D7
Lakelands BT64 . . . . 40 F3
Lake Rd
Armagh BT60 . . . . 113 F2
Craigavon BT64 . . . . 40 F2
Downpatrick BT30 . . . . 108 C3
Keady BT60 . . . . 114 A2
Newry BT35 . . . . 138 F4
Lake St BT67 . . . . 32 A1
Lakeview BT23 . . . . 19 B6
Lake View BT65 . . . . 40 F3
Lake View Ct BT65 . . . . 41 A2
Lakeview Pk BT64 . . . . 40 F2
Lakeview Rd
Castlewellan BT31 . . . . 104 D3
Craigavon BT64 . . . . 40 E3
Lakewalk BT31 . . . . 122 A5
Lakewood Specl Sch
BT19 . . . . 12 F8
LAMBEG (LANN BHEAG)
BT27 . . . . 26 D5
Lambeg Prim Sch BT27 . . 26 E5
Lambeg Rd BT27 . . . . 26 D5
Lambeg Sta BT27 . . . . 26 D5
Lambert Ave BT16 . . . . 17 D6
Lambert Glen BT16 . . . . . . 17 D5
Lambert Pk BT16 . . . . 17 D5
Lambert Rise BT16 . . . . 17 D6
Lána Nabaoise (Folly La)
BT30 . . . . 62 C4
Lanark Way BT13 . . . . 154 A4
Lancaster Ave BT20 . . . . 4 A4
Lancaster St BT15 . . . . 14 D7
Lancaster Wlk BT23 . . . . . . 19 D2
Lancedean Rd BT6 . . . . 22 D7
Lancefield Rd BT9 . . . . 21 A7
Landor Pk BT27 . . . . 38 C8
Landscape Terr BT14 . . . . . 14 B7
Landsdown Ave BT23 . . . . 19 C1
Landsdown Dr BT23 . . . . . . 19 C1
Landsdowne Gdns BT23 . . 19 D1
Landsdowne Ind Est BT23 19 E1
Landsdowne Rd BT23 . . . . 19 D1
Landseer St BT9 . . . . 14 D1
Lane At Manse Rd BT34 . 153 C6
Lane The BT18 . . . . 1 E3
Langley Rd BT24 . . . . 59 C6
Langley St BT14 . . . . 14 A8
Langry Lodge BT67 . . . . . . 34 A2
Langs Cres BT60 . . . . 60 E4
Langs Rd BT60 . . . . 60 E5
Langstane Stablins (Longstone Mews) 4
BT16 . . . . 17 D3
LANN BHEAG (LAMBEG)
BT27 . . . . 26 D5
Lansdowne Pk BT27 . . . . . . 38 D8
Lanyon Pl BT1 . . . . 155 B2
Lany Rd
Craigavon BT67 . . . . 35 E1
Hillsborough BT26 . . . . 46 A8
Lappoges BT25 . . . . 88 F4
Lapwing Pk BT23 . . . . 20 B3
Laragh Pk BT20 . . . . 4 E3
Laraghshankill BT71 . . . 83 D2
Larch Cl BT18 . . . . 9 D5
Larchfield Pk BT33 . . . . 63 C6
Larch Gr BT17 . . . . 27 A8
Larch Hill
Dunmurry BT17 . . . . 27 A8
Holywood BT18 . . . . 1 G2
Larch Hill Ave BT18 . . . . 1 G3
Larch Hill Dr BT18 . . . . 1 G2
Larchmount Pk BT35 . . . . . 64 B8
Larchwood
Banbridge BT32 . . . . 61 B4
Portadown BT63 . . . . 52 C5
Larchwood Ave BT32 . . . . . 61 A4
Larchwood Cres BT32 . . . . 61 A4
Larchwood Ct BT32 . . . . . . 61 B4
Larchwood Mews BT32 . . . 61 A3
Large Park BT26 . . . . 47 D4
Largymore BT27 . . . . 38 E6
Largymore Link
4 Lisburn BT27 . . . . 26 D1
Lisburn BT27 . . . . 38 D8
Largymore Prim Sch
BT27 . . . . 26 D1
Largy Rd BT34 . . . . 121 E4
Larkfield Dr BT4 . . . . 15 E7
Larkfield Gdns BT4 . . . . . . 15 D7
Larkfield Gr BT4 . . . . 15 E7
Larkfield Manor BT4 . . . . . 15 D7
Larkfield Mdws BT65 . . . . . 53 C7
Larkfield Pk BT4 . . . . 15 E7
Larkfield Rd BT4 . . . . 15 E7
Larkfield Sq BT66 . . . . 42 C4
Larkins Rd BT35 . . . . 148 C6
Larksborough Ave BT23 . . 20 A4
Larksborough Cl BT23 . . . . 20 A4
Lassara Hts 3 BT34 . . . . . . 65 B3
Latbirget BT35 . . . . 140 B7
Latmacollum BT60 . . . . . 98 E1
Latmacollum Rd BT60 . . . . 98 E1
Latt BT35 . . . . 131 E7
Latt Cres BT35 . . . . 131 E7
Lattery BT60 . . . . 100 B2
Latt Rd BT35 . . . . 117 D1
Latt Villas BT35 . . . . 131 E7
Laurel Bank BT23 . . . . 25 C3
Laurelbank Ave BT23 . . . . . 19 C5
Laurelbank Pk 7 BT22 . . . 94 D3
Laurelbank Rd BT24 . . . . . . 76 F3
Laurel Cl BT24 . . . . 78 A3
Laurel Dr BT62 . . . . 100 F8
Laurel Gr
4 Craigavon BT62 . . . . . . 100 E8
4 Newry BT34 . . . . 132 A5
Laurelgrove Ave BT8 . . . . . 22 D2
Laurelgrove Cres 6 BT8 . 22 C2
Laurelgrove Ct BT8 . . . . . . 22 D2
Laurelgrove Dale 5 BT8 . 22 C2
Laurelgrove Manor BT8 . . 22 D2
Laurelgrove Pk BT8 . . . . . . 22 D2
Laurel Hill
Dromara BT25 . . . . 86 E4
Newry BT35 . . . . 64 A6
Laurel Hts
Banbridge BT32 . . . . 61 F6
Craigavon BT62 . . . . 100 E8
Downpatrick BT30 . . . . 62 C7
Laurel La BT18 . . . . 1 E2
Laurel Pk
Craigavon BT62 . . . . 100 E8
Newtownards BT23 . . . . 13 A4
Laurel Rd BT24 . . . . 90 B7
Laurels The BT63 . . . . 52 A4
Laurelvale BT4 . . . . 16 A6
LAURELVALE BT62 . . . . 55 D1
Laurel Vale 5 BT30 . . . . . . 92 B5
Laurelvale CC BT62 . . . . . . 55 D1
Laurelvale Rd BT62 . . . . . . 55 B1
Laurel Wlk BT30 . . . . 94 B2
Laurel Wood
Bangor BT19 . . . . 12 E8
Belfast BT8 . . . . 21 F5
Laurencevale (Lawrencevale)
BT63 . . . . 86 C2
Lavery Ave BT67 . . . . 32 A1
Lavery's Bridge Rd
Craigavon BT67 . . . . 35 D1
Hillsborough BT26 . . . . 45 E6
Lawnbrook Ave BT13 . . . . 154 A4
Lawnbrook Dr
Belfast BT13 . . . . 154 A4
Newtownards BT23 . . . . 20 B7
Lawnbrook Sq BT13 . . . . . 154 A4
Lawnmount Cres BT27 . . . 26 D3
Lawnmount St 21 BT6 . . . . 15 A4
Lawns The BT66 . . . . 86 C7
Lawrence Sq BT66 . . . . 42 C4
Lawrence St BT7 . . . . 14 D2
LAWRENCETOWN BT63 . . . . 86 B2
Lawrencevale (Laurencevale)
BT63 . . . . 86 C2
Law's Ct BT1 . . . . 155 A4
Laws La BT32 . . . . 61 D4
Lawson Ave BT22 . . . . 81 D5
Lawson Gdns BT22 . . . . 81 D5
Lawson Pk BT22 . . . . 81 D5
Lawyer Gdns BT12 . . . . . . 154 C2
Leaburn Cl BT32 . . . . 61 B6
Lead Hill BT6 . . . . 22 F8
Lead Hill Pk BT6 . . . . 22 F8
Leadhill Prim Sch BT6 . . . 22 F7
Lead Hill View 2 BT6 . . . . 22 F8
Leamount Pk BT32 . . . . 61 B3
Leansmount Rd BT67 . . . . 32 A5
Leapoges Rd BT25 . . . . 88 F5
Leatham Sq BT16 . . . . 17 A4
Lecale Pk BT30 . . . . 62 D8
Lecale St BT12 . . . . 14 A2
Lecumpher St BT5 . . . . 15 C3
Ledley Hall Cl 10 BT5 . . . . 15 B4
Leeson St BT12 . . . . 154 B2
Lees Pl BT35 . . . . 131 C5
Leestone Rd BT34 . . . . 153 E8
Leeter Rd BT35 . . . . 148 E6
Leeward Cove BT34 . . . . . 146 C3
Legacorry Pk
4 Richhill BT61 . . . . 85 E1
2 Richhill BT61 . . . . 99 E8
Legacorry Rd BT61 . . . . 85 E1
Legacurry BT27 . . . . 39 A1
Legacurry Rd BT27 . . . . 38 C2
Legaghory BT65 . . . . 41 B2
Legaghory Gn BT65 . . . . . . 41 B2
Legahory Ct BT65 . . . . 41 B2
Legahory La BT65 . . . . 41 C1
Legahory Sh Ctr BT65 . . . . 41 B2
Legamaddy BT30 . . . . 124 E8
Legamaddy Prim Sch
BT30 . . . . 124 E8
Legananny
Banbridge BT32 . . . . 102 B3
Castlewellan BT31 . . . . 105 E4
Legananny Dolmen Chambered Grave★
BT31 . . . . 105 C4
Legananny Hall Rd BT31 . 105 C3
Legananny Rd
Banbridge BT32 . . . . 102 B3
Castlewellan BT31 . . . . 105 C4
Craigavon BT63 . . . . 101 F3
Dromara BT25 . . . . 105 B5
Legane BT69 . . . . 82 B7
Legane Rd BT69 . . . . 82 B7
Leganny BT62 . . . . 50 D7
Legarhill BT60 . . . . 60 A5
Legar Hill La BT71 . . . . 84 A8
Legar Hill Pk BT60 . . . . 60 A6
Legavilly BT61 . . . . 99 C8
Leggygowan BT24 . . . . . . 77 E2
Legmore BT67 . . . . 33 F3
Legmoylin BT35 . . . . 139 F1
Legmoylin Rd BT35 . . . . . 139 E2
Leitrim BT31 . . . . 105 E1
LEITRIM BT31 . . . . 121 E8
Leitrim
Newry BT34 . . . . 134 C3
Newry BT34 . . . . 145 B3
Leitrim Rd
Castlewellan BT31 . . . . 121 E7
Newry BT34 . . . . 134 C4
Leitrim St 5 BT6 . . . . 15 B3
Leitrim Upper BT34 . . . . 145 B6
Lelia St BT4 . . . . 15 C5
Lemberg St BT12 . . . . 154 A1
Lemgare 127 B5
Lemnagore BT60 . . . . 96 D4
Lemonfield Ave BT18 . . . . . . 9 E6
Lemons Rd BT22 . . . . 81 D6
Lenaderg BT32 . . . . 86 D2
Lenaderg Rd BT32 . . . . 86 D2
Lenaghan Ave BT8 . . . . 22 A3
Lenaghan Cres BT8 . . . . . . 22 A3
Lenaghan Ct BT8 . . . . 22 A3
Lenaghan Gdns BT8 . . . . . . 22 A2
Lenaghan Pk BT8 . . . . 22 A3
Lenalea BT60 . . . . 99 C4
Lenalea Rd BT60 . . . . 99 C5
Lenamore Pk
Lisburn BT28 . . . . 26 A3
Newtownards BT23 . . . . 19 F4
Lena St BT5 . . . . 15 D5
Lendrick St BT5 . . . . 15 B5
Lenish BT34 . . . . 120 D1
Lennox Ave BT8 . . . . 22 B4
Lennoxvale BT9 . . . . 14 C1
Lennys Rd BT66 . . . . 75 A6
Leode BT34 . . . . 133 D5
Leode Rd BT34 . . . . 133 E5
Lepper St BT15 . . . . 14 D8
Lesh BT35 . . . . 117 B3
Lesh Rd BT35 . . . . 117 A3
Leslie Hill BT21 . . . . 67 A8
Leslie Hill Cres BT21 . . . . . 67 A8
Lessans BT24 . . . . 77 B6
Lessans Rd BT24 . . . . 77 B6
Lester Ave BT28 . . . . 26 B3
Letalian BT34 . . . . 121 A2
Letalian Rd BT34 . . . . 121 C3
Levaghery BT63 . . . . 52 A3
Levaghery Cl BT63 . . . . 51 F4
Levaghery Gdns BT63 . . . . 52 A4
Levalleglish BT61 . . . . . . 85 A5
Levallyclanone BT34 . . 143 C4
Levallymore BT35 . . . . . 140 C6
Levallyreagh
Dromore BT25 . . . . 89 B1
Newry BT34 . . . . 143 A5
Levallyreagh Rd
Dromara BT25 . . . . 89 B1
Newry BT34 . . . . 143 A4
Leven Cl BT5 . . . . 16 E2
Leven Cres BT5 . . . . 16 F2
Leven Dr BT5 . . . . 16 E2
Leven Pk BT5 . . . . 16 E2
Leven Pl BT5 . . . . 16 E2
Leveroge BT8 . . . . 28 D2
Leverogue Rd
Belfast BT8 . . . . 28 E2
Lisburn BT27 . . . . 76 C8
Levin Rd
Lurgan BT67 . . . . 42 B8
Newry BT35 . . . . 130 B5
Lewis Ave BT4 . . . . 15 C5
Lewis Ct BT6 . . . . 15 B3
Lewis Dr BT4 . . . . 15 C5
Lewis Gdns BT4 . . . . 15 D5
Lewis Pk BT4 . . . . 15 C5
Liberty Rd BT24 . . . . 77 E5
Liberty The 4 BT22 . . . . . . 94 D4
Library St BT1 . . . . 155 A4
Lichfield Ave BT5 . . . . 15 D4
Liffey Ct 18 BT14 . . . . 14 B8
Lighthouse Rd BT31 . . . . . 105 B1
Lilac Wlk BT17 . . . . 26 F7
Lilburn Hall BT66 . . . . 42 D4
Lime Ct BT13 . . . . 154 C4
Limefield Rise BT65 . . . . . . 41 B2
Lime Gr
Comber BT23 . . . . 25 C3
Lurgan BT67 . . . . 42 B5
Limehill Rd BT27 . . . . 38 E5
Limehurst Way BT27 . . . . . 26 D2
Limekiln Rd BT35 . . . . 131 D4
Lime Kiln Rd BT67 . . . . 35 D8
Limestone Rd 13 BT15 . . . . 14 E8
Limetree Hill 3 BT30 . . . . 93 C5
Limetree Hollow 2 BT30 . 93 C5
Limetree Hts BT23 . . . . 77 E8
Limewood Gr BT4 . . . . 9 A1
Lincoln Ave BT14 . . . . 14 C7
Lincoln Pl BT12 . . . . 155 A2
Lincoln Sq BT12 . . . . 154 A2
Linden Brea BT34 . . . . 146 C3
Linden Cl BT24 . . . . 77 C3
Linden Gdns BT19 . . . . 4 F3
Linden Pk BT19 . . . . 4 F3
Linden Pl BT23 . . . . 19 C4
Linden St BT13 . . . . 154 A2
Linden Wlk BT17 . . . . 27 A8
Lindisfarne Rd BT30 . . . . . 62 E3
Lindsay Ct BT7 . . . . 155 A1
Lindsay St BT7 . . . . 155 A1
Lindsay Way BT7 . . . . 155 A1
Linehall St BT32 . . . . 61 C4
Linenfields BT32 . . . . 86 D1
Linen Hall St W BT2 . . . . . 155 A2
Linenhall St
Armagh BT60 . . . . 60 D4
7 Banbridge BT32 . . . . 61 C4
Linen Hall St BT2 . . . . 155 A2
Linfield Ave BT12 . . . . 154 C2
Linfield Dr BT12 . . . . 154 C2
Linfield Ind Est BT12 . . . . 154 C2
Linfield Rd BT12 . . . . 154 C2
Link Rd BT28 . . . . 26 A2
Links Cres 17 BT22 . . . . . . 94 D3
Links Dr 7 BT22 . . . . 94 D4
Linkside Pk BT33 . . . . 63 E7
Links Rd BT22 . . . . 81 B2
Links The BT30 . . . . 94 C2
Linley Dr BT23 . . . . 25 E5
Linneybrook Cotts BT19 . . . 4 C1
Linneybrook Ct BT20 . . . . . . 4 C2
Linneybrook La BT20 . . . . . . 4 C1
Linnhurst Pk 5 BT24 . . . . . 91 B1
Linseys Hill 6 BT61 . . . . . 98 F7
Linsey's Hill BT61 . . . . 60 F6
Lintagh Cres BT26 . . . . 89 D8
Lintagh Pk BT26 . . . . 89 D8
Linview Ct BT12 . . . . 154 B2
LIOS NA GCEARRBHACH (LISBURN) BT27 . . . . 26 E2
Lir Gdns BT60 . . . . 114 A2
Lisadell Dr BT20 . . . . 4 B1
Lisadell Pl BT20 . . . . 4 B1
Lisadian
Armagh BT60 . . . . 130 E8
Armagh BT61 . . . . 97 F7
Hillsborough BT26 . . . . 46 D7
Lisagally Rd BT60 . . . . 97 C4
Lisamintry BT64 . . . . 53 A5
Lisamintry Rath★ BT64 . . . 52 F5
Lisamry BT35 . . . . 147 C8
Lisamry Fort★ BT35 . . . . . 147 C7
Lisanally Gdns BT61 . . . . . 60 D7
Lisanally La BT61 . . . . 60 D6
Lisanally Specl Sch BT61 . 60 E7
Lisavague BT62 . . . . 55 B1
Lisavon Dr BT4 . . . . 15 D7
Lisavon Par BT4 . . . . 15 D6
Lisavon St BT4 . . . . 15 D6
Lisbancarney BT71 . . . . . 83 B7
Lisbane
Armagh BT61 . . . . 97 E8
Ballynahinch BT24 . . . . 76 F3
Bangor BT19 . . . . 12 E6
Craigavon BT62 . . . . 101 B5
Downpatrick BT30 . . . . 109 A8
Newtownards BT22 . . . . 80 E3
LISBANE BT23 . . . . 68 D1
Lisbane Dr BT23 . . . . 19 C3
Lisbanemore★ BT35 . . . . 141 D5
Lisbane Pk
1 Mayobridge BT34 . . . . . 133 B4
Newtownards BT23 . . . . 12 F5
Lisbane Rd
Ballynahinch BT24 . . . . 76 E3
Craigavon BT62 . . . . 101 D4
Newtownards BT22 . . . . 80 E3
Newtownards BT23 . . . . 68 F1
Lisbanlemneigh BT71 . . 83 D7
Lisbanoe BT60 . . . . 98 B3
Lisbarnet BT23 . . . . 68 D2
Lisbarnet Ct BT23 . . . . 68 E1
Lisbarnett Rd BT23 . . . . . . 68 D1
Lisbofin Rd BT71 . . . . 84 B5
Lisbon St BT5 . . . . 15 A5
Lisboy BT30 . . . . 93 B1
Lisboy Rd BT30 . . . . 109 B8
LISBURN BT27 . . . . 37 E7
Lisburn Ave BT9 . . . . 21 A8
Lisburn Bsns Pk BT27 . . . . 38 C8
Lisburn Central Prim Sch
BT28 . . . . 38 A8
Lisburn Golf Club BT27 . . . 37 D3
Lisburn Inst of FE & HE
BT27 . . . . 26 B1
Lisburn Leisure Pk BT28 . 38 A8
LISBURN (LIOS NA GCEARRBHACH) BT27 . . . . 26 E2
Lisburn Mus & Irish Linen Ctr★ 3 BT28 . . . . 26 B1
Lisburn Rd
Ballynahinch BT24 . . . . 77 A4
Belfast BT9 . . . . 154 C1
Craigavon BT67 . . . . 34 E4
Hillsborough BT26 . . . . 47 C7
Lisburn BT28 . . . . 36 B6
Lisburn Sq BT28 . . . . 26 A1
Lisburn St BT24 . . . . 59 A6
Lisburn Sta BT28 . . . . 26 B2
Liscalgat BT35 . . . . 148 B7
Liscalgot Rd BT35 . . . . . . 148 B7
Liscorran BT67 . . . . 32 A2
Lisdalgan BT24 . . . . 77 B4
Lisdarragh
Dungannon BT71 . . . . 84 A5
Newry BT35 . . . . 64 B8
Lisdonwilly BT61 . . . . 84 D1
Lisdonwilly Rd BT61 . . . . . 84 C1
Lisdoo Cashel★ BT35 . . . . 141 E5
Lisdoonan BT24 . . . . 77 B8
Lisdoonan Cl BT8 . . . . 29 F1
Lisdoonan Rd
Ballynahinch BT24 . . . . 77 B7
Belfast BT8 . . . . 29 F1
Lisdown BT60 . . . . 97 E7
Lisdown Rd BT60 . . . . 97 E7
Lisdrumard BT60 . . . . 97 E4
Lisdrum Ave 3 BT35 . . . . 131 F5
Lisdrumbrughas BT60 . . 97 F1
Lisdrumchor Lower
BT60 . . . . 116 C3
Lisdrumchor Upper
BT60 . . . . 116 B1
Lisdrum Ct BT35 . . . . 64 B3
Lisdrumgullion
Newry BT35 . . . . 64 C7
Newry BT35 . . . . 131 F5
Lisdrumliska BT35 . . . . . . 64 C4
Lisdrum Pk BT35 . . . . 64 B1
Lisduff
Dungannon BT71 . . . . 83 D6
Newry BT34 . . . . 132 A7
Lisduff La BT71 . . . . 83 D5
Lisfaddan Cres BT12 . . . . 154 B3
Lisfaddan Dr BT12 . . . . . . 154 C3
Lisfaddan Pl BT12 . . . . . . 154 C3
Lisfaddan Way BT12 . . . . . 154 C3
Lisglynn BT60 . . . . 113 C8

LisgobbanⓉ BT71 . . . . 83 D7
Lisgobban Rd BT71 . . . . . . 83 D6
Lisgullion Pk BT35 . . . . 64 C8
Lisieux Ave BT34 . . . . 65 D3
Lisieux Ct BT34 . . . . 65 D3
LisinawⓉ BT30 . . . . 92 F8
Lisinaw Rd BT30 . . . . 78 F1
Liska Ave BT35 . . . . 64 B2
Liska Hts BT35 . . . . 64 B2
Liska Rd BT35 . . . . 64 B2
LiskyboroughⓉ BT61 . . . . . 85 D2
Lislane Ct 9 BT24 . . . . 77 C3
Lislane Dr 10 BT24 . . . . . . 77 C3
Lislane Hill 17 BT24 . . . . . . 77 C3
Lislane Pk 13 BT24 . . . . 77 C3
LislaslyⓉ BT61 . . . . 84 D6
Lislasly Rd BT71 . . . . 84 C5
LisleaⓉ
Armagh BT60 . . . . 98 A1
Armagh BT60 . . . . 113 C3
Armagh BT60 . . . . 114 E7
Newry BT35 . . . . 130 E1
Omeath 142 B2
Lislea Dr BT30 . . . . 92 B5
LisleenⓉ BT23 . . . . 23 E3
Lisleen Pl BT23 . . . . 19 C4
Lisleen Rd BT5 . . . . 23 D6
Lisleen Rd E BT5 . . . . 23 F4
Lisleen Rd S
Moneyreagh BT23 . . . . 30 F8
Newtownards BT23 . . . . 23 F1
Lisleitrim Fort★ BT35 . . . 138 E5
Lisleitrim Rd BT35 . . . . . . 138 E5
LisloonyⓉ BT60 . . . . 96 F3
Lismahon Motte★ BT30 . 123 F8
LismaineⓉ BT67 . . . . 43 E2
Lismaine Rd BT67 . . . . 43 E2
Lismain St BT6 . . . . 15 B2
Lismara BT65 . . . . 41 A1
Lismara Pl BT23 . . . . 19 C4
LismoreⓉ BT30 . . . . 110 A3
Lismore Ave BT20 . . . . 4 B1
Lismore Comp Sch BT65 . 41 C1
Lismore Dr BT16 . . . . 17 E4
Lismore Pk BT35 . . . . 147 F7
Lismore Rd BT30 . . . . 109 F3
Lismore St BT6 . . . . 15 A3
LismulladownⓉ BT68 . . . . 82 B2
LisnabillaⓉ BT67 . . . . 34 E5
Lisnabilla Rd BT67 . . . . 34 E5
LisnabragueⓉ BT35 . . . . . 101 E2
Lisnabreen Cres BT20 . . . . . . 4 B1
Lisnabreen Wlk BT20 . . . . 4 B1
LisnabreenyⓉ BT6 . . . . 22 F3
Lisnabreeny Rd BT6 . . . . . . 22 F4
Lisnabreeny Rd E BT6 . . . . 23 A4
LisnacreeⓉ BT34 . . . . 152 C8
Lisnacree UpperⓉ BT34 . 144 B1
LisnacreevyⓉ BT34 . . . . . 119 C6
LisnacroppanⓉ BT34 . . . . 119 F5
Lisnacroppin Rd BT32 . . . 119 C6
LisnacroyⓉ BT71 . . . . 83 C6
LisnadillⓉ BT60 . . . . 114 E8
Lisnadill Prim Sch BT60 . . 98 E1
LisnafeedyⓉ BT60 . . . . 83 B1
Lisnafeedy Rd BT60 . . . . . . 83 A2
Lisnafiffy Rd BT63 . . . . . . 102 B7
Lisnafiffy (Seapatrick)Ⓣ
BT32 . . . . 86 C1
Lisnafiffy (Tullylish)Ⓣ
BT63 . . . . 102 B8
LisnagadeⓉ BT32 . . . . 102 A5
Lisnagade Rd BT32 . . . . . . 102 A5
Lisnagarvey Dr BT28 . . . . . 26 A3
Lisnagarvey High Sch
BT28 . . . . 37 F8
LisnagarvyⓉ BT28 . . . . 26 B2
LisnagatⓉ BT60 . . . . 115 F6
Lisnagat Rd BT60 . . . . 115 E6
LisnagonnellⓉ BT32 . . . . 118 B8
LisnagreeⓉ BT35 . . . . 117 B5
LisnagreeveⓉ 127 D2
Lisnahilta Rath★ BT34 . . 145 E2
LisnakeaⓉ BT62 . . . . 101 B5
LisnaleeⓉ BT60 . . . . 117 A2
Lisnalee Pk BT60 . . . . 117 A1
Lisnalee Rd BT60 . . . . 117 A1
LisnamaulⓉ BT30 . . . . . . 108 A3
LisnamoreⓉ BT30 . . . . 92 B2
LisnamulliganⓉ BT34 . . . 134 B7
Lisnamulligan Rd BT34 . . 134 B8
LisnareeⓉ
Banbridge BT32 . . . . 103 B6
Newry BT34 . . . . 119 A2
Lisnaree Rd
Banbridge BT32 . . . . 103 A5
Newry BT34 . . . . 118 F1
LisnasallaghⓉ BT8 . . . . 30 B1
Lisnasallagh Rd BT8 . . . . . 30 B2
LisnashankerⓉ BT25 . . . . . 45 B1
Lisnashanker Rd BT25 . . . . 45 A1
Lisnasharragh High Sch
BT6 . . . . 22 D8
Lisnasharragh Pk BT6 . . . . 22 E8
Lisnasharragh Prim Sch
BT6 . . . . 22 D8
LisnasligganⓉ BT32 . . . . 103 C1
LisnastreanⓉ BT27 . . . . . . 39 A4
Lisnastrean Rd BT27 . . . . . 39 A4
LisnasureⓉ BT66 . . . . 87 A7
Lisnasure Rd BT66 . . . . 86 F7
LisnatiernyⓉ BT34 . . . . . . 118 C6
Lisnatruck (Blaris)Ⓣ
BT27 . . . . 26 E1
Lisnatrunk (Lambeg)Ⓣ
BT27 . . . . 26 F2
LisnavaghrogⓉ BT32 . . . . 120 A7
Lisnavaragh Rd BT32 . . . . 102 A4
LisnawardⓉ BT25 . . . . 87 E2
Lisnaward Hill BT32 . . . . . . 87 E2
LisneanyⓉ BT61 . . . . 85 B5
LisniskⓉ
Armagh BT60 . . . . 116 F6
Banbridge BT32 . . . . 120 D3
LisniskyⓉ BT63 . . . . 52 C7
Lisnisky La BT63 . . . . 52 C7
Lisnisky Rd BT63 . . . . 52 C8
LisnodeⓉ BT27 . . . . 76 A7
Lisnode Rd BT27 . . . . 39 F6
LisnoeⓉ BT27 . . . . 38 C3
Lisnoe Pk BT27 . . . . 38 B2
Lisnoe Rd BT27 . . . . 38 D3
Lisnoe Wlk BT28 . . . . 37 E8
LisoidⓉ BT30 . . . . 125 A6
Lisoid Rd BT30 . . . . 125 A6
LisowenⓉ BT24 . . . . 91 E8
LisrawⓉ BT35 . . . . 101 C1
Lisraw Rd
Craigavon BT62 . . . . 101 C4
Newry BT35 . . . . 117 C8
LisroanⓉ BT71 . . . . 72 A2
Lissacashel★ BT35 . . . . . . 150 B7
LissagallyⓉ BT60 . . . . 97 C2
Lissan Cl BT6 . . . . 22 B7
LissaraⓉ BT30 . . . . 92 A4
Lissara Cl 4 BT30 . . . . 92 B5
LissarawⓉ
Newry BT35 . . . . 130 F4
Newry BT35 . . . . 147 E6
Lissaraw Rd
Crossmaglen BT35 . . . . . . 147 F6
Newry BT35 . . . . 131 A4
LisserboyⓉ BT34 . . . . 118 C2
Lisserboy Rd BT34 . . . . . . 118 B2
Lissheagh or Mount IrwinⓉ
BT60 . . . . 97 A2
LissheffieldⓉ BT61 . . . . . . 85 C4
Lissheffield Rd BT61 . . . . . 85 C4
LissizeⓉ BT34 . . . . 119 F3
Lissize Ave BT34 . . . . 119 F2
Lissize Pk 1 BT34 . . . . . . 119 F2
Lissize Rd BT34 . . . . 119 F4
Lissize Villas 3 BT34 . . . . 119 F2
LisslanlyⓉ BT60 . . . . 113 A6
Lissue Cres BT28 . . . . 37 E8
Lissue East Ind Est BT28 . 37 A8
Lissue La BT28 . . . . 36 F8
Lissue Rd BT28 . . . . 37 A8
LissummonⓉ BT35 . . . . . 117 C3
Lissummon Fort★ BT35 . 117 C3
Lissummon Rd BT35 . . . . 117 C1
ListamletⓉ BT71 . . . . 72 B3
Listamlet Rd BT71 . . . . 72 B4
ListarkeltⓉ BT60 . . . . 127 B8
LISTOODER BT30 . . . . 91 E5
Listooder Gdns 12 BT24 . . 77 C3
Listooder Pk 11 BT24 . . . . 77 C3
Listooder Rd
Ballynahinch BT24 . . . . 77 C1
Downpatrick BT30 . . . . 91 D7
Listrakelt Rd BT60 . . . . . . 113 A1
Listullyard Rd BT63 . . . . . 102 C7
ListullycurranⓉ BT25 . . . . 46 B1
Listullycurran Rd
Dromara BT25 . . . . 46 A2
Hillsborough BT26 . . . . 45 F3
Lisvarna Hts BT12 . . . . . . 154 B2
Lisvarna Pl BT12 . . . . 154 B2
Little Barrack St 5 BT60 . 60 D5
Little Charlotte St BT7 . . 155 B1
Little Donegall St BT1 . . . 155 A4
Little Edward St BT1 . . . . 155 B4
Little Forest BT63 . . . . 52 B5
Little May St BT2 . . . . 155 B2
Little Patrick St BT15 . . . . 155 B4
Little Victoria St BT2 . . . . 155 A2
Little Wenham BT67 . . . . . . 34 A3
Little West St BT62 . . . . 51 D4
Little York St
Belfast BT1 . . . . 155 A4
2 Belfast BT15 . . . . 14 E7
Livins Rd BT34 . . . . 145 A4
Lizanne Pk BT66 . . . . 42 B3
Loanda Cres BT35 . . . . 64 B5
LOCH GCÁL (LOUGHGALL)
BT61 . . . . 85 B5
Loch Glen BT20 . . . . 3 E4
Lochinver Ave BT18 . . . . . . 10 A7
Lochinver Dr BT5 . . . . 16 E2
Loch Lao (Lough Lea)
BT5 . . . . 15 A5
Lockside Ct BT9 . . . . 21 D7
Locksley Bsns Pk BT6 . . . . 15 E1
Lockview Rd BT9 . . . . 21 E7
Lodge La BT23 . . . . 19 D5
LOG AN CHOIRE (RICHHILL)
BT61 . . . . 85 E1
Lombard St BT1 . . . . 155 A3
Lomond Ave BT4 . . . . 15 D5
Lomond St BT4 . . . . 15 D5
Londonderry Ave BT23 . . . 25 C4
Londonderry Gdns BT23 . . 25 B3
Londonderry Hill BT23 . . . 25 B4
Londonderry Pk BT23 . . . . 25 B3
Londonderry Pk BT23 . . . . 19 F4
Londonderry Prim Sch
BT23 . . . . 19 C6
Londonderry Rd BT23 . . . 19 E6
Londonderry Rise BT23 . . . 25 B3
London Rd BT6 . . . . 15 A3
London St BT6 . . . . 15 A3
LONEY'S TOWN BT61 . . . . . 85 D1
Longacre BT8 . . . . 22 A5
LongfieldⓉ BT35 . . . . 140 D3
Longfield Hts BT35 . . . . . . 140 D1
Longfield Rd
3 Forkhill BT35 . . . . 149 D8
Newry BT35 . . . . 140 C4
Long Island Dr
Kircubbin BT22 . . . . 80 E7
Newtownards BT23 . . . . 19 F7
Long Kesh BT27 . . . . 37 E4
Long La BT63 . . . . 52 D1
LonglandsⓉ BT23 . . . . 68 E7
Longlands Dr BT23 . . . . 25 E4
Longlands Rd BT23 . . . . . . 68 E7
Long Sheelah Ave 4
BT22 . . . . 80 E7
LongstoneⓉ BT61 . . . . 60 D8
Longstone Ave BT16 . . . . . 17 D3
Longstone Cl 7 BT16 . . . . 17 D2
Longstone Cres 8 BT16 . . 17 D3
Longstone Ct 5 BT16 . . . . 17 D3
Longstone Dr 6 BT16 . . . . 17 D3
Longstone Gn 13 BT16 . . . 17 D3
Longstone Hill BT34 . . . . . 119 D1
Longstone Hospl BT61 . . . 60 D8
Longstone Mews (Langstane Stablins) 4 BT16 . . . . 17 D3
Longstone Rd BT34 . . . . . 146 B4
Longstone Sch BT16 . . . . . 17 D3
Longstone Way 9 BT16 . . 17 D3
Lonsdale Rd BT61 . . . . 60 D6
LooartⓉ 112 A7
Loopland Cres BT6 . . . . 15 B2
Loopland Dr BT6 . . . . 15 B2
Loopland Gdns BT6 . . . . . . 15 C2
Loopland Gr BT6 . . . . 15 C2
Loopland Par BT6 . . . . 15 C2
Loopland Pk BT6 . . . . 15 C2
Loopland Rd BT6 . . . . 15 C2
Lord Moira Pk BT24 . . . . . . 59 B5
Lord St BT5 . . . . 15 B4
Lord Wardens Ave BT19 . . 12 E7
Lord Wardens Chase
BT19 . . . . 12 E7
Lord Wardens Cres 6
BT19 . . . . 12 F7
Lord Wardens Ct BT19 . . . 12 E8
Lord Wardens Dale 3
BT19 . . . . 12 F7
Lord Wardens Dr 4 BT19 12 F7
Lord Wardens Glade
BT19 . . . . 12 D8
Lord Wardens Glen BT19 . 12 E7
Lord Wardens Gn 1 BT19 12 F7
Lord Wardens Gr 7 BT19 12 F7
Lord Wardens Grange
BT19 . . . . 12 E7
Lord Wardens Hollow
BT19 . . . . 12 D7
Lord Wardens Manor
BT19 . . . . 12 E7
Lord Wardens Mdw BT19 . 12 E7
Lord Wardens Mews 2
BT19 . . . . 12 F7
Lord Wardens Mount
BT19 . . . . 12 E7
Lord Wardens Par BT19 . . 12 E7
Lord Wardens Pk 5 BT19 12 F7
Lord Wardens Rd BT19 . . . 12 E7
Lord Wardens Vale BT19 . 12 E7
Lord Wardens View BT19 . 12 E7
Loretto Pk BT35 . . . . 64 C3
Lorne La BT18 . . . . 1 E2
Lorne St BT9 . . . . 14 B1
Lothian Ave BT5 . . . . 16 E3
Louden St Ind Est BT13 . 154 C4
Louden St BT13 . . . . 154 C4
LoughadianⓉ BT35 . . . . . 101 F1
Loughadian Ct BT35 . . . . . 117 E8
Loughadian Rd BT35 . . . . 117 E8
Loughaghery Rd BT26 . . . . 89 E8
LoughansⓉ BT63 . . . . 57 B1
Loughaveely Rd BT35 . . . 148 E7
Lough Beg Pk BT8 . . . . 29 C3
LoughbrattogeⓉ 127 F4
LOUGHBRICKLAND BT32 . . 102 C3
Loughbrickland Prim Sch (No 2) BT32 . . . . 102 D2
Loughbrickland Rd BT63 101 F7
Lough Brickland Rd
BT34 . . . . 119 C4
Lough Brin Pk BT8 . . . . 29 C3
Loughbrook Ind Est
BT35 . . . . 131 D4
Lough Caragh Pk BT8 . . . . 29 C3
Lough Cowey Rd BT22 . . . . 94 C6
Lough Derg Pk BT8 . . . . . . 29 C3
LoughdooⓉ BT22 . . . . 80 E1
Loughdoo Rd BT22 . . . . 80 E1
Loughend Rd BT32 . . . . . . 102 D1
Lough Erne Pk BT8 . . . . . . 29 C2
Lougherne Rd BT26 . . . . . . 76 A1
Lough Fine Pk BT8 . . . . 29 C3
Loughgall FC BT61 . . . . 85 A5
Loughgall Golf Club BT61 85 A4
LOUGHGALL (LOCH GCÁL)
BT61 . . . . 85 B5
Loughgall Rd
Armagh BT61 . . . . 60 C8
Craigavon BT62 . . . . 50 F3
Portadown BT62 . . . . 51 A3
LOUGHINISLAND BT30 . . . . 107 D6
Loughinisland Rd BT30 . . . 92 A1
LoughkeelanⓉ BT30 . . . . 109 F6
Loughkeeland Rd BT30 . . 109 F5
Lough Lane BT66 . . . . 74 A8
Lough Lea (Loch Lao)
BT5 . . . . 15 A5
Lough Leane Pk BT8 . . . . . 29 C3
LoughmoneyⓉ BT30 . . . . 109 E6
Loughmoney Rd BT30 . . . 109 D8
Lough Moss Ctr BT8 . . . . . 29 D2
Lough Moss Pk BT8 . . . . . . 29 C3
Lough Mourne Pk BT8 . . . 29 D2
LoughorneⓉ BT34 . . . . . . 118 E3
Loughorne Rd BT34 . . . . . 118 D1
Lough Quarter Rd BT30 . 108 B5
Lough Rd
Armagh BT60 . . . . 115 F4
Ballynahinch BT24 . . . . 77 F3
Banbridge BT32 . . . . 104 C5
Craigavon BT62 . . . . 100 D4
Craigavon BT63 . . . . 102 A7
Craigavon BT66 . . . . 75 E5
Downpatrick BT30 . . . . 92 D6
Dromara BT25 . . . . 87 B8
Lisburn BT27 . . . . 76 D2
Lurgan BT66 . . . . 41 F7
Newry BT35 . . . . 129 D1
LOUGHRIES BT22 . . . . 20 F2
Loughries Prim Sch BT23 20 E2
Loughries Rd BT23 . . . . 20 F3
LoughriscouseⓉ BT23 . . . 66 A3
Lough Road Learning Ctr
BT67 . . . . 41 F7
LoughrossⓉ BT35 . . . . . . 147 D8
Loughross Rd (Bóthar Loch Rois) BT35 . . . . 147 D7
Loughshore Rd BT22 . . . . . . 94 B6
Loughside Dr BT24 . . . . 59 D4
Loughside Ind Pk BT3 . . . . . 8 A3
Lough Swilly Pk BT8 . . . . . 29 C3
Loughview 8 BT30 . . . . 93 C5
Loughview Ave BT18 . . . . . . 9 D4
Loughview Bsns Pk BT3 . . . 8 E3
Loughview Cl BT30 . . . . . . 107 D6
Loughview Dr BT6 . . . . 22 B6
Lough View Hts BT22 . . . . . 94 D3
Lough View Integrated Prim Sch BT6 . . . . 22 E7
Loughview Pk BT34 . . . . . . 64 E4
Loughview Rd BT23 . . . . . . 68 A1
Lovatt St BT5 . . . . 15 D4
Loverock Cl 3 BT19 . . . . 3 D1
Loverock Dr 2 BT19 . . . . 3 D1
Loverock Way BT19 . . . . 3 E1
Lower BT65 . . . . 41 A2
Lower Aghincurk Rd
BT35 . . . . 129 F8
Lower Balloo Rd BT19 . . . . . 5 D6
Lower Braniel Rd 6 BT5 . 16 A1
Lower Burren Rd BT31 . . 122 C3
Lower Carrogs Rd BT34 . 142 B8
Lower Castlevennon
BT32 . . . . 103 F4
Lower Catherine St BT35 . 64 C6
Lower Clay Rd
Armagh BT60 . . . . 113 D1
Downpatrick BT30 . . . . 79 B2
Lower Clonard St BT12 . . 154 A2
Lower Cres
Belfast BT13 . . . . 154 A3
Comber BT23 . . . . 25 E3
Lower Darkley Rd BT60 . . 114 C2
Lower Dromore Rd BT34 . 65 A4
Lower English St BT61 . . . 60 C6
Lower Foughill Rd BT35 . 141 C4
Lower Garfield St BT1 . . . 155 A4
Lower Kilburn St BT12 . . 154 A1
Lower Knockbarragh
BT34 . . . . 133 E1
Lower Lisdrumchor
BT60 . . . . 116 C4
Lower Mary St 3 BT23 . . . 19 D5
Lower Quilly Rd BT25 . . . . 58 A5
Lower Regent St (Sráid Ríona Íochtir) BT13 . . . . . 155 A4
Lower Rockview St BT12 154 A1
Lower Sq 4 BT31 . . . . 122 C5
Lower Stanfield St BT7 . . 155 B2
Lower Water St BT34 . . . . . 64 D5
Lower Windsor Ave BT9 . . 14 B1
Lowes Ind Est BT8 . . . . 29 D2
Lowes La BT35 . . . . 131 C4
Lowland Ave BT5 . . . . 16 E3
Lowland Gdns BT5 . . . . 16 E3
Low Rd
Lisburn BT27 . . . . 26 D2
Newry BT35 . . . . 140 F2
Lowry Ct BT7 . . . . 21 E6
Lowry Hill BT19 . . . . 3 B4
Lowry's Farm BT19 . . . . 3 B4
Lowry's La BT19 . . . . 3 B4
Lowtown Rd BT66 . . . . 86 B4
Lúb Bholcáin (Vulcan Link)
18 BT5 . . . . 15 A5
Lúb Tullach Phoitinséir (Mountpottinger Link) 36
BT5 . . . . 15 A5
Lucerne Par BT9 . . . . 21 D7
Ludlow Sq
2 Belfast BT15 . . . . 14 D8
4 Belfast BT15 . . . . 14 D8
LurgaboyⓉ BT60 . . . . 99 E2
LurganaⓉ BT60 . . . . 130 C7
LURGAN (AN LORGAIN)
BT66 . . . . 41 E7
Lurgana Rd BT60 . . . . 130 B6
LurganareⓉ BT34 . . . . 118 A1
LurganbaneⓉ BT25 . . . . . . 88 C5
Lurganbane Rd BT25 . . . . . 88 C5
LurgancahoneⓉ BT34 . . . 119 C1
Lurgancahone Rd BT34 . . 119 C1
LurgancantyⓉ BT34 . . . . . 143 A8
Lurgancanty Rd BT34 . . . . 142 F7
Lurgan Coll BT66 . . . . 41 E7
LurganconaryⓉ
Newry BT34 . . . . 152 F4
Newry BT34 . . . . 152 F5
Lurganconary Rd BT34 . . 152 F4
LurgancotⓉ BT61 . . . . 85 F5
LurgancullenboyⓉ BT35 139 C1
Lurgancullenboy Rd
BT35 . . . . 148 D8
LurganearlyⓉ 138 D8
Lurgan Golf Course BT67 . 42 C6
Lurgan Hospl BT66 . . . . 41 F4
Lurgan Jun High Sch
BT66 . . . . 42 B4
LurgankeelⓉ 149 D5
Lurgan Model Prim Sch
BT67 . . . . 42 A6
Lurgan Pk★ BT67 . . . . 42 B6
Lurgan Rd
Banbridge BT32 . . . . 86 D1
Craigavon BT67 . . . . 32 E7
Dromara BT25 . . . . 58 B5
Gilford BT63 . . . . 57 C3
Moira BT67 . . . . 34 A1
Newry BT35 . . . . 139 C1
Portadown BT63 . . . . 52 C7
Seapatrick BT32 . . . . 61 C8
LurganreaghⓉ BT34 . . . . 152 F5
Lurganreagh Rd BT34 . . . 152 E5
LurgansemanusⓉ BT67 . . 33 F7
Lurgan Sta BT67 . . . . 41 F6
LurgantamryⓉ BT66 . . . . . 87 A6
LurgantarryⓉ BT67 . . . . . . 32 A1
Lurgan Tarry BT67 . . . . 42 B8
LurganureⓉ BT28 . . . . 36 D6
Lurganure Rd BT28 . . . . . . 36 E6
LurganvilleⓉ BT67 . . . . . . 45 B7
Lurganville Rd BT67 . . . . . . 45 C6
LurgyrossⓉ BT60 . . . . . . 116 B3
LurgyvallenⓉ BT61 . . . . . . 60 A7
Lurgyvallen Ct BT61 . . . . . . 60 B6
Lusky Rd BT23 . . . . 78 D5
Luxor Gdns BT5 . . . . 15 E4
Lyden Gate BT63 . . . . 52 C5
Lyden Gate Pk BT63 . . . . . 52 B5
Lyle Rd BT20 . . . . 4 E5
LyloⓉ BT64 . . . . 52 E6
Lyndale Dr BT19 . . . . 4 F2
Lyndale Pk 1 BT19 . . . . 4 F3
Lyndhurst Ave BT19 . . . . 3 D3
Lyndhurst Cres BT19 . . . . . . 3 D3
Lynedale Grange BT63 . . . 52 A8
Lynn Ave BT25 . . . . 58 D4
Lynn Cres BT25 . . . . 58 C4
Lynn Doyle Pl (Plás Linn uí Dhúill) BT30 . . . . 62 C4
Lynne Ave BT19 . . . . 3 C2
Lynne Cres BT19 . . . . 3 C2
Lynnehurst Dr BT23 . . . . . . 25 B3
Lynnehurst Pk BT23 . . . . . 25 B3
Lynne Link 5 BT19 . . . . 3 C2
Lynne Rd BT19 . . . . 3 C2
Lynwood Pk BT18 . . . . 9 E5
Lyric Players Theatre★
BT9 . . . . 21 D8
Lysander Pk BT23 . . . . 19 C1

M

M12 Bsns Ctr BT63 . . . . 40 B3
Mabel Ct BT12 . . . . 154 C1
McAdam Gdns BT12 . . . . . 154 C2
McAdam Pk BT12 . . . . 154 C2
McAllister Mews BT4 . . . . . 15 C6
MacantrimⓉ BT60 . . . . 99 F5
McArthur Ct BT4 . . . . 15 B6
McAteer Villas 3 BT34 . . 132 C2
McAuley St BT7 . . . . 155 B2
McCandless St 3 BT13 . . . 14 A7
McCartans Rd BT31 . . . . . 121 E7
McCartney Pl BT67 . . . . 34 C1
McCaughan Pk BT6 . . . . 22 D7
McCaughey Rd BT3 . . . . 8 A1
McCavans Pl BT2 . . . . 155 A2
McCleery St BT15 . . . . 14 D7
McClenaghans Hill BT35 131 C6
McClintock St BT2 . . . . . . 155 A2
McClure St BT7 . . . . 155 A1
McCormack Dr 2 BT66 . . . 41 F3
McCormack Gdns BT66 . . . 41 F3
MCCREADY'S CORNER
BT61 . . . . 84 C2
McDermott's Cnr 150 B5
McDermotts GAC BT12 . . 154 A2
McDonnell Ct BT12 . . . . . . 154 B2
McDonnell St BT12 . . . . . . 154 B2
McDowell's Cnr BT63 . . . . 57 D4
McGoldricks Villas BT34 . 153 C6
McGreavy Dr
Craigavon BT66 . . . . 40 E7
Craigavon BT66 . . . . 40 F7
McGreavy Pk BT66 . . . . 40 F7
McIlwaine La BT19 . . . . 5 E6
Macinish Rd BT31 . . . . 106 A3
McIvor's Pl BT13 . . . . 154 C4
McKays Rd BT31 . . . . 122 C8
McKees Bridge Rd BT26 . . 47 A3
McKenna Rd BT22 . . . . 80 F6
Mackey's La BT25 . . . . 87 E4
McKibben's Ct BT1 . . . . . . 155 A4
MCKINLEY PARK BT35 . . . . 139 B8
McKinstry Rd BT17 . . . . 26 C7
Macleans Cl BT34 . . . . 121 E1
McMaster St BT4 . . . . 15 B5
McMinns La BT33 . . . . 123 C5
McMullans La 2 BT6 . . . . . 15 A4
Macnean Cres BT19 . . . . 4 D1
McQuillan St BT13 . . . . . . 154 A2

McRorys Rd BT35 129 E6
McShanes Rd
Bessbrook BT35 131 C6
Newry BT35 139 C3
Macullagh Rd BT35 129 E2
Maddan Ⓣ BT60 113 D6
Maddan Rd
Armagh BT60 113 F3
15 Keady BT60 114 A3
Maddan Row BT60 113 F3
Madden Rd BT62 101 C7
Madden Row BT60 114 A3
Maddydrumbrist Ⓣ BT34 118 B3
Madison Ave E 3 BT4 15 D5
Madrid Ct (Cúirt Maidrid) 6 BT5 15 A5
Madrid St BT5 15 A5
Magaluf Pk BT23 30 E7
Magaraty Ⓣ BT62 73 D1
Magdala St BT7 14 D2
MAGHABERRY BT67 35 B7
Maghaberry Manor BT67 35 B8
Maghaberry Prim Sch BT67 35 A7
Maghaberry Rd BT67 34 E7
MAGHERA BT31 122 F3
Magherabeg Ⓣ BT25 87 E8
Magherabeg Rd BT25 87 E8
Magheraconluce Ⓣ BT26 89 C8
Magheraconluce Rd
Dromara BT25 89 B6
3 Hillsborough BT26 49 B1
Magheracranmoney Ⓣ BT30 92 C3
Magheradartin Ⓣ BT26 48 D7
Magheradartin Rd BT26 48 C7
Magheradrool Ⓣ BT24 91 A2
Magherageery Ⓣ BT27 37 D5
Magherahamlet Rd BT24 90 B1
Magherahinch Ⓣ BT67 44 D8
Magheraknock Ⓣ BT27 76 C2
Magheraknock Fort* BT24 90 C8
Magheraknock Rd BT24 59 C6
Magheralagan Ⓣ BT30 108 A4
Magheralave Ct BT28 26 A5
Magheralave Grange BT28 26 A5
Magheralave Pk E BT28 26 B3
Magheralave Pk N BT28 26 A3
Magheralave Pk S BT28 26 A3
Magheralave Rd BT28 26 A6
Magheralave (Upper Belfast) Ⓣ BT28 26 B6
MAGHERALIN BT67 43 E6
Magherally Ⓣ BT32 103 C7
Magheralone Ⓣ BT24 91 D1
Magheralone Rd BT24 91 D1
Magheramayo Ⓣ BT31 121 D6
Magheramayo Rd BT31 121 D7
Magheramesk Ⓣ BT67 34 E6
Magheramurphy Ⓣ BT34 153 B7
Magherana Ⓣ BT66 86 B7
Magherana Pk BT66 86 C7
Magherarville Ⓣ BT60 98 B2
Magherarville Rd BT60 98 B3
Magherasaul Ⓣ BT31 122 F6
Magherascouse Ⓣ BT23 68 A1
Magherascouse Rd
Ballygowan BT23 31 F1
Newtownards BT23 68 A3
Magheratimpany Ⓣ BT24 91 A1
Magheratimpany Rd BT24 91 A1
Magherconluce La BT26 48 E1
Magheregh Ⓣ BT34 153 E8
Maghernahely Ⓣ BT35 131 B5
Maghernakill Ⓣ 147 A7
MAGHERY BT71 73 C8
Maghery Ⓣ BT34 152 E8
Magherydogherty Ⓣ BT60 100 B3
Magherydogherty Rd BT60 100 C3
Maghery Kilcrany Ⓣ BT60 97 F3
Maghery Rd BT62 73 D7
Maghery Rural Enterprise Ctr BT71 73 C8
Maghies Pl 1 BT6 15 B3
Maghnavery Ⓣ BT60 116 C7
Maghon Ⓣ BT62 55 D7
Maginnis St BT35 64 C6
Magowan Pk
1 Hillsborough BT26 49 B1
3 Hillsborough BT26 89 D8
Newry BT34 153 A8
Magowan West Sh Ctr BT62 51 D4
Mahee Cl BT8 21 C2
Mahee Island Golf Course BT23 79 D8
Mahee Island Pk BT23 19 F6
Mahon Ave BT62 51 C2
Mahon Cl BT62 51 C1
Mahon Ct BT62 51 C1
Mahon Dr BT62 51 C1
Mahon Ind Area BT62 51 D1
Mahon Rd
Craigavon BT62 55 C6
Portadown BT62 51 C1
MAIGH RATH (MOIRA) BT67 34 C1
Main Ave BT35 64 A7
Main Rd
Carrowdore BT22 66 E1
Newtownards BT22 81 D6
Main St
Armagh BT60 96 E3
Armagh BT60 97 C5
Armagh BT60 116 D3
Armagh BT61 85 A5
Armagh BT61 99 E5
Ballynahinch BT24 59 D5
Ballywalter BT22 71 A6
Banbridge BT32 102 C3
Bangor BT20 4 B4
Bessbrook BT35 131 D5
Caledon BT68 96 D6
Camlough BT35 131 B3
Carrowdore BT22 66 F1
Castlewellan BT31 122 C5
Craigavon BT62 100 E8
Craigavon BT63 101 E4
Craigavon BT66 86 E6
Crawfordsburn BT19 2 F3
Downpatrick BT30 125 D5
Dundrum BT33 123 C4
Dungannon BT71 83 D5
Forkhill BT35 140 D1
Groomsport BT19 5 A7
Hillsborough BT26 47 C6
Hilltown BT34 134 B5
Kircubbin BT22 80 D7
Markethill BT60 116 A8
Millisle BT22 67 A4
Moira BT67 34 C2
Newcastle BT33 63 D4
Newry BT35 130 C4
Newtownards BT22 70 C5
Newtownards BT23 13 A4
6 Richhill BT61 85 E1
1 Richhill BT61 99 E8
Saintfield BT24 77 C4
5 Downpatrick BT30 107 C1
Majestic Dr BT12 154 C1
Major La BT71 72 A3
Majors Hill BT34 146 C5
Major St 6 BT5 15 B5
Makem Pk BT60 114 A2
Mala Chluain Ard (Clonard Rise) 4 BT13 154 A3
Malachy Conlon Pk BT35 147 C6
Malcolm Rd BT66 42 A4
Malcolmson Pk BT67 43 D6
Malcolmson St BT13 154 A2
Maldon Ct BT12 154 A1
Maldon St BT12 154 A1
Malinmore Mews BT35 64 B2
Mallard Dr (Bóthar Mhala Ard) BT30 62 C2
Mallard Rd BT30 62 B2
Mallard View BT23 19 B6
Mallawee Rd BT60 115 D4
Mall East The BT61 60 D5
Mall Sh Ctr The 1 BT60 60 D5
Mall The BT34 64 C5
Mall W The BT61 60 D5
Malon Cres BT30 62 C6
MALONE BT9 21 B6
Malone Ave BT9 14 B1
Malone Beeches BT9 21 A5
Malone Bsns Pk BT9 21 B3
Malone Cl BT30 62 C6
Malone Ct
Belfast BT9 21 A5
Downpatrick BT30 62 C6
Malone Ct Mews BT9 21 A5
Malone (Detached Portion) Ⓣ BT8 21 D4
Malone Dr BT30 62 C6
Malone Golf Club BT17 27 E8
Malone Grange BT9 21 A5
Malone Hill Pk BT9 21 A5
Malone Lower Ⓣ BT9 14 B1
Malone Manor BT15 14 D8
Malone Mdws BT9 21 A4
Malone Pk
Belfast BT9 21 A6
Downpatrick BT30 62 C6
Malone Pk Central BT9 21 A6
Malone Pl BT12 154 C1
Malone Rd BT9 14 C1
Malone Upper Ⓣ BT9 21 A5
Malone Valley Pk BT9 21 A4
Malone Way BT30 62 C6
Malvern Cl BT13 14 B7
Malvern Gn BT19 13 E8
Malvern Hts 10 BT19 13 E8
Malvern Prim Sch BT13 14 C7
Malvern St BT13 14 B7
Malvern Way BT13 154 B4
Manderley Ct BT63 52 A3
Manderley Mews BT63 52 B4
Manderley Pk BT63 52 B4
Manderley Rise BT63 52 B3
Manderson St BT4 15 C5
Mandeville Ave
Lisburn BT27 26 C1
Newtownards BT23 20 C6
Mandeville Dr 12 BT62 101 B7
Mandeville Manor BT64 40 D1
Mandeville Mews BT62 51 D4
Mandeville Rd
Craigavon BT64 40 E1
Portadown BT64 52 C8
Mandeville St BT62 51 D4
Manna Gr BT5 15 D2
Mann's Rd BT23 23 E5
Manooney Ⓣ BT60 97 A5
Manooney Rd BT60 97 A5
Manor BT66 86 C8
Manor Ave BT20 3 E2
Manor Cl BT14 14 B8
Manor Cres BT20 3 E2
Manor Ct
Bangor BT20 3 E2
2 Belfast BT14 14 B8
Donaghadee BT21 67 A8
5 Kilkeel BT34 153 C7
1 Moira BT67 34 C2
Newtownards BT23 19 D5
Manor Dr
17 Belfast BT14 14 B8
Lurgan BT66 41 E5
Manor Farm
Armagh BT61 85 A4
Lisburn BT27 27 C1
Manor Gr BT19 3 E2
Manor Groove BT20 3 E2
Manor Hill BT23 25 D2
Manor Mews 5 BT20 3 E2
Manor Pk
Bangor BT20 3 E2
Comber BT23 25 D2
4 Lisburn BT28 37 F8
Lurgan BT66 41 E5
Newtownards BT23 19 D5
Manor Rd BT23 78 D8
Manor St
Belfast BT14 14 B8
Donaghadee BT21 67 A8
Manor The BT62 51 C2
Manse Cl BT22 70 B8
Manse Ct BT22 66 E1
Manse Dr BT8 29 E5
Mansefield BT66 41 E5
Manse Gdns BT8 29 E5
Manse Gn BT23 19 B5
Manse Hill BT34 118 D2
Manse La BT61 85 D1
Manselton Cl BT20 4 D4
Manselton Pk BT20 4 D4
Manse Pk
Carryduff BT8 29 E5
Newtownards BT23 19 B5
Manse Rd
Banbridge BT32 104 A1
Bangor BT20 3 F3
Belfast BT6 22 F6
Belfast BT8 30 A6
Carrowdore BT22 70 B8
Carryduff BT8 29 E5
Castlereagh BT8 22 A3
Castlewellan BT31 104 D2
Craigavon BT63 57 C8
Downpatrick BT30 78 C2
Downpatrick BT30 107 B2
Dundrum BT33 123 C5
Kilkeel BT34 153 C6
Newtownards BT22 81 A7
Newtownards BT23 19 B5
Newtownards BT23 77 E7
Manse Way 4 BT22 67 A4
Maphoner Ⓣ BT35 140 B4
Maphoner Rd BT35 140 B3
Maple Cres BT17 27 A8
Maple Ct
Holywood BT18 9 D5
Lurgan BT66 41 F5
Maple Dr BT32 102 C3
Maple Gr BT34 64 E2
Maples The BT19 13 E7
Mara Gdns BT18 9 D7
Maralin Ave
Bangor BT20 4 C4
Lisburn BT28 37 E8
Maralin Pl 12 BT15 14 D8
Maralin Village Prim Sch BT67 43 D6
Marcella Pk BT23 19 B3
Marchioness Gn BT12 154 B2
Marchioness St BT12 154 B2
Marcus Sq BT34 64 D5
Marcus St BT34 64 D5
Marcus Ward St BT2 155 A1
Margaret St
Newry BT34 64 D6
Portadown BT62 51 D4
Margretta Cl BT66 41 F3
Margretta Pk
Lurgan BT66 41 F3
Portadown BT63 52 A5
Marguerite Ave BT33 63 C6
Marguerite Cl BT33 63 C7
Marguerite Cres BT33 63 C6
Marguerite Ct BT33 63 C6
Marguerite Dr BT33 63 C7
Marguerite Gdns BT33 63 C7
Marguerite Pk BT33 63 C6
Marian Pk (Páirc Mhúire)
Downpatrick BT30 62 D6
Downpatrick BT30 123 F5
Marian Way 9 BT22 94 D4
Marie Villas BT34 142 D6
Marina Pk BT5 15 E2
Marine Dr BT21 67 A8
Marine Par
Holywood BT18 9 C5
Warrenpoint BT34 65 C2
Marine St 1 BT15 14 E8
Marino Pk BT18 9 F8
Marino Sta BT18 9 F8
Marino Sta Rd BT18 9 F8
Marion Ave BT71 73 C8
Markethill Bsns Ctr 16 BT60 116 A8
MARKETHILL (CNOC AN MHARGAIDH) BT60 115 F8
Markethill High Sch BT60 116 A7
Markethill Prim Sch 15 BT60 116 A8
Markethill Rd
Armagh BT60 115 E2
Craigavon BT62 55 C3
Newry BT35 129 D6
Market La
5 Bangor BT20 4 B4
Downpatrick BT30 62 C5
Market Pl BT28 26 A1
Market Rd BT34 121 F3
Market St Central BT62 51 E4
Market St N BT62 51 E4
Market St W BT62 51 D4
Market Sq
Carlingford 151 C4
Dromara BT25 58 D5
Lisburn BT28 26 B1
Newry BT34 64 D6
Market St
6 Bangor BT20 4 B4
Belfast BT2 155 B2
Crossgar BT30 92 B4
Downpatrick BT30 62 B4
8 Keady BT60 114 A3
Lisburn BT28 26 B1
Lurgan BT66 42 A5
2 Newtownards BT23 19 E4
Portadown BT62 51 D4
Tandragee BT62 101 B7
Mark St
Lurgan BT66 41 F4
Newtownards BT23 19 D5
Markville BT63 53 E5
Marlacoo Beg Ⓣ BT62 100 C5
Marlacoo Beg Rd BT60 100 C4
Marlacoo More Ⓣ BT62 100 B5
Marlacoo Rd BT60 99 F5
Marlborough Ave
Bangor BT19 3 C4
6 Belfast BT9 21 A8
Marlborough Cres BT8 29 C3
Marlborough Ct 5 BT9 21 A8
Marlborough Dr BT19 3 B4
Marlborough Gate 1 BT9 21 B7
Marlborough Gdns BT9 21 B7
Marlborough Hts BT6 22 F7
Marlborough Pk
Bangor BT19 3 B4
8 Belfast BT9 21 A8
Carryduff BT8 29 C3
1 Lurgan BT66 41 F3
Marlborough Pk Central BT9 21 A8
Marlborough Pk Cross Ave BT9 21 B7
Marlborough Pk N BT9 21 A8
Marlborough Pk S BT9 21 A7
Marlborough Ret Pk BT64 40 E1
Marlborough St BT1 155 B3
Marlfield Ⓣ BT22 94 B6
Marlfield Dr BT5 16 C1
Marlfield Rd BT22 94 C6
Marlfield Rise BT5 16 C1
Marlo Cres BT19 4 F2
Marlo Ct BT19 4 F2
Mar Lodge Dr BT23 30 E6
Marlo Dr BT19 4 F2
Marlo Hts BT19 4 F2
Marlo Link BT19 4 F2
Marlo Pk BT19 4 F2
Marmion's Cross Rds 150 A4
Marmont Cres BT4 16 A8
Marmont Dr BT4 16 A8
Marmont Pk 5 BT4 9 A1
Marnabrae BT28 26 B5
Marnabrae Pk BT28 26 B5
Marquis Ave BT20 3 E1
Marquis Gdns BT20 3 F1
Marquis Manor 4 BT20 3 E1
Marquis Rise BT20 3 F1
Marquis St
Belfast BT1 155 A3
Newtownards BT23 19 D5
Marrassit or College Hall Ⓣ BT60 96 E5
Marshalls Rd BT6 15 D1
MARSHALLSTOWN BT30 108 F1
Marshallstown Rd BT30 108 E2
Martello Ave BT18 2 A3
Martello Dr BT18 2 A3
Martello Pk BT18 2 A3
Martindale BT20 3 E3
Martinez Ave BT5 15 D4
Martinpole Rd BT24 90 B2
Martins La BT35 64 A5
Martin St 4 BT5 15 B5
Martinville Pk BT8 22 A2
Maryland Ind Est BT23 23 D2
Marylebone Pk BT9 21 D6
Mary St
Lurgan BT67 42 A6
Newtownards BT23 19 D5
Rostrevor BT34 143 B3
Warrenpoint BT34 65 C2
5 Castlewellan BT31 122 C5
8 Crossgar BT30 92 B5
1 Downpatrick BT30 62 C4
Maryvale Rd BT67 45 B3
Maryvale Wlk BT32 61 D3
Maryville Ave 3 BT9 21 A8
Maryville Cl BT32 61 D3
Maryville Cres BT32 61 D3
Maryville Ct BT7 155 A1
Maryville Dr BT32 61 D3
Maryville Pk
Banbridge BT32 61 D3
Bangor BT20 3 D3
Maryville Pk *continued*
Belfast BT9 21 A6
Newry BT34 64 E6
Maryville Rd BT20 3 E3
Maryville St BT7 155 A1
Maryville Way BT32 61 D3
Mashona Ct BT6 15 B3
Masonic Ave 10 BT22 67 A4
Massey Ave BT4 16 D6
Massey Ct BT4 16 D6
Massey Gn BT4 16 C7
Massey Pk BT4 16 C7
Mass Rock La BT34 132 C2
Matchet St BT13 14 A7
Mater Infirmorum BT14 14 C7
Matilda Ave BT12 154 C1
Matilda Dr BT12 154 C1
Matilda Gdns BT12 154 C1
Mavemacullen (Ballymore) Ⓣ BT62 100 E2
Mavemacullen (Loughgilly) Ⓣ BT62 100 E1
Mavemacullen Rd BT62 100 E2
Mawhinney Pk BT16 17 B3
Maxwell Dr BT20 3 F5
Maxwell Gdns BT20 3 F5
Maxwell La BT20 3 E5
Maxwell Pk BT20 3 E4
Maxwell Rd BT20 3 E5
Maxwell's Pl BT12 154 C1
Maxwell St BT12 154 C1
May Ave BT20 4 B4
Maydown Ⓣ BT71 83 D4
Maydown Rd BT71 83 D2
Mayesfield Villas BT63 52 B3
Mayfair Ave BT6 15 C1
Mayfair Bsns Ctr BT62 51 C6
Mayfair Ct BT14 14 A8
Mayfield Ave BT25 88 F3
Mayfields BT28 26 B5
Mayfield St 2 BT9 21 A8
Mayflower St BT5 15 C4
Maymount St 25 BT6 15 A4
Maynooth Ⓣ BT61 99 E8
Maynooth Hts BT61 99 D8
Maynooth Rd BT61 99 D6
Mayo Ⓣ BT34 133 B2
MAYOBRIDGE BT34 133 B4
Mayobridge GAC BT34 133 B4
Mayo Rd BT34 133 C2
Maypole Hill BT25 58 D6
Maypole Pk BT25 58 D6
Maypole Rd BT25 58 D7
Mays Cnr Rd BT32 119 F7
Maysfield Leisure Ctr BT7 155 C2
May's Mdws BT7 155 C2
May St BT1 155 B2
Maytone Ⓣ BT60 116 C2
Maytone Rd BT60 116 B2
Maytown Ⓣ BT35 131 C6
Maytown Rd
Armagh BT60 117 A1
Newry BT35 131 C7
Maze Ⓣ BT27 36 E4
Maze Pk
Bangor BT20 4 C4
Lisburn BT28 37 E8
Maze Prim Sch BT27 36 D3
Maze Race Course BT27 36 C5
MAZETOWN BT28 36 E6
Mazeview Rd BT26 46 B3
Meadowale BT35 129 C5
Meadow Ave BT23 77 E8
Meadowbank BT32 61 B8
Meadowbank Ave BT21 67 A8
Meadowbank Pl BT9 14 A1
Meadowbank St 1 BT9 14 B1
Meadow Brook BT65 41 D3
Meadowbrook Pk 1 BT35 131 F5
Meadow Cl
Ballygowan BT23 77 E8
Ballywalter BT22 71 A5
7 Belfast BT15 14 D8
Newtownards BT23 20 B4
Meadow Ct
5 Ardglass BT30 125 F6
Ballygowan BT23 77 E8
Newtownards BT23 20 B4
Meadow Dr BT23 77 E8
Meadow Gr BT19 2 E3
Meadow Hill
Downpatrick BT30 62 D7
Dundrum BT33 123 C5
Meadow La
Dromara BT25 58 C8
Dromara BT25 89 D2
Portadown BT62 51 E4
Meadowlands
Bangor BT19 4 D1
Downpatrick BT30 62 C5
Kilkeel BT34 153 C6
Meadowlands Ave BT34 65 C3
Meadow Lands Ave BT34 153 C6
Meadowlands Ct BT19 4 D1
Meadow Mews 1 BT23 77 E8
Meadow Pk
Ballywalter BT22 71 A5
Crawfordsburn BT19 2 E3
Dundonald BT16 17 A4
Meadow Pk N BT19 2 E3
Meadow Pl
6 Belfast BT15 14 D8
Newtownards BT23 20 B4

Meadow Rd
Ballygowan BT23 . . . 77 E8
Craigavon BT67 . . . 35 A4
Meadows Sh Ctr The BT63 . . . 51 F4
Meadows The
Craigavon BT67 . . . 35 A7
Donaghadee BT21 . . . 6 E1
Downpatrick BT30 . . . 62 D7
Dungannon BT71 . . . 72 A5
Newtownards BT23 . . . 20 B4
Meadow The BT19 . . . 5 A7
Meadowvale
Armagh BT60 . . . 98 B4
2 Bangor BT19 . . . 3 E1
Bangor BT19 . . . 12 E8
Lisburn BT27 . . . 38 A6
Newcastle BT33 . . . 63 B7
10 Waringstown BT66 . . . 86 C8
Meadow Vale
Ballynahinch BT24 . . . 59 E4
18 Saintfield BT24 . . . 77 C3
Meadowvale Ave
Bangor BT19 . . . 12 E8
Carryduff BT8 . . . 29 D2
Newcastle BT33 . . . 63 B7
Meadowvale Cl
Bangor BT19 . . . 12 E8
3 Carryduff BT8 . . . 29 D2
Meadowvale Cres BT19 . . . 3 E1
Meadowvale Dr BT19 . . . 12 E8
Meadowvale Gdns
Bangor BT19 . . . 12 E8
1 Carryduff BT8 . . . 29 D2
Meadowvale Link BT19 . . . 12 E8
Meadowvale Pk
Bangor BT19 . . . 12 E8
Carryduff BT8 . . . 29 D2
Newcastle BT33 . . . 63 C8
Meadowvale Rd 4 BT8 . . . 29 D2
Meadowview BT71 . . . 72 B1
Meadow View BT23 . . . 77 E8
Meadowview Drive BT62 . . . 73 A2
Meadowview Pk BT62 . . . 73 A2
Meadow Way
Ballygowan BT23 . . . 77 E8
Crawfordsburn BT19 . . . 2 E3
Meadow Wlk 2 BT23 . . . 77 E8
Mealough BT8 . . . 29 A4
Mealough Rd BT8 . . . 28 C3
Mearne Rd BT30 . . . 62 F8
Medway St BT4 . . . 15 B6
Meenan BT32 . . . 118 B8
Meenan Rd BT35 . . . 102 A1
Meetinghouse La 1 BT23 . . . 19 E5
Meeting House La
4 Kilkeel BT34 . . . 153 C7
Lisburn BT27 . . . 26 D1
Newry BT34 . . . 64 E6
Meetinghouse Point 1 BT21 . . . 67 A7
Meeting House Rd BT32 . . . 61 C4
Meetinghouse St 14 BT22 . . . 94 D3
Meeting House St BT21 . . . 67 A8
Meeting St
Dromara BT25 . . . 58 D5
Hillsborough BT26 . . . 47 C7
Moira BT67 . . . 34 C2
Newry BT35 . . . 117 D8
Warrenpoint BT34 . . . 65 B2
Meganlis Pk BT25 . . . 58 D6
Megarrystown Rd BT67 . . . 45 D5
Megheramesk La BT67 . . . 34 E6
MEIGH BT35 . . . 141 B5
Melbourne St BT13 . . . 154 C4
Melfort Dr BT5 . . . 16 D3
Mellifont Cl BT61 . . . 60 F7
Mellifont Cres BT61 . . . 60 F8
Mellifont Ct BT61 . . . 60 F8
Mellifont Dr BT61 . . . 60 F7
Melmore Dr BT17 . . . 26 D8
Melrose Ave BT5 . . . 15 D4
Melrose Gr BT67 . . . 41 F8
Melrose Pk
18 Kilkeel BT34 . . . 153 C7
Lurgan BT67 . . . 41 F8
Melrose St BT9 . . . 14 B1
Melvin Pk BT19 . . . 4 D1
Menarys Sh Ctr BT20 . . . 4 A4
Mercer Ct 1 BT27 . . . 26 C1
Mercer St BT27 . . . 26 C1
Mercevin Gr BT24 . . . 90 E2
Merchants Quay BT34 . . . 64 C5
Meredi St BT12 . . . 154 A1
Merok Cres BT6 . . . 22 D8
Merok Dr BT6 . . . 22 D8
Merok Gdns BT6 . . . 22 D8
Merok Pk BT6 . . . 22 D8
Merridale Dr BT20 . . . 4 C2
Merrion Ave BT33 . . . 63 D6
Merrion Dr BT66 . . . 42 A3
Merryland Cross Roads BT23 . . . 23 D2
Mersey St Prim Sch BT4 . . . 15 C6
Mersey St BT4 . . . 15 C6
Mervue Ct 18 BT15 . . . 14 D8
Mervue St BT15 . . . 14 D8
Messancy Gr BT60 . . . 60 F1
Messancy Pl BT60 . . . 60 F1
Methodist Coll BT9 . . . 14 C2
Mews The BT21 . . . 6 F1
Michael Mallin Pk (Páirc Mhíchíl uí Mhealláin) 9 BT35 . . . 64 C5
Middle Braniel Rd BT5 . . . 16 D1
Middlepath St BT5 . . . 155 C3
Middle Rd
Ballynahinch BT24 . . . 77 A3
Middle Rd *continued*
Lisburn BT27 . . . 76 A4
Middle Tollymore Rd BT33 . . . 63 A8
MIDDLETOWN (COILLIDH CHANANNÁIN) BT60 . . . 112 D8
Mid Island Pk BT22 . . . 70 B5
Midland Cl 12 BT15 . . . 14 E8
Midland Cres 11 BT15 . . . 14 E8
Milebush Rd BT25 . . . 58 F7
Milecross BT23 . . . 19 A6
Milecross Rd BT23 . . . 18 F5
MILFORD BT60 . . . 98 B4
Milford Cres 7 BT66 . . . 86 C8
Milford Pl BT12 . . . 154 B3
Milford Rise BT12 . . . 154 B3
Milford St BT12 . . . 154 C3
Milfort Dr 6 BT66 . . . 86 C8
Milfort Gdns 8 BT66 . . . 86 C8
Milfort Pk 11 BT66 . . . 86 C8
Millar Hill BT23 . . . 31 E1
Millar's Cl BT16 . . . 17 D2
Millar's Cres 12 BT16 . . . 17 D3
Millar's Ct 14 BT16 . . . 17 C3
Millar's Dr BT16 . . . 17 D3
Millar's Forge BT16 . . . 17 D2
Millar's Forge Link BT16 . . . 17 D2
Millar's Gr 11 BT16 . . . 17 D3
Millar's La BT16 . . . 17 C3
Millar's Pk 10 BT16 . . . 17 D3
Millar St BT6 . . . 15 A2
Millar's View BT16 . . . 17 D2
Mill Ave BT62 . . . 51 E5
Millbank BT19 . . . 5 A2
Millbank Cres BT22 . . . 67 A4
Millbank Ct BT22 . . . 67 A4
Millbank Rd BT22 . . . 67 A4
Millbank View BT32 . . . 103 C5
Millbay Rd BT34 . . . 152 D7
Millberry BT68 . . . 96 C5
Millbrook Ct BT66 . . . 40 E7
Millbrook Dr BT24 . . . 59 F3
Millbrooke Rd BT19 . . . 11 C7
Millbrook Wlk BT27 . . . 26 C2
Millburn Ct BT8 . . . 21 D2
Mill Cottage Pk BT22 . . . 66 F4
Millennium Integrated Prim Sch BT24 . . . 77 A7
Millennium Way BT66 . . . 42 A4
Miller Hill BT21 . . . 67 A6
Miller Pk BT63 . . . 86 B2
Miller's La BT23 . . . 78 F5
Millfield BT13 . . . 154 C4
Millfort Gn BT32 . . . 61 B7
Mill Hill
Castlewellan BT31 . . . 122 C5
Waringstown BT66 . . . 43 A1
Mill Hill Dr BT24 . . . 59 E3
Mill Hill La BT67 . . . 35 E4
Mill Hts BT22 . . . 80 D8
Millicent Pk BT19 . . . 5 A5
Millin Bay Rd BT22 . . . 95 A1
Millington Pk BT62 . . . 51 B2
Millington Prim Sch BT62 . . . 51 D3
Millisle Gdns BT19 . . . 3 D1
MILLISLE (OILEÁN AN MHUILINN) BT21 . . . 67 B5
Millisle Prim Sch 15 BT22 . . . 67 A4
Millisle Rd BT21 . . . 67 A7
Mill La
Crossmaglen BT35 . . . 147 F8
Dromara BT25 . . . 58 D5
Mayobridge BT34 . . . 133 B4
Newtownards BT22 . . . 81 B1
Mill Mews BT26 . . . 47 C7
Millmount Chase BT16 . . . 17 D2
Millmount Rd BT16 . . . 17 D2
Mill Pond Ct 4 BT5 . . . 15 C4
Millrace Cl BT35 . . . 140 D1
Mill Rd
Banbridge BT32 . . . 104 E1
Bessbrook BT35 . . . 131 C5
Carryduff BT8 . . . 29 B6
Downpatrick BT30 . . . 108 B7
Drumaness BT24 . . . 91 B1
Forkhill BT35 . . . 149 D8
Kilkeel BT34 . . . 153 C8
Killinchy BT23 . . . 78 F6
Lisburn BT27 . . . 27 F5
Millisle BT22 . . . 67 A5
Newry BT34 . . . 121 C1
Newry BT34 . . . 146 C6
Newry BT35 . . . 140 B5
Newtownards BT23 . . . 30 E1
Mill Rd W BT8 . . . 29 A7
Mill Row 9 BT20 . . . 4 B4
Mills Rd 1 BT20 . . . 4 B4
Mill St
Caledon BT68 . . . 96 D6
Gilford BT63 . . . 57 D1
Lisburn BT27 . . . 26 D3
Newry BT34 . . . 64 D5
Newtownards BT23 . . . 19 C4
Tandragee BT62 . . . 101 B6
Mill Steet Ct BT23 . . . 19 D4
Millstone Cl BT32 . . . 120 E8
Mill Stream The BT23 . . . 25 C2
MILLTOWN
Banbridge BT32 . . . 86 D1
Banbridge BT32 . . . 119 A5
Craigavon BT62 . . . 73 D8
Craigavon BT62 . . . 100 B7
Dungannon BT71 . . . 83 C4
Milltown BT34 . . . 132 F1
Milltown Ave BT28 . . . 26 B8
Milltown Cres BT28 . . . 26 B8
Milltown East Ind Est BT34 . . . 65 B5
Milltown Gdns BT28 . . . 26 A8
Milltown Hill
Castlereagh BT8 . . . 21 C1
Newry BT34 . . . 132 F1
Milltown La
Ballynahinch BT24 . . . 77 F1
Craigavon BT62 . . . 73 D8
Milltown Pk BT28 . . . 26 B8
Milltown Prim Sch BT32 . . . 86 D2
Milltown Rd
Belfast BT8 . . . 21 B2
Craigavon BT66 . . . 43 B1
Downpatrick BT30 . . . 125 C8
Dungannon BT71 . . . 83 C4
Newry BT35 . . . 130 F1
Milltown Rd Link BT8 . . . 21 C2
Milltown St BT34 . . . 65 A6
Millturn View BT25 . . . 58 B4
Millvale BT34 . . . 153 C8
Millvale Ct BT26 . . . 47 C7
Millvale Pk BT35 . . . 131 D5
Millvale Rd
Banbridge BT32 . . . 103 D1
Bessbrook BT35 . . . 131 D5
Castlewellan BT31 . . . 120 F8
Hillsborough BT26 . . . 47 B7
Newry BT34 . . . 119 E5
Millvale Wood BT26 . . . 47 C7
Mill View BT22 . . . 94 D3
Millview Resource Ctr BT35 . . . 131 D5
Milner St BT12 . . . 154 A1
MINERSTOWN BT30 . . . 124 E5
Minerstown Rd BT30 . . . 125 A5
Miniature Rly★ BT18 . . . 1 D2
Minnowburn Beeches★ BT8 . . . 21 B2
Minnowburn Dr 1 BT8 . . . 21 D2
Minnowburn Gdns 2 BT8 . . . 21 D2
Minnowburn Mews BT8 . . . 21 C2
MINTERBURN BT68 . . . 82 B3
Minterburn Prim Sch BT68 . . . 82 B3
Minterburn Rd BT68 . . . 82 A4
Mission Rd BT34 . . . 145 F3
Mitchell House Sch BT4 . . . 16 A8
Mkt Place Theatre & Arts Ctr The★ 3 BT61 . . . 60 D5
Moat Ave BT21 . . . 6 F1
Moat Entry 4 BT21 . . . 6 F1
Moate Rd BT23 . . . 68 E7
Moatlands The BT22 . . . 81 C8
Moat Rd BT22 . . . 81 C7
Moat St BT21 . . . 6 E1
Moatview Cres BT16 . . . 17 B3
Moatview Pk BT16 . . . 17 A3
Moeran BT62 . . . 51 B2
Moeran Pk BT62 . . . 51 B2
Moira Ct (Cúirt Mhaigh Rath) 5 BT5 . . . 15 A5
MOIRA DEMESNE BT67 . . . 34 B3
Moira Dr BT20 . . . 4 C4
Moira Ind Est BT67 . . . 34 A1
MOIRA (MAIGH RATH) BT67 . . . 34 C1
Moira Mews 2 BT67 . . . 34 B2
Moira Pk
Bangor BT20 . . . 4 C4
1 Lisburn BT28 . . . 37 D8
Moira Prim Sch BT67 . . . 34 B2
Moira Rd
Hillsborough BT26 . . . 46 E7
Lisburn BT28 . . . 36 C6
Moira Sta BT67 . . . 34 D4
Moiry Castle★ BT35 . . . 150 B7
Molly Blayney's Cnr BT30 . . . 109 C2
Molly Rd BT35 . . . 141 C2
Moltke St BT12 . . . 154 A1
Molyneaux St 5 BT15 . . . 14 E7
Monabot Rd BT30 . . . 62 F6
Monaghan Bsns Pk 3 BT35 . . . 64 C6
Monaghan Rd
Armagh BT60 . . . 60 A2
Newry BT35 . . . 129 B4
Monaghan Row BT35 . . . 64 B6
Monaghan St
1 Armagh BT60 . . . 98 B4
Newry BT35 . . . 64 C6
Monaguillagh BT35 . . . 147 C7
Monahoora BT25 . . . 105 E7
Monarch Par BT12 . . . 154 A1
Monarch St BT12 . . . 154 A1
Monascrebe . . . 149 F6
Monaview BT34 . . . 146 D5
Monbrief BT65 . . . 41 E2
Monbrief E Rd BT65 . . . 41 E2
Monbrief Rd BT65 . . . 41 D1
Monclone BT63 . . . 101 D3
Monclone Rd BT63 . . . 101 D3
Monea Cl BT19 . . . 3 E1
Monea Dr BT19 . . . 3 E1
Monea Way BT19 . . . 3 E1
Money BT61 . . . 85 D4
Moneycarragh BT30 . . . 123 A8
Moneycarragh Rd BT30 . . . 106 F1
Moneycree BT61 . . . 84 E3
Moneydarragh Prim Sch BT34 . . . 146 A4
Moneydarragh Rd BT34 . . . 146 C4
Moneydorragh Beg BT34 . . . 146 B3
Moneydorragh More BT34 . . . 146 B5
Moneydorragh More Upper BT34 . . . 146 A7
Moneygore BT34 . . . 120 C2
Moneygore Rd BT34 . . . 120 C2
Moneylane BT33 . . . 123 B6
Moneylane Rd BT33 . . . 123 B5
Moneymore BT34 . . . 118 B4
Moneymore Rd
Newry BT34 . . . 118 B5
Newry BT34 . . . 120 C3
Moneynabane BT25 . . . 90 A1
Moneynabane Rd BT25 . . . 89 F1
Moneypatrick BT60 . . . 98 C3
Moneyquin BT60 . . . 114 B8
MONEYREAGH BT23 . . . 30 F7
Moneyreagh Rd
Moneyreagh BT23 . . . 30 F8
Newtownards BT23 . . . 23 D2
Moneyrea Prim Sch BT23 . . . 78 C7
Moneyrea Rd BT23 . . . 31 B5
Moneyrea St BT6 . . . 15 B3
Moneyscalp BT34 . . . 122 A2
Moneyscalp Rd BT34 . . . 121 F2
MONEYSLANE BT32 . . . 120 E8
Moneyslane Ct BT31 . . . 120 F8
Moneyslane Rd BT31 . . . 104 F1
Moninna Pk 2 BT35 . . . 131 E4
Moninna Villas BT35 . . . 131 E4
Monks Hill Rd BT34 . . . 64 F6
Monlough BT23 . . . 30 D3
Monlough Rd
Ballynahinch BT24 . . . 77 C5
Newtownards BT23 . . . 30 E2
Monlough Rd W BT23 . . . 30 C3
Monog BT35 . . . 148 A8
Monog Rd BT35 . . . 148 A7
Monree BT66 . . . 87 A6
Monreehill 4 BT66 . . . 86 F6
Monree Rd BT25 . . . 87 A6
Monroe Ave BT66 . . . 42 C4
Montague St
Portadown BT62 . . . 51 C5
16 Tandragee BT62 . . . 101 B7
Montagu Pk 11 BT62 . . . 101 B7
Montalto BT24 . . . 59 C4
Monteith Rd BT32 . . . 103 E1
Montgomery Chase BT6 . . . 22 C8
Montgomery Commercial & Bsns Pk BT6 . . . 15 C1
Montgomery Ct
Bangor BT20 . . . 4 F3
2 Belfast BT6 . . . 22 C8
Montgomery Dr
2 Lisburn BT27 . . . 26 C1
Lisburn BT27 . . . 38 C8
Montgomery Rd BT6 . . . 15 E1
Montgomery St BT1 . . . 155 B3
Montrose St S BT5 . . . 15 B5
Montrose St 20 BT4 . . . 15 B5
Monument Pk BT26 . . . 47 B5
Monument Rd BT26 . . . 47 B5
Monuments & Bldgs Record★ BT1 . . . 155 B4
Moodage Rd BT62 . . . 101 B5
Moodoge BT62 . . . 101 A5
Moolieve Cl BT34 . . . 146 D5
Moorcroft Rd BT8 . . . 28 F5
Moore Dr BT19 . . . 2 E5
Moorefield BT32 . . . 61 D6
Moore Island Rd BT61 . . . 84 D4
Moores La BT66 . . . 42 A5
Moorestown Rd BT32 . . . 86 E2
Moorfield Ave BT23 . . . 68 D6
Moorfield Cres BT23 . . . 68 D6
Moorfield Ct BT23 . . . 68 D6
Moorfield Gdns BT23 . . . 68 D6
Moorfield Rd BT25 . . . 58 A8
Moorfield St BT5 . . . 15 D4
Moorgate St BT5 . . . 15 D4
Moor Hill Rd BT34 . . . 64 F3
Moorings The 4 BT21 . . . 67 A7
Moor Rd
Castlewellan BT31 . . . 121 C7
Kilkeel BT34 . . . 153 D7
Moray Ave BT21 . . . 67 A8
Moray Cres BT23 . . . 19 D4
Moray Dr BT21 . . . 67 A8
Moray Hills BT21 . . . 67 A8
Morley Ave BT23 . . . 13 A4
Morningside
Bangor BT20 . . . 4 E5
Lisburn BT27 . . . 38 D6
Mornington BT32 . . . 61 F6
Mornington Mews BT7 . . . 21 E6
Mornington Pl BT7 . . . 21 F6
Morpeth St BT13 . . . 154 B4
Morrisons La
Armagh BT61 . . . 84 F7
Banbridge BT32 . . . 120 E5
Morrowshill BT31 . . . 122 E3
Morstan Pk BT23 . . . 20 A4
Morston Ave BT20 . . . 3 F1
Morston Pk 4 BT20 . . . 4 A1
Morven Pk BT16 . . . 17 C4
Moscow Rd BT3 . . . 8 E3
Moscow St BT13 . . . 154 B4
Moss Bank Rd BT63 . . . 53 B1
Moss Bann Rd BT32 . . . 102 C7
Moss Brook Rd BT23 . . . 30 C7
Mossfield BT60 . . . 116 B2
MOSSFIELD ESTATE BT60 . . . 116 C2
Mosside Bsns Pk BT21 . . . 66 B5
Mosside Mews BT17 . . . 26 D8
Mosside Rd BT17 . . . 26 D8
Moss La BT25 . . . 58 D5
Mosspark
3 Richhill BT61 . . . 85 E1
Richhill BT61 . . . 99 E8
Mosspark Mossgreen 4 BT61 . . . 99 E8
Moss Rd
Ballygowan BT23 . . . 77 F8
Ballynahinch BT24 . . . 59 E7
Banbridge BT32 . . . 118 E7
Belfast BT8 . . . 76 D8
Carryduff BT8 . . . 29 B1
Craigavon BT62 . . . 73 B2
Craigavon BT62 . . . 100 D4
Craigavon BT66 . . . 42 F3
Dromara BT25 . . . 87 E8
Holywood BT18 . . . 9 F2
Lisburn BT27 . . . 26 C6
Lisburn BT27 . . . 76 B8
Newtownards BT22 . . . 66 E4
Newtownards BT23 . . . 78 B7
Waringstown BT66 . . . 42 E1
Moss Row BT60 . . . 128 C8
Mossvale Ave 1 BT23 . . . 77 F8
Mossvale Cres 2 BT23 . . . 77 F8
Mossvale Pk
3 Ballygowan BT23 . . . 77 F8
4 Kilkeel BT34 . . . 153 B7
Mossvale Rd
Ballynahinch BT24 . . . 91 D2
Dromara BT25 . . . 58 E5
Mossview Rd BT35 . . . 117 A6
Motelands 3 BT4 . . . 16 B8
Motte Lodge BT16 . . . 17 B4
Mound Rd
Dromara BT25 . . . 58 F5
Newry BT34 . . . 65 A5
Mountain Lodge Rd BT60 . . . 128 C7
Mountain Pk BT23 . . . 19 D7
Mountain Rd
Ballynahinch BT24 . . . 106 B6
Castlewellan BT31 . . . 104 E3
Kilkeel BT34 . . . 153 C8
Newry BT35 . . . 130 E1
Newry BT35 . . . 131 C2
Newtownards BT22 . . . 94 D5
Newtownards BT23 . . . 12 C2
Mountainside BT23 . . . 19 D8
Mountain Springs 5 BT33 . . . 63 B5
Mountain View
Camlough BT35 . . . 131 B3
Castlewellan BT31 . . . 122 C4
Mountain View Dr BT35 . . . 64 C8
Mountainview Rd BT32 . . . 118 F8
Mount Alexander BT23 . . . 25 D5
Mount Carmel BT34 . . . 153 B7
Mount Charles
Banbridge BT32 . . . 61 D6
Belfast BT7 . . . 14 D2
3 Bessbrook BT35 . . . 131 D5
Mount Con & Bsns Ctr The BT6 . . . 15 A4
Mount Cres BT30 . . . 62 B5
Mount Eden Pk BT9 . . . 21 A5
Mountforde Ct (Cúirt Thulach Forde) 18 BT5 . . . 15 A5
Mountforde Dr (Céide Thulach Forde) 16 BT5 . . . 15 A5
Mountforde Gdns (Garraithe Thulach Forde) 17 BT5 . . . 15 A5
Mountforde Pk 27 BT5 . . . 15 A5
Mountforde Rd (Bóthar Thulach Forde) 23 BT5 . . . 15 A5
Mounthall BT62 . . . 73 D5
Mounthill BT35 . . . 148 E6
Mounthill Rd BT35 . . . 148 F6
Mount Ida Rd BT32 . . . 87 E1
Mountjoy St BT13 . . . 154 A4
Mount Merrion Ave BT6 . . . 15 B1
Mount Merrion Cres BT6 . . . 22 A7
Mount Merrion Dr BT6 . . . 22 B7
Mount Merrion Gdns BT6 . . . 22 B7
Mount Merrion Pk BT6 . . . 22 A7
Mount Michael Dr BT8 . . . 22 B5
Mount Michael Gr BT8 . . . 22 B4
Mount Michael Pk BT8 . . . 22 B4
Mount Michael View BT8 . . . 22 C5
Mountnab Rd BT60 . . . 99 D1
Mountnorris BT60 . . . 116 D4
Mount Norris BT33 . . . 63 B7
MOUNTNORRIS (ACHADH NA CRANNCHA) BT60 . . . 116 D4
Mountnorris Prim Sch BT60 . . . 116 D3
Mount Ober Golf & Ctry Club BT8 . . . 22 E3
Mount Oriel 1 BT8 . . . 22 A4
Mount Pleasant
2 Bangor BT20 . . . 4 A4
Belfast BT9 . . . 21 D8
Newry BT34 . . . 64 E6
Mount Pleasant Pony Trekking Ctr★ BT31 . . . 122 B7
Mountpottinger Link (Lúb Tullach Phoitinséir) 36 BT5 . . . 15 A5
Mountpottinger Rd (Bóthar Thulach Phoitinséir)
7 Belfast BT5 . . . 15 A5
7 Belfast BT5 . . . 15 A5
Mount Prospect Pk BT9 . . . 14 B2
Mount Regan Ave BT16 . . . 17 B5
Mount Royal
3 Bangor BT20 . . . 4 A4
Donaghadee BT21 . . . 67 A8
Lisburn BT27 . . . 38 E8
Mount St Catherine's Prim Sch 1 BT61 . . . 60 B5
Mount St S 13 BT6 . . . 15 A4

Mount St
15 Belfast BT6 . . . 15 A4
Dromara BT25 . . . 58 D5
Mount Stewart BT22 . . . 69 F7
Mount Stewart House & Gdns★ BT22 . . . 69 F7
Mountstewart Rd BT22 . . . 69 E7
Mount The
Belfast BT5 . . . 15 A4
Tandragee BT62 . . . 101 B7
Mountview 1 BT60 . . . 114 A3
Mountview Ct 11 BT14 . . . 14 B8
Mountview Ctr BT30 . . . 62 E3
Mountview Dr
Banbridge BT32 . . . 61 D5
1 Dromara BT25 . . . 58 E6
Lisburn BT27 . . . 26 B5
Mountview Pk
Banbridge BT32 . . . 61 D5
Lisburn BT27 . . . 26 C5
Mountview Rd BT24 . . . 59 A1
Mountview St 9 BT14 . . . 14 B8
Mourne Cres BT23 . . . 30 F7
Mourne District Hospl BT34 . . . 153 C8
Mourne Dr BT34 . . . 65 D3
Mourne Espl BT34 . . . 153 C6
Mourne Gdns 2 BT31 . . . 122 B5
Mourne Gn BT33 . . . 63 D7
Mourne Grange BT25 . . . 58 D4
Mourne Ind Christian Sch BT34 . . . 153 D7
Mourne Mountains East BT34 . . . 135 F2
Mourne Mountains Middle BT34 . . . 144 E7
Mourne Mountains West BT34 . . . 144 C4
Mourne Pk
1 Castlewellan BT31 . . . 122 B5
Newcastle BT33 . . . 63 D7
Mourne Rd BT66 . . . 42 A3
Mourne Rise BT33 . . . 63 C8
Mourne St 16 BT5 . . . 15 B5
Mourneview
Armagh BT60 . . . 115 D4
Carryduff BT8 . . . 29 D5
Mourne View
Ballynahinch BT24 . . . 59 D5
8 Rathfriland BT34 . . . 119 F2
Mourneview Ave BT66 . . . 41 F3
Mourne View Ave BT33 . . . 63 D7
Mourneview Cl BT34 . . . 153 D8
Mourne View Cl BT33 . . . 63 D7
Mourne View Cres BT33 . . . 63 D7
Mourne View Ct BT30 . . . 62 C4
Mourneview Pk
4 Dromara BT25 . . . 58 E6
Kilkeel BT34 . . . 153 D8
10 Tandragee BT62 . . . 101 B7
Mourne View Pk
Newcastle BT33 . . . 63 D7
Newry BT35 . . . 64 D7
Mourne View Rd BT33 . . . 63 D8
Mourneview St BT62 . . . 51 E3
Mourne Wood 1 BT34 . . . 143 C4
Movie House★ BT7 . . . 155 A1
Movilla BT23 . . . 20 A6
Movilla Abbey★ BT23 . . . 20 A5
Movilla High Sch BT23 . . . 19 F5
Movilla Mews BT23 . . . 20 C5
Movilla Rd BT30 . . . 62 D5
Movilla St BT23 . . . 19 E5
MOWHAN BT60 . . . 116 B5
Mowhan Ct 8 BT60 . . . 116 A8
Mowhan Rd
Armagh BT60 . . . 116 B4
Markethill BT60 . . . 116 A8
Mowhan St BT12 . . . 21 A8
Mowillin BT60 . . . 113 F6
Moyad
Newry BT34 . . . 135 D7
Newry BT34 . . . 145 A4
Moyad Rd BT34 . . . 135 D8
Moyad Upper BT34 . . . 145 A6
Moyallan BT63 . . . 57 A6
Moyallan Pk BT63 . . . 57 B3
Moyallan Rd BT63 . . . 57 A5
Moyallon Prim Sch BT63 . . . 56 F7
MOY (AN MAIGH) BT71 . . . 72 A1
Moyard BT71 . . . 83 E4
Moybane BT35 . . . 147 F6
Moybrick Gr BT25 . . . 89 C2
Moybrick Lower BT25 . . . 89 A1
Moybrick Rd BT25 . . . 89 B1
Moybrick Upper BT25 . . . 105 A8
Moydalgan BT25 . . . 89 C3
Moygannon
Craigavon BT66 . . . 86 E5
Warrenpoint BT34 . . . 143 A4
Moygannon Ct BT34 . . . 65 F2
Moygannon La BT66 . . . 86 E6
Moygannon Rd
Craigavon BT66 . . . 86 E5
Newry BT34 . . . 65 F5
Moyle Hill BT22 . . . 71 A5
Moyle Wlk BT8 . . . 21 C2
Moylinn Cl (Clós Maoilinn) BT35 . . . 139 E2
Moymore BT30 . . . 93 C7
Moyne Gdns BT23 . . . 19 F4
Moyne Pk BT5 . . . 16 D2
Moyne Rd BT23 . . . 13 A4
Moyra Cl 2 BT24 . . . 77 C3
Moyra Cres
Dundonald BT16 . . . 17 C2
Saintfield BT24 . . . 77 C3
Moyra Dr BT24 . . . 77 C3
Moyra Pk BT24 . . . 77 C3
Moyraverty BT65 . . . 53 C7
Moyraverty Ct BT65 . . . 53 C8
Moyraverty Mdws BT65 . . . 53 C7
Moyraverty Rd BT65 . . . 41 C1
Moyraverty W Rd BT65 . . . 53 B8
Moy Rd
Armagh BT61 . . . 60 B7
Craigavon BT62 . . . 50 D7
Moy Regional Prim Sch 1 BT71 . . . 72 A1
Moyrourkan BT62 . . . 100 D3
Moyrourkan Rd BT62 . . . 100 D3
Moyrusk BT67 . . . 35 F7
MOYRUSK BT67 . . . 36 A7
Moy Rusk Rd BT67 . . . 36 A7
Muckery BT62 . . . 74 C6
Mulhouse Rd BT12 . . . 154 B2
Mullabrack BT63 . . . 101 E7
Mullabrack Rd BT63 . . . 101 E7
Mullacreevie Pk BT60 . . . 60 A5
Mulladry BT62 . . . 54 B4
Mulladry Rd
Armagh BT61 . . . 85 F2
Craigavon BT62 . . . 54 C4
Mullafernaghan BT32 . . . 87 B1
Mullafernaghan Rd BT25 . . . 87 B3
Mullagh BT30 . . . 93 A3
Mullaghans Rd BT35 . . . 140 A8
Mullaghatinny or Elm Park BT60 . . . 97 C7
Mullaghbane
Armagh BT61 . . . 99 A8
Armagh BT61 . . . 99 F5
MULLAGHBANE BT35 . . . 140 B3
Mullaghbane Rd BT61 . . . 99 B7
Mullaghboy BT71 . . . 83 F7
Mullaghbrack BT60 . . . 99 F3
Mullaghbrack Rd BT60 . . . 99 F2
Mullagh Cl BT34 . . . 146 A1
Mullaghdrin BT25 . . . 89 D5
Mullaghdrin Rd BT25 . . . 89 D4
Mullaghdrin Rd E BT25 . . . 89 D4
Mullaghduff BT35 . . . 138 C5
Mullaghduff Rd BT35 . . . 128 F1
Mullaghgariff Rd BT34 . . . 133 F2
Mullaghglass BT62 . . . 101 C4
MULLAGHGLASS BT35 . . . 131 E6
Mullaghglass Rd BT62 . . . 101 C3
Mullaghmore
Armagh BT60 . . . 116 D5
Armagh BT61 . . . 84 E6
Newry BT34 . . . 133 F3
Mullaghmore Ave 3 BT60 . . . 114 A3
Mullaghmore East BT68 . . . 82 D1
Mullaghmore Pk 2 BT60 . . . 114 A3
Mullaghmossagh BT68 . . . 96 B6
Mullaghmossog Glebe BT71 . . . 83 E8
Mullaglass Prim Sch BT35 . . . 131 E7
Mullahead BT62 . . . 56 D4
Mullahead Rd
Craigavon BT62 . . . 56 C4
Tandragee BT62 . . . 101 A8
Mullalelish BT61 . . . 100 A8
Mullalelish Rd
Armagh BT61 . . . 99 F8
Craigavon BT62 . . . 54 D2
Richhill BT61 . . . 85 E1
Mullaletragh BT61 . . . 85 E3
Mullamore Dr BT24 . . . 91 B1
Mullan BT60 . . . 96 E1
Mullanary
Armagh BT60 . . . 112 F6
Craigavon BT62 . . . 100 F1
Dungannon BT71 . . . 84 B5
Mullanary Rd
Armagh BT60 . . . 112 E6
Craigavon BT62 . . . 100 F1
Dungannon BT71 . . . 84 B5
Mullanasilla BT61 . . . 99 C7
Mullanasilla Rd BT61 . . . 85 C1
Mullandra Pk BT34 . . . 121 C2
Mullan Rd BT60 . . . 96 E2
Mullans Town BT35 . . . 140 B4
Mullanstown Pk BT60 . . . 60 B3
Mullantine
Craigavon BT62 . . . 51 A1
Craigavon BT62 . . . 55 A8
Mullantine Rd
Craigavon BT62 . . . 51 A1
Portadown BT62 . . . 51 A2
Mullantur
Armagh BT61 . . . 83 D1
Craigavon BT62 . . . 101 A5
Mullartown BT34 . . . 146 C6
Mullartown Hts BT34 . . . 146 D4
Mullartown Pk BT34 . . . 146 D4
Mullartown Upper BT34 . . . 136 C1
Mullavat Rd BT34 . . . 142 A8
Mullavilly BT62 . . . 55 E1
Mullavilly Gn BT62 . . . 55 D1
Mullavilly Hts BT62 . . . 55 D1
Mullavilly Prim Sch BT62 . . . 55 E1
Mullavilly Rd BT62 . . . 55 E1
Mullenakill North BT71 . . . 72 F7
Mullenakill Pk BT71 . . . 72 E6
Mullenakill South BT71 . . . 72 F5
Mullenakill West BT71 . . . 72 E6
Mullin Rd BT35 . . . 130 C1
Mullintor BT68 . . . 82 D3
Mullinure BT61 . . . 60 F7
Mullinure Hospl BT61 . . . 60 C7
Mullinure La BT61 . . . 60 E8
Mullinure Pk BT61 . . . 60 F7
Mullurg BT60 . . . 100 A3
Mullurg Rd BT60 . . . 99 F3
Mullyard BT60 . . . 127 B7
Mullyard Rd BT60 . . . 127 C7
Mullyard Standing Stone★ BT60 . . . 127 B8
Mullybrannon Rd BT71 . . . 83 C8
Mullycarnan BT68 . . . 82 B4
Mullyleggan BT71 . . . 84 A4
Mullyloughan BT71 . . . 83 E2
Mullyloughran BT61 . . . 99 A6
Mullyloughran Hts 3 BT61 . . . 98 F7
Mullynaveagh BT68 . . . 82 D1
Mullyneill BT68 . . . 82 C3
Mullyneill Rd BT68 . . . 82 C3
Mullynure BT61 . . . 60 E8
Multyhogy BT5 . . . 15 E2
Munro Villas BT34 . . . 153 B7
Murdock's La BT19 . . . 66 B7
Murlough Bay Ct BT33 . . . 123 C5
Murlough Ct BT33 . . . 63 D8
Murlough Lower BT33 . . . 123 C3
Murlough National Nature Reserve★ BT33 . . . 123 C3
Murlough Quay BT33 . . . 123 C5
Murlough Upper BT33 . . . 63 E8
Murlough View BT33 . . . 123 C5
Murphy Cres BT35 . . . 64 D7
Murrays Hollows BT32 . . . 120 B7
Murrays Rd BT35 . . . 139 C1
Murray St BT1 . . . 154 C2
Murrays Terr BT24 . . . 59 D5
Murraywood BT66 . . . 86 C7
Murvaclogher or Broaghclogh BT30 . . . 107 F8
Musgrave Channel Rd BT3 . . . 15 B8
Musgrave St BT1 . . . 155 B3
Music Hall La BT1 . . . 155 B2
Muskett Ave BT8 . . . 29 C1
Muskett Cl BT8 . . . 29 C2
Muskett Cres BT8 . . . 29 D2
Muskett Ct BT8 . . . 29 C1
Muskett Dr 1 BT8 . . . 29 C1
Muskett Gdns BT8 . . . 29 C2
Muskett Glen BT8 . . . 29 C2
Muskett Mews 3 BT8 . . . 29 C1
Muskett Pk 2 BT8 . . . 29 C1
Muskett Rd BT8 . . . 29 C1
My Lady's Mile BT18 . . . 9 D6
My Lady's Rd BT6 . . . 15 A3
Myra Rd BT30 . . . 93 E1
Myrtledene Dr BT8 . . . 22 B2
Myrtledene Rd BT8 . . . 22 B2
Myrtlefield Pk BT9 . . . 21 A6
Naghan BT30 . . . 107 C2

N

Nairn Ct BT23 . . . 19 D4
Narrow Water BT34 . . . 142 C5
National Arboretum★ BT31 . . . 122 B6
Naul BT60 . . . 97 C4
Naul Rd BT60 . . . 97 D5
Nautilus Ctr★ BT34 . . . 153 D7
Navan BT60 . . . 98 A6
Navan Ct BT60 . . . 60 B4
Navan Fort★ BT60 . . . 98 A6
Navanfortrd BT60 . . . 97 D6
Navanfort Rd BT60 . . . 60 A5
Navan Fort Rd BT60 . . . 97 E6
Navan Pk BT60 . . . 60 B4
Navan St BT60 . . . 60 C4
Navar Ct BT19 . . . 4 D1
Navar Dr BT19 . . . 4 D1
Needham Bridge BT35 . . . 64 C6
Needham Ct BT34 . . . 153 C6
Neills Ave BT60 . . . 116 D6
Neill's Hill Pk BT5 . . . 15 F3
Neills Villas BT60 . . . 116 D6
Nelson Ct BT13 . . . 154 A4
Nelson Pk 10 BT19 . . . 5 B7
Nelson Sq BT13 . . . 154 A4
Nelson St BT1 . . . 155 B4
Nendrum Gdns BT5 . . . 15 D4
Nendrum Monastic Site★ BT23 . . . 79 C8
Nendrum Pk BT30 . . . 62 D5
Nendrum Way BT23 . . . 19 C4
Netherleigh Mews BT4 . . . 16 C7
Netherleigh Pk BT4 . . . 16 C6
Nettlefield Prim Sch BT6 . . . 15 A4
Nevis Ave BT4 . . . 15 D5
New Bridge Integrated Coll BT32 . . . 102 B3
New Bridge St BT30 . . . 62 C6
NEWCASTLE
Newtownards BT22 . . . 95 B6
Newcastle BT33 . . . 63 B6
Newcastle Ctr★ BT33 . . . 63 D4
Newcastle Manor 1 BT4 . . . 15 B6
Newcastle Prim Sch BT33 . . . 63 D6
Newcastle Rd
Castlewellan BT31 . . . 122 D3
Downpatrick BT30 . . . 107 C2
Kilkeel BT34 . . . 153 E8
Newcastle BT33 . . . 123 B4
Newry BT34 . . . 145 F1
Newtownards BT22 . . . 95 C5
Newcastle St
15 Belfast BT4 . . . 15 B5
Kilkeel BT34 . . . 153 C7
New Cl BT22 . . . 81 D5
New Ct BT22 . . . 81 D5
Newforge Ctry Club BT9 . . . 21 C4
Newforge Dale BT9 . . . 21 B5
Newforge Grange BT9 . . . 21 B5
Newforge La BT9 . . . 21 B5
Newforge Pk BT67 . . . 43 D6
New Forge Rd BT67 . . . 43 D3
New Harbour Rd BT22 . . . 81 D4
New Helmsley BT67 . . . 34 A2
New Line
Belfast BT16 . . . 24 C8
Craigavon BT65 . . . 41 E1
Crossgar BT30 . . . 92 C4
Donaghadee BT21 . . . 66 C6
Dundonald BT16 . . . 17 C1
Newry BT34 . . . 119 C3
Newry BT35 . . . 140 F2
Newtownards BT23 . . . 78 A7
15 Saintfield BT24 . . . 77 C3
New Line Lurgan BT66 . . . 86 D7
New Line Rd
Downpatrick BT30 . . . 107 C5
Newry BT34 . . . 134 C5
New Line The BT61 . . . 85 E1
New Line Waringsto BT66 . . . 53 F8
New Lodge Pl 1 BT15 . . . 14 D8
New Lodge Rd BT15 . . . 14 C8
New Mdw Row BT31 . . . 122 D6
NEWMILLS BT63 . . . 57 D8
New Rd
Banbridge BT32 . . . 61 F7
Donaghadee BT21 . . . 6 E1
Newry BT34 . . . 133 E4
Newry BT35 . . . 139 D2
Newry BT35 . . . 149 E6
Newtownards BT22 . . . 67 A1
Newtownards BT23 . . . 19 E4
Portavogie BT22 . . . 81 D4
New Rd The BT26 . . . 49 A4
NEWRY (AN TIÚR) BT35 . . . 64 A5
Newry Bypass BT34 . . . 132 A5
Newry Golf Club BT35 . . . 141 D8
Newry High Sch BT34 . . . 64 D8
Newry Inst (East Campus) 1 BT35 . . . 64 C5
Newry Inst (Model Campus) 1 BT35 . . . 64 C6
Newry Inst (West Campus) BT35 . . . 64 B6
Newry & Mourne Mus★ BT34 . . . 64 D5
Newry Rd
Armagh BT60 . . . 60 E3
Banbridge BT32 . . . 61 B1
Camlough BT35 . . . 131 C4
3 Crossmaglen BT35 . . . 147 F8
2 Forkhill BT35 . . . 149 D8
Hilltown BT34 . . . 134 A5
Newry BT34 . . . 119 B2
Newry BT34 . . . 133 A3
Newry BT34 . . . 152 F8
Newry BT35 . . . 117 D6
Newry BT35 . . . 129 F3
Newry BT35 . . . 139 B1
Warrenpoint BT34 . . . 65 A3
Newry Ret Pk 2 BT35 . . . 64 C5
Newry Sports Ctr BT35 . . . 64 C6
Newry St
Banbridge BT32 . . . 61 C3
Belfast BT6 . . . 15 B3
Kilkeel BT34 . . . 153 C7
Markethill BT60 . . . 116 A8
Newry . . . 151 C4
Newry BT35 . . . 129 D4
Rathfriland BT34 . . . 119 F2
Warrenpoint BT34 . . . 65 C2
Newry Sta BT35 . . . 131 E4
Newry Swimming Pool BT35 . . . 64 C6
Newry Variety Mkt★ BT34 . . . 64 D5
New St
Donaghadee BT21 . . . 67 A8
Lisburn BT27 . . . 26 C2
Lurgan BT66 . . . 41 F5
Newry BT35 . . . 64 D6
Newton Hts BT8 . . . 22 C3
Newton Pk BT8 . . . 22 B4
Newtown
Newry BT34 . . . 143 E5
Newry BT35 . . . 141 D6
Newtownards Airport BT23 . . . 19 E2
NEWTOWNARDS (BAILE NUA NA HARDA) BT23 . . . 19 E3
Newtownards Rd
Bangor BT19 . . . 13 A7
Belfast BT5 . . . 15 A5
Comber BT23 . . . 25 E3
Donaghadee BT21 . . . 66 D8
Newtownards BT22 . . . 70 A5
Newtownards BT23 . . . 13 A5
Newtownards BT23 . . . 68 D7
Newtown Ave BT23 . . . 20 A7
NEWTOWNBREDA BT8 . . . 21 F4
Newtownbreda Ct BT8 . . . 21 F4
Newtownbreda Factory Est BT8 . . . 21 F2
Newtownbreda High Sch BT8 . . . 21 F3
Newtownbreda Prim Sch BT8 . . . 22 A4
Newtownbreda Rd BT8 . . . 21 E2
Newtown Cl BT23 . . . 20 A7
Newtown Cres BT23 . . . 20 A8
Newtown Dr 1 BT23 . . . 20 A7
Newtown Gdns BT23 . . . 20 A7
Newtown Grange BT23 . . . 20 A8
NEWTOWNHAMILTON (BAILE ÚR) BT35 . . . 129 C4
Newtownhamilton High Sch BT35 . . . 129 C5
Newtownhamilton Prim Sch BT35 . . . 129 D5
Newtownhamilton Rd BT60 . . . 60 D1
Newtown Hts 2 BT23 . . . 20 A8
Newtown Pk BT23 . . . 20 A8
Newtown Rd
Newry BT34 . . . 143 E5
Newry BT35 . . . 129 F3
Newtown Upper BT34 . . . 143 E6
Newtown Vale BT23 . . . 20 A8
Newtown Villas 2 BT34 . . . 143 C3
Newtown Way
2 Newtownards BT23 . . . 20 A7
1 Newtownards BT23 . . . 20 A8
Nialls Cresent BT60 . . . 60 B4
Nicholson Gdns BT28 . . . 38 B8
Nicholson's Crossroads BT25 . . . 89 A4
Nicholsons Rd BT34 . . . 153 B5
Ninemile Rd BT35 . . . 129 C7
Ninth St BT13 . . . 154 A4
Nixons La BT19 . . . 5 D7
Nook The BT60 . . . 60 E4
Norbloom Gdns 2 BT5 . . . 15 D3
Norfolk Ave 10 BT21 . . . 67 A7
North Bank BT6 . . . 22 B8
North Boundary St BT13 . . . 154 C4
Northbrook Gdns BT9 . . . 14 A1
Northbrook St BT12 . . . 14 A1
North Circular Rd
Lisburn BT28 . . . 26 A2
Lurgan BT67 . . . 42 A8
North City Bsns Ctr BT15 . . . 14 D8
North Cl BT18 . . . 9 C5
North Down & Ards Inst of FE BT20 . . . 4 B3
North Downs & Ards Inst of Further Ed BT23 . . . 19 E6
North Downs Bsns Village BT19 . . . 13 A7
Northern Ireland Mountain Ctr The★ BT33 . . . 122 B1
Northern Rd 2 BT3 . . . 14 E8
Northfield Rd BT21 . . . 66 F8
Northfield Rise BT5 . . . 16 A1
North Gdns BT5 . . . 15 E3
North Gn BT23 . . . 19 C4
North Hill St BT15 . . . 14 D7
North Howard Ct BT13 . . . 154 B4
North Howard Link BT13 . . . 154 B4
North Howard St BT13 . . . 154 B4
North Howard Wlk BT13 . . . 154 A4
North King St BT13 . . . 154 C4
Northland Ct BT13 . . . 154 A4
Northland St BT13 . . . 154 A4
North Par BT7 . . . 14 F1
North Queen St BT15 . . . 14 D8
North Rd
Belfast BT5 . . . 15 E4
Newtownards BT23 . . . 19 E7
North Side Pk BT23 . . . 19 D6
North Sperrin BT5 . . . 16 D3
North St
Belfast BT1 . . . 155 A4
Lurgan BT67 . . . 42 A6
Newry BT34 . . . 64 D6
Newtownards BT22 . . . 70 C5
Newtownards BT23 . . . 19 D5
Portadown BT62 . . . 51 C4
5 Crossmaglen BT35 . . . 147 F8
North Strangford Lough National Nature Reserve★ BT23 . . . 20 A2
Northumberland St BT13 . . . 154 B4
Northway
Craigavon BT64 . . . 40 C2
Portadown BT62 . . . 51 E5
Northwood BT67 . . . 42 B8
Norton Dr BT9 . . . 21 A5
Norwood Ave BT4 . . . 15 F6
Norwood Cres BT4 . . . 15 F7
Norwood Ct BT4 . . . 15 F7
Norwood Dr BT4 . . . 15 F6
Norwood Gdns BT4 . . . 15 F6
Norwood Gr BT4 . . . 15 F6
Norwood Pk BT4 . . . 16 A6
Norwood St BT2 . . . 155 A2
Norwyn Ave BT21 . . . 67 A8
Notting Hill BT9 . . . 21 B7
Notting Hill Ct BT9 . . . 21 C7
Nottinghill Manor 4 BT9 . . . 21 B7
Nubia St BT12 . . . 154 A1
Nunsquarter BT22 . . . 70 D1
Nun's Wlk BT18 . . . 9 D5
Nursery Dr BT35 . . . 64 A7
Nursery Mews BT60 . . . 60 B4
Nursery Rd
Armagh BT60 . . . 60 B5
Newtownards BT22 . . . 71 B1
Newtownards BT23 . . . 19 C4
Nursery The 7 BT30 . . . 93 C5
Nutgrove Rd BT30 . . . 107 E5
Nuthill Rd BT67 . . . 45 D6

O

Oak Ave BT22 . . . 81 C8

Oak Cl BT35 . . . . **131** E4
Oakdale BT23. . . . . **77** E8
Oakdale Ct
[3] Ballygowan BT23 . . . . . . **77** E8
Banbridge BT32. . . . . **61** E4
Oakdale St BT4 . . . . **15** C5
Oakdene Dr BT4 . . . . **15** D6
Oakdene Par BT4 . . . . **15** D6
Oakdene Pk BT66 . . . . **53** E5
Oakfield Dr BT71. . . . . **72** B1
Oakfield Rd BT60 . . . . . . **115** F3
Oakfields BT65 . . . . **53** B7
Oakfield Terr BT66. . . . . . **41** F6
Oakfield Wlk [4] BT21 . . . . **66** F8
Oak Grange
Waringstown BT66 . . . . **86** C8
Warrenpoint BT34 . . . . **65** B4
Oakhill BT27. . . . . **38** A4
Oakhill Rd BT25. . . . . **88** C3
Oakland Ave BT4. . . . . **15** E5
Oakland Cres BT34. . . . . . . **65** C3
Oakland Gr
Ballynahinch BT24. . . . . **59** C6
Warrenpoint BT34. . . . . **65** C2
Oaklands
Ballynahinch BT24. . . . . **78** A3
Banbridge BT32. . . . . **102** C3
Hillsborough BT26. . . . . **47** B5
Newry BT34. . . . . **64** F1
Waringstown BT66 . . . . **86** C8
Oaklands Cl BT30 . . . . **78** B3
Oaklands Ct BT30. . . . . **78** B3
Oakland Terr [8] BT22 . . . . **94** D3
Oakland Way [2] BT17 . . . . **26** F8
Oakleigh Gr BT67 . . . . **42** A6
Oakleigh Hts BT67 . . . . **42** A6
Oakleigh Manor BT67 . . . . **42** A6
Oakleigh Pk
[1] Belfast BT6 . . . . **15** A2
Portadown BT62 . . . . **51** C2
Oakley Ave BT18. . . . . **9** C5
Oakridge
Armagh BT60. . . . . **60** F1
Banbridge BT32. . . . . **61** E4
Lurgan BT66 . . . . **41** E5
Oakridge Ave BT27. . . . . . . **26** B5
Oakridge Cre BT27. . . . . . . **26** C5
Oakridge Cres BT27. . . . . . **26** B5
Oakridge Gds BT27. . . . . . . **26** B5
Oakridge Pk
Hilltown BT34 . . . . **134** A5
Lisburn BT27 . . . . **26** B5
Oak St BT7 . . . . **155** A1
Oaks The
Bangor BT19 . . . . **13** D8
Craigavon BT62. . . . . **54** E6
Craigavon BT66. . . . . **41** A7
Newtownards BT23. . . . . . . **20** A3
Oaktree Manor [5] BT66 . . **86** C8
Oaktree Pk [10] BT19 . . . . **4** E1
Oakvale BT65. . . . . **53** B7
Oak Vale Ave BT34. . . . . . . **64** F8
Oak Way BT7 . . . . **155** A1
Oakwood Ave
Bangor BT20 . . . . **3** F3
Carryduff BT8 . . . . **29** C1
Oakwood Ct BT9. . . . . **21** A5
Oakwood Gr BT9. . . . . **21** A5
Oakwood Hts BT8. . . . . **29** C1
Oakwood Integrated Prim Sch BT17 . . . . **26** D8
Oakwood Manor [3] BT71. **72** A6
Oakwood Mews BT9 . . . . . **21** A5
Oakwood Pk
Bangor BT20 . . . . **3** F3
Belfast BT9 . . . . **21** A5
Oakwood Pl BT62 . . . . **51** C3
Oberon St BT6. . . . . **15** B2
Obins Ave BT62 . . . . **51** C5
Obins Dr BT62 . . . . **51** C4
Obins Rd BT62. . . . . **51** D5
Obins St BT62 . . . . **51** C5
Obre Ave BT62. . . . . **73** E3
O'callaghan Rd BT35 . . . . **139** F1
Odessa St (Sráid Odúsa) BT13 . . . . **154** A3
O'donaghue Pk [9] BT35 . **131** C5
O'donnell Cl [4] BT31. . . . **122** B4
O'donnell Hts [3] BT31. . . **122** B4
O'donnell Pk [5] BT31 . . . **122** B4
Off Chapel La BT60. . . . . . . **60** D4
Ogilvie St BT6 . . . . **15** B3
Ogle's Fort★ BT66 . . . . **42** E1
Ogles Gr BT27 . . . . **37** C1
Ogle St BT60. . . . . **60** C4
O'hagan St BT34. . . . . **64** C5
OILEÁN AN MHUILINN (MILLISLE) BT21 . . . . **67** B5
Olanrye Pk BT35 . . . . **64** B7
Old Ballybarnes Rd BT23 . **18** D7
Old Ballygowan Rd BT23 . **25** C1
Old Ballynahinch Rd BT27 **39** C3
Old Bangor Rd
Bangor BT19 . . . . **13** A6
Newtownards BT23. . . . . . . **12** F3
Old Bann Rd BT32. . . . . **86** D3
Old Belfast Rd
Ballynahinch BT24. . . . . **59** D8
Bangor BT19 . . . . **3** B1
Downpatrick BT30. . . . . **62** C7
Newtownards BT23. . . . . . . **19** A4
Old Bridge Rd
Castlewellan BT31. . . . . . . **122** C7
[1] Forkhill BT35 . . . . **149** D8
Old Cart Rd BT24 . . . . **77** C5
Old Channel Rd BT3. . . . . . **15** A6
Old Church La BT67. . . . . . **34** B7
Old Coach Rd
Armagh BT60. . . . . **60** E3
Hillsborough BT26. . . . . **47** B4
Old Coach Way BT24 . . . . . **77** D4
Old Course Rd BT30. . . . . . **62** E2
Old Creamery Ret Pk [3] BT35. . . . . **64** C5
Old Crossmaglen Rd BT35 . . . . **140** C7
Old Cross St BT23. . . . . **19** E4
Old Ct Lodge BT65 . . . . **53** D8
Old Ct Manor BT65. . . . . . . **53** D8
Old Ctyd The BT16 . . . . **17** B2
Old Cultra La BT18 . . . . **1** B1
Old Cultra Rd BT18. . . . . **1** B1
Old Dundonald Mews BT16 . . . . **17** B3
Old Dundonald Rd
Belfast BT5 . . . . **16** F3
Dundonald BT16 . . . . **17** B3
Olde Golf Links The BT62. **51** E1
Old Forge
Armagh BT60. . . . . **97** B5
Banbridge BT32. . . . . **61** F4
Magheralin BT67. . . . . **43** D6
Old Forge Ave BT23 . . . . . . **20** C6
Old Forge Cres BT23 . . . . . **20** C6
Old Forge Ct BT23 . . . . **25** E4
Old Forge Dr BT23 . . . . **20** C6
Old Forge Gn BT23. . . . . . . **20** C6
Old Forge La BT23 . . . . **20** C6
Old Forge Mews BT28. . . . **36** E7
Old Forge Pk BT23. . . . . . . **20** C5
Old Forge Way BT23 . . . . . **20** C6
Old Fort BT19. . . . . **2** D7
Oldfort Ave BT67. . . . . **34** A2
Oldfort Gdns BT67 . . . . **34** A2
Old Fort Lodge BT65 . . . . . **53** C7
Oldfort Pk BT67. . . . . **34** A2
Old Gilford Rd
Portadown BT63 . . . . **52** A3
Tandragee BT62 . . . . **101** B7
Old Grand Jury Manor BT24 . . . . **77** D3
Old Grand Jury Rd BT24 . . **77** C3
Old Grange BT61. . . . . **60** B6
Old Gransha Rd BT19. . . . . . **4** D1
Old Hall Ct [6] BT34 . . . . . **143** B3
Old Holywood Rd
Belfast BT4 . . . . **9** C2
Newtownards BT23. . . . . . . **18** D7
Old Kenlis St [5] BT32 . . . . **61** C4
Old Killylea Rd BT60 . . . . . **98** B6
Old Kilmore Rd
Craigavon BT67. . . . . **32** D5
Moira BT67 . . . . **34** A1
Old Lodge Rd BT13. . . . . . . **14** B7
Old Lurgan Rd
Craigavon BT67. . . . . **32** E5
Portadown BT63 . . . . **52** D6
Old Mansegreen BT32. . . . . **61** F3
Old Manse Rd BT32 . . . . . . **61** F4
Old Mill BT62. . . . . **101** B6
Old Mill Cl
Dundonald BT16 . . . . **17** F4
Newry BT34. . . . . **119** D2
Old Mill Cotts BT28 . . . . . . **26** B8
Old Mill Ct
[3] Armagh BT60. . . . . **98** B4
Crawfordsburn BT19. . . . . **2** F3
Newtownards BT23. . . . . . . **19** C4
Old Mill Dale BT16. . . . . . . **17** F4
Old Mill Gr BT16 . . . . **17** F4
Old Mill Hts
Dundonald BT16 . . . . **17** F4
Hillsborough BT26. . . . . **37** B1
Old Mill La BT32 . . . . **103** B5
Old Mill Manor
Craigavon BT62. . . . . **100** E8
Tandragee BT62 . . . . **101** B6
Old Mill Mdws BT16. . . . . . **17** F4
Old Mill Mews BT16. . . . . . **17** F4
Old Mill Pk BT16. . . . . **17** F4
Old Mill Pl BT34 . . . . **121** C2
Old Mill Race The BT23. . . **25** C2
Old Mill Rd
Banbridge BT32. . . . . **102** A3
Craigavon BT63. . . . . **101** F3
Old Mill Rise BT16 . . . . **17** F4
Old Mill The
Castlewellan BT31. . . . . . . **122** E3
Crossgar BT30. . . . . **92** A4
Hillsborough BT26. . . . . **37** B1
Kircubbin BT22 . . . . **80** D8
Old Milltown Rd BT8 . . . . . **21** C2
Old Mount Rd BT35 . . . . . **129** C5
Old Movilla Rd [5] BT23. . . **19** F5
Old Mus Arts Ctr The★ BT12. . . . . **154** C3
Old Navan Fort Rd BT60 . . **60** A5
Old Newry Rd
Armagh BT60. . . . . **60** D4
Banbridge BT32. . . . . **61** B1
Newry BT34. . . . . **119** B1
Oldpark Rd BT14. . . . . **14** B8
Old Pk BT61 . . . . **60** B6
Old Pk Rd
Downpatrick BT30. . . . . . . **107** C7
Drumaness BT24. . . . . **91** B1
Lisburn BT28. . . . . **26** A8
Old Portadown Rd BT66 . . **41** D3
Old Priory Cl BT23 . . . . **19** C4
Old Quarry The BT30. . . . . . **62** C3
Old Quay Ct BT18 . . . . **9** F8
Old Quay La. **151** C4
Old Quay Rd BT18. . . . . **1** E1
Old Rathfriland Rd BT34. **132** E8
Old Rd
Castlewellan BT31. . . . . . . **122** B7
Lisburn BT28. . . . . **35** A8
Newcastle BT33. . . . . **123** B3
Newry BT34. . . . . **133** C4
Newry BT34. . . . . **137** A1
Newry BT34. . . . . **146** E8
Newry BT35. . . . . **117** E6
Newry BT35. . . . . **129** C4
Newry BT35. . . . . **131** A3
Newry BT35. . . . . **140** A6
Newry BT35. . . . . **140** F2
Newry BT35. . . . . **147** D7
Old Rectory Pk
Portadown BT62 . . . . **51** C2
Seapatrick BT32 . . . . **61** C7
Old Rly Cl BT31 . . . . **121** D7
Old Saintfield Rd
Belfast BT8 . . . . **29** C7
Downpatrick BT30. . . . . **91** F7
Old Scarva Rd BT62 . . . . . **101** C6
Old Seahill Rd BT18 . . . . **1** H3
Old Shore Rd BT23. . . . . . . **19** F4
Old Sta Rd BT18 . . . . **1** F2
Old Tandragee Rd [5] BT60 . . . . **116** A8
Oldtowncres BT34 . . . . . . **146** A5
Oldtown La BT34. . . . . **146** A5
Oldtown Rd BT34 . . . . **146** B5
Old Town Rd BT35 . . . . . . **138** F5
Old WarrenⓉ BT28 . . . . . . **38** A8
Old Warrenpoint Rd BT34 **64** E2
Old Warren Prim Sch BT28. . . . . **37** F7
Old Windmill Rd BT19. . . . . . **2** F5
Oliver Plunkett Pk BT35 . **148** F8
Olympia Dr BT12. . . . . **14** A2
Olympia Leisure Ctr BT12 **14** A1
Olympia Par BT12. . . . . **14** A2
Olympia St BT12 . . . . **14** A2
OMEATH **142** D1
Omeath St BT6 . . . . **15** B3
O'neill Ave BT34 . . . . **64** E3
O'neill's Mound★ BT60. . . **98** B5
O'neill's Pl BT18 . . . . **9** D7
O'neill St BT13. . . . . **154** A3
O Neills Villas BT35 . . . . . **131** B3
Onslow Ave [5] BT19. . . . . . **13** E8
Onslow Ct [6] BT19 . . . . **13** E8
Onslow Dr BT19. . . . . **13** D8
Onslow Gdns
Bangor BT19 . . . . **4** E1
Belfast BT6 . . . . **15** B1
Onslow Par BT6 . . . . **15** B1
Onslow Pk BT6 . . . . **15** B1
Open Univ BT7 . . . . **14** D2
Orangefield Ave BT5 . . . . . **15** E3
Orangefield Cl BT60. . . . . . **60** F4
Orangefield Cres
Armagh BT60. . . . . **60** F4
Belfast BT6 . . . . **15** C1
Orangefield Dr
Armagh BT60. . . . . **60** F4
Belfast BT5 . . . . **15** E3
Orangefield Dr S BT5 . . . . **15** E3
Orangefield Gdns
Armagh BT60. . . . . **60** F5
Belfast BT5 . . . . **15** E3
Orangefield Gn BT5 . . . . . . **15** E3
Orangefield Gr BT5 . . . . . . **15** E3
Orangefield High Sch BT5 **15** F2
Orangefield La BT5 . . . . . . **15** E3
Orangefield Par BT5 . . . . . **15** E3
Orangefield Pk
Armagh BT60. . . . . **60** F4
Belfast BT5 . . . . **15** E3
Orangefield Prim Sch BT5. **15** E2
Orangefield Rd BT5 . . . . . . **15** E4
Orange La BT67. . . . . **43** E4
Orby Cl BT5 . . . . **15** E1
Orby Ct BT5 . . . . **15** D3
Orby Dr BT5 . . . . **15** E2
Orby Gdns BT5. . . . . **15** C3
Orby Gn BT5. . . . . **15** C2
Orby Gr BT5 . . . . **15** D2
Orby Grange BT5 . . . . **15** C3
Orby Link BT5 . . . . **15** C3
Orby Mews BT5. . . . . **15** D3
Orby Par BT5 . . . . **15** D2
Orby Pk BT5. . . . . **15** D3
Orby Pl BT5 . . . . **15** D2
Orby Rd BT5. . . . . **15** D3
Orby St BT5 . . . . **15** E1
Orchard Ave BT23. . . . . **19** E5
Orchard Cl
Belfast BT5 . . . . **16** C3
Lisburn BT28 . . . . **38** A7
Orchard Cres
Downpatrick BT30. . . . . **62** C7
Portadown BT62 . . . . **51** C2
Orchard Ct BT4 . . . . **9** B2
Orchard Dr
Armagh BT61. . . . . **85** B5
Newtownards BT23. . . . . . . **79** C6
Portadown BT62 . . . . **51** C1
Orchard Gdns
Downpatrick BT30. . . . . **62** C7
Newtownards BT23. . . . . . . **19** F7
Orchard Grange BT26 . . . . **46** A8
Orchard Hill BT34. . . . . **65** C2
Orchard La
Downpatrick BT30. . . . . **62** C8
Newtownards BT23. . . . . . . **19** E7
Orchard Leisure Ctr BT60 **60** E4
Orchard Pk
Armagh BT61. . . . . **85** B5
Portadown BT62 . . . . **51** C1
Orchard Pl BT23 . . . . **19** E5
Orchard Rd
Armagh BT61. . . . . **85** B5
Downpatrick BT30. . . . . . . **124** C6
Orchard Rise BT8 . . . . **22** A4
Orchard The
Holywood BT18 . . . . **1** C1
Warrenpoint BT34. . . . . **65** E2
Orchard Vale BT6. . . . . **22** E7
Orchardville Ave [6] BT19 . . **3** C2
Orchardville Gdns [7] BT19. **3** C2
Orchardville Pk [1] BT19 . . . **3** C2
Orchard Way
Downpatrick BT30. . . . . **62** C7
Holywood BT18 . . . . **1** C1
Oriel Dr BT30. . . . . **62** D3
Orient Circ BT66. . . . . **42** C4
Orior Pk BT35 . . . . **131** C5
Orior Rd BT35 . . . . **64** B7
Orkney St BT13 . . . . **154** A4
OrlockⓉ BT19 . . . . **5** F7
Orlock Gdns BT19. . . . . **3** D2
Orlock La BT19 . . . . **5** F7
Orlock Rd BT19 . . . . **5** F7
Ormeau Ave BT7. . . . . **155** A2
Ormeau Bsns Pk BT7. . . . **155** B1
Ormeau Emb BT7 . . . . **155** C1
Ormeau Golf Club BT7 . . . **14** F1
Ormeau Rd BT7. . . . . **155** B1
Ormeau St BT7 . . . . **155** B1
Ormiston Cres BT4. . . . . . . **16** A5
Ormiston Dr BT4. . . . . **16** B4
Ormiston Gdns BT5 . . . . . . **16** A4
Ormiston Par BT4. . . . . **16** A5
Ormiston Pk BT4. . . . . **16** B4
Ormonde Gdns BT6 . . . . . . **15** C2
Ormonde St BT62 . . . . **51** D3
Oroory Hill BT25 . . . . **87** C4
Orrs La BT27. . . . . **27** A2
Ortus Bsns Pk BT13 . . . . . **154** B3
Osborne Dr
Bangor BT20 . . . . **3** F3
Belfast BT9 . . . . **21** A7
Killyleagh BT30 . . . . **93** B6
Osborne Gdns BT9. . . . . . . **21** A6
Osborne Pk
Bangor BT20 . . . . **3** F3
Belfast BT9 . . . . **21** A6
Osborne Prom BT34. . . . . . **65** C1
Osman St BT12 . . . . **154** B3
Oswald Pk BT12 . . . . **154** B1
Otterwood BT25 . . . . **58** D4
Oughley Rd BT27 . . . . **76** F5
OuleyⓉ
Ballynahinch BT24. . . . . **77** A7
Newry BT34. . . . . **119** A4
Ouley Rd BT32. . . . . **118** F5
Our Lady & St Patrick's Coll BT5. **16** D2
Our Lady's Gram Sch BT35. . . . . **64** C7
Our Lady's & St Mochua's Prim Sch BT60. . . . . **127** B8
OutlackⓉ BT60 . . . . **98** F1
Outlack Rd BT60 . . . . **98** F1
OutleckanⓉ BT35. . . . . . . **130** B4
Outleckan Rd BT35. . . . . . **130** A4
Oval Ct BT4. . . . . **15** C6
Overdale Bsns Pk BT24. . . **77** D3
Owenglass Rd BT34 . . . . . **134** A5
Owenroe Dr BT19. . . . . **3** D1
Owen's Rd BT31 . . . . **122** A7
Oxford Ave BT28. . . . . **26** B4
Oxford St BT1 . . . . **155** B3
Oyster Cove BT21 . . . . **66** F7
Ozone Leisure Ctr & Belfast Indoor Tennis Arena BT7. . . . . **155** C1

P

Paddock The
Ballygowan BT23. . . . . **77** E8
[3] Newtownards BT23 . . . . **20** A3
Páirc Ard an Lao (Ardilea Pk) BT30 . . . . **62** C2
Páirc Ardchoille (Arkle Pk) BT30 . . . . **62** B2
Páirc Chnoc an Tobair (Springhill Pk) BT30. . . . . . **62** E5
Páirc Ghleann álainn (Glenaulin Pk) BT30. . . . . . **62** D4
Páirc Mhíchíl Uí Mhealláin (Michael Mallin Pk) [9] BT35 . . . . **64** C5
Páirc Mhuire (Marian Pk) BT30 . . . . **123** F5
Páirc Ráh Mr (Rathmore Pk) BT30 . . . . **62** D5
Páirc Shéamais Uí Chonghaile (James Connolly Pk) [7] BT35 . . . . **64** C5
Páirc Shliabh Coimheadach (Commedagh Pk) BT33. . . **63** B3
Páirc úibh Euchaich (Iveagh Pk) BT30 . . . . **62** D4
Páirc Uí Dhálaigh (Daly Cres) BT35 . . . . **139** E2
Pakenham St BT7 . . . . **155** A1
Palace Gr BT18 . . . . **9** D3
Palace Mews BT18 . . . . **9** C3
Palace Stables Heritage Ctr★ BT60. . . . . **60** D3
Palatine Row BT30 . . . . . . **125** D5
Palestine St BT7 . . . . **14** E2
Palmer Ave BT28. . . . . **26** B3
Palmerston Pk BT4 . . . . . . **15** E7
Palmerston Rd BT4 . . . . . . **15** E7
Palms The BT63 . . . . **40** A8
Palmworth Dr BT19 . . . . **5** A5
Pamela Way BT23. . . . . **25** E4
Pandora St BT12. . . . . **154** B1
Pansy St BT4 . . . . **15** B5
Parade The BT21. . . . . **6** G1
Paris St
[10] Belfast BT13. . . . . **14** A7
Belfast BT13 . . . . **154** A4
Park Ave
Ballywalter BT22. . . . . **71** A5
Bangor BT20 . . . . **4** B4
Belfast BT4 . . . . **15** D6
Donaghadee BT21 . . . . **6** F1
Dundonald BT16 . . . . **17** B4
Holywood BT18 . . . . **9** D6
Killyleagh BT30 . . . . **93** B6
Lurgan BT66 . . . . **42** C4
Newcastle BT33. . . . . **63** C5
Park Cres
Comber BT23. . . . . **25** E3
Millisle BT22 . . . . **67** A4
Park Dr
Bangor BT20 . . . . **4** B4
Dundonald BT16 . . . . **17** B4
Holywood BT18 . . . . **9** D6
Parker St BT4 . . . . **15** B5
Parkgate Ave BT4. . . . . **15** D5
Parkgate Cres [5] BT4 . . . . **15** C6
Parkgate Dr [4] BT4 . . . . . . **15** C6
Parkgate Gdns BT4 . . . . . . **15** C6
Parkgate Par BT4 . . . . **15** C6
Park Grange [3] BT4. . . . . . **15** D6
Park Head [4] BT22. . . . . . . **94** D3
Parkhead Cres BT35 . . . . . **64** A7
Park Hill BT25 . . . . **58** D4
Park House Manor BT18. . . . **9** F8
Park La
Belfast BT9 . . . . **14** C1
Craigavon BT63. . . . . **101** E7
Hillsborough BT26. . . . . **47** C5
Newcastle BT33. . . . . **63** D6
Rostrevor BT34 . . . . **143** C4
Saintfield BT24 . . . . **77** D3
Park La Mews BT26 . . . . . . **47** B6
Parkland Cres [3] BT23 . . . **20** A7
Parklands BT67. . . . . **43** E6
Park Lodge BT8. . . . . **21** F3
Parkmore BT64. . . . . **40** E1
Parkmore or DemesneⓉ BT60 . . . . **60** D3
Parkmore St BT7 . . . . **21** F8
Parkmount BT27. . . . . **26** C2
Park Mount BT20 . . . . **4** B4
Parknasilla Cl BT67 . . . . . . **32** F8
Parknasilla Cres BT67. . . . **32** F8
Parknasilla Way BT67 . . . . **32** F8
Park Par
Belfast BT6 . . . . **15** A3
Newcastle BT33. . . . . **63** D6
Park Rd
Belfast BT7 . . . . **14** F1
Dromara BT25. . . . . **89** E2
Portadown BT62 . . . . **51** D5
Parkrow Rd BT25 . . . . **58** F4
Parkside
Dromara BT25. . . . . **58** B5
[3] Warrenpoint BT34 . . . . . **65** D2
Park St
Hillsborough BT26. . . . . **47** C5
Lurgan BT67 . . . . **42** B5
Parkstown La BT63. . . . . . . **57** F4
Park The BT16 . . . . **17** C2
Park View BT35. . . . . **141** D7
Parkview Ct BT67 . . . . **42** B5
Parkview Manor BT5. . . . . . **16** C2
Parkview St BT66 . . . . **41** E5
Parkway BT4 . . . . **9** A1
Park Way BT23 . . . . **25** E3
Parkwood BT27. . . . . **26** C4
Parsonage Cl [2] BT22 . . . . **80** E7
Parsonage Rd BT22 . . . . . . **80** E7
Parson HallⓉ BT22 . . . . . . **94** E3
Pasadena Gdns [2] BT5 . . . **16** A4
PAS AN PHOINTE (POYNTZ PASS) BT35. . . . . **117** D8
Pascali Dr BT23. . . . . **19** B6
Patrick St (Sráid Phádraig) [8] BT35. . . . . **64** C5
Pats Rd BT34 . . . . **153** F8
Pat's Turn BT66. . . . . **86** C4
Patterson's Pl BT1 . . . . . . **155** A3
Pattersons Rd BT67 . . . . . . **45** C3
Paulett Ave [11] BT5. . . . . . . **15** B4
Paxton St BT5 . . . . **15** B4
Pearl St BT6. . . . . **15** B3
Peartree Hill
Belfast BT16 . . . . **24** D8
Dundonald BT16 . . . . **17** D1
Peartree Rd BT24. . . . . **91** C8
Pedens Rd BT32 . . . . **103** E7
Peggy's Loaning BT32. . . . **61** B5
Pembridge Ct BT4 . . . . **16** A6
Pembroke St BT12 . . . . . . **154** B1
Penbrooke Ave BT19. . . . . . **13** D7
Penge Gdns BT9. . . . . **21** D7
Penguin Pl BT34 . . . . **64** E6
Pennington Pk BT8 . . . . **22** B2
Penrhyn Gdns BT23 . . . . . . **20** A6
Penrhyn Pk BT23 . . . . **20** A6
Penrose St BT7 . . . . **14** E2
Percy Pl BT13. . . . . **154** B4
Percy St BT13 . . . . **154** B3
Pernau St BT13 . . . . **154** A4

Perry Ct BT5 15 A4
Perry Dr BT19 5 A1
Perry Pk BT19 5 A1
Perry Rd BT19 5 A1
Peter's Hill BT13 154 C4
Peters Pl (Plás Pheadair) 4 BT35 64 C5
Peters St BT34 65 C2
Phennick Cl 8 BT30 125 F6
Phennick Way 9 BT30 125 F6
Phillip Way BT23 25 E4
Phil's Fort★ BT25 87 D6
Picardy Ave BT6 22 C8
Pickie Fun Pk BT20 4 A5
Pier Rampart BT66 74 E7
Pillar Well La BT30 62 C6
Pilot Pl 4 BT1 14 E7
Pilot St BT1 14 E7
Pim's Ave BT4 15 D6
Pim St BT15 14 C7
Pinebank BT65 41 C3
Pine Crest BT18 9 E5
Pinecroft Ave BT23 20 A6
Pine Gr
Holywood BT18 9 D4
Newry BT35 64 C3
Pinehill BT27 39 C6
Pinehill Ave BT19 5 A1
Pinehill Cres 3 BT19 5 A2
Pinehill Ct 2 BT19 5 A2
Pinehill Gdns BT19 5 A1
Pinehill Gn BT19 5 A2
Pinehill Groove BT19 5 A1
Pinehill Pk BT19 5 A2
Pinehill Rd
Bangor BT19 4 F2
Lisburn BT27 27 F4
Pine Pk BT21 66 F8
Pine Ridge BT21 6 E1
Pines Cl BT66 42 C4
Pines Ct BT66 42 C4
Pines Gr BT66 42 D4
Pines Pk BT66 42 C4
Pine St BT7 155 B1
Pines The
7 Bangor BT19 13 E8
Hillsborough BT26 47 C7
Pine Valley 4 BT34 143 C4
Pineview Ct BT63 101 E8
Pineview Hts BT63 101 E8
Pine Way BT7 155 A1
Pinewood
Bangor BT20 4 E5
7 Rostrevor BT34 143 C4
Pinewood Dr BT61 99 E8
Pinewoodglen BT35 147 F7
Pinewood Hill BT34 65 C3
Pinewood Pk BT27 28 A3
Pinewood View BT33 63 D8
Piney Hill BT24 59 E3
Piney Hills BT9 21 B5
Piney La BT9 21 B4
Piney Pk BT9 21 B4
Piney Way BT9 21 B4
Piney Wlk BT9 21 B4
Pinley Cresent BT32 61 B2
Pinley Dr BT32 61 B2
Pinley Gn
Banbridge BT32 61 A3
Markethill BT60 116 A8
Pinley Mdw BT32 61 A2
Pinley Pk BT32 61 A2
Pipers Cross Roads BT23 30 F8
Pirates Adventure Golf BT16 17 A3
Pirrie Pk Gdns BT6 15 A1
Pirrie Rd BT4 16 A6
Pitcairn Ave BT20 4 C3
Plantation Ave BT27 38 D8
Plantation Cl BT27 38 D8
Plantation Ct BT27 38 E8
Plantation Dr
Bangor BT19 5 A5
Lisburn BT27 38 D8
Plantation Gr BT27 38 E7
Plantation Mews BT27 38 E7
Plantation Pk BT30 62 D6
Plantation Rd
Bangor BT19 5 A5
Craigavon BT63 53 E3
Lisburn BT27 38 E7
Plantation St 1 BT30 93 C5
Planting Rd
Newry BT34 121 F2
Newry BT35 139 F5
Plás an Chaisleáin (Castle Pl)
1 Ardglass BT30 126 A6
4 Newcastle BT33 63 D5
Plás Chluain Ard (Clonard Pl) 2 BT13 154 A3
Plás Linn Uí Dhúill (Lynn Doyle Pl) BT30 62 C4
Plas Merdyn BT18 9 E6
Plás Pheadair (Peters Pl) 4 BT35 64 C5
Plaster 150 C5
Plateau The BT9 21 B4
Plover Gn BT23 20 A3
Plunkett Ct (Cúirt Phluincéid) BT13 155 A4
Plunkett Mews 6 BT35 64 C7
Plunkett St BT35 64 D8
Point Rd BT30 123 F7
Point Rd The BT63 86 C1
Point The BT19 5 A8
Polkone Rd BT35 139 D7
Pollnagh BT60 97 A7
Pollock Dr BT66 42 A3
Pollock Pk★ BT66 42 A3
Pollock Rd BT15 14 E8
Polnagh Rd BT60 97 A7
Pommern Par BT6 15 C2
Pomona Ave BT4 15 D5
Poobles BT67 33 F5
Pool La BT35 64 C4
Poplars The
Bangor BT19 13 E7
Craigavon BT66 86 F6
Portadown Coll BT63 52 A5
Portadown Golf Club BT63 56 C8
Portadown Ind Christian Sch BT63 52 A4
Portadown Ind Est BT66 41 D5
Portadown Intergrated Sch BT63 52 B7
PORTADOWN (PORT AN DÚNÁIN) BT62 51 E3
Portadown Rd
Armagh BT61 60 F6
Craigavon BT62 55 F1
Lurgan BT66 41 D5
Richhill BT61 85 E2
Tandragee BT62 101 A8
Portadown Rfc BT63 51 F6
Portadown Sta BT62 51 E5
PORTAFERRY (PORT AN PHEIRE) BT22 94 D3
Portaferry Rd
Newtownards BT22 69 B8
Newtownards BT22 81 B1
Newtownards BT23 19 F4
Portal Grave★ BT35 140 C5
Portallo St BT6 15 B3
PORT AN BHOGAIGH (PORTAVOGIE) BT22 81 E4
PORT AN DÚNÁIN (PORTADOWN) BT62 51 E3
PORT AN GHIOLLA GHRUAMA (GROOMSPORT) BT19 5 A8
PORT AN PHEIRE (PORTAFERRY) BT22 94 D3
Portavoe BT21 6 A4
PORTAVOGIE (PORT AN BHOGAIGH) BT22 81 E4
Portavogie Prim Sch BT22 81 D4
Portavogie Rd BT22 81 E7
Porthill Rd BT60 116 D3
Portland Manor BT67 42 B8
Portlec Pl BT66 42 A4
Portloughan BT30 93 F3
Portmore St BT62 51 E4
Portnelligan BT60 113 A7
Portside Bsns Pk BT3 8 E4
Portview BT20 4 F5
Portview Ct BT22 81 D5
Portview Hts BT22 81 D5
Portview Trade Ctr BT4 15 C5
Posnett Ct BT7 155 A1
Posnett St BT7 155 A1
Post Office La BT33 63 D4
Pothill La BT27 39 E1
Pottingers Entry BT1 155 B3
Pottinger St BT5 15 B4
Pound Ct BT35 129 C5
Pound Hill BT25 58 D4
Pound La BT30 62 C4
Pound Loanan BT71 84 C6
Pound Rd BT35 64 B6
Pound St
Newry BT34 64 E6
Newtownards BT23 19 D4
Powerscourt Pl BT7 155 B1
POYNTZ PASS (PAS AN PHOINTE) BT35 117 D8
Poyntzpass Prim Sch 1 BT35 117 D8
Poyntzpass Rd BT32 102 B2
Poyntzpass Sta BT35 117 E8
Premier Bsns Ctr BT2 155 B2
Prentice Bsns Ctr BT67 42 A7
Presentation Prim Sch BT62 51 E3
Pretoria St BT9 14 D1
Price's La BT23 19 E5
Priestbush Rd BT60 130 D8
Priests La BT27 37 E7
Priests Rd BT31 122 F6
Priest Town BT22 94 B7
Primacy Dr 5 BT19 13 C8
Primacy Pk BT19 13 C8
Primacy Rd 13 BT19 13 D7
Primary Wlk BT66 86 C8
Primate's Manor BT60 60 C2
Primrose Ave 10 BT20 4 A4
Primrose Gdns BT32 61 B4
Primrose Gdn Village BT28 38 A7
Primrose Hill
Castlereagh BT8 22 B1
Dromara BT25 58 E5
Gilford BT63 101 E8
Primrose St
Bangor BT20 4 A4
Belfast BT7 21 F8
Primrose Way BT25 58 E5
Prince Andrew Gdns BT12 154 B1
Prince Andrew Pk BT12 154 B1
Prince Edward Dr BT9 21 D7
Prince Edward Gdns BT9 21 D7
Prince Edward Pk BT9 21 D7
Prince of Wales Ave BT4 16 D5
Prince Regent Commercial Pk BT5 15 E1
Prince Regent Rd BT5 15 E1
Prince's Cl BT66 41 F7
Princess Anne Rd BT22 81 E4
Princess Gdns
Holywood BT18 10 A7
Portadown BT63 52 B4
Princess Pk BT18 10 A7
Princess St BT34 65 C2
Princes St
Dromara BT25 58 D5
Lurgan BT67 41 F7
Prince's St BT1 155 B3
Princess Way BT63 52 B5
Princeton Ave BT66 42 A3
Princeton Dr BT66 42 A3
Princetoon Ave BT22 81 D4
Princetoon Wlk BT22 81 D4
Princetown Ave 5 BT20 4 A4
Princetown Rd BT20 3 F4
Princetown Terr 8 BT20 4 A4
Priors Lea BT18 9 D3
Priory Ave BT23 20 B6
Priory Cl
6 Bangor BT20 4 A1
Lisburn BT27 26 D5
Newtownards BT23 20 B6
Priory Ct BT23 20 B6
Priory End BT18 9 D5
Priory Integrated Coll BT18 9 D6
Priory Mews BT23 20 B6
Priory Pk BT18 9 E7
Priory Rd BT23 20 B6
Priory The BT25 58 D4
Priory Wlk BT23 20 B6
Proleek 150 E4
Proleek Acres 150 D5
Prospect Cotts 5 BT23 77 E8
Prospect Cres BT23 31 D1
Prospect Hill BT23 31 D1
Prospect La BT23 31 D1
Prospect Pk
Ballygowan BT23 31 D1
Belfast BT14 14 A8
Prospect Rd
Ballygowan BT23 31 D1
Bangor BT20 4 B4
Castlewellan BT31 105 A1
Prospect Way
Ballygowan BT23 31 D1
Lurgan BT66 41 F6
PURDYSBURN BT8 28 D8
Purdysburn Hill BT8 28 C7
Purdysburn Rd BT8 21 F1
Purdy's La BT8 22 A5
Puzzle Walks BT24 90 E2
Pyper's Hill BT22 81 D4

Q

Quadrant Pl BT12 154 C3
Quarry Cotts BT16 17 B3
Quarry Ct
Carrowdore BT22 66 E1
Helen's Bay BT19 2 C5
Quarry Hill BT5 23 A8
Quarry Hts BT23 19 E7
Quarry La BT16 17 B3
Quarry Rd
Banbridge BT32 103 B7
Belfast BT4 16 B8
Newry BT35 130 F3
Newtownards BT22 70 D5
Newtownards BT23 68 F2
Quarter Cormick BT30 108 D3
Quarterland BT23 79 C3
Quarterland Rd BT23 79 C4
Quarterlands Rd BT27 27 C5
Quarter Rd
Bessbrook BT35 131 B5
Downpatrick BT30 125 C8
Newry BT34 146 C6
Newtownards BT22 81 B2
Quay Gate House BT5 155 C4
Quay Mount BT71 84 A5
Quay Rd BT30 108 F8
Quayside BT21 67 A7
Quayside Cl BT35 64 D2
Quayside Office Pk BT3 8 B3
Quay's Sh Ctr The BT35 64 C4
Quay St
Ardglass BT30 125 F6
Bangor BT20 4 B4
Newry BT34 64 D4
Quays The BT71 84 B8
Quay The BT33 123 C5
Queen Elizabeth Bridge BT1 155 B3
Queen's Arc BT1 155 A3
Queensberry Pk BT6 22 A7
Queensbrae BT8 29 C3
Queen's Bridge BT1 155 B3
Queensbury Pk BT20 3 F1
Queens Cres BT8 29 D3
Queensdale BT8 29 C3
Queensfort Ct BT8 29 D4
Queensfort Pk BT8 29 D3
Queensfort Pk S BT8 29 D3
Queensfort Rd BT8 29 D4
Queens Gdns BT63 52 B4
Queenside BT8 29 C3
Queen's Island BT3 15 B8
Queen's Leisure Complex BT18 9 D7
Queens Par BT20 4 A4
Queen's Par
Bangor BT20 4 A4
Belfast BT15 14 D7
Queen's Pe Ctr BT9 14 D1
Queens Pk 14 BT24 77 C3
Queens Pl BT67 42 B4
Queen's Quay BT3 155 C4
Queen's Quay Link BT3 155 C3
Queen's Rd BT3 15 A8
Queens Rd S BT27 26 C1
Queen's Sq
Belfast BT1 155 B3
Newtownards BT23 19 F5
Queen St
Belfast BT1 155 A3
Lurgan BT67 42 B5
Newtownards BT23 19 F4
Portadown BT62 51 D3
Warrenpoint BT34 65 C2
Queen's Univ of Belfast 5 BT9 14 C1
Queensway
Carryduff BT8 29 D3
Dunmurry BT17 26 D7
Queensway Pk BT17 26 D7
Queen Victoria St BT5 15 D5
Quilly BT25 87 E5
Quillyburn Bsns Pk BT25 58 B3
Quillyburn Manor BT25 58 B4
Quilly Rd BT35 140 B2
Quintin Bay Rd BT22 95 A3
Quinton Pk BT23 19 C3
Quinton St BT5 15 C3
Quinville BT18 9 E6
Quoile Brae BT30 62 D8
Quoile Countryside Ctr★ BT30 108 F8
Quoile Pk BT30 62 C7
Quoile Rd BT30 62 D8
Quoile Terr BT24 59 C6

R

Raby St BT7 21 F8
Racarbry BT60 114 A1
Racecourse Cl (Clós An RáschÚrsa) BT30 62 B2
Racecourse Hill BT30 62 C3
Race Course Hill BT30 62 C4
Racecourse Rd (Bóthar An RáschÚrsa) BT30 62 B2
Raceview Terr BT23 19 D4
Rademan BT30 91 F5
Rademon Ave 1 BT30 92 B5
Rademon Cres 2 BT30 92 B5
Rademon Ct 3 BT30 92 B5
Radnor St 28 BT6 15 A4
Rae An Iascaire (Fishermans Row) BT30 125 D5
Raffertys Hill Rd BT26 89 B7
RAFFREY BT30 78 C2
Raffrey Rd BT23 78 C4
Raglan Rd BT20 3 F5
RAHOLP BT30 109 D8
Railway Ave BT35 64 C6
Railway Cres 9 BT60 114 A3
Railway Rd BT35 141 B5
Railway St
Armagh BT61 60 C6
Banbridge BT32 61 C5
Belfast BT12 154 C2
Comber BT23 25 C2
Donaghadee BT21 67 A8
Lisburn BT28 26 B2
Newcastle BT33 63 D6
Newry BT35 117 D8
Railway Terr 8 BT23 77 F8
Railway View St 2 BT20 4 A3
Rainey Way BT7 155 A1
Raleagh BT30 91 C4
Raleagh Rd BT30 91 D4
Raleigh St BT13 14 B7
Ramaket BT68 96 B7
Ramone Pk BT63 52 B7
Rampark BT66 42 E3
Rampart Bsns Ctr BT34 64 E1
Rampart Rd BT34 64 E2
Rampart St
Dromara BT25 58 D5
Lurgan BT66 41 F6
Randall Hts 13 BT34 153 C7
Randal Pk BT9 21 A7
Ranelagh St BT6 15 B2
Ranfurley Rd BT62 51 C4
Ranfurly Ave BT20 3 F4
Ranfurly Dr 8 BT4 15 E6
Rank Rd BT16 17 C3
Rannoch Rd BT18 10 A8
Rann Rd BT30 92 B1
Ranoche Cl 6 BT30 92 B5
Ranton's Cross Roads BT35 131 C8
Raphael St BT2 155 B2
Raskeagh 150 A5
Rassan 148 B4
Ratallagh BT22 81 C3
Ratarnet BT60 99 E4
Ratarnet Rd BT60 99 D2
Ratcliffe St BT7 155 A1
Rathbone St BT2 155 B2
Rathcarbry BT35 131 A8
Rath Caun Hts BT30 62 D6
Rathcillan Ct BT33 63 B6
Rathcillan Wood BT33 63 B6
Rathconvil BT35 116 F7
Rathconvil Rd BT60 116 F6
Rathcool St BT9 21 A8
Rath Cuain BT34 65 C3
Rathcumber BT60 112 F3
Rathcumber Rd BT60 112 F2
Rathcunningham BT30 93 C8
Rathcunningham Rd BT30 93 C8
Rathdrumgran BT61 99 C7
Rathdrum St BT9 21 A8
Rathduff 149 C4
Rathdune Gr BT30 62 B6
RÁTH FRAOILEANN (RATHFRILAND) BT34 119 F2
Rathfriland High Sch 15 BT34 119 F2
RATHFRILAND (RÁTH FRAOILEANN) BT34 119 F2
Rathfriland Rd
Banbridge BT32 61 E2
Dromara BT25 89 C1
Newry BT34 64 E7
Rathfriland St BT32 61 D4
Rathgael Rd BT19 3 C1
Rathgannon BT34 65 F3
Rathgar St BT9 21 A8
Rathgill BT19 12 F8
Rathgill Ave BT19 13 C7
Rathgill Cl BT19 13 C7
Rathgill Cres BT19 13 C7
Rathgill Ct BT19 13 C7
Rathgill Dr BT19 13 C7
Rathgill Gdns BT19 13 B7
Rathgill Glen BT19 13 B7
Rathgill Gn BT19 13 B7
Rathgill Gr BT19 13 C7
Rathgill Link BT19 13 B7
Rathgill Mdw BT19 13 B7
Rathgill Par BT19 13 B7
Rathgill Pk BT19 13 C7
Rathgill Pl BT19 13 B7
Rathgill Way BT19 13 C7
Rathgorman BT23 79 C3
Rathgullion BT35 141 B5
Rath Gullion BT35 141 B5
Rathkeelan BT35 147 E8
Rathkeelan Pk BT35 147 E8
Rathkeltair Pk BT30 62 D6
Rathkeltair Rd BT30 62 E7
Rathmore BT34 65 D3
Rathmore Ave BT19 3 C3
Rathmore Cres BT19 3 C3
Rathmore Pk
Bangor BT19 3 C3
Downpatrick BT30 62 D5
Rathmore Prim Sch BT19 3 C3
Rathmore Rd
Bangor BT19 3 C3
1 Newry BT34 132 A5
Rathmore St 22 BT6 15 A4
Rathmoyle Dr BT60 114 B3
Rathmoyle Pk
Holywood BT18 2 A4
Keady BT60 114 B3
Rathmullan Dr BT23 19 C4
Rathmullan Lower BT30 124 D5
Rathmullan Upper BT30 124 D6
Rathore Sch BT35 64 A6
Rath Rd BT34 65 E4
Rathtrillick Rd BT60 112 D7
Rath View BT32 61 B2
Rathview Pk BT35 147 E8
Raughlan La BT66 75 B5
Rauglan Mdws BT66 75 B5
Ravara BT23 77 E7
Ravara Cl BT23 19 C4
Ravara Dale BT23 77 E8
Ravara Gdns BT19 3 C1
Ravara Rd BT23 77 D7
Ravarnet Gdns BT27 38 B2
Ravarnet Rd
Hillsborough BT26 48 B8
Lisburn BT27 38 B3
Ravelstone Ave BT19 3 B4
Ravenhill Ave BT6 15 A3
Ravenhill Cres BT6 15 A2
Ravenhill Ct BT6 15 A2
Ravenhill Gdns BT7 15 A2
Ravenhill La BT23 19 D1
Ravenhill Par BT6 15 B2
Ravenhill Pk BT6 15 A1
Ravenhill Pk Gdns BT6 22 A8
Ravenhill Rd BT7 15 A2
Ravenhill Reach BT6 155 C1
Ravenhill Reach Ct BT6 155 C1
Ravenhill Reach Mews BT6 155 C2
Ravenhill St 1 BT6 15 A3
Ravenscroft Ave BT5 15 D4
Ravenscroft St BT5 15 C5
Ravensdale Cres 8 BT5 15 B3
Ravensdale St BT6 15 B4
Ravensdene Cres BT6 15 A1
Ravensdene Mews BT6 15 A1
Ravensdene Pk BT6 15 A1
Ravensdene Pk Gdns BT6 15 A1
Ravenswood
Banbridge BT32 61 A5
Bangor BT19 13 F8
Ravenswood Cres BT5 16 B1
Ravenswood Pk BT5 16 A1
RAVERNET BT27 38 B3
Rawdon Pl BT67 34 C1
Rawes BT60 113 A4
Rawe's Fort★ BT60 113 B3
Rawes Rd BT60 113 A3

Raymond Kelly Pk BT35 64 C5
Reagh Island BT23 69 C2
Reagh Island Pk BT23 19 F6
Reaville Pk BT16 17 A4
Rectory Ave
Craigavon BT66 75 A6
Lurgan BT66 41 F6
Rectory Cl BT61 85 A4
Rectory Pk
Kircubbin BT22 80 E7
Lurgan BT66 41 F6
Portadown BT62 51 C2
Rectory Rd BT66 41 F6
Rectory Way BT22 80 E7
Rectory Wood BT22 94 E4
Redbridge Rd BT34 119 E2
Redburn Ctry Pk BT18 9 E3
Redburn Hts BT24 59 D6
Redburn Prim Sch BT18 9 D4
Redburn Sq BT18 9 D7
Redcar St BT6 15 B3
Redcliffe Dr 1 BT4 15 C6
Redcliffe Par BT4 15 C6
Redcliffe St BT4 15 C6
Redcow 150 B3
Redhill Rd BT25 44 F3
Red Lion Cross Roads
BT61 85 F5
Red Lion Rd
Armagh BT61 85 C5
Craigavon BT62 50 B2
Redmonds Cl BT35 130 E1
Redrock Rd BT60 99 C1
Reen BT60 112 E5
Reenaderry Rd BT71 72 E8
Reformed Theological Coll
BT8 22 D1
Regency Ave BT66 42 E5
Regency Ct BT66 41 E3
Regency Dr
Craigavon BT66 42 E5
Newtownards BT23 20 B7
Regency Gdns BT23 20 A7
Regency Manor
Craigavon BT66 42 E5
Newtownards BT23 20 B7
Regency Par BT23 20 B7
Regency Pk
Bangor BT19 4 D1
Newtownards BT23 20 B7
Regency Sq BT19 4 D2
Regent Ct BT16 17 F5
Regent House Grammer
BT23 19 D4
Regents Pk BT66 42 B3
Regent St
Newtownards BT23 19 D5
Belfast BT13 14 C7
Regents Wood BT67 43 D6
Regina Pk BT35 141 C1
Rehaghy Rd BT69 82 A5
Reid St BT6 15 B2
Reilly Ct 1 BT32 61 C4
Reilly Pk BT32 61 C5
Reilly St BT32 61 C4
Reillys Trench BT26 47 A7
Renmore Ave BT62 51 D3
Renwick St BT7 154 C1
Reservoir Rd BT32 102 D4
Reynolds Ct BT62 51 E2
Rhanbuoy Pk BT18 2 A5
Rhanbuoy Pk E BT18 2 A4
Rhanbuoy Rd BT18 2 A4
Riada Cl 2 BT4 15 B6
Ribado BT25 105 D6
Ribadoo Rd BT31 105 F2
Ribble St BT4 15 C5
Richardson St BT6 15 A3
Richdale Dr BT18 9 F8
Richhill Cres BT5 16 A3
RICHHILL (LOG AN CHOIRE)
BT61 85 E1
Richhill Pk BT5 16 A3
Richmond Ave
Belfast BT4 9 B2
Newtownards BT23 20 B7
5 Tandragee BT62 101 B7
Richmond Chase BT62 55 E1
Richmond Cl
Belfast BT4 9 B2
4 Tandragee BT62 101 B7
Richmond Cres BT20 4 F6
Richmond Crt BT27 26 C3
Richmond Ct
Belfast BT4 9 B2
Lisburn BT27 26 C3
2 Newry BT35 64 C7
2 Tandragee BT62 101 B7
Richmond Dr BT62 101 B7
Richmond Gdns 1 BT62 101 B7
Richmond Gn BT4 9 B2
Richmond Gr 3 BT62 101 B7
Richmond Hts
Banbridge BT32 61 E5
Belfast BT4 9 B2
Richhill BT61 99 D8
Richmond Pk BT9 21 D7
Richmond View 6 BT62 101 B7
Richmountgardens BT66 41 E4
Richmount Gdns BT66 41 E4
Richmount or Aghavellan
BT62 50 C7
Richmount Prim Sch
BT62 50 B8
Richmount Rd BT62 50 B7
Richview Hts 6 BT60 114 A3
Richview St BT12 154 B1
Ridgefield Gr BT34 65 B4
Ridge Pk BT28 26 A8
Ridgeway Pk N BT62 51 D3
Ridgeway Pk S BT62 51 D3
Ridgeway St
Belfast BT9 21 D8
Lisburn BT28 26 A1
Ridgewood Ave 14 BT71 72 A1
Riga St BT13 154 A4
Ringawaddy BT30 110 C3
Ringbane
Downpatrick BT30 93 D1
Newry BT34 118 E3
Ringbane Rd BT34 118 E3
Ringbuoy Cove BT22 81 C2
Ringburr Ct 3 BT23 19 F4
Ringclare BT34 118 C5
Ringclare Rd BT34 118 C4
Ringcreevy BT23 68 E6
Ringcreevy Rd BT23 68 D6
Ringdufferin BT30 79 D1
Ringdufferin Golf Course
BT30 79 C1
Ringdufferin Rd BT30 79 C2
Ringfad BT30 125 F5
Ringhaddy BT23 79 D3
Ringhaddy Ave BT23 20 B5
Ringhaddy Dr 3 BT23 20 A5
Ringhaddy Gdns BT23 20 B5
Ringhaddy Pk BT23 20 B5
Ringhaddy Rd BT23 79 C2
Ringmackilroy BT34 65 D3
Ringneill BT23 69 A2
Ringneill Rd BT23 69 A2
Ringolish BT34 118 E4
Ringreagh BT30 108 D4
Ring Sallin Gdns BT30 123 F5
Ringsend Rd
Banbridge BT32 61 A1
Dromara BT25 104 E4
Ripley Mews BT62 51 D2
Ripley Terr BT62 51 C2
Risk BT67 34 B3
Rivercroft BT24 59 C5
River Ct BT17 26 E8
Riverdale
Dungannon BT71 72 D6
Hillsborough BT26 89 D8
Riverdale Cres BT66 86 D8
Riverdale Dr BT34 153 D8
Riverdale La BT24 77 D2
Riverdale Pk BT60 113 D7
Riverfield BT34 65 C4
Riverfields Ave BT34 65 C4
Rivergate La BT27 37 F6
Riverglade Manor BT66 41 D4
River Gr BT17 26 E7
River La 151 C4
River Mews BT17 26 E7
River Pk BT30 93 C5
River Rd
Dunmurry BT27 26 E6
Lisburn BT27 76 A3
Riverside
Banbridge BT32 103 D1
Gilford BT63 57 C1
Holywood BT18 9 E7
Riverside Ave BT20 4 E4
Riverside Commercial Ctr 5
BT27 26 C1
Riverside Cres BT35 131 D5
Riverside Dr
Lisburn BT27 26 C4
Newcastle BT33 63 C6
Riverside Pk
Bangor BT20 4 F4
Kilkeel BT34 153 D8
Riverside Rd
Ballynahinch BT24 59 A5
Bangor BT20 4 E4
Riverside Sq BT12 154 B2
Riverside View BT7 21 E7
River St BT34 64 D4
River Terr BT7 155 B1
Riverview BT63 52 A3
River View BT34 132 A5
Riverview Ct BT32 61 C5
Riverview Dr BT30 62 F7
Riverview St BT9 21 D8
Road Transport Gall★
BT18 1 D2
Robbery Rd BT67 36 A3
Robbs Ct BT16 17 C4
Robbs Rd BT16 17 C4
Robby's Point BT21 66 F7
Robert St
Lurgan BT67 42 B5
Newtownards BT23 19 D5
Robin Hill BT33 123 B5
Robinson Cres BT19 4 F2
Robinson Ctr The BT6 22 E8
Robinson Dr BT61 60 D6
Robinson Rd BT19 4 E2
ROBINSONS TOWN BT62 73 D6
Robinson Way BT19 4 F2
Roche 149 B4
Rochester Ave BT6 22 C8
Rochester Dr BT6 22 C8
Rochester Hts BT23 20 C6
Rochester Rd BT6 22 D7
Rochester St 6 BT6 15 A3
Rock Cotts BT19 5 C3
Rockdene BT19 2 C5
Rockfield BT19 13 E7
Rockfield Dale 1 BT19 13 E7
Rockfield Downs BT60 60 C2
Rockfield Dr
3 Bangor BT19 13 E7
Portaferry BT22 94 E3
Rockfield Glen 2 BT19 13 E7
Rockfield Hts 2 BT34 132 C2
Rockfield Pk BT22 94 E4
Rockland Cres BT23 20 A4
Rockland Dr BT23 30 F6
Rocklands BT26 49 B1
Rockland St BT12 154 A1
Rockmacreany La BT61 99 C7
Rockmacreeny BT61 99 D7
Rock Meeting Rd
Banbridge BT32 118 B7
Newry BT35 117 F7
Rockmore BT32 61 F5
Rockmount BT16 17 B3
Rock Mount Cl BT24 77 B3
Rockmount Gdns BT19 2 D5
Rockmount Golf Club
BT24 76 F6
Rockmount Pk BT19 5 A5
Rock Mount Pk BT24 77 B3
Rockmount Rd BT34 120 A6
Rockport Rd BT18 1 H4
Rockport Rise BT18 1 H3
Rockport Sch BT18 1 H4
Rock Rd
Armagh BT60 114 E3
Dromara BT25 89 A6
Newry BT34 118 D1
Rock Rd The BT60 60 B1
Rocks BT60 99 E5
Rocksavage Rd BT61 84 D4
Rocks Chapel Rd BT30 92 C2
Rocksfield 5 BT30 92 B4
Rocks Rd BT30 110 D2
Rockstown Rd BT60 115 E3
Rockvale BT60 60 B2
Rockview Cl BT32 61 D5
Rockview St BT12 154 A1
Rocky La BT30 107 C6
Rocky Rd BT5 16 D1
Rocky Ridge BT22 66 E1
Roddans BT22 71 B2
Roddans Rd BT22 71 B2
Roddens Cres BT5 15 F1
Roddens Gdns BT5 15 F1
Roddens Pk BT5 15 F1
Roden Pas BT12 154 B2
Roden Sq BT12 154 B2
Roden St
Belfast BT12 154 B1
Kircubbin BT22 80 E7
Roden Way BT12 154 B2
Rodney Pk BT19 4 E2
Rodney Way BT19 4 E2
Roes Gn BT63 86 B2
Roe St BT1 155 A3
Rogers Pk BT8 22 A4
Rogers Pl 2 BT8 22 A4
Rookery Dr BT71 83 D5
Rookery The BT23 79 A5
Rookford Rd BT60 60 A2
Rooney Pk 2 BT34 153 C7
Rooney Rd BT34 153 C7
Roosevelt Rise BT12 154 B1
Roosevelt Sq BT12 154 B1
Roosevelt St BT12 154 B1
Roosley Rd BT34 133 F1
Rosapenna Ct 14 BT14 14 B8
Rosapenna St BT14 14 B8
Rosconnor Pl BT34 120 A2
Rosconnor Terr BT34 120 A2
Rosebery Gdns BT6 15 B3
Rosebery Rd BT6 15 A3
Rosebery St BT5 15 D4
Rose Cotts BT62 51 C5
Rosegarden Cl BT62 100 F8
Rose Gdn BT62 55 E1
Rose Gdn Cl BT62 55 E1
Roseland Pl BT12 154 C1
Roseleigh St 5 BT14 14 B8
Rosemary Ave BT20 3 F2
Rosemary Dr
Bangor BT20 3 F1
Lisburn BT28 38 A7
Rosemary Pk
Bangor BT20 3 F1
Belfast BT9 21 A4
Rosemary St BT1 155 A3
Rosemount BT67 32 B1
Rosemount BT22 70 C4
Rosemount Ave
Armagh BT60 60 E4
Belfast BT5 16 E4
Rosemount Pk
Armagh BT60 60 E4
Castlereagh BT5 22 F7
Rosepark
Belfast BT5 16 E4
Donaghadee BT21 66 F8
Rosepark Ave 5 BT21 66 F8
Rosepark Central BT5 16 E4
Rosepark E BT5 16 E4
Rosepark Mdws BT5 16 E4
Rosepark S BT5 16 E4
Rosepark W BT5 16 E4
Rose Pk
Lisburn BT27 26 B5
Newtownards BT23 19 F5
Rosetta Ave BT7 21 F7
Rosetta Dr BT7 21 F7
Rosetta Par BT7 21 F7
Rosetta Pk BT6 22 A7
Rosetta Prim Sch BT6 22 A7
Rosetta Rd BT6 22 B7
Rosetta Rd E BT6 22 B7
Rosetta Way BT6 22 A7
Rose Vale BT34 153 B8
Rosevale Ave
Lisburn BT27 27 D6
Newtownards BT23 19 F6
Rosevale Gdns BT27 27 D5
Rosevale Mdws BT28 37 C8
Rosevale Pk BT27 27 D6
Rosevale Rd BT32 102 A5
Rosevale St 4 BT14 14 B8
Roseville BT19 3 B4
Roseville Ave BT19 3 B3
Roseville Gdns BT27 26 C2
Roseville Pk
Bangor BT19 3 B3
Lisburn BT27 26 C2
Roseville Wlk BT27 26 D1
Rosewood Pk
Castlereagh BT6 22 F8
Lurgan BT66 42 B3
Roslyn Ave
Bangor BT20 4 C2
Portadown BT63 51 F5
Roslyn St BT6 15 A3
Rosneath Ct BT16 17 E4
Rosneath Gdns BT16 17 E4
Ross BT30 125 F8
Rossconor
Downpatrick BT30 92 A1
Downpatrick BT30 108 A8
Rathfriland BT34 120 A2
Ross Ct BT12 154 B3
Rossdale Gdns 1 BT8 22 C2
Rossdale Glen 2 BT8 22 C2
Rossdale Hts 4 BT8 22 C2
Rossdale Par BT8 22 C2
Rossdale Pk 6 BT8 22 C3
Rossdale Rd
Bangor BT19 5 A5
3 Castlereagh BT8 22 C2
Rosses Quay 5 BT34 143 B3
Rossglass BT30 125 B4
Rossglass Rd BT30 125 C5
Rossglass Rd S BT30 125 B4
Rossinver Gdns 2 BT19 13 D8
Rossmara Pk BT34 65 D3
Rossmore Ave BT7 21 F7
Rossmore Cres BT7 21 F7
Rossmore Dr BT7 21 F7
Rossmore Pk BT7 21 F7
Rossmount Rd BT24 91 A3
Rossmoyle BT65 53 B8
Ross Rd
Belfast BT12 154 B3
Downpatrick BT30 125 F8
Ross Rise BT12 154 B3
Ross St BT12 154 B3
ROSSTREVOR BT34 143 B3
Rosstrevor Mountains
BT34 143 F5
Rosswood Pk 4 BT34 143 C3
Rossyln Pk BT23 20 C6
ROSTREVOR BT34 143 C3
Rostrevor Cl 1 BT19 3 E1
Rostrevor Convent of Mercy
Prim Sch 17 BT34 143 C3
Rostrevor Dr BT19 3 E1
Rostrevor Rd
Newry BT34 134 B3
Warrenpoint BT34 65 E2
Rostrevor Way BT19 3 E1
Rotterdam Ct BT5 155 C3
Rotterdam St BT5 155 C3
Roughal Pk BT30 62 B6
Roughan
Armagh BT60 114 A7
Craigavon BT62 73 F1
Roumania Rise BT12 154 B3
Roundhill St BT5 15 B5
Round Island Pk 1 BT22 80 E7
Round Twr Commercial Pk
BT3 8 A4
Rowallane Cl BT19 13 D8
Rowallane Dale BT24 77 D3
Rowallane House & Gdns★
BT24 77 D2
Rowallane Manor BT24 77 D3
Rowallon BT34 65 F2
Rowan BT60 112 F1
Rowan Coll (Juvenile Justice
Ctr for NI) BT19 12 F8
Rowan Ctr BT27 26 C2
Rowanglen BT32 61 E7
Rowan Glen BT19 13 C8
Rowanmanor BT65 41 B3
Rowanpark BT65 41 B3
Rowan Rd BT60 112 F1
Rowans The BT32 61 E7
Rowantree Dr BT25 58 B3
Rowantree Glen BT25 58 B4
Rowantree Rd BT25 58 A3
Rowan Vale BT32 61 F7
Rowland Way BT12 154 C2
Rowley Cl BT33 63 B5
Rowley Mdws BT33 63 C5
Rowreagh BT22 80 E6
Rowreagh Rd BT22 80 E6
Roxborough Hts 13 BT71 72 A1
Roxborough Pk 10 BT71 72 A1
Roxborough Rd BT35 129 F1
Roxburgh Pl 12 BT34 143 C3
Royal Ave BT1 155 A4
Royal Belfast Academical
Inst BT1 154 C3
Royal Belfast Hospl for Sick
Children BT12 154 A2
Royal Cty Down Golf Club
BT33 63 F7
Royal Irish Fusiliers Mus★
BT61 60 D5
Royal Lodge Ave BT8 22 A1
Royal Lodge Ct BT8 22 A2
Royal Lodge Gdns BT8 22 A1
Royal Lodge Pk BT8 22 A1
Royal Lodge Rd BT8 21 F1
Royal Maternity Hospl
BT12 154 A2
Royal Mews The 6
BT34 153 C7
Royal Oaks BT8 22 A1
Royal Pk La BT26 47 B6
Royal Sch Armagh The
BT61 60 E6
Royal Ulster Rifles Mus★
BT1 155 B3
Royal Victoria Hospl
BT12 154 A2
RUBANE BT22 80 F6
Rubane Mdws BT22 80 F6
Rubane Rd BT22 81 A5
Ruby St BT20 4 B4
Rugby Ave
Banbridge BT32 61 C2
Bangor BT20 3 F3
Belfast BT7 14 E2
Rugby Cres
Bangor BT20 3 F3
Donaghadee BT21 6 E1
Rugby Ct BT7 14 D1
Rugby Gdns BT23 19 D4
Rugby Par BT7 14 D1
Rugby Pk BT20 3 F3
Rugby Rd BT7 14 D2
Rugby St BT7 14 D2
Rumford St BT13 154 B4
Runnymede Dr BT12 14 A2
Runnymede Par BT12 14 A2
Rushfield BT19 2 C6
Rushfield Ave BT7 21 F8
Rushmere Ret Pk BT64 40 E3
Rushmere Sh Ctr BT64 40 F2
Rusholme St BT13 14 B7
Ruskin Hts BT27 38 A6
Ruskin Pk BT27 38 B6
Russel Ave BT24 59 D5
Russell Dr BT66 41 F4
Russell Pk BT5 16 E2
Russell Pl BT2 155 B2
Russell's Quarter BT30 62 F4
Russells Quarter North
BT30 93 D2
Russells Quarter South
BT30 93 D1
Russell St
7 Armagh BT61 60 D5
Belfast BT2 155 B2
Russel Pl 1 BT30 125 F6
Russwood Pk BT63 52 A3
Rutherglen Gdns BT19 3 D3
Rutherglen Pk BT19 3 D3
Ruthven Rise 6 BT30 92 B4
Rutland St BT7 14 E2
Ryan BT34 133 A6
Ryan Pk BT5 23 A5
Ryan Rd BT34 132 F7
Ryans Ct BT27 38 B7
Ryanstown Rd BT34 142 C7
Rydalmere St BT12 154 A1

S

Sabbath Hill BT34 145 F5
Sackville Ct BT13 154 C4
Sackville St 2 BT27 26 B2
Sacred Heart Gram Sch
BT34 64 E8
Sacred Heart Prim Sch
BT33 123 C5
Saelscoil an Lonnain
BT13 154 A3
Sagimor Gdns BT5 15 D4
St Andrew's Sq E BT12 154 C2
St Anne's Cath BT1 155 A4
St Annes Ct BT30 125 D5
St Annes Pk BT34 133 C4
St Anne's Prim Sch BT21 67 A8
St Anthony's Prim Sch
BT65 41 C2
St Bernard's Prim Sch
BT6 22 B6
St Bline's Well★ BT35 140 F6
St Brendan's Prim Sch
BT65 53 C8
St Bride's Prim Sch
4 Belfast BT9 14 C1
Belfast BT9 21 B8
St Bridget's Well★ BT60 60 D4
St Brigid's High Sch 2
BT60 60 B5
St Brigid's Hill BT61 60 C7
St Brigids Pk BT35 131 B5
St Brigid's Prim Sch
Downpatrick BT30 62 D6
Newry BT35 130 F4
Newry BT35 148 D7
St Bronagh's Well★
BT34 143 C4
St Caolan's Prim Sch
BT24 78 A2
St Catherine's Coll BT61 60 B5
St Catherine's Prim Sch
BT12 154 A2
St Clares Ave BT34 64 D6

St Clare's Convent Prim Sch BT34 64 D5
St Colman's Abbey Prim Sch BT34 64 D5
St Colman's Bann Prim Sch BT63 86 B2
St Colman's Coll BT35 64 C8
St Colman's Ct BT35 64 C7
St Colmans Gdns 4 BT34 143 B3
St Colman's High Sch BT24 59 E5
Saint Colmans Pk BT34 64 D5
St Colman's Prim Sch
  Banbridge BT32 103 D1
  Craigavon BT67 45 B7
  Dromara BT25 58 D6
  20 Kilkeel BT34 153 C7
  Lisburn BT27 26 C6
  Newry BT34 132 D5
St Colmcille's High Sch 12 BT30 92 B5
St Colmcille's Prim Sch
  Armagh BT61 84 D3
  Downpatrick BT30 62 C2
St Columban's Coll BT34 153 E8
St Columbanus Coll BT20 4 F4
St Columba's Coll BT22 94 E4
St Columba's Dr 2 BT23 20 A6
St Columbas Vale 1 BT23 20 A6
St Comgall's Parish Ctr BT20 3 F3
St Comgall's Prim Sch BT20 3 F3
St Dallan's Prim Sch BT34 65 D3
St Dillons Ave (Ascaill Naomh Dallan) BT30 62 D4
St Dominic's High Sch BT12 154 A2
St Dympna's Ave BT30 62 D3
St Dympna's Pk BT30 62 D3
St Eda's Prim Sch BT8 22 A1
St Elizabeth's Ct BT16 17 B5
St Ellen Ind Est BT8 27 F8
St Ellens BT8 27 F8
Saintfield Bsns Pk (Spinning Mill) BT24 77 B4
Saintfield High Sch BT24 77 C4
Saintfield Ind Est BT24 77 B4
Saintfield Pk 3 BT27 26 D1
Saintfield Rd
  Ballynahinch BT24 59 D8
  Belfast BT8 22 A6
  Castlereagh BT8 22 A3
  Downpatrick BT30 91 F7
  4 Lisburn BT27 26 C1
  Lisburn BT27 38 E7
  Newtownards BT23 77 E7
SAINTFIELD (TAMHNAIGH NAOMH) BT24 77 B3
St Finian's Prim Sch BT23 19 E5
St Finnian's Well★ BT30 108 D1
St Francis of Assisi Prim Sch 16 BT60 114 A3
St Francis Prim Sch BT66 41 D5
St Francis Prim Sch (Aghaderg) BT32 102 B3
St Gallen Ct 2 BT20 4 A1
St Gallen Pl 1 BT20 4 A1
St Gemma's High Sch BT14 14 A8
St George's Gdns BT12 154 C1
St George's Mkt★ BT2 155 B2
St Helen's Bsns Pk BT18 9 D6
St Ives Gdns BT9 14 D1
St James Prim Sch
  Armagh BT60 99 F2
  Hillsborough BT26 46 B8
  Tandragee BT62 101 A6
St James Rd
  Hillsborough BT26 46 A8
  Lisburn BT27 36 B2
St James St 6 BT15 14 C8
St Jarlath's Prim Sch BT71 84 A5
St John's Ave BT7 21 F7
St John's Ct BT62 51 D6
St John's Pk
  Belfast BT7 21 F6
  Moira BT67 34 C2
Saint Johns Point ⓘ BT30 125 C3
St John's Prim Sch
  Armagh BT60 112 D7
  Gilford BT63 57 D2
  2 Moy BT71 72 A1
  Newry BT34 118 B3
St Johns Rd BT26 45 F6
St Johns Wood Pk BT16 17 B5
St John the Baptist Prim Sch BT62 51 B7
St Joseph's Boys High Sch BT35 64 C8
St Joseph's Coll
  Belfast BT6 22 A8
  Crossmaglen BT35 147 F7
St Joseph's Convent Prim Sch 2 BT35 64 C6
St Josephs Prim Sch
  Belfast BT5 15 F4
  Lisburn BT27 26 C1
  Newcastle BT33 122 E2
St Joseph's Prim Sch
  Ardglass BT30 125 F6
  Armagh BT60 113 E7
  Belfast BT12 154 B2
  Bessbrook BT35 131 C5
  Caledon BT68 96 D5
  Carryduff BT8 29 C6
  Crossgar BT30 92 A5
  Downpatrick BT30 109 E3
  Newry BT34 146 A1
  Newry BT35 117 D8
  Newry BT35 141 A6
St Judes Ave BT7 21 F8
St Judes Cres BT7 21 F8
St Judes Gdns 3 BT34 143 B3
St Judes Par BT7 21 F8
St Jude's Sq BT7 21 F8
St Kilda Ct BT6 155 C2
St Killians Pk 1 BT60 130 C8
St Laurance O'Tooles Prim Sch BT35 130 C4
St Leonards BT34 65 E3
St Leonard's Cres 11 BT4 15 B5
St Leonard's St 12 BT4 15 B5
St Louis Gram Sch BT34 153 A7
St Louis Prim Sch BT60 112 D7
St Luke's Cl BT13 154 B4
St Lukes Hospl BT61 60 D8
St Luke's Wlk BT13 154 B4
St Macartans Ct BT30 107 D6
St Macartan's Prim Sch BT30 107 D6
St Malachys Ave 8 BT31 122 C4
St Malachys Bunga BT34 121 C2
St Malachy's Coll BT14 14 C7
St Malachys Cres 8 BT31 122 C5
St Malachys Dr 7 BT31 122 C4
St Malachy's High Sch BT31 122 B5
St Malachys Pk BT35 131 B3
St Malachy's Pk BT35 131 B3
St Malachy's Prim Sch
  2 Armagh BT61 60 D5
  Bangor BT19 3 E1
  Belfast BT7 155 B2
  Camlough BT35 131 B4
  Castlewellan BT31 122 B5
  Downpatrick BT30 110 C5
  Newry BT34 121 C2
  Newry BT35 64 A5
St Malachy's Well★ BT60 113 B1
St Mark's High Sch BT34 65 C4
St Mary's Boys Prim Sch 16 BT34 143 C3
St Mary's Ct 4 BT13 14 A7
St Mary's High Sch
  Downpatrick BT30 62 D3
  Newry BT34 64 E3
St Mary's Jun High Sch BT66 41 F5
St Mary's La 3 BT33 63 D5
St Marys Prim Sch BT23 25 E2
St Mary's Prim Sch
  Armagh BT60 114 D3
  Ballygowan BT23 77 F8
  Belfast BT12 154 C3
  Craigavon BT66 74 D7
  Downpatrick BT30 110 B1
  Dungannon BT71 73 C8
  Killyleagh BT30 93 C6
  Kircubbin BT22 80 D7
  Newcastle BT33 63 C4
  Newry BT34 117 F1
  Newry BT34 146 D7
  Newry BT35 140 B3
  Portaferry BT22 94 D3
  Rathfriland BT34 120 A2
  Saintfield BT24 77 C3
St Mary's St BT34 64 C5
St Matthew's Ct (Cúirt Naoimh Maitiú) 22 BT5 15 A5
St Matthew's Prim Sch 40 BT5 15 A5
St Matthew's Prim Sch BT31 121 D6
St Michael's Gram Sch BT67 32 C1
St Michael's Pk BT30 110 B1
St Michaels Prim Sch BT35 129 D4
St Michael's Prim Sch
  Armagh BT60 115 D4
  Belfast BT6 15 A1
St Moninna Pk
  Newry BT35 141 B5
  Newry BT35 141 B5
St Nicholas Prim Sch BT30 125 F7
St Oliver Plunkett Pk BT35 131 C4
St Oliver Plunkett's Prim Sch BT61 85 C5
St Oliver's Prim Sch
  Carlingford 151 D4
  Newry BT35 129 F1
St Patricks Ave
  Craigavon BT67 32 F8
  Downpatrick BT30 62 C4
  Newry BT34 64 D6
St Patrick's Ave 8 BT31 122 B4
St Patrick's Cath (C of I) 11 BT61 60 C5
St Patricks Circ BT30 109 B7
St Patrick's Com Enterprise BT1 155 A4
St Patricks Ctr The★ BT30 62 B4
St Patrick's Dr BT30 62 C4
St Patricks Gram Sch BT61 60 C6
St Patrick's Gram Sch BT30 62 D5
St Patrick's Grave★ BT30 62 B4
St Patricks High Sch BT32 61 B4
St Patrick's High Sch 18 BT60 114 A3
St Patricks Pk
  Hilltown BT34 134 B5
  Newry BT35 139 A6
St Patrick's Pk
  Armagh BT60 60 A5
  Camlough BT35 131 B4
  Warrenpoint BT34 65 D4
St Patricks Prim Sch BT66 40 F6
St Patrick's Prim Sch
  Armagh BT61 60 C7
  Ballynahinch BT24 59 D5
  Castlewellan BT31 122 B3
  Craigavon BT67 32 F8
  Craigavon BT67 43 B6
  Crossmaglen BT35 147 E8
  Downpatrick BT30 62 D4
  Holywood BT18 9 D6
  Mayobridge BT34 133 B3
  Newry BT34 119 C1
  Newry BT35 64 B8
  Newry BT35 139 B5
  Newtownards BT22 95 A6
St Patrick's RC Cath BT61 60 C6
St Patrick's Rd BT30 93 E1
St Patrick's (Saul) Prim Sch BT30 109 C8
St Patricks St BT60 114 A3
St Patrick's Stone★ BT32 103 F7
St Patrick's Terr BT34 144 F4
St Patrick's Trian Visitor Complex & Armagh Ancestry★ 4 BT61 60 D5
St Patrick's Way BT30 109 D7
St Patrick's Well★
  Armagh BT60 60 B5
  Portadown BT62 55 C8
St Patrick's Well Grave Yd★ BT21 67 A6
St Patrick's Wlk 2 BT4 15 B5
St Paul's Cl 6 BT31 122 C5
St Paul's High Sch BT35 131 D4
St Paul's Jun High Sch BT66 41 E5
St Pauls Pl BT66 41 E5
St Paul's Prim Sch BT34 120 E1
St Paul's St 5 BT15 14 E8
St Peter's Cath (RC) BT12 154 B3
St Peter's Cl BT12 154 B3
St Peter's Ct BT12 154 B3
St Peter's Prim Sch
  Belfast BT12 154 B3
  Dungannon BT71 84 C8
  Newry BT35 131 D4
St Peter's Sq E BT12 154 B3
St Ronan's Prim Sch 6 BT34 132 B5
Saintsbury Ave BT27 38 A6
Saints & Scholars Integrated Prim Sch BT61 98 F6
St Stephen's Ct BT13 154 C4
St Teresa's Prim Sch
  Armagh BT60 116 D2
  Lurgan BT67 32 B2
Saleen Pk BT18 9 D7
Salisbury Ct BT7 155 A1
Salisbury La BT7 155 A1
Salisbury St BT2 155 A1
Sally Gdns BT33 63 C8
Salmon Leap La BT71 83 D4
Salters Grange ⓘ BT61 84 E1
Salters Grange Rd BT61 84 D3
Salter's Grange Rd BT61 84 E1
Saltpans The BT22 94 D3
Saltwater Cl 3 BT22 71 A6
Saltworks St BT21 67 A8
Sampson's La BT30 62 D4
Samuel St BT13 155 A4
Sancroft St BT13 14 B7
Sandbank Rd BT34 134 C3
Sandbrook Gdns 2 BT4 15 D7
Sandbrook Gr 1 BT4 15 D7
Sandbrook Pk BT4 15 D7
Sandeel La BT19 5 E7
Sandford Ave BT5 15 E4
Sandhill Ct BT63 53 E4
Sandhill Dr BT5 15 E3
Sandhill Gdns BT5 15 F3
Sandhill Gn BT5 15 F3
Sandhill Pk
  Belfast BT5 15 F3
  Lurgan BT66 42 B2
Sandhurst Dr
  Bangor BT20 4 E5
  Belfast BT9 14 D1
Sandhurst Gdns BT9 14 D1
Sandhurst Pk BT20 4 E5
Sandhurst Rd BT7 14 E2
Sand La BT30 123 F5
Sandown Dr BT5 15 F4
Sandown Pk 1 BT5 16 A4
Sandown Pk S BT5 15 F4
Sandown Rd BT5 15 F4
Sandringham BT63 52 A3
Sandringham Ct
  Bangor BT20 4 D4
  Hillsborough BT26 47 C8
  Portadown BT63 52 A4
Sandringham Dr BT20 4 D5
Sandringham Gdns BT20 4 D5
Sandringham Mews BT5 16 B4
Sandringham St 3 BT9 14 B1
Sandy Brae BT34 144 E4
Sandy Hill
  Lisburn BT27 27 B6
  7 Newry BT35 131 F5
Sandy Hill Ave BT27 27 B6
Sandy Hill Gdns BT27 27 B5
Sandy Hill Gr BT27 27 B6
Sandy Hill Pk BT27 27 B6
Sandy La BT27 27 A5
Sandylands BT22 81 E8
Sandymount BT27 27 A6
Sandymount Cl BT27 27 A6
Sandymount Ct BT20 4 C2
Sandymount Rd BT61 85 C2
Sandymount St BT9 21 D8
Sandy Rd BT34 132 D6
Sandy Row
  Belfast BT12 154 C1
  Portadown BT62 51 E4
Sandy's St BT34 64 D6
Sans Souci Pk BT9 21 C8
Sarah Daly's Bridge★ BT35 140 C7
Saratoga Ave BT23 19 C6
Sark St BT4 15 B5
SAUL BT30 109 B7
Saul Brae BT30 109 B7
Saul Bsns Pk BT30 62 F7
Saul Mills Rd BT30 62 F8
Saul Quarter ⓘ BT30 62 E2
Saul Rd BT30 62 E6
Saul St (Sráid Shabhaill) BT30 62 C5
Saul Way 4 BT30 62 C5
Savage's Fort★ BT30 123 A8
Saval Beg ⓘ BT34 132 D7
Saval More ⓘ BT34 132 E8
Savoy La BT33 63 D5
Sawmills Rd BT31 122 D2
SCADDY BT30 92 F2
Scaddy Rd BT30 92 F3
SCARVA BT63 101 E4
Scarva Prim Sch BT63 101 E4
Scarva Rd
  Banbridge BT32 61 B4
  Craigavon BT63 101 E7
Scarva Rd Ind Est BT32 61 A5
Scarva St BT32 102 C3
Scarva Sta BT63 101 E4
Scarva Visitor Ctr★ BT63 101 E4
Sch of Dentistry BT12 154 A2
Schomberg Ave 2 BT4 16 B6
Schomberg Dr BT12 154 C1
Schomberg Est BT63 52 D2
Schomberg Lodge 3 BT4 16 B6
Schomberg Pk BT4 16 B6
School Ct BT4 9 B2
School Hill BT33 123 C5
Schoolhouse Brae 3 BT21 6 F1
School of Ed BT7 14 D2
School of Nursing & Midwifery BT9 14 C2
School Rd
  Ballynahinch BT24 77 E1
  Ballywalter BT22 71 A6
  Banbridge BT32 120 E4
  Belfast BT5 23 C5
  Castlereagh BT8 22 A4
  Downpatrick BT30 106 F1
  Downpatrick BT30 125 D4
  Dromara BT25 88 C3
  Forkhill BT35 140 D1
  Newry BT34 117 F1
  Newry BT34 146 A3
  Newry BT35 129 C6
  Newtownards BT22 66 E5
  Rathfriland BT34 119 F2
Science Pk★ BT3 15 B8
Scolban Rd BT25 87 F2
Scollogs Hill Rd BT30 124 D7
SCOLLOGSTOWN BT30 124 D6
Scotch St
  Armagh BT61 60 D5
  Downpatrick BT30 62 C5
SCOTCH STREET BT62 50 B8
Scots Rd BT67 32 F3
Scott St BT12 154 C1
Scrabo Ctry Pk BT23 19 B1
Scrabo Glen BT23 19 B3
Scrabo Golf Club BT23 19 A1
Scrabo Rd BT23 19 B3
Scrabo St BT3 155 C4
Scrabo View Terr BT23 19 D4
Scrib ⓘ BT24 106 F5
Scribb Rd BT31 106 F4
Scrogg Rd BT34 153 B6
Scroil an Droichid & An Droichead Cultural Ctr BT7 155 B1
Seaboard Sailing Ctr BT30 93 C4
Seaboughan ⓘ BT60 115 F7
Seaboughan Rd BT60 115 F7
Seacliff Cl BT33 63 E1
Seacliff Rd BT20 4 B5
Seacourt BT20 3 F5
Seacourt Gdn BT20 3 F5
Seacourt La BT20 3 F5
Seafields BT34 65 E3
Seafin ⓘ
  Banbridge BT32 120 B7
  Newry BT35 141 B7
Seafin Castle★ BT32 120 C7
Seafin La BT32 120 B7
Seafin Rd
  Banbridge BT32 119 F7
  Newry BT35 141 B7
Seafin View BT34 146 D5
SEAFORDE BT30 107 C2
Seaforde Ct (Cúirt Suí Forde) 20 BT5 15 A5
Seaforde Demesne ⓘ BT30 107 B4
Seaforde Gdns (Garraithe Suí Forde) 19 BT5 15 A5
Seaforde Rd BT30 107 C2
Seaforde St (Sráid Suí Forde) 21 BT5 15 A5
Seaforth Rd BT20 4 C5
Sea Front Rd BT18 1 C2
Seagahan ⓘ BT60 115 A7
Seagahan Rd BT60 99 D1
Seagoe Ct BT63 52 A6
Seagoe Dr BT63 51 F6
Seagoe Gdns BT63 52 A6
Seagoegrove BT63 52 A6
Seagoe Ind Est BT63 40 A1
Seagoe Pk BT63 52 A7
Seagoe Prim Sch BT63 52 A7
Seagoe Rd
  Portadown BT63 40 A1
  Portadown BT63 74 F1
Seagoe Upper ⓘ BT63 52 A7
Seahaven BT22 81 D4
Seahill 8 BT21 67 A7
Seahill Dr BT18 1 H3
Seahill Pk BT21 67 A8
Seahill Rd E BT18 2 A4
Seahill Ridge 7 BT21 67 A7
Seahill Sta BT18 2 A3
Seahill Vale BT21 67 A8
Seal Rd BT3 8 B3
Sean Hollywood Arts Ctr & Newry & Mourne Mus The★ BT35 64 D6
Seapark Ave BT18 9 E8
Seapark Ct BT18 9 E8
Seapark Gr BT18 9 F8
Seapark La BT18 9 F8
Seapark Mews BT18 9 E8
Seapark Rd BT18 9 E8
Seapark Terr BT18 9 E8
SEAPATRICK BT32 61 C7
Seapatrick Rd
  Banbridge BT32 86 E1
  Seapatrick BT32 61 C8
Sea Pk The★ BT19 2 B6
Searce La BT35 117 C1
Seavaghan ⓘ BT30 107 E8
Seavaghan Rd BT24 91 D1
Seavers Rd BT35 141 B8
Seaview
  Ardglass BT30 125 F7
  Warrenpoint BT34 65 D1
Seaview Ave
  14 Kilkeel BT34 153 C7
  11 Millisle BT22 67 A4
Seaview Hts BT34 146 A2
Seaview Terr BT18 9 E7
Second Ave BT35 64 A8
Sefton Dr BT4 15 E6
Sefton Pk BT4 15 E6
Selby Ct BT12 154 B2
Selby Wlk BT12 154 B2
Selshion ⓘ BT62 51 A7
Selshion Manor BT62 51 B7
Selshion Par BT62 51 B5
Sentry Box Rd BT32 103 C1
Sepon Pk BT28 26 A2
Serse ⓘ BT35 117 C1
Servia St BT12 154 B2
Sessiamagaroll ⓘ BT71 83 D6
Sevastapol St (Sráid Seibheástopol) 1 BT13 154 A3
Severn St BT4 15 C5
Seyloran ⓘ BT71 72 A4
Seyloran La BT71 72 A3
Seymour Ave BT19 3 C4
Seymour Hill Prim Sch BT17 26 F8
Seymour La BT1 155 B3
Seymour Pk
  Bangor BT19 3 C4
  Lisburn BT27 38 D8
Seymour Rd BT19 3 C4
Seymour Row BT1 155 B3
Seymour St
  Belfast BT1 155 B3
  Lisburn BT27 26 C2
Seyton Pk BT66 42 E5
Shackleton Wlk BT23 19 C2
Shaerf Dr BT66 42 B4
Shaftesbury Ave
  Bangor BT20 3 D2
  Belfast BT7 155 B1
Shaftesbury Recn Ctr BT7 155 C1
Shaftesbury Sq BT2 155 A1
Shaftesbury Sq Hospl BT2 155 A1
Shaftsbury Rd BT20 3 E3
Shalom Pk BT5 22 F8
Shamble La BT35 129 D5
Shamrock Ct 2 BT6 15 A4
Shamrock Ctr BT62 51 C2
Shamrock Glen 4 BT19 13 E8

Shamrock Pl 8 BT6 15 A4
Shamrock St 5 BT6 15 A4
Shanbally Rd BT30 107 A3
Shandon Dr
  Bangor BT20 4 C5
  Kilkeel BT34 153 C6
Shandon Hts BT5 23 B8
Shandon Pk
  Belfast BT5 16 B2
  Newry BT34 132 A5
Shandon Pk E BT20 4 C5
Shandon Pk Golf Club BT5 16 A1
Shandon Pk W BT20 4 C5
Shandon Sq BT62 51 C3
Shanecrackan Beg BT60 100 D2
Shanecrackan More BT60 100 C1
Shanecracken Rd
  Armagh BT60 100 D2
  Craigavon BT62 116 E8
Shane Dr BT66 42 C2
Shaneglish BT62 101 C2
Shane Pk BT66 42 C3
Shanes Rd BT30 93 A5
Shankill
  Banbridge BT32 118 E7
  Lurgan BT66 41 E6
Shankill Ctr BT13 154 B4
Shankill Leisure Ctr BT13 154 B4
Shankill Par BT13 154 C4
Shankill Rd BT13 154 B4
Shankill St BT66 41 E6
Shankill Terr 6 BT13 154 C4
Shanlieve BT34 134 B5
Shanmoy BT70 82 F8
Shanmullagh or Ballycullen BT71 84 A6
Shannaghan BT31 104 B2
Shannaghan Pk BT30 62 E3
Shannagh Dr BT34 146 D5
Shannaghmore Pk BT66 42 D3
Shannon Ct BT14 14 B7
Shannon Pk BT34 134 C6
Shannon St BT14 14 B8
Shannowen 2 BT34 143 C4
Shanrod BT32 104 B6
Shanrod Crossroads BT32 104 A6
Shanrod Rd BT32 104 A4
Shanroe BT35 140 B2
Shan Slieve Dr BT33 63 C4
Shan Slieve Pk BT23 19 F4
Shantally BT60 112 C7
Shanvally Way 6 BT24 91 B1
Sharman Cl BT9 21 D6
Sharman Dale BT19 3 B3
Sharman Dr BT9 21 D6
Sharman Gdns BT9 21 D6
Sharman Pk BT9 21 D6
Sharman Rd BT9 21 D7
Sharman Rise BT19 3 B3
Sharman Way BT9 21 D6
Shaughan Rd BT35 130 C2
Shaws Bridge BT9 21 A2
Shaw St BT4 15 E6
Shean BT35 140 C1
Shean Rd BT35 149 D8
Sheelagh 148 C4
Sheemore Cres 3 BT34 153 E8
Sheepbridge Rd BT34 118 A1
Sheepland Beg BT30 126 B8
Sheepland More BT30 110 C1
Sheepland Rd BT30 110 B1
Sheeptown BT34 132 D5
Sheeptown Rd BT34 132 D5
Sheetrim
  Armagh BT60 113 B4
  Newry BT35 138 F4
Sheetrim Rd
  Armagh BT60 113 C4
  Newry BT35 138 F5
Sheiland BT35 148 A7
Shelbourne Rd BT6 15 B1
Shelling Ct BT27 38 A3
Shelling Pk BT27 38 B3
Shelling Ridge BT27 38 A3
Shepherds Dr BT35 131 F6
Shepherds Way BT35 131 F6
Sherbey Cres BT34 146 D5
Sherbrook Cl BT13 154 C4
Sherbrook Terr 5 BT13 154 C4
Sheridan Ct
  Bangor BT20 4 E5
  10 Belfast BT15 14 D8
Sheridan Dr
  Bangor BT20 4 D5
  Helen's Bay BT19 2 C6
Sheridan Gn BT63 52 A3
Sheridan Gr BT19 2 D6
Sheridan Manor BT19 2 C6
Sheridan's La BT61 83 F1
Sheridan St BT15 14 D8
Sherwood Gdns BT19 5 A3
Sherwood Pk BT19 5 A3
Sherwood Rd BT19 5 A3
Sheskin Way BT6 22 B8
Shewis BT61 99 D7
Shillington St BT62 51 D4
Shimma Wlk BT66 42 A2
Shimna Cl
  Belfast BT6 22 B8
  Newtownards BT23 19 C3
Shimna Integrated Coll BT33 63 C2
Shimna Par 1 BT33 63 D5
Shimna Pk BT33 63 C5
Shimna Rd BT33 63 C5
Shimna Vale BT33 63 C5
Shimna Ville BT33 63 C5
Shimna Wood BT33 63 C6
Shingle Bay 13 BT21 67 A7
Shinn BT34 118 F2
Shinn Forth Rd BT34 118 F3
Shinn Rd BT34 118 F3
Shinn Sch Rd BT34 118 F1
Shipbuoy St 1 BT15 14 E7
Ship St BT15 14 E8
Shiralee Dr BT23 19 B6
Shore Rd
  Downpatrick BT30 93 C3
  Downpatrick BT30 123 E5
  Holywood BT18 9 D7
  Kircubbin BT22 80 D8
  Millisle BT22 67 A5
  Newry BT34 143 C2
  Newtownards BT22 70 D1
  Portaferry BT22 94 D3
Shore St BT21 6 G1
Shorts La 2 BT35 147 F8
Short St
  Belfast BT1 14 E7
  Newtownards BT23 19 D5
Shortstone East 149 A4
Shortstone West 148 E4
Short Strand BT5 155 C3
Shot La
  Banbridge BT32 104 C7
  Dromara BT25 104 D8
Shrewsbury Dale BT24 77 C2
Shrewsbury Dr
  2 Bangor BT20 3 F2
  Belfast BT9 21 A5
Shrewsbury Hts 8 BT24 77 C3
Shrewsbury Pk BT9 21 A5
SHRIGLEY BT30 93 B6
Shrigley Rd BT30 93 B6
Shuttlefield Fd 1 BT23 19 D5
Sidings Office Pk The BT28 26 A2
Sillis 112 B8
Silverbirch Ave BT19 5 A2
Silver Birch Courts BT13 154 B4
Silverbirch Cres BT19 5 A2
Silverbirch Dr BT19 5 A2
Silverbirch Gdns BT19 4 F3
Silverbirch Glen 1 BT19 5 A2
Silverbirch Groove BT19 5 A3
Silverbirch Pk BT19 5 A2
Silverbirch Rd BT19 4 F2
SILVERBRIDGE BT35 139 E3
Silverbridge Rd BT35 139 E5
Silverstream Ave BT20 3 E2
Silverstream Cres 3 BT20 3 E2
Silverstream Ct 4 BT20 3 E2
Silverstream Dr BT20 3 E2
Silverstream Gdns 1 BT20 3 E2
Silverstream Pk 2 BT20 3 E2
Silverstream Rd BT20 3 E2
Silverwood BT66 41 D7
Silverwood Bsns Pk BT66 41 B6
Silverwood Ct BT66 41 D8
Silverwood Ctr BT66 41 D8
Silverwood Dr BT66 41 E5
Silverwood Gn BT66 41 D8
Silverwood Ind Est BT66 41 C6
Silverwood La BT66 41 B7
Silverwood Rd BT66 41 C6
Silvio St BT13 14 A7
Sinclair Ave BT19 3 B2
Sinclair Dell BT19 3 B2
Sinclair Pk BT19 3 B2
Sinclair Rd
  Bangor BT19 3 B2
  Belfast BT3 8 A1
Sinclair Rd N BT19 3 B2
Sinclair St
  Belfast BT5 15 F4
  2 Newry BT35 64 D6
Sinton Pk BT62 101 B6
Sintonville Ave 4 BT5 15 D5
SIX ROAD ENDS BT19 13 F5
Skateridge Rd BT25 88 F1
Skeagh BT25 88 C3
Skeagh Rd BT25 88 C3
Skegatillida BT35 117 C5
Skeltons Cut BT25 87 B3
Skeltons Rampart BT66 74 E7
Skeltons Rd BT32 87 C2
Skerries BT60 112 E5
Skerriff Rd BT35 128 F1
Skerriff (Tichburn) BT35 138 E7
Skerriff (Trueman) BT35 138 E7
Sketrick Island Pk BT23 19 F7
Sketrick Wlk BT23 79 C7
Skillyscolban BT25 87 E2
Skipper St BT1 155 B4
Skipperstone Ave BT19 4 C1
Skipperstone Dr BT19 13 B8
Skipperstone Pk BT19 4 C1
Skipperstone Rd BT20 4 A1
Skipton St BT5 15 C5
Skyline Dr BT27 26 C4
Slanes BT22 95 B7
Slaney Brae BT30 62 C7
Slaney Pk BT30 62 F6
Slash La BT61 84 D6
Slash Rd BT71 84 D6
Slatady BT35 23 A5
Slatemill Rd BT34 153 B4
Slate Quarry Rd BT35 139 A7
Slaterock Rd BT35 115 A2
Sleepy Valley
  Rathfriland BT34 119 F1
  Richhill BT61 85 E1
Sleepy Valley Ct BT61 85 E1
Slieve 149 B3
Slieve Bearnagh Pk 1 BT23 19 F5
Slievebracken BT35 140 F2
Slievecoole Pk BT33 63 C4
Slievecool Pk BT66 42 A3
Slievecorragh Ave BT33 63 B5
Slieve Cres BT35 140 F2
Slieve Croob Ave 2 BT23 19 F5
Slieve Foy Pl BT34 65 D2
Slievegrane BT30 62 D4
Slievegrane Rd BT30 109 B6
Slieve Gullion BT35 140 D4
Slieve Gullion Rd BT35 64 B7
Slievehanny Rd BT31 106 C1
Slievemore Ave BT23 19 F5
Slievemoyne Pk BT33 63 C4
Slievenaboley BT25 105 B4
Slievenaboley Rd BT31 105 B3
Slievenagarragh BT34 134 A5
Slievenagriddle BT30 109 C6
Slievenalargy BT34 121 D3
Slievenamaddy Ave BT33 63 C5
Slievenaman Rd
  Newcastle BT33 135 D7
  Newry BT34 121 E1
Slievenisky BT31 106 A4
Slievenisky Rd BT31 106 B3
Slieve Shanagh Pk BT33 63 C4
Slieveshan Pk 16 BT34 153 C7
Slieve View Cl BT34 65 C5
Sloan Ave BT66 41 F4
Sloanhill Mews BT66 41 F5
Sloan's Ave BT8 29 D3
Sloans Rd BT35 142 A4
Sloan St
  Lisburn BT27 26 C1
  Lurgan BT66 41 F4
Sloanstown BT22 70 C8
Slopes The BT63 53 F1
Small Park BT26 47 C6
Smalls Rd BT34 65 D4
Smeaton Pk BT67 34 A2
Smithfield Sq N BT1 155 A4
Smithfield St BT28 26 B1
Snugville St BT13 154 A4
Soldierstown Rd BT67 33 F7
Solitude Demesne BT67 42 C7
Solway St 3 BT4 15 B6
Somerset Ave 7 BT20 4 A4
Somerset St BT7 21 F8
Somerton Ind Pk BT3 8 A3
Somme Dr BT6 22 C7
Somme Her Ctr* BT23 12 F2
Sorella St BT12 154 A2
Soudan St BT12 154 A1
South Ave BT20 4 A1
South Bank BT6 22 B8
South Circular Rd BT19 4 B1
South Cl BT18 9 D5
South Cres BT8 21 D2
South Gn BT23 19 C3
Southland Dale BT5 16 A1
South Link BT20 4 A1
South Par BT7 14 F1
Southport Ct 10 BT14 14 B8
South Prom BT33 63 D2
South St Mews BT23 19 D4
South Sperrin BT5 16 D3
South St
  Newtownards BT23 19 D4
  Portadown BT62 51 D3
Southview St 9 BT7 14 E1
Southwell Rd 11 BT20 4 A4
Southwell St BT15 14 D7
Soye Cres BT67 42 A8
Soyegardens BT67 42 A7
Spa Golf Club BT24 59 B2
Spa Grange BT24 90 F2
Spamount St BT15 14 C8
Spa Prim Sch BT24 90 E2
Spa Rd BT24 59 E1
Sparrowhill Bridge BT35 140 C3
Spectrum Ctr* BT13 154 A4
Spelga Ave BT33 63 C5
Spelga Cl (Clós na Speilge) BT30 62 B2
Spelga Dr 4 BT34 119 F2
Spelga Gdns 10 BT34 119 F2
Spelga Pk
  Hilltown BT34 134 B6
  Lurgan BT66 42 A3
Spelga Pl
  17 Kilkeel BT34 153 C7
  Newtownards BT23 19 C4
Spencer St BT18 9 D6
Sperrin Dr
  Belfast BT5 16 E3
  Lurgan BT67 42 A8
Sperrin Pk
  Armagh BT61 60 F7
  Belfast BT5 16 E3
  Lurgan BT67 42 B8
Sperrin Wlk BT5 16 D3
Spier's Pl BT13 154 B4
Spinners Ct BT23 25 C3
Spinner Sq BT12 154 A3
Spirehill Rd BT26 48 D4
Spires Cres The BT23 79 A5
Spires Gr The BT23 79 A5
Spires Ret Pk BT61 60 C6
Spires Sh Mall BT1 155 A2
Spires The
  Dromara BT25 58 D4
  Holywood BT18 9 F5
  Killinchy BT23 79 A5
Spires View The BT23 79 A5
Spittle Ballee BT30 109 C2
Spittle Quarter BT30 109 C1
Splitbog Rd BT31 104 E1
Springburn Pk BT27 38 A6
Springdale Cres 1 BT34 153 B7
Springdale Ct 6 BT34 153 B7
Springfield Ave
  4 Bangor BT20 4 B4
  Warrenpoint BT34 65 D2
Springfield Gdns BT22 81 D5
Springfield Rd
  Bangor BT20 4 B4
  Portavogie BT22 81 E5
  Warrenpoint BT34 65 D2
  Belfast BT12 154 A3
Springfields
  Banbridge BT32 61 B1
  Portadown BT63 51 F4
Springfort Lodge BT66 43 A5
Springhill Ave BT20 3 D3
Springhill Ct 3 BT34 132 A5
Springhill Dr BT34 132 A5
Springhill Hts BT20 3 D3
Springhill Manor BT67 43 B6
Springhill Pk (Páirc Chnoc an Tobair) BT30 62 E5
Springhill Rd
  Armagh BT60 115 F2
  Bangor BT20 3 D3
  Craigavon BT67 43 B5
  Newry BT35 131 F6
Springhill Sh Ctr BT19 3 D2
Spring La BT22 70 A6
Spring Mdws
  Craigavon BT67 34 F8
  Warrenpoint BT34 65 C4
Springmount Rd
  Dromara BT25 89 A3
  Newtownards BT23 31 A2
Spring Pl 18 BT6 15 A4
Spring St 19 BT6 15 A4
Springvale BT22 71 A4
Springvale Dr BT30 62 E5
Springvale Rd
  Ballywalter BT22 71 A5
  Craigavon BT63 86 B1
  Newtownards BT22 71 B3
Springview St BT12 154 A2
Springview Wlk BT13 154 A3
Springwell Ave N 2 BT19 5 B7
Springwell Ave S 1 BT19 5 B7
Springwell Cres BT19 5 B7
Springwell Ct 5 BT19 5 B7
Springwell Dr
  Groomsport BT19 5 B7
  Lurgan BT66 41 E3
Springwell Gdns 9 BT19 5 B7
Springwell Groove 4 BT19 5 B7
Springwell Pk 8 BT19 5 B7
Springwell Pl 3 BT19 5 B7
Springwell Rd BT19 5 C4
Sprucefield Cl BT27 37 F5
Sprucefield Ct BT27 38 A6
Sprucefield Ret Pk BT27 37 E5
Sprucefield Sh Ctr BT27 37 F5
Spruce St BT27 26 D2
Square The
  9 Ballywalter BT22 71 A6
  Comber BT23 25 E3
  Downpatrick BT30 107 C1
  Hillsborough BT26 47 C6
  10 Kilkeel BT34 153 C7
  9 Rostrevor BT34 143 B3
  21 Tandragee BT62 101 B7
  Warrenpoint BT34 65 C2
Sráid an Chaisleáin BT1 155 A3
Sráid an Fhuaráin (Fountain St) 2 BT30 62 C5
Sráid an Tsrutháin (Stream St) BT30 62 C4
Sráid Arann (Arran St) 2 BT5 15 A5
Sráid Bholcáin (Vulcan St)
  10 Belfast BT5 15 A5
  Belfast BT12 154 C2
Sráid Chairlinn (Carlingford St) BT35 147 F8
Sráid Chill Dara (Kildare St) 4 BT13 154 C4
Sráid Earnúin (Arnon St) 3 BT13 154 C4
Sráid Eoin (John St) BT30 62 C4
Sráid Harper (Harper St) 24 BT5 15 A5
Sráid Loch Altáin (Alton St) 1 BT13 154 C4
Sráid Mháire (Mary St) 8 BT30 92 B5
Sráid Mhúire (Mary St)
  5 Castlewellan BT31 122 C5
  1 Downpatrick BT30 62 C4
Sráid na Bhalla (Wall St) BT13 154 C4
Sráid na gCeimiceán (Chemical St) 15 BT5 15 A5
Sráid na Ríona (Regent St) BT13 14 C7
Sráid Odúsa (Odessa St) BT13 154 A3
Sráid Phádraig (Patrick St) 8 BT35 64 C5
Sráid Pháirc na Feá (Beechfield St) 33 BT5 15 A5
Sráid Ríona Íochtir (Lower Regent St) BT13 155 A4
Sráid Seibheástopol (Sevastapol St) 1 BT13 154 A3
Sráid Shabhaill (Saul St) BT30 62 C5
Sráid Sheáin Uí Mháirtín (John Martin St) 5 BT35 64 C5
Sráid Suí Forde (Seaforde St) 21 BT5 15 A5
Sráid Thír Eoghain (Tyrone St) 2 BT13 154 C4
Stanfield Dr BT23 19 F4
Stanfield Pl BT7 155 B2
Stanfield Row BT7 155 B2
Stang BT34 135 A5
Stangate Ave BT23 19 F4
Stangmore (Magee) BT71 83 F6
Stang Rd BT34 134 E8
Stanhope Dr BT13 154 C4
Stanhope St BT15 14 D7
Stanley Ave BT20 4 B5
Stanley Ct BT12 154 C3
Stanley Rd BT20 4 B5
Stanley St BT12 154 C2
Stann's Pk BT34 133 C3
Stanvilla Ave BT23 20 A5
Stanvilla Rd BT23 20 A5
Stanwell Rd BT23 19 F4
Star-of-the-sea Convent Prim Sch BT34 65 C1
Star of the Sea Prim Sch BT14 14 C8
Station Ave BT31 122 C5
Station Cl 6 BT35 131 E4
Station Ct BT19 3 B4
Station Dr BT19 3 C5
Station La
  Ballygowan BT23 77 E8
  Downpatrick BT30 124 E8
Station Mews
  Belfast BT4 15 E7
  Saintfield BT24 77 D3
Station Rd
  Armagh BT61 60 C7
  Bangor BT19 3 B4
  Belfast BT4 15 E7
  Castlewellan BT31 121 B7
  Craigavon BT63 101 E4
  Craigavon BT67 34 D5
  Holywood BT18 1 E3
  Lisburn BT27 26 D5
  Moira BT67 34 C3
  Newry BT35 141 B3
  Ballynahinch BT24 77 F4
  Castlewellan BT31 122 C5
  1 Crossgar BT30 92 B4
  Downpatrick BT30 125 D5
  Saintfield BT24 77 D4
Station Rd Ind Est BT61 60 C7
Station St Flyover BT3 155 C4
Station Sq BT19 2 D5
Station St BT3 155 C3
Station View BT19 3 C5
Station Wlk BT19 3 C5
Steadings The BT27 27 C6
Steam Mill La BT1 155 B4
Steel Dickson Ave 2 BT22 94 D3
Steel Dickson Gdns 1 BT22 94 D3
Steens Hill
  Banbridge BT32 61 F8
  Banbridge BT32 86 F1
Steens Row 5 BT5 15 C4
Stellenbosch Ave 3 BT21 67 A7
Stephen St BT1 155 A4
Steps Rd
  Craigavon BT66 44 B5
  Magheralin BT67 43 E6
Stevenson Pk BT67 42 A5
Stevenson's La BT8 76 E7
Stewart Ave BT63 52 A5
Stewart Cres 5 BT22 71 A6
Stewart Hill BT60 60 E5
Stewart Rd BT23 19 F7
Stewarts Cres BT34 119 F2
Stewart's Pl BT18 9 D7
Stewarts Rd
  Dromara BT25 89 F4
  Newry BT34 146 B3
Stewart St BT7 155 C2
Stiloga BT71 83 A8
Stiloga Rd BT71 83 B8
Stirling Ave
  Belfast BT6 22 D8
  Newtownards BT23 19 C2
Stirling Gdns BT6 22 C8
Stirling Rd BT6 22 C8
Stockbridge Pk BT21 6 B5
Stockbridge Rd BT21 6 A4
Stockingmans Hill BT60 98 F6
STONEBRIDGE BT61 85 F3
Stonebridge Ave BT23 13 B5
Stonegate Sh Ctr BT23 20 C5
Stoney Rd
  Belfast BT16 16 F6
  Dundonald BT16 17 A5
Stonge Ct BT62 51 C2
Stonyford St BT5 15 C5

Stormont Castle★ BT4 ... 16 E6
Stormont Cres 16 BT5 .... 15 B4
Stormont House★ BT4 ... 16 E6
Stormont La 13 BT5 ..... 15 B4
Stormont Pk BT4 .... 16 C5
Stormont Rd BT3 .... 8 A1
Stormont St BT5 .... 15 B4
Stormount Ct BT5 .... 16 D4
Stracam Cnr BT6 .... 22 C7
Stragrane Ⓣ BT68 .... 82 F2
Straiddorn Gn BT23 ..... 25 E4
Straight The BT6 .... 22 B7
Straits The BT23 .... 68 E1
Stramore Pk 2 BT63 ..... 57 C1
Stramore Rd BT63 .... 56 F6
Strand Ⓣ BT30 .... 125 C7
Strand Ave
Holywood BT18 .... 9 E7
Millisle BT22 .... 67 A5
Strandburn Cres 2 BT4 .. 15 E6
Strandburn Ct 1 BT4 .... 15 D6
Strandburn Dr 1 BT4 .... 15 D6
Strandburn Gdns 2 BT4 . 15 D6
Strandburn Par BT4 ..... 15 E7
Strandburn Pk BT4 ...... 15 E6
Strandburn St BT4 ...... 15 D7
Strand Cl (Clós na Trá) 9
BT5 .... 15 A5
Strandfield Ⓣ 150 B3
Strand Mews
Holywood BT18 .... 9 D7
11 Belfast BT5 .... 15 A5
Strand Pk BT22 .... 71 A5
Strand Prim Sch 5 BT4 .. 15 D7
Strand Studios BT4 ..... 15 D6
Strand The 19 BT22 ..... 94 D3
STRANDTOWN BT3 .... 15 E6
Strandtown Prim Sch BT4 15 E5
Strand View BT22 .... 71 A5
Strandview St BT9 ...... 21 D8
Strangford Ave BT30 .... 94 B2
STRANGFORD (BAILE LOCH CUAN) BT30 .... 94 D2
Strangford Ct BT30 ..... 62 D8
Strangford Gate BT23 .... 20 A4
Strangford Gate Dr 1
BT23 .... 20 A4
Strangford Gate St 2
BT23 .... 20 A4
Strangford Hts BT23 ..... 20 A5
Strangford Integrated Coll
BT22 .... 66 E2
Strangford Pk BT23 ...... 20 A5
Strangford Rd
Ardglass BT30 .... 125 F6
Downpatrick BT30 .... 62 C7
Downpatrick BT30 .... 93 D1
Strangford View
Killinchy BT23 .... 79 A5
Newtownards BT22 .... 70 B5
STRANMILLIS BT9 .... 21 C7
Stranmillis Ct BT9 ...... 21 D8
Stranmillis Emb BT9 ..... 14 D1
Stranmillis Embank BT9 .. 21 D8
Stranmillis Gdns BT9 .... 14 D1
Stranmillis Mews BT9 .... 21 C8
Stranmillis Pk BT9 ...... 14 D1
Stranmillis Prim Sch BT9. 21 D6
Stranmillis Rd BT9 ...... 14 D1
Stranmillis St BT9 ...... 21 D8
Stranmillis Univ Coll Campus
BT9 .... 21 C7
Stranmore Ave BT23 ..... 19 F5
Stratford Ave BT19 ...... 13 F8
Stratford Ct 6 BT19 ..... 13 F8
Stratford Dr BT19 .... 13 F8
Stratford Gdns 4 BT19 ... 13 F8
Stratford Glen 1 BT19 ... 13 F8
Stratford Gr 2 BT19 ..... 13 F8
Stratford Rd BT19 .... 13 E8
Stratford Rise 5 BT19 ... 13 F8
Strathearn La BT4 ...... 16 A6
Strathearn Mews 10 BT4 . 15 F6
Strathearn Pk
Bangor BT19 .... 3 C3
Belfast BT4 .... 16 A7
Strathearn Prep Sch BT4. 16 A6
Strathearn Sch BT4 ..... 16 A6
Stratheden Hts BT23 ..... 20 B6
Stratheden St BT15 ...... 14 C8
Strathern Ct BT18 .... 9 C5
Strathleven Pk BT18 ..... 10 A8
Stream St
Newry BT34 .... 64 D6
Downpatrick BT30 .... 62 C4
Streamvale Dairy Farm★
BT16 .... 17 A1
Street The BT62 .... 56 A4
Strickland's Bay BT20 ..... 3 E5
Stricklands Con Ctr BT20 .. 3 F5
Strita's Pk 1 BT34 ...... 143 B3
Strone Hill Ct BT16 ...... 17 E4
Strone Hill La BT16 ...... 17 E4
Strone Pk BT16 .... 17 E4
Stroud St BT12 .... 154 C1
Struell Ⓣ BT30 .... 109 B5
Struell Ave BT30 .... 62 D2
Struell Cl BT30 .... 62 D2
Struell Cres BT30 .... 62 D2
Struell Hts (Ardna na Sruthaile) BT30 .... 62 D2
Struell Pk BT30 .... 62 D5
Struell Rd BT30 .... 62 D5
Struell Wells Rd BT30 .... 62 F4
Stumpa Ⓣ 149 C3
Stump Rd BT22 .... 70 F6
Sturgan Ⓣ BT35 .... 130 F3
Sturgan Brae BT35 ...... 130 F1
Sturgan Rd BT35 .... 130 F3
Sturgeons Hill BT62 ...... 54 A4
Sufficial La BT30 .... 108 B8
Sugarfield St BT13 ..... 154 A4
Sugarhouse Quay 3
BT35 .... 64 D6
Sugar Island BT35 .... 64 D6
Sugar Island Rd BT63 .... 53 D5
Sugartown Rd BT34 ..... 119 C2
Sullivan Cl BT18 .... 9 D7
Sullivan Pl BT18 .... 9 D7
Sullivan Prep Sch BT18 ... 9 D6
Sullivan Upper Sch BT18 .. 9 D6
Summerfield St BT23 ..... 12 F5
Summerhill
Banbridge BT32 .... 61 D3
Craigavon BT66 .... 86 A7
Summer Hill BT34 .... 65 C2
Summerhill Ave BT5 ...... 16 D4
Summerhill Brae BT32 ... 61 D3
Summerhill Ct
Banbridge BT32 .... 61 D3
15 Belfast BT14 .... 14 B8
Summerhill Gdns BT20 ..... 4 E4
Summerhillgreen BT32 ... 61 D3
Summerhill Par BT5 ...... 16 D4
Summerhill Pk
Bangor BT20 .... 4 E4
Belfast BT5 .... 16 D4
Summer Island Rd BT61 .. 84 E7
Summer St BT14 .... 14 B8
Sunbury Ave BT5 .... 15 D4
Sundaywell Rd BT30 ..... 92 E6
Sunderland Pk BT23 ..... 19 D2
Sunderland Rd BT6 ...... 22 C8
Sunmount Pk 4 BT25 .... 58 D6
Sunningdale Ct BT20 ...... 4 C3
Sunningdale Dr BT33 ..... 63 B4
Sunningdale Pk
Bangor BT20 .... 4 C2
Newcastle BT33 .... 63 A4
Sunnydale Ave 12 BT21 .. 67 A7
Sunnyside BT24 .... 59 D5
Sunnyside Cres BT7 ...... 21 E8
Sunnyside Dr BT7 .... 21 E8
Sunnyside Pk 4 BT7 ...... 21 E8
Sunnyside St BT7 .... 21 E8
Sunwich St 4 BT6 .... 15 A3
Surrey St BT9 .... 14 A1
Susan St BT5 .... 15 A5
Sussex Pl BT2 .... 155 B2
Swallow Cl BT23 .... 25 C3
Swallow Field BT62 ...... 55 C8
Sweat House★ BT70 ..... 82 E8
Swift Pl 10 BT6 .... 15 A4
Swift St 12 BT6 .... 15 A4
Sycamore Ct 8 BT24 ..... 91 B1
Sycamore Gr 12 BT4 ..... 15 E6
SYDENHAM BT3 .... 15 F8
Sydenham Airlink Sta
BT3 .... 15 E8
Sydenham Ave BT4 .... 15 F6
Sydenham Bsns Pk BT3 .... 8 F5
Sydenham Bypass BT4 ..... 8 F1
Sydenham Cres BT4 ...... 15 E6
Sydenham Dr 3 BT4 ...... 15 E6
Sydenham Flyover BT5 ... 15 A5
Sydenham Gdns BT4 ..... 15 E6
Sydenham Intake Ⓣ BT3 .... 8 E3
Sydenham Pk BT4 .... 15 E6
Sydenham Prim Sch 6
BT4 .... 15 D7
Sydenham Rd BT3 .... 15 A6
Sydney St W BT13 .... 14 A7
Syenite Pl 14 BT34 ..... 143 C3
Syerla Rd BT71 .... 83 D8
Symons St BT12 .... 154 B1

T

Taafe's Castle★ 151 C4
Tadworth BT19 .... 13 E8
Taghnabrick Ⓣ BT27 ..... 38 C4
Taghnevan Ⓣ BT66 ...... 41 E3
Taghnevan Cl BT66 ...... 41 E4
Taghnevan Dr BT66 ...... 41 E4
Talbot Cl BT19 .... 3 B2
Talbot Dr 4 BT19 .... 3 C2
Talbot Pk BT19 .... 3 B2
Talbot St
Belfast BT1 .... 155 A4
Newry BT34 .... 64 D6
Newtownards BT23 .... 19 D6
Tallbridge Rd BT62 ...... 73 C1
Tamar Bsns Ctr BT4 ...... 15 C5
Tamar Commercial Ctr
BT4 .... 15 B6
Tamar Commerical Ctr
BT4 .... 15 C5
Tamar Ct BT4 .... 15 C5
Tamar St BT4 .... 15 C6
Tamary Ⓣ BT34 .... 133 E7
Tamary Cairns★ BT34 ... 133 D6
Tamary Hill BT34 .... 133 E7
Tamary Rd BT34 .... 133 D5
Tamery Pass BT5 .... 15 B4
TAMHNAIGH NAOMH (SAINTFIELD) BT24 ...... 77 B3
Tamlaght Ⓣ
Armagh BT60 .... 97 F6
Armagh BT60 .... 113 B8
Tamlaghtmore Ⓣ BT71 ... 72 D6
Tamlat Ⓣ 112 B5
Tamnaficarbet Ⓣ BT63 ... 40 C4
Tamnafiglassan Ⓣ BT64 .. 40 D2
Tamnaghbane Ⓣ BT35 ... 141 A8
Tamnaghbane Rd BT35 .. 141 A8
Tamnaghmore Ⓣ BT62 ... 100 E7
Tamnaghmore Rd BT62 . 100 E7
Tamnaghvelton Ⓣ BT62 .. 100 E8
Tamnaharry Ⓣ BT34 ..... 133 A1
Tamnaharry Hill BT34 ... 133 B2
TAMNAMORE BT71 .... 72 D6
Tamnamore Cl BT71 ..... 72 D5
Tamnamore Prim Sch
BT71 .... 72 D6
Tamnamore Rd BT71 ..... 72 E5
Tamnyvane Ⓣ BT67 ...... 33 A6
Tamnyveagh Ⓣ BT34 .... 152 B7
Tanderagee Ⓣ BT60 ..... 114 E5
Tandragee Golf Course
BT62 .... 101 A6
Tandragee Rd
Armagh BT60 .... 100 C2
Craigavon BT62 .... 55 E6
Craigavon BT65 .... 41 E2
Gilford BT63 .... 57 D1
Lurgan BT66 .... 41 F4
Markethill BT60 .... 116 A8
Newry BT35 .... 117 E5
Portadown BT62 .... 51 E2
Tandragee Recn Ctr
BT62 .... 101 B7
Tandragee St
5 Richhill BT61 .... 85 E1
3 Richhill BT61 .... 99 E8
TANDRAGEE (TÓIN RE GAOITH) BT62 .... 101 A7
Tannagh Ⓣ BT69 .... 82 B5
Tannaghlane Ⓣ BT68 ..... 82 C1
Tannaghlane Rd BT68 .... 96 C8
Tannaghmore Ⓣ
Armagh BT60 .... 100 C3
Ballynahinch BT24 ...... 107 B6
Tannaghmore Farm & Gdns★
BT66 .... 40 F5
Tannaghmore Gn BT66 ... 40 F6
Tannaghmore North Ⓣ
BT67 .... 32 A1
Tannaghmore N Rd BT67 . 75 F5
Tannaghmore Prim Sch
BT67 .... 42 A8
Tannaghmore Rd
Armagh BT60 .... 100 B2
Ballynahinch BT24 ...... 107 B5
Tannaghmore South Ⓣ
BT66 .... 42 A4
Tannaghmore West Ⓣ
BT66 .... 40 F5
Tannaghmore W Rd BT66 40 E5
Tanners Ct BT67 .... 34 C2
Tannyoky Ⓣ BT35 .... 117 A7
Tannyoky Rd BT35 ...... 117 B7
Tanvally Rd BT32 .... 103 E2
Tara Ⓣ BT22 .... 95 B1
Tara Cres BT23 .... 19 F7
Tarawood BT18 .... 1 B1
Tarawood Mews BT8 ..... 21 E5
Tareesh La
Ballynahinch BT24 .... 91 E1
Downpatrick BT30 ...... 107 F8
Tarry Dr BT67 .... 42 B8
Tarry La BT67 .... 32 B2
Tarsan Ⓣ BT63 .... 40 A2
Tarsan La BT63 .... 74 F2
Tartaraghan Rd BT62 ..... 73 E3
Tarthlogue Ⓣ BT62 ...... 73 D2
Tarthlogue Rd BT62 ...... 73 E2
Tassagh Ⓣ BT60 .... 114 C5
TASSAGH BT60 .... 114 D4
Tassagh Rd BT60 .... 114 C4
Tassan Ⓣ 127 A4
Tate Rd BT35 .... 130 B1
Tate's Ave BT12 .... 14 A2
Tate's Cross Roads BT25 . 89 D5
Tattintlieve Ⓣ 128 B1
Taughblane Ⓣ BT26 ...... 46 C3
Taughblane Rd BT26 ..... 46 C3
Taughlumny Ⓣ BT66 ..... 44 C2
Taughlumny Rd BT66 .... 44 C2
Taughraine Hts BT67 ..... 42 F5
Taughrane Ⓣ BT67 ...... 42 F6
Tavanagh Ⓣ BT62 .... 51 E3
Tavanagh Ave BT62 ...... 51 E3
Tavanagh Gdns BT62 ..... 51 D3
Tavanagh Ind Est BT62 ... 51 D3
Tavanagh St BT12 ...... 154 A1
Tavanaskea Ⓣ 128 D3
Taylor Cotts BT60 ...... 113 C2
Taylor Sq BT28 .... 37 F8
Teagy Ⓣ BT62 .... 73 C2
Teagy Rd BT62 .... 85 D8
Teal Pk BT23 .... 20 A3
Teal Rocks BT23 .... 20 A3
Teal View BT23 .... 20 A3
Teconnaught Ⓣ BT24 ..... 91 E1
Teconnaught Rd
Ballynahinch BT24 .... 91 E1
Downpatrick BT30 ...... 107 E8
Teemore Ⓣ BT62 .... 100 D6
Teer Ⓣ BT35 .... 138 C3
Teeraw Ⓣ BT61 .... 98 B7
Teeraw Rd BT61 .... 84 A1
Teer Island Ⓣ BT35 ..... 138 C3
Teer Rd BT35 .... 138 D2
Telfair St BT1 .... 155 B3
Templar Ave BT27 .... 38 C8
Templeburn Rd BT30 ..... 78 C1
Templecormick★ BT30 ... 94 A3
Templecraney★ BT22 .... 94 D4
Temple Golf Course BT27 76 D4
Temple Hill Rd BT34 ..... 64 F5
Templemore Ave BT4 .... 15 B5
Templemore Pl 8 BT5 ... 15 B4
Templemore St BT5 ..... 15 B5
Templemoyle★ BT24 .... 106 E7
Temple of the Winds★
BT23 .... 69 F6
Templepatrick Ⓣ BT21 ... 66 F6
Temple St 9 BT5 .... 15 B4
Ten Acres BT23 .... 19 D1
Tennent St BT13 .... 154 A4
Tennyson Ave 6 BT20 .... 4 A4
Teraghafeeva or Lissue Ⓣ
BT28 .... 37 A8
Tern Pk BT23 .... 20 A3
Tern St BT4 .... 15 B6
Terraskane Ⓣ BT61 ...... 98 A8
Terraskane Rd BT61 ..... 84 A1
Terryglassog Ⓣ BT70 .... 82 F7
Terryglassog Rd BT70 .... 82 F7
Terryhoogan Ⓣ BT62 .... 101 D5
Terryhoogan Rd BT62 ... 101 D5
Terryscallop Rd BT71 .... 83 A6
Terryscollop Ⓣ BT71 ..... 83 B7
Teutonic Gdns BT12 .... 154 C1
Thalia St BT12 .... 154 B1
Thanksgiving Sq BT1 .... 155 B3
THE FLUSH BT60 .... 99 C1
Thehawthorns BT34 ..... 146 C4
Themeadows BT62 .... 73 A2
Theodore St BT12 ...... 154 A2
The Point Park Ⓣ BT34 .. 143 D1
THE SPA BT24 .... 90 E2
THE TEMPLE BT27 .... 76 D5
Thiepval Ave BT6 .... 22 C8
Third Ave BT35 .... 64 A8
Third St BT13 .... 154 A3
Thistle Cross Rds 150 D4
Thistle Ct BT5 .... 15 A5
Tholsel St 151 C4
Thomas Russell Pk BT30 . 62 C4
Thomas St
Armagh BT61 .... 60 D4
Belfast BT15 .... 14 D7
Bessbrook BT35 .... 131 C5
Lurgan BT66 .... 41 F5
Newtownards BT23 .... 19 D5
Portadown BT62 .... 51 E4
Warrenpoint BT34 .... 65 C2
Thomastown Ⓣ BT22 ..... 94 D6
Thompson House Hospl
BT28 .... 26 A3
Thompson's Grange BT8 . 29 C2
Thompson Wharf Rd BT3 ... 8 B1
Thora's Fort★ BT23 ...... 12 D5
Thornbrook BT27 .... 38 F2
Thornbrook Rd BT67 ..... 35 B3
Thorndale BT32 .... 61 A3
Thorndale Ave BT15 ..... 14 C8
Thorndale Pk BT8 .... 29 C2
Thorndale Rd S BT8 ...... 29 C2
Thorndyke St 10 BT5 .... 15 B5
Thorn Hill BT19 .... 3 C2
Thornhill Ave 18 BT62 .. 101 B7
Thornhill Cres
Belfast BT5 .... 16 C4
19 Tandragee BT62 ..... 101 B7
Thornhill Dr
Belfast BT5 .... 16 C4
Dromara BT25 .... 58 D6
Thornhill Gdns 3 BT9 .... 21 B7
Thornhill Gr BT5 .... 16 C4
Thornhill Malone BT9 .... 21 B7
Thornhill Par BT5 .... 16 C4
Thornhill Pk
Belfast BT5 .... 16 C4
Lurgan BT66 .... 42 C3
Thornhill Rd BT32 ...... 104 B8
Thorn Hill Rd BT32 ...... 61 B2
Thorn Hts BT32 .... 61 B2
Thornleigh
Armagh BT60 .... 60 F3
Lurgan BT66 .... 41 F5
Newtownards BT23 .... 68 F2
Thornleigh Ave BT23 .... 20 C6
Thornleigh Cres BT23 .... 20 C6
Thornleigh Dr BT23 ...... 20 C6
Thornleigh Gdns BT20 ..... 4 D4
Thornleigh Gr BT30 ..... 107 C2
Thornleigh Pk
Bangor BT20 .... 4 E4
Newtownards BT23 .... 20 C6
Thornwood BT32 .... 61 B2
Thorny Fort★ BT61 ...... 99 D6
Thornyhill Rd BT23 ...... 78 E4
Tides The BT22 .... 81 D4
Tierney Gdns BT12 ..... 154 C1
Tierney Rd BT34 .... 118 D5
Tierny Fort★ BT34 ..... 118 C6
Tievecrom Ⓣ BT35 ...... 149 E8
Tievecrom Rd BT35 ..... 140 E1
Tievenadarragh Ⓣ BT30 . 107 D7
Tievenamara Ⓣ BT60 .... 127 F5
Tievenamara Rd BT60 ... 127 F5
Tieveshilly Ⓣ BT22 ...... 95 A1
Tildarg St BT6 .... 15 B2
Tillysburn Dr 4 BT4 ...... 9 A1
Tillysburn Gr BT4 .... 16 A8
Tillysburn Pk
3 Belfast BT4 .... 9 A1
Belfast BT4 .... 16 A8
Timakeel Cl BT62 .... 50 A8
Timbey Pk
1 Belfast BT7 .... 14 E1
Belfast BT7 .... 21 E8
Timulkenny Ⓣ BT62 ...... 73 E1
Tinto Cres BT19 .... 5 A4
Tipperary La BT33 .... 63 A5
Tireagerty Ⓣ BT71 .... 84 A3
Tirearly Ⓣ BT60 .... 97 F5
Tireggerty La BT71 ...... 84 A4
Tirfergus Ⓣ BT34 ...... 120 B4
Tirgarriff Ⓣ BT60 .... 98 A6
Tirgarve Ⓣ BT61 .... 84 B3
Tirkelly Ⓣ BT34 .... 120 B5
Tirkelly Hill Rd BT32 ... 120 B6
Tirkelly Rd BT34 .... 120 C5
Tirmacrannon Ⓣ BT61 .... 84 E5
Tirmacrannon Rd BT61 ... 84 E5
Tirnascobe Ⓣ BT61 ...... 99 B7
Tirnascobe Rd
Armagh BT61 .... 99 B7
3 Richhill BT61 .... 85 D1
Tirowen Dr BT28 .... 37 D8
Tirsogue Ⓣ BT66 .... 42 C1
Tirygory Ⓣ BT32 .... 120 D4
Tiscallen Ⓣ BT67 .... 32 D7
Tiscallen Rd BT67 .... 32 C7
Titania St BT6 .... 15 B2
Titterington Gdns BT27 ... 28 A2
Tivnacree Ⓣ BT60 ...... 113 B2
Tivnacree Rd BT60 ..... 113 C1
Tobarburr Pk BT30 ...... 62 C2
Tobercorran Ⓣ BT30 .... 124 A8
Tobercorran Rd BT30 ... 107 F3
Tobergill St
9 Belfast BT13 .... 14 A7
Belfast BT13 .... 154 A4
Toberhewny Ⓣ BT66 ..... 42 A2
Toberhewny La Lower
BT66 .... 42 A3
Toberhewny Pk BT66 ..... 42 B3
Tobermesson Glebe Ⓣ
BT71 .... 83 E7
Tobermesson Rd BT71 ... 83 D8
Tobermoney Ⓣ BT30 .... 109 B4
Tobermore Pk BT30 ..... 92 C5
Todd's Hill BT24 .... 77 C4
TÓIN RE GAOITH (TANDRAGEE) BT62 ..... 101 A7
Tollhouse Pk BT34 .... 64 D8
Tollumgrange Lower Ⓣ
BT30 .... 109 F1
Tollumgrange Rd BT30 .. 109 F1
Tollumgrange Upper Ⓣ
BT30 .... 109 F1
Tollymore Ⓣ BT33 ...... 63 B7
Tollymore Park Ⓣ BT33 .. 136 C8
Tollymore Rd BT33 ...... 63 B6
Tomb St BT1 .... 155 B4
Tonaghmore Ⓣ
Ballynahinch BT24 .... 77 A2
Dromore BT25 .... 87 A2
Tonaghmore Rd BT25 .... 86 F2
Tonaghneave Ave 3
BT24 .... 77 C4
Tonaghneave Mews 1
BT24 .... 77 C4
Tonaghneave Pl 2 BT24 . 77 C4
Tonnagh Rd BT60 .... 97 D7
Toragh Pk BT34 .... 64 E3
Tor Bank Specl Sch BT16. 17 B5
Torgrange BT18 .... 10 A7
Toronto St BT7 .... 15 A3
Torwood BT67 .... 34 B2
Tory Brae BT25 .... 88 F1
Tower Cl BT23 .... 12 F4
Tower Ct BT23 .... 19 C4
Tower Hill BT61 .... 60 E6
Tower Hill Cl BT61 ...... 60 E6
Tower La BT23 .... 30 F6
Tower Pk BT23 .... 12 F4
Tower Rd
Banbridge BT32 .... 102 F1
Newtownards BT23 .... 12 F4
Tower St BT4 .... 15 B5
Towerview BT19 .... 5 A4
Towerview Ave BT19 ...... 5 A4
Tower View Cl BT19 .... 5 A4
Towerview Cres BT19 ..... 5 A4
Tower View Ct BT19 .... 5 A4
Towerview Prim Sch BT19 . 5 B4
Town & Ctry Sh Ctr BT8 .. 29 D3
Town Hall La BT21 .... 67 A8
Townhall St BT1 .... 155 B3
Town Parks Ⓣ BT13 ...... 14 C7
TOWN PARKS BT13 ...... 154 C4
Town Parks Ⓣ BT23 ...... 25 C3
Town Parks of Donaghadee Ⓣ BT21 ...... 6 E1
Townsend Ent Pk BT13 .. 154 C4
Townsend St
Banbridge BT32 .... 61 D4
Belfast BT13 .... 154 C4
Townsley St BT4 .... 15 C5
Toy and Kirkland Ⓣ BT30 . 79 B1
Trafalgar St 3 BT15 ..... 14 E7
Traherne Gdns BT27 ..... 38 A6
Trainfield St 5 BT15 ..... 14 D8
Trainor Cres BT35 ...... 139 B1
Trasnagh BT23 .... 79 C6
Trasnagh Dr BT23 .... 19 B4
Trasna Rd BT35 .... 141 A7
Trasna Way BT66 .... 42 A4
Trassey Cl BT6 .... 22 B8
Trassey Rd BT33 .... 135 E7
Tray Ⓣ
Armagh BT60 .... 97 F6
Cullaville 147 C4
Tray Rd BT60 .... 97 F6
Tree Ring★ BT60 .... 98 C1
Trees The BT21 .... 6 E1
Treeyew Pk BT34 .... 64 E5
Trench Rd
Hillsborough BT26 .... 46 F8
Newtownards BT23 .... 69 A2
Trevor Hill BT34 .... 64 D6

Trevor St BT18 9 D6
TrewⓉ BT71 72 B4
Trewmount Rd BT71 72 A5
Trigo Par BT6 15 D2
Trillick Ct 7 BT5 15 B4
Trillick St 4 BT5 15 B4
Trinity Pk BT67 43 D6
Trinity Terr BT28 26 A1
TrooperfieldⓉ BT23 25 A2
Trough La BT63 102 B7
Troughton's Hill BT62 54 C2
Troutbeck Ave BT20 3 E2
TrummeryⓉ BT67 35 A5
Trummery Hts BT67 35 A7
Trummery La BT67 35 A7
Tubber Rd BT22 80 E8
Tudor Abbey BT23 20 A5
Tudor Ave BT6 22 D7
Tudor Ct BT6 22 D7
Tudor Dale BT4 15 F7
Tudor Dr BT6 22 D7
Tudor Gr
Belfast BT13 14 B7
5 Dromara BT25 58 E6
Tudor Grange 1 BT66 86 C8
Tudor Hts BT33 122 C1
Tudor Lodge BT66 86 B8
Tudor Mews BT34 65 C2
Tudor Oaks
Ballynahinch BT24 59 E4
Banbridge BT32 61 E6
Holywood BT18 9 E7
Tudor Pk
Bangor BT20 3 F1
Holywood BT18 9 E7
Tudor Pl BT13 14 B7
Tudors The BT32 61 F4
Tughan Ct BT20 4 C2
Tullamona Pk BT34 144 F4
TullanacrunatⓉ 147 A7
TullindoneyⓉ BT25 88 D3
Tullindoney Rd BT25 88 D3
TullinespickⓉ BT30 125 C5
TulliniskyⓉ BT25 88 D2
TullintanvallyⓉ BT32 103 D2
TullyahⓉ BT35 130 D5
Tullyah Rd BT60 130 D7
TullyallenⓉ BT60 116 C4
Tullyallen Rd BT60 116 B5
TullyanaghanⓉ BT67 42 F7
TullyardⓉ
Armagh BT61 98 D8
Craigavon BT67 45 A4
Lisburn BT27 39 E7
Newry BT35 138 C1
Tullyard Fort★ BT35 138 C1
Tullyard Rd
Craigavon BT67 45 A4
Lisburn BT27 27 F1
Lisburn BT27 39 E6
Tullyard Way (Heichbrae Airt) BT6 22 E8
TullyargleⓉ BT60 98 B6
Tullybeg Fort BT24 59 E3
Tullybletty Rd BT69 82 A5
TullyboardⓉ BT22 94 E2
TullybraniganⓉ BT33 136 C7
Tullybrannigan Ave 2 BT33 63 B5
Tullybrannigan Brae
3 Newcastle BT33 63 B5
8 Newcastle BT33 63 B5
Tullybrannigan Cl 7 BT33 63 B5
Tullybrannigan Cres 6 BT33 63 B5
Tullybrannigan Gdns 4 BT33 63 B5
Tullybrannigan Rd BT33 63 A7
Tullybrannigan Rise BT33 63 B5
Tullybrannigan Rise Spine Rd BT33 63 B5
Tullybrannigan Way 1 BT33 63 B5
Tullybrick Etra or BondvilleⓉ BT60 96 C1
Tullybrick (Hamilton)Ⓣ BT60 112 D8
TullyboneⓉ BT60 114 E4
Tullybrone Rd BT60 114 E4
TullycallidyⓉ BT60 97 D3
Tullycallidy Rd BT60 97 D3
TullycarnⓉ BT25 87 B5
TullycarnanⓉ
Ardglass BT30 125 F6
Newtownards BT22 110 F8
TULLYCARNET BT5 16 D3
Tullycarnet Pk★ BT5 16 D2
Tullycarnet Prim Sch BT5 16 F3
TullyconnaughtⓉ BT32 103 C5
Tullyconnaught Rd BT32 103 B5
TullycoreⓉ BT23 79 B4
Tullycore Rd BT23 79 B3
TullycrossⓉ BT22 80 F1
Tullycross Rd BT22 80 F1
TullydaganⓉ BT67 32 D3
Tullydagan Rd BT67 32 C3
Tullydonnell (Gage)Ⓣ BT35 149 A7
Tullydonnell (O'Callaghan)Ⓣ BT35 149 A8
Tullydonnell Rd BT35 140 A1
TullydoweyⓉ BT71 83 F4
Tullydowey Rd BT71 83 E5
TullyearⓉ BT32 61 D1
Tullyear Ave BT32 61 B1
TullyelmerⓉ BT61 60 B8
Tullyet Rd BT35 129 D4
Tullyfoyle LowerⓉ BT30 110 C5
Tullyfoyle UpperⓉ BT30 110 D4
TullyframeⓉ BT34 144 E2
Tullyframe Rd BT34 144 E1
TullygallyⓉ BT65 41 C4
Tullygally E Rd BT65 41 C3
Tullygally Prim Sch BT65 41 C3
Tullygally Rd BT65 41 B3
Tullygally Sh Ctr BT65 41 C3
TullygardenⓉ BT61 85 C2
Tullygarden Rd BT61 85 D2
TullygarranⓉ BT61 84 B2
Tullygarron Rd BT61 83 F1
TullygarvanⓉ BT23 31 A1
Tullygarvan Rd BT23 31 C1
Tullygeasy Rd BT35 129 B5
TullygivenⓉ BT70 82 F5
TullyglushⓉ
Armagh BT60 128 B8
Banbridge BT32 88 B1
Tullyglush (Kane)Ⓣ BT60 113 B7
Tullyglush (Nevin)Ⓣ BT60 112 E8
Tullyglush Rd BT32 88 B2
TullygoneyⓉ BT71 83 E6
TullygooniganⓉ BT61 84 C2
Tullygoonigan Ind Est BT61 84 C3
TullyhappyⓉ BT35 131 B8
Tullyhenan Rd BT32 87 B1
TullyherronⓉ
Armagh BT60 116 D2
Waringstown BT66 42 F1
Tullyherron Rd BT60 116 D2
TullyhinanⓉ BT32 87 B1
TullyhirmⓉ BT60 113 A2
Tullyhirm Rd BT60 113 A2
TullyhubbertⓉ BT23 31 A4
Tullyhubbert Rd BT23 31 A3
TullyhughⓉ BT62 101 C8
Tullyhugh Pk BT62 101 B6
TullykevanⓉ BT71 84 A6
TullykevinⓉ BT22 70 D6
Tullykevin Rd BT22 70 E6
TullykinⓉ BT30 93 A4
Tullykin Lough Rd BT30 93 A4
Tullykin Rd BT30 93 A4
TullylearnⓉ BT71 83 F4
TullylinnⓉ BT35 117 A8
TullylishⓉ BT63 86 A1
Tullylish Rd BT63 57 F1
TullyloobⓉ BT67 33 B3
TullylostⓉ BT60 98 B5
TullymacannⓉ BT62 101 B4
Tullymacann Rd BT62 101 B4
TullymacarathⓉ BT32 87 D3
Tullymacarette Prim Sch BT32 87 D3
TullymacnousⓉ BT30 93 B7
Tullymacnous Rd BT30 93 B7
TullymacreeveⓉ BT35 140 A6
Tullymacreeve Rd BT35 140 A4
TullymallyⓉ BT22 94 F5
Tullymally Rd BT22 94 F5
TullymoreⓉ
Armagh BT60 98 B5
Armagh BT61 85 E6
Banbridge BT32 118 A6
Newtownards BT23 79 C3
Tullymore AgowanⓉ BT71 83 F3
Tullymore Agowan La BT71 83 E3
Tullymore Downs BT60 60 B4
Tullymore EtraⓉ BT71 83 B4
Tullymore La BT71 83 B3
Tullymore OtraⓉ BT71 83 B4
Tullymore Rd
Armagh BT61 85 E6
Banbridge BT32 118 A6
Tullymore Sch La BT60 83 B3
TullymurryⓉ
Downpatrick BT30 107 E2
Newry BT34 118 C3
Tullymurry Rd BT34 118 D3
TullynacreeⓉ BT30 91 F2
Tullynacree Rd BT30 92 A1
TullynacrewⓉ BT22 95 A3
TullynacrossⓉ
Craigavon BT66 86 E8
Lisburn BT27 26 F4
Newry BT35 117 D8
Tullynacross Rd
Lisburn BT27 26 F4
Newry BT35 117 C7
TullynagardyⓉ BT23 19 B8
Tullynagardy Rd BT23 11 F3
TullynageeⓉ BT23 78 C8
TullynageerⓉ 128 B4
Tullynagee Rd BT23 68 C2
TullynaginⓉ BT60 114 E6
Tullynagin Rd BT60 114 E6
TullynahattinaⓉ 138 C6
TullynakillⓉ BT23 69 A1
Tullynakill Rd BT23 68 F2
TullynamallogeⓉ BT60 114 B4
TullynamalraⓉ 127 F1
TullynashaneⓉ BT68 96 D7
TullynaskeaghⓉ BT30 109 F3
Tullynaskeagh Rd BT30 109 E2
TullynasooⓉ BT34 121 C4
Tullynasoo Rd BT34 121 C5
TullynavallⓉ BT35 139 B4
Tullynavall Rd BT35 139 B5
Tullynawood Rd BT60 114 B5
TullyneaghⓉ BT61 97 E8
Tullyneagh Rd BT61 83 E1
Tullyneill Rd BT35 129 A4
TullynicholⓉ BT61 83 F2
Tullynicholl La BT61 83 F2
TullynoreⓉ BT26 48 C2
Tullynore Rd BT26 48 C3
TullyogallaghanⓉ BT35 130 A1
TullyoriorⓉ BT32 103 D4
Tullyorior Rd BT32 103 C5
TullyquillyⓉ BT34 119 D3
Tullyquilly Rd BT34 119 E3
TullyrainⓉ
Banbridge BT32 103 B7
Craigavon BT63 86 C3
Tullyraine Rd BT32 86 D2
TullyrattyⓉ BT30 94 A1
TullyreeⓉ BT34 121 F1
Tullyree Rd BT34 121 D2
TullyremonⓉ BT68 82 F3
TULLYROAN CORNER BT71 72 F1
Tullyroan Dr BT62 51 B2
Tullyroan Gdns BT62 51 B2
Tullyroan Prim Sch BT71 72 E1
Tullyroan Rd BT71 72 F1
TullyronnellyⓉ BT67 32 E3
TullysaranⓉ BT61 83 E1
Tullysaran Rd
Armagh BT61 83 F1
Dungannon BT71 84 B2
TullytramonⓉ BT22 81 A1
TullyvallanⓉ BT35 129 B3
Tullyvallan (Hamilton) EastⓉ BT35 139 A8
Tullyvallan (Hamilton) WestⓉ BT35 138 F8
Tullyvallan (Macullagh)Ⓣ BT35 139 A7
Tullyvallan (Tipping) EastⓉ BT35 139 B7
Tullyvallan (Tipping) WestⓉ BT35 139 A7
TullyveeryⓉ BT30 93 A7
Tullyverry Rd BT30 92 F7
TullywasnacunaghⓉ BT24 76 F2
Tullywest Rd BT24 76 F1
Tullywill Rd BT60 115 E2
Tullywinney Rd BT35 130 F6
TullywinnyⓉ BT35 130 F6
TullyworgleⓉ BT60 98 A7
Tunnell Rd BT35 117 C3
Turin St BT12 154 B2
TurleenanⓉ BT71 72 B3
Turloughs Hill BT34 146 B4
TurmennanⓉ BT30 92 E3
Turmennan Rd BT30 92 D3
TurmoreⓉ BT34 132 C7
Turmore Rd BT34 132 C7
TurmoyraⓉ BT66 75 E5
Turmoyra La BT66 41 D8
Turnavall Rd BT34 132 E8
Turnberry Gn BT62 101 B8
Turnstone BT23 20 A3
Turnstone Hts BT23 20 A3
Turnstone Mews BT23 20 A2
TurryⓉ BT60 96 F8
Tweskard Lodge BT4 16 C7
Tweskard Pk BT4 16 C7
Twinem Ct BT64 40 D1
Twin Spires Ctr BT13 154 B3
Twiselside BT18 9 E7
TYNAN BT60 96 E3
Tyne St BT13 154 B4
Tyrella NorthⓉ BT30 124 A6
Tyrella Prim Sch BT30 123 F5
Tyrella Rd BT30 123 F7
Tyrella SouthⓉ BT30 124 A4
Tyrones Ditches BT35 117 B4
Tyrones Ditches Rd BT35 117 B6
Tyrone St (Sráid Thír Eoghain) 2 BT13 154 C4
Tyross BT60 60 F4
Tyross or LegagillyⓉ BT60 98 B6

U

Ubi Lurgan (Lurgan Campus) (Upper Bann Inst of Further & Upper Ed) 1 BT66 41 F5
Ulster Ave BT34 119 F2
Ulster Coll of Music BT9 14 B1
Ulsterdale St BT5 15 D4
Ulster Folk & Transport Mus (Ballycultra Town)★ BT18 1 E1
Ulster Hospl The BT16 17 B5
Ulster Mus★ BT9 14 D1
Ulster Sports Club BT1 155 B4
Ulster St
Belfast BT1 155 B4
Lurgan BT67 41 F6
Ulster Transport Mus★ BT18 1 D2
Ulster Villas BT34 64 E2
Ulsterville Ave BT9 14 B2
Ulsterville Dr BT9 14 B2
Ulsterville Gdns
Belfast BT9 14 B2
Portadown BT63 52 A4
Ulsterville Gr BT63 52 A4
Ulsterville Pk BT63 52 A4
Ulsterville Pl BT9 14 B2
Ulster Wildlife Ctr★ BT30 92 C5
UmgolaⓉ BT60 60 A3
Umgola Hts BT60 60 B3
Umgola Manor BT60 60 B4
Umgola Rd BT60 60 B3
Ummeracam (Ball) NorthⓉ BT35 139 E5
Ummeracam (Ball) SouthⓉ BT35 139 D3
Ummeracam (Johnston)Ⓣ BT35 139 D4
Ummeracam Rd BT35 139 D5
UmmerinvoreⓉ BT35 139 D7
UnicarvalⓉ BT23 25 C7
Unicarval Rd BT23 25 E8
Union Bridge BT27 26 C1
Union Ct BT66 42 A4
Uniondale St BT5 15 D4
Union St
Belfast BT1 155 A4
Donaghadee BT21 6 F1
Lurgan BT66 41 F4
Portadown BT62 51 C4
University Ave BT7 14 D2
University of Ulster (Belfast Campus) BT1 155 A4
University Rd BT9 14 C2
University Sq BT7 14 D2
University St BT7 14 D2
University Terr 1 BT9 14 C2
UnshinaghⓉ BT62 55 F3
Unshinagh La BT62 55 E3
UnshogⓉ BT60 112 E6
Uplands Pk BT19 4 F5
UpperⓉ BT34 134 C8
Upper Arthur St BT1 155 A3
Upper Ballydugan Rd BT63 53 D3
Upper Ballygelagh Rd BT22 80 F2
Upper Ballymorran BT23 79 B4
Upper Ballynahinch BT27 39 A1
Upper Bann Inst of FE & HE (Banbridge Campus) BT32 61 E5
Upper Bann Inst of FE & HE (Portadown Campus) BT63 52 A6
Upper Bann Inst of Further & HE BT62 51 D3
Upper Braniel Rd BT5 23 C7
Upper Burren Rd BT34 65 A7
Upper Canning St BT15 14 D8
Upper Chapel St BT34 64 E3
Upper Charleville St BT13 14 A7
Upper Church La
Belfast BT1 155 B3
Portadown BT63 52 B7
Upper Clifton BT20 4 B5
Upper Cres
Belfast BT7 14 D2
Comber BT23 25 E3
Upper Croft Rd BT18 10 A6
Upper Ct St BT23 19 D4
Upper Ctyd BT7 21 E7
Upper Damolly Rd BT34 64 F8
Upper Darkley Rd BT60 114 B1
Upper Dromore Rd BT34 65 B5
Upper Dromore Rd S BT34 65 C4
Upper Edward St BT35 64 C6
Upper English St BT61 60 C5
Upper Fathom Rd BT35 141 F6
Upper Frank St 14 BT5 15 B4
Upper Galwally Rd 3 BT8 22 A6
Upper Gransha Rd BT19 66 A6
Upper Greenwell St BT23 19 F4
Upper Irish St BT60 60 C4
Upper Kiln St BT35 64 B5
Upper Kinghill Rd BT34 120 F1
Upper Knockbarragh BT34 143 A6
Upper Knockbreda Rd BT6 22 E8
Upper Lisdrumchor Rd BT60 116 A1
Upper Malone Rd BT17 27 D7
Upper Malvern Cres 8 BT8 22 C3
Upper Malvern Dr 7 BT8 22 C3
Upper Malvern Pk BT8 22 C3
Upper Malvern Rd BT8 22 C2
Upper Mdw St BT15 14 C8
Upper Mealough Rd BT8 29 A5
Upper Meehan St BT13 14 B7
Uppermourne Rd BT66 42 A3
Upper Movilla St BT23 19 F5
Upper Newtownards Rd
Belfast BT5 16 A4
Dundonald BT16 17 A5
Upper N St BT23 19 D6
Upper Queen St BT1 155 A3
Upper Quilly Rd BT32 87 C3
Upper Ramone Pk BT63 52 B6
Upper Rd BT35 140 C2
Upper Riga St BT13 154 A4
Upper Stanfield St BT7 155 B2
Upper Toberhewny La BT66 42 B2
Uppertown Rd BT32 120 C8
Upper Townsend Terr BT13 154 C4
Upritchard Cres 4 BT19 13 C8
Upritchard Ct 3 BT19 13 C8
UrcherⓉ BT35 148 A8
Urchill 2 BT35 148 B8
Utility St BT12 154 C1
Utility Wlk BT12 154 C1

V

Vail The BT21 6 E1
Valencia Way N BT23 19 B6
Valencia Way S BT23 19 B6
Valentia Pl BT33 63 D5
Valentine Rd BT20 4 B2
Vale Rd BT24 91 C5
Valetta Pk BT23 19 D1
Valley La BT66 86 B7
Valley Rd
Banbridge BT32 87 B2
Newry BT34 146 B3
Valley's La BT61 98 C8
Vauxhall Pk BT9 21 D6
Velton Lawns BT62 55 D1
Velton Manor 1 BT62 100 E8
Vennel The 4 BT20 4 A4
Ventry La BT2 155 A1
Ventry St BT2 155 A1
Vermont Ave BT23 13 A4
Verner St BT2 155 B2
Vernon Ct BT7 155 A1
Vernon Pk BT20 4 E3
Vernon St BT7 155 A1
Vestry Rd
Newry BT35 115 C3
Newtownards BT23 77 E6
Vianstown Hts (Arda Bhaile na Bhfiann) BT30 62 C1
Vianstown Lodge BT30 62 B2
Vianstown Pk BT30 62 C3
Vianstown Rd BT30 62 B1
Vicarage Cl BT63 57 B2
Vicarage Rd BT62 54 D6
Vicar's Carn★ BT60 115 B8
Vicars Hill BT61 60 C5
Viceroy's Wood BT19 3 B1
Vicinage Pk BT14 14 C8
Victoria Ave
Belfast BT4 15 E7
Newtownards BT23 19 E6
Victoria Cl BT23 19 E6
Victoria Coll (Cranmore Campus) BT9 21 B7
Victoria Coll (Richmond Lodge Campus) BT9 21 B8
Victoria Cres
Donaghadee BT21 67 A8
Lisburn BT27 26 C2
Newtownards BT23 19 E5
Victoria Ct
Belfast BT4 15 E7
Richhill BT61 99 E8
Victoria Dr
Bangor BT20 4 B5
Belfast BT4 15 E7
Victoria Gdns
Donaghadee BT21 67 A8
Lurgan BT67 42 A7
Newtownards BT22 81 C8
Newtownards BT23 19 E5
Victoria Gr
Armagh BT61 60 E5
Craigavon BT66 42 F5
Victoria Mews
Armagh BT61 60 E5
Donaghadee BT21 67 A8
Victoria Par BT15 14 D7
Victoria ParkⓉ BT3 15 D7
Victoria Pk
Armagh BT61 60 E5
Newtownards BT23 19 E5
Victoria Pl BT67 42 A7
Victoria Prim Sch
Newtownards BT22 81 C8
Newtownards BT23 19 E5
Victoria Rd
Armagh BT61 60 E5
Bangor BT20 4 B5
Belfast BT4 15 E7
Holywood BT18 9 E7
Newtownards BT22 81 B7
Newtownards BT23 19 E6
Victoria Sq
Belfast BT1 155 B3
15 Rostrevor BT34 143 C3
Victoria St
Armagh BT60 60 E5
4 Banbridge BT32 61 C4
Belfast BT1 155 B3
Keady BT60 114 A3
Lurgan BT66 41 F6
Victor Pl
Belfast BT6 15 A4
Craigavon BT66 42 F5
Victory St BT27 26 D2
Vidor Ct BT4 15 E7
Vidor Gdns BT4 15 E7
Viewpoint Rd BT35 129 B8
Village Ct BT8 21 F4
Village Gn BT67 34 B2
Village Gn The BT6 15 C1
Village La The BT31 122 C2
Village Manor BT33 122 C2
Village Mews 1 BT67 34 B2
Village Wlk BT63 52 B5
Villa Gr BT34 65 B3
Villa Wood Rd BT25 87 C5
Villiers Ave BT66 41 E8
Violet Hill Ave BT35 64 B8
Violet St BT12 154 A2
Vionville Cl BT5 16 F2

Vionville Ct BT5 16 F3
Vionville Gn BT5 16 E3
Vionville Hts BT5 16 F2
Vionville Pk BT5 16 F3
Vionville Pl BT5 16 F3
Vionville Rise BT5 16 F3
Vionville View BT5 16 F3
Vionville Way BT5 16 F2
Virginia St BT7 155 A1
Virginia Way BT7 155 A1
Vistula St BT13 14 A7
Vulcan Ct (Cúirt Bholcáin) 12 BT5 15 A5
Vulcan Gdns (Gairdíní Bholcáinin) 13 BT5 15 A5
Vulcan Link (Lúb Bholcáin) 14 BT5 15 A5
Vulcan St (Sráid Bholcáin)
10 Belfast BT5 15 A5
Belfast BT12 154 C2
Belfast BT12 154 C2

W

Waddel's Hill BT23 68 E4
Walker Ct 7 BT6 15 B3
Walkers Farm BT26 37 B1
Walkers La
Millisle BT22 67 A4
Newtownards BT22 66 F4
Wallace Ave BT27 26 B2
Wallace Gdns BT23 68 E1
Wallace High Sch BT28 26 A3
Wallace High Rd BT30 92 F3
Wallace Pk
Dromara BT25 58 D4
Newtownards BT23 68 D1
Wallace's Pl BT23 19 F5
Wallace's St BT23 19 F5
Wallace Studios 3 BT27 26 B2
Walled Gdn The 2 BT67 44 B8
Wall Rd BT63 57 D1
Wall St (Sráid na Bhalla) BT13 154 C4
Walmer Gr BT19 3 A1
Walmer St BT7 21 E8
Walnut Ct BT7 155 B1
Walnut Hill BT27 36 E1
Walnut Mews BT7 155 B1
Walnut St BT7 155 B1
Walshestown BT30 93 E2
Walshestown Castle* BT30 93 E2
Wandsworth Cres 12 BT4 16 A5
Wandsworth Ct 3 BT4 16 A5
Wandsworth Dale BT19 3 B3
Wandsworth Dr BT4 16 A6
Wandsworth Gdns BT4 16 A5
Wandsworth Glen BT19 3 B3
Wandsworth La BT19 3 B3
Wandsworth Par BT4 16 A5
Wandsworth Pk BT19 3 B3
Wandsworth Pl BT4 16 A5
Wandsworth Rd
Bangor BT19 3 B3
Belfast BT4 16 B5
Wansbeck St BT9 21 D7
Wanstead Ave BT16 17 B2
Wanstead Cres BT16 17 C2
Wanstead Dr BT16 17 C2
Wanstead Gdns BT16 17 B2
Wanstead Mews BT16 17 B2
Wanstead Pk BT16 17 C2
Wanstead Rd BT16 17 B2
Wapping La BT26 47 C6
Ward Ave
Bangor BT20 4 C5
Lisburn BT28 37 F8
Wardsborough Rd 1 BT28 26 B1
Ward The BT30 125 F6
Waringfield Ave BT67 34 A1
Waringfield Cl 4 BT67 44 A8
Waringfield Cres BT67 44 B8
Waringfield Dr BT67 34 A1
Waringfield Gdns 1 BT67 44 A8
Waringfield Grange 3 BT67 44 B8
Waringfield Mews 2 BT67 44 A8
Waringfield Pk BT67 34 B1
Waringmore BT67 34 A1
WARINGSFORD BT25 88 D1
Waringsford Rd BT32 103 B8
Waring St
Belfast BT1 155 A3
Lurgan BT66 41 F5
WARINGSTOWN BT66 86 C7
Waringstown Prim Sch BT66 86 C8
Waringstown Rd
Lurgan BT66 42 D2
Waringstown BT66 86 C8
Warne View Ct BT33 63 E8
Warnock Rd BT22 81 E5
Warnocks Rd BT22 81 D5
Warren Ave BT21 6 F3
Warren Cl
Downpatrick BT30 123 F5
Lisburn BT28 37 F7
Warren Dr BT21 6 E3
Warren Gdns
Donaghadee BT21 6 E3
Lisburn BT28 37 F7
Warren Gr
Bangor BT19 3 F1
Castlereagh BT5 16 B1
Lisburn BT28 37 F7
Warren Hill BT34 64 F1
Warren La BT21 6 D3
Warren Mourn BT28 37 F8
Warren Pk BT28 37 F7
Warren Pk Ave BT28 38 A8
Warren Pk Dr BT28 37 F8
Warren Pk Gdns BT28 38 A8
WARRENPOINT (AN POINTE) BT34 65 B2
Warrenpoint Ent Ctr BT34 65 A3
Warrenpoint Golf Club BT34 65 A4
Warrenpoint Rd
Newry BT34 64 D4
Rostrevor BT34 143 A3
Warren Rd BT21 6 D4
Wateresk BT33 123 A4
Wateresk Rd BT33 122 F4
Waterford Gdns BT13 154 A3
Waterford St BT13 154 A3
Waterfront Hall* BT1 155 B3
Waterloo Rd BT27 38 C4
Watermeade Ave BT22 70 B5
Watermeade Cres BT22 70 B4
Watermeade Pk BT22 70 B5
Waterside BT28 38 B8
Water St
Newry BT34 64 D5
Portadown BT62 51 E5
11 Rostrevor BT34 143 C3
Waterville St BT13 154 A3
Watsons La
Lurgan BT67 42 B5
Portadown BT63 51 E5
Watsons Rd BT35 64 B4
Watson St BT63 51 E5
Watts Pk BT71 72 A5
Watt St BT6 15 A2
Wauchope Ct BT12 154 B1
Waughs Cross Roads BT60 99 D2
Waverley Ave BT28 38 A7
Waverley Dr BT20 4 D5
Wayland St BT5 15 C3
Wayside BT62 101 A7
Wayside Cl 8 BT5 16 A1
Weavers Brook 5 BT35 131 C5
Weavers Ct BT32 61 D5
Weavers Ct Bsns Pk BT12 154 C1
Weavers Gn BT32 61 C5
Weavers Lodge 1 BT66 86 F6
Weaver's Mdw BT32 61 C6
Web Theatre The* 4 BT23 19 E5
Weir Cl BT23 25 D2
Weir La BT24 91 A1
Weirs Row 2 BT25 58 E6
Welland St BT4 15 C5
Wellesley Ave BT9 14 C1
Wellington Coll BT7 21 E7
Wellington Dr BT20 4 E3
Wellington Gdns BT20 4 E3
Wellington Parks BT67 35 A8
Wellington Pk
Bangor BT20 4 E3
Belfast BT9 14 C1
Wellington Pk Ave BT9 14 C1
Wellington Pk Terr BT9 14 C1
Wellington Pl BT1 155 A3
Wellington St
Belfast BT1 155 A2
Lurgan BT67 42 A6
Well La
Downpatrick BT30 62 B6
Newry BT34 64 D5
Well Pl 16 BT6 15 A4
Well Rd
Ballywalter BT22 71 A5
Warrenpoint BT34 65 E3
Wellwood Ave 4 BT4 15 D7
Wellwood Cl 3 BT4 15 D7
Wellwood St BT12 154 C1
Welsh St BT7 155 B2
Wenlock Rd BT66 41 D5
Wentworth Gn BT62 51 E1
Wesley Ct BT7 155 A1
Wesley St
Belfast BT2 155 A1
Lisburn BT27 26 C2
West Acres BT65 41 B1
Westbank Bsns Pk BT3 8 C4
West Bank Cl BT3 8 C4
West Bank Dr BT3 8 C4
West Bank Rd BT3 8 C4
West Bank Way BT3 8 C5
Westbourne St 1 BT5 15 B5
Westburn Cres BT19 3 D4
West Circular Rd BT19 3 E1
Westcott St BT5 15 C4
West End BT35 131 C5
West Gn
Holywood BT18 9 C5
Newtownards BT23 19 C3
West Hill BT19 5 B7
Westland Ave
10 Ballywalter BT22 71 A6
Newcastle BT33 63 D7
Westland Cl 2 BT30 92 B4
Westland Ct 1 BT22 71 A6
Westland Dr
Ballywalter BT22 71 A6
Newtownards BT23 19 C6
Westland Gdns 3 BT30 92 B4
Westland Mews BT62 51 B4
Westland Pk BT22 71 A6
Westland Rd
Ballywalter BT22 71 A6
Portadown BT62 51 B4
Westlands BT30 92 B4
Westlea Dr BT22 81 D4
Westlea Gdns BT22 81 D4
Westlink
Belfast BT12 154 A1
Belfast BT15 14 D7
West Link BT18 9 C5
Westlink Ent Ctr BT12 154 B2
Westminster Ave 1 BT4 15 D5
Westminster Ave N 5 BT4 15 D5
Westminster St BT7 14 E2
Westmoreland Cres BT20 3 E2
Westmount Pk BT23 19 B5
Westpoint BT30 125 D4
Wests Rd BT32 118 C8
West St
Newtownards BT23 19 D5
Portadown BT62 51 D4
WEST WINDS BT23 19 C2
West Winds Prim Sch BT23 19 D2
West Winds Terr
2 Hillsborough BT26 49 B1
2 Hillsborough BT26 89 D8
Westwood BT67 42 A8
Wheatfield BT23 31 E1
Wheatfield Dr BT66 42 C4
Whigamstown BT30 125 A7
Whincroft Rd
2 Castlereagh BT5 15 F1
2 Castlereagh BT5 16 A1
Whincroft Way BT5 16 A1
Whin La BT19 3 B4
Whinland Dr BT34 146 C4
Whinlands Croft BT34 146 C4
Whinney Hill BT16 10 F3
Whinney Hts BT8 22 A3
Whinny Hill
Gilford BT63 57 C1
Gilford BT63 101 D8
Whinnyhill Dr BT8 21 C1
Whinpark Rd BT23 19 D7
Whispering Pines BT6 22 C6
Whitecherry Hill BT23 79 A5
Whitecherry La BT23 79 A5
Whitechurch BT22 71 A7
Whitechurch Rd
Ballywalter BT22 71 A6
Newtownards BT22 67 D1
WHITECROSS BT60 130 C8
White Fort* BT31 122 F7
White Fort Cashel* BT31 106 E5
Whitefort Rd BT31 106 E1
Whitegate Rd BT34 120 A6
Whitegates Sh Ctr BT35 64 C7
Whitehall Gdns BT7 21 F8
Whitehall Mews BT7 21 F8
Whitehall Par BT7 21 F8
Whitehall Rd BT67 32 D7
Whitehill Ave BT20 4 A1
Whitehill Cl BT20 4 A1
Whitehill Dr BT20 4 A1
Whitehill La BT24 91 E7
Whitehill Pass BT20 4 A1
Whitehill Rd BT31 105 D2
White Hill Rd BT32 103 D7
Whitehills BT30 110 A5
Whitehills Rd BT30 109 F5
White House* BT22 95 C7
Whitemill 150 B4
WHITEROCK BT23 79 C6
Whiterock Dr BT30 125 F6
Whiterock Rd
Newry BT35 129 F6
Newtownards BT23 79 B6
Whiteside BT23 19 D7
Whitesides Hill BT62 55 D3
Whitespots BT23 12 E1
Whitespots Ctry Pk* BT23 12 E2
Whitethorn Ave BT23 20 B5
Whitethorn Brae
Dromara BT25 88 F3
Newtownards BT23 20 B5
Whitethorn Dr BT23 20 B5
Whitethorn Mews BT23 20 B5
Whiteways BT23 19 D7
Whitla Cres BT28 26 B4
Whitla Rd BT28 26 B4
Whitla St 6 BT15 14 E8
Whitten Cl BT62 51 D5
Whowhatwherewhenwhy* BT3 155 C4
Whyte Acres BT32 61 E3
Whyte Field BT30 92 C5
Wigton St BT13 154 B4
Wildeen BT27 26 C4
Wildflower Way BT12 14 A1
Wild Forest Cl BT33 63 B8
Wildfowl Obsy* BT23 68 F4
Wildwood BT63 51 F4
Wilgar Cl BT4 15 E5
Wilgar St BT4 15 E5
Willesden Pk BT9 21 D6
William St Ct BT23 19 C5
William St Mews BT23 19 D5
William St S BT1 155 A3
William St
2 Armagh BT60 98 B4
Belfast BT1 155 A4
2 Craigavon BT66 86 E6
William St *continued*
Crossgar BT30 92 B5
Donaghadee BT21 67 A8
Lurgan BT66 41 F6
Newry BT34 64 D5
Newtownards BT23 19 C6
Portadown BT62 51 E4
Willow Ave BT32 61 E5
Willowbank
Armagh BT61 60 B6
Ballynahinch BT24 59 C6
Willowbank Cres BT8 22 C6
Willowbank Dr BT6 22 B6
Willowbank Pk BT6 22 B7
Willowbrook Cres 2 BT19 13 D7
Willowbrook Ct BT19 13 C7
Willowbrook Dale BT19 13 D7
Willowbrook Dr BT19 13 D7
Willowbrook Gdns BT19 13 C7
Willowbrook Gr BT19 13 C7
Willowbrook Pk BT19 13 D7
Willowbrook Pl 1 BT19 13 D7
Willowbrook Rd BT19 13 D7
Willowbrook Rise BT19 13 C7
Willow Cl BT32 61 E5
Willow Cres BT24 59 C6
Willow Ct
3 Dunmurry BT17 26 F8
Lurgan BT66 42 B2
Willow Dean BT60 116 A8
Willow Dr
Banbridge BT32 61 F5
Portadown BT62 51 C1
Willowfield BT62 101 A7
Willowfield Ave 3 BT6 15 B3
Willowfield Cres
2 Belfast BT6 15 B3
Craigavon BT65 53 C7
Willowfield Dr BT6 15 A3
Willowfield Gdns BT6 15 B3
Willowfield Hts 14 BT62 101 B7
Willowfield Par BT6 15 A3
Willowfield St BT6 15 B3
Willow Gdns BT17 27 A8
Willow Gr
Banbridge BT32 61 E5
Newry BT34 64 F8
Willowholme Cres BT6 15 B2
Willowholme Dr BT6 15 B2
Willowholme Par 4 BT6 15 B2
Willowholme St BT6 15 B2
Willow Lodge BT28 35 A8
Willow Pk
Ballynahinch BT24 59 C6
Banbridge BT32 61 E5
Bangor BT20 4 F5
Willow St BT12 154 C2
Willows The
11 Bangor BT19 13 D7
Castlereagh BT6 22 C6
Lurgan BT66 41 F4
Newtownards BT23 20 A4
Portadown BT62 51 C2
Willowvale BT16 17 C4
Wilmar Rd BT27 26 C7
Wilshere Dr BT4 16 A7
Wilson Ct BT1 155 B3
Wilson's Hill Rd BT60 96 F6
Wilson St
Belfast BT13 154 C4
Lisburn BT27 26 C2
Portadown BT62 51 E5
Wilsontown Rd BT60 83 B2
Wilton Ct Mews BT13 154 A4
Wilton Gdns BT13 154 A4
Wilton Gr 5 BT35 131 E4
Wilton St BT13 154 A4
Win Bsns Pk BT34 64 D7
Winchester Ave BT8 29 D1
Winchester Cres BT8 29 D1
Winchester Dr BT8 29 D1
Winchester Gdns BT8 29 D1
Winchester Gr 2 BT8 29 D2
Winchester Pk BT8 29 D1
Winchester Rd BT8 29 D1
Windermere Ave 2 BT8 22 C3
Windermere Cl 3 BT8 22 C3
Windermere Cres
Bangor BT20 4 E2
Castlereagh BT8 22 C3
Windermere Dr
Bangor BT20 4 E3
Castlereagh BT8 22 C3
Windermere Gn 1 BT8 22 C3
Windermere Pk BT8 22 C3
Windermere Rd BT8 22 C3
Windermere Village 4 BT8 22 C3
Windmill Ave
Armagh BT61 60 C5
Ballynahinch BT24 59 E4
Windmill Bsns Pk BT24 77 D4
Windmill Cres BT24 59 E5
Windmill Dr BT24 59 E4
Windmill Gdns
Ballynahinch BT24 59 E5
3 Millisle BT22 67 A4
Windmill Grange 4 BT24 77 C4
Windmill Hill
Armagh BT60 60 B5
Comber BT23 25 D3
Portaferry BT22 94 D3
Windmill Hollow
Newtownards BT23 19 D6
5 Saintfield BT24 77 C4
Windmill Hts 6 BT22 94 D3
Windmill La
Ballynahinch BT24 59 E5
Bangor BT20 4 E4
5 Portaferry BT22 94 D3
Windmill Mdws 11 BT22 94 D3
Windmill Pl BT34 64 E5
Windmill Rd
Bangor BT20 4 E4
Donaghadee BT21 66 E6
Hillsborough BT26 48 C5
Newry BT34 64 E4
Saintfield BT24 77 C4
Windmill Row BT23 19 E5
Windmill St BT24 59 D5
Windmill View BT24 59 E5
Windmill Wlk BT24 59 E4
Windrush 12 BT19 5 B7
Windrush Ave BT8 22 C4
Windrush Pk BT8 22 C4
Windsor Ave
Bangor BT20 3 F4
Belfast BT9 14 B1
Holywood BT18 9 E6
2 Lisburn BT28 37 F8
Lurgan BT67 42 A5
Newry BT34 64 D7
Newtownards BT23 19 C4
Portadown BT63 52 A5
Windsor Ave N BT9 14 C1
Windsor Bsns Pk BT9 14 B1
Windsor Cl
Belfast BT9 21 B8
3 Waringstown BT66 86 C8
Windsor Ct
Belfast BT9 21 B8
2 Waringstown BT66 86 C8
Windsor Dr BT12 14 A1
Windsor Gdns BT20 4 A3
Windsor Hill
Hillsborough BT26 47 E7
Newry BT34 64 E7
Windsor Hill Prim Sch 1 BT34 64 D6
Windsor Lawn Tennis Club BT9 14 C1
Windsor Manor 4 BT9 14 B1
Windsor Mews BT9 21 B8
Windsor Pk
Bangor BT20 4 A3
Belfast BT9 21 B8
Windsor Rd BT9 14 A1
Windy La BT66 42 C3
Windy Rd BT35 141 F6
Windyridge Cotts 7 BT22 71 A6
Winecellar Entry BT1 155 A3
Winetavern St BT1 155 A4
Wingrove Gdns BT5 15 D4
Winona Creston BT66 86 E7
Winona Lodge BT66 86 F7
Winona Manor BT66 86 E7
Winsdor Rd BT63 52 A5
Winston Gdns BT5 16 A4
Winston Pk BT23 25 E4
Witham St BT4 15 C5
Woburn Rd BT22 67 A2
Wolff Cl 32 BT4 15 A5
Wolff Rd BT3 8 C1
Wolf Island Rd BT60 128 E5
Wolf Island Terr BT66 75 B5
Wolseley St BT7 155 A1
Woodbank La BT18 9 F7
Woodbreda Ave BT8 22 A3
Woodbreda Cres 2 BT8 22 A3
Woodbreda Dr 4 BT8 22 A3
Woodbreda Gdns 1 BT8 22 A3
Woodbreda Pk BT8 22 A3
Woodbrook Pk BT34 65 D4
Woodcot Ave BT5 15 D4
Woodcroft Ave BT61 99 E8
Woodcroft Cres BT23 20 A6
Woodcroft Hts BT5 23 A8
Woodcroft Pk BT18 10 A6
Woodcroft Rise BT5 23 A8
Wood End BT18 9 D5
Woodfall Manor BT26 89 E8
Woodford Ave BT25 89 C3
Woodford Cl BT60 60 F1
Woodford Cres BT60 60 F1
Woodford Ct BT60 60 F1
Woodford Dr BT60 60 F1
Woodford Gdns BT60 60 F2
Woodford Gn
Armagh BT60 60 F1
Castlereagh BT8 22 B2
Woodford Grange BT19 4 F1
Woodford Hts BT60 60 F1
Woodford Mews BT60 60 F1
Woodford Pk
Armagh BT60 60 F2
Lurgan BT66 42 B3
Woodford View BT60 60 F2
Wood Gn BT20 3 E2
Wood Gr BT31 122 C4
Woodgrange BT30 108 B6
Woodgrange BT18 9 F7
Woodgrange Rd BT30 108 A6
Woodgrove BT62 51 D7
Woodhall BT67 34 B2
Wood Hill BT35 64 B6
Woodhill Hts BT66 42 C3
Woodhouse St BT62 51 D4
Wood Island Pk BT23 19 F6
Wood La BT66 42 C3
Woodland Ave
Bangor BT19 5 A5
Helen's Bay BT19 2 C5
Lisburn BT27 26 C6
Woodland Cres BT30 93 B6

Woodland Dr BT27 .... **26** C6
Woodland Gdns BT27 .... **26** C6
Woodland Pk BT27 .... **26** C6
Woodland Pk N BT27 ..... **26** C6
Woodlands
Holywood BT18 .... **9** F7
Newry BT35 .... **64** B6
1 Warrenpoint BT34 ..... **65** B4
Woodlands Ave BT18 ..... **10** B8
Woodlands Manor BT62 .. **51** C4
Woodlawn Hts BT61 ...... **99** D8
Woodlee St BT5 .... **15** C4
Wood Rd
Castlewellan BT31 .... **106** C1
Newry BT35 .... **141** A4
Wood Rd The BT71 .... **73** C7
Woodridge BT24 .... **59** B4
Woodrow Gdns BT24 ..... **77** D3
Woodside BT28 .... **38** A7
Woodside Gdns
7 Crossgar BT30 .... **92** B5
Newtownards BT22 .... **67** A3
Woodside Gdns *continued*
Portadown BT62 .... **51** D6
Woodside Gn BT62 .... **51** D6
Woodside Hill BT62 ...... **51** D6
Woodside Pk
Banbridge BT32 .... **102** C3
Lisburn BT28 .... **38** A7
Newry BT35 .... **131** D4
Wood's Quay **151** C4
Woodstock Link BT5 ..... **15** A4
Woodstock Pl 11 BT6 .... **15** A4
Woodstock Rd BT6 .... **15** B3
Woodvale
Banbridge BT32 .... **102** C3
Castlewellan BT31 .... **122** C4
Dromara BT25 .... **89** C2
Woodvale Ave BT25 ...... **89** C2
Woodvale Rd BT27 .... **76** C5
Woodvalle Elms BT67 .... **41** F8
Woodvalle Gate BT67 .... **41** F8
Woodview BT20 .... **4** A1
Woodview Ave BT62 ..... **51** E1
Woodview Cres BT28 ..... **38** A7
Woodview Dr
Castlereagh BT5 .... **16** C1
Lisburn BT28 .... **38** A7
Woodview Pk 15 BT62 ... **101** B7
Woodview Pl BT5 .... **16** C1
Woodview Terr BT5 ...... **16** C1
Woodville Ave BT66 ...... **41** E7
Woodville Gr BT66 .... **41** E8
Woodville Hts BT66 ...... **41** E7
Woodville St BT67 .... **41** F7
Worchester Ave BT19 ..... **3** C4
Workman Rd BT3 .... **8** C1
Wrack Rd BT34 .... **153** F8
Wreck Rd BT34 .... **146** C4
Wrights Arc BT23 .... **19** E5
Wrights Pk BT34 .... **119** F2
Wye St BT4 .... **15** B5
Wylies Gdns 6 BT34 .... **119** F2
Wynard Pk BT5 .... **16** B3
Wynchurch Ave BT6 ...... **22** B6
Wynchurch Gdns BT6 .... **22** B6
Wynchurch Pk BT6 .... **22** B6
Wynchurch Rd BT6 ...... **22** B6
Wynchurch Terr BT6 ..... **22** A6
Wynchurch Wlk BT6 ..... **22** B6
Wyncroft Hts BT32 .... **61** B4
Wyncroft Way BT32 ...... **61** B4
Wyndell Ct BT23 .... **20** A7
Wyndell Hts BT23 .... **20** A7
Wyndel Pk BT23 .... **20** A7
Wynfield Ct BT5 .... **15** E4
Wynford Pk BT27 .... **38** C8
Wynford St BT5 .... **15** D4
Wynfort Lodge BT67 ..... **34** A2

Y

Yard Gall★ BT18 .... **9** D6
Yarrow St BT14 .... **14** A8
Yellow Ford La BT61 ..... **84** D3
Yellow Rd
Hilltown BT34 .... **134** A5
Yellow Rd *continued*
Newry BT34 .... **133** E4
Yewtree Hill Rd BT67 ..... **35** C7
Yorkgate Sh Ctr & Leisure Pk
BT15 .... **14** E8
Yorkgate Sta BT15 .... **14** E8
York La BT1 .... **155** A4
York Link BT15 .... **14** E7
York St BT1 .... **155** A4
Young St BT27 .... **26** C1
Yukon St BT4 .... **15** C5

Z

Zenda Pk BT17 .... **27** B6
Zion Pl BT23 .... **19** F5

Notes

Addresses

Name and Address	Telephone	Page	Grid reference

Name and Address	Telephone	Page	Grid reference